Public Policy and the New European Agendas

NEW HORIZONS IN PUBLIC POLICY

Series Editor: Wayne Parsons
Professor of Public Policy, Queen Mary and Westfield College, University of London, UK

This series aims to explore the major issues facing academics and practitioners working in the field of public policy at the dawn of a new millennium. It seeks to reflect on where public policy has been, in both theoretical and practical terms, and to prompt debate on where it is going. The series emphasizes the need to understand public policy in the context of international developments and global change. New Horizons in Public Policy publishes the latest research on the study of the policymaking process and public management, and presents original and critical thinking on the policy issues and problems facing modern and post-modern societies.

Titles in the series include:

Beyond the New Public Management
Changing Ideas and Practices in Governance
Martin Minogue, Charles Polidano and David Hulme

Public Policy and Local Governance
Institutions in Postmodern Society
Peter Bogason

Implementing European Union Public Policy
Roger Levy

The Internationalization of Public Management
Reinventing the Third World State
Edited by Willy McCourt and Martin Minogue

Political Leadership
Howard Elcock

Success and Failure in Public Governance
A Comparative Analysis
Edited by Mark Bovens, Paul t'Hart and B. Guy Peters

Consensus, Cooperation and Conflict
The Policy Making Process in Denmark
Henning Jørgensen

Public Policy in Knowledge-Based Economies
Foundations and Frameworks
David Rooney, Greg Hearn, Thomas Mandeville and Richard Joseph

Modernizing Civil Services
Edited by Tony Butcher and Andrew Massey

Public Policy and the New European Agendas
Edited by Fergus Carr and Andrew Massey

Public Policy and the New European Agendas

Edited by

Fergus Carr

Head, School of Social, Historical and Literary Studies, University of Portsmouth, UK

Andrew Massey

Professor of Government, School of Social, Historical and Literary Studies, University of Portsmouth, UK

NEW HORIZONS IN PUBLIC POLICY

Edward Elgar

Cheltenham, UK • Northampton, MA, USA

Published by
Edward Elgar Publishing Limited
Glensanda House
Montpellier Parade
Cheltenham
Glos GL50 1UA
UK

Edward Elgar Publishing, Inc.
136 West Street
Suite 202
Northampton
Massachusetts 01060
USA

A catalogue record for this book
is available from the British Library

Library of Congress Cataloguing in Publication Data

Public policy and the new European agendas/edited by Fergus Carr, Andrew Massey.
p. cm. — (New horizons in public policy)
Includes bibliographical references and index.
1. European Union countries—Politics and government. 2. Public administration—European Union countries. 3. Policy sciences. I. Carr, Fergus. II. Massey, Andrew, 1958– . III. Series.
JN30.P932 2006
320.6094—dc22

2005055569

ISBN-13: 978 1 84376 813 5
ISBN-10: 1 84376 813 5

Printed and bound in Great Britain by MPG Books Ltd, Bodmin, Cornwall

Contents

PART IV POLICY SECTORS AND ISSUES

Contributors

Pamela Barnes is Principal Lecturer and Jean Monnet *ad personam* Chair in European Political Integration in the Department of Law, at the University of Lincoln, UK. Her current research interests include the implementation of environmental policy in the new member states, the regional impact of sustainable development policy, nuclear energy policy development in the enlarged EU and EU decision making in an increasingly diverse EU. She has co-authored several books including *Environmental Policy in the EU* with I.G. Barnes, published by Edward Elgar Publishing (hb 1999, pb 2000), and written articles on: enlargement and EU environmental policy; EU environmental management and audit legislation; the environmental impact of CAP reforms; the development of the EU's nuclear energy strategy, EU employment strategy, and EU institutional developments and decision making.

Dr Theresa Callan is Senior Lecturer in International Politics at the University of Portsmouth, UK. Her current research interests include the study of state and nation building in post-conflict societies and security after conflict. She has researched the decommissioning of armaments in the Balkans and Northern Ireland and is currently publishing the findings. Her recent publications include, with Fergus Carr, *Managing Conflict in the New Europe: the Role of International Institutions* (Palgrave, 2002).

Fergus Carr is Head of the School of Social, Historical and Literary Studies and Principal Lecturer in International Politics at the University of Portsmouth, UK. His research interests include the role of international institutions in the management of conflict, contemporary security studies and the external role of the European Union. He has published on NATO, public policy in Europe and British foreign policy. His recent publications include, with Theresa Callan, *Managing Conflict in the New Europe: the Role of International Institutions* (Palgrave, 2002).

Petr Drulák is Director of the Institute of International Relations in Prague. He has published on the theory of international relations, European integration and EU enlargement in a number of Czech and international publications including the *Journal of International Relations* *and Development*, and the *Journal of European Public Policy*. He is author of the first Czech textbook on the theory of international relations (2003). He was Jean Monnet Fellow at the European University Institute in Florence in 2003/2004.

Dr Paul Flenley is Principal Lecturer in Politics and Coordinator of European Studies Masters programmes at the University of Portsmouth, UK. His current research interests are Russia–EU/NATO relations, Russian national identity, and the early development of the Soviet state. He is an editor of the *Journal of Contemporary European Studies* and has edited several special issues, most recently in April 2005. He has published in the areas of Russian nationalism, foreign policy, the media and the Russian Revolution. Recent publications include: 'Nationalism and the National Question in the Soviet Union: Problems of Interpretation', *History Teaching Review Yearbook*, **16**, 2002, pp. 15–21; 'NATO and the Russian Federation: The Founding Act on Mutual Relations', with F. Carr, in the *Journal of Communist Studies and Transition Politics*, **15**, 1999, pp. 88–110; and 'Russia and the EU: A Pragmatic and Contradictory Relationship', *Perspectives on European Politics and Society*, **6** (3), 2005.

Wyn Grant is Professor of Politics at the University of Warwick, UK. He has published extensively in the fields of political economy and comparative public policy. His most recent books are (with William Coleman and Tim Josling) *Agriculture in the New Global Economy* (Edward Elgar, 2004) and (co-edited with Dominic Kelly) *The Politics of International Trade in the Twenty-First Century* (Palgrave, 2005).

Elspeth Guild is Professor of European Migration Law at the Raboud University of Nijmegen, The Netherlands and partner at the London law firm Kingsley Napley. She has researched widely on immigration and asylum in EU law; her most recent book is *Legal Elements of European Identity: EU Citizenship and Migration Law* (Kluwer Law International, The Hague, 2004). She is coordinating, for her university, a European Union Framework Six Project, CHALLENGE, which brings together 23 universities and institutes across the EU to examine the relationship of liberty and security after 11 September 2001 and 11 March 2004.

Dr Barbara Lippert is Deputy Director of the Institut für Europäische Politik, Berlin, managing editor of the quarterly journal *Integration* and Lecturer at Humboldt University, Berlin. Recent publications include: *The Pressure of Europeanization. From post-communist state administrations to normal players in the EU system* (co-author; Nomos Verlag, Baden-Baden, 2005); *Bilanz und Folgeprobleme der EU-Erweiterung* (editor; Nomos Verlag, Baden-Baden, 2004); 'European Politics of the Red-Green

Government: Deepening and Widening Continued', in Werner Reutter (ed.), *Germany on the Road to 'Normalcy: Policies and Politics of the Red-Green Federal Government (1998–2002)* (Palgrave, New York, 2004, pp. 235–52). Current research interests are: EU enlargement policy and its implications for the political system and policies of the EU; processes of transformation and integration in Central and Eastern Europe; European neighbourhood policy and relations with Eastern Europe; and Germany and European integration.

Mike Mannin is the Jean Monnet Chair in European Integration at Liverpool John Moores University, UK and is currently Loewenstein Research Fellow in Political Science at Amherst College. He has published in the fields of European Union, enlargement and monetary, and regional policy. He is presently researching the impact of EU membership on the structure and processes of British government and politics.

Andrew Massey is Professor of Government in the School of Social Historical and Literary Studies, University of Portsmouth, UK. His research interests are in the fields of public policy and public administration, with a special emphasis on reform and modernization. He has worked for several British government departments and is currently a member of a specialist panel on Global Governance for the International Institute for Administrative Sciences, Brussels. His recent publications include *Public Management and Modernization in Britain* with Robert Pyper (Palgrave, 2005); and *Decentralizing the Civil Service: from unitary state to differentiated polity in the United Kingdom*, with P. Carmichael, J. McMillan and R.A.W. Rhodes (Open University Press, 2003).

Dr Paul McVeigh is Senior Lecturer in International (Economic) Relations at the University of Portsmouth, UK. His publications include: 'Is Spain still different? The rise of neo-liberalism in Democratic Spain', in G. Menz, P. Cerny and S. Soederberg (eds), *Internalizing Globalization: the rise of Neo-Liberalism and the Decline of National Varieties of Capitalism* (Palgrave, 2006); 'Introduction' in D. Coates (ed.), *Economic and industrial performance and policy in Europe since the oil crisis* (Cheltenham, Edward Elgar, 1995); and 'Globalization and national economic strategy: the case of Spain', *Journal of European Area Studies*, **7** (1), 1999, pp. 73–90. His research interests include: globalization and neo-liberalism; convergence and divergence of national capitalisms; European economic integration; economic development; and global governance.

Graham Moon is Professor of Health Services Research at the University of Portsmouth, UK. He is a health geographer with current research interests in the geographies of health-related behaviour, primary health care and mental health. He has published five books and over 80 papers in leading journals and collections supported by research funding from the ESRC, the NHS and commercial sources. He is Founding Editor of the journal *Health and Place* and former Chair of the RGS–IBG Geography of Health Research Group. His recent publications include, with Nancy North, *Policy and Place: General Medical Practice in the UK*, Basingstoke, Macmillan, 2000).

Dr Paul Norman is a member of the Centre for European and International Studies Research, and the Postgraduate Programme Area Leader of the Institute of Criminal Justice Studies, University of Portsmouth, UK. His recent publications include: 'The United Nations and counter-terrorism after September 11: towards an assessment of the impact and prospects of counter-terror "spill-over" into international criminal justice cooperation', *Proceedings of the British Society of Criminology Conference 2004*, University of Portsmouth; and 'European Policing Strategies and Transnational Crime', in J. Sheptycki and A. Wardak (eds), *Transnational and Comparative Criminology* (Glasshouse Press, 1995). His current research interests include EU external relations and counter-terrorism after 11 September; terrorism, international security and the United Nations; and African regional criminal justice/counter-terrorism.

Dr Kay Peggs is Principal Lecturer in Sociology at the University of Portsmouth, UK and is a member of the Centre for European and International Studies Research. Her research interests include: pensions; financial planning and risk; and risk and relationship breakdown. Her published work on women, risk and pensions has appeared in the *Sociological Review* and *Research Policy and Planning*. Along with her colleague Richard Lampard she has published work on relationship breakdown in the *British Journal of Sociology*, and has a forthcoming book entitled *Identity and Repartnering after Separation*, to be published by Palgrave Macmillan. Her recent publications include: Kay Peggs and Mary Davies, 'Women's Perceptions of Contributing to a Pension', in Jay Ginn, Debra Street and Sara Arber (eds), *Women, Work and Pensions: International Issues and Prospects* (Milton Keynes, Open University Press, 2001); 'Which Pension?: Women, Risk and Pension Choice', *Sociological Review*, **48** (3), 2000, pp. 349–64; and 'Researching Women and Pensions: empowerment and sharing "expert" knowledge', *Research Policy and Planning*, **18** (3), 2000, pp. 3–12.

Frank Schimmelfennig is Professor of European Politics at the Swiss Federal Institute of Technology, Zürich. He is the author of *The EU, NATO and the Integration of Europe: Rules and Rhetoric* (Cambridge University Press, 2003) and co-editor with Ulrich Sedelmeier of *The Europeanization of Central and Eastern Europe* (Cornell University Press, 2005) and *The Politics* *of EU Enlargement. Theoretical Approaches* (Routledge, 2005). His work on the international politics and integration of Europe has appeared, *inter alia*, in *Comparative Political Studies*, the *European Journal of International Relations*, *International Organization*, the *Journal of Common Market Studies*, and the *Journal of European Public Policy*.

Acknowledgements

We would like to thank the Centre for European and International Studies at the University of Portsmouth, UK, under whose auspices research for this book was undertaken. Particular thanks go to Peter de Lara for technical assistance and Carolyn Carr and Lou Brand for all their help with the manuscript and its preparation.

Chapter 10 is reprinted with permission from Kluwer Law International © 2003, Elspeth Guild, 'International Terrorism and EU Immigration, Asylum and Borders Policy: The Unexpected Victims of 11 September 2001', *European Foreign Affairs Review*, **8** (3), 331–46.

Abbreviations

AC10	Estonia, Latvia, Lithuania, Poland, the Czech Republic, Hungary, Slovakia, Slovenia, Malta, Cyprus
ACP	African Caribbean and Pacific countries
CAP	Common Agricultural Policy
CE8	Central and Eastern European and Baltic states of Estonia, Latvia, Lithuania, Poland, the Czech Republic, Hungary, Slovakia, Slovenia
CEC	Commission of the European Communities
CEECs	Central and Eastern European countries
CFSP	Common Foreign and Security Policy
CIS	Commonwealth of Independent States
CMEA	Council for Mutual Economic Assistance
CO_2	carbon dioxide
COREPER	Committee of Permanent Representatives (of the EU)
CSCE	Conference on Security and Cooperation in Europe
EAP	Environment Action Programme
EC	European Community
ECHR	European Convention on Human Rights
ECCP	European Climate Change Programme
ECSC	European Coal and Steel Community
EC-T	Treaty on the European Community
ECx,	EC with a number of 'x' member states
EEA	European Environment Agency
EEB	European Environment Bureau
EFTA	European Free Trade Area
EMS	European Monetary System
EP	European Parliament
EPC	European Political Cooperation
ERDF	European Regional Development Fund
ESDP	European Security and Defence Policy
EU	European Union
EU15	Austria, Belgium, Denmark, Finland, France, Germany, Greece, Ireland, Italy, Luxemburg, the Netherlands, Portugal, Spain, Sweden, UK

EU25	EU-15 plus Estonia, Latvia, Lithuania, Poland, the Czech Republic, Hungary, Slovakia, Slovenia, Malta, Cyprus
G8	Group of Eight (most industrialized countries of the world)
GATT	General Agreement on Tariffs and Trade
GDP	gross domestic product
GNI	gross national income
ICC	International Criminal Court
IGC	Intergovernmental Conference
IMF	International Monetary Fund
IPPC	Integrated Pollution Prevention and Control
JHA	Justice and Home Affairs
MDG	Multi-Disciplinary Group (on Organized Crime)
MLG	Multi-level Governance
NACC	North Atlantic Cooperation Council
NATO	North Atlantic Treaty Organization
NGO	non-governmental organization
OECD	Organisation for Economic Cooperation and Development
OSCE	Organization for Security and Cooperation in Europe
PHARE	Poland and Hungary: Assistance for Economic Reconstruction
ProEuroJust	Provisional-Eurojust
QMV	Qualified Majority Voting
RandT	Research and Technology
SAPARD	Special Accession Programme on Agriculture and Rural Development
SDS	Sustainable Development Strategy
SEA	Single European Act
SF	Structural Funds
TACIS	Technical Assistance for the Commonwealth of Independent States
TCE	Treaty Establishing a Constitution for Europe
TEC	Treaty of the European Community
TEU	Treaty on European Union
UNFCC	United Nations Framework Convention on Climate Change
WCED	World Commission on Environment and Development
WEU	Western European Union
WSSD	World Summit on Sustainable Development
WTO	World Trade Organization

Introduction

Fergus Carr and Andrew Massey

In 1999 Edward Elgar published our *Public Policy in the New Europe: Eurogovernance in Theory and Practice*, which sought to analyse the institutions and processes of multi-level governance in Europe. The text addressed a number of theoretical approaches to European integration, government and governance followed by an empirical analysis of key policy areas in European politics. The primary focus of the book was the European Union (EU), although the wider Europe and the influence of the USA were acknowledged. The focus of this text, *Public Policy and the New European Agendas*, is similar to its predecessor but places a far greater emphasis upon Europe's new policy agendas. We see two key themes as of particular salience for policy makers: the enlargement of the European Union; and the place of Europe in international politics.

Enlargement challenges virtually all aspects of existing EU policy from agriculture to security. Enlargement does not just expand the single market but places new demands upon public policy developed for a constituency now eclipsed, as 15 member states have become 25. Reform is therefore predicated but carries its own challenges as the balance of interests inherent in existing policy provisions, for example, in agricultural subsidies or social welfare, has to be unpacked. This in turn leads to the questions of what reform programme Europe is going to adopt and the degree of liberalization that will be introduced into social and economic policy, and what models Europe will follow and how electorates perceive change. Enlargement also has implications for the *de facto* and *de jure* constitutional organization of the Union.

The rejection by the French and Dutch electorates in 2005 of the proposed European Constitution effectively ended its political viability, questioned the direction of the European project and its relevance to voters. The enlargement agenda is therefore far from concluded and has, in prospective Turkish membership, a highly contentious postscript.

The role of Europe in international politics is also a fundamental question for the Union, for its identity, and for its relationship with the USA. The degree to which the European project remains compatible with transatlanticism permeates debates on the development and institutional setting of defence and security policy in Europe. Approaches to security in the wider international system, epitomized by the 'war on terror', have also revealed divergences both within Europe, and between Europe and the USA. The war in Iraq divided 'old' and 'new' Europe over endorsement for the US strategy and revealed the constraints facing the European commitment to a Common Foreign and Security Policy (CFSP). At the same time Europe's counter-terrorism measures have largely been conducted in partnership with Washington in recognition of common threats. Beyond security policy the place of Europe in economic policy, development aid, environmental policy and human rights raises more questions about relations with Washington. Russia's role in the wider Europe and in relation to the USA also affects the EU. Moscow's impact is not as dramatic as in the Cold War but is still significant in policy sectors such as counter-terror, in international organizations such as the UN and in a developing raft of economic engagements.

This book has dedicated sections on enlargement and the place of Europe. The section devoted to enlargement has three chapters. It begins with Petr Drulák's study of enlargement through 'East European eyes'. The chapter examines the theories of enlargement and the motivation of the Central and Eastern European countries (CEECs) to join the EU. The transition process is shown to associate democratization with a 'return to Europe', although accession is revealed to be far from uncontested. The chapter details the impact of accession in different states and the intended and unintended aspects of Europeanization. Frank Schimmelfennig's chapter follows, providing a general analysis of the EU socialization process in Central and Eastern Europe. His study assesses the mechanisms and strategies the EU has used to promote its rules and examines their effectiveness. Three stages of the socialization process are identified and analysed: political conditionality; *acquis* conditionality; and finally the new member states' implementation of and compliance with *acquis* rules. Schimmelfennig points to the pattern of EU 'intergovernmental reinforcement by reward' and the critical importance of a 'credible membership perspective' for the export of norms. The Turkish case is considered in this context and linked to the variables of domestic politics. The pervasive nature of *acquis* conditionality is underlined but so too is its technical and élitist transfer. Conclusions are drawn about the overall nature of socialization and its prospects post conditionality.

Barbara Lippert concludes the section by analysing the political and constitutional implications of enlargement for existing and new members. The chapter provides an overview of past enlargement, treaty revision and the development of the European project. This analysis demonstrates that enlargement was neither the cause nor the key leverage to improve the governance capacities of the EU but has made reform more urgent and complicated. Lippert then turns to the institutions of the Community, examining the impact of enlargement upon the Commission, the Council/ European Council and the European Parliament. The final section of the chapter assesses the implications of enlargement for the budget and key policy areas including agriculture. The conclusion looks to the problematic future of enlargement and the Turkish case.

The section on the place of Europe also has three dedicated chapters. Fergus Carr and Theresa Callan examine the relationship of Europe and the USA in security and defence policy. The chapter analyses the erosion of transatlanticism in the post-Cold-War era, the development of EU security institutions and their relationship to NATO. It reviews the changing nature of security and contrasts European and US perspectives of threat and responses. The challenges of the new security environment from the Balkans to the Gulf are analysed and specific coverage given to the war against terror. The European divide with Washington over the invasion of Iraq, the role of the UN, and American willingness to pursue unilateral strategies are examined. The chapter is complemented by Paul McVeigh's analysis of European and US relations in trade, finance and development. The study begins by placing European integration within the broader context of the evolving international political economy. The degree to which the EU will develop as a 'counter and rival' to the USA is questioned. The potential modalities of the integration project as a 'European market', a 'Social Europe', a 'state-led' model and an 'Anglo-Saxon' model are compared and contrasted. They provide the basis for McVeigh's exploration of the reform agenda and its contemporary direction. The EU's external trade policy and relations with the US are also examined. The key features of Europe's development policy and relations with the developing world are reviewed. The chapter concludes with an analysis of the EU and global finance. In contrast to the first two chapters of the section, Paul Flenley looks beyond the EU to Russia's role. His chapter considers Russia's relations with Europe in the context of Moscow's overall foreign policy, especially with the USA. The post-Cold-War Yeltsin era in Russian policy forms the backdrop for an analysis of Putin's strategic reassessment. A particular emphasis is given to Russian responses to terrorism and the post-9/11 relationship with Washington and its domestic reception. A detailed examination of Russian relations with the EU concludes the chapter. Flenley argues that Putin's 'Westernism' marks a new pragmatism in Russian policy which reflects mutual interests and shared threats but also the Russian desire for sustained economic development.

Like its predecessor, *Public Policy and the New European Agendas* has a substantive section on specific policy areas. The majority of original chapters have been retained but updated, and, where relevant, include material on enlargement and/or Europe's external role. New chapters have been added to include material on agriculture, human rights, and pensions and ageing.

The policy section begins with Paul Norman's work on Justice and Home Affairs (JHA). Norman demonstrates that the impact of 9/11 and the EU adoption of counter-terrorism as a major policy objective constitute a significant turning point in the attainment of EU internal security objectives and their external projection. Following an analysis of third-pillar governance from 1993 to 2001, Norman details the scale and pace of change in European cooperation. His analysis reveals the links between JHA and CFSP and concludes with a study of external relations with Washington and Moscow. This chapter is complemented by Elspeth Guild's study of terrorism, EU immigration, asylum and borders policy. The chapter originally appeared in *European Foreign Affairs Review*, **8** (2003) and is reprinted here by kind permission of Kluwer Law International. Guild argues that there is no direct relationship between forced migrants, normally seen as asylum seekers or refugees, coming to Europe and the risk of terrorism in the EU. The impact of 9/11 was, however, to focus attention on borders. Security was increasingly perceived in a territorial framework. EU action in enhancing visa requirements, reinforcing border controls and working through third countries is shown to have hit migrants hard. Guild reviews the rights of migrants, the significance of the Geneva Convention and the provisions of the European Convention on Human Rights. Against this legal provision the association of terrorism with foreigners and the prevailing trend of forced migrants coming from Muslim countries is analysed. The chapter concludes with the observation that non-nationals of the state seeking to cross its borders inadvertently become the face of menace, and if they are from a Muslim country the threat is heightened.

The protection and promotion of human rights is the subject of Theresa Callan's chapter. It begins with an outline of human rights regimes at the systemic and the European level. The chapter then analyses the specific EU commitments to human rights integral to the enlargement process. Contemporary challenges to human rights, particularly the effects of fighting the war on terror, are then examined. In this analysis the role of the USA is given clear attention. The tension between the pursuit of security and the protection of rights is explored. The chapter concludes with a warning that counter-terrorist strategies can run the risk of undermining human rights and, therefore, become self-defeating.

While enlargement has implications for nearly all aspects of the EU, agriculture can be seen as a key sector. Wyn Grant examines current EU agricultural policy, the 2004 enlargement and the prospects for reform. He explains the 'productionist' philosophy of the Common Agricultural Policy (CAP) set up to reward farmers to increase production. Grant then looks at the disproportionate share of the EU budget consequently devoted to agricultural subsidies and the wider impact of CAP upon the developing world. He analyses past EU agricultural reforms, including the failure of 'Agenda 2000' to undertake radical action and agree a real annual reduction in subsidies. 'Optimistic' and 'pessimistic' interpretations of the current reform agenda are provided and the constraints, for example in a sector such as sugar production, analysed. The 2004 enlargement is reported to have added 4 million farmers to the EU's existing 7 million, some 38 million hectares of farmland but only a 6 per cent rise in the value of agricultural production. The potential costs of this enlarged CAP have not, Grant argues, produced the expected reforms. Instead the budgetary 'crunch' has been stalled by the accession countries receiving a lower subsidy than existing EU members until 2013. Grant concludes with analyses of future challenges to CAP. He provides studies of Hungarian and Polish agriculture under CAP and the potential impact, including environmental factors, on Europe.

Environmental concerns are the subject of Pamela Barnes's chapter. Environmental policy is shown to be highly Europeanized and the accession process an effective driver of national policies for new member states. Barnes reviews the extensive environmental *acquis* and the EU's Environmental Action Programmes. The EU commitment to sustainable development is assessed and the threats posed by climate change and global warming analysed. The EU's role in promoting global agreements is examined, as are the consequences of Washington's resistance to environmental measures such as Kyoto. The chapter then undertakes a substantive analysis of the impact of enlargement on EU environmental policy. The need for the accession states to be part of the policy process, the involvement of civil society and the qualities of national administrations are examined. The concluding analysis considers the overall consequences of enlargement, potential alliances among 'laggards' and 'leaders' and the overall probability of a slowing of the EU environmental dynamic.

Mike Mannin looks at the challenges confronting regional policy in the EU after enlargement. His analysis begins with a review of the objectives of EU regional policy (EURP), the constraints – political, financial and administrative – facing the reduction of disparities in regional economic performance and the role of structural funding as the main financial driver. The chapter outlines in detail the development of regional policy from principles in 1957 to a policy framework in the 1970s. The 1988 reforms and subsequent initiatives, policies and objectives are examined. The concept of 'cohesion' is unpacked and its relationship to the single market assessed. The components of Structural Funding policy are identified in depth and a comparative analysis of sub-state policy undertaken. Enlargement is then specifically considered and the scale of the task facing new member states in 'catching up'. The potential costs for EURP are depicted, linked to the budgetary implications of a non-reformed CAP and possible time scales for change in Central and Eastern Europe outlined.

The final two chapters of the book concern social policy. Graham Moon examines health policy and concentrates upon two issues: emergent diseases and tobacco. His chapter begins with an analysis of the EU role in health protection and its evolution from Maastricht to proposals in the draft constitution. The focus then turns to emergent diseases and the salience of public health matters given HIV/AIDS, SARS/Asian flu. Moon links public health to security concerns and the notion of outside 'threats' to Europe's well-being. Enlargement, he argues, has brought some of the 'outside' inside while migrants and asylum seekers 'threaten' by crossing borders. Moon also examines a second linkage of health and security – the threat of bio-terrorism. The formation of the Health Security Committee in 2001 and post-9/11 developments are reviewed. As the EU moves to a cross-sector approach in protection Moon tests its consistency with an analysis of the tobacco industry in Europe. The health effects of tobacco, the significance of consumption in Central and Eastern Europe and the tobacco lobby in Europe are analysed. The challenges facing the EU are assessed as the contradiction between economic and social priorities for policy makers is depicted.

Europe's demographic profile, with older people comprising an increasing proportion of the population, is the subject of Kay Peggs's chapter. Peggs traces how societal ageing has been allied with discourses of individual and collective risks. Concerns about the viability of pensions have led to worker and pensioner demonstrations in Europe and governments to change policy. Enlargement can be seen to have further exacerbated the situation, with additional ageing populations being supported by what are perceived as unsustainable pension systems. The chapter begins with an analysis of theoretical perspectives of risk associated with pensions and ageing. The study reveals how marketization and individual responsibility have been posed as a solution. The study then examines the nature of societal ageing in European member states. The combination of weak birth rates and declining mortality rates as sustained trends are shown to shape current and future demographic structures. Within this overall profile variations between states are examined and specific attention given to the ageing profile of the accession countries. The negative consequences for state provision of pensions, the main source of income for older people, are analysed and the implications of alternative occupational and private pensions for Europe's population are assessed. The limits of EU policy effectively leaves individual states responsible for pension provision. The prospect for reform is seen as problematic, with pensioners fearing change that seems to erode their benefits and states unable to sustain responsibly. In conclusion the chapter points to the presentation of ageing as a burden and the specific consequences for women, who make up the majority of older people.

The book is introduced by two chapters, one concerning the nature of public policy and the other, the place of Europe in the international system. Andrew Massey's study of public policy is designed to provide an analytical setting for the subsequent empirically based policy chapters. Massey's purpose is to provide a framework for understanding the making of policy in states that are subject to the focus of globalization, members of the European Union and international organizations. The chapter considers the relationship between domestic politics and government in this context. The approach adopted is to examine the utility of the concept of governance as a means to explain the process of governing in a multi-level political system and, as Massey terms the EU, a differentiated polity. The chapter analyses how a wide range of actors beyond the core executive are involved in the policy process, albeit in unequal measure. Policy networks inform this approach and Massey reveals the complexity of contemporary multi-level governance. This process of managing interdependence can be seen as inevitable but, as Massey argues, raises questions of democratic accountability. This leads to an analysis of the democratic deficit in the EU, of policy as a process remote from the citizen and without clear lines of accountability. The chapter looks at the nature of the Europeanization of policy, the specific consequences of regional management of interdependence and integration. The consequent impact of the EU on national administrations, domestic political systems and governments is examined. In the final section of the chapter attention is given to the importance of ethics to the public sector particularly in light of problems of democratic accountability. The conclusion warns of the dangers of contemporary governance: that European institutions may be perceived as authoritarian or politically irrelevant to citizens. The rejection of the draft European Constitution by the French and Dutch electorates in 2005 can be seen to be a case in point, underlining the need for reform in the management of governance.

The chapter 'Whither Europe?' investigates the place of Europe in the international system. Fergus Carr asks if the EU has an external influence commensurate with its economic base and what form of actor the Union constitutes. The chapter begins with a review of the breadth of EU external relations comprising pillar-one competencies in trade, finance and development and pillar-two provisions for a Common Foreign and Security

Policy (CFSP). The evolution of these roles is analysed and treaty revisions detailed. The constraints facing CFSP are discussed and illustrated with reference to Europe's response to the break-up of the former Yugoslavia and the crises in the Gulf. Enlargement is linked to the challenge of finding consensus in this intergovernmental framework. European security strategy is analysed and its linkages to development, human rights and 'good governance' explored. The role of enlargement in the stabilization of the European political space is discussed and the importance of new border regions beyond the accession countries identified.

The EU role in the Middle East is examined as a case study of external relations. EU motives to promote stability on its southern flank, ensure energy access, develop trade and address migratory pressures are identified and the process of engagement with the actors concerned, evaluated. A particular focus is given to EU relations with the Palestinians. The fate of EU policy in seeking to underpin and legitimize the peace process is examined under the post-9/11 conditions in the region. The impact of terrorism, the 'closure' of Palestinian territories and rising violence are seen to undermine a strategy based upon 'soft power' and the export of norms. EU policy after 9/11 and solidarity with the USA is examined. The erosion of transatlanticism as Washington pursued its 'axis of evil' agenda is discussed and European divisions over Iraq analysed. The schism of 'old and new' Europe is examined and the policy of the accession states outlined.

The chapter concludes with an examination of the role of the EU, the variable nature of Europeanization in foreign and security policy and the impact of institutionalism in this sector. Carr argues that CFSP has failed to eclipse national policy but member states have recognized that common strategies may be the only appropriate response to contemporary security challenges such as terrorism. The result is an actor uneven in performance, difficult to categorize but significant to third parties, not least in economic affairs.

Carr and Massey conclude the book seeking to draw out the implications of each chapter for Europe's new policy agendas and the overarching themes of the text.

PART I

Public Policy and the Place of Europe

1. Public policy and administration in Europe[1]

Andrew Massey

Today, political leaders throughout Europe are facing a real paradox. On the one hand, Europeans want them to find solutions to the major problems confronting our societies. On the other hand, people increasingly distrust institutions and politics or are simply not interested in them. (Commission of the European Communities, European Governance: a White Paper, 2001, p. 3)

'Now, what I want is, Facts. Teach these boys and girls nothing but Facts. Facts alone are wanted in life. Plant nothing else, and root out everything else. You can only form the minds of reasoning animals upon Facts: nothing else will ever be of any service to them. This is the principle on which I bring up my own children, and this is the principle on which I bring up these children. Stick to Facts, sir!' (Thomas Gradgrind, in Charles Dickens's *Hard Times* (1854), London: Hazel Watson)

The fictional Thomas Gradgrind represents a vivid portrayal of the positivistic approach to the pursuit of knowledge, a belief that reality exists and its laws and manifestations may be discovered through empirical observation and experimentation. It has long been recognized within social science, however, that 'pure' 'empirical knowledge of how institutions work is impossible and thus not very meaningful. It is *impossible* since the representation of empirical facts is always based on particular concerns, and assumptions' (Diez and Wiener, 2004, p. 4). It has become almost a cliché, therefore, to point out that 'facts' are understood and interpreted via the use of theory, that reality itself is socially, or theoretically, constructed (Berger and Luckman, 1967). There are at least three main functions of theory:

1. Theory as explanation or understanding; these seek to discover why and how things occur, they tend to be explanatory;
2. Theory as description and analysis; these approaches focus on the development of definitions and concepts with which to grasp particular developments, practices and institutions:

3. Theory as critique and normative intervention; these approaches either problematize a given development or seek to develop an alternative. (Diez and Wiener, 2004, p. 17)

Attempts to explain developments in the European policy process utilize each of these approaches. Indeed, the sophistication and multiplicity of theories attempting to explain the policy process in Europe is matched only by the complexity of policy making itself.

The approach taken by the other chapters in this book reflects the different perspectives of the authors, with those from a public administration/social policy background tending towards a more applied social science stance. At this juncture it is worth inserting the magisterial rebuke Philippe Schmitter reserves for many of the newer theories developed to explain European integration. He notes:

> Hardly a year passes without someone coming up with a new theory and, even more surprisingly, managing to convince a group of other scholars to produce a collective volume extolling its virtues. … Most of these 'novelties' turned out not to be theories at all, but just more or less elaborate languages for describing what the authors thought had taken place in the recent past – devoid of any discreet and falsifiable hypotheses about where the process might be heading in the future. (2004, p. 46)

Such 'theory-building' he sceptically describes as *déjà vu* all over again. Much that purports to be new is in fact a reworking of existing theory (where there is a theoretical basis for the analysis) and this theory is often rooted in neo-functionalism (ibid., pp. 43–75). In this chapter, indeed in this volume, it is generally approaches derived from a theoretical perspective (such as governance, which is essentially a bounded neo-pluralist approach – bounded in the sense of being restricted to élite actors within the polity) rather than new theories that are discussed.

In an earlier work we noted the different perspectives used to interpret developments in European integration and governance. This was attempted while seeking to explain the basis of the policy-making processes from the perspective of public policy and administration (Carr and Massey, 1999, pp. 27–42). The subsequent expansion of the academic corpus of work addressing these issues has kept pace with the explosion of EU and more general European policy initiatives and developments in the intervening years. To simply list them all would not aid understanding of the policy process, and to simplify them in an attenuated literature survey would not do justice to them.

It is intended that this will provide a useful link into the subsequent issue and policy chapters, providing a basic guide for readers in their understanding of the *facts*. While not trying to unduly simplify complex matters, in order to do justice to them, it should be noted that the European Commission is itself concerned about the opacity resulting from its activities and the subsequent lack of interest shown by the European citizenry in the Commission and European politics, a concern greatly exacerbated by the results of the vote on the proposed EU Constitution in France and the Netherlands in the summer of 2005. In response to this it has established a screening process aimed at simplifying over 170 directives and regulations in 20 policy sectors (Commission of the European Communities, 2003, p. 3). In the light of Schmitter's comment, reproduced above, an informed reader of European public policy may wonder if it is not time to establish a similar approach to the cornucopia of academic theories that abound. Whilst accepting that no single theory will suffice, rather the 'simultaneous presence of antithetic and conflictive ones' (Schmitter, 2004, p. 70), the sheer complexity of often transitory approaches seeking to explain small parts of the policy process may benefit by recognizing their theoretical roots. The study of European public policy is necessarily and properly a multidisciplinary one, and that means that we are often using different terms to mean the same thing. Wherever possible we need to recognize this and clarify the genuine connections as well as the genuine differences between the approaches taken.

Accordingly, in this chapter we attempt the more modest aim of defining and explaining the concept of 'governance'; placing this within a context of the 'differentiated polity', which is itself linked to notions of 'multi-level governance'; discussing the concept of 'Europeanization' as a form of 'modernization', before concluding with some brief observations on ethical and accountable policy making. This is done in order to set out a framework within which the understanding of public policy, as it is applied to the real problems and issues confronting Europe, may be understood. That said, readers should keep in mind the purpose of theory, as set out above, and Schmitter's warning about an abundance of novel theory.

THE CONCEPT OF GOVERNANCE

The term governance has become increasingly used in both official and academic publications. Although its usage in English may be traced back to 1399 and the English Wars of the Roses (Richards and Smith, 2002, p. 14), for the most part academic and practitioner discussions have addressed the respective roles of the governed and government, or the state and civil society. The concept of governance has evolved and entered general usage; it is a part of the intellectual currency as perceptions about the role of the state and notions of the limited role of governments to govern have developed. There are clear distinct national academic traditions that reflect the usage of the term, both between the Anglo-American and European traditions and within the European traditions (Wallace, 2003 cited in Jachtenfuchs and Kohler-Koch, 2004, p. 98).

In part this also reflects the contrasting approaches to the role of the state and civil society. The continental European tradition of public administration is one that sees it as existing largely for the purposes of the state, based upon a legalistic deductive approach to government (Stillman, 1999, p. 258). By contrast, the Anglo-American approach induces the state from public administration; it is a more institutionalist approach than the European one (Massey and Pyper, 2005). For the latter (non-Marxist) tradition, the concept of the state is itself problematic; writers within this perspective tend to discuss and analyse institutions and government, but not the state. For many continental European writers, public administration and its constituent institutions are the product of state direction and its activities are prescribed and limited within administrative law (Stillman, 1999, pp. 247–59; Massey, 1993; Price, 1983). The (non-social-democratic) Anglo-American tradition views the state as a necessary evil, something to be controlled and constrained; in this explanation there is a need to constantly seek ways to make government accountable and responsive to the citizenry. But one ought not to take this dichotomy too far; to do so would be to fall into the pit of normative theorizing. As the work of Rose has demonstrated, there is much in both traditions that borrows from the other and we need to retain sight of this vibrant, fuzzy reality (Rose, 2005).

Governments govern and governing may be seen to be

> The totality of interactions, in which public as well as private actors participate, aimed at solving societal problems or creating societal opportunities; attending to the institutions as contexts for these governing interactions; and establishing a normative foundation for all those activities. (Kooiman, 2003, p. 4)

This is a somewhat elastic definition, stretched from more traditional views. These may be summarized by arguing that

> We use the term 'government' to denote those core institutions of the state, that is, executive, legislative and judicial, that carry out the state's functions, which increasingly today may in fact be done through private and/or non-profit entities, yet ultimately serve the state's interest(s). (Kickert and Stillman, 1999, p. 15)

The study of government *per se* has traditionally had a strong political science and public administration perspective and includes the study of the machinery of government, local and regional government, public service staffing and public corporations, as well as an element of the differing theories of the state (Dunsire, 1973, p. 206).

Kooiman's definition and that of Kickert and Stillman recognize the limitations to the more traditional approach and prepare the way for a definition of 'governance', which for Kooiman may be considered 'as the totality of theoretical conceptions on governing' (2003, p. 4). But it may also be defined as

> a descriptive label that is used to highlight the changing nature of the policy process in recent decades. In particular it sensitizes us to the ever-increasing variety of terrains and actors involved in the making of public policy. Thus, governance demands that we consider all the actors and locations beyond the 'core executive' involved in the policy-making process. (Richards and Smith, 2002, p. 15)

'Governance', therefore, means the inclusion of civil society and the economic and social interests into the networks of government policy formulation and service delivery. Thus, 'governing' is what governments do, but 'governance' is an attempt to explain, describe and analyse the ways in which they do it. Given this explanation, it is clear why in different political traditions and theoretical perspectives the word 'governance' often has a somewhat different meaning when applied to the policy process. As with most things of a political nature, it is the context in which they are set that is important. The Mr Gradgrinds of this world may seek their 'facts', but the facts of public policy lie embedded within a cultural, historical, political and economic context.

The process of governing through governance, therefore, is complex. It is a complexity born of many parents. These include the fruits of globalization, new public management, new technologies and the remorseless remodelling of the structures of the state. These changes are wrought by the demands of consumerist societies and modernizing politicians; all are responding to the market logic of a world now bereft of the certainties previously engendered by the existence of the bi-polar ideological division that crumbled with the fall of the Soviet empire (Massey and Pyper, 2005; Gray, 2004). Furthermore, as Chapter 2 in this volume makes explicit, the events in New York and Washington during 11 September 2001 transformed the problems of modernization and globalization into a paradox; the paradox being that just as the triumph of liberal democracy appeared assured (Fukuyama, 1992), the atavistic forces of those opposed to modernization and all that it stands for provoked a continuing discourse about what it means to be liberal and about how the values of the West may be protected in a way that is in accord with notions of individual rights, due process and the rule of law (Gray, 2004).

Part of this debate must include a discussion about what we understand the concept of the 'nation-state' to mean, both within and outside of Europe. We discuss 'modernization' in a later section of this chapter, but it and governance exist within a context of multi-level governance and, along with other paradoxes of liberalism, modernization provides:

> The contradictory coexistence of universalisms of global economics and telecommunications and particularisms of different contemporary social movements, especially ethnic and religious ones, cause problems for modern states at the domestic level and international order at the interstate level. The modern nation-state, emerging in the nineteenth century as the fundamental unit to which domestic social, political and economic action is bound on the one hand and on the other hand as the primary actor in international relations, is no longer able to answer the challenges of globalization and localization. The changing nature of the nation-state amidst the globalizing features of contemporary politics is perhaps one of the most important aspects of 'post-modern' geopolitics. (Gruber, 2002, pp. 202–3)

While we may debate what is meant by 'post-modern' geopolitics, the point that Gruber makes regarding the complexities of understanding the role of the modern nation-state in its current global context is well made. Even the largest and most powerful states are now situated within a changing context of multi-level governance, which we now address.

MULTI-LEVEL AND DIFFERENTIATED GOVERNANCE

If governance represents the inclusion of civil society (including the economic, professional and social interest groups) into the networks of the policy process, that inclusion is not comprehensive and neither is it on an equal basis as some groups and networks are exclusive and/or dominant. That is, some groups exercise leadership, or hegemony, or they retain control over scarce or valuable resources such as knowledge, in the case of professional groups (for example lawyers and doctors), and the power to raise money through taxation, in the case of governments. The point is that these multifarious groups interact in a fluid, dynamic way that reflects their position in the policy process. This situation raises questions regarding the democratic legitimacy of some policies and the means by which both national governments and civil society may hold those involved in governance to account (Massey, 2005, pp. 3–17). The growth in the number and activities of non-governmental organizations (NGOs) is a particular issue here, especially when sovereignty and therefore effective (that is enforceable) law is located at the level of the nation-state, but the efficacy of national systems within a global context is at best variable. Smaller states and polities are often open to penetration of their policy process by larger states and powerful interest groups. These groups may be commercial, industrial, or indeed criminal.

A core concept of governance is the recognition that bureaucratized, that is hierarchical, centralized government is no longer the dominant method of organizing public administration. With the demise of

> old fashioned command systems has come a more pluralistic concept of power and service delivery. But although it may be pluralistic, it is not immune to being dominated by powerful coalitions of interests. This diversity and complexity is sometimes explained as the *differentiated polity*; or to use another expression, *governing without government*. (Massey, 2005, p. 6)

This perspective argues that the role of the state has been transformed into an enabling role whereby the purpose of government is to 'create the conditions in which other organizations, most notably those located in the private sector, can prosper' (Richards and Smith, 2002, p. 20). In other words:

> a nation's core executive is less able to depend upon giving orders to ensure the effective implementation of its policies, but must rely instead on diplomacy and negotiation to ensure it gets its way. States' membership of international organizations and their corresponding international commitments and obligations, has accelerated the dependency of governments across the globe upon these skills and underlined the interdependency of even global superpowers upon regional powers and also upon small nations (Rhodes, *et al*, 2003, pp. 23–35). Furthermore, this perspective recognizes the expansion and strengthening of the private sector, especially those NGOs and international corporations engaged in performing a role in the delivery of previously government-owned and run services; an example being the contracting by several governments of the US company EDS to deliver and run revenue and welfare software systems for government departments (Margetts, 1997, pp. 87–104; Dunleavy, 1997, pp. 16–46). Such relationships create interdependency, indeed dependency by governments upon internationally operating corporations for the delivery of their policies, where previously there was no such relationship. (Massey, 2005, p. 6)

It may be argued from these points that government and governance are multi-levelled and differentiated, with the location of sovereignty, power and legitimacy being a shifting, negotiated, multi-centred set of entities.

The differentiated polity perspective may be applied to a variety of political systems within the European (and broader international) community, with its emphasis on governance rather than government. It addresses issues of power dependence and exchange relationships within and between networks and the actors that comprise those networks. Policy networks are seen as a medium of policy making where there is a segmented, even fractured, executive (sometimes referred to as the 'hollowed-out' state) and intergovernmental relations are conducted with an emphasis on diplomacy and negotiation (Rhodes et al., 2003, pp. 151–67; Richards and Smith, 2002, p. 6). Multi-level governance exists in several forms in different contexts and is more than simply recognizing the fact of the limitations to national sovereignty. States voluntarily limit their sovereignty in a number of ways:

> and the notion of the differentiated polity recognizes the role of regional political organizations, devolution, federalism, professional groups, international corporations and other transnational organizations in governance. As a neutral model, it neither approves of this, nor disapproves of it; it simply draws attention to the reality of the situation. (Massey, 2005, p. 7)

In any discussion of how policies are made, implemented and evaluated within the modern European context, there needs to be recognition of the disparities of power, that is, the relative weakness of some nations (and groups of nations) to address wider issues. These issues may include crime, economic and social deprivation, health care issues and the problems of an ageing population, among others. But we need to recognize that multi-level governance

> takes place at the supranational level, both global and regional; the national level, where sovereignty remains legally located, but from which much has migrated, and at the sub national level. Through policy networks powerful actors criss-cross the interstices that comprise the gaps around and between these levels and it is often difficult to track them, let alone to hold them to account. (Massey, 2005, p. 7)

It is the notion of *accountable* government that is at the core of democratic government, the notion that public officials must account for their actions and be accountable in the sense that they must provide for the redress of legitimate grievance. In order for this to take place there needs to be an effective culture of political legitimacy, and this has traditionally been contingent upon national sovereignty: the ability of governments to exercise power in a geographically defined area and for them to be held to account for their actions therein.

At the global level, or beyond the level of pure national sovereignty, there has been a focus on

> examining the evolving mechanisms of political coordination among states and private agencies that seek to resolve collective problems or realize common or complementary interests in an era of globalization (Held and McGrew, 2002a).

> Advocates of global governance contend that its domain includes states, international governmental organizations (IGOs), multinational corporations (MNCs), and international nongovernmental organizations (INGOs) – all of which seek to advance common international activities through regulation (Cutler, 1999; Held and McGrew, 2002b). Global governance marks the acceptance of regulations at the global level out of a conviction that such regulations will enable actors to seek wealth in an orderly fashion and in accordance with the norms of the international system. (Halabi, 2004, p. 21)

In this perspective global governance as an attempt to 'manipulate the forces of globalization' in order to 'mitigate globalization's negative effects, and privilege states that follow global rules' and globalizations effects and long-term consequences 'are often beyond the control of states that can merely react to them' (ibid., p. 23).

For most states globalization is something external: it happens to them and they are affected by it. The gradual development of global governance is an attempt to deal with the challenges raised by globalization through a series of mechanisms to govern and mediate its impact, to coordinate 'among various local and global actors (states, MNCs, INGOs and so on)' (Halabi, 2004, p. 23, quoted in Massey, 2005, p. 8). It is something

> internalized by states both individually, through their adherence to new rules, regulations and laws, and collectively, through the adoption of these new rules together as a concerted and coordinated attempt to deal with the issues of globalization; global governance thereby being intentionally created to address the impact of the unintended and often unforeseen consequences of globalization.

As such it may be seen to have a close approximation to the process of Europeanization addressed in the next section of this chapter; indeed Europeanization is itself fuelled by globalization and may be considered a regional variant of it.

National governments are wary of losing their ability to control the policy process within their own borders, but this is precisely what has happened to an accelerating extent. Governments have responded by reforming the intergovernmental organizations responsible for dealing with the more prominent policy areas such as the World Trade Organization and the World Bank, as well as the (regional) institutions of the European Union, among others (Halibi, 2004, p. 25; Howse and Nicolaidis, 2003). But the erosion of states', or more precisely, national governments' ability to control the policy process has

> made policy coordination among states an important but difficult task. Decision-makers and even bureaucrats are in many ways unqualified to cope with the range of problems. Moreover, some global concerns such as those of global warming,

> HIV/AIDS, and contagious financial crises are affecting domestic politics. Much of this political void has been filled by INGOs, each specializing in one issue area and consulting with states on strategies for coping with that set of concerns. The elevation of INGOs to this prominent role in world affairs has often been referred to as the creation of a global civil society (Lipschutz, 1996). (Halabi, 2004, pp. 24–5)

There remains an obvious problem, however, sometimes referred to as a 'democratic deficit', but it could also be seen as a crisis of popular citizen confidence in terms of holding to account the policy makers in national and international/supranational institutions.

Attempts to address this issue have been tried through the institutional reform of international organizations *per se* (Howse and Nicolaidis, 2003), and through efforts to develop global civic society in order to nurture good governance. Examples of attempts to define what is meant by the term 'global civic society' are provided by, among others, Omelicheva. Most such definitions are really descriptive lists of traits or actors. Omelicheva's descriptive definition makes it a useful tool for understanding the institutions, issues and civil society actors involved. She argues

> that global civil does not have territorial boundaries in the way states do, but operates globally through NGOs and complex networks of civil society actors and institutions. 'Global civil society is composed of various interacting units that are often referred to as "agents" or "actors"', but it is neither defined by international law nor given a legal status (Omelicheva, 2004, p. 5). She specifically excludes those institutions created by intergovernmental treaty from the realm of civil society, but this is perhaps an area open for debate. (Massey, 2005, p. 8)

Taking these points into account, Omelicheva argues global civil society actors may be considered to be:

1. non-governmental, i.e., institutionally separate from the system of states, uncontrolled by a governmental entity, and not established by an intergovernmental agreement;
2. not-for-profit, meaning that profit making plays a secondary and subsidiary role in a spectrum of activities of global civil society organizations; and profits received from commercial activities are not distributed for the benefit of the members, boards, staff or shareholders;
3. voluntary, i.e., the human and material resources come from voluntary contributions of time and money, membership is not legally required, and the members can leave the organization at any time;
4. having some institutional presence and structure expressed through the relative persistence of goals, activities, and/or a legal charter (bylaws, a

> written constitution etc.,) that demonstrate intent of (the) organization to continue in existence. (2004, p. 6)

This definition, or perspective, of what we mean by global civil society is the one that locates the actors within the wider policy process and the institutions of governance.

Global civil society clearly developed partly as a response to the imposition of the liberal economic agenda following the fall of the communist bloc of the former Soviet Union and its satellites. The resulting social and economic dislocation in more vulnerable societies

> meant that their governments were unable to supply vital health, education and welfare functions and 'civil society actors came forward to take over the functions reserved for the states and to advocate for harnessing processes of globalization by placing checks and controls on the global market' by seeking to introduce good governance in the form of 'accountability, transparency and democracy on the global scale' (2004, pp. 6–7). Organizations that must be included in these activities, however, include UNHCR and a welter of EU initiatives, suggesting that we are witnessing something more akin to Rhodes' version of the differentiated polity and multi-level governance. (Massey, 2005, p. 9)

In order to understand the impact of this on policy making in democratic societies, it is necessary to explore individual policy areas, and that is the important contribution supplied by the policy case study chapters in the rest of this book.

'MODERNIZATION' OR REFITTING?

Whilst all Western governments seek to portray themselves as modern, in Europe this concept is located within the context of the 'Europeanization' of European governance. It is

> a process that impacts upon members of the European Union and those aspiring to join, as well as other states that may be said to be affected by what some analysts have argued amounts to a form of international socialization (Schimmelfenig, 2000). An understanding of modernization, then, must take cognisance of developments in public administration and an understanding of the modernization of public sector institutions within contemporary Europe requires the concept and process of *Europeanization* be addressed. (Massey, 2003, pp. 59–60)

As Chapters 1 and 6 in this book show clearly, the Europeanization of governmental and quasi-governmental institutions aligned to or part of governance policy networks has its roots in the post-Cold-War global economic liberalism that is outstripping the political capacity of states adequately to deal with its consequences. In Europe this is referred to as Europeanization and it reflects (as noted in a preceding section) the European (but not British) perspective of the existence of public administration as emanating from reasons of state (Stillman, 1999, p. 258). The Anglo-American approach, by inducing the state from public administration, is a more institutional and institutionalist approach than the European one based as it is upon a corpus of administrative law (Stillman, 1999, pp. 247–59; Massey, 1993; Price, 1983). Despite the different British and continental European traditions, there is a convergence in the policy-making and institutional decision-making structures and procedures.

As we have noted elsewhere, though now largely out of fashion the functionalists and neo-functionalists of the 1950s and 1960s performed a useful analytical role when their analysis was deployed to describe and make sense of the evolving structures in Western Europe, especially those of the young European Communities (Adshead, 2002; Chryssochoou, 1999; 2001). In other words, as a descriptive tool of analysis, indeed a stylized map of the political and administrative terrain, their approach assisted understanding of the political processes at work (Massey, 2003, pp. 62–3). Neofunctionalism is sometimes wrongly associated with the gradualist approach to European unity adopted by Monnet and his successors, a kind of 'functionalist federalism' (Chryssochoou, 2001, p. 53). Neofunctionalism adopts an abstract conception of politics and sees it as an inherently conflictual process in terms of allocating values in the community. It may be seen that there is throughout this perspective an administrative flavour to the political process: institutions are established to advance the political goals of a federal, integrative and politically élitist process (ibid.). Both here and within the intergovernmentalist perspective may be found the infamous democratic deficit of the EU, a deficit neofunctionalism not only does little to address, but would also actually perceive as a necessary price for European integration (Massey, 2003, pp. 63–4). It is this politically élitist view that has come in for so much criticism in recent years.

Indeed, the neofunctionalists went further than this and advocated

> a deepening of the elite socialization, 'the process by which influential actors of policy- and decision-making from different national settings learn to work with each other within a larger management setting' (Chryssochoou, 2001, p. 54). Such an approach engendered criticism from various observers for its 'supranationally biased image of Community arrangements and dynamics, (and) underestimating the role of "summit diplomacy" in putting together complex package deals', it also generally overestimated the importance of the Commission and other supranational institutions and institutional actors (Chryssochoou, 2001, p. 57). (Massey, 2003, p. 63)

By the late 1990s, theory building had advanced to take account of these realities and included the construction of elaborate theories of 'confederal consociation', the belief that the EU is best understood as

> a compound polity whose distinct culturally defined and politically organized units are bound together in a consensually pre-arranged form of union for specific purposes, without either losing their national identity or resigning their individual sovereignty to a higher authority. (Chryssochoou, 1999, p. 25)

It is this intergovernmentalist approach, replete with several varieties, that has found most favour with analysts. It may be further refined to state 'the distribution of preferences and the conduct of bargaining among the governments of the member states broadly explain the nature, pace and scope of integration (Sandholtz and Stone Sweet, 1998, p. 3, quoted in Massey, 2003, p. 64).

The development of the concept of Europeanization reflects the sheer complexity of supranational governance in the EU and the global situation in general. For example, the World Trade Organization and a host of international NGOs are organizations designed to bring a measure of order and predictability to global governance. Within the EU

> the nature and extent of supranational governance varies along a number of dimensions. In some sectors, the competence to govern is held exclusively by the Community; in others, national institutions are the primary sites of policymaking; and in many domains, the transfer of power from the national to the supranational level has been only partial. Within the same policy sector, the answer to the question 'who governs?' has changed over time. And in those areas in which (EU) institutions have become sites of policy innovation and change, one finds variation in the relative capacity of the member state governments. (Sandholtz and Stone Sweet, 1998, p. 4, quoted in Massey, 2003, pp. 63–4)

It may be argued that at its grandest Europeanization resurrects some of the neofunctionalist dynamic for supranationalism through institutional integration (with EU law as represented through the Union's own court (and national courts' compliance) being a key element (Stone Sweet, 2000)). Europeanization, through European (supranational) integration

> is the process by which the EC (EU) gradually but comprehensively replaces the nation-state in all of its functions … (rejecting) … the comparative statics of intergovernmentalists as a mode of analysis incapable of capturing crucial temporal elements of European integration. … The expansion of transnational exchange, and the associated push to substitute supranational for national rules, generates pressure on the EC's organizations to act. ... [EU] organizations, such as the Commission and the Court, respond to this pressure by working to extend

> the domain of supranational rules, in order to achieve collective (transnational) gains. (Sandholtz and Stone Sweet, 1998, p. 4, quoted in Massey, 2003, p. 64)

We can see this in action across a range of strategic policy areas, such as competition policy (Dunford et al., 2001), the Common Agricultural Policy (Tarditi and Zanias, 2001) and structural policies (Mairate and Hall, 2001) and as outlined in the case study chapters in this volume. But it is also apparent in more low-level areas such as the toy directive, the machine directive, and directives and rules on medical devices and construction products, which impose common European standards and regulations in these arcane fields (Egan, 2001).

Despite the wry warning by Schmitter, with which we began this chapter, academics developing theoretical and empirical work on Europeanization have evolved a range of definitions to take into account the supranational nature of the policy process and its impact on domestic structures. Yet we may state it simply as a 'situation where distinct modes of European governance have transformed aspects of domestic politics' (Buller and Gamble, 2002, p. 17). This most closely reflects the reality of the policy process in the supranational polity and is as good a place to start as any. Governance in this usage is the process of governing which brings about conditions for ordered rule and collective action (ibid., p. 18). This definition allows a linkage to Stone Sweet and Sandholtz's attempt to create a general theory of supranational governance and takes account of the impact of institutional changes designed to accelerate the demise of national institutions at odds with the integration programme in the Treaties of Rome, Maastricht and Amsterdam. It also, crucially, defines Europeanization

> not as a process, but as a situation, 'where certain effects can be shown to have occurred' (Buller and Gamble, 2002, p. 17). An implication of this is not that Europeanization is inevitable, but is contingent upon social, political and economic interactions, while giving 'analytical primacy to the impact of European developments at the domestic level' (Buller and Gamble, 2002, p. 18). Thus, 'in its crudest sense, Europeanization [is used] to denote a condition of becoming "like Europe"' and the term implies change or transformation in domestic politics and institutions that may be 'through "positive", "negative", or "framing" integration' (Buller and Gamble, 2002, p. 18). (Massey, 2003, pp. 64–5)

Europeanization therefore impacts upon and takes place at several levels to induce the 'modernization' of Europe, both of EU members and others in the region. It does this at the level of supranational integration and that of a domestic transformative dynamic. It may be explained by noting that

> as transnational exchange rises in any specific domain (or cluster of related domains), so do the costs, for the governments, of maintaining disparate national

> rules. As these costs rise, so do the incentives for governments to adjust their policy positions in ways that favour the expansion of supranational governance. Once fixed in a given domain, European rules – such as relevant treaty provisions, secondary legislation, and the ECJ's case law – generate a self-sustaining dynamic, that leads to the gradual deepening of integration in that sector and, not uncommonly, to spillovers into other sectors (Stone Sweet and Sandholtz, 1998, p. 5). (Massey, 2003, p. 65)

Examples include monetary union, regional policy, and the development of civil nuclear fusion technology (Massey, 1999).

At the global level environmental law (Wildavsky, 1995; Spragia, 1998) and world trade and consumer legislation illustrate similar incentives to supranational rules. In the European context, the domestic impact of modernization is institutionally

> greater because of the existence of more (and more binding) treaty obligations and the corresponding incentives to conform and comply. 'In a fundamental sense, governments are reactive, constantly adjusting to the integration that is going on all around them' (Stone Sweet and Sandholtz, 1998, p. 12). Europeanization is often a fundamental constituent of analyses that argue the power of national governments and the nation state are being hollowed out and transferred up to supranational institutions and down to the regions (Rhodes, 1994; Rhodes, Carmichael, McMillan and Massey, 2003). But there is no reason, as Stone Sweet and Sandholtz strongly imply (1998 pp. 5–12), why intergovernmental approaches such as Moravcsik's (1991; 1993) are in conflict with this view of Europeanization. Indeed, intergovernmental approaches may be seen as a sub-set of the institutionalist approach adopted in supranationalism. (Massey, 2003, p. 66)

Integration varies over time, place and policy area and may rely as much on intergovernmental diplomacy and multi-level governance as on grand treaties, and all approaches appear as likely or unlikely to succeed in different times and different contexts and all 'are as evasive of the control of individual national governments' (ibid.).

Lodge (2002, pp. 48–9) identifies four dynamics to the Europeanization of the policy process:

1. Coercive triggers. These include at least three subsets; requirements to comply with European legislation; rulings by the European Court of Justice; European Commission executive acts.
2. Mimetic triggers. There are two sub-sets within this group; increased interaction among civil servants leading to the adoption of 'best-practice'; national co-ordination networks through things like peer-group review for the implementation of EU employment policy and monetary policy, among other fields.

3. Professionalization as a trigger. The two sub-sets here include policy networks as part of the transnationalization of societal actors leading to the 'logic of exchange' in areas such as regulatory agencies for telecommunications; the emergence of policy communities, following on from the work of Sabatier (1988).
4. Domestic politics as a trigger. There are three sub-sets here, which include strategic competitive adjustment, whereby domestic institutions and regulations are adjusted to comply with European standards to ensure protection of domestic markets. Secondly there is the way Europeanization shapes domestic policy opportunities through legitimizing particular policy beliefs and options. Finally, domestic triggers are found in the lobbying of élite groups to force the adjustment of domestic laws, regulations and institutions to the European model in order to ensure access to resources and the global 'playing field'. (Quoted in Massey, 2003, p. 66)

A review of the implementation of regulatory reform in various EU jurisdictions, including Britain, illustrates all these triggers in action and what constitutes integration or Europeanization activity differs according to a complex constellation of factors (Lodge, 2002, pp. 48–60). For example:

> in Sweden's case, it was the desire of that country's political and economic elite to join the EU that led to major reforms of its public administration (Lodge, 2002, pp. 58–60). In other words it was change engendered by the domestic elite in anticipation of what was required for entry that was the dynamic, a process being repeated by each tranche of aspirant nations. (Massey, 2003, p. 67)

It may be argued, then, that the practical impact of Europeanization is a process of federalizing and we also need to recognize the temporal aspect of Europeanization. In other words, address what the entity is becoming and how space for national decision making is being compressed chronologically as well as institutionally (Ekengren, 2002). But the problem with any federal system is that it is a compromise between the centralizers and the devolutionists; each official will have an allegiance somewhere and it may not always be where governments would wish. For example, the devolution that has occurred in the UK

> has created separate institutions for Wales, Scotland and Northern Ireland and it is clear the allegiance of officials in those countries has markedly shifted away from London (Rhodes, Carmichael, McMillan and Massey, 2003). Indeed, devolution combined with Europeanization has conspired to bypass the 'heart' of national government in London for the devolved countries to an extent that calls into question the continued ability of national government to perform its

> traditional role. This is a pattern repeated elsewhere and represents modernization as Europeanization. (Massey, 2003, p. 67)

Whilst institutions are changed through Europeanization, it is the changing of the governance 'software' of a country that has a greater impact on the policy process. That is, Europeanization changes domestic beliefs and expectations. Even the language and comprehension of governance, and a nation's policy-making timetable, are structured by the EU in that the EU's meetings and directives structure domestic policy making: the concept of 'European competence', and the need for European education and socialization, are all implicit in national public administrations (Ekengren, 2002, pp. 3–60). It may be seen that

> the daily reality for the national policy-makers of member states is a European one (Greenwood, Pyper and Wilson, 2002, pp. 186–192). Elected ministers spend a large proportion of their time shuttling to and from meetings in Brussels deliberating and negotiating with EU Commissioners and fellow ministers from other states, all national policy decisions are benchmarked against EU law and policy (Egan, 2001; Hall, Smith and Tsoukalis, 2001). All member governments and administrations are 'severely constrained by policy outputs from the EU system' (Greenwood, Pyper and Wilson, 2002, p. 189). ... Even when new institutions themselves are not created as a specific result of EU measures, the existing institutional actors have had their behaviour substantially modified by the EU reality. It is a continuing example of new wine in old bottles. (Massey, 2003, p. 68)

Given these points, returned to frequently in one guise or another in the case study chapters of this volume, it may be argued that aspects of the modernization process have run ahead of the institutionalization of democratic accountability.

Thus

> officials at all levels have their lives structured by this reality, in taking into account EU rules and practice. With regard to the environment, for example, everything from the environmental impact of a new power station to the application of building regulations in individual cases of privately owned dwellings are located within their EU context. From national treasuries to local town halls, officials are influenced, guided and constrained by the Europeanization of public administration in the way in which they carry out their duties. To neglect this reality is to risk the invocation of the judicial review of a decision and it is here through the juridicalization of public administration, government by judges, that the imposition of Europeanization is keenly felt (Stone Sweet, 2000). Officials modify their behaviour to avoid the risk of such judicial review, ensuring that even when the EU's laws and doctrine are not being explicitly applied, their application is nonetheless omnipresent. (Massey, 2003, p. 70)

The problems encountered by member states in attempting to obtain the consent of their citizens to the ratification of the EU Constitution, and singularly failing to do so in several cases, do not reflect a simple mistrust of the EU, a misunderstanding of the EU or even a sense of anomie. The problems reflect all these things and very much more: a complexity of citizen response to reflect the complexity of the EU. But clearly those who disapprove of the Constitution on the grounds that it advances the process of European integration, of federalism, have missed the point. That process has already advanced to the extent that the EU is a functioning political entity in its own right. National politics take place within that context and the EU's Constitution would merely have recognized what has become a political, administrative and legal reality. Politics within the EU and indeed within Europe is now Europeanized.

SOME OBSERVATIONS REGARDING ETHICS AND ACCOUNTABILITY

This section can be no more than a brief 'nod' towards the broad corpus of work on public sector ethics, drawing attention to some of the salient points of importance for understanding the policy process in Europe. One way in which governments and EU bodies are seeking to address the democratic deficit inherent to 'governance' is through the imposition of 'ethics' in the public sector, often via a new regulatory (or oversight) framework. This new 'ethical' approach, or perhaps it should be termed a new approach to ethics, is part of the modernization process. Work on public sector ethics is produced from several perspectives and is therefore a growing and innovative contribution to understanding the policy process. There is not room to go into detail in this chapter, but it is important to note the impact upon issues of accountability from a public sector ethics perspective. The notion of an accountable public sector, accountable that is to civil society and its citizens, is intrinsic to broader notions of democracy and is in turn partly realized through the particular notion of a public service ethic and public sector ethics (the two terms are used here interchangeably, although that is not always the case in some parts of the literature) (Plant, 2003; Salway, 2001).

In one sense and again as a result of the process of political 'modernization', the epistemology of ethics is becoming far reaching, with the word becoming a commonplace suffix, for example to 'business', 'professional', 'medical' and so forth. The significant expansion across Europe (and elsewhere) of the engagement of the private sector in the delivery of public services, however, has given rise to some alarm that these increasingly embedded developments could in some way 'erode the public sector's service ethics and ethos' always supposing that such a thing exists (Plant, 2003, p. 560). The imposition by governments of a regime of 'ethical' dimensions and targets to the policy process for institutions is a way they have sought to address this.

The concept of a public service ethic, allied to ethical behaviour, has its roots in the development of US and European public administrations throughout the nineteenth century, and is closely linked to the (modern) rise of the professions and the delivery of services often mediated through those professions and guided by their adherence to a code of professional ethics; indeed the very term 'service' denotes that the products, the outputs, of the state are deemed to be different to those of commerce and industry (Plant, 2003, p. 561; Massey, 1988). The concepts have always been and remain deeply contested, if not within individual states, then certainly 'across' them, reflecting the different approaches to the concept of the state as discussed in the preceding sections. The concepts of a public good, a public interest and a notion of public service may be traced via Hegel's *The Philosophy of the Right*, back to Plato's Guardians and the belief that the state is a body with a moral purpose (Plant, 2003, pp. 561–2). A summary of the arguments for this perspective, as set out by Plant, distils the characteristics of the traditional public service ethic to be:

1. Motivation: people enter public service to 'do good' or to serve their community, not to advance their individual wealth or position.
2. Professionalism: again, this is linked to motivation and is sometimes referred to as a 'vocation'; the individual is guided by a set of professional values and ethics.
3. Trust: trust is essential for the proper accountability of public officials; they must be trustworthy and the citizenry must be able to endow them with their trust. This is because an effective public sector embodies a degree of political agreement to provide a set of services funded from taxation; thus those involved in the delivery of those services have to be trusted to do so without self-interest and must reflect broader social and community values to do so. This trust extends further than simply trustworthiness, in that the citizens must be able to trust the state's officials, but so must the government and policy makers generally. As the strategic policy setters for a society, governments must trust that their instructions are lawfully and faithfully carried out. There must also, in this age of governance, be trust between the different partners within the public sector and between the public and private sectors.
4. Impartiality: a part of trust, this notion implies that officials will behave without a personal or sectional interest, that is without bias. It is a central tenet of the rule of law.

5. Judgement: this last element, Plant argues, is to fill the gap between a rule and its application; the officials should apply judgement, or rather good judgement, and act in a just way in order to maximize the public good (summarizing Plant, 2003, pp. 564–5).

If the public sector is believed to emphasize these traits, or at least to aspire to them, then it follows that it is distinguished from the private sector or the world of commerce and business, where profit, partiality and self-interest are the motivating forces.

To collude in this simple dichotomy would be to set up a straw man and ignore the substantial body of work of the New Right and Public Choice theorists and would therefore be foolish (Buchanan, 1999; Massey, 1993; Plant, 2003, pp. 569–70). The reality is far more complex than the traditional perspective in that there is a multiplicity of motivations for people to seek work in the public sector, and trust, as implied in contracts, remains as it has been since ancient times an essential ingredient of private contracts. Indeed, in many professions such as law and medicine the primary mode of employment is a private contractual agreement between the professional and the client, whether that client is an individual or a state institution purchasing a service on behalf of society. The nature of the public service ethic and public sector ethics, then, must often lie in a difference of emphasis on outputs (in terms of the honest, efficient, timely, accountable and impartial delivery of services) as well as the 'inputs' that go into providing that service in the form of professional ethics and the other traits identified by Plant. When the Public Choice perspective is added to the mix, we can also see the importance of including institutional, indeed legal, mechanisms for constraining bureaucratic and political self-interest, as a way of shoring up the ethical imperative. The problem for European civic society is in identifying the location for these entities if the process of Europeanization and the reality of government through governance mean that multi-level governance is the new political norm. The growth of the voluntary sector and NGOs further complicates the process of identifying where responsibility within the policy process lies (European Policy Forum, 2003; Plant, 2003, pp. 566–7).

Plant begins to address these issues when he argues that the notion of trust be mitigated down into one of confidence, given that civic society cannot really know if an institution is trustworthy or, given the Public Choice critique, if bureaucrats are entirely (or largely) self-interested (Plant, 2003, pp. 578–9). The belief that we should move to an entirely contractual state (or states) with governments setting the standards and then contracting for delivery within a budget misses the very real differences between the public and private sectors (Massey, 1993) and overlooks the deep flaws within the Public Choice perspective (Plant, 2003, p. 579; Hay, 2004). But trust can only really function on a more personal and narrowly focused level; thus Plant's concept of seeking broad confidence in the institutions and officials that comprise the state is a useful way to proceed in order to understand what is meant by a new public service ethic; it has to be a public sector, and a process of governance, that inspires confidence. That must mean confidence in its ability to deliver services to civil society in an honest, transparent, efficient, timely and accountable manner, and it is precisely the lack of popular belief in this, partly for reasons outlined in the previous sections, that the system of governance engendered by the process of Europeanization suffers a crisis of confidence.

In groping for a remedy to these ills, there is a growing recognition of the need to develop both value-based ethics and rule- (or law-)based ethics. That means in order to inspire and build civic confidence (especially in Europe) there is a need to ensure there is a moral imperative through codes of ethics and the effective training of individuals. The development and production of professionals imbued with a sense of public service, and the training and continuing professional education and development of officials are central to this goal. Alongside this is the need for rule-based ethics; this is achieved through the implementation of a regulatory and audit framework, a legal basis of oversight and reporting that results in wrong-doing being detected, the perpetrators punished and grievances redressed in a transparent and timely manner. Both approaches ought to take place to a greater or lesser extent (depending on circumstances) alongside each other and the increased marketization of government services, which provides a competitive alternative to the employment of state officials for the provision of public goods. An example of where just such an approach has been attempted, albeit with some mixed success, is the Public Sector Management and Employment Act in Victoria, Australia, although given that this takes place in one sparsely populated state in the Commonwealth of Australia, which is based upon the British Westminster style model of government, this example has a limited (but none the less useful) applicability for the EU (Salway, 2001).

The Australian example has limited applicability as it is taken from a largely politically homogeneous entity. Indeed, although the work of Haynes and Melville Jones demonstrates that in the 1980s the states of Queensland and Western Australia went through 'an ethical Dark Age', with a significant number of major political and business scandals (1999, p. 70), the point here is that all concerned knew they were doing wrong and tried to cover it up. Often behaviour considered reprehensible in some regions of Europe is 'business as usual' elsewhere. The limitation to Plant's concept of confidence begins when we explore the common application of laws, norms and rules:

there is little evidence to suggest it takes place, rather the contrary is the experience of observers. The difficulties experienced by European countries lie with their heterogeneity; the sheer diversity of polities from ancient kingdoms to recent constructs new to democracy provides the hurdles to a common appreciation or understanding of an uncontested perspective of ethical behaviour. There is no concept, beyond a mere statement of intent from time to time in various treaties and Council minutes, of what is meant by a shared ethical climate, that is what Maesschalck (quoting Victor and Cullen) refers to as the 'shared perceptions of what is ethically correct behaviour and how ethical issues should be handled' (2004, p. 2). The fall of the Santer Commission and the findings of the subsequent investigations, reviews and reports (Massey, 2003) provides eloquent testament to the lack of a shared ethical climate. A comprehensively shared climate, where (or should) it exist(s), includes an understanding of the role of the individual, laws and rules. From this follows a need to establish an uncontested 'template' for 'ethical' policy making and implementation. Where there remain contested values, as in the EU and its hinterland, it will prove difficult to evolve a common public sector ethic. Without such a common ethical currency it remains difficult to foresee a time when the European civic society *per se* will have broad confidence in the governance and governing structures. From that it follows that the crisis of confidence, combined with a corrosive anomie, will continue, with unpredictable results for the whole.

CONCLUSION

The whole concept of ethical policy making (which, as noted in an early section of this chapter, may be traced in some parts back to Plato) is in its modern guise integral to the success of building public trust in the political and policy processes of the EU and a wider Europe. Without that trust, certainly within the EU, the European experiment will not succeed, at least as a democratic entity. The Europeanization, modernization and hollowing out of the state engendered through governance and the dynamics behind this process act in ways that place the policy process beyond the ken of ordinary citizens. Institutions become remote and authoritarian or simply irrelevant in terms of ordinary citizens' understanding of their role and function.

This chapter began by discussing the role of theory in making sense of the momentous changes taking place within Europe after a long period of bipolarity-induced sclerosis in at least half its political landmass, but with Schmitter's caveat that not all theories purporting to be novel, or indeed properly 'theoretical', should be seen as such. Indeed, we need to remain as wary of grand theories of explanation (or a more normative invocatory nature) as we do of unquestioning ideologies in favour of, or opposed to, some kind of European 'ideal'. A reasonable set of questions may help us with this. It may be useful when reviewing a particular policy or policy *per se* to ask:

- How is this policy made?
- Who makes policy?
- Who, therefore, has power?
- How did they get that power (to make policy)?
- How may they be held to properly account for the exercise of that power, including redressing grievances and experiencing sanctions, where appropriate?

A sceptial concern with and use of theory assists with this, including those theories that appear most currently applicable to Europe: 'governance' and 'multi-level governance', within a framework of modernization and Europeanization. Issues of broader accountability, regulation and ethics feed into these concerns. As noted above, we need to look at the formal and informal institutions, structures, procedures and political cultures in order to understand public policy in Europe (Christiansen and Piattoni, 2003). Politics, policy, law and ethics all play a part in this quest for understanding.

The rest of this volume explores these issues from a variety of different perspectives and case studies.

NOTE

1. Some limited sections of this chapter are adapted from 'Modernization as Europeanization', in Butcher and Massey (eds) 2003, *Modernizing Civil Services*, Edward Elgar Publishing (pp. 59–73) and 'Multilevel Governance: Administering Global Governance in a Differentiated Political Context', in G. Fraser Moleketi (ed.), *Administering Global Governance*, Administering Global Governance Working Group, Amsterdam: IOS Press, 2005. I am most grateful to the other members of this International Institute of Administrative Sciences' working group for their insights.

2. Whither Europe?

Fergus Carr

INTRODUCTION

On 1 May 2004, with the accession of ten new states, the European Union (EU) grew from 15 to 25 members with a combined population of 459 million (Eurostat, 2004). The ten newcomers included eight Central and East European countries: the Czech Republic, Estonia, Hungary, Latvia, Lithuania, Poland, Slovakia and Slovenia plus Cyprus and Malta. Bulgaria and Romania are scheduled to join the Union in 2007, while Turkey and Croatia began membership negotiations in 2005. The Union consequently is now truly pan-European and constitutes the largest economic area in the world. It generates a quarter of global wealth and its currency, the euro, is second only to the US dollar in world financial markets (European Commission, 2004, p. 2). In global terms the EU is the second largest economy in the world (Young, 2004, p. 201). For the European Commission, the 'sheer size of the European Union in economic, trade and financial terms makes it a world player' (European Commission, 2004, p. 1).

This chapter examines the Union's capacity and record in international politics. It asks whether the EU performs as a major international actor if the Union has an external influence commensurate with its economic base and what sort of actor represents 25 member states. The chapter argues that the Union's internal dynamic for integration has had a significant external impact, and to focus exclusively on the 'classical' elements of foreign policy, including security, provides only a partial appreciation of the EU. The Union's attempt to forge a Common Foreign and Security Policy (CFSP) will be analysed but set against the wider impact of the EU in the international system.

The chapter begins with an overview of the development of the Union's external roles and competences. It then examines EU policy towards the Middle East as a case study. It concludes with an analysis of the EU as an international actor.

THE DEVELOPMENT OF THE UNION'S EXTERNAL ROLES

The EU has a number of external roles that have developed in different phases with separate decision-making procedures. As the European Commissioner for External Relations has explained, 'in Brussels jargon, external relations or "external action" as it is called ... is a much wider concept than CFSP. It encompasses the so-called "first pillar" policies such as development cooperation and technical assistance, trade, environmental, visa and asylum policy and other areas, plus "classical" foreign policy or CFSP' (Patten, 2003).

The policy areas within the first pillar of the Maastricht Treaty have a lineage dating from the foundations of the European Community in 1957. Decisions in this sphere are taken in the Council by Qualified Majority Voting (QMV) following Commission initiatives and under the auspices of the European Parliament. CFSP provisions are placed within Maastricht's second pillar and were developed from the member state system of intergovernmental consultation set 'outside' the Community method known as European Political Cooperation (EPC). CFSP, like EPC, is intergovernmental in character and requires the unanimous consent of all member states for action. CFSP provisions have been developed in the Union since Maastricht in 1992 and enhanced in Treaty revisions in Amsterdam in 1997, and Nice in 2001. The proposed European Constitution agreed at member state level in 2004 would, if ratified, take CFSP coordination a stage further.

The Treaty of Rome to Maastricht

The first-pillar provisions have their precedents in the commercial and trade roles of the European Coal and Steel Community (1951) and the European Economic Community (EEC) (1957). The establishment of the Common Market led its six member states to coordinate external economic relations. Articles 18 to 29 of the EEC Treaty established a Common Customs Tariff and Articles 110 to 116 provided for the Common Commercial Policy. The Commission was entrusted with negotiations with third countries and 'was almost immediately involved in developing its role as a trade actor, as its trading partners sought to negotiate on the effects of the Customs Union' (Brotherton and Vogler, 1999, p. 49). The Common Agricultural Policy (CAP) (Articles 38–47) had similar external consequences for third parties. The Community's development role was based upon the colonial interests of the six, in particular France. The Treaty provisions for Association offered preferential trade relations and financial assistance.

Enlargement and consolidation of the Community widened the significance of its external role. British membership in 1973 led to the inclusion of additional third-world partners. The Lomé Convention in 1975 linked the EU and African, Caribbean and Pacific countries (ACP). The Community's reach became global:

> By 1978 the Union had concluded Association Agreements or Cooperation Agreements with all the states of the Mediterranean basin not covered by earlier Association Agreements (excluding Libya and Warsaw Pact member states); concluded the third Lomé Convention with 75 states in Africa, the Caribbean and the Pacific; had established Cooperation Agreements under Article 113 and 235 with the States of the Andean Pact and the states of Central America, the ASEAN states and the Gulf Cooperation Council; and created framework bilateral agreements with other Asian and Latin American countries. (Whitman, 1998, p. 47)

The Single European Act (SEA) in 1986 set the end of 1992 for completion of the internal single market and made Economic and Monetary Union (EMU) an objective of the Community. The SEA had a number of political implications for member states as a 'Europe without frontiers' was created. Externally the dynamics of the new market led first to European Free Trade Association (EFTA) members seeking access via the creation of the European Economic Area (which linked the EC and EFTA markets) and then membership for Austria, Finland and Sweden in 1995.

The collapse of communism in Europe and the reunification of Germany set the seal on the commitment to a new Union. Two Intergovernmental Conferences (IGCs) were launched, one on EMU and one on Political Union. The outcome was the Treaty on European Union agreed at the Maastricht European Council Summit in December 1991. The Treaty was seen to mark 'a new stage in the process of European integration …' and tasked the Union with a number of objectives, including 'to assert its identity on the international scene, in particular through the implementation of a common foreign and security policy including the eventual framing of a common defence policy, which might in turn lead to a common defence' (TEU, 1992, Title I, Article B).

The record of EPC was an extensive policy network between member states, declarations and common positions (Nuttall, 1992). In terms of output the results were mixed and at times modest (White, 2001, pp. 71–93). The Community's response to the Iraqi invasion of Kuwait in 1990 encapsulated the difficulties inherent in EPC. While the Community took sanctions against Saddam Hussein's regime, as the prospect of military action increased, divergence and discord among member states grew. Jacques Delors, President of the European Commission, saw the crisis as an 'object lesson – if one were needed – on the limitations of the European Community' which 'had neither the institutional machinery nor the military force which would have allowed it to act as a community' (Delors, 1991). Reform became imperative but at the IGC a key issue was whether CFSP should be subsumed under Community procedures. Although the strictly governmental nature of EPC had been eroded in practice and by the provisions of the SEA (White, 2001, p. 77), France, the UK, Denmark, Greece and Portugal opposed EPC integration into the Community (Nuttall, 2000, p. 10). The result was the separate-pillar approach adopted at Maastricht and the retention of intergovernmentalism.

The objectives of the new CFSP were:

> to safeguard the common values, fundamental interests and independence of the union; to strengthen the security of the Union and its member states in all ways; to promote peace and strengthen international security, in accordance with the principles of the United Nations Charter as well as the principles of the Helsinki Final Act and the objectives of the Paris Charter; to promote international cooperation; [and] to develop and consolidate democracy and the rule of law, and respect for human rights and fundamental freedoms. (TEU, Article J.1)

The European Council was to 'define the principles of and general guidelines for common foreign and security policy' (TEU, Article J.8.1). CFSP was to be taken forward on the basis of 'common positions' and 'joint actions'. When the Council defined a 'common position' member states were to ensure that their national policies conformed (TEU, Article J.2.2) and to 'coordinate their action in international organizations and at international conferences' (TEU, Article J.2.3). When the Council decided to take a 'joint action' it was to 'lay down the specific scope, the Union's general and specific objectives in carrying out such action, if necessary its duration, and the means, procedures and conditions for its implementation' (TEU, Article J.3.1). Decision making for the CFSP was to be on the basis of unanimity (TEU, Article J.8.2); except when a 'joint action' has been adopted the Council 'shall, when adopting the joint actions and at any state during its development, define those matters on which decisions are to be taken by a qualified majority' (TEU, Article J.3.2).

Following Maastricht, the development of the European security identity followed two avenues: that concerning defence (which is the subject of Chapter 6); and the enhancement of political coordination. The European Council in 1993 asked the Council of Ministers to define the conditions and procedures for joint action in the following five areas: the promotion of stability and peace in Europe; the use of the Union's financial, political and economic resources in support of the Middle East peace process; support for the transition towards multiracial democracy in South Africa through a programme of assistance including preparation and monitoring of elections; contribution to the implementation of a peace plan for the former Yugoslavia and support for humanitarian action; and support for the democratic process in Russia by providing observers for parliamentary elections (European Council, 1993a). These initiatives focused Union action and practice. The first area for joint action, for example, was taken forward by a 'Stability Pact' for Eastern Europe to 'consolidate their borders and to resolve the problem of national minorities ...' (European Council, 1993b). The Pact was developed by conferences with participating states, regional 'round tables', Commission involvement, and ultimately the prospect of enlargement (Ueta, 1997).

Association Agreements known as 'Europe Agreements' were concluded with the Central and East European Countries (CEECs) in the wake of the Cold War. The agreements consisted of preferential, asymmetrical tariff reductions for CEEC access to the EU, a commitment on the part of the CEECs to make their competition policy and state aid compatible with the EU, and recognition that accession was the final objective of the country concerned (Nuttall, 2000, pp. 91–2). Conditionality was central to EU strategy and enlargement became a powerful means to create a stable and institutionalized wider European space. The Copenhagen EU Council in June 1993 accepted the principle of admission for the Europe Agreement countries and adopted three key principles for membership. Each candidate country had to achieve

> stability of institutions guaranteeing democracy, the rule of law, human rights and respect for and protection of minorities, the existence of a functioning market economy as well as the capacity to cope with competitive pressure and market forces within the Union. Membership presupposes the candidate's ability to take on the obligations of membership including adherence to the aims of political, economic and monetary union. (European Council, 1993c, p. 13)

The European Council in Essen in 1994 agreed to adopt a pre-accession strategy to set out the requirements for accession. In July 1997, the Commission recommended in its 'Agenda 2000' paper that accession negotiations should begin with Estonia, the Czech Republic, Hungary, Poland and Slovenia. The Commission believed negotiations could start with Bulgaria, Latvia, Lithuania, Romania and Slovakia when they were deemed to have met the Copenhagen criteria.

The success of the Union in exporting its norms to Eastern and Central Europe was not matched by its intervention in the crises resulting from the break-up of the former Republic of Yugoslavia. The dissolution of Yugoslavia transcended the IGC that led to CFSP but soon became its first major test and failure. The EU in theory sought to uphold the integrity of the former Yugoslavia in line with the Helsinki Final Act, but in practice, member states moved towards recognition of its constituent parts. As the inevitable conflict progressed to war, the EU offered 'good offices', and tried to broker a peace among the factions but did not take preventive action on the ground. It fell to the United Nations and NATO to mount an intervention (see Chapter 6). The EU failure needs to be set against the record of the international community, which wrestled with the problem of intra-state conflict until the Dayton Agreement of 1995. None the less, the Union's 'limited competence in security and defence matters and, more importantly, its member states' disparate foreign policy objectives together ensured that the EU's ambition to assert its presence as an international actor was impaired by its inability to maintain common positions' (Kintis, 1997, p. 164).

In 1995 Jacques Santer, President of the Commission, questioned the will of member states to work together in CFSP, the adequacy of the intergovernmental pillar and the unanimity rule for decision making (Santer, 1995). The Commission proposed an extension of QMV to foreign policy areas excluding defence and the integration of the Western European Union (WEU), the pre-NATO European defence alliance, into the EU. France sustained its position on the need for a second intergovernmental pillar, while Britain led the opposition to an extension of QMV and opposed France and Germany over the integration of the WEU. The resulting Amsterdam Treaty in 1997 did not, consequently, fundamentally alter arrangements for CFSP.

From Amsterdam to the European Constitution

The 1997 Amsterdam Treaty restated the significance of the European Council in CFSP and the principle of unanimity in decision making, although it did allow for 'constructive abstention' whereby a member state will 'not be obliged to apply the decision, but shall accept that the decision commits the Union' (Article 23.1). The instruments of CFSP were refined with the adoption of Common Strategies in addition to Common Positions and Joint Actions.

The key innovations of Amsterdam were, however, in terms of representation. A new high representative for CFSP was instituted as a secretary-general within the Council Secretariat. The high representative, or 'Mr CFSP', was to work with the Presidency of the Council of Ministers and a senior member of the Commission. This 'troika' replaced the former system of representing CFSP by past, present and future presidencies. The high representative was to be supported by a new policy planning and early warning unit to be established in the General Secretariat of the Council consisting of staff drawn from the General Secretariat, member states, the Commission and the WEU.

Union development policy changed after the Amsterdam Summit. It had been built upon preferential trade relationships and financial assistance either delivered bilaterally, or multilateral in geographical and thematic approaches. The Community budget had provided aid and the European Development Fund (EDF), funded by member states, as well as grants, risk capital and loans to the private sector. The impact of EU policy was significant. In 2000 the Union was the third largest donor of Official Development Aid (ODA) and its member states were the developing countries' largest trading partners (Matthews, 2004, pp. 471–92). The Union's preferential trade regime for ACP countries was, however, in contravention of World Trade Organization (WTO) non-discrimination norms. The EU could not indefinitely seek WTO exemptions and in any case there were perceived failings in the Lomé model. Its inability to 'produce visible progress in standards of living had seriously undermined the credibility of the EU as a leading actor on development issues' (Babarinde and Faber, 2004, p. 45). The result was the Cotonou Agreement of June 2000, which ended non-reciprocal trade preferences. Cotonou embodies financial assistance, priority for poverty reduction, a political dimension and liberalized trade between the two parties. Negotiations on new regional economic partnerships began in 2003 and are to be completed by 2008. The new trading arrangements were seen as 'crucial to improving the ACP countries' capacity to trade and to attract international private investment' (Nielson, 2000). The balance of responsibility in the Agreement was clear: 'each country must own and be accountable for its policies' (Cotonou Agreement, 2000). The political dimension of Cotonou encompasses: dialogue, respect for human rights, peace-building and good governance. The parties reaffirmed 'that democratization, development and the protection of fundamental freedoms and human rights are interrelated and mutually reinforcing' (ibid.). Cotonou integrates conditionality and provides for review and termination subject to the political pillar.

The EU's development policy was also reformed in light of the United Nations (UN) Millennium Summit in September 2000. The UN General Assembly adopted the Millennium Declaration setting eight Millennium Development Goals (MDGs) to be realized by 2015 (United Nations Millennium Declaration, 2000). The European Community's Development Policy Statement by the Council and the Commission in November 2000 identified six areas for action:

> The link between trade and development; regional integration and cooperation; support for macro-economic policies and the promotion of equitable access

> to social services; transport; food security and sustainable rural development; and institutional capacity-building. (The European Community's Development Policy, 2000)

The policy made clear, like Cotonou, that 'attention will consistently be given to human rights, to the environmental dimension, to equality between men and women and to good governance' (ibid.). The objective was to reduce and eventually eradicate poverty and provide support for 'sustainable economic and social and environmental development, promotion of the gradual integration of the developing countries into the world economy and a determination to combat inequality' (ibid.). For the world's 48 poorest countries (LDCs) the EU adopted the 'Everything but Arms' (EBA) proposal in February 2001. The EBA provides for duty-free access into EU markets for all goods except arms (bananas, rice and sugar were subject to a progressive scale of tariff reduction) (Council of Ministers, 2001). The EU has called on other developed sectors of the world economy to adopt EBA strategies and looked to reform its own policies to realize the MDGs. In 2005, following the Council's request, the Commission prepared proposals on three aspects: finance for development, policy coherence and focus on Africa. The Commission's proposals aim to

> set new intermediate targets for growth in official aid budgets by 2010 for both the EU as a whole and the individual member states with a view to achieving the overall target of 0.7% of the gross national income (GNI) by 2015; speed up reforms that will improve the quality of aid; re-think the way that the EU, through its own model of sustainable development and its internal and external policies, influence the conditions for development; ensure that Africa is the number one beneficiary of these new approaches and seize new opportunities for partnership between the two continents. (Commission of the European Communities, 2005a, p. 5)

The Commission's analysis was comprehensive in scope and identified sectors for reform. In terms of policy coherence the Commission identified a number of priority areas including: trade, environment, security, agriculture, fisheries and migration, where the challenge of attaining synergies with development policy objectives is considered particularly relevant (Commission of the European Communities, 2005b, p. 5). The link to security strategy reflects the European integrated approach to conflict prevention and crisis management. The breadth of security conceptualization embodied in the European Security Strategy adopted in 2003 (see below) meant that the EU was committed to 'security and development as complementary agendas, with the common aim of creating a security environment and of breaking the vicious cycle of poverty, war, environmental degradation and failing economic, social and political structures' (ibid., p. 10). The Commission saw the need to increase the amount of international aid, enhance the quality of aid (Commission of the European Community, 2005a, pp. 5–8) and pursue Coherence for Development Commitments in the context of MDGs (Commission of the European Communities, 2005b, p. 6). The challenges to the Commission agenda include: sustaining reform of the Common Agricultural Policy (CAP); and enlargement. Enlargement in the case of the CEECs means a transition from aid recipients to donors, limited resources for ODA and the need to identify poverty reduction as an aid strategy (Migliorsi, 2003).

The Nice Treaty of 2001 was designed to reform the EU in anticipation of enlargement. With regard to CFSP the major work was in respect of ESDP (discussed in Chapter 6) to enable the EU to assume responsibility for crisis management. The Nice European Council recognized that if 'it is to play fully its role on the International stage, the EU must be in a position to have at its disposal the whole range of instruments required for a global approach to crisis management, and in particular: – develop a coherent European approach to crisis management and conflict prevention; ensure synergy between the civilian and military aspects of crisis management; and cover the full range of Petersberg tasks' (European Council, 2000a, p. 41).

To manage this process Nice formalized a committee structure initiated at Helsinki in 1999. The new Political and Security Committee (PSC) consisting of ambassadors from member states is seen as the 'linchpin of the European security and defence policy (ESDP) and of the common foreign and security policy (CFSP)' (European Council, 2000a, p. 63). The PSC was to

> keep track of the international situation in the areas falling within the common foreign policy and security policy, help define policies by drawing up "opinions" for the Council, either at the request of the Council or on its own initiative, and monitor implementation of agreed policies … (Ibid., p. 64)

In a crisis situation the PSC is the body which 'examines all the options that might be considered as the Union's response …' and 'exercises "political control and strategic direction" of the EU's military response to the crisis' (ibid., pp. 64–5). The PSC was complemented by the creation of the EU Military Committee (EUMC) comprising Chiefs of Defence and the European Union Military Staff Organization (EUMS) which was to provide early warning and strategic planning for the 'Petersberg tasks'.

As the Union moved to make its CFSP more proactive and cohesive, it also adopted an overall strategy for foreign and security policy. The 'European Security Strategy', published in December 2003, envisaged a multi-level and multi-issue agenda for the Union. The security environment was seen as 'one of increasingly open borders in which the internal and external aspects of security are indissolubly linked' (European Security Strategy, 2003, p. 2). Large-scale aggression was seen as improbable and 'instead, Europe faces new threats which are more diverse, less visible and less predictable' (ibid., p. 3) including: terrorism; proliferation of weapons of mass destruction; regional security; state failure and organized crime. In contrast to the Cold War none of the new threats was seen as purely military and 'in an era of globalization, distant threats may be seen as much a concern as those that are near at hand' (ibid., p. 6). The Union's approach was to be multilateral:

> in a world of global threats, global markets and global media, our security and prosperity increasingly depend on an effective multilateral system. The development of a stronger international society, well functioning international institutions and a rule-based international order is our objective. (Ibid., p. 9)

The objectives for the EU were to 'promote a ring of well governed countries to the East of the European Union and on the borders of the Mediterranean …' (ibid., p. 8).

Consolidation of stability in the Balkans was seen as a test of Union credibility, a more active interest in the problems of the Southern Caucasus was advocated and the resolution of the Arab–Israeli conflict was identified as a strategic priority. The European Security Strategy heralded the European Neighbourhood Policy (ENP) adopted by the Council in June 2004. The Commission had advocated a new Neighbourhood Instrument in 2003 in light of enlargement and the challenges of managing new borders with new neighbours (Commission of the European Communities, 2003). ENP offers regional economic integration linked to political reform and conflict prevention. The initiative brought Eastern Europe and the Mediterranean into the same policy framework and the EU offers a similar relationship as the EEA (Aliboni, 2005, p. 2). The Union's strategic interest in its hinterland is not surprising but the consequences will be increasing CFSP involvement in the volatile politics of the Middle East and the Caucasus.

The European Security Strategy had recognized that the Union needed to be 'more active, more coherent and more capable' (ibid., p. 11). In a similar vein the Laeken Declaration had posed the question, 'does Europe not, now that it is fully unified, have a leading role to play in a new world order, that of a power able both to play a stabilizing role worldwide and to point the way ahead for many countries and peoples? (European Council, 2001a).

The proposed Constitution for Europe adopted in July 2004 by member state governments had been hoped to address these questions. Its provisions were not, though, radical departures from the existing CFSP mandate and were, like past Treaty reforms, more incremental in nature.

The draft Constitution saw CFSP as being based upon the 'development of mutual political solidarity among member states, the identification of questions of general interest and the achievement of an ever-increasing degree of convergence of member states actions' (Article 1–40). Decision making was to remain based on the principle of unanimity except where the European Council instructed the Council of Ministers to proceed by QMV (Article 1–40) and where the new Union Minister for Foreign Affairs (see below) has presented a proposal following a specific request from the European Council (Article 111–300). If a member of the Council declares that 'for vital and stated resources of national policy, it intends to oppose the adoption of a European decision to be adopted by a qualified majority, a vote shall not be taken' (Article 111–300). Abstention was retained from the Amsterdam Treaty and unanimity was required for all decisions with military or defence implications (Article 111–300–4).

An important innovation was the creation of a new post, the Union Minister for Foreign Affairs, 'who shall chair the Foreign Affairs Council, shall contribute through his or her proposals towards the preparation of the common foreign and security policy and still ensure implementation of the European decisions adopted by the European Council and the Council' (Article 111–296–1). The Minister for Foreign Affairs is to represent the Union in matters concerning CFSP, conduct political dialogue with third parties and express the Union's position in international organizations (Article 296–2). The Minister effectively replaces both the High Representative for CFSP and the post of External Relations Commissioner. The Minister will be one of the vice presidents of the Commission (Article 1–28–4) while at the same time having a pivotal role in the Council of Ministers' policy process. The new post therefore spans and links the hitherto separate policy areas of pillar one and pillar two. The Union Minister for Foreign Affairs is to be assisted by a European External Action Service, which will comprise officers from relevant departments of the General Secretariat of the Council; from the Commission and staff seconded from member state diplomatic services. The Political and Security Committee is retained to monitor international politics, contribute to the definition of the CFSP and take strategic direction of crisis management operations under ESDP (Article 111–307). The Minister is further to consult and inform the European Parliament, as are special representatives if appointed to cover a specific policy issue (Article 111–302 and Article 111–304–1).

The draft Constitution proposes that the CFSP should be conducted by '(a) defining the general guidelines; (b) adopting European decisions defining (i) actions to be undertaken by the Union; (ii) positions to be taken by the

Union; arrangements for the implementation of the European decisions referred to in points (i) and (ii); (c) strengthening systematic cooperation between member states in the conduct of policy' (Article 111–294–3). The European Council is to define the general guidelines of CFSP and the Council will adopt the European decisions necessary for their definition and implementation. Member states are to ensure their national policies conform to the positions of the Union, and 'shall refrain from any action which is contrary to the interests of the Union or likely to impair its effectiveness as a cohesive force in international relations' (Article 111–294–2).

The final innovation of the Constitution was the introduction of a 'solidarity clause' which states, 'the Union and its member states shall act jointly in a spirit of solidarity if a member state is the object of a terrorist attack or the victim of a natural or man-made disaster' (Article 1–43). The Union is to mobilize 'all the instruments at its disposal, including the military resources made available by the member states' (ibid.), to respond to such a crisis.

The draft Constitution reaffirmed the principles of the Common Commercial Policy and confirmed the role of the Commission in negotiation with third parties and international organizations once authorized by the Council (Article 111–315–3). Except where agreements relate exclusively to CFSP the Council will conclude the agreement by obtaining the consent of the European Parliament in cases including association agreements; Union accession to the European Convention for the Protection of Human Rights and Fundamental Freedoms; agreements establishing a specific institutional framework by organizing cooperation procedures and agreements with important budgeting implications for the Union (Article 111–325–6).

Union development policy was declared to have as 'its primary objective the reduction and, in the long term, the eradication of poverty' (Article 111–316–1). The Union and member states are to coordinate their development policies and consult on aid programmes including in international organizations. The Union is also to provide humanitarian aid as 'ad hoc assistance and relief and protection for people in third countries who are victims of natural or man-made disasters, in order to meet the humanitarian needs resulting from these disasters' (Article 111–321–1). The Constitution provides also for the termination, in part or completely, of economic and financial relations with one or more third countries when the Council acts by a 'qualified majority on a joint proposal from the Union Minister for Foreign Affairs and the Commission' (Article 111–322–1).

If past history is a guide, the development of CFSP instruments and Union external relations competencies clearly will continue beyond the provisions of the draft Constitution. None the less the current array of policy provision is comprehensive and with ESDP (discussed in Chapter 6) offers the Union the capacity to act in economic and political spheres. The degree to which this confers the status of a true 'international actor' will be discussed below after consideration of the Union's role in the Middle East case study.

THE EU AND THE MIDDLE EAST

The Middle East poses a complex challenge for the security interests of the European Union. It combines the politics of energy dependence with the Arab–Israeli conflict and the question of Palestine. The Cold War polarized the region, enhanced its strategic significance and compounded local conflicts. Secular nationalism has competed with Islamic movements to lead Arab politics and respond to Israel and Western intervention. Radical and revolutionary forces have also contested the legitimacy of states and traditional authority. After 9/11 the region's local politics have global consequences predicating an enhanced strategic interest by the Western powers. The US response to the threat of terrorism and weapons of mass destruction (WMD) has divided Europe and sustains concern with regard to Iran and other regional powers.

The Development of the European Role

The EU has looked to promote stability on its southern flank, ensure energy access and supply, develop trade, and address migration pressures. The EU contribution to conflict management and resolution in the region, however, has been constrained by the predominant role of Washington, the seemingly intractable nature of the conflict and the limitations of CFSP.

The EEC did not have an agreed common position on the Arab–Israeli conflict when EPC was inaugurated in 1969 (Dosenrode and Stubkjær, 2002, p. 83). In 1972 the Community adopted its 'Global Mediterranean Policy' (GMP) which provided a framework for commercial relations with individual Mediterranean states and was a precursor of later initiatives. It was the oil crisis of 1973, and Europe's oil dependence on the Middle East, that stimulated a political initiative and a declaration which referred to the 'legitimate rights' of the Palestinians (ibid., p. 86). The significance of this statement can be gauged by comparison with UN Security Council Resolution 242, which had set the prevailing norms for resolution of the Arab–Israeli conflict. Resolution 242 spoke only of a 'just settlement of the refugee problem' (Laqueur and Rubin, 1984, p. 365) and did not place Palestinian rights into its equation for settlement. Arab states promptly recognized the significance of the European position and sent a delegation of ministers to the EC Copenhagen Summit in December 1973. This was the birth of the 'Euro-Arab dialogue', which reflected a simple balance of interests: European concerns about oil and Arab desires to see Europe support the Palestinian cause.

Israel first called upon the EEC to remain neutral (Dosenrode and Stubkjær, 2002, p. 82) but 'several EU actions, positions and declarations on the MEPP (Middle East Peace Process) so adversely affected Israel's vital national security interests that Israel never accepted the EU as a mediator' (Ginsberg, 2001, p. 107). While the EEC signed an Association Agreement with Israel in 1975 the European Council in 1977 called for Palestinian representation in the peace process and a Palestinian 'homeland' (Aoun, 2003, p. 291). Washington's response was to try to maintain the autonomy of Camp David in the peace process and pressure Europe to modify its stance (Dosenrode and Stubkjær, 2002, pp. 96–7). None the less the Community's Venice Declaration of June 1980 stated that a 'just solution must finally be found to the Palestinian problem which is not simply one of refugees ...'. The Palestinian people, it further declared, 'must be placed in a position, by an appropriate process defined within the framework of the comprehensive peace settlement, to exercise fully its right to self determination'. The Community also saw the need for the Palestine Liberation Organization (PLO), not recognized by the USA or Israel, to play a part in the settlement (European Council, 1980). In Israel virtually the whole political spectrum condemned the Declaration (Alpher, 2000, p. 196) and the government clung to the American-brokered process which eventually de-linked Palestinian autonomy from a settlement with Egypt.

Europe may not have become a significant peacemaker (Aoun, 2003), but it did make an important contribution to how the conflict was defined. The USA and UN had predominantly focused on the relations of states and the consequences of the 1967 War in their approach to the diplomatic resolution of the conflict. After the oil crisis Kissinger had sustained the bargaining process that linked return of Arab land for peace and oil. President Carter had sought a more comprehensive settlement but allowed Palestinian autonomy to be relegated to a letter of intent in the Camp David negotiations. It was Europe that had placed the Palestinians and their right to self-determination at the centre of any potential conflict resolution.

Oslo and Beyond

Following the Gulf War of 1990 the USA, with the Soviet Union as co-sponsor, convened the Madrid Conference to negotiate a peace agreement between Israel and the Arab states. The European community attended as an observer following Israeli objections to full participation. The EC did chair the working group on Regional Economic Development (REDWG) and 'between 1993 and 1997 allocated $15.2 million for preparation of feasibility studies of infrastructure and the establishment of communication networks between cities, universities and media' (Dosenrode and Stubkjær, 2002, p. 122). This heralded the EU's role in seeking to financially and diplomatically underpin the peace process. This role was intensified after the historic breakthrough in Oslo between Israel and the PLO leading to the Declaration of Principles (DoP) signed in Washington in 1993 by Yitzhak Rabin and Yasser Arafat. The EU now 'concentrated its efforts on supporting the creation of an environment that would make possible lasting peace in the region rather than contributing directly to a political solution between the conflicting parties' (Asseburg, 2003, p. 11). The EU and its member states quickly became the largest donors of financial and technical aid to the new Palestinian Authority agreed in the DoP. Between 1994 and 1998 the EU provided over 50 per cent of the international assistance for Gaza and the West Bank (ibid., p. 12). European aid was focused on infrastructure projects including Gaza harbour and airport, hospitals and schools. In addition specific assistance was provided for Palestinian state building, such as the 17 million ECU for the 1996 elections (Dosenrode and Stubkjær, 2002, p. 136).

The EU has also invested in the promotion of regional multilateral frameworks. The 1995 Barcelona Conference brought together the EU with Algeria, Cyprus, Egypt, Israel, Jordan, Lebanon, Malta, Morocco, the Palestinian Authority, Syria, Tunisia and Turkey. The Conference agreed to create a Euro-Mediterranean Partnership (EMP). The three main chapters of the EMP covered the promotion of security, the creation of shared prosperity and the development of understanding between cultures. The participants agreed to establish a regular political dialogue, to develop the rule of law and democracy in their political systems and to respect human rights (Barcelona Declaration, 1995). The economic objectives were to be realized through the progressive establishment of a free trade area, regional cooperation and financial assistance from the EU. The EMP looked to regular meetings, exchange agreements, education and the media to develop the dialogue between cultures and societies. Specific meetings were convened to address the issue of migration which sought to enhance job creation to reduce migratory pressures. The EMP adopted a work plan for each chapter and conducts its business via annual meetings of Foreign Ministers.

In June 2000 the European Council adopted a Common Strategy on the Mediterranean which endorsed the Barcelona Declaration but made more explicit the political and security aspects of the EMP. Specific objectives in the field of justice and home affairs including migration were also added (European Council, 2000b). The Valencia Action Plan in April 2002 committed EMP members to further cooperation in the sectors of migration, reform of the judiciary and the fight against criminality. This reflected the general emphasis of EU external relations upon good governance and the specific need to respond to the 'internationalization of criminal networks, of terrorism and of modern management of migratory flows …' (EMP, 2005–6, p. 21).

The Impact of EU Policy

The EU's policy towards the Middle East has been critically affected by the deepening conflict between Israel and the Palestinians, the polarization of the region after 9/11 and the Iraq War of 2003. Following Ariel Sharon's 'visit' to the Temple Mount in Jerusalem on 28 September 2000, the second intifada, the 'Aqsa Intifada', began. Violence and unrest spread through the West Bank and Gaza. Palestinian suicide bombings targeted Israelis, whose government responded by reoccupying territory ceded to the Palestinian Authority, imposing curfews and restricting movement. Israel 'closed' the occupied territories and began building a 'separation barrier' in the West Bank. By the beginning of 2004 some 3300 people had been killed in the conflict and 24 000 injured (European Commission, 2005).

In an attempt to halt the cycle of violence the Clinton Administration called for a summit which in turn led to the appointment of a fact-finding commission chaired by US senator George Mitchell and included the EU High Representative Javier Solana. Mitchell reported to the incoming President, G.W. Bush, who showed little enthusiasm to commit the USA to a resolution of the conflict. The impact of 9/11, however, provided a new impetus in Washington to address the crisis. In 2003, the USA with its 'Quartet' partners (UN, EU and Russia) published a 'Roadmap' to peace. The 'Roadmap' identified a number of stages to a comprehensive settlement by 2005 based upon a 'two-state' solution. Events on the ground, though, took a different course and despite appeals from the Quartet, violence continued.

The closure of the Palestinian territories has had a specific impact upon EU policy. The EU commitment to Palestinian development was designed to win popular support for the peace process, to 'drain the sea' from the radicals and help create a state that would be in Israel's security interest (Asseburg, 2003, p. 12). Closure has meant the opposite of EU aims, poverty has increased and a humanitarian crisis has developed. The immediate effect of closure was the reduction by 'approximately 70 per cent employment of Palestinians in Israel, Israeli settlements and industrial zones' and the consequent lower demand for goods 'caused an almost 20 per cent contraction of domestic employment' (United Nations, 2002). By

2002 Palestinian gross national income 'mounted to 40 per cent less than in 2000', real per capita incomes were 'only half of their September 2000 level' and unemployment equalled '53 per cent of the workforce' (World Bank, 2003). If a poverty line of US$2 per day is used, some 21 per cent of the Palestinian population were poor before the intifada began but by December 2002 that figure had risen to 60 per cent (World Bank, 2003). Real per capita food consumption had declined by 30 per cent, resulting in 9.3 per cent of Palestinian children suffering from acute malnutrition (DFID, 2004, p. 5). The severe decline of the Palestinian economy meant that the EU had to refocus its assistance to humanitarian and emergency aid. The EU has also provided critical funding for the Palestinian Authority, without which it would collapse. Accusations have been levied that this assistance has been used to fund terrorist activity. The EU has rejected these claims, finding no conclusive evidence (OLAF, 2005) but has pressed the Palestinian Authority for greater budget transparency and reform. The most likely factor fuelling Palestinian extremism is the consequences of Israeli closure policy, not EU assistance. The derailment of EU policy points to the limits of 'soft power' and norm setting without a clear momentum to conflict resolution in the peace process. As the Arab world has long recognized, only Washington can deliver Israel and a concerted Western approach is needed. The basis for a common transatlantic understanding to the Middle East was, however, set back in the Iraq War, which also opened deep fissures in CFSP.

From 9/11 to the Axis of Evil

The immediate European reaction to 9/11 was to stress partnership, solidarity and cooperation with the USA. The joint EU–US Ministerial Statement on Combating Terrorism adopted on 20 September 2001 spoke of 'acting jointly', in a 'broad coalition to combat the evil of terrorism' (*European Union Bulletin*, 2001). The European Council declared it 'would cooperate with the United States in bringing to justice and punishing the perpetrators, sponsors and accomplices of such barbaric acts' (European Council, 2001B). Tony Blair saw a battle 'between the free democratic world and terrorism' (*The Guardian*, 12 September 2001).

President Chirac pledged to do everything that 'appears useful or necessary' to eradicate terrorism. In policy terms Europe supported new anti-terror resolutions at the United Nations and the European Council criminalized the wilful collection of funds for terrorist activity, defined terrorist acts and groups and introduced a Europe-wide arrest warrant (Duke, 2002).

On the military front, Operation Enduring Freedom began on 7 October 2001 with strikes against al-Qaeda and the Taliban in Afghanistan. European support was forthcoming but the forces employed were predominantly American with some British assets. The USA saw allied support as valuable but not essential. The Bush Administration did not want the coalition to tie their hands; the ethos was that 'the mission should define the coalition, not the other way around' (Woodward, 2002, p. 48). Transatlantic solidarity ended, however, when the focus of the 'war on terror' switched to Iraq.

In his State of the Union Address in January 2002, President Bush spoke of an 'axis of evil', identifying regimes such as Iraq which sought WMD and 'could provide these arms to terrorists, giving them the means to match their hatred' (Bush, 2002). The speech alarmed Europe, and Javier Solana warned against the 'global unilateralism of the American leader's conflation of Iran, North Korea and Iraq as his next targets' (*The Guardian*, 14 February 2002). France and Germany warned that any strike against Iraq could be justified only by a mandate from the United Nations. Chancellor Schröder, facing re-election, turned to outright opposition in line with German public opinion. President Chirac pressed for the resumption of UN weapons inspectors to ascertain the WMD case.

Franco-German opposition to American military intentions was made public at the United Nations on 20 January 2003. The French Foreign Minister told Colin Powell 'today nothing justifies considering military action' and that France would 'not associate ourselves with military intervention that is not supported by the international community' (Shawcross, 2003, p. 125). In opposition to the Franco-German position, the leaders of Britain, Spain, Italy, Portugal, Hungary, Poland, Denmark and the Czech Republic signed a letter supporting the US campaign to disarm Iraq and calling for the UN Security Council 'to face up to its responsibilities' (*The Guardian*, 30 January 2003). The Vilnius Group of Albania, Bulgaria, Croatia, Estonia, Latvia, Lithuania, Macedonia, Romania, Slovakia and Slovenia also declared their support for Washington in February 2003 (see Croci, 2003, p. 470). With eight of the above (the Czech Republic, Estonia, Hungary, Latvia, Lithuania, Poland, Slovakia and Slovenia) due to join the European Union, President Chirac reportedly rebuked their behaviour while US Secretary of Defence Rumsfeld seized on the division, contrasting 'an old and a new Europe'.

The differences between European and US policy approaches to the Middle East can be seen as a dichotomy between multilateralism and unilateralism. While the divide is not absolute, American power does grant Washington the ability, if it chooses, to resist the constraints of multilateral rules and institutions. In a 'uni-polar' international system the USA is afforded unprecedented opportunities to exercise military power and follow a strategic doctrine that emphasizes pre-emptive action (The White House,

2002). Europe's approach, in contrast, reflects a desire for a rule-based regional and international order (Cooper, 2003).

In the Middle East context, this is typified by the Barcelona process. Chris Patten, EU External Relations Commissioner, hoped 'that our friends across the Atlantic are recognizing that our long-term consensus-building approach has some value, based as it is on building common agendas that respect differences of approach in different countries and regions' (Patten, 2004a). The 'axis of evil' agenda stands in stark contrast and sustains European concern, exemplified after Iraq, with the Iranian case.

The USA has a long-standing antipathy towards the Iranian regime following the Islamic revolution of 1979 and the seizure of American hostages (Bill, 1988; Hiro, 1985). Washington imposed sanctions and designated Iran a state sponsor of terrorism in 1983 after Teheran was linked to attacks on US forces in Lebanon (Marr, 2000, p. 274). In 1995 Iran began negotiations with Russia and China for the construction of nuclear power plants. Although the proposals fell under the Non-Proliferation Treaty (NPT) regime, Washington feared that Iran was seeking to procure WMD. In the US Senate two bills were introduced, one to prevent US trade and investment in Iran and one to impose sanctions on foreign companies that were doing so. A final version of the law embodied sanctions against foreign companies that involved US$40 million or more in Iran's oil industry (Marr, 2000, p. 276). The EU protested as Britain, France, Germany and Italy (plus Japan) were Iran's main trading partners (Ehteshami, 2000, p. 298). On the eve of the invasion of Iraq US officials claimed that Iran was pursuing a secret nuclear weapons programme (*The Guardian*, 14 December 2002). In 2003 the Iranian President, Mohammed Khatami, announced that Iran was mining uranium ore and intended to take control of the fuel cycle (*The Guardian Unlimited*, 22 November 2004). Under NPT rules countries may develop enrichment but must place the full process under International Atomic Energy Agency (IAEA) safeguards to ensure civilian use. Washington suspected an illicit programme under the guise of civilian production and intensified its coercive strategy. The USA has sought to politically isolate Iran, demanded vigorous action by the IAEA and the UN and escalated pressure on Teheran with reports of potential airstrikes and regime change circulated in the media (*The Guardian*, 20 June 2003 and 22 November 2004). Iran has rejected Washington's claims and Foreign Minister Kharrazi has claimed that Iran wanted enrichment facilities to 'produce fuel for our plants and we are not after nuclear weapons' (*The Observer*, 1 August 2004). In a statement of principle, Kharrazi informed the United Nations, 'it is unacceptable that some tend to limit access to peaceful nuclear technology to an exclusive club of technologically advanced states under the pretext of non-proliferation' (Kharrazi, 2005).

In contrast to the USA, the EU has pursued a strategy of 'constructive engagement' with Iran. This diplomatic approach has encompassed a number of areas: nuclear power; a human rights dialogue; trade; and investment. The EU has tried to link these areas with Patten's warning, 'we cannot simply ignore problems in one area and think that we can move rapidly in all the others' (Patten, 2004b). Britain, France and Germany have represented the EU in negotiations with Iran concerning its nuclear programme. The 'EU Three' have promised access to civilian nuclear technology in return for Teheran suspending uranium enrichment and agreeing to short-notice IAEA inspections. In 2003 the EU looked to have secured Iranian agreement but, in August 2004, Teheran announced that it had restarted the building of uranium enrichment centrifuges (*The Observer*, 1 August 2004). Former President, Ali Akbar Hashami Rafsanjani, declared that Iran could not give up its enrichment programme, but indicated that a diplomatic solution could be found to assure its civilian use (*The Guardian Unlimited*, 11 February 2005).

The EU has pursued a difficult course seeking to secure measures that will lead to international confidence in the Iranian nuclear programme. Iranian politics have constrained the process and IAEA concerns about Teheran's transparency are shared in both Europe and Washington. Europe's engagement strategy would be more effective if directly supported by the USA. President Bush indicated a willingness to reconsider the European position in early 2005 but did not agree to a change of policy (FT.com, 24 February 2005). Despite these constraints EU engagement policy has remained consistent and, unlike on Iraq, held as a common position. Patten has summarized European thinking: 'One only has to look at its neighbourhood to see how important it is and to recognize that we cannot have a credible policy for the wider Middle East that does not embrace and include Iran' (Patten, 2004b).

THE EUROPEAN UNION AS AN INTERNATIONAL ACTOR: CONCLUSIONS

The evidence of this chapter points to the mixed record of the EU as an international actor. In terms of CFSP, Treaty provisions provide member states with the means and procedures to act as one. In areas falling under pillar one the Commission filters, forms and provides consistency to European policy. In the Middle East the EU has sustained a common position with regard to the Arab–Israeli conflict, Palestinian rights, the peace process and Iran. Development strategy for the region has clearly been integrated with European security, and Europe's voice has been distinctive from that of the USA. At the same time Europe has not been a mediator in the dispute and does not have the leverage of the USA over Israel or the capacity to guarantee outcomes. Europe remains predominantly an economic power despite ESDP projected commitments. The European failure to find common ground in key crises such as the break-up of the former Yugoslavia, the Iraqi invasion of Kuwait and the Iraq War of 2003 also points to serious political flaws in the making of European foreign policy. The issue is clearly about political will and consensus. The challenge for analysis is that the EU has gone beyond the 'false dilemma of omnipotence or inexistence on the international scene' (Gnesotto, 2002, p. 5) and has a 'variable and multi-dimensional presence, which plays an active role in some areas of international interaction and a less active one in others' (Allen and Smith, 1990, p. 20).

The interpretation of the EU's international role has, unsurprisingly been contentious. In the early 1970s François Duchêne suggested that the European Community could become a 'civilian power':

> the European Community's interest as a civilian group of countries long on economic power and relatively short on armed force is as far as possible to *domesticate* relations between states, including those of its own members and those with states outside its frontiers. This means trying to bring to international problems the sense of common responsibility and structures of contractual politics which have in the past been associated almost exclusively with 'home' and not foreign, that is *alien*, affairs. (Duchêne, 1973, p. 20)

Hedley Bull, in contrast, asked whether 'civilian power Europe' was a contradiction in terms, asserting that 'the power or influence exerted by the European Community and other such civilian actors was conditional upon a strategic environment provided by the military power of states, which they did not control' (Bull, 1982, p. 151). In accord with the realist tradition, Bull saw states as the primary actors in international politics. International organizations were but secondary bodies where states conducted their affairs:

> 'Europe' is not an actor in international affairs, and does not seem likely to become one; the Europe with which I am concerned is the actual one of state governments, in which a minor role is played, chiefly as instruments of cooperation among governments, by various committees, assemblies and secretariats bearing the designation 'European', including those of the EC among others. (Ibid)

In this vein of thinking, intergovernmentalism, as in CFSP, may be seen as a constraint on the EU attaining the autonomy necessary for a true international actor. Hill, following Sjöstedt (1977), states, 'an international actor can be said to be an entity which is (1) delimited from others, and from its environment; which is (2) autonomous, in the sense of making its own laws and decisions ...; and which (3) possesses certain structural prerequisites for action on the international level, such as legal personality, a set of diplomatic agents and the capability to conduct negotiations with third parties' (Hill, 1993, p. 309).

The EU does, in part, meet these criteria. It has a legal personality in specifically defined policy areas (Brotherton and Vogler, 1999, pp. 16–18). It has representation, conducts negotiations and has detailed decision-making procedures. It is at best, however, quasi-autonomous in that the 'Europeanization' of foreign policy is a matter of degree and affected by policy area.

Institutional theory points to the instrumental character of international organizations and regimes as a means to solve collective action problems (Young, 2002, p. 176). The state is seen as self-interested (as per realist theory) but preference is given to joint action given that independent policy could lead to 'undesirable or sub-optimal outcomes' (Stein, 1993, p. 120). The typical approach is to see regimes less as 'centralized enforcers of rules than as facilitators of agreement amongst governments' (Keohane, 1984, p. 238). If institutionalism becomes embedded over time, as in the EU, policy networks can, however, establish norms and develop shared perceptions of political order. The propensity for cooperation in EU external relations has been seen as the result of institutional mechanisms which 'have *pre-empted* the formation of fixed national foreign policy preferences on an expanding number of issues and *socialized* its elite participants into articulating a common European policy on these issues' (Smith, 2004, pp. 99–100). In this context it is important to emphasize that the EU has been seen as 'less than a state, but more than a conventional intergovernmental organization …' (Hill, 1993, p. 309). It has been argued that while the EU shares with regimes qualities such as establishing common expectations, it is 'much more centralized and institutionalized than an international regime and receives a much higher level of commitment from its members' (Keohane and Hoffmann, 1991, p. 10). The difficulty of categorizing the EU arises because it is 'essentially organized as a network that involves the pooling and sharing of sovereignty …' (ibid., p. 13). In foreign policy terms Hill has suggested that Europe should be seen as a 'system (ie: not a single actor) which generates international relations – collectively, individually, economically, politically …' (Hill, 1993, p. 322). In this way member states simultaneously conduct 'their persistently vigorous national policies, their sophisticated co-ordination and common initiatives through EPC (now CFSP); and the highly structured political economy dimension of collective commercial and development policies' (ibid.). Crises such as the Iraq War expose the multi-level nature of European external policies but do not end

CFSP (Hill, 2004). The propensity to collaborate in security politics remains despite disagreement in specific issue areas.

The degree to which foreign policy is 'Europeanized' therefore varies according to issue areas and their sensitivity for member state governments, in turn affected by domestic politics. This is not to suggest direct lines of accountability for foreign policy; indeed the multi-level nature of decision making weakens the often tenuous relationship between executives and publics. Legitimizing European decisions poses a significant challenge for member states and one that will grow with ESDP. The political history and capabilities of member states also affect the degree to which their foreign policy is Europeanized. For Britain and France, with their extensive networks of external relations outside the EU, membership can represent a 'constriction or simply a means to amplify national foreign policy' (Manners and Whitman, 2000, p. 263). Moreover, such states and other EU members have special interests, such as Britain's relationship with the USA, which are kept separate from CFSP. For states without an extensive external network or with historical reasons to place national initiatives in a multilateral framework the EU represents an opportunity (ibid.). In this orientation 'the member state involved often seeks to work with the EU or defers most foreign policy prerogatives to the Union' (ibid.).

The post-Cold-War security environment has provided a powerful impetus to coordination of foreign policy in the EU and underlined the relevance of the European rationale. As contemporary security understandings have broadened to include political, economic and societal elements, the international environment is 'uniquely conducive to EU actorness' (Brotherton and Vogler, 1999, p. 257). The challenges of global finance, trade, poverty and terrorism can arguably require international and multilateral responses. For the European Union's High Representative for CFSP, 'not even the most powerful country can confront on its own the challenges the international community is facing. Our security and prosperity increasingly depend on an effective multilateral system' (Solana, 2004). The EU's contribution has been to seek to anchor political and economic stability for its members through 'Association Agreements', 'Stability Pacts', regional strategies and neighbourhood policy. Human rights and good governance also have become core criteria in EU external relations. The EU's ambition is the 'development of a stronger international society, well functioning international institutions and rule based order' (Solana, 2004). The EU can, therefore, be seen to be a 'normative power' in security provision.

> After a century in which the European State system produced conflicts of catastrophic proportions, it is not surprising that European countries value an environment in which states operate within a legal framework and conflicts are

> settled peacefully. The desire to spread this to the rest of the world is both natural and praiseworthy. (Cooper, 2003, p. 160)

Norm setting is fundamental to the European project embodied in treaty law and directing external relations. It has been argued that by 'refocusing away from the debate over either civilian or military power, it is possible to think of the ideational impact of the EU's international identity/role as representing normative power' (Manners, 2002, p. 238).

The normative direction of EU external relations is closely associated with its soft power attributes. Soft power, 'getting others to want what you want ...' (Nye, 2002/3, p. 552), is essentially the notion of 'co-optive power' rather than 'coercive' or 'command power': 'Soft power is also more than persuasion or the ability to move people by argument. It is the ability to entice and attract. And attraction often leads to acquiescence or imitation' (ibid.). Soft power can be seen as a relevant and an important instrument of diplomacy.

> If a country can make its power legitimate in the eyes of others, it will encounter less resistance to its wishes. If its culture and ideology are attractive, others more willingly follow. If it can establish international rules that are consistent with its society, it will be less likely to have to change. If it can help support institutions that encourage other countries to channel or limit their activities in ways it prefers, it may not need as many costly carrots and sticks. (Ibid., p. 553)

The potential of the EU to influence others on the basis of soft power has been optimistically interpreted in some quarters. Leonard, for example, has asserted that 'the strength of the EU ... is broad and deep: once sucked into its sphere of influence, countries are changed forever' (Leonard, 2005, pp. 4–5). The 'outreach' of the EU is, however, variable, with degrees of influence permeating outwards from accession countries to the wider borderlands. The Middle East case study demonstrated that intense local conflicts are not swayed by norms codified in the EMP or EU association agreements. The point is that soft power has its limits: while it is not to be derided, it is important to recognize that 'foreign policy is about war and peace, and countries that only do peace are missing half of the story – perhaps the more important half' (Cooper, 2003, p. 162). The EU's weakness in 'hard power' has been recognized by the European Council with its consequent commitment to ESDP. The planned investment in military resources should provide the means to significantly redress the current deficiency in capabilities. Europe will not be a match for the USA but will be able to deploy forces in support of a range of CFSP objectives, including crisis management roles. The parallel requirement is for political coherence and coordination to ensure effective use of resources. The draft European

Constitution sought to address this, but while institutional provision can facilitate outcomes, political will and consensus remain key elements in the successful attainment of European policies. Enlargement of the Union provides additional challenges to the process of attaining coordination and will make the establishment of consensus a harder exercise.

In conclusion, it can be argued that the European Union is a significant international actor even though it defies straightforward categorization by being neither a state nor a regime. The EU constitutes a new type of actor: it may be uneven in performance, at times inconsistent, but it remains important. It is the breadth of European external relations, reflecting the internal integration of member states, and not just CFSP, that gives the EU political gravity. The constraints within the CFSP system – capabilities, consensus and political will – mean that it has not replaced national policy. At the same time it remains in the interests of member states to pursue common strategies when Union initiatives are seen as appropriate. It is this multi-level and multi-issue nature of European foreign policy making that limits the EU to a partial or quasi-international actor role. This does not mean the role is insignificant, and when account is taken of the impact of the EU on third parties, when its 'presence' is measured, (Allen and Smith, 1990) the perspective of 'outsiders' confirms the salience of the Union's external role. The pattern is variable, as would be expected from Union external policy, but clearly demonstrable in international organizations, the diplomacy of political economy, the developing world and Europe's 'borderlands'. In a study of the EU's external political impact in the 1990s, Ginsberg found the evidence undermined the conventional dichotomy of the EU as an 'economic superpower–political dwarf' (Ginsberg, 2001, p. 278).

Although not a 'dwarf' in political affairs, the EU is unlikely to complete a transition from civilian power to fully fledged international actor in the immediate future. ESDP will alter the balance of its policy instruments but elements of the current 'imperfect union' are likely to persist. The challenge for Europe's élites is not only to manage this process – but to legitimize it.

PART II

The Enlargement of the European Union

3. Enlargement and Central and Eastern Europe

Petr Drulák

This chapter looks at the eastern enlargement of the European Union (EU) through Central European eyes. It focuses on the costs and benefits which the Central and Eastern European countries (CEECs) associate with their EU membership. However, the chapter tries to avoid a standard, economic cost–benefit analysis, which would quantify all the items, summarize them and present the bottom line as the final result. Even though this kind of analysis can provide valuable findings (see e.g. Majcen, 1999), it is bound to miss the bigger picture of institutional and ideational changes in the CEECs related to EU accession.

Therefore, I start by pointing to the asymmetry in the theorization of EU enlargement that leads to the underestimation of the ideational factors in the analysis of the CEECs, even though these factors are usually taken into account in the analysis of the EU. Following this, I look into how Europe is constructed in relation to the national identities of the CEECs, arguing that these constructions represent frameworks within which the accession practice has been embedded. The accession practice itself is addressed by the analysis of accession negotiations and the development of good governance in the CEECs. I argue that these two areas represent the accession practice very well. As for the former, the most contested issues in the accession negotiations provide us with an idea of how the costs and benefits of accession were perceived. Concerning the latter, good governance became the key issue of accession preparation, on which the fulfilment of other conditions depended. Finally, I deal with the CEECs' perspective on two vital issues of the EU's future: its institutional framework and its relations with the USA.

THE THEORETICAL ASYMMETRY OF THE RESEARCH ON EU ACCESSION

The research on EU enlargement suffers from a theoretical asymmetry. Whereas the conduct of the CEECs seems to fit into the thick rationalist framework, the decisions of the EU members can be understood only in thin rationalist, or constructivist, terms.

On the one hand, it has been rightly pointed out that the economic and security benefits of enlargement for the EU members do not provide a satisfactory explanation for their support to the enlargement process. Therefore, the decision of the EU to enlarge eastwards has been repeatedly analysed in the literature, and the investigation of its motives required theoreticians either to leave the prevailing rationalist framework, taking a more reflectivist position (Fierke and Wiener, 1999), or to try to enrich rationalism with norms and ideas (Schimmelfennig, 1998). In both respects, the EU's decision to enlarge was explained with reference to the norms on which the EU was built, and which prevented EU members from saying no to the CEECs' plea for membership, no matter how it compared with their own material self-interests.

On the other hand, the motivation of the CEECs has usually been taken for granted. Even though it is acknowledged that the CEECs' desire to enter the EU 'conforms with both constructivist and rationalist explanations' (Schimmelfenning and Sedelmeier, 2002, p. 519), the constructivist explanation is usually forgotten for the sake of much-valued parsimony. It has usually been assumed that these benefits would be so large for the CEECs that no other explanation for their efforts to join the EU was needed than the rationalist reference to their pursuit of material self-interests (Moravcsik, 1998). Why bother with ideas if material interests seem to do all the necessary explanatory hard work?

Even though this asymmetry rests on fragile grounds, it can be misleading in political practice. The asymmetry results from two factors – a quest for parsimony, and a lack of knowledge about the CEECs. Neither of these make it inevitable. First, the explanatory parsimony is embraced by rationalists (Ray, 1992, p. 191) but criticized by reflectivists. Second, lack of knowledge about the CEECs is due to the shortage of West European or American researchers who study the CEECs and due to shortage of researchers in the CEECs who are able to present their arguments in a form in which the social sciences are practised in the EU and USA. Therefore, while during the previous round of enlargement the literature focused on the candidate countries, it is EU politics that is the main focus of the literature on the Eastern enlargement (Schimmelfenning and Sedelmeier, 2002) and the current enlargement is seen in terms of the EU politics rather than in terms of the candidate countries' politics.

Importantly, the quest for simplistic solutions and the lack of knowledge about the CEECs also shapes much of the political practice. Thus the implications of the theoretical asymmetry can be misleading in political practice, leading to a short-cut conclusion that the enlargement was possible only due to a combination of Eastern European self-interest and Western European self-denial in the name of European norms. Assuming this, some old EU members expected the CEECs to be grateful for the invitation to their inner circle. They then felt cheated when the CEECs supported the Bush Administration during the Iraq crisis in 2003. In contrast, the leaders of the CEECs were surprised both by the ferocity of the criticisms coming from the EU and by the fact that they were expected to be grateful. This misunderstanding points to the deeper problems stemming from the simplified picture of self-interest and self-denial, which ignores the constitutive function of ideas in the accession efforts of the CEECs. It is the analysis of identities which helps understand why.

THE RETURN TO EUROPE: PRO-EUROPEAN IDENTITIES, EUROSCEPTICISM AND POLITICAL DYNAMICS

The project of EU accession was deeply embedded in the particular construction of the national identities of the CEECs, which also provided the framework for the whole transition from totalitarianism or authoritarianism to democracy. In all of the CEECs, the transition was understood as a 'return to Europe' (Drulák, 2001), which was one of the slogans of the democratic revolutions in 1989. This move established a firm link between the national and European identities of the CEECs, which merits a closer look.

The concept of a return to Europe implies two ideas (Drulák and Druláková, 2004). First, there is the idea of belonging to Europe, since people can only return to places which they have previously occupied. Second, the return refers to the process by which people proceed from one point to another. Both the static idea of belonging and the dynamic idea of process reveal Europe as a foundational framework for the very constitution of the CEECs as sovereign political agents.

In the political discourse of the CEECs a variety of references can be found whose goal is to demonstrate the European, or if possible the West European, credentials of the country. There are several types of these arguments based on geography, religion and history, which resonate with the national mythologies of the countries, and which contribute to the narratives on the basis of which people understand themselves and their place in the world (Drulák, 2001; Drulák and Druláková, 2004). Despite the diversity of these narratives, two features are shared across all the countries. First, the CEECs are constructed as naturally European from time immemorial. Second, they are also constructed as victims for the well-being of Europe.

To start with, geographical arguments have been very popular, particularly the ones that represent a given country as a true centre or heart of Europe. Thus the current Czech president, Václav Klaus, who is one of the most Eurosceptic of EU leaders, has recently argued (Klaus, 2003) that his country has 'always been in the heart of the continent and it is inconceivable that the multi-national organism in making could do without its heart or that the heart could do without the body'. Similar claims have also been made by Slovakia. To drive their point home, the Lithuanians erected a monument marking the geographical centre of Europe near their capital Vilnius, as well as changing the time zone of Lithuania by switching to Central European time in the 1990s (Vinogradnaite, 2001).

Besides geography, religious and cultural arguments have frequently been emphasized. In this connection, belonging to Western Christianity, the Roman Catholic and Protestant Churches has been equated with belonging to Western Europe. Similarly, historical events and institutions from the distant past have been evoked to show the links with Western Europe. Hence the Hanseatic League (Poland, the Baltics), the Holy Roman Empire (Czech Republic, Hungary, Slovakia and Slovenia), and early experiences of statehood (medieval kingdoms) were turned into favoured reference points.

All these readings of history also share a sense of victimhood (Krzeminski, 2001). They concentrate on particular historical events which are supposed to remind the West of its historical debts to CEECs. Therefore the Yalta agreement in 1945, the Munich agreement in 1938, the nineteenth-century struggles for national autonomy or the fights against Turks in the sixteenth and seventeenth centuries are often evoked as instances when Central and Eastern Europeans put their lives and freedom on the altar for West European security and freedom.

While the idea of belonging is conservative, emphasizing stability, the idea of process is inherently dynamic, stressing change (Drulák and Druláková, 2004). This change can be broadly characterized as modernization. The EU became a symbol of economic and political modernity. Looking at the shop windows of German and Austrian department stores was a shocking experience for citizens who grew up in conditions of constant shortages of all kinds of consumer goods. For many, this experience was the ultimate argument against communism and central planning, which always used to boast about its superior economic efficiency over capitalist countries. It was especially the fact that European integration was primarily perceived in terms of the economic community harvesting all the possible benefits of capitalist efficiency while also keeping a strong social dimension that turned it into an example seen as worthy of emulation. Therefore the experience of the EU countries was used as an important reference point when discussing the transition.

To sum up, the concept of a 'return to Europe', within which transition and EU accession, as a key element of transition, has been embedded, has been connected with at least three ideas: a return to time-tested relations, the repayment of the old debts of Western Europe to the CEECs, and economic and social modernization as well as democratization. Despite the political dynamics and despite the changes in attitudes towards the EU, these three elements have been remarkably stable since 1989.

Euroscepticism

Although the general mood in the CEECs was supportive towards EU accession, the accession was far from uncontested. Indeed, in many countries there were several groups which either rejected EU membership or at least did not support it. A closer look at the Eurosceptic positions reveals what various groups perceive as the costs of EU membership. Therefore I look into the arguments on which their rejection of the EU is based. In this respect, I do not make the potentially useful distinction between Euroscepticism and EU scepticism (Beichelt, 2004; Kopecký and Mudde, 2002), instead addressing Euroscepticism as a broad variety of attitudes.[1]

Most Eurosceptic groupings fit into the traditional classification of ideologies (conservative, liberal and socialist) each assuming an extreme position (Gyárfášová, 2001; Brusis, 2001; Kopecký and Mudde, 2002; Beichelt, 2004). Hence there are groups of die-hard nationalist conservatives who argue that the EU threatens national sovereignty and national values. Sometimes this has been linked with Catholic fundamentalists warning against the godless Europe, such as the network around Radio Maryja in Poland which inspired a successful oppositional political party, the League of Polish Families, or the conservative wing of the Slovak Christian Democratic Movement which has been a part of the ruling coalition. However, the nationalist groupings often lacked any religious links embracing rightist populism or extreme right ideology such as the Republican Party of Czechoslovakia, the Slovak National Party (which was part of the Mečiar coalition in the 1990s), the Slovenian National Party or the Hungarian Justice and Life Party, all of which had some parliamentary presence throughout the 1990s.

On the other hand, there are also liberal critics who see the EU as a socialist project which burdens the economic activity with overly heavy regulation. For example, former Czech prime minister Václav Klaus and his Civic Democratic Party argued that there was a danger that the Czech Republic would again import a planned economy from the EU. In contrast, leftist populists argue that the EU is too liberal, giving free rein to transnational corporations and the exploitation of workers (Gyárfášová, 2001). This was the case with the Czech and Slovak Communist Parties. However, this argument also found adherents among some leftist opponents of globalization, for whom European integration was a part of capitalist globalization.

However, apart from these three ideational streams, there are other kinds of Eurosceptic movements which are more country specific and which do not easily fit into the scheme. I look into two of these: sector-based groupings and minority-based ones. First, in Poland, Andrzej Lepper organized a successful political movement called Self-Defence which campaigned against the EU in the name of Polish peasants. However, while Self-Defence is on the extremist fringe on the Polish political scene, parts of its agenda are shared with the more moderate Polish Peasant Party, which was part of the ruling coalition during the final stage of accession. This was connected with the idiosyncrasies of the Polish agricultural sector – its enormous size and the tenure of the land by a large number of smallholders. This condition made agriculture both less efficient and more politically sensitive in Poland than in other countries, while also providing a breeding ground for populist leaders.

Second, minority-based Euroscepticism looms large in the Baltic countries, where there is a marked absence of other Eurosceptic groupings or political parties (Beichelt, 2004). It is especially the case in Latvia and Estonia, where support for EU accession is quite low among the large Russian minorities. Now this may seem puzzling at first glance, as the EU pushed hard for the minority rights of Baltic Russians, and thus it could be seen as their natural ally. However, the puzzle can be understood if we take into account that in the Baltic countries, the pro-European discourse was at the same time sharply anti-Russian (Freiberga, 2001). The Latvian and Estonian readings of EU membership as the ultimate shelter against Russian dominance led to the construction of the EU as anti-Russian in the eyes of Russian minorities.

To sum up, most accession countries have Eurosceptic parties and movements which are politically significant. Not only do they reflect traditional ideologies (conservatism, liberalism and socialism) but they also draw on the specific attributes of the CEECs.

Political Dynamics

Both pro-European identities and Euroscepticism have so far been discussed in synchronic terms. And, indeed, the issues on which I have focused have been remarkably stable throughout the whole period. Nevertheless, within this stable framework the interpretation of the return to Europe has been evolving, mainly in response to political dynamics. Three stages of the evolution can be distinguished (Drulák and Druláková, 2004; Plavšak, 2001): idealism, disenchantment and pragmatism.

Idealism was the prevailing mood of the early 1990s in the period immediately after the democratic revolutions. On the one hand, it was believed that the countries could return to Europe with the same speed with which communism had fallen. The optimistic statements of European leaders about building a common Europe were taken at face value, and nothing seemed impossible. On the other hand, knowledge about 'Europe' was very patchy. Europe was simply seen as 'an opposition to what people were trying to escape from' (Ivanov, 2001). Hence, not only EU membership but also the memberships of the IMF, WTO, Council of Europe, OECD and NATO were associated with the return to Europe (Drulák and Königová, 2005), frequently without the élites being able to tell these organizations apart.

Inevitably, after this euphoria a painful sobering period followed. Tough negotiations of the first association agreements in 1991 taught people that the grand talk about European unity does not prevent EU leaders from defending the interests of their agricultural or steel industries (Mayhew, 1998). Moreover, apart from NATO, the attention focused on the EU, which looked distant and difficult to reach. In 1993, Václav Havel (1993/1999, pp. 162–71) bitterly complained that the West likes to use the label 'formerly communist' to get rid of any responsibility and solidarity. However, it was only at this stage that the learning process of the élites about the EU started, even though it was only at the very basic level, such as clarifying the distinction between the European Council and the Council of Europe.

As the accession talks, which started in 1998, drew closer, a more pragmatic, bargaining mood prevailed. The relationship with the EU was increasingly seen in terms of give-and-take, and the general balance was evaluated as positive for the candidate countries. Nevertheless, it would be wrong to conclude that the return to Europe boils down to a financial cost–benefit analysis, even if the bargaining process of accession talks may support such a perspective. However, the very act of bargaining presupposes common ground among the participants defined by shared ideas and a shared language, especially if the bargaining takes place in as complex a system as the EU. Without such common ground, it would hardly be possible to compare in cost–benefit terms, for example, the costs of limitations of national autonomy with the benefits of participation in the EU decision making. This common ground was to a large extent defined during the idealist period of the early 1990s, thus constituting the framework in which the nitty-gritty of accession talks was embedded.

ACCESSION TALKS: (UN)REAL NEGOTIATIONS AND BROKEN PROMISES

It has sometimes been argued that the accession talks were not real negotiations, being rather a process of the simple transfer of norms. First, the candidate countries were obliged to take over the whole of the *acquis communautaire*, without the possibility of any opt-outs. The only thing that could be negotiated was a transition period which could temporarily postpone the incorporation of some EU norms. Second, the asymmetry of bargaining power worked so greatly to the benefit of the EU that the CEECs were left with no choice.

Now, even though these two arguments are relevant, this does not diminish the importance of the accession talks. They represented the most intensive experience of mutual learning between the EU and the CEECs. They shaped the perception of the EU in the final stage of the accession process. And they also involved real negotiations, especially when the EU itself asked for transition periods.

The review of the accession talks proceeds in three steps. First, general problems which touched on all the CEECs are addressed. Following this, some country-specific issues are reviewed. Finally, the lack of mutual cooperation between the CEECs is dealt with.

Issues

The *acquis communautaire* was divided into 31 chapters, such as agriculture, transport and competition policy, and the negotiations proceeded from the least controversial chapters to more difficult ones. A closer look into some of the most contested issues provides us with a more specific idea about the costs and benefits as they were perceived by the actors.

From the very beginning it was obvious that areas such as agriculture and the budget would be especially difficult to deal with because of their redistributive nature which turned talks about them into a pure zero-sum game. Whereas candidate countries tried to maximize the financial inflows from the EU into their budgets, the EU tried to minimize them. Both parties were able to present respectable arguments for their positions. While the candidates argued that in line with the *acquis* they should get the same treatment as current EU members, the EU pointed to the limited capacity of the candidates to absorb the funds, and to the lower levels of prices in the candidate countries.

Therefore, both the budget and agriculture were left until the very end of the fierce negotiations in the final hours of the Copenhagen Summit, when the enlargement process was closed and the bills were signed. The accession countries pointed out that the EU was enlarging on the cheap. The whole enlargement package cost the EU a bit more than EUR 13 billion per year for the period 2004–6, representing about 0.05 per cent of EU GDP (Ludlow, 2004, p. 345) which, on the other hand, represents quite a decent gain of more than 1 per cent of the GDP for the ten accession countries each year. However, the accession countries also seemed to be quite concerned with their relative gains. This was especially the case with the Visegrad countries and Slovenia, which got much less per capita than the Baltic countries (ibid., p. 241).

However, there were other issues which did not have such a clear redistributive character but which also proved controversial. Except for Slovenia, most EU candidates (especially Poland), fearing a cheap sell-out of their assets, asked for transition periods in the chapter on the free movement of capital, which touched upon the purchase of real estate. Hence transition periods were agreed which constrained the right of non-residents to buy agricultural land and secondary residences in the accession countries ranging from seven to twelve years after accession. On the opposite side, many EU members (particularly Germany and Austria) were afraid that their labour markets would be flooded with cheap labour from the CEECs if the free movement of persons were allowed from the first day of accession. Unusually, it was the EU which asked for the transition period in this case. Eventually, a transition period of up to seven years was agreed during which the old EU members can protect their labour markets against the inflows of labour from the new EU members.

The cases for transition periods in both chapters were based on political sensitivities rather than on objective evidence. Therefore, it was quite easy for the EU negotiators to link these two issues in the accession talks, presenting them as a trade-off between two politically sensitive packages (Boruta, 2002). On this basis, it was possible to disregard a host of studies which pointed to the low migratory potential of the CEECs and, hence, to the absence of the threats to the EU labour markets. Compared to this, the chapter on environment, which was often mentioned as one of the more difficult chapters, was relatively easy to conclude. Despite the high costs of implementation of the measures for environmental protection, there was a consensus about its benefits for the badly damaged environments in accession countries.

However, some chapters were more specific to the countries involved. It was the case that the more difficult the chapter was for a given country, the longer it took to finish the negotiations. Therefore the review of these late chapters, disregarding agriculture and budget which were intentionally left for the very end of the negotiations, provides us with an insight into where the greatest challenges were.

To start with, Lithuania was the only CEEC which had closed all of the chapters before the Danish presidency started (Ludlow, 2004). However, the last of these chapters was energy. This was sensitive for Lithuania as the country was forced to close its nuclear power plant in Ignalina, based on Chernobyl technology. In exchange, Lithuania was able to gain significant financial assistance from the EU.

On the other hand, Latvia put off the closure of the institutional chapter as it felt underrepresented in the Council. Latvia was offered four votes there, being put in the same category as Luxembourg or neighbouring Estonia. Disagreeing with this, Latvia argued that, on the basis of its population, it should get somewhat closer to the seven votes of neighbouring Lithuania. However, the EU did not budge on this issue and, eventually, Latvia had to accept the original offer. In contrast, Slovenia had troubles in regional policy. Being relatively rich and small, Slovenia could not tap into the EU money for underdeveloped regions. Therefore it came up with a new administrative division of the country into two regions, the poorer of which would qualify for EU funds. However, the EU rejected this. Estonia could not close the energy chapter for some time as it tried to delay the liberalization of its energy market, being afraid of Finnish competition. It was thanks to Finnish generosity that Estonia was able to get a lengthy transition period at the end of the day (Ludlow, 2004, p. 116).

Like Lithuania, Slovakia agreed to shut its nuclear power plant in Jaslovské Bohunice. However, it still had two chapters to close on the eve of the Danish presidency. First, there was regional policy, where the EU had doubts about the Slovak administrative capacity for handling EU funds. Second, there was competition, where Slovakia extended generous tax breaks to foreign investors, which some EU countries saw as unfair subsidies which threatened their own competitiveness. Eventually, Slovakia was given the benefit of the doubt concerning its administrative capacity, and it was agreed that the tax breaks had to be phased out.

Similarly, the Czech Republic also struggled with competition policy. However, it was state aid to the steel industry rather than tax incentives for foreign capital that was the main stumbling block. The EU did not oppose the state aid as such; however, it insisted that the aid had to be one-off and not repeated in future (Telička and Barták, 2003, pp. 102–19). In this respect, it took some time before the Czech government produced a plan which the EU found convincing. Like the Latvians, the Czechs also had objections to the institutional chapter. They pointed out that they were underrepresented in the European Parliament, being offered two fewer seats than Belgium or Portugal, which had the same population. However, unlike the Latvians, they were able to drive their point home by the end of the accession talks. Moreover, the Czech Republic hesitated with the closure of the chapter on transport, where the EU, under pressure from Germany and Austria, insisted on a transition period constraining the access of hauliers from the CEECs to the single market. Eventually, the Czech negotiators had to give in.

Poland had troubles with the competition policy as it had to phase out tax breaks, like Slovakia, and, like the Czech Republic, to reinvigorate its steel industry in a way that would be compatible with EU rules. Again like Slovakia, Poland did not seem able to cope with administrative requirements for the distribution of regional aid; however, it was eventually given the benefit of the doubt. Unlike the other candidates, Poland struggled with justice and home affairs due to its long borders with Belarus and Ukraine (Ludlow, 2004, p. 119). While the EU countries asked Poland for information about the protection of the border which the Poles considered too sensitive to provide, the Poles asked for funds for the maintenance of the border which were not foreseen in the enlargement package.

Hungary had similar problems as Slovakia with competition policy and regional policy, and it had the very same problem as the Czech Republic with underrepresentation in the European Parliament. Therefore Hungary also closed all three chapters with similar results as was the case with Slovakia and the Czech Republic. In addition, the EU raised some concerns in the areas of culture and audiovisual policy when the government of Prime Minister Orbán interfered with the media, preventing a successful closure of the chapter until a new media law was passed (Ludlow, 2004, p. 120).

To sum up, as expected, issues connected with financial flows (agriculture, budget, free movement of capital) and the movement of people proved to be the most controversial in the accession talks, as it was in these areas where the important costs and benefits were expected in all of the countries. Moreover, these issues were easy to quantify, which often allowed the boiling down of their complexity to a single number, making the issues presentable in media discourse, although at the price of a gross distortion. However, there were also other issues which accession countries had to struggle with, such as competition policy, which was to constrain their ability to attract foreign capital by tailor-made tax incentives as well as their ability to subsidize ailing companies, or regional policy where the accession countries' administrative capacity had to be developed. Nevertheless, despite these overlaps, each accession country had to deal with its own unique configuration of issues distinct from others.

The Absence of Mutual Cooperation

The CEECs were often perceived as a block of very similar countries, which raised both hopes and fears of their coordinated march into the EU.

However, such a march failed to materialize. First, the accession countries considered one another as competitors rather than as partners (Boruta, 2002), and the EU encouraged this kind of attitude. Second, despite sharing some interests, each accession country was very much in a unique position. On the one hand, there were several fora in which accession countries tried to coordinate their position towards the EU. These included the ten fast-track countries (all the candidates except for Bulgaria and Romania), the first-wave countries (Estonia, the Czech Republic, Hungary, Poland, Slovenia), and the Visegrad countries (the Czech Republic, Hungary, Poland, Slovakia). These networks provided the framework for regular consultations, but only rarely were any common positions agreed, and even then one or more countries defected from the common position at the earliest possible opportunity.

The EU encouraged this mutual competition using an 'icebreaker tactic' (Friis, 2002, p. 17), which consisted of trying 'to break the ice with one country and then hope that others will follow suit by accepting more or less the same deal'. It usually worked. Thus, it was Slovenia that broke the ice in the environmental chapter, the Czech Republic was the first to conclude the free movement of capital, and Hungary was the quickest to accept the free movement of persons (Friis, 2002). Obviously, this kind of icebreaking undermined any potential for cooperation. The last attempt at it came on the eve of the Copenhagen Summit when the heads of governments of the Visegrad countries agreed to press for a higher share of direct payments in the financial package than offered by the EU. However, Poland and the Czech Republic made separate deals with the Danish presidency in the final hours of the summit, to the great disappointment of Hungary and Slovakia (Ludlow, 2004, pp. 109–10).

The only example of successful cooperation among the candidate countries is that between the Czech Republic and Slovakia after Slovakia was invited to the accession talks in 1999. Prague supported the Slovak effort to catch up with the first-wave countries by providing intensive consultations and the transfer of the accession-related know-how.

However, there was more successful cooperation between some candidate countries and some EU members. Hence Poland had very close links with Germany (Lippert et al., 2001b, p. 21), and Germany repeatedly let it be known that without Poland no enlargement was possible. Similarly, the Baltic countries benefited from the support of the Nordic countries. More specifically, Finland felt itself to be a sponsor of Estonia while Denmark felt strongly pro-Lithuania (Ludlow, 2004, p. 105).

To sum up, experience from the accession talks does not point to any blocks of CEECs in the making, apart from the special relationship between the Czech Republic and Slovakia, whose role in EU governance would be comparable to, for example, Benelux or the Nordic countries. In contrast, one can expect the development on patterns of cooperation which cut across the border between old and new member states, such as cooperation between Germany and Poland, or between Nordic and Baltic countries.

GOOD GOVERNANCE: EUROPEANIZATION RIGHT OR WRONG

Even though there was no chapter on administrative capacity in the accession talks, the quality of national administration became one of the central and least tractable issues of the whole accession process. Its importance was somewhat underestimated in the early stage of the accession. However, since the mid-1990s it has become obvious to all concerned that a functioning administration was a key precondition for fulfilling each of the three Copenhagen criteria: the rule of law, market economy, and the ability to implement EU law. It was the European Council in Madrid in 1995 that introduced administrative capacity as the *de facto* fourth criterion, without which no enlargement is possible (Dimitrova, 2004). In connection with this, the Commission has refocused its pre-accession financial assistance towards administrative reform in candidate countries since the late 1990s (Bailey and De Propris, 2004). Moreover, in the candidate countries, an improved administration was seen as one of the most important accession-related benefits.

Nevertheless, the development of administrative capacity was far less tangible than the transposition of the *acquis communautaire*, which seemed to dominate the accession. While the latter consists of the thousands of specific regulations which had to be translated and incorporated into national legal systems, the former does not provide any clear blueprint for action. The EU does not prescribe any model for national administration; the only thing that the EU requires is the ability to implement nationally what was agreed at the EU level. Therefore the impact of the EU on national administrations in member states has traditionally been moderate and there has been no EU model of national administration. Even though there is a growing evidence of a Europeanization of national administrations in EU members, their national administrations still remain distinct systems working by their own rules. However, there are several reasons why Europeanization is likely to have a much stronger impact on the national administrations of the new members (Grabbe, 2001; Goetz, 2001).

First, the communist institutions lost their legitimacy and the new organizational framework has not been strongly institutionalized. Hence the institutions have been in development and thus susceptible to external influences. The return to Europe turned the EU into the most important external influence in this respect. Second, some of the institutions were non-existent and the EU has been a natural source of templates for their creation. Third, the EU targeted the national administrative capacities to a greater extent than ever before, making candidates initiate important administrative reforms. Not only has it addressed the executive branch of the central government but it has also been involved in the reforms of legislature, judiciary and sub-national state structures. Moreover, these reforms took place at an enormous speed, as they had to be at least partly in place before accession itself.

Despite these favourable conditions, the process of Europeanization of national administrations has been far from smooth, as it had to struggle with the communist legacy. This legacy consisted of the under-politicization of the state administration in policy terms, and of its over-politicization in personnel terms (Goetz and Wollmann, 2001). On the one hand, the state administration was under-politicized in the sense that it was not involved in policy formation, only serving for the implementation of decisions made by the Communist Party. On the other hand, it was over-politicized as all the important appointments were subject to the approval of the Communist Party. Therefore, after the fall of communist rule a thorough overhaul of all the state institutions was needed to create the administrative backbone of the state, where decisions would be taken and implemented efficiently. This overhaul concerned all three branches of the state's central power – executive, legislature, and judiciary – as well as local and regional structures.

Intended Europeanization

In discussing the role of the EU in the Europeanization of national administration in candidate countries, one can distinguish between its intended and unintended effects. Interestingly, the latter tend to be stronger than the former, and sometimes they run up against each other. To start with, the EU, together with other international organizations (the OECD, World Bank), aimed at specific administrative reforms to improve administrative capacity. At the macro level, the EU used the accession negotiations and regular evaluation reports to signal what issues it saw as vital to successful administrative reforms. In this respect, three issues stood out: the professionalization of the central administration, regionalization, and the enhanced efficiency of the courts.

First, professionalization was supposed to overcome the over-politicization of appointments. Apart from Hungary (Meyer-Sahling, 2001), candidate countries started their civil service reforms under pressure from the EU, and often with great reluctance. For example, the Czech Republic keeps delaying the implementation of its Civil Service Act, whose approval the EU considered as indispensable for the conclusion of the accession process, and which would deprive the political élite of much of its control over appointments in the civil service. Second, regionalization is connected with the EU system for development assistance (Structural Funds), which is distributed on a regional rather than on a national basis. Therefore several candidate countries had to establish new regional structures to become eligible for EU funds. In this respect, for most CEECs, with the exception of Poland, regionalization was a top–down process motivated by the EU, taking place in the absence of any bottom-up pressures for regionalization (Marek and Baun, 2002, p. 896). Third, the inefficiency of the judicial system became notorious in most candidate countries. The average length of the judicial process took several years, thus hampering law enforcement and the very rule of law. Repeated criticisms by regular reports put the reform of the judiciary high on the domestic political agendas.

However, besides these interactions at the macro level, the EU also tried to shape the national administrations at the level of specific procedures. The most important tool of this micro management was twinning (Bailey and De Propris, 2004), a programme within which civil servants from EU countries' administrations (so-called 'twinners') were invited by the accession countries for up to two years to assist their administrations with the implementation of the *acquis*. The Commission launched twinning in 1998 as its key programme of institution building. It did not aim at the transfer of any specific procedures, its goal was more general, namely to build an efficient national administration which would be able to implement the *acquis*. Therefore, most twinners were in the areas that presented the greatest challenges for implementation, such as public finance, justice and home affairs, and agriculture (ibid., p. 87).

Preliminary findings suggest that the results of twinning have been mixed (Königová, 2004). It usually failed whenever twinners rigidly stuck to the model of their own national administration, trying to export that model. Moreover, it was often difficult to overcome the distrust and the lack of interest on the part of the local civil servants, which was a particular problem at the start of the twinning programme. However, it was successful when, on the basis of argumentative interactions, CEEC civil servants were able to reflect on the existing procedures and to learn from the experience of the twinners. In the Czech Republic, it was, for example, in the areas of public–private partnerships in social services, environmental education, and health care for non-residents that twinning brought substantial added value (ibid., p. 20).

Unintended Europeanization

As suggested, the impact of the accession process has often given birth to unintended consequences. I focus on four groups of these effects: professionalization; the rise of the executive; bureaucratization; and centralization (Grabbe, 2001; Lippert et al., 2001a). First, the preparations for membership presented an enormous challenge for the civil services of candidate countries. Each administration set up a special EU unit which was responsible for the preparation for membership in the given area of competence. Moreover, all of these units were coordinated at the governmental level (Lippert et al., 2001a). This brought benefits in two regards at least. To start with, the governments were forced to invest in the modernization of their institutional structures, and to tackle long-standing problems such as inter-agency and interministerial coordination. Moreover, civil servants within these structures had to be able to communicate in English, and to absorb and implement new knowledge. These civil servants were then exposed to the EU in a very intensive way. On this basis, a highly professional group of civil servants emerged, standing out 'from overall public administration organs in quality and efficiency' (Nunberg, 2000, p. 20, quoted in Goetz and Wollmann, 2001, p. 878). Thus islands of professionalism inside the national administrations were created from which the know-how of efficient administration is likely to spread into others.

Second, the accession process privileges the executive over the legislature (Grabbe, 2001). The executive plays a key role in the preparations for and negotiation of membership, while the legislature is expected to rubber-stamp the EU laws without any deliberation. On the one hand, this rise of the executive helps to establish strong central state institutions, thus overcoming the totalitarian legacy. On the other hand, it can contribute to the weakening of the role of parliaments in democratic decision making, thus creating a democratic deficit.

Third, the technical nature of most accession issues makes them largely intangible to the political élite, which is then heavily dependent on the expertise of civil servants. Therefore a significant part of the decision making gets de-politicized and bureaucratized (Lippert et al., 2001a). The bureaucratization refers to two processes. On one hand, it reduces the over-politicization of personal appointments within the state institutions, strengthening the principle of meritocracy; for example, most chief negotiators were professionals rather than politicians. This brought the advantage of stability, as the chief negotiators did not change with every change in government. In this connection, bureaucratization provides a shelter against political interference in contributing to institutional autonomy (Drulák et al., 2003).

On the other hand, bureaucratization may further deepen the under-politicization of the state administration in policy formation in the sense that the administration is fully absorbed by implementation of Brussels' rules and procedures without developing any capacity for autonomous policy making. Therefore bureaucratization is a mixed blessing: it provides a remedy for the problem of over-politicization while deepening the problem of under-politicization.

Fourth, even though the accession process gave rise to a wave of decentralization at the constitutional level, it often led to centralization at the practical level. This centralization is again connected with the technocratic nature of the accession process. As Marek and Baun (2002, pp. 913–14) observe, 'the Commission's demands for efficiency and expediency in accession preparations and the implementation of EU programmes have had a contrary effect, reinforcing the centralist preferences of national government authorities and undermining the Commission's nominal support for decentralization'. Therefore, even though sub-national units came into being at the insistence of the EU, the practice of EU accession was not favourable to their empowerment.

To sum up, the accession process helped to improve the administrative capacity of CEECs, thus contributing to their better governance. In this respect, it was beneficial to the stabilization of their young democracies. However, the accession also encouraged centralization, the weakening of parliaments, and further under-politicization of policy making; these are detrimental to good democratic governance.

THE FUTURE OF EUROPE: KEEPING THINGS AS THEY ARE

EU enlargement has coincided with another important project of European integration, namely, the debate on the future of the EU. This debate has developed along two key dimensions. First, there is the institutional dimension, within which institutional and constitutional issues such as distribution of competencies between the EU and its members or the division of competencies among the EU institutions themselves were discussed. Second, there is the dimension of the EU as an actor on the world stage, which addressed the development of EU capabilities and relations with the USA.

The accession countries were not too active in these discussions, and they mostly refrained from taking clear positions on the issues discussed. There are several reasons for this (Drulák, 2002). First, the élites focused on accession-related issues, and had little attention left for other EU issues.

Second, there was some fear that by expressing their preferences the accession countries could alienate important actors in the EU and jeopardize smooth accession. Third, there was a general lack of policy-making capacity both on the administrative and political levels due to the communist past. Fourth, there was an understandable absence of insider experience with the EU, without which it was difficult to address many of the raised issues.

Nevertheless, the discussion about the EU's future could not be totally avoided, and leaders from the accession countries were motivated to contribute to the discussion to prove their European credentials. Vague though these contributions are, they provide us with some interesting insights. Reviewing the speeches by the leaders from the accession countries (Drulák, 2004), several general observations about the institutional dimension can be made, even though the positions of individual countries differ significantly from one another.

To start with, the idea of a European federation is almost universally rejected, and proposals for a radical deepening of the EU are usually met with a higher scepticism in accession countries than in the EU (Drulák, 2004). This is very much due to the bad historical experience with communist federations and unions. Similarly, the accession countries have been hostile to the idea of a hard core or avant-garde, referring to a smaller group of EU members engaged in a deeper integration (Drulák, 2002). They have expressed fears that such initiatives would leave them out of the centre of the integration process, creating within the enlarged EU a new community from which they would be excluded. On the contrary, most accession countries seem to like the EU as it is, especially if small improvements in supranational directions are made. Most of them have appreciated solidarity as an important European value, which might have mitigated some mistrust towards supranational authorities.

All the accession countries have also argued for more EU agency in world politics. However, they have been quite concerned lest the new EU role weaken the links between the EU and the USA. These concerns were connected with the fact that it was NATO and its US-led enlargement rather than the EU that was seen as a key security guarantee in the region (Bilčík, 2002, pp. 93–4). Hence NATO accession topped the agenda of the EU accession countries for some time. Moreover, the interpretation of twentieth-century history which dominates in the region considers the USA as a saviour of Europe in two world wars and the Cold War. On this basis, CEECs are warned against exclusive reliance on the West European powers in security matters. Therefore the position of candidate countries on European Security and Defence Policy (ESDP) was somewhat hesitant at the start (ibid.). On the other hand, British participation served as a litmus test which proved the compatibility of the ESDP with a strong transatlantic partnership, and which mitigated Central European suspicions. However, these suspicions were re-awoken before the Iraq War in 2003, when all the candidate countries supported the Bush Administration, for which they were publicly chided by the French president.

To sum up, the accession countries' positions have been oriented towards the status quo: keeping the EU basically as it is, and preserving the transatlantic alliance. This conservative position is above all related to their particular reading of history, and to the lack of insider experience which prevented the accession countries from a reflection on the strengths and weaknesses of the current system.

CONCLUSIONS

EU accession touched upon all dimensions of public life in the CEECs. This chapter could briefly review only a few of them. Subsequently, it tried to focus on the questions which cut across specific issue areas and which, therefore, provide general insights into what the most important challenges of the EU membership have been, and how these have been perceived by the CEECs. In this respect, six insights can be identified as especially important.

First, the accession of the CEECs to the EU has been part of a 'return to Europe'. In this respect, it has been, among other things, understood as a repayment of the historical debts that Western Europe had towards the CEECs. This dimension has usually been ignored by the EU, leading to several misunderstandings between EU members and candidates. Second, despite the dominance of the idea of a 'return to Europe', the CEECs have been providing fertile ground for a variety of Eurosceptic movements.

Third, across all of the CEECs, the most contested issues in the accession talks were those that were easy to quantify, or which were reducible to yes-or-no questions (e.g. the budget, agriculture, free movement of persons, free movement of capital, state aid to industry). At the same time, each country had to address its particular set of issues. Fourth, this particularity, as well as mutual rivalry between the CEECs, prevented any cooperation *vis-à-vis* the EU. However, patterns of cooperation emerged which cut across the division between member countries and accession countries.

Fifth, even though, in general, the EU helped to improve the governance structures in the CEECs, it also contributed to centralization and the weakening of democratic control. Finally, the CEECs were quite reluctant to take sides in the debates on the future of the EU. When pressed by their partners and allies, the CEECs have favoured the status quo: keeping the EU basically as it is, and preserving the transatlantic alliance.

NOTE

1. While Euroscepticism rejects European integration as such, EU scepticism supports integration, yet it objects to its current shape within the EU.

4. EU enlargement and international socialization

Frank Schimmelfennig

After the end of the Cold War, the European Union (EU)[1] embarked on a large-scale process of international socialization in the post-communist Central and Eastern European countries (CEECs), in which it inducts the CEECs to its general political rules of liberal democracy and to its specific rules of the *acquis communautaire*. When the first eight CEECs became full members of the EU in May 2004, the socialization process came to a first, formal conclusion. This chapter presents a general analysis of EU socialization policy in Central and Eastern Europe. Which mechanisms and strategies has the EU used to promote its rules? What effects did they have, and under which conditions and to what extent have they been successful?

The EU mainly relies on intergovernmental reinforcement to promote its rules in the CEECs; its core instrument is accession conditionality. The effectiveness of this instrument depends both on the credibility of the membership perspective and on the domestic costs of adopting EU conditions. Depending on the nature of EU conditions and conditionality three stages of EU socialization can be distinguished

1. The first stage is characterized by political conditionality. At this stage the focus is on the basic political standards of liberal democracy as a precondition for opening accession negotiations. The effectiveness of political conditionality is mainly determined by the credibility of the membership perspective and the domestic power costs that the target governments expect to incur from adapting to the liberal democratic rules of the EU. Political accession conditionality has been most successful in producing compliance with regard to low-cost issues and in locking in democratic consolidation in countries with alternating liberal and authoritarian governments. It has been largely redundant in the democratic front-runners of the region and ineffective in the autocratic systems of Eastern Europe.
2. *Acquis* conditionality becomes dominant after CEECs have adopted the basic political norms of the EU and accession negotiations start.

At this stage the focus of socialization is on the adoption of the specific rules of the *acquis communautaire*. The prospect of EU membership is highly credible and domestic power costs are lower than at the political conditionality stage. They affect the speed but not the success of rule adoption. This stage ends with formal accession to the EU. *Acquis* conditionality has generally been effective in the formal transposition of EU rules. However, rule implementation is still lagging behind.

3. The challenge of post-socialization accession then consists in the implementation of and compliance with the *acquis* rules. However, the EU can no longer rely on the power of accession conditionality. Successful socialization at this stage would be indicated by high and habitual compliance with EU rules in the absence of external inducement.

In the first two sections of the chapter, I describe the EU as an international socialization agency – the community rules it promotes and the strategies it uses for this purpose. The following sections explain the outcomes of political and *acquis* conditionality. Since the third stage of socialization has only just begun for the new members of the EU, I conclude with a brief outlook.

RULES: LIBERAL DEMOCRACY AND THE *ACQUIS*

International socialization is generally defined as the process of inducting states to the norms and rules of an international community (Risse and Sikkink, 1999, p. 11; Schimmelfennig, 2000, pp. 111–12). If international socialization is successful, the target state internalizes the community rules, that is, it reliably complies with them in the absence of external incentives and sanctions, and becomes a member of the international community. This definition triggers two sets of questions. First, what is the relevant international community in the context of the enlargement process of the EU, and which are the relevant rules? Second, how does the EU induct states to its rules and which conditions determine the success of its efforts?

The EU is part of the Western international community, with which it shares basic liberal rules of international and domestic conduct. In addition, it has its own EU rules, which only apply to EU candidates and member states.

Community rules are interrelated with the collective identity of an international community. The Western international community is an interstate community with a post-national collective identity based on liberal rules of domestic and international conduct (Schimmelfennig, 2003, pp. 77–89). Liberal human rights – individual freedoms, civil liberties and political rights – are at the core of the Western community's identity. They are the 'constitutive values that define legitimate statehood and rightful state action' in the domestic as well as in the international realm' (Reus-Smit, 1997, p. 558). In the domestic realm, the liberal principles of social and political order – social pluralism, the rule of law, democratic political participation and representation, private property and a market-based economy – are derived from and justified by these liberal human rights. Only a state that bases its domestic political system on these principles and reliably follows them in its domestic politics is regarded as fully legitimate by the Western international community.

As a consequence of the end of the Cold War, the breakdown of the communist systems and the beginning transition to democracy, the community rules of the Western international community became the 'standard of legitimacy' for the entire European system of states. The symbolic turning point was the adoption of the Charter of Paris for a New Europe in 1990, in which the European governments declared that 'we undertake to build, consolidate, and strengthen democracy as the only system of government for our nations' and that 'full respect' for human rights 'is the bedrock on which we will seek to construct the new Europe'.[2] Although few (if any) of the CEECs qualified as democratic countries and community members at the time, the Charter of Paris established a declaratory consensus to which all European countries formally committed themselves. It served as a normative basis for international socialization and for evaluating the legitimacy of the CEECs.

The liberal political principles are also constitutive for the international organizations of the Western community, such as the EU, NATO or the Council of Europe. They define the collective identity and the membership of these organizations. In the EU case, Article 6 of the Treaty on European Union (TEU) represents the most authoritative and clear statement of its liberal identity: 'the Union is founded on the principles of liberty, democracy, respect for human rights and fundamental freedoms, and the rule of law, principles which are common to the Member States'. Its membership rules in Article 49 TEU are explicitly linked to this identity: 'Any European state which respects the principles set out in Article 6(1) may apply to become a member of the Union.'

By contrast, specific rules regulate behaviour in individual issue areas and organizational procedures. In the EU these specific rules are mainly defined by the *acquis communautaire*, the accumulated EU policies and the rules that govern them. The *acquis* has to be accepted and adopted by all candidate countries. Except for transitional periods, during which the old or new member states are exempt from applying some of its rules, it is not subject to negotiations and modifications.

The two sets of rules correspond to two stages in the enlargement and international socialization process of the EU: democratic consolidation and *acquis* transfer. Support for democratic consolidation started immediately with the democratic transition of the CEECs at the end of the Cold War in 1989. Together with the other organizations of the Western international community, the EU mainly promoted the adoption of liberal-democratic political and economic institutions during this stage. *Acquis* transfer has become more prominent since the mid-1990s, when the EU began to spell out in increasingly explicit terms the content of legislation that the CEECs had to adopt as preconditions for membership. The 1995 Commission White Paper on regulatory alignment was the most visible example. The formal transition to *acquis* transfer comes with the opening of accession negotiations (in 1998 for the first group of CEECs). Functioning liberal-democratic institutions are the main prerequisite for the Commission's recommendation to start accession talks. The focus of socialization then shifts from general liberal rules (which continue to be monitored and assessed, however) to the *acquis*.

SOCIALIZATION STRATEGY: CONDITIONALITY

There are various potential mechanisms of international socialization through which states can be inducted to the norms and rules of an international community. On the one hand, externally driven socialization processes, in which the socialization agency plays an active role in exporting its norms to non-member states, can be distinguished from domestically driven socialization, in which domestic actors have an interest in importing external norms and the community organizations remain a passive source or model. On the other hand, socialization may follow different logics of action (March and Olsen, 1989, pp. 160–62). According to a 'logic of consequences', the socialization process is driven by cost–benefit calculations of instrumentally rational actors and, if successful, leads to sustained behavioural adaptation and compliance. In contrast, the 'logic of appropriateness' assumes that actors are motivated by identities, values and norms. Among alternative courses of action, they choose the most appropriate or legitimate one. Successful socialization results in a change of interests and identities. A combination of these distinctions yields the typology of socialization mechanisms and strategies depicted in Table 4.1 (adopted from Schimmelfennig and Sedelmeier, 2005a).

In reinforcement, the socialization agency seeks to condition the behaviour of the socializee through external incentives and disincentives; in persuasion, it tries to convince the socializee of the appropriateness of the community norms. In lesson-drawing, the socializee adopts community norms and rules for instrumental reasons – to replace failed institutions or enhance the effectiveness of domestic policies. Finally, imitation is characterized by the adoption of community norms regardless of their perceived utility. They are taken for granted and copied as 'the way things are done' in the international community.

Table 4.1 Socialization mechanisms

		Logic of action	
		Logic of consequences	Logic of appropriateness
Role of socialization agency	Active	Reinforcement	Persuasion
	Passive	Lesson-drawing	Imitation

This is an analytical typology. In reality, various socialization mechanisms are at work simultaneously and socialization agencies pursue different strategies in combination. It is possible, however, to distinguish a dominant strategy for each socialization agency, which may vary in different historical and geographical contexts. Before the end of the Cold War, the EU played a predominantly passive role in Central and Eastern Europe. With the exception of Yugoslavia, the EU had not established formally institutionalized relations with the CEECs or their economic organization, the Council for Mutual Economic Assistance (CMEA), and it did not have an explicit policy to transfer its norms and rules to the East (van Ham, 1993). However, it served as a model of regional organization for the anti-communist opposition in these countries. When the opposition came to power in the democratic transitions of 1989/90, they defined the 'return to Europe' as their core foreign policy orientation and immediately declared EU membership their central foreign policy objective.

In a parallel move, the EU gave up its predominantly passive role and defined support for the liberal-democratic transformation of the CEECs, and the establishment of close institutional relations with them, as a core task for the post-Cold-War era. The main strategy it chose to pursue this task was conditionality. Conditionality is a socialization strategy based on the mechanism of reinforcement. EU conditionality sets the adoption of the community and *acquis* rules as a condition for reaping the benefits of support by and institutional relations with the EU – such as financial aid, technical expertise or trade preferences. With each step in the deepening of institutional relations, the benefits increase – but so do the conditions attached to them. Full membership in the EU comes at the end of the conditionality ladder, including open access to the internal market, entitlement to subsidies such as payments from the Common Agricultural Policy and the Structural Funds, and participation in EU decision making. By granting these benefits to countries that fulfil the conditions and excluding countries that do not, the EU creates selective external incentives for sustained compliance with its rules.

Already in January 1989, the European Parliament demanded that 'reference to human rights should figure' in the Trade and Cooperation Agreements the EU was beginning to negotiate with the CEECs and should be mentioned specifically in the negotiating mandates given to the Commission.[3] In April, the Council made resumption of the negotiations with Romania conditional upon this country's compliance with its human rights commitments in the CSCE (Conference on Security and Cooperation in Europe) framework.[4]

In May 1992, the Council underscored that 'respect for democratic principles and human rights ... as well as the principles of a market economy, constitute essential elements of cooperation and association agreements between the Community and its CSCE partners'.[5] Henceforth, the EU added a clause to the agreements, which stipulated a suspension of the agreements if CEECs fail to comply with these principles. In November of the same year, the Council approved guidelines for its PHARE (Poland and Hungary: Assistance for Economic Reconstruction) assistance programme, which made aid conditional upon the 'state of advance of the reforms in each of the beneficiary countries'.[6] In July 1993, the new TACIS (Technical Assistance for the Commonwealth of Independent States) regulations strengthened conditionality, too: 'The level and intensity of the assistance will take into account the extent and progress of reform efforts in the beneficiary country.'[7]

At its Copenhagen Summit in June 1993, the European Council established the 'stability of institutions guaranteeing democracy, the rule of law, human rights and respect for and protection of minorities' as the *sine qua non* political condition of accession to the EU. The importance of minority rights was underscored by the 'Pact on Stability in Europe' launched in May 1994 at the initiative of French prime minister Edouard Balladur, which called upon all EU membership candidates to settle their border and minority conflicts and provide for minority protection in a series of bilateral negotiations and treaties. The concrete terms of the treaties were left to the negotiating parties but it was understood that without such a settlement, the road to accession would be blocked.

In its 1997 Opinion on the applications for membership and in subsequent annual progress reports, the Commission has regularly evaluated the political conditions in all candidate countries. Based on these opinions and reports, the Commission made recommendations on the beginning of accession negotiations and later pointed out reforms that needed to be undertaken before the conclusion of accession negotiations.

Conditionality also shapes the *acquis* transfer. The EU sets the adoption of the *acquis* rules by the applicant countries as the central condition of membership and links accession to progress in the transfer and implementation of EU rules. In 1997, the Commission stated that 'the actual timetable for accession will depend primarily on the progress made by individual countries in adopting, implementing and enforcing the *acquis*' (quoted in Avery, 2004, p. 37). Correspondingly, the EU refused to set a date for the end of negotiations and for accession until the end of 2000.

The EU's socialization strategy can be further characterized more precisely as intergovernmental reinforcement by reward. Under a strategy of reinforcement *by reward*, the socialization agency withholds the reward if the target government fails to comply with its conditions, but does not intervene either coercively or supportively to change the cost–benefit assessment of the target government by inflicting extra costs (reinforcement by punishment) or offering unconditional assistance (reinforcement by support). In the EU case, countries that fail to meet the criteria are simply denied assistance, association or membership and left behind in the competition for EU funds and the 'regatta' for accession. Only in a few early and minor cases did the EU suspend existing agreements (Romania 1989, Yugoslavia 1991), and it has never invoked the 1992 'human rights clause' in Central and Eastern Europe to terminate agreements that had already been in force. The EU generally thus does not inflict extra punishment (in addition to withholding the conditional reward) on non-compliant governments. Although EU members have participated in UN sanctions and NATO military interventions against Yugoslavia, the EU as an organization has not been prominently involved in these coercive measures.

On the other hand, the EU does not give extra support to those who fail to meet the conditions either. Rather, the EU regularly exhorts the CEEC governments that it is their own responsibility to create the conditions to be rewarded. To be sure, the EU does provide funding for projects designed to promote democracy and human rights in Central and Eastern Europe directly. In 1992, both a PHARE Democracy and a TACIS Democracy Programme were launched; both were merged in 1997 as the PHARE and TACIS Democracy Programme (PTDP). Since 1999, the European Initiative for Democracy and Human Rights (EIDHR) has been the most important EU programme to promote liberal democracy in third countries. In comparison with the rewards-based technical and financial assistance under the main PHARE and TACIS programmes, however, direct support was rather marginal. According to Karen Smith (2001, p. 49), only 1 per cent of the EU's total aid budget was dedicated to the direct support of democratization in the CEECs. The typical biennial budget for PTDP in the 1990s was in the range of €40 million, and according to the Programming Document of EIDHR for the years 2002–4, Bosnia–Herzegovina, Serbia–Montenegro, Russia, Turkey and Ukraine have been allotted a total of €12.8 million.[8] Yet the 1997–98 PHARE budget alone was €1.6 billion.

In addition, EU conditionality is predominantly intergovernmental. It targets governments directly and seeks to influence their material and social cost–benefit calculations, rather than interacting with non-governmental actors in the target countries such as social movement organizations, interest groups, parties or business actors. Governments are the recipients of financial and technical assistance, and agreements and treaties are also negotiated and concluded with governments. Bureaucratic actors, intergovernmental or interbureaucratic relations, and a top–down process of rule transfer also dominate the process of *acquis* transfer. The EU mainly relies on intergovernmental bargaining and privileges central governments and bureaucracies in the CEECs that it charges with implementing EU rules (Grabbe, 2001). Even in social policy, where transnational networks were in place and societal actors should have played an important role, they had no input (Sissenich, 2002). By providing assistance to civil society and education projects, the EU uses the transnational, societal channel of socialization mainly for its secondary and complementary strategy of reinforcement by support.

How can we explain the choice of this strategy? Why did the EU focus on intergovernmental reinforcement by reward? I suggest that this choice has to do with the specific capabilities and cost–benefit calculations of the EU and its member states and with the specific conditions of socialization in the CEECs.

First of all, the focus on rewards has to do with the specific capabilities of the EU: economic incentives of market integration, protection and subsidies are the EU's main assets. In contrast to NATO, it does not have the military power to intervene militarily against massive human rights violations; in contrast to the OSCE (Organization for Security and Cooperation in Europe) or the Council of Europe, it lacks specific expertise in democratic institution building.

Most importantly, however, reinforcement by reward is generally a low-cost strategy. First, the cost of sanctioning non-compliance is usually lower than in the case of punishing and supporting. If target states do not comply, reinforcement by punishment requires inflicting extra costs and reinforcement by support requires the transfer of extra assistance, whereas under reinforcement by reward, the socialization agency just waits and sees.

Second, in reinforcement by reward, the rewards are paid only after the successful adoption of norms, whereas reinforcement by punishment or support requires costly coercive and supportive engagements the success of which is uncertain. Third, a strategy of reinforcement by reward avoids the 'moral hazard' problems of reinforcement by support: governments cannot count on receiving EU assistance by just remaining 'needy' and not adapting to EU rules. For these reasons, a socialization agency prefers, *ceteris paribus*, rewarding to punishing or supporting. It will only engage in the more costly strategies if it is vulnerable to negative externalities from developments and policies in the target states and if reinforcement by reward is not sufficiently effective to control these negative externalities.

Yet EU vulnerability is low. First, the EU's economic stakes in the CEECs are low in general; the CEECs pose no military or economic threat. CEECs do not possess strategic resources and their share of foreign trade has remained below 5 per cent for the EU as a whole throughout the 1990s. The material effects of war as well as political and economic deterioration in Central and Eastern Europe on the West have been small and manageable. Western countries have been able to protect themselves effectively against a massive inflow of refugees or migrants (see Lavenex, 1998). Second, the international socialization of the CEECs is generally regarded as a low-priority issue in EU societies. No Western government had to fear domestic pressure if it was miserly with support to the CEECs and if it opposed or sought to put off enlargement.

The predominance of *intergovernmental* reinforcement can be attributed both to the nature of the rules and the state-centric domestic structures in the CEECs. First, the adoption of general liberal rules and the EU *acquis* require changes in the organization and the laws of the target state. Therefore intergovernmental reinforcement is the more direct channel of influence. Second, the domestic structure of the CEECs is in general characterized by the weakness of society *vis-à-vis* the state. This is obvious in the presidential systems of government that prevail in the former Soviet republics but also applies to the parliamentary democracies of Central Europe. Even here, political parties have been organized top–down, have no or weak roots in society and social organizations, and depend on the state for their resources. A powerful civil society has failed to emerge despite promising beginnings in the revolutions of 1989. Rather, levels of political participation have declined. This domestic structure gives both governments and parties ample space for discretionary decision making and strongly limits the influence of societal actors on day-to-day policy making (see, e.g., Ágh, 1998, pp. 52, 106; Kaldor and Vejvoda, 1999, pp. 11, 19–22).

To be sure, candidate governments are generally subject to the most powerful sanctioning mechanism of society – electoral confirmation and defeat. Yet if elections are to serve as a reliable instrument of conditionality, a majority of the electorate must either identify itself strongly enough with 'Europe' or be sufficiently concerned with the opportunity costs of non-compliance to make a conscious choice for reform-oriented political parties. However, it seems that actual voting behaviour is more strongly shaped by immediate concerns with personal security and welfare than by concerns about the government's compliance with European norms. Most often, changes in government have been caused by societal dissatisfaction with the hardships of economic shock therapy, economic mismanagement by the incumbent government, and corruption scandals. Dissatisfaction has turned against both reform-friendly and reform-adverse governments (Jasiewicz, 1998, p. 186; Pravda, 2001, pp. 26–7).

THE IMPACT OF POLITICAL CONDITIONALITY

Political conditionality constitutes the first stage of EU socialization policy in Central and Eastern Europe. What impact did it have on the democratic consolidation of the CEECs? Under which conditions was it effective? In this section, I will analyse the impact both on compliance with specific EU demands and on the longer-term political development of the CEECs.[9]

Comparative analysis shows that a credible EU membership perspective and low domestic power costs for the target government have been both necessary and jointly sufficient conditions of compliance with EU political conditionality. Norm-violating Central and Eastern European governments only complied with the political conditions of the EU if these conditions were explicitly linked to a credible perspective of opening or completing accession negotiations with the EU. In the absence of such a credible linkage, legislative and behavioural change did not occur. Thus the impact of the EU was low before it committed itself to eastern enlargement in 1993. But even then it was not clear when and how the EU would make concrete decisions to open accession negotiations with individual countries. Highly credible accession conditionality was only fully in place in 1997 when the Commission prepared the first set of Opinions on the applicant states and recommended the start of accession talks with five of them that fulfilled the political conditions. The selective decision to begin accession negotiations signalled, first, that the EU was serious about enlargement, thus increasing the credibility of the promise of membership, and second, that it was serious about the political prerequisites, thus strengthening the credibility of the threat to withhold the reward from non-compliant countries.

A credible membership perspective was not sufficient, however. Governments that relied on illiberal and non-democratic institutions and practices to preserve their power, and risked losing power after changing these institutions and practices, generally failed to comply. They preferred jeopardizing their accession chances to risking domestic power. Two cases may serve to illustrate this configuration of conditions.

Slovakia during the Mečiar government (1994–98) represents a combination of a credible accession perspective with high domestic power costs. Although Slovakia had long been named together with the Czech Republic, Hungary and Poland as a strong candidate for early EU enlargement and had received repeated and consistent signals that the authoritarian practices of the Mečiar government would be an obstacle to opening accession negotiations in 1997/98, that government did not comply with the demands of the Western community for respecting the constitutional rights of the parliament, the president, and the judiciary and for granting improved rights to the Hungarian minority. Compliance with some of these demands was strongly opposed by the extreme nationalists on whom Mečiar depended to remain in power. Others would have undermined the centralized control of the Slovak state that the Mečiar government established to limit the competences of the parliament and the president, which had worked together to bring down the previous Mečiar government. Slovakia only complied with the Western demands after a broad anti-Mečiar coalition came to power in the parliamentary elections of 1998. Thus even a highly credible membership perspective did not produce compliance in the presence of high power costs.

In contrast, the case of Turkey demonstrates the necessity of a credible membership perspective. Although Turkey had been associated to the EU since 1963, the absence of a credible commitment to full Turkish membership undermined the effectiveness of the EU's demands for a thorough liberalization of the Turkish state. When, however, the EU decided to accord Turkey 'candidate status' in 1999 and treat it like the Central and Eastern European applicants, it triggered a massive reform of the Turkish legal system, an improvement of rights for the Kurdish minority, and a far-reaching disempowerment of the military in anticipation of the EU's decision to open accession negotiations with Turkey in 2005. At the same time, the power costs of reform for the Turkish government were significantly reduced after the end of the anti-terrorist warfare in the Kurdish region of Turkey and after the decisive victory of the AK Party in the parliamentary elections of 2002, which was not part of the old Kemalist élites and stood to gain from curbing the military's political competences.

Comparative analysis also shows the crucial role of EU political conditionality compared to the efforts of other Western organizations. For instance, the OSCE and its High Commissioner for National Minorities had urged Estonia and Latvia to reform their citizenship law and improve the rights of the large Russian-speaking minorities in their countries since the early 1990s. However, the governments and parliaments of both countries only complied with these demands when the EU took them up in the late 1990s and linked them explicitly to accession. The same applies to the long-standing concerns of the Council of Europe with regard to the death penalty and the rule of law in Turkey.

However, under the condition of electoral volatility in the CEECs, the long-term prospects for democratic socialization not only depend on the cost–benefit calculations of the government currently in power but on those of potential future governments as well. All major parties – that is, all parties that are able to form a government or will be dominant in any feasible coalition government – must therefore make the same basic cost–benefit assessment in favour of rule adoption. Therefore the effectiveness of international socialization depends on the party constellations in the target countries.[10] Three basic types can be distinguished: liberal, anti-liberal and mixed-party constellations.[11]

If all major parties base their legitimacy claims and programmes on liberal reform and integration into the Western organizations (liberal party constellation), the conditions of intergovernmental reinforcement by reward are favourable because the perceived costs of adaptation are low and do not change after a change of government. Whenever a government is dismissed or voted out of office, its successors follow the same basic parameters of political change. This not only applies to the parties of the centre and the moderate right but also to the reconstructed post-communist parties that came to power through democratic elections only a few years after the communist breakdown in Hungary, Lithuania and Poland. Accordingly CEECs with a liberal party constellation (which include the Baltic countries and most Central European countries) went through a quick and smooth socialization process and reached a high level of democratic consolidation.

The independent contribution of the EU and other Western organizations to this outcome was small, however. These CEECs had made significant progress before accession conditionality was in place and would probably have continued on the path to democratic consolidation without it. Nevertheless EU political conditionality had two kinds of positive impact. First, it reinforced and stabilized democratic consolidation through a virtuous circle. It rewarded initial reform steps with material assistance and a strengthening of institutional ties. These rewards strengthened the norm-conforming government domestically, created incentives for further adaptation, and raised its stakes in integration. Second, it furthered compliance with particular rules not generally shared by liberal parties. In

Central and Eastern Europe, this has mainly been the case with minority protection (above all in the Baltic countries).

In contrast, if the major parties base their legitimacy claims and programmes on nationalism, communism, populism and/or authoritarianism (anti-liberal party constellation), the political costs of adaptation to liberal norms are always high. As a consequence, the conditions for successful reinforcement are unfavourable in the long term. Whereas governments may agree to cosmetic changes or tactical concessions to reap the political benefits of Western rewards, adaptation to liberal norms would undermine the basis of their rule. In these CEECs, such as Belarus, Russia, Serbia under Milošević or Ukraine, reinforcement by reward has little impact; autocracy rather than democracy is consolidated. These countries are excluded from the benefits of assistance and membership. In the absence of increasing EU integration, the stakes in reform and democratization do not grow, the political gap between these countries and the rest of the CEECs widens, and the prospect of EU accession becomes ever more distant. Thus a vicious instead of a virtuous circle operates. Only a domestic revolution (such as in Serbia in 2000) can reverse this dynamic.

In mixed-constellation countries with both major liberal and anti-liberal parties, there is no élite consensus on liberal-democratic reform and Western integration. Liberal parties or coalitions have been able to come to power in these systems but did not exclusively shape their post-communist development. Either superficially reconstructed communist parties initiated (but also slowed down and distorted) democratic transition from above (such as in Romania), or reform-adverse nationalists and populists benefited from the failure of reform-oriented parties to provide for economic recovery or efficient governance. In some of these countries (Bulgaria, Croatia, Romania, Slovakia), governmental authority has shifted more than once between the two camps.

Over time, however, these countries still made significant progress on the way to democratic consolidation and political conditionality was a major factor in this development. When liberal parties were in government, the liberal domestic changes they institutionalized led to progress in EU integration, and the benefits of EU integration subsequently raised the stakes in democratic consolidation and increased the costs of any future reversal. Populist parties therefore adapted their political goals in order to preserve the achieved benefits of integration. After the major nationalist-authoritarian parties of Croatia (HDZ), Romania (PDSR) and Slovakia (HZDS) had been voted out of government, Romania and Slovakia started accession negotiations with the EU, and Croatia became an EU associate and applied for membership. During the same time, these parties modified their programmes and presented themselves as unequivocally pro-integration. When the PDSR and the HDZ were back in power in 2000 and 2003, they stayed the course of reform and integration. Thus the lock-in effects of Western integration create path-dependency across changes in government and, eventually, change the party constellation from mixed to liberal. Accession negotiations with Bulgaria, Romania and Slovakia started in 2000 and with Croatia in 2005.

THE IMPACT OF *ACQUIS* CONDITIONALITY

Acquis conditionality takes centre stage during the accession negotiations between the EU and the applicant states. The success of political conditionality depended on both the credibility of the membership perspective and low domestic costs, and its impact was mainly felt in CEECs with mixed-party constellations. In contrast, the impact of *acquis* conditionality has been highly pervasive in all countries that passed the threshold of accession negotiations and covered not only basic political institutions but the whole range of EU policies.[12] As one EU official reportedly joked, 'once a country applies to join the EU, it becomes our slave'.[13]

Studies in this area show that the key condition for the success of EU rule transfer is the high credibility of *acquis* conditionality. There was some adoption of *acquis* rules even before the EU's conditionality was spelled out, but it was patchy and selective. For instance, whereas EU environmental rules against long-range air pollution were adopted in the Czech Republic but not in Poland (Andonova, 2005), the Czech Republic, in contrast to Hungary, resisted regionalization and public service reform ahead of accession negotiations (Andonova, 2005; Jacoby, 2005). In addition, CEEC governments often adapted EU rules or mixed EU rules with other models. However, once a given issue area became subject of the accession negotiations and the *acquis* conditionality, rule adoption increased dramatically and became a consistent feature across countries and issue areas. The massive benefits of EU membership being within close reach, the fulfilment of EU *acquis* conditions became the highest priority in CEEC policy making, crowding out alternative models and domestic obstacles.

The importance of domestic power costs thus contrasts sharply with political conditionality. As *acquis* conditionality does not concern the political system and bases of political power as such, governments generally do not have to fear that the costs of rule adoption in individual policy areas will lead to a loss of office. Costs are thus unlikely to be prohibitive. Moreover, once a credible membership perspective has been established, adoption costs in individual policy areas are discounted against the (aggregate) benefits of membership, rather than just the benefits in this particular policy area. For example, in the area of social policy, the CEECs even adopted the more costly rules relating to secondary legislation (such as health and safety at the workplace) more fully than the less costly rules relating to the Social Dialogue (Sissenich, 2005). Similarly, concerning the free movement of persons, rule adoption was more pronounced for the more costly Schengen rules than for the internal market rules (Grabbe, 2005). This may be explained by the differential salience the EU attaches to particular areas. Whereas EU actors clearly communicated to the CEECs that the Schengen rules were a key condition for membership, parts of the Commission and some member states indicated that rather superficial alignment would not present an obstacle to concluding negotiations in the areas of EU social policy.

In other cases, adoption costs explain variation in the *speed* of rule adoption across issue areas and countries. In the Czech Republic, regionalization only increased after the reticent Klaus government had lost office (Jacoby, 2005). In Slovakia, rules for decentralization were eventually adopted after the election victory of the anti-Mečiar coalition, but the divergent preferences within the coalition that related to ethnic minority politics still made for protracted negotiations (Brusis, 2003). In the area of environmental policy, opposition from the energy sector in Poland prevented the adoption of control-and-command instruments that the EU prescribed to combat air pollution. In contrast to the Czech Republic, EU rules were thus only adopted in the late 1990s once the EU's conditionality set in (Andonova, 2005).

The pervasiveness of *acquis* conditionality, the sheer quantity of rules that had to be transposed (the oft-quoted '80,000 pages of the *acquis*') and the enormous time-pressure of the accession process made *acquis* transfer a highly technocratic process. On the part of the EU, it is the Commission bureaucracy that specifies, explicates and monitors the demands on the applicant states. On the side of the accession countries, it negotiates with the chief negotiators and their teams, delegations of line ministries or only with interministerial coordination units, which were specifically created for the accession negotiations. Thus the accession processes further contributed to the centralization and strengthening of the executive; societal interest groups and parliaments were marginalized (Grabbe, 2001, pp. 1016–18; Bruszt and Stark, 2003, p. 78). During the accession negotiations, the parliamentary agenda was primarily shaped from the outside. The applicant states introduced accelerated procedures for adopting EU rules and were under pressure to pass – and often rubber-stamp – the *acquis*-related legislation at high speed to provide for accession in time. The Hungarian parliament, for instance, did not even debate 152 out of 180 laws passed in June 1999, because they were part of the *acquis*.[14]

The technocratic tendencies of *acquis* transfer were strengthened by the implantation of the 'regulatory state' in the CEECs. The expansion of the regulatory state is a typical feature of the development of Western democracies but even more characteristic of the political system of the EU (Majone, 1996). It is the main purpose of the regulatory state to correct 'market failure' through regulation – in contrast with the politics of redistribution of the 'welfare state' and the politics of macroeconomic stabilization of the 'intervention state'. Correspondingly, the *acquis* transfer to the CEECs consisted predominantly in the transfer of organizations and rules for market regulation that had no roots there. Numerous regulatory policy areas such as environmental and consumer protection, product safety, regional policy and competition policy were either added to the portfolio of traditional policies or at least strongly expanded. At the same time, *acquis* conditionality led to a mushrooming of the technocratic agencies of the regulatory state: independent central banks, competition authorities, offices for environmental protection, transport and food safety agencies, and many more (Grzymala-Busse and Innes, 2003, pp. 70–71; Maniokas, 2002).

CONCLUSIONS: AFTER ACCESSION

Socializing the new or transformed countries of Central and Eastern Europe to the community rules of the Western international community and the specific rules of the *acquis communautaire* has been a core task of the post-Cold-War EU. The main instrument used by the EU to accomplish this task was conditionality. After 15 years, what can we say about the effects and limits of this policy?

In order to promote the democratic consolidation of the CEECs, credible EU (and, in some cases, NATO) accession conditionality proved to be a necessary condition of producing domestic change in norm-violating countries – and a more effective instrument than the softer methods and less sizeable carrots used by the Council of Europe or the OSCE. Its effectiveness was circumscribed, however, by the domestic power costs of incumbent governments. EU accession conditionality was most relevant in locking in democratic change in the fragile transformation states with a mixed constellation of major liberal-democratic and nationalist-authoritarian parties. But it was largely redundant in the democratic front-runners and largely ineffective in the authoritarian or autocratic systems of Central and Eastern Europe.

By contrast, the impact of *acquis* conditionality has been pervasive in all applicant countries and across a wide range of policy areas. The high and imminent benefits of EU membership put the domestic costs of policy adaptation into perspective and generated a tremendous amount of EU-conforming legislation in a short time-span. This top–down effectiveness, however, might come at the cost of undermining the bottom–up democratic process in the CEECs. Electoral choice and party competition on socioeconomic issues were undercut by the fact that whoever was in government had to work towards adopting EU rules (Grzymala-Busse and Innes, 2003). Parliamentary activity was to a large extent determined by the schedule of the accession process and the need to formally transpose EU legislation. In sum, the EU might have the same ambivalent impact on democracy as in some of the older member states, which have emerged from a non-democratic past: firmly anchoring democratic institutions at the national level while undermining them at the supranational level.

Moreover, socialization does not end with accession. First, rule adoption consists primarily of formal transposition into national legislation, with implementation and effective enforcement in everyday policy making lagging behind. Second, the entire EU socialization process has been dominated by the direct use or at least the shadow of accession conditionality. We cannot know at this point whether the CEECs will continue to follow community and *acquis* rules of their own accord and in the absence of external incentives and sanctions. This would be the ultimate test of successful socialization, and this test comes after accession when the power of conditionality will have waned. There are reasons to be sceptical (Schimmelfennig and Sedelmeier, 2005b). Those domestic interests and concerns that were pushed away to ensure that EU membership might come to the fore again. In addition, many of the policy makers or 'core executives' responsible for the quick transposition of EU rules and knowledgeable in EU affairs – and those with the most EU-friendly attitudes – will move to Brussels to assume the posts in the European organizations allotted to the new member states. Third, the new member states might not be willing to further accept the rules of the 'enlargement *acquis*', for instance with regard to minority protection, which were specifically designed for accession candidates but are not binding on full members. Moreover, as we know from British and Spanish experiences, accession deals that are considered unfair impositions lead to disgruntled newcomers that spend much of their early accession years trying to renegotiate perceived wrongs. Under all these circumstances, the short-term effectiveness of rule transposition in the context of conditionality might well be compromised by medium-term ineffectiveness of implementation.

NOTES

1. At the time the European Union was still the European Community. For the sake of simplicity, however, I will use 'EU' throughout the chapter.

2. http://www.osce.org/docs/english/1990–1999/summits/paris90e.htm.
3. *Agence Europe*, 20 January 1989.
4. Ibid., 24/25 April 1989.
5. Ibid., 14 May 1992.
6. Ibid., 16/17 November 1992.
7. Ibid., 24 July 1993.
8. http://europa.eu.int/comm/external_relations/human_rights/doc/eidhr02_04.pdf.
9. The findings I present are based on a research project on the international socialization of Central and Eastern Europe that combines a detailed process-tracing analysis of the impact of European organizations on compliance in nine cases of rule-breaking CEECs (Belarus, Estonia, Latvia, Macedonia, Romania, Serbia and Slovakia in addition to Cyprus and Turkey) with a qualitative comparative analysis of the conditions of effective political conditionality. For a more detailed presentation of the preliminary results, see Schimmelfennig et al. (2003; 2005). For concurrent results, see Kubicek (2003) and Kelley (2004).
10. To be sure, this variable only qualifies as a proximate cause: the party constellation depends in turn on deeper factors such as ethnic cleavages, political culture, socioeconomic structures or transition trajectories.
11. See McFaul (2002) for a similar three-way categorization of transition countries and explanation of transition outcomes based on the domestic balance of power between democratic parties and supporters of the *ancien régime*.
12. The findings presented are based on a collaborative project on the Europeanization of Central and Eastern Europe in a great variety of countries and issue areas (see the conclusions in Schimmelfennig and Sedelmeier, 2005b).
13. *The Economist*, 25 September 2004, p. 9.
14. *Magyar Nemzet*, 19 June 1999, quoted in Kopstein and Reilly (2000, p. 27).

5. Enlargement: the political and constitutional implications

Barbara Lippert*

INTRODUCTION

The history of European integration from the 1960s to the present has often been told with a general reference to the widening of its membership (Dinan, 1999; Brunn, 2002). Widening and deepening are considered to go hand in hand although coincidence in timing does not necessarily indicate a cause–effect relationship (Nugent, 2003, pp. 22–53). However, a tension between the two processes is widely acknowledged. Enlargement is perceived either as an incentive for deepening and institutional change (Keohane and Hoffmann, 1991, p. 22) or as the natural enemy of deepening (Pinder, 1991, p. 51; see also Maurer, 2000, p. 57). All through the 1990s and up to the present, the EU has been facing serious problems sequencing deepening and widening, so that the enlargements of 1995 and of 2004 happened although intended reforms were still lagging behind. This is particularly true with regard to institutions and decision-making procedures. Thus in December 2001 at the European Council in Laeken a catalogue of questions was put forward to be tackled by a European Convention. Its task was to increase the enlarged EU's efficiency, to enhance its capacity to act and improve its legitimacy. On the basis of the draft European Constitution tabled by the Convention, the Intergovernmental Conference (IGC) finally agreed on a thorough revision of the treaties and signed a Constitutional treaty that is now awaiting ratification (Conference of the Representatives of the Governments of the Member States, 2004). Some even speak of a 'constitutional turn' (Wiener, 2004, p. 179) and a period of 'politicization' of the integration process that was initiated in the 1990s by the prospect of the biggest enlargement of the EU (to the East). Enlargement became an incentive to address the ambiguous *finalité politique* of the Union (Fischer, 2000; Joerges et al., 2000; Jopp, 2002). In 2004 neither enlargement nor the constitutionalization of the EU polity were completed. Both processes will be continued, including the challenge of an accession of Turkey.

What lessons can we draw from the past for the future agenda of the EU with regard to the relationship between enlargement and treaty as well as policy reform?

FROM THE HAGUE TO THE EUROPEAN CONSTITUTION – AN OVERVIEW ON TREATY REFORM AND ENLARGEMENT

The summit of The Hague in 1969 and its famous slogan 'completion, deepening and widening' indicates that the member states which – through Intergovernmental Conferences and the European Council – take decisions on constitutional reforms as well as enlargement consider these two dynamic processes as mutually reinforcing and hence not as exclusive. At the beginning of the 1970s the EC set out to complete agricultural policy, deepen political integration and enlarge to northern EFTA countries, taking in the UK as a new member state. Ever since then the Community/EU has confirmed its belief in a smooth relationship between further constitutionalization towards an 'ever deeper Union' (Article 1 TEU and Article 48 TEU) and growth in membership (Article 49 TEU).

When it comes to causal factors, enlargement has never been sufficient to trigger treaty revisions or to fundamentally reshape policies and decision-making rules in the Union. A far more complex constellation of actors, interests and challenges is needed to boost deepening of the EU. So my main thesis is that enlargement is rather an incentive and opportunity to push forward the deepening and refining of the constitutional order of the EU through piece-meal reforms. This is often tried in anticipation but mostly done in retrospect after enlargement has already taken place, accepting the risk of sub-optimal and inadequate solutions. The reform project, however, has to coincide with other factors that reflect essential interests and preferences of the member states. Prospects for constitutional reform and policy development were regularly considered when the Community was confronted with applications for membership or while already negotiating with candidates. Governments of the member states usually act and decide on the accession of new members without a clear picture of the effects on the constitution and policies of the EU and its functioning. The growing complexity of the *acquis* has considerably increased the problem of impact assessment. Given the fact that we do not know an optimal size of the EU, and given the normative decision of the Union to be principally open to European states that fulfil membership criteria (Article 49 EU Treaty, formerly 237 EC Treaty, now even explicitly in Art. I (2), I-58 TCE), the EU's approach towards enlargement remained basically reactive and pragmatic (European Commission, 1992). The Community aims at controlling effects on the existing state of integration and resorts to protective measures (for example through the terms laid down in the Accession treaties and the doctrine of full application of the *acquis* on behalf of the newcomers). Interestingly, enlargement was never accepted as an argument to slow down constitutional or policy development and freeze the *acquis*. The so-called Copenhagen criteria for membership also concerned the EU and its 'capacity to absorb new members, while maintaining the momentum of European integration' (European Council, 1993, point 7). So on the contrary, at least some member states, the Commission and the European Parliament are interested in using the momentum of enlargement for boosting deepening and policy development. They refer to enlargement as a challenge to improve the efficiency, the capacity to act, and the legitimacy of the EU. Against this background the impact of enlargement on the constitutional order, namely institutions, and policies of the EC/EU will be reconsidered.

One can easily see that in terms of timing the two processes of enlargement and treaty reform do not run in sync. This observation is backed up by the simple fact that in the history of the Community, enlargement came first. The first and second rounds (1973 and 1981) took place without a significant revision of the treaties of Rome. The changes in the institutional configuration, of policies and tasks during the next rounds of enlargement were widely interpreted as an adaptation and extrapolation of the given constitutional order and the set of institutions and structures. A path-dependent evolution of the institutional system of the EU prevails (Nugent, 2003). However, in the run-up to the fifth enlargement, the enlargement towards the East and the Eastern Mediterranean in 2004, the argument was put forward that – at last – it was high time for a radical reform of the institutions and procedures of the EU. Otherwise the EU of 25 member states would have to function on the basis of the institutional architecture of the EC6 and probably collapse (European Commission, 1997a, pp. 5–6; Dehaene et al., 1999; Redmond and Rosenthal, 1998, p. 4).

Looking at the relationship between enlargement and treaty reform from the first enlargement in 1973 up to the present, we get the following broad picture. Even without treaty revisions in the period covering the northern and the first southern enlargement of 1981 important changes occurred with respect to three central categories of constitutionalization: governance, legitimacy and policies (see Appendix). Shortly after the accession of the UK, Denmark and Ireland the European Council was formally established in 1974 and started to meet on a regular basis. This purely intergovernmental institution – originally outside the treaties but gradually incorporated – became the umbrella and top steering and decision-making institution for all activities, not only with regard to deepening and widening. The first direct elections of members of the European Parliament in 1979 can be regarded as some sort of supranational counterweight. Neither institutional innovation was induced by enlargement but by the demand for a *relance* of European integration (after the empty chair crisis and de Gaulle's refusal of British membership in the 1960s) and a fulfilment of a long-standing political goal. However, the accession of the UK affected the political balance in the EC. Also smaller countries saw advantages in having a formalized exchange between the heads of state and government in the European Council instead of the emergence of an implicit *directoire*.

The creation of the system of own resources and a renewed budgetary procedure (starting in 1970) went hand in hand with the new albeit politically less visible institution, the Court of Auditors established in 1975. Moreover, even before the three Northern countries joined the EC it had extended its competencies to new policies such as fisheries. The first enlargement involved the creation of a modest regional policy which should also parallel plans for an economic and monetary union and increase transfers from the EU budget to the UK (Preston, 1997, p. 139). In 1975 the ERDF was established using Article 308 EC-T (then Article 235) as the legal basis to further an objective not covered by a specific treaty article. The Werner Plan for a monetary union and the more restricted project of a European Monetary System (EMS) were also launched in response to external challenges such as the breakdown of the system of Bretton Woods, the oil price crisis and the end of détente in the second half of the 1970s. The accession of the UK – a permanent member in the Security Council of the United Nations and a country with strategic foreign policy interests and outlook – improved the basis for the EC9 to play a more substantial role in international politics and reinforced attempts to coordinate foreign policy in the Community framework. So in the 1970s, new members and institutional players as well as new policy areas came into the realm of the Community without a formal revision of the treaties. The proliferation of policy studies such as the reports of Tindemans in 1975[1] and of the Dooge Committee on institutional affairs (1985), as well as political initiatives such as that of Genscher and Colombo (1981/82),[2] and the White Paper on the internal market (European Commission, 1985) all signalled the mounting pressure for reform of EC governance and policies (Bengel et al., 1983). A strengthening of the European Council and a reform of the decision-making system towards more majority voting were key proposals.

The reforms of 1986 had a long incubation period and produced their own momentum, to which the second southern enlargement was successfully linked. In terms of timing and substance this round of enlargement coincided with the first big reform of the treaties of Rome of 1957, the

Single European Act (SEA) in 1986. It is widely acknowledged that the SEA, which brought together the treaty changes, depended on a conjunction of events of which the expansion of membership was only one element (Keohane and Hoffmann, 1991, p. 25). Other factors which point at the complexity of constellation and the need to find a package solution were the agreement on the rebate for the UK, a legacy of the first round of enlargement which had paralysed EU decision making for some years. The agreement of Fontainebleau in 1984 to introduce compensatory payments for the UK allowed progress with regard to other imminent projects. In order to meet the challenge of increased competition with countries of Asia and the USA and in order to reinvigorate the sluggish European economy, the Commission proposed the completion of the single market up to 1992 on the basis of an indicative programme. Policy development (completion of the four freedoms) should complement the reform of EC governance. A package was agreed upon that could transcend cleavages between intergovernmentalists and supporters of a stronger community method/communitarization. So, even the sovereignty-minded British government under Prime Minister Thatcher supported the introduction of Qualified Majority Voting (even if limited to areas concerning the internal market) and of the cooperation procedure which also involves a stronger engagement of the European Parliament in law making. Other constitutional changes through the SEA were the right of assent of the European Parliament to the accession of new members and also to association agreements, the legal recognition of the European Council and the stronger institutionalization of EPC which was put on a legal basis and which should become more operational through a small secretariat in Brussels. Moreover, a new Court of first instance was established to cope with a growing workload and growth in membership. Directly related to enlargement were provisions in the Single European Act on economic and social cohesion (new title V in EC-T) which was also mirrored in the budget. Other new policies such as environment or research and technology were seen as flanking policies but also held a signal for closeness to the EC citizens. To finance both the new policies and also enlargement, the SEA was linked to the first ever agreement on a multi-annual financial perspective for the EC, the so-called Delors I package for the years 1988 up to 1992. Interestingly, this reform package – SEA, completion of the internal market and Delors I – was driven by diverse preferences of the member states' governments but by a clear economic programme and neoliberal ideology. The approach of economic deregulation was paralleled by the strengthening of distributive politics, so that negative and positive integration (structural/cohesion policy) were combined in a comprehensive political project initiated and chaired by the European Commission and supported by the big member states. Thus significant expansion of the spending on structural policy was due to bargains over a wider agenda (including constitutional reform). Moreover, structural funds developed as a reservoir for side payments in order to facilitate broader compromise and buy off reluctant players. For example this was the case with the introduction of an Integrated Mediterranean Programme for Italy, Greece and France before the second Southern enlargement.

As a follow-up to the Single European Act and against the background of the momentous German unification, two IGCs – on European monetary union and on political union (1990/91) – were called in. They agreed on the establishment of a European Union as part of the so-called Maastricht Treaty. Reforms concerned both governance and policies and again the treaty revision was followed by an agreement on a seven-year financial perspective for the EU (1993–99), the so-called Delors II package. Innovations such as the introduction of the co-decision procedure, the extension of qualified majority voting, the formal acknowledgement of the principle of subsidiarity, the creation of a committee of the regions and of an ombudsman were only in a very general way linked to the prospect that the Community would more than double its original membership. The schedule for a staged introduction of a single currency, a major step in the history of European integration, as well as the establishment of the second and third pillars of the EU, for Common Foreign and Security Policy (CFSP) and Justice and Home Affairs (JHA), took up projects such as the European Political Community and the European Defence Community of the early 1950s or the Schengen agreement of the 1980s. So we observe a functional spill-over and widening of tasks and competencies of the EC. The introduction of the cohesion fund in 1993 was directly linked to the two Southern enlargements. For the poorer member states which have to cope with the challenges of the single market and the strict criteria for the monetary union all at the same time special payments were earmarked for the improvement of infrastructure and the environment. The opt-out for the countries of the first northern enlargement of parts of Justice and Home Affairs and the British opt-out of the social policy, however, indicated the wide range and spread of interests in the EU12. Heterogeneity of preferences as well as of basic orientations towards European integration increased with every round of enlargement. Already the first enlargement set off a debate (Dahrendorf in 1973,[3] Brandt in 1974;[4] the Tindemans report of 1975) on differentiation in the governance of the EU and discussed concepts such as *l'Europe à la carte*, '*abgestufte Integration*' (Scharrer, 1984) or multi-speed Europe. However, steps towards a permanent differentiation among the willing and able were rejected (Grabitz, 1984; Wallace, 1985).

The IGC of Maastricht did not succeed in updating the European Union to the challenges and new constellations after the end of the cold war. Moreover, the ensuing problems in ratifying the Maastricht Treaty in some member states (such as Denmark, France and Germany) slowed down ambitions for further deepening. The European Parliament initially threatened to withdraw its assent to enlargement without prior reform of the institutions and decision-making procedures. But the EU decided to start negotiations with the four EFTA countries (originally also Norway) even before the ratification of the Maastricht Treaty was completed albeit after having ratified the Delors II package. The smooth enlargement of 1995 added three net payers that were already closely integrated into the internal market. It increased reform pressure because of the unsatisfactory depth of reforms in the Maastricht Treaty as far as the political union was concerned. In order to make up with EFTA enlargement and in anticipation of the impending and big eastern enlargement, 'enlargement' became the rationale for the next IGC 1996/97 (Sedelmeier, 2000, p. 223; Dinan, 1998, p. 36). However, exactly those problems which the EU15 intended to solve in order to be prepared for enlargement to the East were again postponed to a next IGC that should take place before accession of new members. The 'leftovers of Amsterdam' concerned the reweighting of votes in the Council, the size and composition of the Commission (the size of the European Parliament), and the extension of majority voting to new areas as well as the extension of the co-decision procedure. The most memorable change in the governance of the European Union connected with the Amsterdam Treaty was the introduction of enhanced cooperation and the incorporation of the Schengen *acquis* as core provisions of a novel Area of Freedom, Security and Justice. The need to have an inbuilt possibility of differentiation in an ever bigger and more complex European Union was acknowledged. Including the TCE, provisions on enhanced cooperation have always been designed as a last resort. They are neither foreseen as a standard procedure to cope with diversity nor as a means to establish a community of concentric circles around a core group of member states (Schäuble and Lamers, 1994; Wallace and Wallace, 1995; Fischer, 2000). Its key purpose is to circumvent veto positions and to give a group of avant-garde states the opportunity to stimulate further integration and open up new policy fields.

Adaptation and reform of policies, namely of the CAP and structural policy, that were possible without treaty reform were de-coupled from the IGC of Amsterdam and dealt with under the so-called 'Agenda 2000'. It also contained proposals for a financial perspective that covered the period 2000–2006 and hypothetically took into account enlargement of the EU in 2002. The political link between the treaty reforms of Amsterdam and Nice and Agenda 2000 (which was tabled in 1997, agreed only in 1999 and adapted to the accession negotiations in 2002) was far looser than in the case of the SEA. However, initially, in the mid-1990s the EU had the ambition to accommodate constitutional and political reforms and enlargement in a coherent strategy. Agenda 2000 (European Commission, 1997a; 1997b) was the first attempt at a comprehensive analysis of the implications of enlargement for the EU institutions and in particular its policies and the budget. The aim of the Commission was to control the process and to get a grip on probable effects of enlargement, so that widening would not take over while reforms were lagging behind. The Commission was concerned that the process of enlargement would get carried away (European Commission, 1997a, p. 5), and rightly so. Adherents of deepening before widening, such as Belgium, France and Italy, who attached a declaration on the necessary strengthening of the institutions in view of enlargement to the Amsterdam Treaty, were unable to make substantial reforms a precondition for enlargement and so used enlargement as a leverage for reforms. Adherents of widening and deepening, mainly Germany, shied away from a rigid linkage between the processes because they came to realize that there was no solid majority inside the EU for enlargement, not to speak of a consensus on burden sharing and depth of reforms. The EU had committed itself to start negotiations with Cyprus and Malta six months after the end of the IGC of Amsterdam. Given the haphazard rate of institutional reforms under the Amsterdam and Nice summits on treaty reforms, enlargement was moving in the fast lane. The slogan 'erosion or integration' (Fischer, 2000) echoed concerns as to whether the EU after a big bang enlargement that was now scheduled for 2004 would be capable of governing a Union of 25 effectively. In his speech at Humboldt University German Foreign Minister Fischer outlined his idea that 'enlargement will render imperative a fundamental reform of European institutions' (Fischer, 2000) and the vision of a European federation of nation-states, while PM Blair insisted on a 'superpower, but not a superstate' at the Polish stock exchange (Blair, 2000).

The restricted agenda of the IGC 2000 was focused on the leftovers of Amsterdam mentioned above which concerned the balance of power between big, and between small and big member states. The principle of the equality of sovereign states and the principle of representative government and democratic representation had to be balanced in a new definition of the qualified majority. Moreover, for the first time in the history of European integration the parity between Germany and France in the Council was at stake and led to serious conflicts between the two countries. At the summit in Nice, an – albeit inconsistent – shift of power from the small to the bigger member states was agreed upon by reweighting of votes in the Council. A new formula defined qualified majority as a majority of states, of weighted votes and – on request – of 62 per cent of EU population. This rule increased complexity and intransparency of decision making. The decisions of Nice on the reform of institutions and decision making were regarded as unconvincing or even harmful, and the whole IGC as a failure in treaty making (Jopp et al., 2001). At the turn of the century the EU had run into the trap of a major enlargement with too few reform achievements.

This gave a boost to a new procedure for preparing a treaty revision – the European Convention, dominated by parliamentarians. The Convention soon pursued the ambitious project of a European Constitution, thus going beyond the restricted agenda of Nice. While policy development was excluded from the agenda of the Convention and of the subsequent IGC, the focus was on governance and legitimacy of the enlarged EU. The project of a constitution(al treaty) was an attempt at freeing the Union from immobilism and backlog of reform. The TCE, if eventually ratified, will bring major changes in decision making and as far as institutions and the balance within the power triangle are concerned. The introduction of double majority voting is a break with the decision-making rules of the past. It demonstrates – within the Council – the two principles on which the EU is based, the states and the citizens, and is expected to improve efficiency as well as legitimacy of the Council. Other institutional innovations such as the EU foreign minister or the president of the European Council were accepted with hesitation by many, mostly smaller, countries. The stronger role for national parliaments is a clear tribute to the member states and the aim is to reduce the legitimacy gap in the course of both widening and deepening. The TCE provides elements for more flexibility for further constitutional development. It will simplify procedures for treaty revision (Article IV-444 TCE), it confirms the so-called flexibility clause to widen EU competencies (Article I-18 TCE, present Article 308 EC-T), streamlines provisions on enhanced cooperation (Article I-44), and introduces permanent structured cooperation in ESDP (Article I-41, 6 TCE). Absolutely new is the provision of a voluntary withdrawal from the Union (Article I-60 TCE), which runs against the understanding of belonging to a community of fate while emphasizing the treaty character of the Union. The TCE does not give a conclusive answer to the question of the *finalité*. There is no predetermination of the future direction either towards supranational or intergovernmental solutions. Interpretations range from a '*fédération d'etats-nations*' (Chirac) to 'Europe ... is not a superstate, not a federal state but a group of nations' (Blair).[5] The Constitution thus confirms the *sui generis* nature of the Union that also entails the unfinished process of building a transnational polity.

PRELIMINARY CONCLUSIONS

Overall, in the course of enlargement no roll-back and deterioration of the constitutional *acquis* evolved. Enlargement added to the increased complexity of the EU system and the constitutional order because of a greater heterogeneity of interests and capacities of its members. The proliferation of actors and also veto players characterizes the architecture of the enlarged EU. Enlargement was neither the cause nor the key leverage to improve the governance capacities of the EU but it accentuated and sometimes aggravated the weaknesses of the constitutional order. Thus enlargement made reform more urgent. The evolutionary development of the constitutional order and the bargains over concrete choices led to a precarious balance and very specific provisions which were challenged by each new member state. The doctrine that newcomers have to accept the entire *acquis* when joining was an essential precondition for the preservation of the status quo and dynamic inside the Community. The interest constellation was modified with every enlargement and stimulated adaptation. However, development and change were built on the existing *acquis* and were bound to decisions taken before. This path-dependency led to ever more baroque and complex provisions and solutions that made streamlining and more transparency almost as difficult as fundamental reforms. The basic tension between intergovermentalists and integrationists was maintained up to the Convention and the IGC 2003/04. It is difficult to come to a clear view of how far supranationalization, and intergovernmentalization, illustrated in the bicephal presidencies of the European Council and Commission, hold a balance in the TCE (Wessels, 2004). As a long-term trend we can observe that the member states delegate tasks and decisions to the level of the EU in order to manage complex interdependence. Pooling of sovereignty increased across policy fields. With growing complexity and decreasing transparency as well as acceptance of European integration in public opinion, the problem of legitimacy has become more crucial for the EU.

Moreover, in the course of enlargement and integration the French–German engine lost some of its power to shape reforms and package deals. This is partly due to tensions and non-convergence of preferences between them but also because the range of interests in the bargaining process is widening and the large number of small states stimulate an anti-hegemonic attitude in the enlarged EU. Despite the fact that many of the originally joint French–German proposals can be found in the Draft TCE of the Convention and the final outcome of the IGC, the leadership question remains high on the agenda. The EU25 searches for a centre of political gravity beyond France and Germany to structure decision making and provide political impetus.

INSTITUTIONS AND DECISION MAKING

Each enlargement had an impact on the institutions of the Community. It affected the size, composition and working practice of the respective institution. Adaptations and cautious innovations prevailed over any radical changes or a complete overhaul of the institutional architecture. We look at the institutional triangle of Commission, Council/European Council and the European Parliament.

The Commission

Enlargement affected the Commission mostly in terms of its size, organization and the principle of collegiality (Dinan, 1998). The EC6 started with nine Commissioners; the Commission of the EU25 counts 25 members. Up to 2004 bigger member states (EC6 France, Germany, Italy; EC9 plus UK; EC12 plus Spain) nominated two Commissioners (Table 5.1).

Table 5.1 Commission and enlargement

Commission	Members	Vice presidents	Directorate general
EC6	9 (14)*	2–3	9
EC9	13	4–5	19/20
EC10	14	5	
EC12	17	6	23
EU15	20	2	23 (May 2002)
EU25	30**/25	5	
EU27 TCE	27***/18		

Notes:
* Transitory period 1967–70 following the merger treaty.
** Between 1 May 2004 and 30 October 2004.
*** Until 2014, thereafter two-thirds of member states.

Source: Own compilation.

Only the enlargement of 2004 introduced a change in the composition of the Commission which is now made up of one national per member state. An extrapolation of the status quo would have led to a Commission of 30,[6] which was only the case in the period between the accession date 1 May and the date the new Commission took office in November 2004. The Commission of 25 in an EU25 was however only a halfway success for those who had advocated, like France since the Amsterdam IGC, for a smaller Commission which would not be based on the 'representation of all member states at one time. Since the seventies proposals for a smaller Commission were put on the agenda, not in the least by the Commission itself' (Dinan, 1998, pp. 22–5). Against the background of a comparatively small and stagnant *acquis* the Community already had some problems in defining meaningful portfolios for an increasing number of commissioners (Commission of the EC, 1979) after the first enlargement. The Spierenburg report of 1979 proposed ten (stable) portfolios for the EC12 and favoured limiting the number of commissioners while the president should be strengthened and supported by a vice president who would be responsible for coordinating the work of the commissioners and so improve coherence.

The provision of the Nice Treaty and the common position of the EU15 in the accession negotiations of 2002 to allow for only one national per member state in the next Commission was part of a broader compromise. The big member states that would 'lose' one of two posts in the Commission achieved a reweighting of votes in the Council in their favour. The link between a reform of the Commission and the Council was already laid down in the protocol on the institutions to the Amsterdam Treaty (No. 7). As far as the Commission was concerned, efforts for a permanent restriction of its growth failed again. Proponents for a fixed size of 15, 12 or even fewer members argued that a smaller Commission would be more efficient, more independent and hence more supranational. Others, among them many small and all new members of 2004, argued that one commissioner per member would improve communication with the countries 'they know best' and enhance the legitimacy of the Commission and the Union as a whole. Consequently the IGC of 2003/04 refused to accept the provision of the draft European Constitution of the Convention which foresaw to limit the size to 15 European commissioners (including the president and vice president) with voting rights and include other commissioners without voting rights from the countries not represented among the 15 (Article I-25 Draft TCE). The TCE now provides for a limitation of the members of the Commission to two-thirds of the member states which shall be elected through the European Council on the basis of a system of equal rotation. This rule shall apply from 2014 unless the European Council does not decide otherwise and sticks to the status quo (Article I-26, 6 TCE).

Linked to the problem of the size of the Commission is the trend towards a stronger hierarchization and differentiation among the commissioners, who are supposed to be equal. Although the principle of collegiality persists, the position of the president, who is also member of the European Council, was strengthened over the years, in particular as far as political guidance and organizational power (design and distribute portfolios; dismiss members of the Commission) were concerned. The number of the vice presidents and their role depend on the decision of the president (see Table 5.1). The TCE will bring change through the double-hatted EU Foreign minister who acts as a (fixed) vice president with responsibility for external relations. Informally a core group of commissioners holding key portfolios (budget, single market, trade, competition, external affairs, economic and monetary policy, CAP, regional policy) has emerged so that there are heavyweights and less important portfolios/commissioners in the college. Neither nationals of small nor new member states were relegated to the insubstantial posts in the Barroso Commission. Ms Hübner of Poland as a new member state and Ms Boel of Denmark as a small member state are responsible for regional policy and CAP, which account for 80 per cent of the EU budget. However, up to the Prodi Commission 1999/2004 nationals of the big member states were responsible for at least one of the key portfolios. The European Council in Brussels (June 2004) upheld the principle of collegiality and rejected the proposal of the European Convention to formally create junior commissioners or any other differentiation with regard to the status of the members of the Commission. It can be expected that informal groups will emerge in the Commission of 25 and more. Fragmentation and groupings can follow different patterns and criteria, such as geography and culture, interests of member states, party or other political affiliation, or thematically linked portfolios (Wessels, 2004, p. 172).

Occasionally, the creation of portfolios was inspired by interests and preferences of new members. In connection with the southern enlargement, President Delors established a portfolio for Mediterranean policy and North–South relations. President Prodi was the first to create a portfolio for enlargement to deal with the exceptionally high number of applications and candidates. President Barroso maintains this portfolio, while he resisted any attempts to single out relations with the 'new neighbours' in a European neighbourhood portfolio but adds it to the external relations commissioner. Enlargement necessarily leads to a proliferation of portfolios and departments. Hence under the Barroso Commission portfolios were split, for example fisheries from CAP or budget control from budget in order to reach the number of 24 portfolios. Horizontal tasks are mostly taken over from the five vice presidents, which then is not merely a honorific title. President Barroso regroups all commissioners and their cabinets together and bases them centrally in the Berlaymont building, hoping this will strengthen team spirit and smooth coordination.

As far as administrative cultures were concerned, the accession of the UK was most influential and long term. The British administrative culture, including the spread of the English language, challenged the French, which had dominated and shaped the administration of the EC from its origins in terms of structures, procedures and styles. Membership of Finland

and Sweden added a Northern dimension and generally strengthened the Anglo-Saxon and Germanic administrative traditions. Key concerns of the Northern countries were transparency, access to information, the post of the ombudsman and so on, which highlight deficits in terms of accountability and legitimacy of the EU. It is quite an open question whether the new member states from Central and Eastern Europe, who largely belong to the administrative traditions already represented in the EU, will add specific features to the EU administration as post-communist states (Lippert and Umbach, 2004).

The Council, the European Council and Decision Making

The Council 'suffers' most from enlargement because the range of interests and preferences widens and makes decision making more difficult (Kerremans, 1998; Edwards, 1998). To accommodate heterogeneity and diversity is particularly difficult when unanimity is explicitly required or when the Council tries – as is common practice – to produce consensus among all member states. Thus enlargement makes EU decision making potentially less efficient. That is one reason why areas where unanimity is the rule were gradually reduced in favour of Qualified Majority Voting (Figure 5.1).

Before proposing the allocation of votes to candidates in the accession negotiations the member states have a chance to review and revise the existing system of weighted votes. Up to the enlargement of 2004 the EC pursued a conservative approach and extrapolated the status quo. It adapted the existing formula to a growing number of members. The threshold for QMV settled down around 71 per cent and increased to 72.3 in the EU25 and even 73.9 in the EU27 according to the Nice Treaty. After the first enlargement only countries of relatively small size of population joined the EC9 which aggravated the implicit and intended imbalance in favour of small countries.[7]

The TCE introduces a double majority of states and population that will replace the entire system of weighted votes. This innovation was the most controversial issue at the IGC 2003 and led to the first failed summit on the TCE in December the same year. Finally the IGC raised the threshold which the Convention had proposed from 50 to 55 per cent of member states and from 60 to 65 per cent of the population. The double majority in combination with an extension of the areas where this procedure can be applied shows a way towards more efficiency and improved capacity to act. Under the TCE, countries with a population around 10 million (such as Hungary or the Netherlands) will lose power compared to the rules on qualified majority in the Nice Treaty while the big countries and Germany in particular gain

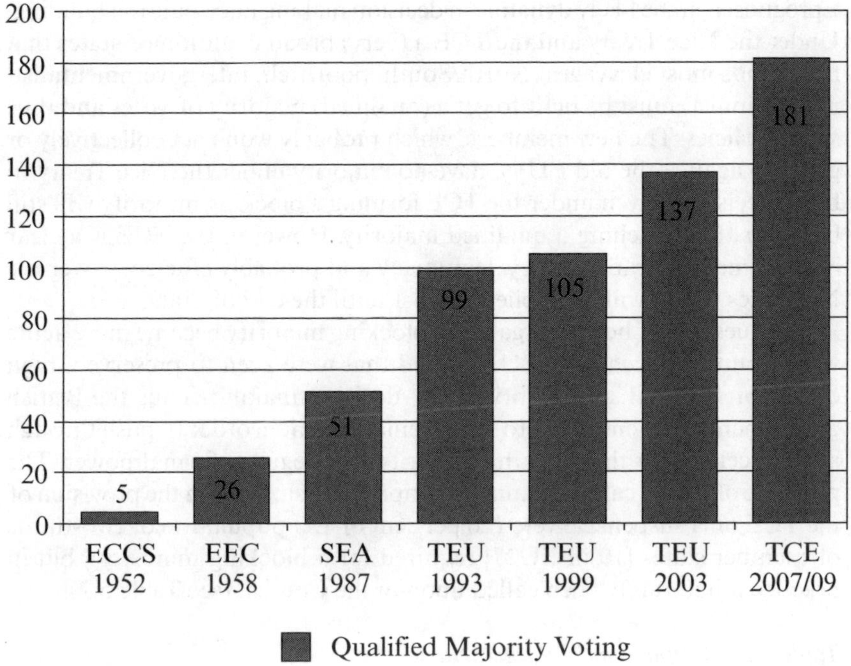

Source: Wessels (2004), p. 166.

Figure 5.1 Growth areas where Qualified Majority Voting in the Council is provided for by the treaties (in absolute figures)

in power (Baldwin and Windgrén, 2004). The new rule for double majority would give Turkey as the probable most populous member state in the EU after 2014 a powerful stance in both making and blocking decisions. Interestingly, at the Nice IGC the EU15 only agreed on a list of 12 new members and their integration into the EU institutions. The newcomer Turkey will have the combined size of population of all ten countries that acceded in 2004 and could – together with Germany – dominate the Council and large parts of policy making. Turkish accession will affect the entire balance of power between the big member states and also affect the power constellations between the big and all other members. The membership of Turkey would have implications for institutions and decision making like none of the five previous rounds of enlargement. Scenarios and speculations like these show how delicate and probably transitory these arrangements are.

Where a qualified majority is needed for a decision, the effects of enlargement on voting coalitions is of particular interest. It is difficult to make a prognosis on the likely dynamic in decision making and coalition building. Under the Nice Treaty and the TCE a (very) broad coalition of states that transcends most cleavages (North/South, poor/rich, intergovernmentalist/integrationist) must be built to get a (qualified) majority of votes and thus shape policies. The new members, which probably won't act collectively or gang up against the old EU15, have no majority under the Nice Treaty to block decisions. Even under the TCE forming a blocking minority will still be easier than reaching a qualified majority. However, the TCE is a clear improvement in transparency, legitimacy and probably efficiency over the Nice rules which will be applied at least until the end of 2009.

The question of how to organize a blocking minority became more acute when countries such as the UK joined that were keen to preserve a high degree of national sovereignty in EU decision making. Thus the British government threatened to veto EFTA enlargement in order to push through a lower ceiling for the blocking minority to safeguard formal power. The principle of the so-called 'Ioannina compromise' survived in the provision of the TCE on a suspensive veto (26 per cent of EU population or two-thirds of member states [10 in EU27] required for a blocking minority), but in practice it had rarely been called upon in the Council (see Table 5.2).

Table 5.2 Council and enlargement

Council	Total vote	Spread of votes	QMV*	QMV threshold (%)	Blocking vote
EC6	17	1–4	12	70.6	6
EC9	58	2–10	41	70.7	18
EC10	63	2–10	45	71.4	19
EC12	76	2–10	54	71.0	23
EU15	87	2–10	62	71.3	26**
EU25 (1 November 2004)	321	4–29	232	72.3 plus 62% EU population	90
EU27 TCE (1 November 2009)	27	1	15	55 (minimum 15 MS) plus 65% EU population	14 member states or more than 35% of the pop. of at least 4 member states

Notes:
* Decisions after proposal of Commission.
** 23–25 according to Ioannina compromise.

Source: Own compilation.

From the origins of the EC votes were weighted in favour of the smaller countries who feared a dominance of the big, notably France and Germany. According to the TCE a minimum of four states is needed to block a vote because some countries wanted to make sure that Germany, France and Italy could not build a blocking minority. For countries such as Poland and initially also Spain the rules for blocking decisions were a crucial point in the negotiations.

The reform of the Council and its configurations was another point of concern. The need for better coordination and hierarchization of the Council formations was emphasized in recent rounds of enlargement. Some changes in the organization were possible without a change of the primary law and lengthy ratification. Thus, at the European Council in Seville in 2002 the EU decided to reduce the configurations of the Council from 16 to 9. However, more radical reforms were again turned down. The draft TCE of the Convention stipulated the creation of one single super Council dealing with all legislative acts. The TCE preserves the old system of mixed legislative and executive tasks but strengthens the coordinating role of the General Affairs Council which is separated from the new Foreign Affairs Council (former external relations) of foreign ministers. This might well lead to a strengthening and creation of European ministers who are located close to the heads of government in their capitals and would certainly also affect COREPER (the Committee of Permanent Representatives).

Another issue linked to enlargement was the rotating presidency. In a larger EU member states would only hold the presidency every 12 or 15 years for six months. Concerns over administrative capacities of the many small countries had already led to a manipulation of the alphabetical order of the presidencies so that a smooth sequence of small and big states holding the presidency was possible. Also the composition of the troika for CFSP was changed so that it is now made up of the Presidency, the High Representative and the President of the Commission. As a real improvement, the TCE foresees permanent and elected chairs only for the Foreign Affairs Council which is held by the newly created post of a European Foreign minister. Moreover, the president of the Euro-Council is elected for a term of two and a half years. Small countries were particularly interested in preserving the principle of rotation. In the TCE only a shallow compromise was found which remains close to the status quo. For the other Council configurations a team presidency of three member states shall chair at all Council levels for a period of 18 months and based on a joint work programme. The old system is continued because each member state in the team shall chair for a period of six months. This does not seem a real improvement in terms of efficiency, continuity and visibility.

The European Council steadily enlarged and strengthened its power and gradually got locked into the institutional system of the EU. Over the years but not only as a result of enlargement, the European Council lost its original informality and confidentiality. According to the constitutional treaty of 2004, the European Council will become a proper organ (however, outside the jurisdiction of the European Court of Justice). The TCE confirms and even extends the role of the European Council as the highest and ultimate centre of decision making in the EU, not only for the history-making decisions (for example on constitutional and financial questions) but also for elections and nomination for key posts in the EU and many everyday decisions which could not be solved otherwise. Even earlier some members made an effort to refocus the agenda of the summit meetings on crucial questions, reduce the size of the delegations and so on (Schröder and Blair, 2002). The TCE now provides for a permanent president of the European Council who shall prepare, chair and coordinate the work and also represent the Union externally. The TCE opens the possibility for a future merging of the President of the European Council with the President of the Commission.

THE EUROPEAN PARLIAMENT

The European Parliament seems least affected by enlargements (Neunreither, 1998). The youngest institution within the power triangle increased its competencies as a co-legislator over the last decades each time the treaties were revised but quite independent of enlargement. Most obvious was the increase in seats of the EP when new members joined. The Assembly of the EC6 counted 142 delegates, and after the accession of Denmark, the UK and Ireland 198 seats. Following the first direct elections to the EP the number of seats doubled and amounted to 412, modestly increased after the Greek entry (434). While the next Southern enlargement followed the traditional pattern and brought in 84 more MEPs, German unification provoked some political debate about the right balance, most notably between the bigger countries. For political and psychological reasons seats for Germany (which increased its population by more than a quarter) increased from 81 to 99; that is just below the sensitive mark of 100. At the same time more seats were allocated for the other big countries. However, for the first time the 'enlargement without accession' (Spence, 1991) introduced a differentiation between the big four; stronger representation of Germany as the biggest member state was finally accepted. All in all the changes did not establish a more transparent and proportional distribution of seats. While the EP itself wanted to limit its size to 700 (European Parliament, 1992 – 'de Gucht Report'; European Parliament, 1995 'Bourlanges–Martin Report'), a proposal taken up in the Amsterdam Treaty (Article 189 EC-T), the parliament soon crossed the threshold in the next rounds of enlargement. In the EU15 the EP had 626 seats; in the EU25 it already had 732. If Romania and Bulgaria have joined the Union up to the elections in 2009 the EU27 will temporarily have 782 seats (see Table 5.3).

Table 5.3 European Parliament and enlargement

EP	Seats	Minimum/maximum of seats per member state	Languages
EC6	142*	6–36	4
EC9	198*	6–36	6
	412**	6–81	
EC10	434	6–81	7
EC12	518	6–81	9
	564***		
EU15	626	6–99	11
EU25	732	5–99	20
EU27	782	5–99	22
TCE	750	6–96	

Notes:
* National delegates.
** First directly elected.
*** Since 1994 as a result of German unification.

Source: Own compilation.

The TCE defines a maximum of 750 seats with a maximum of seats per member state reduced to 96. Imbalance in the proportional representation increased with every new round of enlargement. The degressive proportionality is still not convincing. The number of the minimum seats was again redefined and increased the threshold from five to six in the TCE.

Languages are of course a key problem for the working procedures in Parliament. Plenary and most committee work is translated simultaneously into all official languages, which increased from four in the EC6 to 20 in the EU25.

OVERALL CONCLUSIONS

Institutional spill-over from enlargement remained limited. Key concerns were the decision making and the widening of competencies and tasks at the EU level to deal with the challenge of diversity. On the whole, the development shows that in the course of widening and treaty reform unanimity was reduced and nearly abandoned as the principal decision-making procedure and majority voting is about to become the norm, at least on paper. Interestingly, in the past, qualified majority voting was only used in about one-fifth of possible cases. However, since 2000 the trend to make use of QMV has increased (Maurer, 2004, p. 12). So over the last decades the community method has spread across policies. The tension between intergovernmental and supranational solutions has been maintained. Reforms reveal an effort to ensure the institutional balance in the power triangle. However, the creation of the European Council introduced a permanent change that limits federal aspirations. New members have generally supported the precarious balance between further communitarization of problem solving and the preservation of the superseding role of the member states in the European Council and Council. The TCE will particularly strengthen the European Parliament as co-legislator and the Council through the introduction of double majority voting. It upgrades the paramount role of the European Council and strengthens the President of the Commission. If the Council gets its act together; that is if double majority is used and works in decision making, it can become the key driver of the integration process.

BUDGET AND POLICIES

Enlargement has important policy and financial implications for the EU. The majority of countries that joined after the first enlargement were poorer than the Community average and had strong interests in agriculture. Therefore we will concentrate on the budgetary implications and then look at regional policy and CAP, the two biggest categories of expenditure of the EU budget while leaving out other implications, most notably geopolitical and foreign policy implications (Hill, 2000).

For reasons pointed out above, the scope of reform intended and achieved did not correspond with the number of countries joining or the economic and political potential they added to the Union (Table 5.4).

THE BUDGET AND ENLARGEMENT

The budget is affected by enlargement on the revenue and on the expenditure side. However, enlargement only was one reason for the growth of the EU budget over the last decades. It was also due to the extension and expansion of policies and the introduction of new budgetary lines (e.g. aid). The EU

Table 5.4 Impact of successive enlargements of the EU

(Based on 1995 data)	Increase in area (%)	Increase in population (%)	Increase in total GDP[1] (%)	Change in per capita GDP (%)
EC9/EC6	31	32	29	–3
EC12/EC9	48	22	15	–6
EU15/EC12[2]	43	11	8	–3
EU25/EU15	25[3]	22[3]	9[4]	–14[4]

Notes:
1 In purchasing power parities.
2 Including German unification.
3 GD enlargement: Eurostat (2000).
4 Statistisches Bundesamt: Europäische Union 2004, Wiesbaden, 2004.

Source: European Commission (1997b), p. 22, updated.

budget grew from 1970 to 2004 from 3.5 bn to 99.7 bn EUR (Figure 5.2). The dominance of CAP over the budget was already established in the EC6 and was maintained in every round of enlargement and financial package. The average share of the CAP developed from 66 per cent (Delors I) to 51 per cent (Delors II) to 43 per cent (Agenda 2000). It will, according to the Commission's proposal (European Commission, 2004a and Table 5.6 below), reach 47 per cent in 2008 before going back to a share of 40 per cent in 2013. Overall expenditure for CAP slowly decreased over the years and money was saved for other tasks, namely to finance cohesion policy which developed as the most dynamic and also most 'wanted' fund on the part of acceding countries. The southern enlargements of 1981 and 1986 led to a doubling of the expenditure on Structural Funds (Allen, 2000, p. 249) which made up around 32 per cent of the budget in 1993. The average share of the structural policy remained the same for Delors II and Agenda 2000 period (35 per cent of the overall budget). Following the Commission's proposal it will increase significantly in the next financial perspective 2007–2013 and reach 51 per cent on average (European Commission, 2004a and Table 5.6 below), and will be the most dynamic category of expenditure. Special arrangements such as the cohesion fund to improve capacities to join the euro zone were prolonged because no explicit rules for graduation were established. In the Agenda 2000 Structural Funds for the new member states are twice as high as for CAP.[8] They were limited with the help of an absorption threshold of 4 per cent of national GDP as maximum transfers from the EU to national budgets. This approach was, however, contested by the candidates. While they had to accept it in the course of accession negotiations they will cause controversy between cohesion countries and net contributors in negotiations over the next financial perspective 2007.

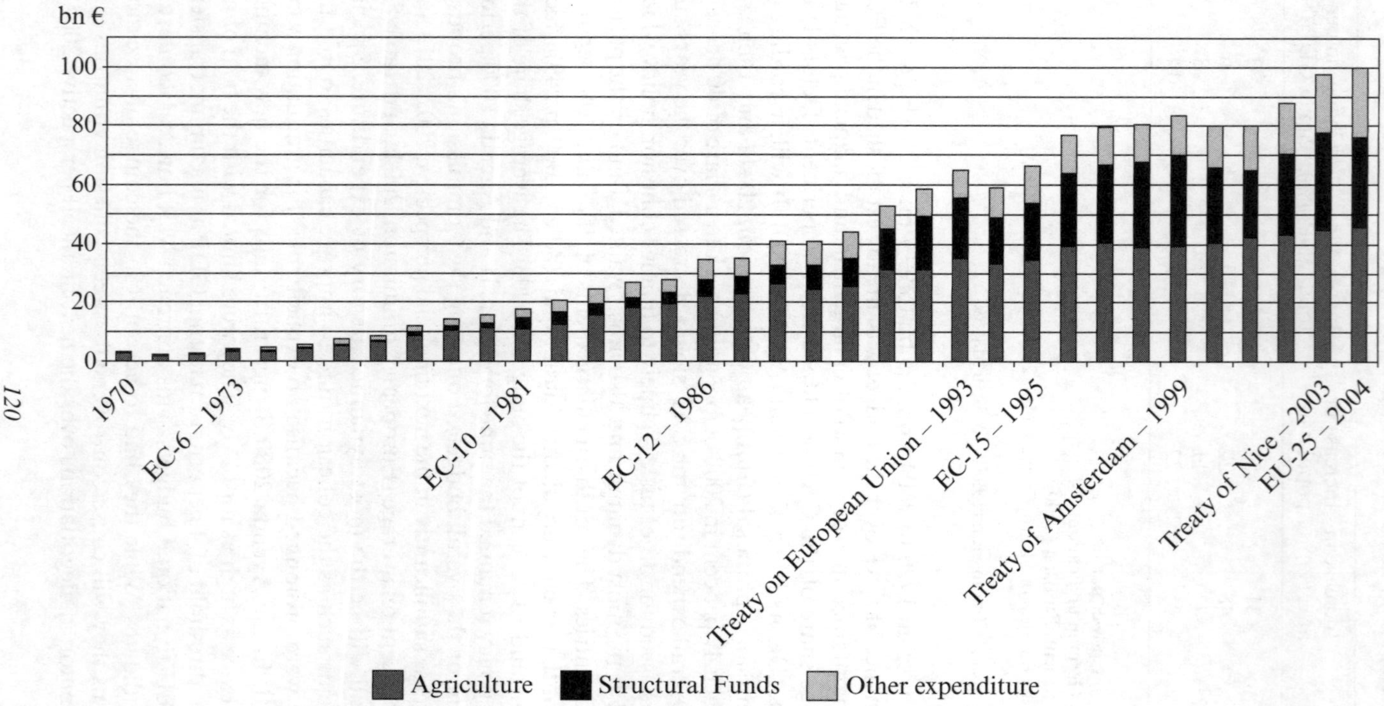

Source: EU Commission: Financial Report 2002/German Ministry of Finance, 2004.

Figure 5.2 Growth of budget/growth of EU membership and treaty revision, 1970–2004

Table 5.5 Development of own resources ceiling (million ECU)

	1988	1989	1990	1991	1992	1993	1994	1995	1996	1997	1998	1999	2000*	2001*	2002*	2003*	2004*	2005*	2006*
Total appropriations for commitments	45.303	46.885	48.900	50.950	52.800	69.177	69.944	72.485	75.224	77.989	80.977	84.089	92.025	93.475	93.955	93.215	91.735	91.125	90.660
Total appropriations for payment	43.779	45.300	46.900	48.600	50.100	65.908	67.036	69.150	71.290	74.491	77.249	80.114	89.600	91.100	98.360	101.590	100.800	101.600	103.840
Appropriations for payments as % of GNP	1.12	1.14	1.15	1.16	1.17	1.20	1.19	1.20	1.21	1.23	1.25	1.26	1.13	1.12	1.18	1.19	1.15	1.13	1.13
Margin for unforeseen expenditure (%)	0.03	0.03	0.03	0.03	0.03	n.a.	0.01	0.01	0.01	0.01	0.01	0.01	0.14	0.15	0.09	0.08	0.12	0.14	0.15
Own resources ceiling as % of GNP	1.15	1.17	1.18	1.19	1.20	1.20	1.20	1.21	1.22	1.24	1.26	1.27	1.27	1.27	1.27	1.27	1.27	1.27	1.27

Note: * Total appropriations including appropriations for payments available for accession.

Source: EU Commission: Financial Report 2002/German Ministry of Finance, 2004.

The own resources ceiling developed from 1.15 per cent of GDP in 1988 (EC12) to 1.20 in 1992 to 1.27 per cent of GDP in 2004 (EU25), which equals 1.24 per cent of GNI (Table 5.5).

While the budget grew steadily in absolute figures, the battles between the member states concerned the own resources ceiling and their financial contributions as well as the expected transfers they receive from the budget. Thus the perspective of the so-called net payer or net recipient shapes preferences of member states in the bargaining process on financial and reform packages. The return from the EU budget depends on the design of the policies. That is why the financial perspective is directly linked to a reform of policies. The Delors I package (1988–92) had to take into account the Southern enlargement, the Delors II package (1993–99), the EFTA and Agenda 2000 (2000–2006) the eastern enlargement (Laffan and Shackleton, 2000). Agenda 2007 will, however, be the first financial perspective that must be agreed by consensus among 25 member states and will thus reflect also the new constellation of interests and proliferation of actors and potential veto players. While the Convention had proposed to decide on the next but one multi-annual financial framework by Qualified Majority Voting (article I-54, 4 Draft Treaty of a Constitution for Europe), the TCE now only foresees that the European Council may decide by unanimity to use Qualified Majority Voting (Article I-55, 4 TCE). Thus each member state retains its power to veto decisions.

The own resources ceiling maintained the level of 1.24 GNI from the EU15 to the EU25 and according to the Commission proposal, even beyond in an EU27 (Tables 5.5 and 5.6). The difference lies in the real spending of money. In 2003/04 appropriations for payments totalled only 0.98 per cent of GNI. The Commission now foresees a higher ceiling for the next seven-year period (on average 1.14 per cent). In particular net payers reject this financial perspective. They want to limit payments to 1.00 per cent; that is, continue the status quo from the EU15 to the EU25/27. However, in this scenario the budget would also grow in absolute figures because of GDP growth in the EU. According to the Commission proposal (European Commission 2004a and Table 5.6 below), payments should increase from 116.5 bn euro in 2006 to 143 bn euro in 2013, which amounts to an increase of 22.8 per cent (payments) and even 31 per cent (commitments reaching 158 450 bn in 2014). This projection is based on an optimistic annual growth rate of 2.3 for the EU (2.2, for EU15; 4.1 per cent for ten new members).

On the revenue side the system of own resources was considerably affected by the introduction of the so-called British rebate which amounts to 66 per cent of the UK's annual net contribution. It should compensate for the disadvantages the UK had. Because of the structure of its agriculture it could benefit only little from CAP payments that dominated the EU budget. Thus

Table 5.6 Agenda 2007 (million € at 2004 prices)

Appropriations for commitments	2006 (a)	2007	2008	2009	2010	2011	2012	2013
1. Sustainable growth	47582	59675	62795	65800	68235	70660	73715	76785
1a. Competitiveness for growth and employment	8791	12105	14390	16680	18965	21250	23540	25825
1b. Cohesion for growth and employment	38791	47570	48405	49120	49270	49410	50175	50960
2. Sustainable management and protection of natural resources	56015	57180	57900	58115	57980	57850	57825	57805
Of which: Agriculture – market-related expenditure and direct payments	43735	43500	43673	43354	43034	42714	42506	42293
3. Citizenship, freedom, security and justice	1381	1630	2015	2330	2645	2970	3295	3620
4. The EU as a global partner (c)	11232	11400	12175	12945	13720	14495	15115	15740
5. Administration (d)	3436	3675	3815	3950	4090	4225	4365	4500
Compensation	1041							
Total appropriations for commitments	120688	133560	138700	143140	146670	150200	154315	158450
Total appropriations for payments (b)(c)	114740	124600	136500	127700	126000	132400	138400	143100
Appropriations for payments as % of GNI	1.09	1.15	1.23	1.12	1.08	1.11	1.14	1.15
Margin available (%)	0.15	0.09	0.01	0.12	0.16	0.13	0.10	0.09
Own resources ceiling as % of GNI	1.24	1.24	1.24	1.24	1.24	1.24	1.24	1.24

Notes:
(a) 2006 expenditure under the current financial perspective has been broken down according to the proposed new nomenclature for reference and to facilitate comparisons.
(b) Includes expenditure for the Solidarity Fund (1 billion in 2004 at current prices) as from 2006. However, corresponding payments are calculated only as from 2007.
(c) The integration of EDF in the EU budget is assumed to take effect in 2008. Commitments for 2006 and 2007 are included only for comparison purposes. Payments on commitments before 2008 are not taken into account.
(d) Includes administrative expenditure for institutions other than the Commission, pensions and European schools. Commission administrative expenditure is integrated in the first four expenditure headings.

Source: European Commission (2004a), p. 29.

the accession of the UK accentuated the imbalance of the EC budget, which was driven by French preferences in CAP. The agreement of Fontainebleau in 1984 was not achieved through a reduction and reform of CAP. Instead, on the revenue side a special correction mechanism for the UK was introduced so that the balance between British receipts and contributions improved. The example is also typical in that accession negotiations are not the arena for changing the *acquis*. The only hope is that reforms are pursued in parallel. The continuation of the British rebate is challenged in each negotiation on the financial perspective. The constellation is one country against all others who have an interest in abolishing the mechanism. Agenda 2000 established better conditions for net payers like Germany and the Netherlands because their share in financing the rebate was reduced, at the disadvantage of all others, including the new members of 2004 who have to pay more. Against this background the Commission proposed the introduction of a general correction mechanism (as presented in the Commission's report on the own resources system in 1998 and as unsuccessfully proposed by the German government in 1997/98 with regard to the Agenda 2000 negotiations) and phase-out of the British rebate between 2008 and 2011 (European Commission, 2004a, pp. 36–8 and *Agence Europe*, 15 July 2004, p. 9). Any member state with a net contribution beyond 0.35 per cent of its GDP would benefit from a 66 per cent reduction in the contribution. However, as the UK would lose from this arrangement compared to the status quo it will be difficult to reach a consensus, while the Commission tries to split the front of net payers by isolating the UK. One of the main advantages of a general correction mechanism would be fairer burden sharing and probably a more transparent system. Another improvement in terms of transparency could be achieved through a tax-related revenue system, for example on VAT, corporate income or energy. The ECT also leaves open the option of a genuine EU competence in taxation.

Traditional cleavages also persist as regards Agenda 2007: between the net contributors and the net beneficiaries, for example over the own resources ceiling and between reform-oriented countries and adherents of the status quo, for example with a view to regional policy and CAP. This translates into a differentiated constellation of interests in the EU25: the six net payers (Germany, France, the UK, the Netherlands, Austria and Sweden) who have already signed a letter[9] in favour of limiting the budget to 1.00 per cent of GNI (payments) as well as Denmark and Finland are opposed by the cohesion countries of the EU15, namely Greece, Spain and Portugal, while Ireland is in a phase of graduating from this status and redefining its mid-term interests. Other countries, such as Belgium, Italy, Luxembourg, and the richer new members Malta and Cyprus, have not yet taken a decision on the own resources ceiling. The new members from Central and Eastern Europe oppose the 1 per cent ceiling and also want to abolish or increase the 4 per cent absorption quota on transfers from the EU budget for structural policy. As this was a key provision to limit costs of eastern enlargement, the net payers will certainly defend this absorption rate. It also reflects the preference of the net payers for a top–down approach while the cohesion countries – supported by the Commission and wide parts of the EP – favour a demand-driven, bottom–up approach. Again a compromise has to be found between the hard liners on both sides.

At the Berlin Summit in 1999 the financing of the CAP was far more controversial than it will be in the case of Agenda 2007. As part of the internal EU bargaining over a common position in the accession negotiations – in October 2002 a compromise on the CAP was agreed that reaches far into the future and very much reflects French interest in preserving the *status quo*. The European Council had fixed CAP expenditure up to the year 2013. Expenditure for market support and direct payments would increase from about 45.5 bn EUR in 2006 to around 50.5 bn EUR in 2013; in real terms (measured in constant prices 2004 and with an assumed inflation rate of 2 per cent) expenditure would even decrease from 43.7 bn EUR in 2006 to 42.3 bn EUR in 2013 (Ahner, 2004). As a result of tough accession negotiations the new members (and later on also Romania and Bulgaria) are phased into the system of direct payments up to 2013, although the EU had originally denied their eligibility. The principle of equal treatment of all members – new and old – is upheld. Reform proposals to co-finance direct payments through national budgets were rejected, most vocally by France. It is very unlikely that this agreement will be questioned. This, however, means that the bargain on the distribution of funds in the next budget as well as proposals for saving money will be centred around the second biggest category of expenditure, that is structural policy. In this regard the cleavage exists between countries which want to concentrate funds to the relatively poorest countries and regions, that is, the new members and others falling below the 75 per cent threshold of the per capita GDP and those who cross this level as a result of their improved relative position in a larger and poorer EU (statistical effect) and insist on a continuation of transfers in absolute terms (under old Objective 1 and 2). The Commission proposes to spend around 78.5 per cent on the convergence objective, including the statistical effect regions, namely in Spain, the UK, Germany, Finland, Portugal and Austria (European Commission, 2004b, p. 12). Roughly 52 per cent of the funds (objective 1 and 2) would go into the new member states (*Agence Europe*, 13 February 2004). This shows again the strong political bias for the old member states. The Commission presents a new approach and puts the so-called Lisbon objectives under the sub-category 'competitiveness for growth and employment' alongside the cohesion policy. In 2013 one-third of the funds for sustainable growth shall be spent under this sub-heading. This is opposed by some member states which insist on the aim of regional policy as laid down in Article 158 EC-Treaty to reduce 'disparities between the levels of development of the various regions and the backwardness of the least favoured regions, including the rural areas'. At a time when social and regional disparities in the enlarged Union significantly widen,[10] the

Commission seems to be concerned that the old EU15 countries would lose interest in regional policy once funds are really concentrated on the poor new members. Therefore long phasing out and horizontal programmes (community initiatives) are included in the proposals.

Negotiations on Agenda 2007 will be difficult because of the controversial issues and the new constellation of actors and interests in the enlarged EU but also because of timing: the calendar for elections in key member states, such as the UK (first half 2005) and Germany (autumn 2006) and the calendar for referenda on the TCE in ten or more member states (!) will only leave a narrow time window. The intention of the heads of state and government is to agree on the package up to June 2005, which would be after a referendum on the TCE in France, and before a referendum in the UK. Domestic politics will reduce the room to manoeuvre and negotiations might run into deadlock.

CAP AND REGIONAL POLICY

Overall the impact of new members and enlargement on the content and design of policies is difficult to estimate. Of course preferences and specific conditions of the newcomers had to be taken into account. This was the case with a new 'objective 6' for Arctic and thinly populated areas when Sweden and Finland joined and with the introduction of market regulations for Mediterranean products when Southern countries joined. The biggest reform process – the MacSharry reforms of 1992 – were a result of efforts that started under the Delors I package to reduce spending on CAP. In 1992 direct payments were introduced which shifted CAP from price support to direct income subvention. Although this turned out to be costly, even enlargement towards countries with huge agricultural sectors and a high rate of (however unproductive) workforce[11] did not bring about fundamental change. In CAP the combination of international competition, in particular the WTO negotiations, and the objectives of environmental protection and rural development were more effective in policy development than enlargement. The very nature of accession negotiations under the imperative of an un-negotiable *acquis* and the strong bias towards the insiders (Preston, 1997, p. 84) mostly led to expensive status quo oriented policies.

CAP and regional policy survived the five rounds of enlargement as the biggest and also most bureaucratic policy fields (Josling, 1998). Warnings that the budget would implode and policies could not be continued unless fundamental changes happen before enlargement turned out to be less threatening than initially feared or predicted. So we see that new member states contribute their preferences within a path-dependent development of policies. Normally the new members accentuate existing cleavages and join one or the other camp. As interests between old and incoming members are not so clear cut it was difficult for the EU to agree on fundamental reforms before the actual enlargement. That was the case with Agenda 2000, when many issues were postponed to a later stage.

In the financial framework for 2007–2013 the Commission proposes a new classification and reduction of expenditures. The biggest category is called 'sustainable growth' (structural policy and Lisbon goals), followed by the CAP-dominated category 'sustainable management and protection of natural resources'; third and smallest is 'citizenship, freedom security and justice', fourth concerns external relations 'the EU as a global partner' and last is administration. The headings rather show a political language than give a clear idea of the contents. The Commission thus wants to indicate that a restructuring of the budget is under way. However, the EU is miles away from spending money on public goods like internal and external security, environment or research and development.

PERSPECTIVES

With deepening and widening, the EU has become more complex as far as the decision-making provisions, the number of institutions, and law making were concerned. As a complementary development, flexibility formally was acknowledged by way of enhanced cooperation but also through new procedures such as the open method of coordination. Still, the single institutional framework was maintained. In the future bargaining and coalition building among more stable groupings of member states will be more likely, while in the past occasional voting coalitions that were linked to concrete issues dominated. Moreover, the possibilities the treaty offers for taking votes might be used more extensively, at the expense of a lengthy search for an overall consensus. One can only speculate about new dynamics and use of new opportunity structures as a result of both further constitutionalization and widening of membership. The revision clauses in the treaties and the TCE indicate uncertainties and the need for trial-and-error processes. External pressures and incentives play an increasingly important role for further integration and the development, notably enlargement, of the European Union. In the light of the cumbersome decision making in the EU it is increasingly difficult to keep pace with the changes in international relations and pressures of globalization.

Ratification of the TCE will interfere with and influence negotiations on Agenda 2007. This might lead to blockages and will certainly add to the path-dependent and piecemeal reform approach instead of any more systematic change. In the past the price of enlargement has been a higher complexity of problems and solutions. The larger the EU, the more difficult the accommodation of preferences becomes in the framework of treaty and policy reforms, as well as budgetary questions. In connection with the negotiations on Agenda 2007, solidarity and burden sharing will be prominent topics on the EU's future agenda. As a lesson from past enlargements, one can say that cautious readjustments dominate over revolutionary changes or reversal of current trends. The mantra that enlargement shall not happen at the expense of deepening proved difficult to realize. Only the SEA reform package and Southern enlargement turned out to be mutually reinforcing. Even if the TCE will be ratified, which is regarded as a minimum condition to govern the enlarged EU, many uncertainties and fluidity of constellations (Redmond and Rosenthal, 1998, p. 4) exist. The unbroken attraction of the EU *vis-à-vis* third countries proves that European welfare states regard the EU as the best available system to pool instruments, power and financial resources to manage complex interdependence. With regard to the following enlargements and in particular the controversial membership of Turkey, one must conclude from the history of deepening and widening that the EU will not find a scope and depth of change to meet the challenge of integrating a poor, populous, largely agrarian country that borders on a crisis region.[12] In the past the EU got away with limited reforms and long periods of belated digestion of the consequences of enlargement. The constitutional, financial and political implications and the risk of overstretch are enormous in the case of Turkey and further expansion to the East. Compromises on these issues were always the result of intergovernmental bargains. Countries such as Germany, that in the past were willing and able to pay the bill for enlargement, are economically too weak to continue with this strategy. Moreover, with a view to candidates such as Turkey or the Ukraine, the material interests and probably also those linked to the collective identity (Schimmelfennig, 2003) of the EU which gave momentum to eastern and also previous rounds of enlargement are comparatively weak (Lippert, 2004). The EU was often said to be at the crossroads (European Council, 2001/Laeken Declaration). Next time this might be felt more acutely.

NOTES

* The author is grateful to the Otto Wolff-Foundation for its support in the framework of the IEP programme 'Dialogue Europe der Otto Wolff-Stiftung', to which this chapter contributes.

1. Report on the European Union, by Leo Tindemans, *Bulletin of the European Communities*, Supplement 1/76.

2. Reprinted in *Europa-Archiv*, Bonn: Verlag Internationale Politik, Vol. 36, No. 6/1981, p. D164 and Vol. 37, No. 2/1982, pp. D 50–55.
3. Taken up in Dahrendorf (1979).
4. Quoted after Scharrer (1984), p. 6–9.
5. Quoted after Wessels (2004), p. 175.
6. Or even 31 if Poland had been treated like Spain.
7. Out of 16 acceding countries Spain and Poland were the only two with a population of 40 million; the others ranged between 400 000 and 11 million.
8. In the period 2004–2006 the ten new members will receive 9.8 million EUR from CAP and 21.8 from structural funds (appropriations for commitments). Cf. the Treaty of Accession of the Czech Republic et al., signed in Athens on 16 April 2003, AA 2003 final, Art. 29/30 and Annex XV.
9. Cf. for a summary: *Agence Europe*, 17 December 2003, p. 8.
10. The Commission states that 'the gap between the average GDP per head in the EU-15 and the level in the least prosperous member states is currently just under 30% (Greece and Portugal have levels almost 30% below average), the gap will double when the new member states join in 2004 (Latvia has a GDP per head which is over 60% below the EU average) and is likely to widen even more once Bulgaria and Romania enter' (European Commission, 2004c, p. I-11).
11. The Commission states that 'The new Member States will add about 38 million hectares of utilized agricultural area to the 130 million hectares of the current Member States, an increase of 30 per cent, while production in the EU will expand by about 10–20 per cent for most products. The gross value added of agriculture will only increase by 6 per cent' (European Commission, DG Enlargement and Agriculture, 2004d).
12. Given demographic development, Turkey will be the biggest member state in the EU with a population of 82 million in 2015 and 87 million in 2025. In 2002, Turkey's GDP accounted for 26.9 per cent of the average EU GDP (PPS). Cf. Hughes (2004), p. 8–9.

APPENDIX: ENLARGEMENT AND TREATY REFORM/CONSTITUTIONALIZATION AND EXTERNAL CHALLENGES

Enlargement and treaty reform / Constitutionalization	Governance	Legitimacy	Policy development	External challenges
Northern and first southern enlargement	European Council Court of Auditors Budgetary procedure and powers Directly elected EP	EP direct elections	Fisheries regional policy EPC EMS	Breakdown of Bretton Woods Oil price crisis End of détente
Southern enlargement *SEA plus* Delors I (88–92) Maastricht Treaty Delors II (93–99)	QMV Cooperation procedure Assent procedure Legal recognition of European Council EPC Secretariat New Court of First Instance *Co-decision procedure* *Opt-outs* *Subsidiarity* *Committee of the Regions* *Ombudsman* *Revision clause IGC 1996*	European citizenship Improve efficiency *Subsidiarity*	Completion of single market 1992 Economic and social cohesion Environment, R&T, EPC Treaty based EMU JHA CFSP *Cohesion fund* *Social protocol*	Eurosclerosis Recession Japanese/Asian challenge End of war Cold War ↓

EFTA enlargement ↑ *Amsterdam Treaty* 'Agenda 2000' *Nice Treaty* ↓	Extension of co-decision, abandoning cooperation procedure Extension QMV Enhanced cooperation Enhanced status commission president Revision clause *Amsterdam Leftovers: size Commission, weighted votes in Council, extension QMV and co-decision, new ceiling and redistribution seats EP* Revision clause	Charter of fundamental rights Enhancing openness and transparency Simplification, consolidation of treaties	Schengen; Tampere JHA Employment policy ESDP	New world order Globalization
Eastern/Mediterranean enlargement ↑ *European Convention* *Draft Constitution* *plus* *Rome Constitutional Treaty* Agenda 2007	Convention Constitution Double majority EU Foreign Minister President of the European Council National Parliaments Elected president of Commission		European Neighbourhood policy Lisbon agenda	'War' against terrorism

PART III

The Place of Europe

6. Europe and the USA: security and defence policy

Fergus Carr and Theresa Callan

INTRODUCTION

The collapse of the Soviet Union marked not just the end of the Cold War, but also the threat system that was a fundamental element of the political cohesion of the transatlantic relationship. Moscow's policies had cemented the Atlantic community and provided the focus for its strategic rationale. In the aftermath of the Cold War international actors were offered 'a relatively blank sheet of paper on which to write the outlines of a new world order' (Howorth, 2004a, p. 211). In the process of rethinking and redefining security new policy preferences and approaches developed on both sides of the Atlantic. The antecedents of this divergence of interests can be found in the past history of European and American relations but the policy disputes, which fractured openly over Iraq in 2002–2003, heralded a far stronger potential for divorce than past rifts.

This chapter examines the erosion of the Western security community amidst the challenges of the post-Cold-War era. It analyses the impact of the reconceptualization of security upon NATO and the European Union (EU). It reviews the role of the Western Alliance in the new Europe and the international system. It concludes with an analysis of Europe and America after 9/11 and considers the future cohesion of transatlantic relations.

TRANSATLANTIC RELATIONS IN THE COLD WAR

The basis of the transatlantic alliance lay in the European and American mutual recognition of security dependence. Both sides responded to 'powerful incentives to cooperate and avoid discord in the face of a monolithic Soviet threat' (Peterson and Pollack, 2003, p. 1). At the centre of the Atlantic community was NATO, which committed members to collective defence and 'entangled' the USA in the affairs of Europe. Washington also provided economic assistance through the European Recovery Programme and encouraged the integration of the West European economies (see Crockatt, 1996, pp. 76–80). American enlightened self-interest and European need were joined in a security agenda that interwove economic, political and military concerns. This agenda became increasingly militarized as the European perception of Soviet threat grew and Washington lost its monopoly of atomic power. American strategy formally recognized that without 'superior aggregate military strength, in being and readily mobilizable, a policy of "containment" – which is in effect a policy of calculated and gradual coercion – is no more than a policy of bluff' (NSC68, 1950, p. 290). When the Cold War turned 'hot' in Korea, NATO began its transformation from a 'transatlantic mutual assistance treaty into an integrated military alliance run by the United States' (Calleo, 1970, pp. 25–6). The Atlantic relationship consequently became an unequal partnership dependent upon American resources and power. As the defence of Western Europe increasingly turned to nuclear deterrence the centrality of Washington's leadership was further underlined. The partnership in practice reflected what one observer has seen as 'dependence and not interdependence, hegemony and not integration' (Calleo, 1970, p. 28). Alliance tensions grew over a number of issues such as German rearmament, and decolonization provided another contested theme as the locus of power shifted from Europe to the superpowers. It was de Gaulle, however, who challenged American leadership and the cohesion of NATO in 1966 by terminating the assignment of French forces to international commands and calling for the transfer of Alliance Headquarters from France (see Menon, 2000, pp. 7–13). As tension in Europe had declined with the development of superpower détente, Kissinger had anticipated that 'defence against a military threat will soon lose its force as a political bond' (Kissinger, 1965, p. 10). He saw the challenge for the Alliance as 'polycentrism' which did not 'reflect so much new centres of physical power as the attempt by allies to establish new centres of decision' (ibid., p. 17). European economic recovery underpinned this potential and the significance of the European Community as a political organization was recognized by the six member states at the Hague Summit in 1969.

None the less the Alliance survived its 'enduring crisis' (Joffe, 1981). Its resilience has been explained by the notion of common interests which have overridden particular disputes; these are seen as 'family fights, often sharp but contained in a web of common interest' (Treverton, 1985, p. 2). The transatlantic bargain is seen to have worked because 'the bargaining goes on within a framework of common interest, perceived and acknowledged' (Cleveland, 1970, p. 5). This was facilitated by a decision-making process which combined the principle of consensus with the reality of American power. For Stanley Hoffmann the Atlantic Community has rested on two myths. One was 'the absence of any necessary conflict between European integration and the Atlantic community – a myth that served both to help contain de Gaulle's ambitions for a generally autonomous "European Europe" and to reassure Atlanticists on both sides of the ocean that European integration could be seen as a subset of the Atlantic community' (Hoffmann, 2003, p. 1030). The second myth was that, 'Europe remained, for the United States, the most crucial diplomatic and strategic theatre, one with which the US was linked not only by vital economic and security interests, but also by a common culture and common values' (ibid.). When the Cold War ended, these myths were increasingly exposed and importantly no longer buttressed by the overarching security rationale provided by the Soviet threat.

THE CHANGING SECURITY AGENDAS IN EUROPE

The process of change within the Atlantic community since the end of the Cold War has been gradual, episodic and contested. Advocates of a new European approach to security have, for example, been challenged by member states of the EU, such as Britain, which have sought to maintain the compatibility of the European project with transatlanticism. Successive American administrations have also asserted Washington's interests in an era when the power position of the USA is unmatched in the international system. The consequences in the European arena can be seen in terms of institutional developments and policy issues.

The transformation of European politics since the end of the Cold War led to fundamental changes in security understandings. The dominant notion of 'threat' gave way to the idea of 'risks', which NATO saw as 'multi-faceted in nature and multi-directional' (North Atlantic Council, 1991a, p. 237). The security agenda was broadened from a military perspective to include political, societal and economic stability. In this new conceptualization a range of issues became securitized, including: human rights; the plight of minorities; migration; democratization; the rule of law; and environmental concerns. Security was now a 'diffuse concept ... in which economic integration and assistance and the internal democratization of states became as important as traditional military defence ...' (Wörner, 1991, p. 8). The new agenda was also multi-level, ranging from societal groups to states, regions and global considerations. The events of 9/11 added a new dimension to this equation and enhanced the complexity facing security providers.

In the new security environment the potential role for international institutions was recognized as actors accepted the limits of state-level policy.

The breadth of the agenda, moreover, invited a new approach to security that involved several 'interlocking' institutions.

> The challenges we will face in this new Europe cannot be comprehensively addressed by one institution alone, but only in a framework of interlocking institutions tying together the countries of Europe and North America. Consequently, we are working toward a new European security architecture in which NATO, the CSCE, the European community, the WEU and the Council of Europe complement each other. (North Atlantic Council, 1991b)

The institutionalization of security concerns became a key feature of the new Europe. Institutions sought to enhance their relevance, adapt to the new order and develop new roles. Within this process functional overlap and competition for missions resulted and reflected conflicting strategic visions of the key players. The most sensitive issue area was NATO's relationship with the European Union.

NATO AND THE EUROPEAN UNION

While Britain sought to ensure NATO remained the keystone of European security (Deighton, 1997), Paris claimed the 'end of the Cold War had removed the need for integrated military structures' (Menon, 2000, p. 41). Both states recognized the need for an enhanced European contribution to post-Cold-War European security but differed in their vision of its autonomy. The USA warned its allies of the 'danger that positions which seem to emphasize European over transatlantic solidarity or institutional changes which diminish the centrality of the Alliance could pose for American opinion on and support for the transatlantic partnership' (Bartholomew, 1991). German policy saw continued membership of NATO as 'essential to the stability of a post-Cold-War Europe' (Anderson and Goodman, 1994, p. 29), while European integration was at the 'heart of its grand strategy' (Hyde-Price, 2000, p. 180). Germany saw 'no inherent contradiction between NATO and an autonomous European defence capability' (ibid., p. 195) and Chancellor Kohl joined with President Mitterrand to press for a new European Union. These positions met with some turbulence within the NATO reform process and the Intergovernmental Conferences underpinning the Maastricht Treaty.

Anglo-American interests were invested in NATO's attempt to anchor its position by: declaring it would adapt (North Atlantic Council, 1990); adopting a 'New Strategic Concept' in 1991 (North Atlantic Council, 1991) which stressed a 'broad approach to security', including conflict prevention and crisis management; and developing a new dialogue with its former adversaries through the North Atlantic Cooperation Council. At the same time NATO declared the 'new environment does not change the purpose or the security functions of the alliance' (North Atlantic Council, 1991a). But within a month of launching its New Strategic Concept the Soviet Union collapsed, opening the question of the need for collective defence. If crisis management was to be the new rationale for transatlanticism, then 'out of [Treaty] area' roles beckoned – and problems of legitimacy. The latter were in part resolved when the North Atlantic Council declared itself ready, in 1992, to support on a case-by-case basis peacekeeping operations under the Conference on Security and Cooperation in Europe (CSCE) or United Nations (UN) auspices. But the need for political will and cooperation to mount such missions remained and, as we shall see in the case of the former Yugoslavia, placed real constraints on the new NATO.

The Franco-German agenda resulted in the Maastricht Treaty in 1992 which marked a new stage in the development of the European project. Among its commitments was the creation of a Common Foreign and Security Policy (CFSP). The CFSP structure was intergovernmental, though the Commission was to be fully associated, and decision making was to proceed by unanimity. CFSP was to 'include all questions related to the security of the Union, including the eventual framing of a common defence policy, which might in time lead to a common defence' (Art. J.4.1). The Treaty did not, following British insistence, create an EU force structure but looked to the Western European Union, the European alliance whose origins pre-dated NATO, to 'elaborate and implement decision of the Union which have defence implications' (Art. J.4.2). The nine member states of the WEU, including Britain, who were also EU members, declared that the WEU would be developed as the 'defence component of the European Union and as a means to strengthen the European pillar of the Alliance' (Maastricht Declaration on Western European Union).

The pivotal role of the WEU, between NATO and the EU, became the basis of the compromise between the Atlanticist and Europeanist agendas. It sustained the myth that the European project was compatible with transatlanticism by placing European defence cooperation with the Alliance framework.

The compromise was sustained by the North Atlantic Council meeting in Brussels in 1994 which declared its willingness to

> stand ready to make the collective assets of the Alliance available on the basis of consultations in the North Atlantic Council, for WEU operations undertaken by the European Allies in pursuit of their Common Foreign and Security Policy. We support the development of separable but not separate capabilities which could respond to European requirements and contribute to Alliance security. (North Atlantic Council, 1994)

To implement this process NATO looked to the development of Combined Joint Task Forces (CJTF) to facilitate both peacekeeping missions and cooperation with the WEU. The North Atlantic Council formally endorsed the concept in Berlin in 1996. NATO envisaged the identification of 'separable but not separate' assets for WEU missions, including headquarters, 'double hatting' appropriate personnel in the NATO Command structure and military planning for illustrative WEU missions (see North Atlantic Council, 1996). For NATO, CJTF meant a sharing of assets to ensure 'as far as possible that Europe's CFSP effectively complements rather than compares with the transatlantic security structures' (Schake et al., 1999, p. 22). France, under Chirac's leadership, moved closer to the Alliance but insisted that 'NATO's new missions implied the need for a fundamental reform of its decision-making structures and procedures' (Menon, 2000, p. 50). Paris looked for a European Deputy SACEUR to be given authority to command European missions and for Europeans to be given command of two regional European commands (Wijk, 1997, p. 135). The role of Deputy SACEUR was agreed but Washington insisted that an American would command AFSOUTH in Naples. As Chirac's aim to enhance the Europeanization of NATO was only partly realized, French enthusiasm for an EU alternative was revitalized.

In the debate preceding the EU Amsterdam Treaty (1997), France, Germany and the Commission advocated the integration of the WEU into the EU. Britain rejected this proposal and led the opposition to an extension of Qualified Majority Voting (QMV) to CFSP. The resulting Treaty enhanced the use of QMV when the European Council agreed and a new office, a High Representative for CFSP, was to be appointed. While the possibility of integrating the WEU into the Union was voiced in the Treaty, it was subject to the 'blocking' clause 'should the European Council so decide' (Art. 17.1). This impasse was dramatically lifted by the British Prime Minister, Tony Blair, in the Anglo-French declaration on European Defence in St Malo in December 1998. The St Malo declaration called for the European Union to 'have the capacity for autonomous action backed up by credible military forces, the means to decide to use them, and a readiness to do so, in order to respond to international crises' (Foreign and Commonwealth Office, 1998). Blair believed that 'Europeans should not expect the United States to have to play a part in every disorder in our backyard' (Blair, 1999, p. 3). Robin Cook, then Foreign Secretary, explained that 'Bosnia, Albania and Kosovo have all shown that crisis management requires a joined up approach which brings together the economic, financial and humanitarian resources of the European Union with the military assets of the European countries in NATO' (Cook, 1999, p. 6). Despite the initiative originating in London, the USA still warned the Europeans not to 'decouple' from or duplicate the Alliance (Howorth, 2000, p. 45). The London Anglo-French Summit in November 1999 sought to placate Washington with the assurance that the EU would only seek to act 'where the alliance as a whole is not engaged' (*The Times*, 26 November 1999).

The European Union took its defence policy forward in the Cologne and Helsinki European Council meetings in 1999. The operational role of the WEU was to be transferred to the EU by December 1999. The EU was to have the capabilities to perform the so-called 'Petersberg Tasks': 'humanitarian and rescue tasks; peacekeeping tasks; tasks of combat forces in crisis management, including peacemaking' (WEU, 1992). The Helsinki European Council set the target of creating by 2003 a force 50 000–60 000 strong which could be deployed in 60 days and sustained for a year (European Council, 1999, p. 3). The EU further instituted new decision-making bodies within the framework of CFSP to execute its European Security and Defence Policy (ESDP).

NATO sought to maintain the line that ESDP was a reinforcement of the European pillar of the Alliance. The Washington NATO Summit in April 1999 acknowledged 'the resolve of the European Union to have the capacity for autonomous action so that it can take decisions and approve action where the Alliance as a whole is not engaged' (North Atlantic Council, 1999).

The devil, however, remained in the detail. As consideration of the planning process of EU-led operations proceeded, American misgivings grew. Lord Robertson, NATO Secretary General, pledged to work to ensure ESDI (European Security and Defence Identity) 'is based on three key principles, the three Is: Improvement in European defence capabilities; inclusiveness and transparency for all Allies; and the indivisibility of Trans-Atlantic security, based on our shared values' (Robertson, 1999, p. 4). Washington endorsed these principles but stressed the lessons of Kosovo for European armed forces. The US Secretary of Defence William Cohen warned:

> We simply cannot continue with a posture in which one member of NATO conducts virtually two thirds of all air support sorties and half of all air combat missions; in which only a handful of countries have precision munitions that can operate in all kinds of weather; and, in which some pilots had to communicate over open frequencies in a hostile environment. (Cohen, 2000a, p. 3)

The USA looked to the implementation of NATO's Defence Capabilities Initiative (DCI) launched at the Washington Summit in 1999 and saw Europe's emphasis on new structures as at best a distraction and at worst a threat to Allied cohesion. Cohen demanded that 'we have to pay real attention to function and capabilities as opposed to façade' (Cohen, 2000b, p. 2).

He explained that the USA supported ESDI because 'a strong European pillar will mean a stronger NATO …' but 'here is the caveat … provided that we make sure that the capabilities that are now being discussed and debated and, hopefully, fulfilled, will be consistent for both the EU and also for NATO. The last thing we want to see is separate capabilities developed or weak capabilities developed and bigger bureaucracies' (Cohen, 2000b, p. 3). On the eve of the EU Nice Summit in December 2000 which was to develop ESDP, Cohen proposed a 'common defence planning process involving all 23 NATO and EU countries as the only logical, cost effective way to ensure the best possible coordination of limited forces and resources' (Cohen, 2000c, p. 2). Cohen warned that if 'NATO and the EU with its ESDP are seen as autonomous and competing institutions rather than integrated, transparent and complementary ones, then NATO and collective security are likely to suffer, leaving North America and Europe alike to rely on uncoordinated, inefficient and ad hoc responses to destabilizing threats' (ibid.).

The Nice Summit did not adopt Cohen's proposal for joint planning but did recognize that 'NATO remains the basis of the collective defence of its members and will continue to play an important role in crisis management' (Nice, 2000, Presidency Report on ESDP, Introduction). The Summit endorsed detailed arrangements for the management of ESDP. The EU sought an 'autonomous capacity to take decisions and, where NATO as a whole is not engaged, to launch and conduct EU-led military operations in response to international crises' (ibid.). EU relations with NATO were to 'respect the autonomy of EU decision-making', a regular dialogue was to 'ensure consultation, cooperation and transparency', and in times of crisis meetings would be increased so the 'two organizations can discuss their assessments of the crisis …' (ibid., Annex VII). Nice further outlined the EU's expectations of guaranteed access to NATO's planning capabilities and, in accord with NATO's Washington Summit Communiqué, pre-identified Alliance capacities and assets for EU use. Operations requiring recourse to NATO assets and capabilities operational planning 'will be carried out by the Alliance's planning bodies, and for an autonomous EU operation it will be carried out within one of the European Strategic level headquarters' (ibid., Annex VI). For the six non-EU NATO members Nice envisaged consultation on the use of NATO assets and involvement in NATO planning bodies. For EU autonomous operations the six would be invited to send liaison officers to the European Military staff bodies at strategic level (ibid.). For one observer this approach 'was backwards: it should be joint planning first, then deciding who would undertake an operation (NATO or the European Union), then considering whether

NATO assets would be needed and hence transferred, and then undertaking any subsequent planning ...' (Hunter, 2002, p. 12).

The primacy of NATO was of concern to the incoming Bush Administration. The new President reported that he had been reassured by Tony Blair that 'NATO is going to be the primary way to keep the peace in Europe ...' and that 'there would be a joint command, that planning would take place within NATO' (Bush, 2001a, p. 3). The President, speaking at NATO, stressed that 'a strong, capable European force integrated with NATO would give us more options for handling crises when NATO, as a whole, chooses not to engage' (Bush, 2001b, p. 2). If 'autonomy' was to be reconciled with 'NATO first', the issue of deciding when NATO was not to be 'engaged' remained central. The difficulty of EU and NATO negotiations was matched by the parallel concern of non-EU NATO members about their potential involvement in non-Alliance missions. Turkey sought particular safeguards, which, when finally accommodated, led to objections from Athens which, in turn, delayed matters further.

The EU–NATO negotiations were conducted by working groups covering a number of issue areas including: security of information; permanent arrangements for consultation and cooperation; modalities for EU access to NATO assets; and EU capability goals. The working groups were supplemented by meetings of the North Atlantic Council and the European interim Political and Security Committee of the EU. The Foreign Ministers of both organizations began meetings in May 2001. The process finally resulted in the December 2002 EU–NATO Declaration which led in turn to the 'Berlin Plus' agreement of 17 March 2003 which covers: EU guaranteed access to NATO planning; EU use of listed NATO assets and capabilities; and NATO European Command options for EU-led military operations with Deputy SACEUR as a primary candidate for EU operation commander. The 'Berlin Plus' agreements enabled the transfer of responsibility for peacekeeping from NATO to the EU for operations in the former Yugoslav Republic of Macedonia and Bosnia in December 2004.

As agreement between the EU and NATO appeared to be solidifying, the convergence process was challenged by Washington's response to the 9/11 attacks (see below). The initial solidarity of Europe and the USA was lost as Washington's agenda moved from al-Qaeda and the Taliban to Saddam Hussein's Iraq. When President Bush spoke of an 'axis of evil' in his State of the Union address in January 2002 the French Foreign Minster described the approach as 'simplistic' and urged Europeans to speak out against a Washington that 'acts unilaterally, without consulting others, taking decisions based on its own view of the world at its own interests' (Vedrine, 2002). France and Germany refused to endorse British support for the Bush Administration's demand for regime change in Iraq. Germany made clear its resolve to oppose war and France looked to the United Nations to be given more time for weapons inspections. Chris Patten, European Commissioner for External Relations, spoke on behalf of the EU when he argued that there was 'no real alternative to the UN system of values and international rules ...' as 'it offers the best hope of avoiding the potentially disastrous consequences of a spread of unilateral action allegedly to "solve" regional disputes' (Patten, 2002). Washington, however, did not feel bound to accept UN constraints. President Bush warned the General Assembly that America would work with the Security Council for the necessary resolutions but asked whether the UN would serve its purpose or be deemed irrelevant (Bush, 2002, p. 3). When the UN could not furnish a resolution authorizing the use of force, the USA, supported by the UK, invaded Iraq.

The implications for NATO and the EU were complex. Despite NATO invoking Article 5 for the first time in its history, the USA conducted its own military operations with 'coalitions of the willing'. When Washington requested that NATO dispatch Patriot missiles and surveillance aircraft to defend Turkey, the proposal was blocked by France, Germany, Belgium and Luxembourg (*The Times*, 30 January 2003). Donald Rumsfeld, US Defense Secretary, in response said it was 'breathtaking' (*The Economist*, 12 February 2003). On 29 April 2003 the same four European states met in Brussels and agreed a number of measures for defence cooperation including the establishment of an EU operational planning staff in Tervuren. The initiative was seen to breach the consensus of 'Berlin Plus' and for Geoff Hoon, British Defence Secretary, 'risks sending a message of division about the creation of a defence policy separate from NATO' (*Times Online*, 28 April 2003). The US Ambassador to NATO hoped that 'this new brand of European unilateralism will be repudiated by the majority of European countries that want to preserve NATO as the pre-eminent security organization on the continent' (Burns, 2003, p. 4). Tony Blair, excluded from the Brussels Summit, moved swiftly to heal the rift with Washington and reassert the British role in European defence cooperation. When he met President Chirac and Chancellor Schröder in Berlin in September 2003 a compromise was reached that the EU would set up an operational planning cell at SHAPE, NATO's planning headquarters. There was also to be a new planning unit with civil/military components to join the existing EU military staff.

Despite Blair's unimpeachable transatlantic credentials, Washington still demanded reassurance that NATO retained its primacy. The issue became compounded with debates on the new European Constitution and the possibility of a mutual defence clause (*International Herald Tribune*, 17 October 2000). Blair contended that 'nothing whatever must put at risk our essential defence guarantees within NATO ...' (Blair, 2003a, p. 1) but

NATO had to hold an extraordinary meeting to address Washington's concerns. In November Blair and Bush issued a joint statement that they sought 'a dynamic, mutually-reinforcing relationship between NATO and the EU, without duplication and divisiveness, and grounded in the essential NATO–EU agreements which underpin it' (Blair and Bush, 2003, p. 1).

In late November, Britain, France and Germany appeared to be close to a consensus which US Defense Secretary Donald Rumsfeld said would not duplicate the work of NATO (*The Guardian*, 2 December 2003). Lord Robertson described exchanges as 'robust' (ibid.) but in public the Western powers spoke of a 'common success' and 'common vision' (Joint Press Statement by the NATO security general and the EU Presidency, 4 December 2003) and the EU declared 'the transatlantic relationship is irreplaceable' (European Security Strategy, 12 December 2003). On 12 December, Blair confirmed that a deal had been struck, 'in a way that is completely consistent with NATO as the cornerstone of our alliance' (Blair, 2003b). The European project, however, had not made defence an integral part of its future; as President Chirac put it, 'we think there will not be a Europe without a defence capacity' (*International Herald Tribune*, 21 October 2003).

The proposed European Constitution adopted by member states in June 2004 makes a number of provisions to enhance the EU's external role, including: a Union Minister for Foreign Affairs; a redefinition of the Petersberg Tasks; the creation of a European Defence Agency; and specific measures to enhance 'flexibility' in ESDP. In addition, member states agreed to a solidarity clause in respect of terrorist attack or man-made disasters (Art. 1–43). The Union Minister for Foreign Affairs combines the responsibilities of the High Representative for CFSP and the Commissioner for External Relations (Art. 1–28). The new post therefore links the Commission and the European Council, providing a much-needed focus for external relations. The minister will represent the EU in international organizations and preside over a European External Action Service (Art. 111–296). The Petersberg Tasks now reflect the breadth of the European security strategy and include the fight against terrorism and post-conflict stabilization (Art. 111–309). The European Defence Agency, whose role is to provide coordination and cooperation in European armaments policy and procurement, was launched in advance of the Constitution being ratified (Art. 111–311). Member states had recognized in the European Capability Action Plan in 2001 the need to remedy shortfalls in the commitment process to the Helsinki headline force goals for ESDP. In May 2004 the European Council adopted the 2010 headline goal which superseded Helsinki and included new commitments to rapid reaction battle groups which could cover the breadth of crisis management tasks envisaged in the new Constitution. The EU's ambition was to launch an operation within five days of the approval of the Crisis

Management Concept by the Council. The battle groups are to be credible, rapidly deployable stand-alone forces with global deployability from 2007. Finally the Constitution envisages 'flexibility' to ensure the delivery of ESDP in light of enlargement and the vagaries of member states' policies and capabilities. Howorth has identified six instruments of flexibility in the Constitution, with the most important being 'structured cooperation' (Howorth, 2004b, p. 485). Structured cooperation (Art. 111–312) builds on the Amsterdam provisions for closer or 'reinforced cooperation' among member states who wish to develop deeper policy mutuality. The Constitution reflected Franco-German desires to build a core Europe in defence matters and British concerns regarding NATO compatibility. The outcome was to identify structured cooperation in defence capability, investment, development and acquisition. Member states who pledged closer cooperation in this regard were those who made a commitment to contribute to the new battle groups discussed above. EU military operations were to remain subject to unanimous vote in the Council and not subject to the procedures of QMV associated with structured cooperation.

In February 2005 President Bush and his Secretary of State, Condoleezza Rice, toured Europe seeking to rebuild transatlantic bridges and move beyond 'a partnership based on common threats' to focus instead 'on common opportunities, beyond the transatlantic community' (Rice, *The Guardian*, 9 February 2005). The idea of a reinvigorated partnership was welcomed in Europe but the critical issue of balance awaited resolution. While France for the first time in 40 years hosted a meeting of NATO Defence Ministers, the French Minister of Defence looked to a new balance of responsibilities:

> It is important, today, to readjust American and European responsibilities in terms of security and defence. It is that goal which Europe of Defence aims at. It must be consolidated, and its autonomy guaranteed, in order to make the European Union a credible actor on the international scene. (Allot-Marie, 11 February 2005)

Chancellor Schröder also looked for change and called for the reform of NATO as he claimed it was 'no longer the primary venue where transatlantic partners discuss and coordinate strategies' (*The Guardian*, 14 February 2005).

The debate over the nature of transatlantic relationships is clearly not over and its institutional representation in EU–NATO relations is an unfinished story. The deployment of the EU 'battle groups' will stand alongside the NATO Response Force (NRF) agreed at Prague in 2002. While the units will in all probability be complementary force allocations, NATO exclusivity or 'first call' will not be guaranteed. Real European military assets will in effect open up a new round of intra-Alliance diplomacy. However, the issues concern not only roles and capabilities, but, critically, leadership. Despite a common security agenda, perceptions of risk and policy preferences have divided the Atlantic community leading to the ongoing significance of EU–NATO relations.

THE CHALLENGES OF THE NEW SECURITY ENVIRONMENT

The dominant paradigm of Cold War inter-state conflict has been replaced by the phenomenon of conflicts within malfunctioning states. The durability and dispersal of these wars has undermined initially optimistic findings that 'the local carnage of the 1990s was a kind of aftershock – terrible but temporary' (Allin, 2004, p. 659). Instead, failing states have persisted 'as orphans dumped on the doorstep of the international community', presenting continuing challenges to global stability (Howard, 1995, pp. 293–4). Initially policy makers and analysts focused on their associated risks such as 'spill-over' in terms of refugee flows stoking ethnic tensions in neighbouring states with diasporas. In time, concern spread to include the interrelationship of failing states with international terrorist and criminal networks. It became accepted that such states afforded a permissive environment for terrorists to plot and, sometimes, execute their plans. This 'superterrorism' (Freedman, 2000) differs from more traditional predecessors in several ways, notably its utilization of indigenous criminal networks and its willingness to commit acts of unlimited violence with mass casualties. While terrorists previously seemed to include media and popular reaction in their calculations, contemporary international terrorism appears perversely committed to acts spectacularly lacking in restraint. This raises the spectre of international terrorists acquiring WMD to add to their arsenal and emphasizes the need for robust arms control regimes especially concerning collapsing states. Following the 9/11 attacks, much attention was given to the location of such states as the 'zone of instability', gave way to 'the arc of crisis', and thence to 'the axis of evil'. A consensus seemed to emerge on the strategic necessity of the Western liberal democratic community to 'drain the swamp' via the extension of democratization. As the preponderant power within the international system, the USA was well placed to ensure the promotion of this agenda and to act as 'the global security provider of last resort' (Allin, 2004, p. 650).

The USA had its first opportunity to demonstrate its role as defender of law and order with the Gulf crisis in 1990 when, in what may prove to be the last major manifestation of a traditional inter-state conflict, Iraq invaded neighbouring Kuwait. This action constituted a clear violation of international law and such clarity facilitated a common response on the part of the international community. Under the aegis of the United Nations, whose series of resolutions for withdrawal was ignored, the USA led a military force of 700 000 troops from a coalition of 28 countries. In the face of overwhelming military power, beginning in mid-January 1991, Kuwait was liberated within six weeks. Significantly for later US foreign policy, the capitulation of Iraq did not culminate with the collapse of the Saddam regime. American policy makers did not pursue the goal of regime change via military means believing that such an objective, unsanctioned by the UN, would deleteriously affect the unity of the coalition. The strength of the international response to this first Gulf War was created and sustained by the legal clarity of the *casus belli* and the voluntary multilateralism of the coalition:

> It was directed against a clear and particularly ruthless case of cross-border aggression. The UN Security Council, with the active support of Russia and China, explicitly sanctioned it. It was carried out by a 'coalition of the willing' that included a number of Arab states … (Allin, 2001, pp. 163–4)

Ironically, while restoring the *status quo ante* held this coalition together, later it would prove to be a core source of dissension between the USA and its allies. The success of this war appeared to endorse claims that the community of liberal democratic states could extend the zone of stability through concerted action. It seemed that American primacy or 'hyper-power' could be effectively and best exercised within a multilateral context. This common strategic vision was given expression through the then Bush Administration's Transatlantic Declaration in November 1990.

In the wake of this conflict, however, the compatibility between American 'hyper-puissance' and the multilateral order seemed less assured. As more complex security challenges arose, so too did the degree of confusion concerning the best response to them. The starkness of the inter-state threat to Westphalian norms ceded to murky multifaceted threats from imploding states.

THE BALKAN CRISES

The implosion of Yugoslavia into a morass of secessionist conflicts in the early 1990s corresponded with the closing phase of the Bush Administration. In the run-up to presidential elections, the Administration was reluctant to respond to such intra-state conflict. Instead the UN and the EU sought to settle contending claims through the use of diplomatic pressure. These efforts, however, were undermined by their inability to speak with one voice in their diplomatic dialogue. Germany's decision in late 1991 to recognize claims to independent statehood by the constituent republics damaged the EU's ability to influence the concerned parties. Additionally, Mitterrand's 1992 trip to persuade the Bosnian Serbs to lift their siege of Sarajevo was a unilateral move that unquestionably undermined claims of a commonality in European foreign policy. Thus despite the labour of the EU, not least its Hague Peace Conference of September–December 1991, its 'soft' power proved insufficient when 'the conflict grew too complex and dangerous for civilian diplomacy to remain effective in the absence of the involvement of any other credible international authority' (Ginsberg, 2001, p. 75). The EU scrambled to present some sort of unity, however superficial, when it announced that it would recognize the independence of Slovenia and Croatia on 15 January 1992, despite an earlier warning by Lord Carrington and Cyrus Vance that such a move would 'trigger a chain reaction culminating in war in Bosnia' (taken from Holbrooke, 1999, p. 31).

The coming to office of the Clinton Administration did not occasion a change in US policy towards the Balkans, despite Clinton's campaign emphasis on the importance of the Bosnian question and support for the use for a 'lift-and-strike' policy – to lift the arms embargo on the Bosnian Muslims and the use of air strikes to break the siege of Sarajevo. Once he was in office, support for the use of military force abated. The cautionary tale of the US experience in Somalia weighed heavily. The initial US military deployment by Bush in December 1992 was aimed at creating a stable environment for food delivery and distribution. This sort of mission appeared tailor-made for a Democratic administration that 'believed in the use of military force to advance humanitarian aims' (Schulzinger, 2002, p. 359), and Clinton initially supported its continuance while allowing the UN to assume greater responsibility for relief provision. The operation was dogged with difficulties, not least concerning command-and-control matters between the USA and the UN and reached its nadir with the downing of a US 'Black Hawk' helicopter, the deaths of 18 US marines and the dragging of a dead marine through the streets of Mogadishu – shown to American viewers courtesy of CNN. The 'CNN factor' among other things led to Clinton's withdrawal of American troops by the end of 1993. This experience militated against involvement in the Balkans, and a policy of inaction held until July 1995 and an attack by the Serbs on the Bosnian Muslim enclave of Srebrenica. Despite its status as a UN 'safe area', the Bosnian Serbs took over this town, killing anywhere between 4000 and 7000 Bosnian Muslim men and boys. Inaction no longer seemed viable in what Vulliamy has termed the West's 'final chance to rescue a battered credibility in Bosnia' (1994, p. 262). In August, the US Congress voted to end the arms embargo on Bosnian Muslims and NATO launched air strikes on Serbia. All the deliberation and delay had sorely affected the Atlantic Alliance, with then US Secretary of State Christopher Warren expressing his despair at the 'indifference, timidity, self-delusion and hypocrisy' among the European Allies (taken from Vulliamy, 1994, p. 284). Even the attainment of Serbian, Croatian and Bosnian signatures on the Dayton Accords at the end of the year could not eradicate the fact that 'lack of strategy and political will to settle on a common course of action in Bosnia inflicted a serious blow on European–American relations and established a pattern of mutual suspicion in crisis-management' (Stevanova, 2001, p. 85). The negotiations and contents of the Dayton Accords were an exclusively American exercise, thereby reinforcing 'in Europe the worst apprehensions of the unilateral way of crisis management' (ibid., p. 86).

Europe was not the only omission. The Accords' failure to address the nascent conflict between Albanian and Serb Kosovars spurred its exacerbation and militarization. The Serbs in Kosovo sought to reverse what they perceived to be the 'Albanization' of Kosovo through a raft of discriminatory legislation. This radicalized Albanian opinion helped fuel demands for political independence from Yugoslavia rather than greater autonomy within the federation. This shift in sentiment was mirrored in the growing significance of the Kosovo Liberation Army and the onset of clashes between it and both Serb militias and the JNA (Thomas, 1999; Judah, 1999; 2000). In the wake of the other Balkan wars, Milosevic played the 'Kosovo card' to demonstrate his nationalist credentials and so shore up his domestic political position. The conflict became increasingly overt and by the winter of 1998/99 commanded global media attention. The distressing tales of ethnic cleansing, accompanied by pictures of mass graves and the mass migration of displaced persons, led to popular pressure on the governments of the West to 'do something'. As diplomatic pressure alone proved unable to secure a Serb withdrawal from the province, the decision was taken to authorize NATO air strikes. 'Operation Allied Storm' that began in March 1999 highlighted splits within the international community and within the European Union. This was NATO's first intervention into the affairs of a sovereign nation-state without a prior request for involvement by an indigenous party. Foreshadowing later developments over the Gulf, the legality of NATO action was contested due to the lack of a UN mandate. Russia and China had both stated their intention to veto the operation should it come before the UN Security Council. Within the EU, there were high levels of domestic opposition to the operation, especially within Greece, Italy and Germany. Whilst the capitulation of Milosevic and the eventual signing of the Rambouillet Accords ended the military action, concern about the legality of the operation persisted. In the actual fighting the USA played the central role with the Allied contribution having 'primarily a political effect' (Duke, 2003, p. 5), while in the post-conflict reconstruction efforts it is the EU's 'soft power' that is at the fore.

UNILATERALISM AND MULTILATERALISM

Despite its stated commitment to assertive multilateralism in the pursuit of humanitarian goals, the Clinton Administration represented the emergence of another trend in American foreign policy – that the USA would follow a unilateral path if necessary to safeguard its strategic interests. This trend was supported too during the Clinton years with increased defence expenditure and further development of military technology. The capabilities gap between the USA and its European allies was becoming ever wider. This situation combined with US reluctance to eschew involvement in areas not deemed significant to its interests – witness events in Rwanda in 1994 – and Europe's paralysing divisions over the Balkans led to renewed European efforts to accelerate cooperation on defence and security policy. Despite such apparently diverging trajectories, or indeed perhaps because of them, 'A New Transatlantic Agenda' (NTA) was announced at the US–EU Madrid Summit of December 1995. The NTA and its accompanying Joint Action Plan (JAP) was designed to strengthen the ties between the USA and the EU. It built on the earlier Transatlantic Declaration of 1990, which had proved unsatisfactory due to its unidirectional nature – US officials were required merely to brief their European colleagues and so it 'lacked the necessary synergy and European output' (Mettler, 2001, p. 4). In the NTA/JAP, the partners noted their 'common strategic vision of Europe's future security', reaffirmed the primacy of NATO while welcoming the development of ESDI, and committed the Allies to a series of common political and economic objectives. These included: implementing the Dayton Accords within Bosnia–Herzegovina; consolidating democracy around the world; meeting transnational security threats; enhancing the multilateral economic order and further developing social, cultural and scientific ties between the USA and the EU. There was an emphasis on the coordination of foreign policy, and an institutional network for regular meetings was established, including at the executive and parliamentary levels. Such declarations notwithstanding:

> the US and the EU have rarely found themselves capable of defining a common agenda, let alone pursuing joint action, on pressing economic and transnational issues, as they equipped themselves to do so on most hard security issues during the Cold War. (Peterson, 2004, p. 618)

The arrival of George W. Bush in the White House further tested such attempts to solidify the transatlantic Alliance as it appeared to promise a unilateralist US foreign policy at best and an isolationist one at worst. During the 2000 presidential election campaign, Bush suggested the US troop withdrawal from Bosnia and Kosovo, a reduction in nation-building involvement and instead a concentration on domestic politico-economic affairs. Foreign policy was to focus on strengthening relations within Latin America, especially with Mexico. Once Bush was in office, this trend seemed manifest in US withdrawal from or neglect of international treaties such as the Kyoto Protocol, the ABM Treaty, a land mine treaty and the imposition of a tariff on steel imports. The cumulative effect of such acts 'sent the clearest possible message across the Atlantic that the skinheads of international politics seemed to have taken over the White House' (Cox, 2003, p. 527). It appeared that the 'assertive multilateralism' of Clinton had been supplanted by an 'imperious unilateralism' (Calleo, 2001, p. 15). More accurately, perhaps, US foreign policy had entered an increasingly nationalist phase – the seeds of which were contained within Clintonite foreign policy. Clinton had overseen increased defence expenditure and military hardware development. It was Clinton's Defence Counterproliferation Initiative of 1993 that signalled the possibility of pre-emptive strikes against 'rogue states' making or storing WMD. It was Clinton too who authorized a missile strike on an alleged chemical weapons plant in Sudan in August 1998 and on some targets in Iraq four months later.

THE WAR AGAINST TERROR

This trend to the pre-emptive use of military force was strengthened by the atrocities of 11 September. In a Special Address to a Joint Session of Congress on 20 September, Bush attributed culpability for the attacks to al-Qaeda and warned the Taliban regime in Afghanistan to deliver all the al-Qaeda leaders present there to the USA or 'share in their fate'. Bush served notice on the American people that the USA was waging a 'war on terror' that would end only when 'every terrorist group of global reach has been found, stopped and defeated'. The message to the rest of the world was uncompromising: 'either you are with us or you are with the terrorist … [and] regarded by the United States as a hostile regime'. The European response to the events of 11 September was prompt and perhaps best articulated by the *Le Monde* headline: '*Nous Sommes Tous Americains*'. NATO invoked Article V of the Washington Treaty treating the attacks as an attack against them all and pledging support for the USA in 'such action as it deems necessary'. The EU High Representative for the CFSP declared 'the European Union stands firmly and fully behind the United States'. Such offers of multilateral support and assistance were received warmly by the Bush Administration but were barely called upon in the subsequent war in Afghanistan. It was 'very much the case of the dog that did not bark, or at least was not allowed to bark by the United States' (Cox, 2003, p. 527). This exclusion may be attributed to the exigencies of the situation and the 'novelty of both the theatre and the type of warfare contemplated' (Makins, 2003, p. 10) but it was clear that the USA wanted the fluidity of 'coalitions of the willing', not the potential straitjacket of multilateralism.

The war in Afghanistan – or, more accurately, its initial phase – was quickly expedited. Military action began on 7 October with Kabul falling within a week. Within another month al-Qaeda fighters within the Tora Bora caves had escaped into bordering Pakistan and in due course an interim government under Hamid Karzai was established. While this opening engagement in the 'war on terror' was satisfactorily undertaken, the wider war remained. In his State of the Union Address of 2002, President Bush noted the 'axis of evil' of regimes allegedly sponsoring terror, specifically North Korea, Iran and Iraq, and linked their activities with WMD proliferation. It was Iraq that commanded the Administration's attention and energies. Regime change in Iraq was necessary not only for US strategic security interests but for 'the interest of the world'. In September 2002, the National Security Strategy or 'Bush Doctrine' was published. It claimed that America's 'enemies have openly declared that they are seeking weapons of mass destruction and evidence indicates that they are doing so with determination' and pledged pre-emptive action 'against such emerging threats before they are fully formed'. While espousing a commitment to multilateral institutions, the doctrine held that 'we will not hesitate to act alone if necessary' as such unilateral pre-emption was nothing less than 'a matter of common sense'. The prospects for war with Iraq grew firmer throughout the spring of 2003. By August, Vice President Cheney declared that Iraq constituted a 'mortal threat' to the USA and the White House Iraq Group (WHIG), comprising policy makers and political advisers, was set up to frame the issue of Iraq for public consumption. In early September, the Sunday *New York Times* quoted anonymous officials of the Iraqi nuclear programme: 'the first sign of a "smoking gun" may be a mushroom cloud'. The link between Iraq, WMD and international terrorism was explicitly enhanced: 'Disarming Iraq and the war on terror are not merely related. Disarming Iraq … is a crucial part of winning the war on terror' (Deputy Secretary of Defence Wolfowitz, taken from Gellman and Pincus, 2003, p. A9). Such language and insistence were used by the Administration to secure support from the American public and Congress and from the wider world. The Administration made it clear that while domestic support was essential, international support was desirable but ultimately unnecessary: 'We will consult. But let there be no misunderstanding: If Saddam Hussein does not fully disarm, for the safety of our people and for the peace of the world, we will lead a coalition to disarm him.' The UN Security Council and some of the European allies proved resistant to the veracity of American 'evidence' and reluctant to sanction a pre-emptive strike on a sovereign state. The UNSC did unanimously pass Resolution 1441 in November 2002 condemning the Iraqi regime's failure to comply with previous Resolutions and reinstating the UN weapons inspectors. The failure of the inspectors to discover any substantive weaponry was interpreted by the US Administration not as evidence of Iraq having disarmed and desisted from its nuclear programme, but of the inspectors' gullibility in the face of Iraqi deceit and, ultimately, of the weakness of the UN. While Blair's Britain pledged to stand 'shoulder to shoulder' with the USA, disquiet and dissent characterized the responses of the majority of EU member and accession states. The UN became convulsed by what has been termed 'a political disaster which pitted the US against France, Germany and Russia, a number of the "new" states in Europe against a few of the "old" ones, and European opinion against … "Bush's War"' (Cox, 2003, p. 528). There had been acquiescence to the passing of UNSC Resolution 1441 'because the other members of the Security Council were convinced that the US would go to war alone if they didn't pass it' (Allin, 2004, p. 653), but many believed that it alone was insufficient to provide a legal basis for war. UNSC Resolution 1441 offered Iraq 'a final opportunity to comply with its disarmament obligations' and threatened 'serious consequences' if it failed to do so. In the case of continued non-compliance, however, it facilitated a recovening 'to consider the situation'. Opponents to the war argued that UNSCR 1441 was insufficient to mandate military action, and thus another resolution was needed. British attempts to break the deadlock by drafting a second resolution were abandoned in the face of implacable resistance, especially from France. France, Russia and China all stated their intention to reject any second resolution that should come before the UNSC. The divisions led to a paralysis of the ESDP, leaving its architecture and the Political and Security Committee 'entirely at arms length from what was probably the most significant foreign and security policy issue of the entire five year period since Saint Malo' (Howorth, 2003, p. 180). Once again, Europe failed to speak with a common voice on foreign policy.

In this rancorous environment, the US-led coalition of American, British, Australian and Polish forces went to war against Iraq in March 2003. At the start of May, Bush declared that `Operation Allied Freedom' was complete in that the allied forces had prevailed albeit 'difficult work' remained to be done.

AMERICAN GUNS AND EUROPEAN BUTTER?

In the immediate aftermath of the military action in Iraq, there was a clear effort to restore the unity of the EU and to rehabilitate the transatlantic relationship. There were some grounds for cautious optimism for reconciliation with the USA. Despite the generally unilateralist tenor of the National Security Strategy, it acknowledged that 'little of lasting consequence that the US can accomplish in the world without the sustained cooperation of its allies and friends … in Europe' (NSS, 2002, p. 25). While the legality of the military action and the ongoing occupation remains contested, legitimacy possibly may be increased through the multilateral construction effort and the deployment of soft security support. This division of labour, 'if the United States can provide the "guns" for peace-enforcement, the European Union is better placed to provide the "butter" for reconstruction after the bombing', already has occurred in Bosnia–Herzegovina and Afghanistan. In 1999, the EU adopted a regional approach to reconstruction in the Balkans and South East Europe via its Stability Pact. In this approach, recipients in the region must meet economic and political criteria for aid, trade preferences and contracts. The states covered by the Dayton Accords must demonstrate their active implementation. The EU is a primary contributor of reconstruction aid to Afghanistan despite the difficulties inherent in working in a conflict theatre. While international focus has shifted to the war in Iraq, Afghanistan remains characterized by ongoing violence, an interim government whose legitimacy is contested, and a president who, more accurately, may be regarded merely as the Mayor of Kabul. The interim government of President Karzai is supported by the UN-sanctioned International Security Assistance Force (ISAF), whose troops are drawn mainly from France, Germany, Italy and Britain. In light of the worsening security situation, since August 2003 ISAF has been under NATO authority and has been steadily augmented to facilitate an environmental hospitable for national elections. The EU has pledged approximately €2 billion for Afghanistan for the three-year period from January 2002; again this aid is 'conditional on a positive contribution by all the parties of Afghanistan to the process and goals agreed in Bonn' (European Commission, 2002). Thus all the indigenous parties must sign up to the democratization programme and commit to the elimination of terrorism and drug production and trafficking. The EU has pledged €200 million for the reconstruction efforts within Iraq. At the Madrid Donors' Conference of October 2003, Commissioner Patten stressed the multilateral nature of this reconstruction: 'Whatever the disagreements earlier this year we have now all come together with a shared determination to work with the people of Iraq to build a better future for them and their region.'

Through UN Security Council Resolution 1500 of 14 August 2003, the UN Assistance Mission for Iraq (UNAMI) was established for a year in the first instance and renewed for a further year 12 months later. Following the bombings of the UN headquarters in Iraq in August and September 2003, UNAMI was withdrawn from Iraqi territory and now operated mainly from the neighbouring states of Jordan, Kuwait and Cyprus. The withdrawal of the UN and most foreign NGOs and INGOs reflects the deteriorating situation within Iraq. Whilst sovereignty technically has been transferred to President Al-Yawer's caretaker government since June 2004, its writ, like that of the Karzai Administration in Afghanistan, is heavily circumscribed. Despite the stated end of the occupation in June 2004, a US-led multinational military force remains engaged in peace-enforcement activities in the hope that national elections may be facilitated in January 2005. Since Bush's speech that the war was over in May 2003 until mid-September 2004, there have been 1163 coalition deaths, of which 1028 have been Americans. Insurgent control, wholly or partially, of volatile areas of the country, hostage taking and beheadings bear testimony to the dubious prospects for inclusive elections. In late September US Secretary of Defence Rumsfeld seemed to recognize the difficulties when he claimed that partial elections would be better than none at all. Nevertheless, President Al-Yawer, addressing the UN a few days later, called for greater international military and economic assistance and stressed that full elections would take place at the start of 2005.

The continuing casualties and instability in Iraq are undermining popular support for the war within the USA. As of mid-September 2004, 39 per cent of those polled believed that the USA had been wrong to use military force in Iraq – an increase from 22 per cent in March 2003. Additionally, 55 per cent of those polled believed that Bush possesses no clear plan for a successful disengagement from Iraq (Pew Research Centre for the People and the Press, 2004). The initial satisfaction at the seemingly quick 'victory' in Iraq has matured into a more ambiguous appraisal: 'We know we're killing a lot, capturing a lot, collecting arms. We just don't know yet whether that's the same as winning' (Rumsfeld, 11 December 2003, quoted in Loeb, 2003). The continuing absence of reliable intelligence on the insurgency builds upon the intelligence deficit that lay behind the case for war. In July 2004, the Select Committee of the US Senate produced its Report on the Intelligence Community's Pre-War Intelligence Assessments on Iraq (Select Committee on Intelligence, 2004). A damning indictment of failures by US intelligence bodies, it held that internal 'group think' led to worst-case interpretations of Iraqi behaviour and a systematic exaggeration of evidence to justify war. The threat posed by Iraq to US national and international security was overblown and given greater urgency than it actually merited.

Assumptions were made that Saddam clearly was duplicitous and dangerous, and intelligence was tailored to fit conclusions already made. The Report clearly gave the lie to Secretary of State Powell's address to the UN Security Council on the case for war: 'Every statement I make today is backed up by sources, solid sources. These are not assertions. What we are doing is giving you the facts and conclusions based on solid intelligence' (Powell, 2003). Rather, the Report concluded that the intelligence, especially that from the CIA, on Iraq's reconstitution of its nuclear programme, its possession of chemical and biological weaponry and its delivery capacity for biological warfare 'was overstated, misleading or incorrect'. The supposed link between al-Qaeda and Saddam was totally refuted, as Senator Jay Rockefeller of the Committee explained: 'leading up to September 11, our government didn't connect the dots. In Iraq, we are even more culpable because the dots themselves never existed' (Borger, 2004). Although the Report ultimately found that there had been no political pressure for this manipulation of evidence, CIA Director George Tenet resigned albeit allegedly for 'the well-being of my wonderful family – nothing more and nothing less' (Tenet, 2004). In the face of this Report, many in Congress claimed that they doubted they would have voted for war if they had been aware of the true facts. The case for war was weakened still further by UN Secretary General Annan's statement of its illegality: 'I have indicated it is not in conformity with the UN Charter, from our point of view, and from the Charter point of view, it was illegal' (Annan, 2004).

Annan has expressed his hope that 'we do not see another Iraq-type operation for a long time – without UN approval and much broader support from the international community' (ibid.). The costs of reconstruction, in terms of economics and human lives, in both Afghanistan and Iraq undoubtedly provide grounds for such hopes. Regime change in 'rogue' states continues to be an aim of the Bush Administration, but the willingness to effect it through military power has waned. A combination of 'deterrence and reassurance' is seen as more preferable when dealing, for example, with Iran and North Korea (Litwak, 2003/04, p. 19). The divisions over the war in Iraq undoubtedly hurt the transatlantic relationship, but it was not fatally wounded. Even at the height of the public rancour, cooperation continued on a host of security-related issues such as policing and judicial affairs. Indeed, the Iraq crisis may have been 'possibly even salutary' for the EU as it seeks to develop its security and defence presence. ESDP has become operational in Bosnia and Herzegovina through the EU Policy Mission (EUPM) there since January 2003 for a three-year period. In March 2003, Operations Concordia occurred with the EU sending a small military force to FYROM (the former Yugoslavian Republic of Macedonia) to create a hospitable environment for the implementation of the 2001 agreement between the Macedonian government and the Albanian insurgents. From June to September 2003, Operation Artemis was launched in the Democratic Republic of Congo to keep the peace between the government and rebels there (Menon, 2004). The EU and the USA appear to share a vision of the world order in terms of their commitment to the spread of democracy and the combating of transnational threats, such as WMD proliferation, human and drug trafficking and international terrorism. Through the deployment of its 'soft' power with the 'hard' power of the USA, the EU can play a role in international security provision despite the immense difference in capability between it and the USA. It can bring a degree of legitimacy to state building that the USA acting alone cannot. In this way, there can be an accommodation of American power within the international system. It is, however, a fragile one and there are no guarantees as to its durability. The EU appears to be learning, however painfully, the ramifications of American dominance while the USA is taking longer to learn the value of partnership over primacy.

CONCLUSIONS

This chapter has examined some of the key issues in contemporary transatlantic relations. It has been argued that while Europe and the USA share the same security agenda and have a significant commonality of interests, there is also a propensity for division.

It is accepted that political conflict and crises within the Atlantic community are not new but it is asserted that they are more profound in their consequences in the post-Cold-War era. In the new security environment Europe and the USA have differed over perceptions of threat, and the means of response, not just in Iraq, but in the European theatre. The complex and labyrinthine development of EU–NATO relations also represents a divergence among the Western powers which, at its heart, is about leadership. NATO embodies American leadership while the EU pursuit of a credible ESDP heralds alternative decision-making processes. This was instigated in part by Washington's chosen disengagement from crises affecting European security, in part from European recognition of the EU's weakness to project its influence, and in part by the growth of European identity in the community of Western powers. The West is no longer simply a transatlantic construct.

The preservation of division as multipolarity versus unipolarity conveys some of the current problems in the Western Alliance. The Iraq war did emphasize differences in approach but the issue is really one of degree as Europeans can also act without UN blessing, as shown in Kosovo. The trend of American policy from Clinton to Bush, though, does demonstrate a resistance to multilateral constraints (Pollack, 2003, p. 123). The European stress upon multilateralism is seen by some as a product of the EU's own construction (Cooper, 2003, p. 168) and 'Europe's experience of successful multilateral governance has, in turn, produced an ambition to convert the world' (Kagan, 2003, p. 60). Whether we see this as the product of 'modern' and 'postmodern' worlds (Cooper, 2003, pp. 21–54) or as between the realities of 'hard' and 'soft' power (Nye, 2002–2003), the implications are of division. For Kagan, 'America did not change on September 11, it only became more itself' (Kagan, 2003, p. 85). The Bush Administration's response to the terrorist attacks emphasized the gulf between European and American capabilities. Washington's power was, and is, decisive in strategic intervention, leaving Europe with 'secondary' roles of reconstruction. The contrast, moreover, between Washington's ability to act and division and impasse in Brussels was striking.

In Kagan's analysis 'the task, for both Europeans and Americans, is to readjust to the new reality of American hegemony' (Kagan, 2003, p. 97). For transatlanticists in 'New and Old Europe', acceptance of American leadership has been an implicit part of the Alliance bargain. For Europeans, the gulf in power projection with the USA is not necessarily the issue; rather it is the substance and manner of American leadership. The division is not 'just because Europe is weak and the US strong, but because many people outside the United States simply do not trust America to use its enormous power wisely or well' (Cox, 2003, p. 532).

The stage is set for 'optimistic' and 'pessimistic' analyses of the transatlantic relationship (Moravsik, 2003) in which there is potential for 'divorce, partnership or drift' (Daalder, 2001, p. 563). What is not in question is that the Cold War transatlantic balance of interests is over and a new bargain has yet to be realized. Europe is now less strategically important as the locus of threat moved from the continent, with dramatic interest after 9/11, and other regions demand Washington's attention. Parallel to that process and, of equal significance, is the construction of the European project. The challenge for Washington is to accept a Europe which seeks to be a credible actor on the world stage. The challenge for Europe is to realize its ambition and rely less on the USA for its security. The process of adjustment is under way but its conclusions are yet to be realized.

7. Europe and the USA: trade, finance and development

Paul McVeigh

INTRODUCTION

Since its foundation, there has been intense academic and political speculation regarding the nature of the European Union. Much attention has focused in particular on whether the development of the EU obeys the logic of a liberal intergovernmental bargain between sovereign states (Moravcsik, 1998) or whether it contains its own internal functionalist dynamics towards federalism (Haas, 1958). Aside from debates over 'form' there has been significant speculation also about the content and outcome of integration.

A recurring theme in the literature is the thesis that the EU will develop as a 'counter' and 'rival' to the USA through the translation of its undoubted economic muscle on to the world political stage (Haseler, 2004). Often this is accompanied by an implicit belief that Europe represents a different type of capitalism to the USA, and that competition between the two regions will necessarily open up divergences on a range of fundamental global issues (Redwood, 2001).

On the other hand, liberal intergovernmental theories imply limits to the process of integration arising in the control exercised over the process by European nation-states and divergences in interest between them, precluding certain integrative steps (Moravcsik, 1998).

This chapter argues that these two views of the EU offer only partial explanations of the integration process. The first suggests a coherence, universality and consensus within the EU which does not exist and to which the second is a welcome antidote. There is a danger of exaggerating the strategic and geo-political impact of Europe's undoubted economic muscle or the impact this may have on transatlantic and international relationships. Most importantly, however, both perspectives overlook the transformations and trends within European political economy, which, if anything, suggest some convergence towards a more 'neoliberal' or 'Anglo-Saxon' model of economic governance both within and beyond the EU. These developments owe much to the role of social forces within and across member states and undercut the state-centric assumptions of the intergovernmental thesis.

This chapter therefore seeks to analyse the nature and content of the European Union within the broader context of the evolving international political economy since 1945. The process of European integration is located within the wider framework of the evolution of international capitalism since the Second World War and, in particular, processes of globalization and transnationalization. Following van Apeldoorn (2002), we apportion a critical role to the dynamics of transnationalism in constructing a dense and evolving network of political, ideational, cultural and social interactions between a range of European, trans-European and global private and public actors. These interactions have thus far privileged the interests of transnational capital in the integration process with consequences both internally for the European economy and the member states' economies and externally for the EU's role in international economic governance.

Whilst it is true that during the phase of the postwar boom, most of the EU countries developed models of capitalism fundamentally at odds with Anglo-Saxon and American models, the period of intense global restructuring since the 1970s has led to gradual and uneven erosion of these models. This has been reflected and reinforced by the type of market integration achieved at the EU level, intensifying competitive pressures and capital mobility. Given these dynamics and the remaining challenges around European unemployment and the demographic time-bomb, the European 'social model' has undergone some erosion with the likelihood of further reform. Yet there is little evidence that at the EU level a consensus exists to embed it through further integration. In that context, the broader dynamics of globalization and liberalization are progressively undermining both the notion of a clearly differentiated 'common' European social model of capitalism and any sense of consensus between member states necessary to embed it through EU-level policy initiatives in areas such as tax, welfare and labour market harmonization.

The notion of the EU as projecting an alternative vision of capitalism to that of the USA must therefore be open to doubt. Indeed, in the EU's external economic relations, participation in and commitment to the broad globalization agenda of the WTO and division over issues of development cast further doubt on the EU's capacity to play the role of a coherent strategic counter to the USA or even to project and represent a vision of a clear and coherent alternative global economic agenda.

The chapter begins with a sketch of the broader context of the postwar global political economy and Europe's place within it before considering more specifically the process of market and monetary integration within

Europe. This leads to consideration of the impact of integration on European social models. Attention is then focused on the external impact of the EU in international economic governance within the fields of trade, development and finance.

THE INTERNATIONAL ECONOMY SINCE 1945: THE POSTWAR BOOM

European integration evolved within the context of the Bretton Woods system and institutions designed by the USA and the UK in 1944. The Bretton Woods system in part reflected the need for a more stable international financial framework so as to facilitate a liberal trading order between capitalist economies. This was deemed necessary in response to the international economic crisis of the interwar years and particularly the 1930s in which the collapse of international financial markets paved the way for an upsurge in economic nationalism, protectionism and extremism ultimately unleashing imperialist and militarist rivalries between the major capitalist powers (Dinan, 2004, pp. 2–5). In this way, the lack of an appropriate international financial architecture and the corresponding lack of economic cooperation between states was a major cause of instability and insecurity in world politics. The postwar settlement would therefore be characterized by attempts to promote and systematize international economic cooperation in the developed capitalist world at least, through a set of international institutions designed to foster and facilitate world trade.

The Bretton Woods institutions adopted a liberal approach to the governance of international economic relations. The postwar settlement established the role of the US dollar as the world's reserve currency through the dollar standard. The General Agreement on Tariffs and Trade (GATT) created a forum for successive rounds of trade liberalization. The International Monetary Fund (IMF) was established to recycle trade surpluses and provide lending to deficit nations so as to lubricate world trade. The International Bank for Reconstruction and Development (the World Bank) was established to tackle long-term issues of reconstruction – and later development – to underpin an expanding world trade system. At the same time, decolonization destroyed imperial trading networks, allowing the opening of markets on a multilateral basis (Tsoukalis, 1997, pp. 9–10; Burchill, 2001a, p. 53). US aid to Western Europe for reconstruction was predicated on commitment to the longer-term, US agenda of liberalization (Dinan, 2004, pp. 13, 19–22). Hence Marshall Aid not only served the interests of reconstructing Europe but also enabled the USA to kick-start European integration on liberal premises in line with the broader agenda of

US hegemony (ibid., p. 21). The subsequent development of the European Coal and Steel Community strengthened this development, particularly as the more supranational ambitions and proposals of Monnet were gradually diluted (ibid., pp. 51, 57–62).

Both Bretton Woods and the EU (then EEC) itself were implicitly predicated on the liberal contention that open markets promote peace, democracy and prosperity. The liberal ideological underpinnings to the postwar settlement remain enormously controversial in terms of both their coherence and their actual purpose (Burchill, 2001a). Realists, structuralists and critical theorists all point to the deployment of ideology as a veneer for the pursuit of national or class interests and more or less explicitly question the 'economics' which posits free trade as the optimal policy for all nations (Burchill 2001a; 2001b; Linklater, 2001; Gilpin, 1995). In this context, then, the Bretton Woods settlement may be seen as responding to the interests and preferences of the US state in particular and/or a set of national and increasingly transnational class (Gill and Law, 1998). Bretton Woods represented a 'hegemonic project' centred around the US state while stimulating the formation of an incipient transnational class (van der Pijl, 1984; 1998).

The postwar economic boom permitted a graduated process of economic liberalization. International liberalism was, however, very firmly 'embedded' at the level of national economies where there remained considerable scope for the pursuit of national strategies of legitimation through the consolidation of national models of economic governance striking a balance between the interests of organized labour and capital. These models are analysed in more detail later, but it is important to note at this stage that they represented an accommodation between market liberalization and social protection – the 'de-commodifying' role of the social model, as Esping-Anderson (1990, p. 37) puts it – allowing the creation of a new hegemonic bloc tying together financial and industrial capital *and* organized labour (van Apeldoorn, 2002; Gill and Law, 1998; Davis, 1984).

The development of the EU (then EEC) and the postwar reconstruction of Europe therefore took place within this context. This period of reconstruction saw a boom in the economies of Western Europe with the consolidation of developed, industrial capitalism across the then EEC. The spread of American multinationals facilitated the diffusion of Fordist production models to Europe, stimulating productivity. The development of Keynesian welfare models ensured the necessary demand infrastructure to soak up the output of Fordist mass production (Arrighi, 1982; Boyer, 1978).

Trade, mainly intra-industrial, expanded between the EEC members. Along with the spread of American capital, American cultural influences penetrated Europe. These developments consolidated transnational exchange and the formation of transnational interests and orientations within sections of European national capitalisms. While not joining the 'original six' EEC members, other West European countries participated in the same broad processes of Fordist reconstruction, development and liberalization, and ultimately most became formally integrated into the EU.

Over time a variety of contradictions assailed the postwar boom (Armstrong et al., 1991; Boyer, 1978; Callinicos, 2001, pp. 81–2; Cerny, 1993, pp. 163–6). The very success of the Bretton Woods system tended to promote such contradictions. The recovery of the European and Japanese economies placed pressure on the exchange rate system. Growing deficits, in US trade and public finances, fed by the Vietnam War and the Great Society programmes of the 1960s, prompted Nixon to devalue the dollar in 1971, leading to instability on international financial markets. Through the late 1960s, and across the developed world, organized labour, emboldened by buoyant economic conditions and low unemployment, pressed for a greater slice of the economic cake, disturbing the class compromise on which the boom was founded. Their success in securing higher wages stoked inflationary pressures while encouraging further radicalism. The social radicalism of the 1960s reflected a dissatisfaction with the excessive routine and standardization of Fordism. Inflationary pressures grew across the capitalist world, fuelled by devaluations and growing industrial unrest. The quadrupling of oil prices in 1973 delivered the *coup de grâce*.

The crisis of Fordism upset the delicate compromise of the postwar period; but also that between competing fractions of capital in which those externally oriented and transnational fractions of capital have tended to hold the upper hand over more internally oriented and fractions (van Apeldoorn, 2002, pp. 29–30). Along another cleavage within 'capital', the interests of finance and money capital have tended to win out over those of productive capital (ibid., pp. 27–9; Grahl, 2003, pp. 36–41).

Despite a tendency in some of the literature to downplay the continuities between the post-1945 and post-1973 periods, the seeds of this struggle were sown with the internationalization accompanying the postwar boom (Lochner, 1999). This promoted the development of transnational capital and, critically, also began to unleash the power of international financial markets in ways which impinged upon both states and productive capital (Strange, 1986; Cerny, 1993). The development of increasingly liberalized capital markets can be traced back to the Bretton Woods system itself, its focus on full currency convertibility, international trade and the dollar standard which created the conditions for an accumulation of dollar balances in the hands of an array of private financial actors (ibid., pp. 165–6).

The destabilization of currency markets and the transfer of significant dollar balances to the OPEC oil producing countries accelerated the consolidation of a significant volume of footloose money capital seeking rapid return, encouraging the creation of financial markets and instruments seeking to accommodate it. Rapid technological change and intense capital market liberalization have fed this development, transmitting short-termist and internationalizing pressures to both the productive sector and domestically oriented banking systems (Nolke, 1998; Grahl, 2003, pp. 28–30; Cerny, 1993).

At the same time these pressures also impinge upon states with the power of speculation, imposing neoliberal discipline on governments fearful of the consequences of capital flight (Gill, 1998, pp. 412–15; Grahl, 2003, pp. 34–6). But although financial capital has an increasingly systematic transnational bent, the growth of transnational productive capital has also been significant (van Apeldoorn, 2002, pp. 55–60). Again, this growth was partially a corporate response to the crisis of Fordism. The exhaustion of national markets stimulated the search for new, external markets and led business to pressure national governments to bargain for access to other markets (Hanson, 1998). Overcapacity triggered more intense international competition in many industries as firms, encouraging strategies of relocation to cheaper production environments, stimulated the growth of transnational networks of supply and production. A major transformation took place away from standardized mass production to more flexible, customized and leaner production strategies featuring closer inventory control, rationalization, subcontracting, downsizing and relocation offshore (Amin, 1994; Jessop, 1991). At the political level, this began to erode organized models of capitalism (Lash and Urry, 1987).

Across the Western economies, the immediate need to curb inflation in the wake of the oil crisis floored the Keynesian consensus. Policies of tight money and financial orthodoxy were increasingly adopted, creating additional constraints in terms of domestic demand and competitiveness, further encouraging corporate strategies of internationalization. The demise of Keynesianism was reflected in a general revival in liberal economic ideas and their ascent to political and intellectual hegemony. The emergence of neoliberalism was symbolized within the Bretton Woods institutions and their global pursuit of the Washington Consensus (Stiglitz, 2002). Within the EU, the Single European Market and the case made for it in terms of specialization, efficiency and competition are likewise built on neoliberal premises. Europe's economic crisis was located in the sclerosis of internally oriented and excessively regulated national capitalisms and the 'distributional coalitions' they sustained (Olson, 1982). Removing protection from these coalitions and enforcing competition would stimulate trade, specialization, efficiency and virtuous cycles of growth (Cecchini, 1989).

MARKET EUROPE

European integration has so far revolved around the construction of a unified single market with a shared currency promoting dense economic interactions between European economies. This pattern of integration conformed to the strictures of neoliberal political economy and those of the Bretton Woods settlement: that is, European peace would be fostered by promoting economic and cultural interactions across the Continent and negative economic integration through the removal of economic barriers would bind the member states together in terms of shared interests and aspirations, making conflict between them counterproductive and obsolete (Burchill, 2001a). Similarly, the logical result of such an agenda is to draw more capital into Europe-wide competition and therefore progressively deepen the transnational bases and influences on the European Union. Hence the dynamics of integration continue to bear the heavy imprint of American influence and interests in terms of a broad agenda of economic liberalization both within Europe and between Europe and the USA.

Regardless of the tensions this has at times created with national traditions, ideological predilections and possible future integrative steps, the European project explicitly embraces the economic orthodoxies of neoliberalism as a fundamental building block in Europe's framework of economic governance. It should be remembered that two key influences impelling Europe towards this path were constituted by the American influence in the postwar period (prompting the creation of the European Payments Union to facilitate freer trade and exchange) and a prevailing tradition of internationalism and trans-Europeanism which preceded the Second World War (Tsoukalis, 1997, p. 9; Dinan, 2004, pp. 2, 13, 19–22). The seeds of a transnational and liberal influence on the European project are discernible from its outset.

But also discernible at the outset and still redolent is the notion of a politically united Europe (Dinan, 2004, p. 23). From the founding fathers of the European Community to modern-day Federalists, a constituency within the European political élite had seen integration as a process that would produce political unity. The logic of functionalist spillover is often applied to uphold the eventual inevitability of full integration. Habermas's (1999) contribution to the debate can be located on the margins of this broad current and within the transformationalist thesis and cosmopolitan democratic vision of Held et al. (1999). Habermas argues for further political integration at the EU level. The consequences and tensions posed by market integration make the traditional European nation-state an inadequate vehicle through which to exercise political and democratic control over the potential pathology arising from unrestrained market forces. The removal of national-level control and sovereignty over markets implied by market and monetary integration requires the construction of an alternative, supranational mechanism for the exercise of control over the excesses of market forces, implying closer political integration and union.

This call for greater political mediation of the market corresponds to two key currents within the debate regarding the nature and content of Europe (van Apeldoorn, 2002, pp. 78–82). The first is 'neo-mercantilism', defined in terms of the creation of a protected European economy. The internal market would be offset by external protection. This protectionist aspiration of 'Fortress Europe' has commanded support from fractions of capital and labour within the EU vulnerable to extra-EU competition. The second current is the appeal of 'Social Europe', in which the de-commodifying aspects of European national models of capitalism are protected and 'locked in' through appropriate integration, harmonization and standardization of a range of welfare and labour market policies, providing security for European workers and citizens. Both views contest the validity of a neoliberal Europe and on a variety of issues may make common cause. Both views represent an approach in which the market integration achieved thus far is simply a necessary step in the creation of a more complete and comprehensive union. From differing perspectives, van Apeldoorn (2002) and Moravcsik (1998) both demonstrate that, as yet, neither view has been able to assert itself over neoliberalism.

The Single European Market (SEM) has successfully removed a variety of non-tariff barriers to the movement of goods, services, capital and labour within Europe. Active national industrial policies have been largely abandoned save for EU-sanctioned 'exceptions' focusing on key regional and sectoral problems. EU competition policy has further curtailed the role of the state and public enterprise as conduits for national industrial and economic strategies (Petitbò, 1993). For this reason the SEM was an important milestone on the way to enforcing and spreading a neoliberal framework of economic governance throughout the Union.

This initial shift in the direction of neoliberalism was pressed further in the critical process of convergence for membership of the single currency which privileged financial rather than real convergence, driving public sector and welfare reform across Europe (Gill, 1998, p. 414; van Apeldoorn, 2002, pp. 167–75; Grahl, 2003, pp. 32–4). The resulting monetary union based on an independent European Central Bank, with a clear brief to ensure price stability and monitor member state finances, 'locked in' fiscal constraints and budget orthodoxy to the political options of the members, reducing their room for manoeuvre in fiscal policy and providing a permanent pressure for reform of the social model. While the new currency modelled itself on the Deutsche Mark, no equivalent to the redistributive policies or elaborate social model of Federal Germany was engineered at a European level, thus mirroring Habermas's argument surrounding the need for political structures to catch up with market forces (Tsoukalis, 1997, p. 221).

It is important to recognize the fundamental voluntarism with which member states entered this new framework. Liberal intergovernmentalism effectively captures the role of such voluntarism in the construction of the European single market and monetary union. Nevertheless, its concentration on the state tends to beg questions about how national interests are formed and how they shift over time. Whilst the 'visible' site for the political realization of the single market was constituted by the intergovernmental level of the EU, it is nevertheless important to acknowledge the deeper currents promoting the agenda of market Europe: the balance of social forces arising from the contingencies of the collapse of the postwar boom and an activist supranational Commission and Court of Justice (van Apeldoorn, 2002, p. 40).

As Van Apeldoorn (ibid., pp. 89–100, 115–57) demonstrates, the role of the European Roundtable of Industrialists, its shifting perspectives and personnel, reveals much about the social bases for, and conflicts over, integration. The case is very clearly made that different fractions of capital pushed for alternative agendas, that these fractions represented very closely their (competing) sectoral, national-institutional and geographical interests and bases; and that with the intensification of transnationalizing and globalizing forces, the ranks of those possessing and reflecting such interests grew, increasing the pressure for a neoliberal interpretation and implementation of both the SEM and EMU.

EUROPEAN INTEGRATION AND THE SOCIAL MODEL

Despite the achievements of the Single European Market (SEM) programme, a fully integrated market complete with social dimension or external protection has not yet come to pass, nor has a system of political authority and democratic accountability analogous to that of the traditional nation state been developed at the centre of the European Union (Habermas, 1999; Streeck and Schmitter, 1991). Neither the project of Fortress Europe nor that of Social Europe has come to fruition.

While conforming to neoliberal principles, the creation of the SEM and EMU can also be interpreted as necessary steps in the construction of a politically united Europe. From such a perspective, building Social or Fortress Europe requires the same kinds of integrative steps as were necessary in the formation of the nineteenth-century European nation-state.

Market integration is not necessarily therefore an end in itself and could yet pave the way for further integration in which the distinctive features of Europe's social model would be enhanced and extended through the whole Union. From here we see the continuing controversy as to what 'Europe' is or should be, a controversy represented throughout the EU's existence in both political and academic debate. Of great significance here, then, is the *actual* impact of integration on the national models of governance. Is there convergence towards the neoliberal model?

The literature presents anything between two and four stylized models of economic governance (Hutton, 1995, p. 282; Albert, 1993; Esping-Anderson, 1990; Hart, 1992; Coates, 1999; Schmidt, 2002; Grahl, 2001, pp. 140–41). Arguably three models are visible in the European Union.

1. The Anglo-Saxon model prevailing in the UK and, particularly during and after its high Thatcherite period, holding much in common with neoliberalism and advocating a *relatively* low-tax–low-social-spending, deregulated market resulting in a market-driven allocation and distribution of resources and wealth (Hutton, 1995; Coates, 1999). Within this more market-driven system, British labour wields less power than most of its continental counterparts and capital has traditionally been composed of more internationalized and transnationalized fractions than other European economies. The role of financial markets as opposed to banks within the UK capital market also implies a traditionally stronger orientation towards money capital than productive capital, whilst the *laissez-faire* leanings of the model have created similar orientations away from state interventionism. The existence of this approach within the UK – though in a less extreme form than in the USA – is a key factor differentiating the UK from its European partners, and British fears over integration are often related to a perceived threat to the Anglo-Saxon model arising from more statist and social-democratic currents in the EU (Portillo, 2005; Redwood, 2001).
2. The state-led model, normally associated with the Far East but a model with which the French tradition of *dirigisme* and planning would appear to provide a European counterpart, featuring a strong economic bureaucracy, exercising ultimate control over market access and over the allocation and distribution of resources; and planning these in line with national economic priorities, as defined by the élite (Wade, 1990; Hall, 1986; Hayward, 1986). In this system, national capital is largely nurtured and developed precisely through state sponsorship and protection. However, having successfully developed, and facing an increasingly globalizing environment, this dependence is theoretically open to erosion. With the arrival of the single market, the traditional protectionist tools

of the state-led approach were simply removed at a stroke from the arsenal of policy instruments available to member states.

3. The social model, a rather amorphous term given to describe the prominence of social partnership within an array of different national contexts across the rest of the EU, but always resulting in tendencies towards corporatist governance and a high degree of social cohesion and equality (Therborn, 1987; Hutton, 1995; Streeck, 1999; Meidner, 1992; Katzenstein, 1985). Within such models the balance between state leadership and social partnership differs. 'Corporatist' traditions differ in the extent to which they are 'top–down' or 'bottom–up', with Southern European models demonstrating more bureaucratized and state-led models than most of their Northern and Alpine counterparts, where the role of organized labour has a longer tradition of institutionalized participation in economic governance and where communist influence within the labour movement was less pronounced at an earlier stage. Indeed, Swedish and Danish Euroscepticisms, in direct contrast to their British counterpart, coalesce around fears that the EU carries a neoliberal threat to the highly developed Nordic social model. Lacking that level of institutionalization, South European variants are to some extent a hybrid of the state-led and the corporatist, making them more vulnerable to neoliberal reform (McVeigh, 1999).

The argument is often posited that under the pressures of globalization and European integration, convergence is taking place between these models, with the second and third models undergoing reform towards the Anglo-Saxon model (Streeck, 1999; Coates, 1999; Dore, 2000; Crouch and Streeck, 1997). It is sometimes alleged that this process, if unchecked, will logically produce a 'race to the bottom' as levels of social protection and welfare provision are pruned further and further back to provide the flexible and competitive labour markets required to attract more mobile and demanding capital (Grahl, 2001, p. 159; Rodrik, 2003; Bauman, 1998, pp. 65–9). Taxes and regulations have to be reduced to allow competition with firms locating in 'cheaper' model countries. Capital in all locations is pulled into an international- and global-level competition as the search for more markets logically requires penetration of foreign markets and the search for more capital requires interaction with the more 'short-termist' circuits of finance capital represented by international investors and global equity markets (Grahl, 2003, pp. 28–30).

The opening up of economies since the oil crisis, in which Europe has been centrally involved, is therefore seen as at once essential to the re-launch of 'exhausted' organized national models of economic expansion but at the same time removing that critical insulation which allowed a balance between the goals of growth and those of redistribution, equity, social inclusion and cohesion (Streeck, 1999). With market barriers removed, high- and low-cost models come more directly and systematically into competition with the presumption that footloose capital will then use its 'exit' power of relocation to cheaper business environments to undermine existing labour–capital relations at the national level (Grahl, 2003, p. 30). Organized capital, itself under pressure to produce faster returns in order to secure capital on increasingly integrated and short-termist global markets, presses for reductions in regulation, social charges and labour market rigidity with the implicit threat of relocation (Grahl, 2003, p. 30; Rodrik, 2003; Streeck, 1999).

To what extent this has driven a fundamental reform of social models is less obvious (Schmidt, 2002). In the case of the Nordic countries, in which the social model of capitalism has had its strongest political roots and much success, the literature indicates that aspects of the model have undergone reform but without any wholesale adoption of the Anglo-Saxon/neoliberal model or substantive abandonment of core principles (Kuhnle, 2000, pp. 213–18). However, Jochem (2000, p. 115) find that inroads have been made into collective bargaining, the centralization of wage setting and social insurance principles of welfare provision, leaving the models in a 'state of flux'.

Likewise, in the French case, Palier (2000) and Beland and Hanson (2000) demonstrate erosion of social insurance principles and an increased focus on policies of (re-)activation in the French labour market (*Economist* Survey, 1999, pp. 5–10). In Germany, the difficulties of reunification and the attempt to transfer the German model to the east has produced significant stresses in terms of unemployment, leading to reform of the social insurance system (Streeck, 1991). In several cases the literature points to a shift in the burden of social charges away from business and on to labour and/or the state. The convergence process for membership of the monetary union did create pressures for reforms and reductions of state spending across the EU, with retrenchment of unemployment provision, reforms to pension systems and the privatization of state industries and assets all featuring across the EU in the strategies of member governments as they sought to qualify for membership (Ferrera and Gualmini, 2000; Grahl, 2003; Perez, 2000, p. 445–53; Salmon, 2000, pp. 35–9; McVeigh, 1999).

The organization of capital has also been affected, with traditionally opaque patterns of interlocking, cross-ownership and family holdings, bank engagement and corporate governance all undergoing some (uneven) erosion over the last decade, while the single market also promoted further concentration of capital through mergers and acquisitions (Grahl, 2001; 2003, pp. 42–5; Nolke, 1999; *Economist* Survey, 2000).

In spite of these common trends in the direction and nature of reform, there remains considerable divergence in the depth and pace of such changes (Schmidt, 2002). This is barely surprising given the sheer number of differentiating variables within national capitalisms. Within economies generally adopting social-corporatist approaches to national wage bargaining, for instance, the density of union membership, the degree of centralization of bargaining, the issues covered in national accords, the existence of bi-partisan or tripartite models of bargaining and the internal organization of the social partners are all variables affecting the evolution and outcome of the social model, and all differ significantly from country to country (Therborn, 1987). With respect to welfare models, there are continued divergences in tax rates, in the degree of universalism and means-testing, the replacement rate, the extent of insurance-funded or tax-funded social provision (Grahl, 2001). In corporate governance there remain differences in the level of worker representation, of bank participation, and of debt–equity ratios which influence the nature of national capitalisms (*Economist* Survey, 2000). For all of these myriad of variables to 'converge' is clearly unlikely in a short period of time, particularly as many are deep-rooted both institutionally and culturally; but all do have an impact on the exact nature and outcomes of national capitalism (ibid., p. 159).

This diversity is also reflected in the process by which reform takes place. In several countries, social partnership was actually encouraged by the process of monetary union rather than unhinged by it. In Ireland, Italy and Spain national social accords were (re-)discovered in the run-up to EMU as a means by which to ensure that convergence criteria were met (*Economist* Survey, 2004a, pp. 4–5; Ferrera and Gualmini, 2000, p. 204; Perez, 2000, p. 445). The Dutch Pohldermodel inspired much optimism about the capacity of social dialogue to resolve the tensions brought about by the collision of global forces on national structures and encouraged the development of Third Way discourse (van Apeldoorn, 2002, p. 183; Green-Pederson, 2001).

It is important to look at the substance and content of such accords. The existence of national accords is by no means inimical to reform, and may enable labour and capital to accommodate to market forces in an organized way though not, in the classic German model described by Streeck (1999), to control, govern and de-commodify market forces. This 'accommodation model' of social partnership takes place within the context of a power imbalance between mobile capital and immobile labour, and consequently has necessitated more accommodation from labour than from capital (van Apeldoorn, 2002, p. 183).

Nevertheless, where consensus and social concertation have deep cultural roots and institutionalized bases, they are not quickly or easily torn up

(Katzenstein, 1985; Menz, 2003). Whereas, in France the national model and its 'de-commodifying' implications have been deeply rooted in constructions of national identity and as a counterpoint to the brutality of Anglo-Saxon market forces, the pattern of reform is inevitably uneven and gradual (*Economist* Surveys, 1999, pp. 10–12; 2002, pp. 13–15).

We can conclude that some convergence is taking place in the direction of a more market-based capitalism but that national variations remain an obstacle both to the full economic and social integration of the market (Schmidt, 2002, pp. 141–7, 303–11). In much of the Union, there is considerable resistance to rapid convergence and dismantling of the social model among labour and capital. This is reflected within political parties and élites; and in the continued commitment, at the very least rhetorically, to a Europe whose model of economic governance is clearly differentiated from that of the Anglo-Saxon model (Portillo, 2005; *Economist* Survey, 1999, pp. 1–5).

For some this has spurred the search for political integration of the key areas of the social model, perhaps even the construction of a single European social model to be applied across the EU and responding to the need to ensure a social dimension to Market Europe and a means of differentiating European from Anglo-American capitalism. As we argue below, this project faces obstacles in the institutional framework of the Union, implying the persistence of national interests and strategies undermining the thesis of inevitable political union (Atkinson and Divoudi, 2000, p. 442).

For proponents of the liberal intergovernmental thesis, the development of the single European market and monetary union required interstate bargaining whose success depended upon a community of shared interests in the opening up and integration of the European economies (Moravcsik, 1998). Despite and perhaps because of the integration of the European market on neoliberal principles, the achievement of a similar consensus around the social model, considered broadly to cover labour–capital relations, labour market regulation, taxation and welfare provision, seems unlikely.

It is this continuing diversity of national contexts, and its functionality at the national level, which makes both market-led convergence gradual and uneven, and yet an agreed EU-level harmonization unlikely (Schmidt, 2002, pp. 141–7). Having given up key macroeconomic controls through market and monetary integration, states are now more reliant on their powers over tax, welfare and the labour market. These policy areas provide much of the remaining scope for flexible national-level responses to the threats posed by international market forces. In the context of the competition state, one would anticipate that such micro-level areas of economic strategy and policy in these key areas would constitute critical policy instruments for states in their attempts to attract capital and pursue growth (Cerny, 1996).

It is unsurprising, therefore, that the project of 'Social Europe' has not been advanced successfully to date: there are key differences in approach and desired outcome between the member states which make it difficult to create the required consensus for further integration in these areas. Underneath this, of course, these divisions reflect and overlap with the struggle between the competing interests of national and transnational social forces (van Apeldoorn, 2002, pp. 183–4).

Any major initiatives in the 'social dimension' would require approval in the Council of Ministers. Even with the progressive extension of Qualified Majority Voting and occasional Commission activism, this is unlikely to occur. We have alluded earlier to the failure of the Delors' Commission's proposals in which an activist stance was taken by the Commission in pursuit of building the European Social Model through integration. The failure of the Delors Plan revealed that even among countries committed to the idea of the social model, there was disagreement as to how it was to be attained at an EU level, the French predilection for a centralized, statist solution tending to jar against German preferences for the decentralization of power to the social partners. This latter view has been better reflected in the social chapter and on issues such as European works councils. Commission activism continued with the working time directive and parental leave legislation, and the establishment of the European Social Policy forum. In spite of this activism, the social chapter did not result in the development of a Commission-engineered social model. The lack of consensus has left Delors' goals to develop the social dimension largely unmet (Atkinson and Divoudi, 2000, pp. 428–31; van Apeldoorn, 2002, pp. 146–9; Grahl, 2001; Tsoukalis, 1997, p. 137).

What is striking here is that the mechanisms for decision making on key economic issues in the Union still rely heavily on intergovernmental consensus at the European Council and Council of Ministers and, facing diversity, they often do not yield consensus. The institutional set-up of the Union therefore appears to operate systematically in favour of negative integration through the removal of barriers and against positive integration via the creation of common policies at the European level. The possibilities for development of common policies are further prejudiced by the difficulties of achieving agreement on financing such policies and creating redistributive mechanisms between member countries beyond the rather limited development of regional and budgetary policies (Tsoukalis, 1997, p. 221). On the one hand, it would seem that the EU remains a union of nation-states where legitimacy is delivered at the national level, placing significant limits on the nature and pace of integration. On the other hand this institutional set-up privileges negative integration and thereby the restricted agenda of neoliberal market integration.

There is no immediate prospect of a significant embedding of Social Europe. Given the even greater diversity introduced by the new members of the EU in terms of social provision, national interests and fiscal and institutional capacities, it is difficult to see a coherent EU-level approach emerging. The recent development of employment policy through the Lisbon process is a case in point. Decentralized to the national level and concentrated around an enterprise, opportunity and activation agenda, the process operates through benchmarking, facilitating policy transfer across the Union (van Apeldoorn, 2002, pp. 175–80). It does not involve the mobilization of resources nor the creation of common labour standards, and despite its rhetorical commitment to avoiding the 'race to the bottom', does not integrate labour market issues of employment with the wider 'de-commodification' agenda of social protection in concrete terms (European Commission, 2003, pp. 8–9). Its results so far have been modest. (European Commission, 2004, pp. 10–11).

Without integration in these areas, there will remain 'imperfections' in the single market as well as a 'gap' in the European project between the economic and the social. Accommodation to market forces will continue to take place largely at national level, with the possibility of an informal convergence taking place over time, driven by the market but mediated by national state structures and transnational social forces.

THE EU'S EXTERNAL TRADE POLICY

So far we have argued that, internally, the EU has not developed a single, coherent conception of European capitalism going significantly beyond a commitment to neoliberal principles of monetary stability and open markets. This suggests that the EU may lack the unity to forge a coherent alternative to American capitalism and that although committed in principle to their social models, member states wish to retain the political space for domestic reform and accommodation of those models to the needs of accumulation in the more competitive environment that their own project of market integration has helped to create.

In its external economic relations we will again see reasons to question the notion that the EU has developed a coherent world-view and policy which diverges significantly from neoliberalism although, in agriculture, its failure to live up to the rhetoric of open markets has arguably frustrated the needs of the developing world in the one area where freer trade would be of unambiguous benefit to it.

In global terms, world trade was worth $6272 bn in 2002 (WTO, n.d.). Within that global figure, the West European region accounted for 42.4

per cent. An additional 5 per cent of world trade was accounted for by the Central and Eastern European countries (CEECs), several of whom have since joined the EU. The Asian region followed in importance with around a quarter of world trade, leaving North America in third place with 15 per cent. The three regions as a whole concentrated 80 per cent of world trade, indicating their central place and the marginalization of the developing world (WTO, n.d.). However, much West European trade is intra-regional – largely due to the process of European market integration discussed above, with Western Europe absorbing 67 per cent of the EU's exports and providing an almost identical proportion of its imports. Again, if we include the CEECs, the proportion rises to almost three-quarters (WTO, n.d.). Of the remainder, only North America, with 10 per cent of EU exports and 7 per cent of imports, and Asia, with the percentages reversed, constituted significant proportions. In sum, the EU is indeed a major player in world trade but does trade largely with itself and its geographical hinterland.

These figures tend to underestimate the overall degree and pace of globalization. As Dicken (2004, p. 35) points out, world trade increased 20-fold between 1950 and 2000, four times faster than the growth of world output. And in more recent times, the acceleration in foreign investment flows has outstripped both trade and output, with flows of foreign direct investment (FDI) growing at four times the rate of output during the 1980s (ibid., p. 53). The author goes on to demonstrate that during the 1990s flows of FDI grew at three times the level of output in the first half of the decade and then at an astonishing rate of 40 per cent per annum between 1996 and 1999. Unsurprisingly, this was accompanied by intense cross-border merger and acquisition activity, with EU economies well represented (ibid., pp. 53–4). Overall, then, these figures demonstrate the EU's key role in world trade and investment flows, and an accelerating expansion in transnational economic linkages over recent decades. This process has been facilitated by the Bretton Woods settlement and accelerated by the manner of its breakdown, as discussed earlier.

Since the 1960s the EU has been a customs union, operating a single commercial policy featuring a common external tariff against non-members. This policy has developed within the context of successive rounds of GATT trade negotiations and now within the 'rules-based trading order' of the WTO. Two highly significant trends are visible within the GATT/WTO system over time (*Economist* Survey, 1998, pp. 6–7). The number of participating countries in world trade accords has grown consistently since the 1940s to encompass 149 countries in the current WTO. With this growth of participating states, there has been a concomitant expansion in the number of trade barriers covered by GATT/WTO agreements. The initial emphasis was on the negotiation of tariff reductions essentially in the industrial sector (with the exception of textiles). Over time and especially since the Uruguay Round, which led to the formation of the WTO, the scope of world trade agreements has grown to cover most non-tariff barriers such as quantitative restrictions and customs procedures, and traditionally 'difficult' sectors such as services, agriculture and textiles (*Economist* Survey, 1998). In addition, the WTO provided the impetus for agreements in trade-related investment measures (TRIMS) and intellectual property (TRIPS) which significantly liberalize transnational investment.

The Uruguay Round established a significant liberalization of world trade, with reductions in a wide range of barriers to trade and investment and the institution of permanent procedures of dispute settlement with the force of international law. In one sense, then, the global agenda has followed the European agenda, with an initial focus on tariff reductions leading to the removal of non-tariff barriers and the formation of a single market. The core principle of WTO agreements is (theoretically) that of multilateralism: signatories to WTO agreements commit to treating all trading partners equally, i.e. offering all other member states the same access to their markets as those granted to the most favoured nation. Likewise, the principle of non-discrimination commits member states to equal treatment of domestic and foreign corporations within their borders. Taken together, these reforms in the world trade system constitute a highly significant and controversial development in global economic governance, sparking resistance and protest within civil society and the development of the 'anti-globalization movement' (*Economist* Survey, 2001). It is therefore critical to understand that the opening of world trade could not have taken place without the EU's explicit commitment: indeed, the Uruguay Round succeeded only after several years of tough negotiation between the EU, the USA, Japan and the Cairns Group, largely over agricultural issues, and that this extensive liberalization has dramatically opened up the European market, frustrating the interests for a Fortress Europe (Hanson, 1998).

The philosophy behind this substantial and rapid liberalization of world trade is clearly neoliberal, based on the notion that freer trade globally will advance the prosperity of all nations and ensure a more optimal allocation of resources (*Economist* Survey 1998, pp. 4–5; Krugman, 1996; Smith, 2003). Beyond the rarified atmosphere of broad sections of the economics profession, these liberal assertions are highly contestable. What for liberals constitute trade barriers are for many realists (mercantilists) and structuralists the necessary policy tools to promote domestic industrial development (Hamilton, 2003; Gerschenkron, 1962; Burchill, 2001a). A large literature exists positing the necessity of protectionist measures to promote the national economic cause. The evidence from the East Asian tiger economies heavily implies the importance of effective and interventionist state strategies of industrial support, encompassing strategic management of trade for successful economic catch-up (Wade, 1990; Henderson, 1993; Johnson, 1982; Dore, 2000; Krugman, 1986). Including within the EU itself, it is difficult to identify a single developed nation achieving its critical economic breakthrough without resort to protectionism. Nevertheless, the legacy of 1930s protectionism and its rhetorical value lie at the heart of transactional capital's discourse over the desirability of free trade.

It is of no little relevance to note the conversion of the EU to a more open economic agenda more in keeping with that of the USA (Hanson, 1998). This does not mean that the EU does not wield important power in global trade negotiations, nor that the EU consistently operates an open policy. On the contrary, the exceptions to openness are instructive. The EU – and the USA – have operated relatively protectionist policies in agriculture and in some specific industrial sectors such as textiles. Before the WTO, however, European protectionism extended to more industrial sectors such as services, electronics, steel, shipbuilding and cars (Hanson, 1998; van Apeldoorn, 2002, pp. 81–2, 130–32, 136–41). These industries were precisely those left most vulnerable to international competition and/or seen as 'strategic' and hence the focus of national efforts of industrial promotion. Protection therefore reflected successful lobbying and pressure from a set of specific industrial sectors at national and European level whose strategy was a defensive one of market protection. Hanson (1998) demonstrates the shifting of influence towards outward-looking export interests, coinciding with the single market project, and reflected in the WTO agreement underscoring again the role of the more transnationally focused fractions of capital in the EU's recent trajectory. In consequence, it comes as no surprise to see the decline in protectionism during the 1990s and the retreat from Fortress Europe.

Given this shift towards a more neoliberal approach to world trade, EU–US trade relations are substantially more stable and cooperative than is often presumed to be the case. Both parties have been responsible for the development of the WTO, with its wide-ranging impact in trade and investment liberalization, and both are committed to its core principles. This does not preclude the possibility of specific trade disputes but we should remember that the WTO was established to formalize and legalize the handling of such disputes. For all of the furore created over specific disputes such as those over the EU banana regime, US steel and hormone-injected beef, both the USA and the EU have simply sought to maximize their bargaining positions and strategically delay the dispute settlement process before ultimately accepting the WTO's jurisdiction. This suggests that both parties take full advantage of dispute settlement procedures in pursuit of their interests but are also committed to the WTO process.

Clearly there is scope for more trade rows and rivalry, especially if the USA adopts a more unilateral stance towards world trade, but given the scope of the WTO's agreements, these are by no means as important as the general consensus over the WTO process. Indeed, the USA and the EU have in addition deepened their dialogue through the Transatlantic Economic Partnership, which has already launched further cooperation between regulatory agencies in several sectors (Europa, a). In sum, the economic ties between the two regions, their joint stake in globalization, and the role of transnational forces and networks in their policy-making processes all operate as important constraints on protectionist excess.

In addition to its general WTO commitments the EU operates additional bilateral agreements with a variety of regions around the globe. These additional relationships focus on the specific issues around interregional trade and include the Mediterranean region, the Andean and MERCOSUR economies, the African Caribbean and Pacific countries (ACP – see below the section on development), the Gulf States, China, Turkey, Russia and so on (Europa, b). Taken together, these relationships constitute an ongoing process of dialogue regarding further trade liberalization, going beyond the formal commitments made under the WTO but increasingly integrated within WTO rules and negotiating rounds. Short of a major global economic collapse, it is difficult to see how such a wide-ranging and deeply embedded agenda of trade liberalization could be overturned in the short term. The EU's embrace of neoliberalism and the rules-based trading order of the WTO appear to constitute a definitive rejection of Fortress Europe in favour of a focus on the opening of markets to trade and investment, with all of the opportunities this brings to transnational capital.

In response to the assorted and sometimes contradictory concerns of the anti-globalization movement and developing countries over the excessive neoliberalism of the initial WTO agreements, the Doha Round of trade negotiations was launched in 2002 (Ainger, 2003). The Doha agenda reflects disillusion with the uncompromising neoliberal premises of WTO agreements among developing countries and the anti-globalization movement.

Alongside the developing countries' demands for reform, the deregulatory bias of WTO accords has raised significant issues for countries operating high domestic environmental and labour standards. Non-discrimination principles extend to the WTO's treatment of the way that products are produced, leading to the allegation that they disconnect the theoretical economic gains from trade and investment from their distributional and social consequences by transforming national environmental, health and safety and labour regulations into potentially unsustainable trade barriers (Burbach, 2004; Elwood, 2004). Equal access applies also to the treatment of foreign capital and inward investment, reducing, in practical terms, control and sovereignty over key national assets, infrastructures and development strategies. This opens up the possibility of a democratic deficit within the WTO, with nationally agreed and democratically determined systems of regulation laid open to challenge through their potential conflict with principles of non-discrimination and equal access (Ledebur, 2004; Ransom, 2000).

In response, the EU is currently taking forward initiatives in areas such as corporate social responsibility and labour standards (Europa, c and d). The Doha Round has involved major clashes of interest between developed and developing nations, pushing back the timetable for agreement to the next Ministerial Conference of the WTO in December 2005. Despite the EU's willingness to engage in this round and a bevy of proposals on many of the issues, the underlying neoliberal principles of the WTO remain intact (Ainger, 2003). These principles are perceived by many as advancing the 'race to the bottom' without genuinely tackling the intractable issues of international development, to which we now turn.

DEVELOPMENT POLICY

Development policy cannot be considered without an appreciation of Europe's colonial past and the dysfunctional economic and political inheritance this has created for many post-colonial states. This has been reflected in the very centrepiece of Europe's development policies with its focus on the ACP countries, mostly former colonies of France or the UK. This legacy includes the creation of artificial states not contiguous with ethnic divisions and identities, creating major challenges for state building and the avoidance of ethnic conflict; and the economic legacy which has placed most of these economies in peripheral positions within the world economy, producing a portfolio of exports such as raw materials, primary commodities and cash crops in line with the needs and preferences of the core (Ainger, 2004; Amin, 1977, pp. 103–16, 126–8; Rodney, 1982; Dos Santos, 1970; Frank, 1978).

This division of labour is held to militate against industrialization and development, creates structures of dependence and unequal exchange, and tends to concentrate the accumulation of capital by an assortment of pre-capitalist and rentier classes or old colonial élites and corporations (Dos Santos, 1970). The simple operation of free trade tends to embed and freeze this division of labour and the dysfunctional pattern of specialization it reproduces for the developing country. Liberalization does not contain a dynamic of its own by which the necessary blockages to development, in agriculture, in property rights and in the need to concentrate scarce capital into priority sectors such as infrastructures and education, can be addressed. Critics contend that globalization and liberalization, far from advancing the interests of developing economies, rather lock them in to a spiral of deficit, debt and adjustment (Burbach, 2004). Taking the argument further, it is contended that in fact those structures of dependence crystallize the historical roots of globalization and a long-existing pattern of trade relations loaded in favour of the core (Frank, 1978). Globalization is not new (Modelski, 2003). Thus for some, post-colonial policy and neoliberal globalization simply continue and adapt a pre-existing pattern of imperialism (Ainger, 2004; Loomba, 1998; Biel, 2000).

On the other hand, a rival literature posits that it is the *lack* of economic relationships with the West and various internal blockages to such relationships that is diluting and deterring the otherwise progressive role of Western capital and technology (Krugman, 1996; Warren, 1980; *Economist* Surveys 1998; 2001, pp. 10–15; 2004b, pp. 4–5, 11–12).

Without doubt, there is a distance between the EU's rhetorical commitments to development and its record. The persistence of literally enormous gaps in living standards between the developed and developing world – whether measured by GDP per capita or the Human Development Index – illustrate the limitations of the EU's development policy to date. With the emergence of the WTO and the perceived failures of policies of development aid in the past, the EU's development policy has seen a switch of emphasis from aid to trade and the opening of markets.

This is reflected in the evolving relationship between the EU and the ACP countries (Europa, e, f, g and h). The EU has operated a series of agreements with the ACP countries through successive Lomé conventions which sought to provide the African, Caribbean and Pacific economies with a mixture of aid and mechanisms for stable and preferential access to the European market in their key export sectors (Europa, f and g).

Of course, this very focus on key existing specializations may, as suggested above, have deterred precisely the economic diversification and modernization that was necessary for development. Considerable evidence suggests that the focus on the export of cash crops and commodities across the developing world has been self-defeating, directly contributing to oversupply, environmental degradation and a worsening of the terms of trade (Anon., 2003).

At the same time, aid packages were much criticized for their implication of the EU in support for regimes which failed to protect basic human and civil rights and/or which fed corruption and militarization (Ainger, 2004; *Economist* Survey, 2004b, pp. 4–5, 12).

The Cotonou agreement reflected the neoliberal focus on trade not aid, while still providing resources for the building of trade capacities. Seventy-eight countries signed the agreement, which paved the way for new, separate economic partnership agreements for each of the African, Caribbean and Pacific regions (Europa, h). These agreements will come into force in 2008 as the transitional Lomé IV agreement runs out. The new accords fit into the WTO framework, unlike Lomé, which, in providing guaranteed access to the EU market for ACP bananas, was successfully challenged by the US and Latin American states, prompted by several major US agro-corporations (Ransom, 1999).

Key features of the new EU development policy are the concession of complete market access to the least developed countries (41 ACP countries qualify for this) under the 'Everything but Arms' initiative and targeted tariff reductions in textiles, clothing and footwear (Europa, h). In textiles, the EU has removed all quantitative restrictions (Europa, i).

Additional concessions have been made available under the 'Generalized System of Preferences' for developing countries meeting certain international environmental and labour standards (Europa, f). The EU has also made some limited moves on the social and labour agenda which are not explicitly included in the Doha Round (Europe, c and d). Finally, the EU is 'committed' to ensuring that developing nations' interests are taken into account in the Doha negotiations around competition laws (Europa, l).

These initiatives are welcome, if rather limited. They do not directly address many of the issues around sustainability, labour treatment and social responsibility through 'hard' regulatory and legal measures; and the thrust remains towards the opening of markets and extending the liberalization of trade and investment. Whilst acknowledging critiques of WTO liberalization, the EU is not proposing a pulling back of the liberalization agenda.

At the same time, the EU continues to operate policies in the field of agriculture and agro-industries which not only directly reduce market opportunities for developing countries in the export of basic foodstuffs and cash crops, but also the export of semi-manufactured goods, restricting the opportunities for developing countries to consolidate more remunerative upstream industries in the processing of goods such as sugar, coffee and chocolate The EU's protection of agriculture has contributed to a major dislocation of world trade and a severe squeezing of opportunities for developing countries, arguably maintaining the market structures of dependence, unequal exchange, monopsony, oligopoly and corporate control which are held by some to reduce the effectiveness of trade liberalization as a tool of development (Bunsha, 2003).

In this way, the EU's external trade policies closely match its economic interests, pushing for an opening of developing countries' markets on the grounds of economic liberalism without then offering access in sectors where it stands at a competitive disadvantage. Much the same can be argued in relation to the USA, leading to growing demands from the G-77 group of developing countries for movement on the agricultural issue in the current Doha Round. The EU has responded to this agenda with further reform of the CAP which, while improving market access and cutting tariff and other barriers, has the effect of maintaining heavy subsidy of the sector through the repackaging of support to farmers (Europa, j, k). European farmers will receive a single payment, breaking the link between subsidy and production but transferring much CAP support into the 'blue' and 'green' categories of farm support deemed to be less 'trade-distorting' and hence meeting WTO rules. It remains to be seen whether this will fully address the concerns of developing nations over the protection of European agriculture and the consequent squeezing of their already scarce opportunities to generate export earnings.

THE EU, EMU AND THE GLOBAL FINANCIAL ARCHITECTURE

A key constraint on the growth of developing economies arises from the global financial architecture and its economic governance. Primarily, governance here has resided with the IMF, in which voting rights correlate with national financial contributions, hence promoting US dominance. This has resulted in the emergence within the IMF of the 'Washington Consensus', leading not only to the imposition of fundamentalist neoliberal packages to borrowers but to severe criticisms of the IMF's role in managing international financial crises (*Economist* Surveys, 2001, pp. 27–9; 2003, pp. 3–5, 16–18, 25–6; Stiglitz, 2002). With respect to its role in development, the IMF is accused of imposing drastic structural adjustment conditions on loans to debtor nations, resulting in excessively rapid liberalization, the privatization of strategic national assets and excessively restrictive and deflationary fiscal policies necessitating cuts in social expenditure including subsidies in health and, most counterproductively, public education (ibid., pp. 43–52). These programmes impose painful adjustment on debtor nations and without apparent long-term success in relaunching their economic development (Burbach, 2004). At the same time, the IMF's policies have partially promoted the interests of international financial stability in that they secure the interests of financial institutions, though in other ways provoke the spread of crises (Stiglitz, 2002, pp. 106–9, 115, 199–200). Here again we see the supremacy of the neoliberal agenda and its correspondence to the interests of transactional capital, especially finance capital (ibid., pp. 67–73).

These policies have been roundly condemned, with calls for greater international financial coordination and the reimposition of effective control over the large volumes of speculative financial capital whose rapid movements not only distort national development strategies but also create sources of instability in an increasingly interconnected and interdependent global economy, raising the spectre of financial contagion. It is in this context of a deeply rooted process of global financial liberalization that we must place the external role of the euro (Grahl, 2003).

Against this backcloth, the case that the euro transforms the prospects for more effective international governance is heavily overstated, as is its pretension, in the medium term at least, to emerge as a genuine rival reserve currency to the dollar. The initial arrival of the euro on international markets was not auspicious as externally it suffered a persistent fall in value which was greeted by successive interest rate rises by the ECB, with deflationary implications for the internal European economy. In general, this accorded with the models of financially driven disciplinary liberalism put forward by Grahl (2003) and Gill (1998), with implications for European labour markets and social models.

Despite these structural deficiencies in the design of the Euro, which have been partially addressed by the flexible interpretation of the Stability Pact by European Finance Ministers and its subsequent loosening, the euro has recovered after its unsteady start, largely due to a waning dollar. Its use in international financial markets is by no means negligible though still not rivalling the dollar (HSBC, 2003; European Central Bank, 2005; Padoa-Schioppa, 2002). The euro's shares of the various international markets are relatively stable and where it does rival the dollar, in trade and in financing trade, much of its usage arises from intra-EU transactions. This distorts the figures, as does the greater use of the Euro by accession countries, including those in the Balkans and in Europe's 'Near Abroad'. Once these geographical aspects are taken into account it is clear that the dollar dominates. According to an HSBC study (HSBC, 2003, p. 7), the dollar dominates in bond markets (60 per cent to 40 per cent), equity markets (74 per cent to 26 per cent), foreign exchange trading (70 per cent to 30 per cent) and overall (55 per cent to 45 per cent). The study concludes that for the Euro to seriously rival the dollar would take a quite massive sale of US dollars, which the USA itself cannot afford to happen (ibid., pp. 7–9). While this suggests a potential conflict between the USA and EU, it is also argued that there is no mechanism by which the EU could engineer such a situation even if it wanted to (Padoa-Schioppa, 2002, p. 7; Grahl, 2003, pp. 23–4).

Indeed, the dominance of the dollar is heavily embedded in the power of inertia and the growing risk aversion of official institutions for whom the dollar is a safer bet in volatile, deregulated capital markets (Padoa-Schioppa, 2002, p. 4).

So, if not currently able to rival the dollar in the medium term, does the euro contribute to an improved governance of the international economy? Unfortunately, the answer seems to be in the negative here also. Although scope for greater coordination exists between the USA and the EU, there has been only 'incremental' change in international financial governance despite a succession of crises in East Asia, Russia, South America and technology stocks (Padoa-Schioppa, 2002, p. 6). The current global financial framework signals the supremacy of finance capital backed by US hegemony and diffused through the 'Washington Consensus' which has seen little reform despite Stiglitz's stinging critique and the various mobilizations against globalization (*Economist* Survey, 2003, pp. 3–5; Stiglitz, 2002, pp. 53–4; 73–4).

The project of progressive financial and trade liberalization is heavily embedded. Its social bases are located in a dense transnational network which, as we have seen, has driven neoliberal integration in the EU and which operates on the global stage through a variety of other institutions including the WTO, the World Economic Forum, the OECD and the G8. According to Grahl (2001, p. 35), EMU may not even insulate Europe against the forces of speculation and mobile transnational capital unleashed by the deep-rooted liberalization of global financial markets (see also Cerny, 1993, pp. 167–74). The power of global finance is therefore a defining force in productive restructuring and in national economic strategies, posing a real and genuine threat to the European social model and the shift towards the competition state (Cerny, 1993, 1996). For Grahl, only major and global reform can counter these forces. The analysis here indicates that the EU lacks the power to pursue any such strategy independently and, more importantly, lacks the internal consensus to do so. The same globalizing currents have exerted critical influence over the shape of European integration, and the contemporary EU therefore constitutes at worst a mildly critical junior partner to the USA, particularly in the field of economic governance.

CONCLUSIONS

This chapter has sought to relate developments in the EU's internal and external economic agenda, capacities and roles to the wider context of the course of capitalism since the Second World War. In so doing, it has located the EU within a broader transnational hegemonic bloc which has successfully engineered a neoliberal transformation of the world and European economy. Within that context, both the Fortress Europe and Social Europe challenges to the neoliberal project have been increasingly marginalized. In so far as the EU does wield influence in international economic governance, it does so in a largely complementary fashion to the USA. This does not preclude some degree of competition between the USA and EU, but it does contain that rivalry within the parameters of a globalization process bearing the heavy imprint of US leadership and in which structural and ideological dimensions of power are at work to constrain and dilute competition from states and civil society alike. Internally, this raises increasing questions for the future of social models of capitalism within Europe, which remain vulnerable to deregulation and erosion.

8. Russia and the West: the new pragmatism

Paul Flenley

Relations between Russia and the West have undergone substantial changes since the initial period after the collapse of the Soviet Union and the years of the Yeltsin presidency. This is in part due to the development of a more assertive and pragmatic foreign policy in Russia under Vladimir Putin from 2000 onwards and in part due to a reassessment in the West of Russia's relative stability and significance. In particular there has been a move away from a relationship based on the memories of the Cold War involving mutual suspicions over such issues as NATO expansion and where 'partnership' often involved pro forma commitments and the need to bolster a fragile Russian democracy against the internal threat of communist or nationalist opposition. The contemporary relationship is much more based on a realistic appreciation of mutual interests and needs, whether it is in 'the war on terror' or in working out the consequences of EU enlargement to the benefit of both sides.

This chapter seeks to explore the origins and nature of the new pragmatism in the relationship between Russia and the West and considers Russia's relations with Europe in the context of its overall foreign policy, especially in relation to the USA. The chapter examines such issues as the changing relations between Russia and NATO and the effects of the 11 September terrorist attacks. It also looks at the different dimensions and determinants of the relationship with the EU. Throughout the chapter it will be seen that beneath the rhetoric of partnership and building common spaces with the EU lie very specific issues of mutual self-interest. In addition a key argument of the chapter will be that there are certain contradictions, especially between the EU and Russia, which prevent full integration. As will be seen this is partly to do with continuing structural problems in the economy but is more substantially to do with different overall agendas in terms of future development. Putin's desire to reassert central control and stability in Russia does not sit easily with the EU's agenda. In addition Russia's new pragmatism and assertiveness means a foreign policy which demands the right to maintain a free hand in dealing with the West, particularly between the EU and the USA.

A NEW PARTNERSHIP AFTER THE END OF THE SOVIET UNION?

In the immediate period after the collapse of the Soviet Union in 1991 the previous ideological and political divisions between East and West which had characterized the Cold War seemed to disappear. Under Boris Yeltsin a leadership was in power in Moscow which was committed to the same values as those of Western leaders, that is, democratization and the free market. On Christmas Eve 1991 George Bush senior spoke of a future partnership between Russia and the USA (Burns et al., 1995, p. 296). Yeltsin talked of realigning Russia with the West and the policies of the Russian government aimed at integrating Russia as quickly as possible into the main global political, economic and security institutions. Very soon, however, the new relationship ran into difficulties. Within Russia the economic reforms of 1992, including liberalization of prices and privatization, had adverse social consequences which led to disillusionment with radical market reform. There was a popular backlash against Westernization (Utkin, 2003, p. 555). In addition, the pain of opening up the economy and realigning with the West was not rewarded by the expected integration into Western institutions. Full membership of the G7 was not forthcoming and the reality of the new relationship appeared to be that Russia was sidelined as a junior partner. The dilemma for the West was that while governments were keen to support Yeltsin and democratization in Russia against increasing internal criticism from communists and nationalists, the weakness of the Russian economy and the relative instability of Russian democracy precluded full membership of organizations such as the G7.

A key area in which the relationship began to turn sour was in that of security. In the post-Cold-War era the Russians had expected to see the development of a new security architecture for Europe which would cross the Cold War divide. The obvious basis for this was the Organization for Security and Cooperation in Europe (OSCE; founded as the CSCE – Conference on Security and Cooperation in Europe – in the 1970s). This could operate as the political umbrella since it had included both NATO and Warsaw Pact countries. The coordination of military activity could be undertaken by the North Atlantic Cooperation Council (NACC) established by NATO in November 1991 and which the former Soviet successor states, including Russia, had joined by the spring of 1992 (Mihalka, 1994, pp. 35–7). NATO, the CIS and the WEU could be subordinated to this.

For the West there were major problems with this proposal. It could dilute the European–Atlantic alliance and would confine European integration to the Western part of the continent. Also it did not address the fears of the Central and East European states on their future security. The USA in particular argued for the expansion of NATO eastwards, not least because it had an effective integrated command structure unlike the OSCE – NACC. The idea was sold to Russia as providing an extension of stability to areas of Europe which had previously been a source of conflict, hence adding to Russia's security as well. Unfortunately the Russians did not interpret it in this way. Opposition to NATO expansion united Russian opinion across the board for a whole range of reasons (Plekhanov, 1999, p. 178). Many, especially in the military, saw the West exploiting Russian economic and military weakness to expand and threaten their security further. Others felt that understandings surrounding Russia's cooperation in ending the Cold War had been betrayed. For the communist and nationalist opposition to Yeltsin it confirmed their views of the dangers of Westernization and boosted their popularity at the polls. For much of the population it fed into traditional suspicions of the threat from the West.

NATO had attempted to assuage Russian fears by asserting that it had changed its functions and was not a threat to Russia. The Partnership for Peace (PfP) programme had been extended to all former Soviet bloc countries in 1994 and Russia had joined in June 1994. However, even here Russian sensitivities had been hurt. At first it seemed Russia was expected to participate in the programme alongside other former Soviet states on an equal basis rather than as a former superpower. Western lack of consultation over operations in Yugoslavia in 1994 added to resentment (Flenley, 1998, pp. 110–12). In 1995 NATO recognized that the future of European security and the success of NATO expansion would require treating Russia as more than just another European country. In May 1995 an individual programme for NATO–Russia cooperation beyond PfP was worked out and in November 1995 Russia gained membership at ambassadorial level of the consultative committee of the NATO Council. Finally, on 27 May 1997 Russia and NATO signed 'The Founding Act on Mutual Relations, Cooperation and Security'. This was presented as the beginning of a new full security partnership It set up a structure for cooperation in the form of the NATO–Russia Permanent Joint Council and a permanent Russian mission to NATO. The Act also identified a range of areas for consultation and cooperation such as crisis management, conflict prevention and arms control. For the Russian leadership it was seen as not only averting the threat posed to Russian security by the expansion of NATO but marked a new era in international relations (Carr and Flenley, 1999, pp. 98–102).

At the end of the 1990s, however, Russian–Western relations declined yet again as a number of specific grievances accumulated on the Russian side. These included NATO's declaration at its Washington NATO Summit of April 1998 of the strategic goal to operate out of area. In addition to this, NATO's resolve to continue expansion eastwards seemed to confirm Russian critics' views of NATO's ultimately hostile intentions. The Russians also complained that the NATO–Russia Permanent Joint Council had simply turned into 'a mere debating club with no decision-making power'. Instead of operating at 19+1 it was more and more operating at 19 versus 1 as NATO members appeared to arrive at agreed positions before meeting with the Russians (Kozin, 2000, p. 13). In addition, Russia resented Western criticism of policy in Chechnya. The final break came with the beginning of NATO bombing of Serbia on 24 March 1999. Practically all ties with NATO were frozen, the exception being the peacekeeping operations in Bosnia (Kelin, 2004, p. 18). 'All of a sudden, the apocalyptic scenarios of a Third World War ... returned to the table as practical policymaking and military operational planning issues ... reviving the worst instincts and stereotypes of the Cold War' (Arbatov in Wallander, 2002, p. 9).

REASSESSING RUSSIA'S FOREIGN AND SECURITY POLICY

As in the case of the heightened tension that preceded Gorbachev's Perestroika and 'New Thinking' in foreign policy in the mid-1980s, the 1999 crisis concentrated minds. In response, a reassessment of Russia's security needs began in 2000. As in the case of Gorbachev, such new thinking coincided with a change in leadership. On 31 December 1999 Yeltsin resigned as president and was replaced by Vladimir Putin. Along with him, 'new forces emerged in the Russian political scene in late 1999' (Kozin, 2000, p. 17).

For Sergei Karaganov, chair of the Russian Council for Foreign and Security Policy in 2000, the real sources of danger for Russia were not Europe and the USA but along the southern belt. The likelihood of radical transformation of regimes in the Middle East, the instability of states on the territories of the former Soviet Union, the tension in nuclearized southern Asia, the unpredictability of North Korea and the spread of weapons of mass destruction in countries close to Russia were now more worrying (Karaganov, 2002, p. 39; Averre and Cottey, 2002).

The problem was that much of the military budget was spent on resources which reflected the old threats. In 1997 strategic nuclear forces took up some 80–90 per cent of the projected military budget. This meant that there was little money left over to meet real existing needs. The problems of the armed forces in Chechnya in 1994–96 and 1999 to the present were seen to be due in the main to the disintegration of the forces deployed there (Umbach, 2003, p. 54). In August 2000 the sinking of the *Kursk* nuclear submarine, the pride of Russia's Northern Fleet, symbolized the dire state of the Russian military and its lack of funds (Herspring, 2003, p. 166). Economic constraints meant that Russia had to make clear choices about where its security interests and threats ultimately lay. A dispute developed within the military over perceptions of threat. Kvashnin, the Chief of the Defence Staff, argued against the Defence Minister Sergeyev at the time in 2000 that the threat came from ethno-nationalist conflict and Islamic fundamentalism. It was Putin's intervention at the National Security Council meeting on 11 August 2000 to resolve this dispute which marked the precise timing of the shift in Russia's policy towards a new pro-Western position (Umbach, 2003, p. 54). The 11 September terrorist attacks on the USA, one year later, accelerated that decision.

The initial strategic decision in 2000 was followed by a series of unilateral actions spurred on by economic necessity. In summer 2001 the Kremlin announced the closure of Russia's last two overseas military bases – Cam Ranh Bay, Vietnam and Lourdes, Cuba. Moscow was paying some $4 million in rent to Cuba, and Vietnam was about to request a similar sum. It was decided to reduce the Russian military from a total of 1.2 million in 2001 to between 800 000 and 850 000 by 2005 (Herspring, 2003, pp. 170–71). In this Putin was also signalling an end to a key feature of Russian and Soviet foreign policy – rivalry with the USA (Trenin, 2003, p. 48).

Reassessment of security threats did not just mean an end to the last vestiges of Cold War rivalry, but also the realization that there were areas in which Russia shared the same security threats with the West. If anything, Russia was far more at risk from the current sources of terrorism than the West. Russia's long and porous southern borders lacked natural barriers and defence fortifications, and were difficult to control. At a conference in Moscow on Russia and the New World Order on 12 May 2001, Igor Ivanov, the Russian Foreign Minister, complained that Russia had had to face the war on terrorism on its own and that it had long been aware of the new security threats while the West's vision was clouded by the 'Cold War Victory Syndrome'. (Ivanov, 2001). The Russians had already identified links between groups fighting in Chechnya and Osama bin Laden's al-Qaeda. Terrorist networks operating in Afghanistan had been identified as operating in Central Asia, threatening instability in Uzbekistan, Tajikistan and Kyrgyzstan on Russia's southern borders (Wallander, 2002, p. 126). In September 2000, one year before the attacks on New York, Sergei Yastrzhembsky, Putin's senior adviser, called for 'pre-emptive strikes' against terrorist camps in Afghanistan which had become 'a hotbed of international terrorism' (Gedmin, 2002). He called for a common front with the USA. Indeed, in spite of the coolness in relations between Russia and the USA before 11 September, in practice cooperation was under way on the terrorist front, including moves against the drug trade which finances the terrorist networks (Wallander, 2002, p. 126). In June 2000 Putin proposed that NATO, Europe and Russia should jointly develop a missile defence system (Umbach, 2003, p. 55).

A further reason for reassessing policy towards the West was the realization that Yeltsin's policy of rejectionism had generally been counterproductive. Russian opposition to NATO expansion had not succeeded in stopping the process. Indeed Yeltsin's protests at NATO expansion and threats to restore the old Soviet space in retaliation (Sherr, 1996, p. 12) had, if anything, convinced the aspiring members of NATO of a continuing Russian threat and therefore of the urgency of tying their security to the West (Herd and Moroney, 2003, p. 193). Similarly, opposition to NATO operations in Kosovo had not prevented NATO action. At best Yeltsin's tactics had created tension and suspicion of Russia's lingering imperial ambitions, and at worst their failure had shown Russia's powerlessness. The Russian reaction to the Iraq war displayed Putin's new realism. When it appeared that the USA was set on the invasion of Iraq, Putin appeared to understand 'the senselessness of protests against the inevitable, preferring to extract from the inevitable the maximum dividend' – in the case of Iraq, US assurances over Russian economic interests (Bovt, 2002, p. 2).

Reassessment was also provoked by an apparent change in US policy to Russia in the later years of the Clinton presidency and even more so under the new Republican Administration from 2001 onwards (Legvold, 2001, pp. 72–5; Stent and Shevtsova, 2002/2003). A security system based on mutual nuclear deterrence increasingly appeared outmoded now that Russia was no longer a threat. While Putin could agree with the latter, the Russians were not prepared for the unilateral nature of the conclusions which the Republican Administration drew from the analysis (Shevtsova, 2003, p. 198), for example the abrogation of the 1972 ABM (anti-ballistic-missile) Treaty in December 2001. Even when Bush and Putin at the Crawford Summit in November 2001 agreed to mutual deep cuts in their arsenals of nuclear weapons, Bush later explained that he was cutting America's stockpile regardless of anything Russia did because the decision was taken 'on the basis of America's security needs alone' (*The Economist*, 17 November 2001, p. 51). The USA now clearly wanted freedom of action in its defence planning. The problem for Russia was that the relationship with the USA had been the one which gave it a sense of significance. Bilateral summits and especially nuclear arms control helped to maintain the idea of a superpower.

Yeltsin had demanded the right for Russia to be treated as a 'strategic partner' of the West. 'Russia is a big country, a superpower, and should be treated as such, not as just any other European country' (Lepingwell, 1994, p. 6). The West had generally been sensitive to this view largely to prop up the Russian leadership and Boris Yeltsin in particular. The fear was that if the Russian democrats were not supported, then Russia could fall prey to a nationalist reaction or the return of the communists. Either of the latter could have produced a Russia which was more difficult for the West to deal with. Now Russia was no longer a security threat and, after ten years of reform, capitalism of a sort was firmly embedded. The Russia–USA relationship could be downgraded. Lines of communication were kept open and cooperation projects continued, but little effort was put into the relationship (Legvold, 2001, p. 72). Moreover, in a new world of one superpower it was not obvious what Russia had to offer in terms of US security.

It was against this backdrop that the Putin leadership began to break with the foreign and security assumptions of the past ten years and to redefine Russia's relationship with the West. In particular it was realized that Russia could no longer rely on Western sympathy or the kind of appeals to past 'debts' that Yeltsin had made (Lepingwell, 1994, p. 2). The priority now was to show what Russia could practically bring to any partnership with the West and in this, 11 September provided the superb opportunity.

THE NEW RUSSIAN FOREIGN AND SECURITY POLICY

The 2000 shift in policy was reflected in the Russian Foreign Policy and Security Concept published that year. According to Igor Ivanov, the Foreign Minister, the policy identified three key tasks for foreign policy – ensuring reliable security, the creation of favourable external conditions for socio-economic development and protecting the rights of Russian nationals abroad (State Council of Russia, 2003, p. 11). This was reflective of the 'Pragmatic Nationalism' which was to become the 'central tenet of Russian foreign policy' under Putin (Puglisi, 2003, p. 63). After a decade of internal chaos and loss of external influence the overwhelming priority now was to rebuild the strength of the Russian state. A key purpose of the strengthening of the state was to rebuild the economy. Putin was returning to a traditional Russian formula – a strong state presiding over the modernization of the economy. The role of foreign and security policy in this was to promote Russia's economic growth. In pursuing this, Putin marked a historic shift in the Russian perception of foreign policy. Soviet and tsarist foreign policy had sought broader goals whether exporting revolution, supporting ideological or religious orthodox allies, or imperial competition and expansion. Even in the post-Soviet period under Yeltsin much of military expenditure and foreign policy effort had been geared to maintaining status rather than meeting immediate threats and needs. This was a drain on the nation's wealth. Maintaining 'empire' was expensive. Now Putin wanted a foreign and security policy that would be a resource for internal reconstruction and development. Russia should grow internally rather than externally (Trenin, 2003, p. 52). As Putin explained to a meeting of his Russian ambassadors at the Foreign Ministry on 12 July 2002, there was now to be a direct link between foreign policy and Russian business – 'carefully calculated, well thought-through diplomatic moves, the ability to rally allies – all of this contributes to enhancing the country's authority, facilitating economic growth and strengthening the position of domestic business' (Stepanov, 2003, p. 175). According to Ivanov, the Foreign Minister in 2002, 'the bulk of the Russian president's negotiations deal with concrete economic issues' (Puglisi, 2003, p. 64). Some have referred to the 'commercialization of foreign policy' under Putin (Shevtsova, 2003, p. 199). By 2003 Ivanov considered that Russia was well on the way to achieving the required relationship between security and the needs of the economy – 'On the whole the situation in the security area is now shaping in a way enabling us to concentrate our efforts on the solution of the main strategic task – providing maximally favourable conditions for the country's sustained socio-economic development' (State Council of Russia, 2003, p. 11).

The new pragmatism informed the 'new Westernism' now pursued by Putin. The newspaper *Izvestiya* remarked on how the US–Russian relationship had changed by 2002 – 'Putin and Bush junior play more pragmatic games than Gorbachev and Bush senior. They do not need global alliances and head-spinning plans of Russian–US friendship. They need concrete agreements' (*Izvestiya*, 23 November 2002, p. 2). For Putin, pragmatism also meant that Russia had the right to develop relations with other states, such as China, North Korea, Iran, also on the basis of economic and security needs, even if the USA objected. In August 2002 Iraq offered Russian companies engineering and construction contracts worth at least $40 bn. This was welcomed by an official Russian news agency, saying it 'conformed with the foreign policy principle advocated by President Putin – "yes to pragmatism, no to ideology"' (Cottrell, 2002). Russia's pursuit of relationships with such countries as Iraq, Iran or North Korea is not necessarily motivated by the desire to assert independence of the dominant Western relationship or even some kind of retaliation for US unilateralism. All these 'rogue' states lie close to Russia's borders and their stability is of direct concern for Russia's security. Some form of economic relationship with them is also seen as necessary, not least for Russia's southern regions. Russia and Iran share an interest in the development of the Caspian Sea (Guzhvin, Governor of Astrakhan, at State Council of Russia, 2003, pp. 15–18). Putin's meeting with Kim Jong-Il, the North Korean leader, in Vladivostok in August 2002 enabled him to push forward Russia's plan to rebuild the main railway line across North Korea to link the Trans-Siberian railway with South Korea and offer exporters there a land route to Europe (Cottrell, 2002).

A greater assertion of Russia's interests as different from those of the USA and Europe had indeed already developed earlier when Primakov became Foreign Minister under Yeltsin in January 1996. He put forward the idea that Russia should pursue a multi-polar foreign policy and that Russia should develop its relations with the CIS and Eastern Europe in particular (Parrish, 1996, p. 33). Even as early as 1993 Yeltsin had declared that 'the recent series of visits to South Korea, China and now India is indicative of the fact that we are moving away from a Western emphasis' (Crow, 1994, p. 3). However, Primakov's views had been based on the developing influence of Eurasianism within the Foreign Ministry. This idea had posited the view that Russia's foreign policy should reflect its geopolitical and geocultural position as both a European and an Asian state. Russia should pursue relations with all the countries along its border, the former Soviet states, China, India as well as the USA and Europe equally (Kerr, 1995). Indeed, it was felt that Russia could provide a bridge between East and West.

Putin's multi-vectored foreign policy is, however, not the same as the policy of multi-polarity pursued by Primakov the former Foreign Minister under Yeltsin. The idea of Eurasianism, which informed policy then, is no longer in the ascendancy in the Foreign Ministry. For Putin the relationship with the West is primary rather than being on an equal status with others. The economic advantages for Russia of developing closer relations with the EU and the USA far outweigh those derived from other relationships. Building up alliances as a counterweight to the USA and/or Europe would therefore be very damaging to Russia's interests. The Russian commentator Fedor Burlatsky noted, 'some leaders of Russia, I remember, have nurtured the idea of a triple alliance: Russia–China–India as a counterweight to American hegemony. During Putin's visit (to India and China in 2002) not one of the powers expressed enthusiasm or even interest for any triangle and preferred a deepening of relations on a bilateral basis' (*Izvestiya*, 11 December 2002). Putin's pursuit of a closer relationship with China was based on specific economic and security interests. The 2001 Sino-Russian Treaty – the first in 50 years – provided for increased arms sales to China and hence essential support for the survival of the still large military–industrial sector in Russia. In addition, the 'Shanghai Five' regional grouping of China, Russia, Kazakhstan, Kyrgyzstan and Tajikistan is concerned with maintaining stability in the region where borders are porous and in particular enforcing regional anti-terrorism measures (Ivanov, 2003, p. 37).

SEPTEMBER 11 AND THE END OF THE COLD WAR

September 11 was not the initial cause of the change in Russia's foreign policy direction (Primakov, 2004, p. 26). It accelerated the pace and in particular it meant Putin could now justify his plan to domestic critics (Fritch, 2002, p. 2). First, it gave the opportunity to identify Russia explicitly with the USA – 'in the moments of truth, when the very existence of our nations were at stake Russia and the US have always stood together. I am sure now that our destiny meets history again. We shall be friends and partners' (Putin speech, Washington, November 2002, *Independent*, 15 November 2001).

Second, he used the opportunity to show just how useful Russia could be as a partner in the 'war on terror'. In this he asserted his increasing authority as president. On 14 September the Defence Minister, Sergei Ivanov, had rejected the possibility of a NATO military presence in Central Asia. On 22 September 2001 Putin held a key meeting with the power ministers at which he broke the resistance of his generals and the Defence Minister to allowing the USA/NATO to use military bases in Central Asia – i.e. Uzbekistan, Tajikistan and Kyrgyzstan (Shevtsova, 2003, p. 206).

Third, Putin was able to draw a clear link between Russia's war in Chechnya and the US war on terror. They were facing a common enemy and for some time at least the West toned down its allegations of Russian human rights violations in Chechnya. The concept that Russia is fighting a similar 'war on terror' has continued after 11 September. The school hostage crisis faced by Russia in Beslan, North Ossetia in early September 2004 saw Putin gain support from the international community in the form of a UN Security Council statement expressing determination to combat 'all forms of terrorism' (Steele, 2004a).

For Bush and Putin at least, 11 September and the 'war on terror' meant a clear end to the Cold War and a genuine realignment based on mutual security threats (Wallander, 2002, p. 127). At the summit in Washington in November 2001 they agreed that the shared threats were terrorism, proliferation of weapons of mass destruction, militant nationalism, ethnic and religious intolerance and regional instability. Old adversaries could now be of practical help to each other. Anatolii Safonov, Deputy Russian Foreign Minister, has talked of the need for a 'global antiterrorist system' in the face of 11 September and the Moscow October 2002 theatre siege. Rather than seeing NATO as hostile, now 'NATO can make the weightiest contribution to the strategy of struggle against international terrorism – not only as a striking military force but also within the format of NATO strategy under revision. One cannot exclude that the process of revision will produce "specialized antiterrorist capabilities"' (Safonov, 2003, p. 33) For Russia the US action in Afghanistan and the US presence in Central Asia have actually helped their own security problem in the south. They enabled them to clamp down on activity in Chechnya, liquidating terrorist training camps and disrupting channels of financial support. It also generally weakened the position of Islamists in the Central Asian republics. According to Primakov, the former Foreign Minister, Putin's support for US action was entirely within the national interest (Primakov, 2004, p. 26). For Russia's fight against terrorism the only alternative to cooperation with the USA is to build up its own military responses in competition with the West and in partnership with weak states along the south, who make unreliable allies (Pavlovskii in Yasmann, 2002). As one Russian comedian has put it, 'Better the Americans in Uzbekistan than the Taliban in Tatarstan' (Yasmann, 2002).

As a consequence of Russia's practical help in Afghanistan a number of benefits flowed which cemented the new realignment. The Russian economy was recognized as a market economy by the EU in May and by the USA in June 2002. Support for Russia's membership of the World Trade Organization was expressed by the USA and the EU. Russia was granted full membership of the G8. In May 2002 a Russia–USA nuclear agreement was signed and in the same month Russia reached a new accord with NATO in the form of the NATO–Russia Council of 20.

RUSSIA AND NATO

With respect to NATO–Russia relations in particular, the unfreezing of contacts after the dispute over Kosovo also occurred before 11 September. In any case, throughout the freeze, cooperation had continued in the area of peacekeeping in the Balkans. Russia maintained its contribution to the Stabilization Force (SFOR) in Bosnia and in July 1999 Russian troops were deployed in KFOR in Kosovo. On 23 July 1999 the Permanent Joint Council met, solely devoted to evaluating the situation in Kosovo and Bosnia. If anything, the talk was of upgrading the cooperation between Russian and NATO contingents in this area (Kozin, 2000, p. 17). While 'the going was gruellingly hard' (Kelin, 2004, p. 18) in maintaining the dialogue during this period, the experience provided lessons for both sides. In particular NATO became less sceptical about the chances of working with Russia and aware of the practical benefits of working jointly on key security issues. 'Close cooperation between NATO and Russia in the Balkans has been critical in improving relations and building trust between the Russian and Allied militaries, both on the ground and at higher command levels' (NATO, 2002, p. 3). Putin's new, more pragmatic approach and reassessment of Russia's security needs facilitated the rebuilding of NATO–Russia relations in 2000. In February 2000 George Robertson, the new NATO Secretary General appointed in October 1999, visited Moscow with a clear commitment to stabilizing NATO–Russian relations. 'Moscow and Brussels share the view that the visit became the first stage on the way to the restoration of their ties' (Kozin, 2000, p. 18). May 2000 saw a ministerial-level meeting of the Permanent Joint Council, the first since the formal break, and in February 2001 NATO opened an Information Office in Moscow. The events of 11 September further cemented the new relationship. Putin and Robertson met in Brussels in October 2001 and again in Moscow in November. At their summit in Crawford, Texas in November 2001, Bush and Putin's joint statement declared that Russia and the USA would 'work together with NATO and other NATO members to improve, strengthen and enhance the relationship between NATO and Russia, with a view to developing new effective mechanisms for consultation, cooperation, joint decisions and coordinated/ joint action' (Matser, 2001/2002, p. 21).

The 'new relationship' which Bush and Putin talked about was cemented at the Russia–NATO summit in Rome on 28 May 2002 with the signing of the Rome Declaration 'Russia–NATO Relations: A New Quality'. This established a new Russia–NATO Council to replace the old Permanent Joint Council. It was to meet monthly at the level of ambassadors and military representatives to NATO and twice a year each at the level of foreign ministers, defence ministers and chiefs, and occasionally at summit level (NATO, 2002, p. 1). Within it NATO and Russia would work 'at 20' on the basis of consensus i.e. without pre-coordinated NATO positions, on those areas where NATO and Russia had common ground (Matser, 2001/2002, p. 21; Babaeva, 2002, p. 1). This was to be clearly different from the former Permanent Joint Council where there was little joint decision making (Fritch, 2002, p. 2). The new agreement, however, left NATO's core functions of mutual defence and military action untouched. Moscow had no right of veto over the alliance (Traynor, 2002). The main areas of cooperation and joint decision making included the struggle against terrorism; crisis regulation and developing joint peacekeeping operations; tackling the spread of weapons of mass destruction; weapons control; military reforms, including the development of an integrated centre of military training; search and rescue at sea; planning and reacting to civil emergencies (Babaeva, 2002, p. 1). In practical terms the Council meant that the normal team of the Russian ambassador, and the military delegation at NATO headquarters was added to by specialists and military and diplomats who would work with the Alliance on a permanent basis. Within the first six months experts working 'at 20' had evaluated threats coming from al-Qaeda and the safety of peacekeeping forces in the Balkans. 'For sides which only recently came out of half-a-century of opposition – a breakthrough' (*Izvestiya*, 10 December 2002). One Russian diplomat involved declared that 'they were surprised at how much had been achieved' (*Izvestiya*, 23 November 2002). The new arrangement fitted Putin's new agenda of building the relationship with the West on pragmatic rather than purely symbolic bases. The Chief of the General Staff, General Kvashnin, was positively disposed to 'at 20', saying that 'We do not see a threat from the West' (*Izvestiya*, 29 May 2002, p. 2).

One group who had resisted the new council had been NATO's new members, Poland, Hungary and the Czech Republic. Having just sought refuge in NATO from Moscow's grasp, they had not expected to be sitting again at the same table so quickly (Shevtsova, 2003, p. 214). A diplomatic effort was put into calming their fears. On 14 February 2002, Robertson on a visit to Poland spoke of the need to reinforce NATO–Russia relations:

> I recognize that there are quite a few people who get nervous whenever we talk about closer cooperation with Russia. Many in Russia feel the same way about closer cooperation with NATO … The real threats to our security, from regional instability to the proliferation of ballistic missile technology and nuclear, biological and chemical agents, to terrorism, to cyber-warfare, to organized crime, do not recognize borders and are faced by NATO allies and Russia alike. Isolating or ignoring Russia would only hobble our response to these dangers. (NATO Update, 14 February 2002)

A key test of the new NATO–Russia relationship came with the further expansion of NATO at the Prague Summit in November 2002. This included the sensitive issue of the incorporation of Lithuania, Latvia and Estonia. Much of the Russian anger at the first wave of enlargement had been to draw a line in the sand and prevent a second round which would have included these former soviet republics (Carr and Flenley, 1999, pp. 102–3). The first round of NATO enlargement had been seen by the military as extending the degree to which NATO could strike at the heart of Russia.

This second round also led to similar debates in the military. Yurii Baluevskii, first deputy chief of the General Staff, argued that Moscow would be totally deprived of its buffer zone – 'that means in case of aggression the armed forces of the Alliance would take 24 hours to get to the important nerve-centres of Russia and planes and winged rockets only minutes' (*Izvestiya*, 23 November 2002). The reaction by Putin was, however, starkly different from that of Yeltsin to the first round. Whereas the latter had threatened in 1995 that enlargement would lead to a restoration of the two-bloc system in Europe (Sherr, 1996, p. 12), Putin's position was to be 'calmly negative' (Kelin, 2004, p. 21). While there was nothing good in the enlargement for Russia, Sergei Ivanov, Minister of Defence, declared that 'Russia relates calmly to the expansion of NATO in so far as it is not a member of this organization and does not intend to join it' (*Izvestiya*, 22 November 2002, p. 2).

The key reasons for the change in attitude are, first, Putin's policy of avoiding futile and counterproductive confrontation with the West over issues which cannot be blocked. Second, it has been realized that actual membership of NATO and eventually the EU may reduce the insecurity felt by the former soviet bloc countries and facilitate a more constructive relationship between them and Moscow. Third, in Russia there has been a reassessment of NATO and its 'threat' over the last few years. As one Kremlin official noted, 'The wider NATO, the more complicated it is to take a decision' (*Izvestiya*, 29 May 2002, p. 2). Enlargement could actually make NATO less of an effective military organization. Some see NATO turning from a military into more of a political organization (*Izvestiya*, 21 November 2002, p. 1). There is a realization that NATO itself is undergoing a transformation responding to new threats facing its members. This gives ample opportunity for Russia to feed into the accompanying debate and develop a special relationship without being a formal member (Kelin, 2004, p. 23). Moreover, in the case of both Iraq and Afghanistan the USA effectively made the running without NATO. In the eyes of Russians it seems that NATO is losing its significance (Shevtsova, 2003, p. 210). According to Anatolii Utkin, soon 'NATO will be seen as a dinosaur of past times' (Utkin, 2003, p. 558). Nevertheless, NATO enlargement still has the capacity to cause friction. The prospect that the 1 000 000 US troops stationed in Germany might now be moved to NATO's new border countries, Poland, Romania and Bulgaria, was considered by Sergei Ivanov, the Defence Minister, as provoking 'totally understandable anxiety' (Dempsey, 2003).

DOMESTIC POLITICS AND FOREIGN POLICY

In Russia, Putin's critics have pointed out the downsides of all the policy 'successes' of the last few years. In particular, it is argued that the new Westernism has not in practice brought Russia many results. Nationalist and communist opponents still see a continuing process of concessions to the USA with little in return. In spite of the support given after 9/11, the USA still withdrew unilaterally from the ABM (anti-ballistic-missile) Treaty and there is no constraint on the US missile defence programme. NATO enlargement still continued unchecked. The view among many is that the new NATO–Russia Council was little more than a sop to buy off Russian acquiescence to expansion in the same way that the Founding Act and the Permanent NATO–Russia Joint Council were used at the time of the last round of expansion in 1997 (Zyuganov in RFE/RL Newsline, 12 November 2002).

For some conservatives in Moscow the dramatic increase in US security assistance to Central Asia following 11 September has also been a cause for concern (Kleveman, 2003, pp. 188–93). The continuing US presence has countered the traditional role of Russia, and many observers now talk of the new 'Great Game' in the area, i.e. renewed competition between the powers – now Russia, the USA and China – in particular for control of oil and gas reserves (*Diplomaticnet*, 16 January 2002). Uzbekistan has become the US key strategic partner, in spite of its human rights record (Moroney, 2003, p. 198).

So far these concerns have not developed into the kind of opposition that undermined Boris Yeltsin. For much of his period in office Yeltsin was plagued by a communist- and nationalist-dominated Duma critical of government policies. The rapid market reforms and attached social consequences meant that Yeltsin's brand of Westernism in foreign policy was associated with the idea that the country was being sold to the West. This was accentuated by the presence of powerful oligarchs in the circle around Yeltsin who benefited from the privatization programmes of the early 1990s. In dealing with Russia, Western policy makers were aware that Yeltsin had to be careful not to alienate the nationalists. Putin, however, has benefited from the general perception that he has broken with the chaos of the Yeltsin years. As Kasyanov, the former Prime Minister, remarked, 'ten years ago in the country there was economic chaos, society stood on the verge of civil war and over ten years we have succeeded in overcoming this' (*Nezavisimaya Gazeta*, No. 265, 8 December 2003). Second, in rehabilitating pride in the Soviet past and yet believing in rebuilding Russia's strength, Putin has been able to appeal to that Red–Brown alliance of communists and nationalists which Yeltsin had alienated by his rejection of the Soviet era and by the privatization and corruption of the 1990s. Finally, he has been able to recentralize power at the centre. This has led to what many have called a 'managed democracy' (McFaul, 2003). It has involved the biased use of the media to promote government parties such as United Russia in the December 2003 elections and tactics to undermine and weaken opposition parties such as the communists, thus producing a compliant Duma (ibid.). Particularly popular has been the harassment and, in the case of Khodorkovksy, the boss of the Yukos oil company in November 2003, the arrest of rich businessmen who attempt to use their vast wealth to indulge in opposition politics. Moving against Yeltsin-era oligarchs has also facilitated more control over the media. The regions have also felt the extension of central power. Putin's creation of seven super-regional executives answering directly to him was an attempt to reverse the political autonomy of the regions which had developed under Yeltsin. This went hand in hand with the removal of the regional governors and heads of regional legislatures from the Federation Council, the higher chamber of parliament. The war on terror has facilitated these centralizing tendencies. The school hostage crisis in Beslan in September 2004 led to the announcement that regional governors would no longer be directly elected locally but appointed by the Kremlin and approved by regional parliaments. There is even some discussion of restoring Russia as a unitary state (Coalson, 2004). The key to power at the centre now is said to be the 'siloviki', those in the power ministries, particularly the security organs (Piontkovski, 2003).

For many in the West these moves have been greeted with disquiet about the trends in Russian 'democracy'. US reaction to the Yukos affair was to assume the worst. US state department spokesman Richard Boucher commented that it 'raised serious questions about the rule of law in Russia and we've noted that it sparks concerns among domestic and international investors about respect for ownership rights in Russia' (*Russian Foreign Policy and Security Watch*, 5 November 2003). Putin tried to reassure foreign investors by telling the visiting IMF Managing Director Horst Koehlers that 'there is no basis to suppose that the use of laws is selective or will be selective' (*Russian Foreign Policy and Security Watch*, 21 November 2003).

The Yukos case points to one of the key contradictions in the relationship between domestic policy and the new Westernism in foreign policy. On the one hand Putin's greater assertion of central control has had a number of positive benefits for foreign policy. There is less chaos in actual policy making itself. One of the key features of the Yeltsin period was the conflict between different ministries and between them and the presidential administration (Parrish, 1996, pp. 30–33). Putin has been able to assert greater discipline in the process of foreign policy making. 'President Putin and a narrow circle of his colleagues shape the Russian course without any substantial effort to institutionalize this process or to involve a broader range of actors' (Polikanov and Timmins, 2004, p. 228). As we have seen, after 9/11 Putin has even been able to use his authority to overrule ministers and generals to the benefit of a Western-oriented policy. It has been Putin's greater authoritarianism that has delivered Russia as a more coherent reliable Western ally. Putin's dominance of the political scene and control of the Duma have meant that Russia can now project itself outwards as a confident coherent actor on the world stage. For much of the Yeltsin period the government was consumed with internal conflict and the West had to be mindful of the need to prop up Yeltsin against his internal critics. The collapse of the communists at the December 2003 elections and the fragmentation of the nationalist parties has meant the end of the 'it's me or chaos' card which Yeltsin used to play in foreign policy. Western policy makers can deal with Russia more in terms of the issues than with a fearful eye on Russian instabilities. Finally, the greater assertion of central power has enabled a more stable atmosphere for foreign investment to develop. Putin's commitment to enforcement of the law and his desire to push through administrative, tax and financial reforms are the kinds of developments the EU in particular needs if the economic relationship with Russia is to grow closer.

The paradox, however, is that the greater authoritarianism which has produced this new Westernism has also produced developments which are increasingly worrying to Western observers, especially in the area of rights and democracy. The Yukos affair displayed the capacity of the state to be selective in targeting businessmen. This makes investors unsure of the long-term security of investments. Biased media coverage, suspicious attacks on journalists, and policy in Chechnya are a number of areas where the EU in particular is concerned about the trends in Russian democracy. It is almost as if the central control which will deliver a Russia able to operate as a reliable partner of the West will also prevent it integrating fully as a Western country following Western norms.

Even in terms of the Westernist foreign policy there is also a degree of instability. Putin has been able to deliver Russia, in part because of his authority and in spite of the political élite and the population. Central control has meant that there has been little need to explain foreign policy to the population at large or to justify the current trends of integration with the EU and so on. In this sense, even more so than in the West, foreign policy is a very élitist exercise (Polikanov and Timmins, 2004, p. 229). This makes the current policy very vulnerable to changes in leadership. The 2003/4 parliamentary and presidential elections showed that most Russians were concerned with domestic issues and in particular their social and economic welfare. As we have seen, Putin has justified his pro-Western foreign policy in these terms. However, this makes it vulnerable to any change in economic fortunes. A report from the European Commission in 2004 noted that the reliance of the economy on natural resources, especially oil and gas, meant that the economy was 'vulnerable to any sudden collapse of oil prices' (European Commission, 2004d, p. 10). Foreign direct investment is still low. Overall, most investment has been in the oil and gas sector and construction, leaving most of the infrastructure and manufacturing untouched (ibid., p. 11). Businesses are suffering a chronic shortage of capital as the latter leaves the country at the rate of some $30 billion per year. Exports, apart from oil and gas (60 per cent of total), are falling as imports rise (Stratfor Analysis, 2003).

RUSSIA AND THE EU

The Framework of the Relationship

The initial relationship between the EU and Russia after the fall of the Soviet Union was largely incoherent and concentrated on issues of technical and economic assistance. This centred in particular on the TACIS (Technical Assistance for the Commonwealth of Independent States) programme established in 1991 to encourage institutional, legal and administrative reform and help in the transformation to a market economy. From 1991 to 2003 some 2.6 billion euros were allocated to Russia under TACIS (European Commission, 2004e, p. 2). Aid also involved programmes developed by the individual member states, such as Germany's TRANSFORM programme established in 1993.

This low-key approach derived from the attitude of both sides. The Russian leadership in the 1990s still saw international relations in terms of relations with individual states. The EU was regarded as an economic agency (Gower, 2004, p. 236). The EU's development of a Common Foreign and Security Policy and the proposals for expansion of the EU meant, however, that the latter was beginning to exert a powerful identity in its own right and one that would impact directly on Russia itself. 'The Foreign Policy Concept of the Russian Federation' of July 2000 rather belatedly recognized the significance of European integration and expansion (*Diplomaticheskii vestnik*, No. 8, 2000, p. 8) and hence the need for Russia to develop a coherent response to the EU in its own right.

The EU also only began to develop a coherent policy towards Russia in the 1990s. The Partnership and Cooperation Agreement with Russia (PCA) which still forms the basis for EU–Russian relations was adopted in 1994 but did not come into force until 1997 due to EU disquiet over Russian actions in Chechnya. On paper it covered broad areas of cooperation including a political dialogue on issues such as democracy and human rights. However, its main emphasis in practice initially was on trade and economic cooperation (European Commission, 2004e, p. 1). A more strategic view towards Russia began to be developed by the EU from 1995 onwards with the 'Strategy for Future EU/Russia Relations' adopted at the Madrid European Council in which political reform, security issues and foreign policy occupied equal place with economic cooperation (Webber, 2001, p. 409). This was followed up by an 'Action Plan for Russia' in May 1996. However, much of this was of a pro forma and speculative character designed to bolster the 'democrats' in Russia. In practice individual member states tended to pursue their own bilateral relations with Russia (Gower in Webber, 2000, p. 80). The first real attempt to deal with Russia more coherently at an EU level comes with the Common Strategy of the European Union on Russia adopted at the Cologne European Council in June 1999 (European Commission, 2004e, p. 2). This was spurred on by the realization that EU membership of former Soviet bloc countries was now becoming a realistic proposition in the near future. The EU was aware of the mistakes made by NATO in initially not considering the Russian dimension as it had expanded eastwards (Webber, 2001, p. 409). However, unlike NATO expansion, this was not just a question of being sensitive to Russian pride. Successful EU enlargement necessitated a closer relationship with Russia for very practical reasons. There was a range of concrete issues which needed to be solved quickly, such as the status of Kaliningrad, cross-border crime and immigration from the East. Being next door to the EU, Russia's stability and cooperation could also seriously affect the success of the EU itself. As the Common Strategy recognized, Russia and the EU shared a common space (European Commission, 2004e, p. 2). In addition, the Cologne European Council also committed the member states to a European Security and Defence Policy. This meant not only clarifying relations on security with US and NATO but also with European 'third parties' outside the EU, especially Russia (Webber, 2001, p. 407).

The institutional framework for EU–Russia relations set up by the PCA consists of two summits a year including the President of the Council of the EU supported by the High Representative for the CFSP, the President of the European Commission and the Russian President. The first summit was held in May 1998. A Cooperation Council involved senior ministers from Russia and the member states, usually foreign ministers. At first the summits were seen as an exercise in 'political dialogue' (EU–Russian Federation Summit, 6 November 2003). For their part, Russian officials expected little from them. They were an opportunity for a 'loosening up of the European bureaucracy' in its attitudes to Russia after the Cold War (Babaeva, 2002). Gradually, however, they became occasions to review an 'entire "inter-pillar" sphere of collaboration' (EU–Russian Federation Summit, 6 November 2003). As cooperation began to intensify, it was decided in May 2003 to turn the Cooperation Council into a Permanent Partnership Council, meeting more frequently and now including different levels of ministers, for example justice and home affairs, environment. A Cooperation Committee meets at senior official level and there are nine sub-committees covering a whole range of technical issues in such areas as agriculture, transport, financial and economic issues, customs and cross-border cooperation (European Commission, 2004e, pp. 3 and 6).

Democratization and the Spread of EU Norms

From 2000 onwards the growing extent and detail of EU–Russian cooperation reflected the view that closer cooperation between the EU and Russia essentially meant bringing Russia as closely as possible into line with EU practice and regulations. From the EU's perspective this derived from a vision of its new role internationally as a coherent foreign and security policy actor. While the EU is unable to compete with the USA in terms of the provision of military hardware, the EU sees itself as making a contribution to global security through the prevention of the implosion of states and the promotion of democratization. The strategy document of the EU Brussels Summit, 2003 talked of 'preventive engagement', helping countries to build democracy (Steele, 2004b). One of the goals of the EU's Common Foreign and Security Policy is 'to develop and consolidate democracy, the rule of law and respect for human rights' (Olsen, 2000, p. 143). This was seen as part of the EU's long-term agenda in its relationship with Russia and was outlined explicitly at the start of the EU's 'Common Strategy on Russia' published in 1999.

The case of the East European states joining the EU gave hope that the engagement between the EU and Russia would have a normative effect on Russia. The prospect of EU membership had promoted internal reform in Central and Eastern Europe. Countries such as Estonia and Latvia had been pressed to rethink their treatment of national minorities. However, in the case of Russia there has been some questioning whether this is a realistic possibility in view of recent political trends outlined above. There is an awareness that in itself the EU has limited influence over the encouragement of democracy in Russia and the former USSR (Olsen, 2000, p. 150). Central and Eastern Europe is perhaps an exceptional example of the EU's normative effects in that these states had a realistic possibility of joining the EU. In the case of Russia today, EU membership is not on the cards. Indeed, current opinion among the political élite in Russia is clearly against any idea of actual membership precisely because EU norms and regulations would be too inhibiting politically and economically, and would involve a loss of sovereignty (Yasmann, 2004, p. 1). Nevertheless, in the case of Russia there are internal domestic, particularly economic, reasons which make some acceptance of EU norms necessary in the long term. However, as in the case of the rest of Putin's assertive new Westernism, it will be the practical necessity of Russia's economic interests which will drive this rather than any lecturing by the EU on human rights or democracy (Arbatova et al., 2003).

The Common European Economic Space

Bringing Russia closer to the EU economically is seen as being in the practical interest of both sides. At the EU–Russia Summit of May 2001 discussions were launched on the establishment of a common European economic space. This envisaged the elimination of trade barriers between the EU and Russia, mostly through regulatory convergence. The benefits of common rules were seen as opening up a market of 600 million consumers (European Commission, 2004c, p. 3). The acceptance of this idea by the EU was a major achievement by Putin. As he came to realize the significance to Russia of the EU, one of his main goals has been to develop an organic relationship with the EU for a variety of reasons. First, for Russians generally the relationship with the EU is not as problematic as that between Russia and the USA/NATO. The Cold War psychology of competition and threat does not infect the relationship. In addition Putin sees the economic benefit for Russia of an even closer relationship with its main trading partner. Before enlargement the EU accounted for some 46 per cent of Russia's foreign trade turnover. With enlargement it will be 54 per cent (*Izvestiya*, 24 February 2004). He is also keen to show the value of Russia as a key supplier of energy to the EU and one that is politically more stable in the long term than the Middle East. At the EU–Russia Summit in Paris in October 2000 an 'energy dialogue' was agreed on and the need for the 'definition of an EU–Russia energy partnership' identified. Russia already supplies over 20 per cent of the EU's needs in imported fuel (European Commission, 2004c, p. 2). Not surprisingly, therefore, in the 'Mid-Term Strategy for Developing Relations between the Russian Federation and the EU (2000–2010)' Putin urged the opening up of EU markets to Russia, called for a Russian/EU free trade zone and posited the idea of an all-European economic and legal infrastructure. In addition he called for all-European security to make sure Russia was not left out of the thinking on ESDP (Gower, 2004; Webber, 2001).

The key impulse to building a common economic space has been the eastward expansion of the EU. As the countries of Central and Eastern Europe themselves adopt EU regulations and norms and reorient their trade to the EU, Russia is faced with being cut off from traditional trading partners in the West. Trade with Central and Eastern Europe will be difficult if Russia does not also move closer to EU standards. As the joint statement issued after the first meeting of the Permanent Partnership Council on 27 April 2004 stated, 'the interdependence of the EU and Russia, stemming from our proximity and increasing political, economic and cultural ties will reach new levels with the enlargement of the EU' (European Commission, 2004b, p. 1). The EU and Russia agreed to extend the Partnership and Cooperation Agreement between them to the newly enlarged EU as of 27 April 2004 (European Commission, 2004a).

The St Petersburg EU–Russia Summit held in May 2003 also identified three other areas apart from the economy for the building of 'common spaces', that is, freedom, security and justice; research and education; and external security.

Border Security

In the area of the common space of freedom, security and justice the issue of border security has been seen as urgent in the light of EU expansion. The challenge here is to maintain secure but transparent borders between the expanding EU and Russia. This means allowing legal trade but cooperating against illegal migration and combating cross-border crime such as trafficking in human beings and drugs. This has meant joint work under the Justice and Home Affairs pillar of the EU and includes the Action Plan on combating organized crime of June 2000 and a Europol–Russia agreement. Putin's aim has been to move towards visa-free travel between Russia and the EU. For many Russians the extension of Schengen to the new EU members will mean raising barriers where they had not existed before. Speaking in July 2003, A.I. Denisov, a deputy minister of foreign affairs, pointed out that it would affect 'millions of our citizens, businessmen, students, tourists etc.' (Denisov, 2003), especially those Russians who had long-term links particularly with Eastern Europe and areas such as the Baltic States. The immediate practical significance of this issue was highlighted by the problem of Kaliningrad, the Russian enclave which is cut off from the rest of Russia by Poland and Lithuania, now EU members. Expansion of the EU meant a solution had to be found to the problem of travel for Russian citizens between Kaliningrad and the rest of Russia. On 1 July 2003 a specific transit regime based on facilitated travel documents came into effect (European Commission, 2004e, p. 4; Kortunov, 2003, p. 126).

Terrorism and the Problem of Chechnya

A second area of cooperation within the common space of freedom, security and justice is terrorism, especially after 9/11. The EU–Russia Summit of 3 October 2001 decided to exchange information on the activities and movements of individuals or groups belonging to terrorist networks, supplies of arms and explosives, financial transactions which support terrorism and new forms of terrorist activity. It was agreed to freeze the financial accounts of terrorists. This cooperation again was of an urgent, practical nature. 'Russia is the main point of transhipment for drug trafficking via Central Asia to Eastern and Western Europe. A substantial part of the proceeds from the sale of Afghan opiates goes to support terrorist groups both within and outside Afghanistan' (Trubnikov, 2003, p. 43). There has been a shared view on the threat of terrorism, its global nature and the link with organized crime. However, the one area of disagreement has been over the issue of Chechnya. While Putin has been successful in establishing Chechnya as a terrorist issue in the eyes of the West, the EU has differed from the USA in its assessment of the Russian reaction to the problem, arguing that allegations of human rights abuses in Chechnya need to be investigated (European Commission, 2004e, p. 5). As one Russian policy-making think-tank concluded in 2003, 'Russia will have to acknowledge that European states, unlike the US and Israel, are less concerned with the war on international terrorism than they are to point out the humanitarian and legal aspects of that war' (Foundation for Prospective Studies and Initiatives, 2003, p. 14). The EU has not accepted that the label of 'terrorist' applies to all those identified as such by Moscow. Particular anger was expressed by the Russian government against the Danish and British governments in 2003 for allowing entry into their countries of Akhmed Zakaev, the representative in Europe of Aslan Mashkhadov, a former elected president of Chechnya who was a key leader of the secessionist movement there. Moscow condemns Zakaev as a terrorist. Trubnikov, the Russia First Deputy Foreign Minister, complained in 2003 that 'even now we are confronted with manifestations of political shortsightedness and lack of statesmanship or appeasement of terrorists and double standards' (Trubnikov, 2003, p. 39). Even the school hostage crisis in Beslan, North Ossetia in early September 2004 became a source of friction with the EU. The call by the Dutch Foreign Minister, Bernard Bot, during the Dutch presidency of the EU, for an explanation of 'how this tragedy could have happened' was regarded by the Russian Foreign Minister Sergei Lavrov as 'insolent' (EUPolitix.com, 2004). The area of terrorism is one in which Russia is generally closer to the USA than it is to the EU (Grigor'evna, 2002).

FOREIGN AND SECURITY POLICY AND THE IRAQ WAR

The idea of a common space of external security was largely based, according to Romano Prodi, former President of the EU, on the idea that the views of Russia and the EU converged on many international problems such as the Middle East and the proliferation of weapons of mass destruction. The potential here was to enhance cooperation within international fora (Prodi, 2004) such as the UN, to which Russia with its depleted power now attaches greater significance than it did in the Soviet era. The Iraq war seemed to indicate that such common fronts might be possible. The Russian, French and German governments tried to come to a common position on the role of the UN in resolving the Iraq crisis

(Joint Declaration by Germany, France and Russia on Iraq, 2003). With the apparent increasing unilateralism of the USA, many saw the value of Europe and Russia coming together as a possible counterweight (Young, 2002). Indeed some Western observers have argued that hoping to drive a wedge between the USA and the EU is part of Russian security strategy (Light et al., 2000, p. 501). However, Iraq also showed the dangers of this for both Russia and the EU. First, the EU itself did not have a common position on Iraq given the differences between the UK and several new members states such as Poland on the one hand and France and Germany on the other. Second, being seen to exploit divisions between Europe and the USA could backfire on Russia badly. While labelling US actions in Iraq as a 'gross historical mistake', Moscow has been careful not to slip into anti-Americanism, realizing that many of its broader security concerns on terrorism and proliferation of weapons of mass destruction cannot be tackled without US support (Primakov, 2004, p. 29). Third, given the new direction of Russian foreign policy, Russia has no intention of locking itself into a bloc with the EU (Yasmann, 2004). As we have seen, foreign policy decisions are made on the basis of Russia's interests at the time, especially economic. The Iraq war was to highlight this above all. Russia was faced with a dilemma – 'to support the close alliance with the US and the West in the struggle with terrorism and not to argue with the Arab world. Also we have our own strategic and economic interests' (Burlatskii, 2002). Iraq owed $8 billion to Russia and the business and political élite feared that any successor regime to Saddam Hussein may not honour that debt. Moreover, a war imperilled Russia's investments, including its oil contracts. Any new government could review all oil contracts and Russian companies, especially Lukoil, could lose out (Tikhonov, 2002). In addition, it was feared that war would destabilize an already volatile region close to Russia's borders and disrupt the collective defence against Islamic extremists in Central Asia (Burlatskii, 2002). These were issues that made Russia seek a potential common line with France and Germany but not establish any form of bloc to oppose the USA. After all, it was recognized that the USA would ultimately determine whether Lukoil would be allowed to maintain a share in the extraction of oil in a postwar Iraq. 'Unofficially Russian diplomats recognize that the question of Russian oil contracts in post-Saddam Iraq stands on the order of the day in all consultations with the US on Iraq' (*Izvestiya*, 23 November 2002, p. 2). Ultimately Putin received assurances about Russian interests at the Bush–Putin Summit on 22 November 2002 (*Izvestiya*, 23 November 2002, p. 2). In any case the USA understood that the period when Moscow was siding with Germany and France over Iraq was precisely when it needed their support during the negotiations with the EU over the status of Kaliningrad (Yasmann, 2004).

The Russians have generally been positive to the development of a European Security and Defence Policy. This contrasts with their view of NATO, which they see as ultimately a vestige of the Cold War (Mahncke, 2001, pp. 430–32). This, however, was conditional on it being separate from NATO and pursuing a more pan-European dimension to security, which should include a partnership with Russia (Webber, 2001, pp. 414–15). There has been some EU–Russia security cooperation, such as Russian participation in the EU-led police mission in Bosnia at the beginning of 2003. Much work has been done on developing the practical and legal aspects of future cooperation in the areas of conflict prevention, crisis management and post-conflict reconstruction. The EU has also offered itself as a potential partner to settle conflicts in areas such as Transdnestr and the South Caucasus (Prodi, 2004, p. 6). The problem is that much of the 'work' has been of a pro forma quality. There has been a lack of real practical coordination between the EU and Russia in crisis prevention in the former Soviet Union and the Balkans. For some observers the problem has been Moscow's preference for keeping any Russian role distinctive (Gomart, 2003), and in particular it has insisted that in the former Soviet space it leads the way rather than engaging in joint moves. In November 2003 it unilaterally proposed a settlement to the Transdnestr conflict to which the EU objected (Yasmann, 2004). Any systematic cooperation will depend on the way in which the larger security architecture for Europe is developed over the next few years, including the future of NATO and its relationship with the EU's ESDP. Russia's interest in a European security dialogue at present is to influence the debate and ensure that the Europeans take Russia's interests into consideration (Webber, 2001).

Regional Integration

While it is difficult to see all 89 regions and republics of Russia being affected by EU norms, EU expansion has raised the possibility that those bordering the EU would be allowed to integrate more with their EU neighbours. The concept of the Northern Dimension was informed by this agenda. In 1997 the Finnish government prompted the EU to develop a cooperative relationship with Russia in the Barents–Baltic region (Archer, 2000, p. 208). The Dimension attempts to engage such regions of Russia as the city of St Petersburg, Novgorod, the Leningrad Region and the Republic of Karelia in cooperation with adjoining EU states. At present it involves a number of infrastructural projects, environmental protection, cooperation on organized crime and interregional exchanges. However, Russia has complained of the scheme's 'overwheening focus' on environmental issues and the lack of funding for it (Ivanov, 2001). Nevertheless such a 'dimensionalist' approach to EU–Russian relations, involving greater regional devolution and encouragement of transnationalism, could also provide a way for the Kaliningrad enclave to integrate with the surrounding Baltic states and thereby prevent it becoming an island of underdevelopment surrounded by the EU (Makarychev, 2003). EU aid, albeit with limited effect, has been extended for specific projects, for example tackling the environmental problems of the region (Babkin, 2002, p. 4). The Russian government in 1996 established Kaliningrad as a 'Special Economic Zone within which many legal procedures have been simplified to attract foreign and Russian investors'. However, a conflict of laws between the region and the centre and the frequency with which the centre would change its mind about local concessions meant a lack of continuity and stability which has actually inhibited foreign investment (Kortunov, 2003, pp. 115–17). In this way the idea of greater regional autonomy which could facilitate integration with the EU still conflicts with the arbitrariness of central authority and the desire of Moscow to keep the centrifugal forces of regionalism in check lest they lead to the break-up of Russia. Although the present political tendency is towards centralization of political control, Russia's regions have always been able to exert a degree of autonomy. Currently, 'the élite's support for both stronger central government and regional and local self-governance reveals a rather hybrid approach to the federation under Putin' (Steen, 2003, p. 116). However, although regionalism may be seen as a way to greater integration with the EU, it will always be vulnerable to the historic tension between the centrifugal and centripetal forces in Russia.

In any case it would be a mistake to assume too Eurocentric a view of Russia's regions. While Moscow may prioritize the Euro-Atlantic relationship, many regions of Russia are focused elsewhere. For many, full integration with the EU and the adoption of EU regulations would actually be inhibiting economically. Those regions in the south and east of the Russian Federation are concerned to remain free to undertake trade with neighbours across their borders unhindered by regulations which are geared to trading with the EU. At a State Council meeting in 2002, Guzhvin, the governor of Astrakhan, urged on the government a closer regional association with Iran, a fellow littoral partner on the Caspian Sea (State Council of Russia, 2003, p. 15–18). While the making of official foreign policy is highly centralized in the Kremlin in practice, through economic relations in particular the regions do play an influential role in the actual conduct of foreign relations (Herd and Aldis, 2003).

KEY PROBLEMS OF THE RUSSIAN–WESTERN RELATIONSHIP

One problem for Russia in dealing with the EU is that it still does not speak with one voice in foreign and security policy. This makes it difficult for strategic partners (Prodi, 2004). In particular it is difficult for Russian officials to distinguish those issues on which the EU is speaking as a coherent actor and the European Commission makes the running and those issues on which it is the views of specific member states that count. It is therefore difficult for a Russian diplomatic corps to know how to influence decision making in the EU. Their experience is still one of dealing with individual states (Bordachev, 2000).

There is also disappointment in Russia at what appears to be sluggishness of decision making towards Russia within the EU (Shevtsova, 2003, p. 210). This slowness is to some extent an aspect of delays associated with the whole enlargement process. For much of the 1990s the initiative for enlargement came from the Commission itself and was not a priority for individual member states. Member states concentrated on the project of further integration more than widening to the East. Even so, as the enlargement process moved to the fore towards the end of the 1990s, the EU has become consumed with the intricacies of incorporation of so many new states and the need to reform its own institutions to accommodate them. Attention to the detail of how to create 'the common spaces' with Russia therefore moved along on the piecemeal basis of dealing with very specific problems affected by enlargement such as Kaliningrad rather than building anything broader. This slowness is not helped by the fact that within Europe the political and public constituency that championed Russia and its integration into Europe has declined since the Gorbachev and Yeltsin days.

Much of the EU–Russia relationship is also hampered in practice by a mutual lack of understanding and cultural distance. As a high-ranking employee in the Russian Cabinet of Ministers complained, 'the mentality of European officials is stuck in the mid-1990s, they do not know anything about Russia, do not want to do anything and only when you sit them opposite a Russian colleague, do they thaw and begin to say how important this cooperation is for both sides' (Babaeva, 2002). In addition, there are still cultural differences over the processes of negotiation between officials and diplomats. The operation of the NATO–Russia Permanent Joint Council had been problematic because NATO's culture of consensus had conflicted with Moscow's more top–down approach to collaboration and fear of its own officials 'going native' (Matser, 2001/2002, p. 20).

The development of cooperation is also affected by a whole range of practical problems. In the case of security, joint actions are hampered by the technical differences between Russian and NATO/EU forces. The problem of reliability and interoperability limits the possibilities of Russian contribution to joint operations (Webber, 2001, pp. 418–22). In the area of business the building of a broader vision of the common economic space with the EU and Russia's membership of the WTO is hampered by a lack of structural reform and lack of competitiveness. A key feature of the Russian economy is the predominance of governmental–private forms of ownership. Almost two-thirds of all assets belong to this form of ownership. In addition Russian business is dominated by integrated business groups which have established their own financial structures – banks, marketing organizations, insurance companies and so on. These replace the standard institutional and financial structures which operate in developed economies. A 'virtual economy' exists in Russia which is based on a vast web of barter relationships between business and between them and government. While competitiveness is increasing, some 40 per cent of business still runs at a loss. Many are sustained by informal relationships and survival networks. All this undermines the operation of a market economy and limits the potential for integration with the EU (Jones and Fallon, 2003). From the Russian side there is also suspicion of Western economic intentions. EU anti-dumping measures are suspected of being a case of EU protectionism, as are the standards imposed by the EU on imports of Russian machinery, chemical and agricultural goods (Ivanov, 2001).

In addition, behind the image of increasing state power the continuities with the Yeltsin 'system' are still there. Organized crime and corruption are still endemic and reach the higher levels of the system. As of 2003, 93 of the Duma's 450 members were under criminal investigation at the time of their election. Estimates suggest that some 10 000 organized crime groups have divided the country up and take protection money from state and private and foreign businesses (Stratfor Analysis, 2003). Although Putin is known for taking on the 'oligarchs' from the Yeltsin era, in fact new oligarchs have been created that are close to him (Hoffman, 2002). As a European Commission report noted in 2004, 'The recent spectacular moves against the leaders of some of these groups (large financial–industrial groups) are very popular with domestic public opinion but do not necessarily mean that the Kremlin is committed to moving away from the current model of 'oligarchic' capitalism' (European Commission, 2004d, p. 11).

CONCLUSION

Since 2000 there has been a qualitative change in the relations between Russia and the West. The earlier declarations of intent about partnership tended to mask suspicions and resentments that were vestiges of the Cold War. Now both Russia and the West recognize areas of mutual interest and have come together against shared threats. However, the relationship is based on practical need and national interests, and is largely confined to dealing with specific issues. The capacity and will to go beyond this and build something broader, such as the full integration of Russia into the EU, is limited. This is not simply a consequence of Putin's 'pragmatic nationalism' or the EU being consumed by the need to settle immediate problems arising out of the expansion of the EU. It derives from the fact that Russia is now on a different path of development from the rest of Europe. While the EU project is concerned with developing new types of governance – eliminating borders, transnationalism, multi-level governance, the hollowing out of the state and even the dilution of the functions of the nation-state – Russia for the time being is concerned with reconstructing the central state after almost 15 years of chaos (Shevtsova, 2003, p. 266).

Putin's new Westernism is also derived from Russia's greater assertiveness, which means independence in foreign policy choices. Integration with the EU would mean an unacceptable loss of sovereignty (Yasmann, 2004). As this chapter has shown, the relationship with the EU needs to be considered within the overall framework of Russia's foreign policy. While Russia seeks a closer relationship with the EU, it also asserts the freedom to pursue other relationships in line with its own interests. In particular, the relationship with the USA continues to be important, not only because of the specific area of security and terrorism, but also because it accords with Russia's perception of itself as not just another European country but a power which also operates on the world stage. In view of this, the likely scenario for future relations between Russia and the West is one of cooperation, adaptation and mutual dependence where beneficial to both parties on the basis of shared interests. It is unlikely that the talk of creating 'common spaces' in Europe will turn into anything like a unified Eurasian mass, but rather will consist of agreement to play by similar rules in those areas where mutual benefits require it. In this way Russia will remain perhaps what it has always been – part of Europe but also apart from it (Baranovsky, 2000).

PART IV

Policy Sectors and Issues

9. Governing the third pillar: institutional development and external relations in Justice and Home Affairs before and after 11 September

Paul Norman

INTRODUCTION

This chapter examines the developing governance of the third pillar and how the Justice and Home Affairs (JHA) dimension of European Union (EU) external relations has been affected by the events of 11 September 2001. The EU's legal and strategic policy frameworks for integration in JHA had already been established, respectively within the Treaty of Amsterdam and at the Tempere European Council (European Council, 1999a); however these were substantially unrealized despite a number of innovations that sought to overcome the limits of governance within JHA cooperation (Norman, 1999). The innovations included greater strategic continuity for the multi-annual planning of work programmes but also the development of meso-level policy communities within and outside the EU, to implement to the strategic objectives of the European Council (and the Group of Eight – G8) particularly in action against 'organized crime'. But the participation of the EU in the 'war on terrorism' in the aftermath of 11 September, and the consequent elevation of counter-terrorism as a 'major policy objective', proved to be a significant turning point for comprehensive attainment of the EU internal security objectives and its projection externally.

The EU's 'roadmap' against terrorism agreed in the aftermath of 11 September was ambitious. Internally, the EU and its member states launched a significant programme to realize a diverse range of criminal police and judicial policy initiatives, operational action and institution building, with political agreement on contentious issues such as the abolition of extradition and the establishment of the judicial cooperation agency

EuroJust. The speed and cross-pillar breadth of this response following the attacks was remarkable given the discontinuous pattern of crises and institutional inertia that had characterized EU–JHA cooperation since its inception (Norman, 1999). However, more than this, den Boer and Monar also highlight that 'September 11 must be regarded as the first truly "cross pillar" test of the Union's role as a security actor' (2002, p. 11). Therefore 11 September provided an opportunity to the EU for radical action to implement strategic objectives in the field of criminal police and judicial cooperation, in the name of counter-terrorism, but extending into the EU's Common Foreign and Security Policy (CFSP) and with a more structured deployment of external relations instruments to support achievement of JHA policy objectives. This second focus, on the field of JHA action in the EU's 'external relations' in relation to third states, will be examined in relation to the USA and Russia.

The reinvigoration of the external relations dimension of JHA highlighted, albeit obliquely, one of the main limitations of EU–JHA cooperation up to that point – a strong focus upon the internal security of the Union and the challenge of ten new entrants in 2004 (Monar, 2000). Tackling international and transnational offending, whatever its form, requires a broad scope of action, and one not hindered by the policy silos of specific Councils of Ministers. As will be seen below, EU counter-terrorism has required a reappraisal of strategy across the pillars of the Union, and in relation to EU external relations with third states and other international organizations. Despite the forging of ambitious plans in 2002 and 2003, the 2004 train bombings in Madrid again highlighted some loss of momentum within the EU JHA field after a hiatus of political agreement on the development of policies and institutions to tackle cross-border crime and terrorism. Madrid refocused the minds of Heads of States within the European Council (European Council, 2004), with a recognition that despite the internal and external rancour over the invasion of Iraq the threat was not just 'out there' and that concrete sustained action was still required to implement political agreements and undertakings. Therefore to provide a broad overview of governance in the third pillar this chapter will examine the EU's third pillar, but in relation to both counter-terrorism and external relations.

THIRD-PILLAR GOVERNANCE, 1993 TO 2001

The development of third-pillar governance during this period can be regarded as a number of integration phases where treaty changes or presidency initiatives have overcome 'legislative blockages'. Many of the Council presidency initiatives have been the most politicized attempts to move the Union forward in the field of JHA, the stimuli often being responses to unplanned events, with the EU's response to 11 September being the latest. The main 'pushes' commenced with the decision, anticipating ratification of the Maastricht Treaty on European Union (TEU), to create the hierarchical Council formation for intergovernmental[1] cooperation for police, customs and immigration services in 1992. The pressure for such change came from the abolition of internal border controls in the Single European Act and realization that security and law enforcement coordination across a range of criminal investigation and border control agencies was critical to secure the 'external frontiers' of the Union and to maintain the perceived levels of internal security (Home Affairs Committee, 1990). The ratification of the TEU in November 1993 formalized a process under way to create a hierarchical and more transparent system of governance (Hayes-Renshaw and Wallace, 1997, p. 94) but fractured by the three 'pillars' – the community method within the EC treaties (first pillar) and intergovernmental cooperation within the Common, Foreign and Security Policy (second pillar) and Justice and Home Affairs (third pillar). The TEU introduced a formal framework for EU cooperation and a justicable legal basis for international agreements between the member states of the EU (Art. K.6). For the inaugural third pillar, the model was overwhelmingly intergovernmental, reliant upon unanimous agreement, with an attenuated role for the Commission and no meaningful practical role for the European Parliament, let alone national parliaments, in the scrutiny of legislative initiatives (Art. K.11). This new policy domain of JHA cooperation was capped by the collective political authority of the justice and interior ministers from the member states in a new JHA Council.

The first JHA governance arrangements proved to be disappointing. The early decision-making processes of the third pillar were characterized by tortuous negotiations and extended delays, exemplified in the drafting of two key legal texts, the Europol Convention and the Convention on Mutual Legal Assistance. Decision making based on principles of unanimity resulted in a lack of agreement on the appropriate role of the European Court of Justice, the inability to agree uniform standards of data protection, the demand for meaningful external accountability mechanisms, and ultimately no common view of which way Europol should develop in the future.[2] The growing crisis in third-pillar governance was exacerbated by the UK's obstructionism during the BSE crisis (Statewatch, 1996), and its ideological predilections against the European Court of Justice (Duff, 1997, pp. 186–7). It was widely seen that a flawed system of JHA governance had encumbered member states where a single 'Eurosceptic' administration could exploit the weaknesses of intergovernmental cooperation, prevent agreement and ultimately the attainment of the objectives of the Union.

The Treaty of Amsterdam introduced a revised legislative process with a number of attractive innovations that forged links between the JHA Council with other EU institutions, including a formal consultation role for the European Parliament (Art. 39.1). The political will to improve what had become a dysfunctional JHA policy process spurred the Irish presidency in the latter half of 1996 to initiate change in advance of ratification of the Treaty of Amsterdam. But the focus of the second major policy push came weeks afterwards, in the Irish presidency's response to the seemingly domestic issue of the assassination of an investigative journalist Veronica Guerin early in the presidency period (International Press Institute, 2000). That event spurred the Irish government to promote domestic legislation, but also broad-based EU action against 'organized crime', the creation of the EU's first JHA High Level Group (on organized crime) and subsequent EU Action Plan Against Organized Crime (Norman, 1999) with its enhanced focus on the achievement and implementation of agreed policy outcomes. This novel but sustained Irish presidency initiative uniquely established the institutional space for the General Secretariat of the Council, servicing national member states cooperating in the Council of the EU, to develop ongoing specific expertise in the field with the seconding of 'eight national experts and practitioners' (Council of the EU, 1997, p. 6), thereby providing the technical prerequisites for increased continuity between, and support for, the rotating Presidencies in the JHA sphere – a role performed by the Commission under the first pillar.

Crucial to the success of this second JHA policy push by the Irish presidency was the effective depoliticization of policy formation, legislative development and institutional construction in the decisive move to selective horizontal policy integration, underpinned by the informal devolution of executive responsibility to the 'High Level' group. This provided for the first time strategic orientation to the third pillar, but at the operational level also ensured concrete action on a wide front. The 1996 Irish presidency, in the name of action against 'organized crime', was key to changing third-pillar governance and gained high level endorsement at the European Council (Dublin II) in December 1996. This important outcome somewhat unconventionally circumvented the problematic third-pillar structures – in creating the 'High Level Group on Organized Crime' – and provided the temporary policy 'cement' for the coordination of JHA policy development and implementation across the three pillars. The Council's review of the effectiveness of the Action Plan on Organized Crime (updated at Vienna in December 1998) acknowledged that 'the Plan of Action helped to create the political and professional climate required on both the EU level and the national level to take and implement the necessary decisions' (Council of the EU, 2000, p. 2). This expedient corralling of a wide range of stalled legislative initiatives in the ordinary criminal police and judicial cooperation sphere in terms of concerted EU action to combat 'organized crime' proved to be a deft presidency ruse that assuaged the anticipated domestic political opposition to deepening JHA integration and brought much needed strategic direction to the JHA Council in the Action Plan's 15 Political Guidelines. The JHA Council sanctioned a successor to the High Level Group, the Multi-Disciplinary Group (MDG) on Organized Crime, in July 1997 providing for a continued focus on strategy and its implementation and crucially in external relations, principally with reference to the accession states.

The MDG signalled a nascent strategy focus on external relations in JHA, developing a close working relationship and ultimately a meso-level policy community with the 'Group of Eight' (or G8) Senior Experts Group on Transnational Organized Crime facilitated by the UK's concurrent presidency of both the EU and the G8 (Norman, 1999, pp. 110–14; Wrench, 1997). Focusing on 'transnational organized crime', and later 'cyber crime', the resulting overlapping networks of state actors 'possessing specialist skills and expertise' empowered within the transnational context of EU G8 (Norman, 2001; 1999). Remarkably, some of the EU 'working methods' during this interregnum entailed tabling G8 agreements at JHA Councils for adoption, once again bypassing the third-pillar policy-making processes entirely (Norman, 1999, p. 113).

The move from the formal intergovernmentalism of the original third pillar, to a reliance on non-treaty-based mechanisms designed to enhance effectiveness and efficiency of the JHA policy domain, thereby increased its 'output legitimacy' (Horeth, 1999, p. 251) but also had a clear transnational impact. The EU's growing orientation towards globalized crime concerns keyed into the Transatlantic Partnerships with the USA and Canada, to the G8 and to a lesser extent the Council of Europe (Norman, 1999, pp. 114–17). This period, mediated by the Irish then UK presidencies, was the precursor to the development of a more systematic and gradated network of transnational relationships that moved from informality to more of a formal basis with a number of 'Common Strategies'[3] and the development of six monthly presidency work programmes concerning external relations in JHA, and regular monitoring of these by the European Council. This developing external orientation significantly broadened the scope of the EU–JHA integration vision, particularly with ratification of the Treaty of Amsterdam and the special Justice and Home Affairs European Council (Tempere) in October 1999 focusing upon cross-border crime issues and relations with other states. Given the above Council mechanisms focused upon organized crime, the overall coherence of third-pillar policy development, implementation and institution building was now underpinned by two parallel tracks of activity, that on organized crime on the one hand and on an Area of Freedom, Security and Justice on the other (Monar, 2001, pp. 758–60). In reality, there was significant overlap in the criminal police and judicial cooperation components of the Action Plans, ultimately resulting in a decision to merge the twin-track approach with a new Strategy for the Beginning of the New Millennium published in May 2000. In common with the original High Level Group's approach, this sought to provide overall strategic coherence to the governance of JHA cooperation with a series of Political Guidelines, specific recommendations and delineated institutional responsibilities. Further, the Commission's new-found cross-pillar role under the provisions of the Treaty of Amsterdam introduce a formal pressure point to ensure member state implementation of JHA policies. Most visible was the transparent six monthly Commission 'Scoreboard' of measures outlining progress made towards the attainment of the 'Area of Freedom, Security and Justice' (Commission, 2002a).

This period of dynamic development of third-pillar governance was recognized tangentially in the Commission's White Paper on European Governance (Commission, 2001a) via proposals on strategic guidance for the third pillar, consultation in legislative processes and the discipline of an 'impact assessment' for legislative proposals. Clear strategic guidance to the JHA Council on the Union's ultimate integration ambitions come to the fore with the High Level Group on Organized Crime and latterly in the ambitions in the Treaty of Amsterdam. Contrary to the second pillar (TEU, Art. 13), the European Council is not formally cited in the provisions of the TEU and thus does not have a routine obligation to provide strategic guidance to the third pillar/JHA Council (Curtin, 1993, p. 27; O'Keefe, 1995, pp. 895–7). This 'omission', rectified in the Constitution for Europe, had placed greater responsibilities upon the rotating presidency, most particularly in the phase before the Treaty of Amsterdam when the Commission had limited powers of legislative initiative (excluding police and judicial cooperation in criminal matters and customs cooperation, TEU, Art. K.2). Elsewhere it has been argued that this 'depoliticized' and thereby facilitated EU action but at some cost to transparency and accountability (Norman, 1999, pp. 106–10), which Anderson and Burns have characterized as 'an instance of post-Parliamentary governance' (1998, p. 227) where 'negotiations, policy making and implementation takes place in thousands of specialized policy settings' (ibid., p. 229). In this case, they were also conducted in an increasingly transnational context, placing a greater weight of responsibility upon national political executives to provide strategic guidance (and *de facto* legitimacy) (Commission, 2001a).

By the time of the June 2002 Seville European Council it was clear that the Council's own efforts to reform its institutional arrangements in advance of enlargement (European Council, 2002, Annex II) had been accepted with immediate effect. For the European Council this entailed a 'substantial change to present practices in the direction of enhancing the efficiency of the institution' (European Council, 2002, p. 2). Specifically the reforms to governance of the third pillar included the development of a 'multi annual strategic programme' dovetailed to the 'annual operating programme of activities' for each of the Councils but, crucially, agreed by the next two presidencies. In JHA external relations this innovation had already been in place since January 2001 with an annual presidency work programme for external relations in JHA being endorsed by three Presidencies (Presidency of the Council of the EU, 2001, p. 1). Before examining this deepening and developing external relations focus to JHA across a broader geographic terrain, the specific impact of 11 September on JHA governance will now be briefly assessed.

THE EVENTS OF 11 SEPTEMBER 2001 AND THIRD-PILLAR GOVERNANCE

Throughout the period of 1993 to 2001 the profile of EU counter-terrorism was extremely low but 11 September changed all that. Overnight the domain of EU counter-terrorist cooperation became one of the most high-profile areas of cooperation between EU member states and, as will be seen below, perhaps one of the most effective accelerators to JHA integration. Within days of George Bush declaring 'war on international terrorism' the Commission prepared two key proposals on combating terrorism setting common EU definitions of terrorist offences, and the European Arrest Warrant effectively abolishing extradition between EU member states (Commission, 2001b; 2001c). The JHA Council met on 20 September to agree the 'EU counter-terrorism roadmap', endorsed on 21 September by a special European Council meeting (European Council, 2001a). The unprecedented speed and breath of the EU response merits detailed assessment in light of the above analysis of third-pillar governance. The EU's actions were a major step change in decision taking and the tight timetable set out in the 'roadmap' required an 'accelerated consultation procedure' to be put into place to meet its formal consultation obligations to the European Parliament. It was seen above that implementation is now one of the key impediments to effectiveness in third-pillar governance and this aspect will be addressed in considering the EU's response to 11 September.

The JHA Council Conclusions of 20 September set out a far-reaching 'roadmap' of EU action in four main areas: counter-terrorism within the EU, cooperation between EU police and intelligence agencies, the financing of terrorism and EU–US cooperation (JHA Council, 2001). The roadmap is now continuously updated[4] with allied initiatives and actions, recording progress made by the EU institutions and the member states (Presidency of the Council of the EU, 2002). The main elements will be examined with reference to actual EU action and the analysis of third-pillar governance affecting three main areas relevant to the current focus: the effectiveness of policy formation, institution building and the legislative process.

In examining the effectiveness of policy formation there has been a substantial deepening of criminal legal integration allied to concerted efforts to secure member state implementation of a wide range of international legal commitments (for example signed but unratified EU, Council of Europe and UN agreements) as part of efforts 'stepping up the fight against terrorism within the EU'. The EU responded both to early indications of European links to the al-Qaeda terrorist suspects, as well as to ambitious plans to secure unanimous agreement on the replacement of the current extradition arrangements between EU member states with a 'European Arrest Warrant', ratification of two EU extradition conventions[5] and agreement on 'common definition of terrorism and penalties' (JHA Council, 2001). Agreeing a definition of terrorism is key to the whole strategy and this Framework Decision was adopted on 13 June 2002, albeit six months after political agreement (Presidency of the Council of the EU, 2002, p. 13). The EU-wide definition of terrorism set the basis for facilitating extradition of suspects between EU member states and so on, but it also raised the problem of distinguishing between 'internal' domestic terrorist groups (which may be offending internationally or transnationally) and 'international terrorism'. The extent of the Commission's suggested common list of terrorist groups showed that 'internal terrorism' had been initially excluded and that the list was also dominated by Arab groups (Commission, 2001d, Annex 1). While understandable in the immediate aftermath of 11 September, the initial focus on Arab groups did fuel criticism of the measures by not encompassing other groups deploying political violence from around the world, partly assuaged by the final Council Decision (Council of the EU, 2001). Further, the scope of the definition of terrorism appeared to include environmental and animal rights activists (Commission, 2001b, Arts 3f. and 3h) despite the European Council's laborious presentation of the measures as a response to UN Security Council Resolution 1373 passed in the immediate aftermath of 11 September (European Council, 2001b, para. 17).

The EU extradition conventions of 1995 and 1996 demonstrate how member state implementation of EU conventions has been problematic, with extended delays in securing national ratification. On 11 September only two-thirds of member states had ratified both, but by July 2002 progress had been made, with 13 member states ratifying both, with France and Italy still outstanding on both conventions. These conventions have now come into force between those ratifying member states who 'made a declaration to that effect' (European Council, 2001b, para. 17). The UN Security Council's focus upon the financing of terrorism after 11 September resulted in EU agreement on measures that cut across all pillars with, for example, the 'automatic information transfer between national financial intelligence units' and the EU extension of the freezing of assets to those charged with terrorist offences (JHA Council, 2001; Presidency of the Council of the EU, 2002, p. 13). Further, in EU's foreign and external relations portfolios the roadmap spurred efforts to increase third state ratification of UN legal instruments, with the threat of 'measures' against those states failing to comply with Financial Action Task Force orders relating to money laundering legislation and enforcement, etc., a strategy reminiscent of G8 action during the 1990s against organized crime and money laundering (Norman, 1999). In the event COREPER did agree a common text to be included in all EU third-party agreements but recoiled from the use of sanctions, instead favouring dialogue and assistance in building capacities in individual states including through regional agreements such as EuroMediterranean Partnership (Commission, 2002b; Council of the EU, 2002d).

In examining the third-pillar institution-building measures included in the roadmap the immediate priority was extension of the remit of EU's nascent judicial cooperation institution (or 'ProEuroJust') from criminal policing to counter-terrorism (by 15 October 2001) with full operation of the EuroJust (JHA Council, 2001) achieved in February 2002. In practice it was July before rules of procedure and agreement on Community funding had been settled (Presidency of the Council of the EU, 2002, p. 12). The more operationally oriented investigative measures to facilitate 'cooperation between the police and intelligence services' focused upon the creation of institutional structures between the EU bodies of Europol and EuroJust and the members states' authorities. These included the Tempere counter-terrorism Joint Investigation Teams composed of police and magistrates (European Council, 1999a, para. 43) agreed in June 2002 and anticipating Article 13 of the unratified EU Convention on Mutual Assistance in Criminal Matters (Council of the EU, 2002c).

In assessing the legislative process during this period it is seen that many of the political agreements made and announced in December 2001 by the Council were successfully translated into third-pillar legislative instruments during 2002. The apparently facilitative environment established by the EU's response to 11 September has perhaps extended mutual recognition most significantly with the introduction of the European Arrest Warrant and the establishment of EuroJust (Monar, 2002, pp. 129–32). But increasingly attention is being focused upon further powers for Europol – such as the power to request that member states initiate criminal investigations – and even the replacement of the Europol Convention with a Framework Decision (the legal basis for EuroJust) so that amendments could be made more expeditiously without the need for national ratification.[6] It could be said that the measures put into place after 11 September have finally resulted in the death of the EU third-pillar convention for institution building – a keen intergovernmental brake on JHA integration – with a consequent shift in the balance of powers between the JHA Council and national legislatures.

Evaluation of the implementation of EU member states' third-pillar agreements was seen above in the 'peer evaluation' mechanisms as part of a Council strategy, mediated by the General Secretariat of the Council, to ensure member state compliance with third-pillar agreements and commitments. Perhaps indicative of the qualitative change in the operation and working culture of the third pillar, the counter-terrorism roadmap extends these mechanisms to national counter-terrorism efforts a somewhat ambitious foray into a nationally sensitive area of policing (JHA Council, 2001), with all member states being examined by the end of 2002 (Presidency of the Council of the EU, 2002, p. 18).

The extension of the additional formal legal and investigative powers within the counter-terrorism roadmap was great, and many of the ambitious political agreements have resulted in successful legislative outcomes in 2002. These have significantly deepened integration on mutual recognition in the 'security' aspects of the EU's creation of an area of freedom, security and justice (Monar, 2000, pp. 140–41; Grabbe, 2001, pp. 73–5) and also transformed the EU's JHA external relations vision into an increasingly practical reality between the EU's 'privileged partners' and increasingly its near neighbours and its trading partners. This area will now be examined in relation to the development of JHA external relations.

DEVELOPING IMPACT OF EXTERNAL RELATIONS IN JHA

Both the USA, a 'traditional partner', and Russia have been selected to illustrate how JHA external relations have developed before and after 11 September. Writing soon after the attack on 11 September, den Boer and Monar highlighted how the reaction of the EU would be seen as a cross-pillar security test for the EU. However, this had also to be seen in relation to preceding efforts to develop the external impact of EU JHA policies, so that context will also be reviewed. Before examining each example, it is relevant to note that the EU's counter-terrorism 'roadmap' required significant cross-pillar coordination by the General Affairs Council and since the attacks the EU has issued its own (cross-pillar) European Security Strategy (European Union, 2003). Its drafter, the High Representative for CFSP, now also has counter-terrorism responsibilities (overseen by a new Terrorism Intelligence Coordinator) and the position of JHA external relations has been reinforced to the extent that the Council's Three-Year Strategic Programme 2004–2006 aims for complete integration of JHA concerns in all external relations policies (Presidency of the Council of the EU, 2004, p. 3). Further, the 2004 accession of ten new countries has concurrently shifted the proximate boundaries of concern closer to Russia and the Mediterranean, notwithstanding the increased importance *per se* of these areas, which are witnessing upsurges in politically motivated violence.

The United States of America

The basis for cooperation with the USA is the EU's 'Transatlantic Dialogue' under the provisions of the 1996 New Transatlantic Agenda and accompanying Action Plan (EU USA, 1995, pp. 7–8). Since then, six monthly EU-US Summits have provided the focal point cooperation with ministerial and official meetings taking forward the JHA agenda. In the criminal policing field this contact has principally concerned organized crime and the coordination of the substantial work programme in this area within the G8 (Norman, 1999). Since 11 September the frequency of contacts, and the breadth and depth of cooperation, between the USA and the EU has changed dramatically (Council of the EU, 1999; 2004a). The EU's counter-terrorism roadmap identified EU–US cooperation as one of the four key areas of activity both at an operational and at a strategic level (JHA Council, 2001). For example, this resulted in formal agreement for US participation in EU Counter-Terrorist Task Forces and the counter-terrorist cooperation unit established at Europol in the aftermath of the attacks, but also the informal encouragement of immediate exchange of intelligence with the US authorities in anticipation of a formal agreement. This was later realized, extending to all forms of serious crime for non-personal, but also personal, data in December 2002 (Peers, 2003). In the judicial sphere, agreements based on Article 38 of the TEU on extradition and mutual legal assistance, the first of its kind in the JHA field, were again extended beyond terrorism to serious crime in general (Statewatch, 2002). The legal agreements were widely regarded as controversial given the death penalty in the USA, but were again envisaged at Tempere (European Council, 1999a, para. 60). By June 2003 negotiations had been completed and detailed work is now being undertaken to implement these agreements (Council of the EU, 2004a, p. 19).

In examining contemporary EU–US cooperation, it is clear that high-level cooperation and liaison now routinely takes place specifically on counter-terrorism, as well as the traditional agenda of action on organized crime. The commitments made in 2001 were further enhanced at the 2004 EU–US Summit following the Madrid bombings (EU USA, 2004). Aside from the summits, high-level joint meetings now take place with US Attorney General, the Secretary for Homeland Security and, on the EU side, the EU Counter-terrorism Coordinator and European Commission (ibid.). At the practical level, joint training programmes between criminal police and judicial practitioners were launched in 2004, presaging implementation of the EU–US agreements on extradition and mutual legal assistance, but also intelligence exchange between US law enforcement authorities and Europol.

Overall it is seen that after 11 September the JHA external relations between the USA and the EU have now undertaken a step change and become embedded in JHA specific joint legal agreements, and deepened into the cooperation agreements on practical police and judicial cooperation criminal matters. This range of strategic, legal and operational EU third-country agreements with the USA clearly sets the pace and tone in terms of the EU JHA external relations with its partners, with similar agreements likely with Canada in due course (Presidency of the Council of the EU, 2004, pp. 19–20). However, the key to understanding the possibilities, limits and ultimately impact of EU external relations in JHA is how the gradated relationships are now being formally established, not only with transatlantic partners but also other third countries. To help illustrate these differing dimensions to EU external relations in JHA, EU cooperation with Russia will now be examined.

The Russian Federation

The first formal basis for cooperation between the EU and Russia was the 1999–2004[7] Common Strategy. Within the joint aims to tackle 'common challenges' in Europe, including those on 'organized crime, money laundering, illegal trafficking in human beings and drug trafficking' (European Council, 1999b, Pt 1), the focus in JHA external relations has been upon judicial and police cooperation against organized crime, and administrative and judicial reform, but strategically linked to the external relations ambitions set out in the Tempere European Council Conclusions (Council of the EU, 2002e, s. 1). The parameters of police and judicial cooperation are set out in an action plan on organized crime signed in 2000 (ibid.), including the enhancement of cooperation between Europol and member states' liaison officers with the Russian authorities (European Council, 1999b, Pt I 4e). Even after 11 September, and joint statements on terrorism in October 2001 and November 2002, practical results in the JHA field have been stalled by a range of issues, including apparent economic bargaining and coupling of 'dossiers' by the Russian authorities, and increased tensions from the Russian side over the newly imposed visa regime for Russians entering the Eastern and Central European countries now in the EU, in particular the impact on Russians in the enclave of Kaliningrad (Council of the EU, 2003).

It is clear that there is a strategic determination on the part of the EU, despite ongoing concerns over political violence in Chechnya, to develop its relationship with Russia, including the JHA field (Council of the EU, 2004b, p. 5). Since 2004 this has been focused upon the 'four spaces' within the EU Russia Permanent Cooperation Council, established to increase the frequency of interaction and boost official cooperation at all levels, ensuring it is both 'efficient and transparent' (EU Russia, 2003, p. 2). In this reinvigorated political context moves 'towards the common space of freedom, security and justice' now promise 'vigorous' implementation of the Action Plan on Organized Crime, now some four years old, and attempts to realize the practical benefits of the 2003 agreement between the Russian Federation and Europol (ibid.).

CONCLUSION

This chapter has examined third-pillar governance through the policy sectors of counter-terrorism and JHA external relations. It was evident that the mid-1990s marked the development of transnationalization of JHA in general, but in particular with the traditional partners and the G8. However, this should be regarded as an informal precursor to the accelerated formal development of JHA in external relations after 11 September. What is now observed is the development of gradated transnational networks of cooperation, policy development and operational action at various stages of maturity and strategic intent. Whilst the vision was set out in 1999 at Tempere, the practical political realization and institutional infrastructure to support the longevity of strategic alliances is now being constructed. This change has also seen JHA develop into a genuine cross-pillar endeavour spurred by the counter-terrorism policy and institutional development and the increased transnational soft security role and responsibilities of the EU's foreign policy coordinator.

The progressive realization of the JHA external relations vision has also increased the importance of technocratic policy groups *vis-à-vis* parliamentary settings, and in particular at the national level in relation to JHA. Institution building, as has been seen after 11 September with EuroJust, now requires no national ratification procedures, in stark contrast to the genesis of Europol in the 1990s. Multi-annual strategic planning now provides long-term continuity and impetus between presidencies – key in JHA – but also limits intrusion of oversight, debate and accountability over this increasingly important transnational policy domain. While the benefits of international cooperation in JHA can now be increasingly realized in advance of the European Constitution, it is also clear that the EU and its member states need to realize the benefits of enhanced democratic accountability not only within an expanded Union, but also in its transnational engagements in the name of EU external relations and counter-terrorism.

NOTES

1. As noted by O'Keefe, this is not strictly intergovernmental as Title VI cites connections between the third pillar and other European Union institutions such as the European Parliament, the Commission and the Court of Justice. In addition, expenditure under this pillar may be charged to the Community budget (O'Keefe, 1995, pp. 903–4).
2. The Treaty of Amsterdam only partly addressed this bind by allowing conventions to come into force when half the member states have completed their national ratification procedures (Art. K.6.2.(d)).
3. These included Russia, Ukraine, the Mediterranean region and the western Balkans (Presidency of the Council of the EU, 1999, p. 1).
4. By COREPER. Versions include those of October 2001 (12800/01 REV 1), April 2002 (7686/02), May 2002 (8547/02), July 2002 (10773/02 REV 2), June 2004 (10586/04) and November 2004 (14330/04).
5. 1995 Convention on Simplified Extradition between member states of the EU (covering 'voluntary' agreement to extradition) and the 1996 Convention relating to Extradition (covering 'involuntary' extradition).
6. Amendment of the Europol Convention was required, for example, to allow Europol to participate in the Joint Investigation Teams.
7. The 1999 Common Strategy expired in June 2003, but was extended for one year until June 2004 (Council of the EU, 2003).

10. International terrorism and EU immigration, asylum and borders policy: the unexpected victims of 11 September 2001

Elspeth Guild

INTRODUCTION

What is the relationship between forced migration and terrorism in the European Union after the terrorist attacks of 11 September 2001? I will argue here that there is no direct relationship between forced migrants coming to Europe and the risk of terrorism in the EU. In so far as a relationship exists, it is indirect, the result of a displacement of linkages made at the political level about security and borders. Forced migration is only one form of border crossing, but it is the one which engages international human rights commitments directly. Forced migrants are normally classified by EU member states as asylum seekers and refugees.[1] In none of the 11 September and subsequent terrorist-related attacks have asylum seekers been directly or indeed indirectly implicated.[2] Movement by persons across borders has, however, been central to the 11 September 2001 US terrorist attacks in the form of foreign students, tourists and possibly irregular migrants.[3]

The first EU Justice and Home Affairs Council meeting following the US attacks took place on 20 September 2001 with an agenda exclusively devoted to the EU response on security and other measures to combat terrorism.[4] Four types of measures were adopted: first measures on judicial cooperation,[5] cooperation between police and intelligence services, cooperation with the USA, and measures at the border. Specifically the JHA Council agreed to strengthen the controls at the external borders of the EU; increase surveillance measures under Article 2(3) Schengen Implementing Agreement 1990,[6] reinforce checks on identity documents; extra measures regarding the issue of visas and cooperation at local consular offices; a network for information exchange on visas; more systematic entry of persons considered undesirable aliens in the Schengen Information System; a request to the Commission to re-examine the relationship between safeguarding internal security with human rights obligations, including those towards refugees; and examination of the risk of large-scale population movements as a result of heightened tensions.

The significance of the border and border controls as a mechanism for combating terrorism was thus firmly established in EU policy by 20 September 2001. By placing security in a territorial framework, the right to cross borders becomes a security issue. Citizens have the right to enter their state of nationality – it is for their security that the borders are being drawn. As borders are secured, so those individuals who have a claim to cross borders to seek protection become the victims of border-related anti-terrorism measures. Enhanced visa requirements, reinforced border controls, the displacement of border controls into third countries – these efforts are the ones which hit forced migrants most directly as those persons least able to obtain visas, and most vulnerable to border controls and their displacement.[7]

FORCED MIGRATION AND NATIONAL SECURITY

Immigration, asylum and national security have traditionally had an uneasy relationship. The right of citizens to the limitation of arbitrary exercise of state power is rarely extended in full to non-nationals. It is never extended as regards the right not to be expelled.[8] Among the principles which inform national security is the link which citizenship represents between the state and the individual as one of allegiance. The failure of the individual to respect this link in its most extreme form may result in an allegation of treason, one of the crimes for which the most severe penalties have traditionally been reserved.[9] A foreign national does not owe this duty of loyalty to the state; thus in the logic of national security he or she does not enjoy an equivalent protection from arbitrary state action based on security concerns.

This perception of the foreigner as outside the field of loyalty takes on another perspective when the foreigner is someone who has sought asylum. By seeking asylum, the individual makes an allegation against his or her country of origin that that country has broken the duty of protection towards its citizens as embodied in the asylum seeker him or herself. Such a claim is a challenge to the assessment which the host state (where the individual finds him or herself) makes in respect of the home state. Where the host state takes the view that the home state is perpetrating human rights abuses or sponsoring terrorism, there may be a convergence of the assessment of the host state and the asylum seeker, as in autumn 2002, in the case of Iraq. The host state may of course consider that the individual is not being truthful and in fact is closely associated with his or her state of origin and thus constitutes a national security threat. On the other hand, where the host state has good relations with the state of origin, to acknowledge the validity of the protection claim will be, in effect, to challenge the human rights record of the state of origin. In order to signal clearly which states will be protected against their disloyal citizens' claims of persecution, in the European Union in particular, the concept of a safe country of origin has been developed which sets out in a list of countries described as safe in law.[10] Nationals of those countries who seek protection are thus defined as probable tellers of lies and untruths, disloyal to their state and unworthy of protection. They are then, by this form of definition, presented as a security threat. Their acts are construed as the result of hidden motives. Hidden motives are suspect.[11] Their act of seeking protection is then categorized by the host state as showing a disregard for the obligations and duties of citizenship. From here the connection between treason and terrorism becomes a close one.

BORDERS, SECURITY AND TERRORISM

When, following the 11 September 2001 attacks in the USA, it became apparent that the persons suspected of perpetrating the attacks were foreigners in the USA, the issues of immigration and asylum became engaged. The fact that the alleged perpetrators of the attacks were of Arab origin, apparently nationals of countries outside the USA and European Union, created a link between foreignness and threat which would be central to the response in many ways. The focus encompassed the interaction of terrorism, borders and movement of persons. The transformation of US internal security by the new concept of homeland security is central. In the EU it was the focus on borders and border controls. The convergence of sovereignty, territory and security is the essence of the US strategy in the war against terrorism and has had important implications for the EU. The letter of 16 October 2001 from President Bush to the President of the European Commission, Romano Prodi, regarding the security imperatives of the USA as regards action in the European Union, demonstrates this interest clearly. Many of the areas where the US President requests action are related to the securing of EU borders as regards the movement of persons to and from the USA.[12]

Those foreigners who present the greatest challenge to the concepts of sovereignty and integrity of the border are forced migrants. Through the development of customary international law to the Geneva Convention relating to the protection of refugees 1951 and its 1967 protocol, the principle of non-refoulement of protection seekers has become defined by interior ministries as the central weakness of the border regime.[13] If a state no longer has the power to reject an alien seeking protection at the border and to refuse to permit him or her entry to the state, then the integrity of a system of national security which is hinged on the border is impaired. By reconfiguring national security as territorially placed, the USA and the EU member states have placed the forced migrant and his or her security at the centre of the debate about national security.

The forced migrant becomes the one individual (other than citizens) who has a right in international law to breach the security of the border. Thus the forced migrant is the individual who must be kept as far as possible from ever arriving at the border. For him or her, the border must be moved, by preference of the EU, within his or her state of origin through the application of visa requirements. Where this is not possible, agreements with surrounding countries are negotiated which place the question of patrolling the border on them so that persons should not be permitted to arrive at the state's borders unless fully equipped with every document that might be needed for entry.[14] The field of insecurity in a vision of security which is territorially bound relates to the breaching of the border's security. Those whose plight as protection seekers gives them a right to breach such security boundaries are dangerous by definition.

There are many aspects of the response to terrorism which indicate a dislocation. The 2003 campaign in respect of Iraq is only one example of a response which does not answer the question posed: was there a credible link between the regime of Saddam Hussein and terrorism, particularly in the form of al-Qaeda? Similarly there is a dislocation at the centre of the national security and sovereign border linkage. It is at odds with the realities of New York's Twin Towers, the Bali bombings[15] or the Mombasa, Kenya, attacks. In all cases the movement across the borders which occurred was entirely and completely lawful by persons who had all the correct and necessary documentation, issued by the state of origin and accepted as valid for entry into the host state. But the emphasis on national security as a borders-related issue becomes diverted away from the reality of who is lawfully crossing borders into an issue about the security threat which protection seekers present to the integrity of borders.

BORDERS, SECURITY AND A WAR ON INDIVIDUALS

There has been a further change in the nature of security which engages the nexus of territory, movement of persons and terrorism. A sovereign state, the USA has declared war on terrorism, an activity which is primarily non-state in nature.[16] Thus instead of a state enemy, the USA is faced with individuals working more or less closely together but not encompassed in the trappings of statehood. Thus the offensives on the one side at least in this war are attacks by or on individuals subject to immigration controls. The framework of movement of persons, in particular of Arab origin, across borders is no longer the natural manifestation of trade, commerce and tourism. Rather it is the field of threat both criminal and military. The definition of the border as a place of danger as regards criminal activity and military invasion takes on increased importance. Hence immigration controls take on a new significance in the war on terrorism.[17] The link among these individuals is no longer perceived as based on nationality or the fact of belonging to one state, but rather ethnicity and religious conviction. This transformation of the face of the enemy into an individual identifiable on the basis of racial profiling has been one of the most controversial of the post-11 September effects.

But the majority of the EU's forced migrants from 1992 to 2001 are persons coming from countries that are primarily Muslim. Of the top ten countries of origin of asylum applicants in the EU, seven are either predominantly Muslim, as in the cases of Turkey, Iraq, Afghanistan, Iran and Somalia, or a large proportion of the persons fleeing to the EU are Muslims, as in respect of the Former Republic of Yugoslavia, Bosnia and Herzegovina. These nationalities account for almost a quarter of the asylum seekers in the EU over the ten-year period.[18] Protection seekers are already often perceived as a security risk by definition because they alone among aliens are able to breach the border because of international commitments by states.

The 11 September 2001 attacks transformed the face of the foreigner into a *prima facie* face of terrorism. President Bush's declaration of war against terrorism had the consequence of placing the foreigner firmly on the territory of a military threat in addition to a police threat. The identity threat came directly from the Muslim specificity which was placed on the foreigner. Thus the political will for closure against foreigners as threats of high magnitude was apparent in the USA and throughout Europe personified by Muslims. However, against this designation of the border as a place of danger and the foreigner as the manifestation of threat, two logics create a contrary tension, those of economic liberalism and international human rights. So while the construction of the foreigner as a threat justifies the adoption of action and measures to close the border and expel foreign nationals, so industrial and commercial interests in freer borders and human rights obligations have been pushing in the other direction.

Before considering these alternative logics, one further observation on consequences of a response in the form of a war on terrorism is required. Terrorism is an activity, which is in essence carried out by individuals working together. The link between them in this case is religion, radical Islam, rather than citizenship or some other attribute. War is an interstate activity in which the soldier is the extension of the state and the means by which the state carries out its hostile action. A US war on terrorism, in effect, is the US state (in coalition with other states) carrying out hostile activities abroad against individuals. In this way of looking at the issue, the state where the hostile activities are carried out is not necessarily engaged in the war. It is only the place in which the war is carried out. This is one way of looking at the CIA killings in Yemen. In a policing framework this would be categorized as extra-judicial killing, which is condemned in international human rights law. In the alternative, if this is war, then this is military action which may be justified. Into this uneven contest between a state or group of states and a group of individuals, states not engaged in the conflict may be categorized as having lost their sovereignty. The concept of a state which is harbouring terrorists has become part of the furniture of this war. The difference between a state harbouring terrorists and a state granting asylum to protection seekers is not necessarily an easy one to define.[19] As nineteenth-century European history has amply demonstrated, one man's terrorist is another man's hero.

HUMAN RIGHTS AND PRINCIPLES OF OPEN BORDERS FOR FORCED MIGRANTS[20]

Principles of fundamental human rights place an imperative on open borders in certain circumstances. First, the Geneva Convention relating to the status of refugees 1951 and its 1967 Protocol place substantial limitations on state sovereignty as regards the closure of borders. The Geneva Convention obligation is not to expel any person back to a country where he or she fears persecution on the basis of race, religion, nationality, membership of a social group or political opinion. This means that anyone seeking protection who arrives at the territory of a state cannot be sent back to his or her country of origin (or persecution) until and unless an examination of any claim to asylum has been determined. However, the Geneva Convention states that its provisions do not apply to any person with respect to whom there are serious reasons for considering that he or she has committed a crime against peace, a war crime, or a crime against humanity, as defined in the relevant international instruments; or he or she has committed a serious non-political crime outside the country of refuge before his or her admission; or he or she has been guilty of acts contrary to the purposes and principles of the United Nations. This exclusion clause is contained in Article 1F of the Geneva Convention. A second provision, Article 33(2), states that protection against refoulement (i.e. return to the country where persecution is feared) may not be claimed by refugees in respect of whom there are reasonable grounds for regarding them as a danger to the security of the country in which they are or who, having been convicted by final judgement of a particularly serious crime constitute a danger to the community of the host country.[21]

The discussion regarding prosecution of refugees for crimes against humanity or war crimes has been spurred, primarily by Mary Robinson, UN High Commissioner for Human Rights, in particular in her statement to the UN Human Rights Commission on 20 March 2002. Her contention is that respecting human rights is a core component of enhancing security. Her vision of a world in which rule of law plays a central role in security through the international pursuit of those who commit crimes by the enforcement of law creates a very different framework for the anti-terrorism fight. The cooperation of states in the fight against terrorism does not take as its starting place the exclusion from the territory of alleged or feared terrorists, but rather their arrest and trial in the interests of international security and solidarity.[22] Her voice, together with that of the UN High Commissioner for Refugees and the OSCE Commissioner for the Protection of Minorities, has not yet had much echo at the EU or member state level. The vision of territorial protection, for the moment at least, appears to be informing the relationship of terrorism, borders and movement of persons.

However, the obligations of states in the human rights field relating to movement of persons across borders do not stop at the protection of refugees under the Geneva Convention. The European Convention on Human Rights (ECHR) also creates obstacles to the exclusion and expulsion of foreigners from the territory of signatory states. As regards persons who fear torture, inhuman or degrading treatment in their country of origin, the ECHR places an absolute prohibition on their return (Art. 3 ECHR) irrespective of whether they are international terrorists or not.[23] This obligation is in addition to the duties on states contained in the Geneva Convention and is wider, as there is no exceptional proviso like Article IF or 33(2) to permit states to derogate.

The ECHR also creates duties on states not to expel foreign nationals where such an expulsion would constitute an interference with their right to family and private life in the host country. Here the jurisprudence of the European Court of Human Rights (ECHR) has developed rapidly over the ten years, primarily in relation to young criminals, nationals of North African countries who have lived most of their lives in Belgium or France have most of their family connections in those countries.[24] This line of jurisprudence has increased the security of residence of foreign nationals in Council of Europe countries against which those states may not offend. The decision of the ECHR in June 2002, on the right of a foreigner not to be expelled, confirmed the priority of the right to family life even where allegations of terrorist activities are made by the state.[25]

TERRORISM AND BORDERS

Terrorism is by no means a clear category in law, let alone in practice. In fact, the UN Special Rapporteur on Terrorism and Human Rights notes that studies show there are some 109 different legal definitions of the term 'terrorism' which have been put forward between 1936 and 1981.[26] While some countries have a long history of anti-terrorism legislation, such as the United Kingdom, others have none. The European Union has now adopted a common position on terrorism which includes a definition, but that definition tends to be circular.[27] In Europe, the field I know best, terrorism has been very much a national concern which has engaged own nationals and perhaps nationals of a neighbouring country. It relates to the designation of certain crimes which are already defined as crimes in the normal statute books as terrorist crimes. For example, murder, which is a crime according to the criminal law of all European countries, when it is accompanied by certain other attributes relating to political motivation, can in some countries be designated as terrorism under different criminal law provisions.

The designation of criminal activities as 'terrorist' permits the state to act in ways which would otherwise not be countenanced: for instance, the rights of the defence are abrogated, the right to question witnesses for the Prosecution is subject to limitations or may indeed be removed, and so on. One enters the field of exceptionalism, which acts like a magnetic field drawing those within its sphere ever deeper into a logic of state security which accepts no limitations. Once the drift from rule of law commences, all too often it ends in the state's complicity in torture, extra-judicial killings and subversion of democracy.

For example, one of the most intractable of terrorist concerns in the EU at the moment is the situation in the Basque country, primarily a concern of Spain but also to a lesser degree of France. This situation has led to very substantial concerns about the rule of law in Spain in particular. The development in the 1980s of the GAL, a group based within the Spanish ministry of the interior which engaged in extra-judicial killing of ETA members (the Basque separatist movement), resulted in the conviction and imprisonment of a former Minister of Interior in 1995.[28] The political framework of the response to terrorism permitted so wide a margin of action by the state that constitutional norms were disobeyed, the rule of law was disregarded and in the name of national security the state commenced extra-judicial killing.[29]

Another important source of terrorist concerns in Europe arises in the UK as a result of the long-standing disputes in Northern Ireland. The political result in the UK of designating the IRA as terrorists appears, unfortunately, to be surprisingly similar to that in Spain. The revelation in the BBC programme *Panorama* in June 2002 regarding the Stevens 3 Inquiry[30] into the killing of human rights solicitor Patrick Finucane in Belfast in 1989 indicates that the British state was implicated in the killing.[31] Again, the rule of law appears to have broken down in the face of the allegation of terrorism. An outstanding victim is also the democratic state itself.

Although terrorism is perceived as a threat related to movement of persons, in the EU context it does not often result in measures closing the borders. For instance, in the mainland UK–Northern Ireland situation, one of the constant complaints of the security services was that terrorists moved back and forth across the UK–Irish border to escape. The degree of cooperation provided by the Republic of Ireland was subject to substantial criticism particularly as regards the flight of suspected terrorists across the border. However, at no point did the UK government reintroduce systematic passport controls at the border between the UK and the Republic of Ireland. This is not to diminish the importance both in law and practice of the permanent roadblocks and identity checks at some of the land border crossing points between the countries. Although the UK maintains its border controls with all the other EU member states on the grounds that entry into the Schengen arrangements on abolition of border controls would have negative effects on security in the UK, the main border source of security issues in the UK, the UK–Irish border, is not the site of systematic identity checks.

Turning to Spain and France: this border too has been the subject of substantial friction around the issue of terrorism and movement of persons. The Aznar Protocol to the Amsterdam Treaty provides that subject to various conditions, nationals of one member state may not be refugees within the territory of another member state. This Protocol is a direct result of the movement of Spanish nationals from Spain and in particular the Basque region to other member states, notably Belgium and France, and seeking asylum there.[32] Thus the post-11 September 2001 linkage of borders and national security is not as self-evident as many governments present it.

MAKING THE TERRORISM–ASYLUM LINK

Asylum has dominated Western policy making on movement of persons for the last 25 years. The rise in numbers of asylum seekers entering the EU reached a high in 1992 of 675 460, and had consequences in policy which were still being felt in 2003. The fact that UNHCR felt it necessary to issue a press release on 31 May 2002 to remind the EU member states that, in 2001, the number of asylum applications received within the territory was only a little more than half what it had been in 1992 indicates just how far public perceptions about asylum have drifted from the realities.

The thrust in Europe of the terrorism–asylum linkage has been to seek to exclude protection seekers from any sort of status or even a determination of their status on the basis that they are, or are linked with, terrorists. This takes form in the European Commission working document on safeguarding internal security and international protection obligations of December 2001,[33] which raises for further discussion the principle that a person seeking protection from persecution can be excluded from refugee status on the grounds of active voluntary membership of terrorist organizations. The central problem with this approach is that refusing to determine an asylum application does not relieve states of their protection duties under other human rights obligations such as Article 3 of the UN Convention against Torture (UNCAT), which prohibits the return of persons to countries where there is a serious risk they will suffer torture, or Article 3 ECHR (see above, p. 239). Thus if a state refuses to consider an asylum application but the individual comes within the category of Article 3 UNCAT, then the state cannot remove the individual. If the state considers that there are security reasons for refusing asylum, it is none the less left with an individual against whom expulsion is not an option.

In the UK, the government considered it necessary to detain indefinitely persons whom they considered a security risk but against whom expulsion action could not be taken.[34] The logic of this result is apparent – there are individuals who are dangerous; their claims for protection mean that they cannot be expelled. Thus to protect society they must be detained indefinitely. In order to pursue this line of logic the UK was required then to derogate from the right of liberty of the person in both the ECHR and the International Covenant on Civil and Political Rights, as these international obligations prohibit indefinite detention. The flaws in the logic are equally impressive. The first, which applies to all issues of expulsion and terrorism, is that by expelling an individual, national security is enhanced. If the individual is expelled to a country that permits him or her to carry on terrorist activities without hindrance, then no country's national security is enhanced by the expulsion. Indeed, the opposite may be true. More problematic for the international community in general was the example of yet another Western state failing to take seriously its international obligations. The arguments regarding the US obligations under the UN Charter as regards the war against terrorism have been set out elsewhere.[35] The UK approach of derogating from inconvenient human rights guarantees sets at least an equally poor example for the rest of the world. This point was amply, and forcefully, made by the UN High Commissioner for Human Rights, Mary Robinson, in March 2002 (see above, p. 239).

ASYLUM, SECURITY AND TECHNOLOGY

Asylum also became increasingly linked with terrorism through the new technologies. The EU regulation establishing a common database of fingerprints for asylum seekers which had been adopted two years earlier[36] was awaiting agreement on implementing measures[37] when 11 September 2001 became a date tied to terrorism. At the member state level, the gathering of information, including fingerprints, on asylum seekers was intensified and the controls on exchange of information were loosened. Nowhere was this more evident than in Germany, where the whole emphasis of the fight against terrorism in the post-11 September 2001 legislation revolves around tracking individuals, knowing who people are, where they are, being able to manipulate this information through searches by profile, and sharing the results.[38] In the Netherlands the step was taken to permit, under restricted circumstances, the use of asylum seekers' fingerprints, taken in pursuit of the asylum application, in relation to criminal investigations.[39] This may allow the police to resolve criminal matters in which an asylum seeker is involved as they have access to a tool – fingerprints – that is not available in respect of the general public. The proportion of clear-up rates of crimes by asylum seekers is likely to increase in relation with the rest of the population, thus confirming the belief that asylum seekers are criminals. Other technological projects were also presented as part of the solution to terrorism. In the Netherlands and Germany biometric data collection was strongly promoted as the way forward. This was then generalized to the population at large when the UK Home Secretary strongly promoted the inclusion of biometric data including fingerprints and iris recognition information in British passports for all nationals, and recommended this extension to all G8 states.[40] Similarly the rules on destruction of data regarding asylum seekers after their use have been relaxed. Foreigners, and in particular asylum seekers, no longer have the benefit of removal of their data from the databases once their files are completed. All the time periods for retention of data have been substantially extended.

Great emphasis has been placed on the creation of lists of terrorists, a phenomenon which has proliferated. The consequences of databases of suspected terrorists are by and large unclear. The intentional lack of clarity on the legal status is nowhere more clearly illustrated than in the list of terrorists whose funds must be frozen. This was implemented in the EU by Regulation 2199/200 listing the persons and groups whose funds were frozen. The first challenge to the regulation before the European Court of Justice (ECJ) (T-306/O1R *Aden*) relates to a naturalized Swedish woman of Somali ethnic origin (possibly an asylum seeker in former times) whose funds are frozen and is refused any social benefits to feed herself and her children. A claim for interim relief was rejected by the ECJ when the Swedish authorities provided information that they had found a way of taking care of the woman and her family.[41] The substantive case has yet to be determined. The UN Resolution 1373 includes the list of persons and organizations whose funds must be frozen. In response, a plethora of lists have come into existence, few with the clear legal basis of the Regulation. The consequences of being on other terrorist lists are cloaked in legal uncertainty, the hallmark of national security. In the linking of terrorism, asylum and immigration the normal legal security which derives from the right of freedom of the person is excluded. The state can detain people on terrorism grounds without a duty to bring criminal charges which carry with them all the civil liberties protections central to constitutional settlements. Because these are foreigners, fundamental rights are no longer necessarily subject to adjudication in the criminal courts. They are shifted into the limbo of immigration and asylum-related procedures, not least because of this shadowland where immigration and asylum procedures, terrorism allegations and criminal law fail to intersect.

SECURITY, IDENTITY AND FORCED MIGRATION

Control over identity is at the centre of much of the EU discussion. Most third states are no longer considered capable of identifying security risks among their own nationals or taking action. Instead, in the EU in particular, other countries are seen as permitting their nationals who are potential security risks to move from their borders elsewhere. It is now the document issued by an EU member state that defines the identity of the individual, the visa, not the document on which the visa is placed, the passport. The inclusion of photographs on the EU common visa is indicative of this move. Documents issued by non-member states are no longer definitive for determining identity. The document issued by the member state – the visa – contains all the information required to establish identity. The Union takes over the task of identifying all persons who seek to come to the Union and determines where they belong. Thus a database on visas and their status becomes increasingly relevant to the issue. The EU as a whole is then able to track third-country nationals' movements and control where they go and what they do.

Protection seekers arriving without documents, either because they could not get them in the first place or because to have documents is only to provide the state where the individual seeks protection with a means of expelling them swiftly, offend fundamentally against this regime. The image of state control at the frontier is undermined. The state may consider that its security is undermined by the arrival of protection seekers claiming to be nationals of one state but whom the host state suspects of being nationals of another country. In the development of the EU's Justice and Home Affairs *acquis* on asylum, the emphasis on false documents as a ground for refusing to consider an asylum claim has become increasingly insidious.[42]

CONCLUSIONS

What is the map of terrorism? The definition of protection against terrorism as a geographically placed one inside the Schengen border draws theoretical lines around the geography of terrorism. The enemy outside will be kept out by border controls; the enemy inside will be hunted down by the security services. For all of the claims and insistences of EU leaders that the war against terrorism is not a crusade against Islam,[43] the topology of terrorism undermines these claims. It is not that George Bush or Tony Blair are insincere when they assure the world that the war on terrorism is not about Islam in itself; the issue is in the definition of security and insecurity as placed inside and outside a border. A map of the states from whose nationals the EU demands visas for short stays and those it does not is never officially published. It is too stark a reminder of who is excluded and who is not, in particular as it shows the extent of convergence of exclusion, colour and religion.[44] By defining terrorism as something that comes from somewhere else (i.e. outside the border), one must then look at where outside the border it comes from. This then engages a military response, as external threats are the responsibility of the army. The definition of terrorism as something against which war can be declared positions terrorism outside the borders in the field of military defence and leads inexorably to adventures in Afghanistan and Iraq.

The border then takes on a new sacred symbolism as the line of security. Activity taking place at the border is charged with great importance. The exercise of state control at the border becomes the embodiment of the task of the state in providing protection to its citizens. Those who have a right to cross the border but who are not nationals of the state by contrast become the symbol of the threat – protection seekers, through their right in international law to cross borders, inadvertently become the face of the menace. Where the protection seeker is from an Islamic country, the geography of terrorism acts in such a way as to heighten the threat that such a person is seen as constituting for the state.

NOTES

1. The category of asylum seekers and refugees is, however, determined to a substantial degree by the state. For example, when the British Home Secretary and the French Minister of the Interior agreed on the closure of the camp at Sangatte where non-EU nationals were housed by the Red Cross as they apparently waited to cross to the UK to apply for asylum, the press and members of parliament on both sides of the Channel referred to the persons at Sangatte as asylum seekers. However, when 1400 of them were admitted to the UK under the ministerial agreement, they were admitted as labour migrants. The form letters from the UK Immigration and Nationality Directorate advised them that if they applied for asylum in the UK their status as labour migrants would be withdrawn (including their residence right). This is a particularly clear example of how the state is central in determining whether a specific individual is categorized as an asylum seeker or some other type of migrant.
2. The situation in Israel and the Palestinian Authority is excluded for the purposes of this discussion.
3. P. Buchanan, 'Immigration Law Developments in the United States since September 11', in E. Brouwer, P. Catz and E. Guild (eds), *Immigration, Asylum and Terrorism: A Changing Dynamic in European Law*, Nijmegen: CMR, 2003, pp. 149–68.
4. Conclusions of the Extraordinary Council Meeting – Justice, Home Affairs and Civil Protection, Brussels, 20 September 2001.
5. Leading to the adoption of the European Arrest Warrant.
6. Incorporated into the TEU and EC Treaty by the Schengen Protocol to the Amsterdam Treaty and related measures.
7. 'The Border Abroad – Visas and Border Controls', in K. Groenendijk, E. Guild and P. Minderhoud (eds), *In Search of Europe's Borders* (The Hague: Kluwer Law International, 2003), pp. 87–105.
8. Except in some highly particular categories where the foreigner is considered as if a national because of such strong political links.
9. Indeed, in the UK this was among the last crimes for which the death penalty was abolished.
10. *Proposal for a Council Directive on minimum standards for the qualification and status of third country nationals and stateless persons as refugees or as persons who otherwise need international protection*, COM (2001) 510 final.
11. For a very interesting discussion of the ethical ground for this suspicion see M. Frost, *Ethics in International Relations: A Constitutive Theory* (Cambridge: Cambridge University Press, 1996).
12. For full text of letter see www.statewatch.org/news/2002/feb/useu.PDF7
13. A clear example of this was the reaction of the Australian interior minister, Mr Ruddock, to the prospective arrival of the Afghan refugees on the Norwegian ship, the *Tampa*, in August 2001. He sent the Australian navy to prevent the arrival of the ship in Australian waters.

14. The mechanism is readmission agreements which make third states responsible for receiving back any individual who is found in the EU without proper entry documents or seeking asylum and has passed through a third state en route to the EU. The EU has settled such agreements with Hong Kong, Sri Lanka and Macao. Further agreements are under negotiation with Russia, Albania and the Ukraine. For an analysis of the contents of the agreements see Professor S. Peers, www.state~watch.org/news/2003/may/12readmission.htm.
15. According to press reports, these appear to have been quite local in organization and execution.
16. Of course there is much discussion on the use of the discourse of war in this context; see A. Cassese, 'Terrorism is also Disrupting Some Crucial Legal Categories of International Law' and A. Pellet, 'No, This is not War!', *European Journal of International Law*, www.ejil.org/forum-wtc
17. The House of Lords Sub-Committee F on the European Union: Inquiry into Proposals to Establish a European Border Guard, March 2003.
18. UNHCR, *Statistical Yearbook 2001*, Geneva, 2002, p. 118.
19. This is the centre of much legal discussion about the meaning of Article 1F of the Geneva Convention, which permits states to withhold protection from an individual on the basis that he or she has committed very serious crimes.
20. This section and the section on Making the Terrorism–Asylum Link are heavily indebted to my chapter in Bulent Gokay and R.J.B. Walker (eds), *September 11, 2001. War. Terror and Judgement* (London: Frank Cass, 2003).
21. For a comprehensive and detailed review see N. Blake, QC, 'Exclusion from Refugee Protection: Serious Non Political Crimes after 9/11', *European Journal of Migration and Law*, 2002, pp. 1-23.
22. None the less, the Dutch authorities have devoted increasing resources to screening asylum applicants for potential war criminals since the Bosnia conflict in 1992. However, not one criminal action has been commenced. Report on the Netherlands, ELISE Consortium (European Liberty and Security in Europe), April 2003.
23. *Chahal v. UK* (1996), 23 EHRR 413.
24. See for instance *Beldjoudi v. France* (1992), 14 EHRR 801.
25. *Al-Nashif v. Bulgaria* (50963/99), ECtHR, 20 June 2002.
26. Working Paper by K. Koufa, 26 June 1997 (E/CN.4.Sub.2/1997/28), para. 17.
27. Council Common Position of 27 December 2001 on the application of specific measures to combat terrorism OJ L 344. 28/12/2001 PP 0093–0096.
28. José Barrionuevo, Minister of the Interior from 1982 to 1988 under the Gonzalez government in Spain, was convicted by a court of first instance in 1995 for his involvement in the GAL affair on 26 November 1995. He was thereafter also convicted of kidnapping and imprisoning Segundo Màrey (part of the GAL operations) on 17 July 1998.
29. J.-P. Hanon, *Étude comparé des concepts et des doctrines de maintien de l'ordre et d'intervention anti-terroriste en Europe (Allemagne, Espagne, Italie, Grèce et Irlande du Nord) et aux Etats Unis*, DAS/CPGN, June 2002.
30. UK Metropolitan Police Deputy Commissioner John Stevens was invited to conduct an independent inquiry into the murder of Patrick Finucane, a Belfast solicitor, by the Royal Ulster Constabulary in 2000. Mr Stevens had already conducted two investigations into police irregularities in the RUC in Northern Ireland.
31. Report from the Stevens Inquiry, www.statewatch.org: the leaked texts have been placed in their entirety on the Statewatch website. Also see BBC *Panorama*, 19 June 2002.
32. See for instance C-100/01 *Olazabal*, ECJ, 26 November 2002.
33. Commission Working Document, *The Relationship between Safeguarding Internal Security and Complying with International Protection Obligations and Instruments* COM (2001) 743 Final, 6 December 2001.
34. Anti-terrorism. Crime and Security Act 2001. This meant that the UK had to derogate from its obligation to protect liberty of the person in Article 5 ECHR and Article II International Covenant on Civil and Political Rights; SI 2001 No 3644 The Human Rights Act 1998 (Designated Derogation) Order 2001.

35. M. Byers, 'Terrorism, the Use of Force and International Law after 11 September', (2002), 5I ICLQ. pp. 401–14.
36. Regulation 2725/2000 OJ 2000 L 316/1.
37. Regulation 407/2002, OJ 2002 L 62/1.
38. E. Brouwer, 'Germany', in Brouwer et al., *Immigration, Asylum and Terrorism*.
39. P. Catz, 'The Netherlands', in ibid.
40. Passport iris chip plan wins backing from G8 ministers, *Guardian Weekly*, 8–14 May, p. 9.
41. Order, 7 May 2002.
42. As note 10.
43. This is dealt with at some length in each country chapter in Brouwer et al., *Immigration, Asylum and Terrorism*.
44. The map is published for the first time to my knowledge in *Cultures et Conflits* (2002).

11. Human rights and civil rights

Theresa Callan

INTRODUCTION

This chapter discusses the challenges facing the protection and promotion of human rights in the contemporary international system. It starts with an outline of the human rights regimes at the systemic and the European level, noting the UN provisions and procedures and those within the European space. It looks at the centrality of a commitment to human rights and fundamental freedoms to the political criteria for EU enlargement, yet notes the difficulty of ensuring this commitment once accession is granted. The chapter then investigates the impact of the prevailing international system on the provision and protection of rights and freedoms. It looks specifically at the effects of fighting the 'war on terror' in terms of the cost to rights both at home and abroad. Ultimately, the chapter argues that the upholding of human rights and fundamental freedoms – either at a regional or a systemic level – depends on the political will of sovereign states to honour their commitments to international law. It reflects that the reassertion of realpolitik in international affairs bodes ill for the security of one and all.

SYSTEMIC AND REGIONAL HUMAN AND CIVIL RIGHTS REGIMES

Contemporary human rights regimes have their roots within the horrors of the Nazi period. In the wake of the Second World War, the UN was established to assist in the prevention of systemic war and to tackle the systematic and mass violations of human rights and the rights of the state, notably to defend territorial sovereignty. From the inception of this nascent human rights regime, therefore, there was an inherent tension in terms of the duality of the security referent – both the individual and the state were to have their rights and sovereignty protected in the execution of the UN's primary function, specifically the maintenance of international peace and security (Art. 1 of the UN Charter). The centrality of human rights to the UN Charter is explicit in the exposition of the UN's purposes: 'to achieve international cooperation in solving international problems of an economic, social, cultural or humanitarian character, and in promoting and encouraging respect for human rights and for fundamental freedoms for all without distinction as to race, sex, language or religion …' (Art. 1). Initially in the immediate aftermath of the Second World War, it seemed that this commitment to the rights of the individual would take precedence over the rights of the state. The prosecution of war criminals at the International Military Tribunal at Nuremberg and its counterpart at Tokyo held individuals liable under the prescripts of international law for actions taken in the name of the state. The charges of war crimes, crimes against peace and crimes against humanity were upheld, the defendants found guilty and duly sentenced. The legal personality of the state could not supplant the legal responsibility of the individual. The principle of non-interference in the domestic affairs of a state could not be observed should universal norms and rights be systematically violated. This belief in the universalist nature of human rights was strengthened and advanced in the Universal Declaration of Human Rights (1948) and two further international covenants in 1966 on Civil and Political Rights and on Economic, Social and Cultural Rights respectively. These latter covenants made the Declaration's provisions more explicit and enhanced its enforceability. Such universal rights are seen to derive from natural law and to prevail over any values and norms that may be specific to particular cultures. These central documents enshrine such fundamental rights as those to life, liberty and security, equality before the law, protection against arbitrary arrest and detention, the right to a fair and public trial and so on. In short, 'these legal pillars articulate the human rights, civil liberties, and fundamental freedoms to which all people are entitled' (Joyner, 2004, p. 241). The UN also sought to further prohibit the practice of torture, genocide and racial discrimination. Additionally, specific measures were introduced to protect targeted groups such as refugees, women and children. In this wide remit of measures, then, the UN may validly be seen as 'the institutional vehicle through which international laws are codified into international agreements' (ibid., pp. 242–3).

Whilst the UN offers a global human rights regime, the Council of Europe offers 'the most developed system of protection for human rights at the regional level' (Smith, 2003, p. 92). Founded in 1949 with ten original member states, the Council of Europe now has 45 member states as the result of eastward expansion in the wake of the Cold War. The Council of Europe's principal document on human rights is the Convention for the Protection of Human Rights and Fundamental Freedoms (1950), wherein its members committed to the right to life, prohibition of torture, prohibition of slavery and forced labour, right to liberty and security, right to a fair trial, no punishment without law, right to respect for private and family life, freedom of thought, conscience and religion, freedom of expression, freedom of assembly and association, right to marry, right to an effective remedy and prohibition of discrimination. The Convention also established enforcement mechanisms at the regional level via the European Court of Human Rights. This forum hears petitions from both states and individuals. This enforcement machinery has proven highly effective, with member states almost always abiding by Court interpretation of the Convention and, if necessary, amending their national legislation to ensure compatibility with European practice. Over time, the Convention's realm of rights has been extended through the Protocols. These have added further rights concerning education, free elections, the peaceful enjoyment of property (all Protocol 1), and outlaw imprisonment for debts (Protocol 4). They further enhance the freedom of movement within and between states, prohibiting the expulsion of nationals and the collective expulsion of aliens (Protocol 4). Abolition of the death penalty is provided through Protocol 13, superseding Protocol 6 that had allowed it in times of war and national emergency only. Protocol 7 makes provision concerning the right to appeal, to avoid double jeopardy and the right to recompense for wrongful conviction in criminal affairs. It also provides for equality between spouses in private law matters. Protocol 12 provides for anti-discrimination on the grounds of sex, race, colour, language and religion but remains short of the ten ratifications needed to come into force. In May 2004, Protocol 14 was opened for signature and immediately signed by 18 states. It is designed to reinforce the effectiveness of the European Court of Human Rights in light of the ever-increasing volume of individual complaints coming before it. It hopes too to improve the implementation of the European Convention on Human Rights at the national level and to strengthen regional mechanisms to ensure the expeditious delivery of justice. As yet Protocol 14 has not received the required ten ratifications to facilitate enforcement.

There are further measures to enhance the provision and protection of rights within the European space, such as the European Social Charter (1961) guaranteeing social and economic rights; the European Charter for Regional and Minority Languages (1992); the Framework Convention for the Protection of National Minorities (1997); the European Convention on the Exercise of Children's Rights (1996); and the Convention of Human Rights and Biomedicine (1997).

The Council of Europe has a sophisticated institutional structure, of which some is involved in the promotion and protection of this array of human rights. The Secretary General heads the Secretariat, which is the depository for the state responses to the Council's measures. The Council of Ministers, comprising the foreign members from the respective member states, includes within its remit the monitoring of the states' observation of their obligations under the Convention and the other strictures. In this way, it is hoped that good governance will be provided within the member states on issues such as human rights, the rule of law and democratic practice. This monitoring system, however, is firmly cooperative in nature and confidential, leading some to question its efficacy. Since 1999, there has also been a European Commissioner on Human Rights whose office is an independent institution within the Council and whose mandate is to promote education on human rights within the member states; identify any deficits in human rights law and practice; and to promote the full enjoyment of human rights within all the states of the Council of Europe. Elected by the Parliamentary Assembly, the Commissioner serves a non-renewable term of six years.

The codification of human rights within a wider Europe stretching from Vancouver to Vladivostock may be found too in the 'baskets' of the Helsinki Final Act of 1975. This Act led to the establishment of the Conference on Security and Cooperation in Europe (CSCE). Its efforts to promote and realize effective human rights protection were limited during the Cold War, largely defeated by the geo-political realities of the time. In its aftermath, however, the CSCE, like many international organizations, reviewed its remit. At the Second Meeting of the Conference of the Human Dimension in Copenhagen in June 1990, the primacy of a liberal-democratic polity – with all attendant human rights responsibilities – was accepted (Buergenthal, 1990, p. 217). Later that same year, the CSCE declared a new start for both Europe and itself within the 'Charter of Paris for a New Europe'. To embed itself within this 'new era of democracy, peace and unity within Europe', the CSCE started to institutionalize and consolidate its processes. The Paris Charter facilitated the establishment of several bodies within the CSCE: a Council of Foreign Ministers; a Committee of Senior Officials (CSO); an office for free elections (OFE – in January 1992, it became the ODIHR, the Office for Democratic Institutions and Human Rights); a Conflict Prevention Centre (CPC); and an Administrative Secretariat. The Charter also referred to the OSCE Parliamentary Assembly which was established later in the Madrid Declaration of 1991.

In its Helsinki Review Conference (1992) and Budapest Review Meeting (1994), the CSCE continued its institutional augmentation. At Helsinki, it established the post of High Commissioner on National Minorities (HCNM) and the Forum for Security Cooperation. At Budapest, it changed its name to the Organization for Security and Cooperation in Europe (OSCE), effective from 1 January 1995 and consolidated the roles of the Chairman in Office (CIO) and the Office for Democratic Institutions and Human Rights.

In its Paris Charter, the CSCE declared that 'ours is a time for fulfilling the hopes and expectations our peoples have cherished for decades: steadfast commitment to democracy based on human rights and fundamental freedoms; prosperity through economic liberty and social justice; and equal security for all our countries'. To this end, the OSCE has been heavily involved in post-conflict peace building in places such as Kosovo and Bosnia–Herzegovina. The OSCE has been particularly concerned to address 'frozen' conflicts within Europe, notably those within the Caucasus. In other areas of Europe, it has concentrated much effort and resources on integrating minorities. It is noteworthy, however, that the OSCE's HCNM refers to the High Commissioner 'on' rather than 'for' national minorities. The emphasis is on the regulation of intra-state conflict rather than the advocacy of national minorities' rights. The Commissioner's remit covers the whole OSCE region but attention has been concentrated on matters within the recent EU accession states. Chandler (1994, p. 68) explicitly notes a 'qualitatively different level of intrusiveness into the affairs of the states of Eastern Europe'. In effect, then, the OSCE has worked in tandem with the EU in the spread of liberal-democratic norms and practice and so is equally open to the charge that it has concentrated its fire on the weakest targets: 'the high commissioner knows that any recommendation given to Western countries would be summarily ignored' (Johns, 2003, p. 687).

At the Nice Summit of December 2000, the European Union adopted the text of the Charter of Fundamental Rights of the European Union. This Charter upholds basic civil, political, economic and social rights, most of which are contained in other earlier documents. The Charter is not yet legally binding as its incorporation into the Nice Treaty was stymied by opposition from some of the member states (The Charter of Fundamental Rights of the European Union, 2000). In 2002, however, a new Convention was established to focus on the constitutional future of the EU and to consider the inclusion of the EU Charter within EU treaties. Subsequently, in June 2004, a draft EU Constitutional Treaty was agreed. In legal terms, the Constitution confirms the status quo, namely that EU human rights law has primacy over national legislation and incorporates the Charter of Fundamental Rights of the European Union within its Part II.

EU ENLARGEMENT AND HUMAN RIGHTS

The abundance of treaties, covenants and declarations, combined with the array of instruments and mechanisms, attests to the commitment to rights within the European space. This commitment was evident too in the 'conditionality' attached to the accession of new states in the recent enlargement of the European Union, as Pinelli (2004, p. 355) has noted: 'conditionality is the main instrument through which human rights discourses and practices are being diffused'. The political criteria for accession to the EU were made explicit at the European Council in Copenhagen in June 1993. These 'Copenhagen criteria' included the 'stability of institutions guaranteeing democracy, the rule of law, human rights and respect for and protection of minorities'. The Amsterdam Treaty of 1997 (entering into force in May 1999) reaffirmed the principle of respect for human rights and other fundamental freedoms and established a procedure for instances when these rights and freedoms were not observed. In cases of a 'serious and persistent breach' of its obligations, the rights of the state concerned, including possibly its voting rights, in the Council would be suspended. Although the Amsterdam Treaty did not mention the need for respect and protection for minority groups, the Commission began to monitor the candidate states' progress on democratization and human and minority rights in a series of annual reports. In 1997, the Commission held that Estonia, Poland, Hungary, Slovenia and the Czech Republic had met the requisite democratic standards, whilst others – Bulgaria, Romania, Lithuania and Latvia – were making considerable progress to do so. It adjudged, however, that Slovakia had made insufficient progress and so it was excluded from the accession talks at that time. At the Helsinki Summit of the European Council in December 1999, however, Slovakia was accepted as a candidate for membership because the new government of Dzurinda was deemed to have made substantial progress in many areas.

The enlargement process therefore can be seen as a method of transmitting democratic and liberal norms between and within states (Risse-Kappen, 1996). It facilitated the augmentation of domestic democratic forces within the accession states. Moravcsik (2000, p. 220) explains why the most recent democratizing states are so keen to limit their domestic sovereignty by subscribing to such international regimes as the ECHR: 'self-binding is of most use to *newly established democracies*, which have the greatest interest in further stabilizing the domestic political *status quo* against non-democratic threats'. This endogenous pressure in democratizing states is supplanted by an exogenous pressure on more established democracies. Their self-limitation of sovereignty is made explicable by 'an incentive to promote such arrangements for others – in order to bolster the "democratic peace" by fostering democracy in neighbouring countries' (ibid., p. 229). Thus the newly democratic polities become 'locked into' the liberal project. Once they are part of the project, however, there appears to be a lack of political will to monitor the observance of commitments to human rights and fundamental freedoms and to employ sanctions in cases of default. Despite the European institutional architecture concerned with human rights, 'there is no comprehensive human-rights monitoring in the EU at the moment' (Sadurski, 2004, p. 380). Arguably, indeed, the complex nature of the architecture with 'all the actors in the EU … involved at some time or another in making decisions and perfecting practices that have a human rights dimension' serves to adversely affect the EU's human rights policy (Williams, 2003, p. 659). The augmentation of the EU's competency in human rights could be achieved through a widening of the applicability of the Charter of Fundamental Rights to the member states' institutions, but this is unlikely at the present time. The draft EU Constitutional Treaty, contrary to much public 'understanding' within the UK, applies the Charter solely to EU laws and institutions and consequently cannot be used to negate national laws.

HUMAN RIGHTS AND THE 'LONELY SUPERPOWER'

While the complexity of human rights as an issue-area contributes to the difficulties in making focused and coherent policy in the EU, the nature of the international system itself exacerbates the matter further. A system dominated by a 'lonely superpower' (Huntington, 1999) is one in which the demands of international law and the demands of that predominant state appear to be incompatible. While other states view some 'self-binding' behaviour as in their interests, the USA seems impervious to such calculations. The Bush Administration's seemingly inherent indisposition to multilateral arrangements was clearly signalled in its initial period in office. Its rejection of the Kyoto Protocol and the Ottawa Mines Convention, and its 'unsigning' of the Rome Statute of the International Criminal Court (ICC), demonstrated a tendency to unilateralism that has only become still more pronounced in the wake of the 9/11 attacks. The 'unsigning' of the Rome Statute in May 2002 reflected the Bush Administration's fears that US troops and officials would be at risk of politically motivated prosecutions. However, in fact, the ICC would exercise its jurisdiction only when two conditions were met: that the acts are of sufficient gravity to necessitate international attention; and when the state with national jurisdiction failed to investigate or prosecute the acts. Thus the ICC is complementary to national legal structures and processes rather than aiming to supplant them. The renunciation of the Statute by the USA has been interpreted by some as further evidence of the USA's rejection of multilateral arrangements in favour of the most narrow-minded view of national interest. In addition to its own 'unsigning', the USA is actively seeking to persuade other states to take the same course of action. It wants other states to sign Article 98 agreements thereby agreeing not to surrender or transfer US nationals to the ICC. This position was supported by the UK in 2002 and led the EU to agree that member states could sign such agreements as long as the US Administration agreed to bring Americans suspected of war crimes before its national courts (Davis, 2003, p. 5). More recently, in July 2004, the Republican leaders within the House of Representatives approved the so-called Nethercutt Amendment. This Amendment bans certain forms of economic aid to states that refuse to sign an Article 98 agreement. This Amendment was passed despite the Administration's opposition to it and its recognition of its potentially adverse effects upon the 'war on terrorism'. Republican Jim Kolbe, the Chairman of the House Foreign Operations Subcommittee, noted that under the Amendment 'we would have to cut off all economic assistance to Jordan. I don't see how that will help us in the war against terrorism' (Lobe, 2004). It would appear that the Administration's tendency to unilateralism and the 'new sovereigntists' in the USA who regard the ICC as a threat to democracy have bedfellows that may prove tough to control (Spiro, 2000).

The ultimate paradox is a superpower dedicated to the spread of democracy and freedom yet arguably undermining this very project through the prosecution of its ongoing and potentially endless 'war on terror'. The 'exceptionalism' of America, then, may be understood as 'a belief that the United States has a unique mission to lead the world, but ought logically to be exempt from the rules it promotes' (Hathaway, 2000, p. 121).

The prosecution of the 'war on terror' raises significant challenges to the promotion and protection of human rights and international law and 'a core security dilemma ... How far should human rights and civil liberties of citizens be abridged by a government for the avowed stake of protecting that state's nations security?' (Joyner, 2004, pp. 240–41). The current stress on the exigencies of national security has effectively changed the primary referent of security from the individual to the state. Indeed, the very notion of the individual is up for reconsideration and redefinition. In what Roberts has termed 'axes of discrimination', a distinction is now drawn both by the USA and its allies, most notably the UK, between citizens and non-citizens. This distinction represents 'a movement away from universal human rights towards a person's rights being tied to their membership of particular groups' (Roberts, 2004, p. 722). The security of the 'nation' then appears to involve the insecurity of the non-national, eroding any sense of the indivisibility or comprehensiveness of human security. In the wake of 9/11 the rights of non-citizens especially are sacrificed on the altar of 'national security'. In the USA, this sacrifice is especially evident in the detention camp at Guantanamo Bay. In his 'Detention, Treatment, and Trial of Certain Non-Citizens in the War Against Terror' of 13 November 2001, President Bush authorized the indefinite detention of non-citizens and their trial by military commission. Throughout 2002, hundreds of individuals from Afghanistan and elsewhere were transported to Guantanamo Bay. The majority of these detainees are without access to lawyers or courts. Instead, they are all to be tried by military commissions, the Star Chamber Tribunals, where the usual rules of evidence do not apply. Neither will any detainee have recourse to appeal to a civilian court. Rather their appeals will be heard by another military panel and its decision will be reviewed either by President Bush or Vice President Cheney. Should a detainee be found not guilty, release is not assured as the Department of Defense has stated that they may still be detained if they are still regarded as a security threat. A further distinction is made between types of non-citizens too. The country of origin of the detainees becomes crucial in terms of the treatment they may expect. The Bush Administration has agreed not to seek the death penalty or listen to any consultation with legal representation for British and Australian detainees leading Roberts to observe: 'The United States has clearly adopted preferential policies toward non-citizens from certain countries, in the same way as it bestows trade benefits under the "most favoured nation" policy' (2004, p. 727). Conversely, those from Arab and Muslim countries that are accorded 'least favoured detainee status'. There have been challenges to such blatant violations of human rights and international law. In July 2004, the US Supreme Court ruled that US courts have jurisdiction to hear cases disputing the legality of detaining both citizens and non-citizens in Guantanamo. The legal basis of its ruling was that *habeas corpus* does not differentiate between Americans and non-Americans. The Bush Administration has consequently established a Combatant Status Review Tribunal so that detainees can challenge their status as combatants, just as American citizens can.

The evidence of the torture of US prisoners in Abu Ghraib raises still further concerns that the prosecution of the 'war on terror' is undermining its very goals, with grave consequences as 'the one government whose power can be decisive in stopping human rights abuses' is complicit in the continuance of such abuses (Ignatieff, 2002, p. 7).

Within the USA itself, the Bush Administration has enacted the 'United and Strengthening America by Providing Appropriate Tools Required to Intercept and Obstruct Terrorism Act', more commonly known as the Patriot Act (2001) (The Century Foundation, 2004). This legislation has facilitated the widening of police powers, especially in surveillance. 'Sneak and peak searches' no longer require that the suspect be informed of searches before they happen. The powers of prosecuting authorities too are expanded, notably those of the Foreign Intelligence Surveillance Court. This Court, which reviews the government's surveillance orders, uses a lower burden of proof than is used in criminal courts and much of its activity is difficult to chart as information is scarce. The new crime of 'domestic terrorism' is ill defined and can be used to include some forms of political and civil disobedience. Certainly, there are implications for the Fourth Amendment to the US Constitution. Indeed, Amnesty International (2004) has charged that the Patriot Act 'undermines the human rights of Americans and non-citizens, and weakens the framework for promoting rights internationally'.

The UK, too, has adopted a differentiated approach to citizens and non-citizens in the name of national security. The Anti-Terrorism, Crime and Security Act 2001 was commended to the House of Commons by the Home Secretary, David Blunkett, as 'legislative measures which … will protect and enhance our rights, not diminish them' (taken from Jimeno-Bulnes, 2004, p. 241). This Act allows the Home Secretary to detain a non-citizen if it is suspected that the individual is a terrorist or is linked to an international terrorist group. Indefinite detention of 'suspected international terrorists' (a term which is not clearly defined) is allowed if they cannot be deported from the UK – because of either legal or practical impediments. The detainee has leave to appeal to the Special Immigration Appeals Commission (SIAC) and then to the Court of Appeals. There is, however, no requirement for either the detainee or their solicitors to be at the hearings, nor for them to be informed of all the evidence supporting the state's case. These anti-terrorist measures required the UK to derogate under Article 15 of the ECHR. The UK is the only state within the European Union to use the derogation clause and so suspend its obligations under the Convention. Article 15 (1) states that:

> In time of war or other public emergency threatening the life of the nation any High Contracting Party may take measures derogating from under its obligations under this Convention to the extent strictly required by the exigencies of the situation, provided that such measures are not inconsistent with its other obligations under international law.

Thus, in the 'war on terror', an asymmetrical and non-traditional form of 'war', the British government holds that the 'life of the nation' is under threat. Arguably, however, the British state is not struggling for survival. It is more accurate, perhaps, to say that there is a prevailing 'public emergency' but the urgency and immediacy of such an emergency is not reflected in the open-ended chronic threat of a terrorist incident. There arguably is no sense of imminence.

REALPOLITIK AND HUMAN RIGHTS

Other states have also brought in legislation to combat perceived threats. In 2002, both India and Pakistan passed legislation to facilitate the detention of individuals suspected of terrorist links and/or activities. India's Prevention of Terrorism Act permits the detention of such individuals for up to 90 days without charge, another 90 if a judge grants permission, and 30 days' detention before facing a court. Pakistan's Anti-Terrorist Ordinance permits the detention of terrorist suspects for up to a year. Certain states are clearly exploiting the threat of international terrorism to repress domestic opposition and dissent. Indeed, the speed of Pakistan's reversal of fortunes has been astonishing. General Musharraf's non-democratic regime is seen as at the frontline in the 'war in terror' and promptly gained significant US economic aid in thanks for its stance. Egypt has augmented its prevailing 'emergency' laws – an 'emergency' of over 20 years' duration – and suspects may be held for rolling 45-day durations without any charge being made against them. In cases where defendants were brought to trial, they faced military courts. Its prime minister stated that the West should 'think of Egypt's own fight against terror'. Israel too sought to place its campaigns against the Palestinians within the context of the wider war, not least in Prime Minister Sharon's regular description of President Arafat as 'our bin Laden'. The Malaysian government has used its Internal Security Act to repress the pro-democracy movement and supporters of the imprisoned former Deputy Prime Minister Answar Ibrahim (Human Rights Watch, 2002; 2004a; 2004b). One of the most disturbing situations, however, was the self-perpetrated 'terrorist attack' by Macedonian authorities in April 2004. This act, resulting in the deaths of seven immigrants, was staged to prove to the USA that Macedonia was a stalwart ally in the 'war on terrorism'.

The 9/11 attacks provided a pretext for some states to satisfy a domestic political agenda under the guise of robustness against international terrorism. Uzbekistan allowed the USA to use air bases within its territory for the prosecution of the war in Afghanistan. In return for this cooperation, its government has been afforded a greater degree of latitude in its repression of Muslim activists and religious freedom. Additionally, the USA gave it $160 in aid. The Putin Administration in Russia explicitly linked the conflict within Chechnya to the wider phenomenon of international terrorism, stating that there were links between the rebels and the Taliban and Osama bin Laden (Human Rights Watch, 2002). US policy on Russia's handling of the Chechnya crisis significantly changed when Putin offered the USA the opportunity to use its airspace and bases when necessary. President Bush thanked the Putin Administration by adopting its stance on the secessionist war, demanding that the Chechnyan fighters sever links with 'international terrorist groups' and participate in negotiations with Russia (Fitchett, 2001, p. 10). Additionally, the fortunes of the Chinese Administration have taken a turn for the better. Its support for the US 'war on terror' and specifically the action taken in Afghanistan was not without a price tag: 'China, like Russia, expects new understanding for its brutal repression of a Muslim minority, the Uighurs, on the grounds that it is also counterterrorism. And, as with Russia, the Bush Administration appears to be ready to make important concessions' (*Washington Post*, 2001, p. 8).

In the present international order, realpolitik dictates a reconfiguration of international relations. The 'axis of evil' appears to be counter-balanced with an axis of allies – many of whom have a poor track-record of protecting fundamental freedoms, as Bishara (2001) notes: 'the members of the unwritten alliance are undemocratic regimes that grossly violate human rights'.

In the wake of the 11 September attacks, the EU offered total support for the USA in the initial stages of its 'war on terror'. Within the EU too, there is a commitment to combat the challenge of international terrorism at both the Community and intergovernmental level. At the Community level, the EU passed Council Regulation No. 2580/2001. This Regulation facilitates such measures as the freezing of all economic assets of individuals or groups designated as terrorists. It also obligates financial institutions, such as banks, to provide data on accounts and transactions of those designated as terrorists. Council Regulation No. 881/2002 facilitates the application of these measures specifically to individuals or groups suspected of links to bin Laden, al-Qaeda, and the Taliban. These rulings are updated regularly in light of amendments and additions to the listings of those designated as terrorists.

This legislation is accompanied by measures taken in the second pillar, or the CFSP. At this intergovernmental level, there is significant interstate cooperation in the form of Common Positions. In Council Common Position 2001/930/CFSP, the member states can take different measures to restrict the activities of those involved or intending to be involved in the commission of terrorist acts. These measures can include the freezing or sequestration of economic assets, the denial of safe haven, and the prohibition of free movement across borders. Council Common Position 2001/931/CFSP offers definitions of 'persons, groups and entities involved in terrorist acts', 'terrorist act' and 'terrorist group'. On the basis of such interpretations of these terms, it provides a list of both individuals and groups considered 'terrorists'. This listing is updated regularly. In Council Common Position 2002/402/CFSP, these measures were targeted specifically on bin Laden, al-Qaeda, the Taliban and any individual or groups held to be associated with them. There have been Decisions as well as Framework

Decisions made under the third pillar, Justice and Home Affairs (JHA) taken to combat the threat of terrorism. One of the most important, Council Framework Decision 2002/475/JHA, reiterates much of the contents of Council Common Position 2001/931/CFSP in terms of defining terrorist groups and offences. It, however, introduces minimum penalties to apply to terrorist offences, including extradition, and permits the extension of a state's jurisdiction to the sovereign territory of another member state. Council Decision 2003/48/JHA provides for police and judicial cooperation between member states in information gathering and dissemination on investigations of terrorist activities and offences. This Decision also alludes to the potential for 'joint investigation teams in order to carry out criminal investigations into terrorist offences involving any of the listed persons, groups or entities'. Council Framework Decision 2002/684/JHA facilitates cooperation between the member states in the fight against terrorism via a European Arrest Warrant and a 'system of surrender' of arrested persons suspected of terrorism.

Notwithstanding the close alliance between the UK and the USA in the military response to the threat of international terrorism, the 'old'/'new' Europe debate, and the measures outlined previously to tackle terrorism, most European states prefer a strategy of prevention, as articulated by German Foreign Minister Joschka Fischer (2002):

> Tough action and repression alone do not ... constitute a satisfactory response to the threat posed by modern terrorism. We will only be able to combat it through a policy of prevention, if we manage to take a new joint approach to effectively fighting its many different causes. This includes new strategies against hunger, poverty and lack of opportunities as well as the socially just management of economic globalization. But this includes above all protection of human rights, civil, political as well as socio-economic and cultural rights.

Nevertheless, given the capability and the will for the USA 'to go it alone', such a strategy of prevention exists in rhetoric only. States that have opposed the US policy and its erosion of human rights could have worked together within the UN General Assembly for a condemnatory resolution but signally failed to do so. Instead the USA pursues its endless 'war on terror' almost exclusively with military means. There is an attempt to bring former leaders of 'rogue' states to justice before international tribunals. An Iraqi Special Tribunal exists but it differs significantly from the International Criminal Tribunal for the Former Yugoslavia (ICTY). The latter is established under the aegis of the UN Security Council and Resolution 771. This Resolution held that those who had committed or ordered the commission of grave breaches of the Geneva Conventions were individually responsible for these breaches. Its authority thus comes from the UN and its writ is legitimate within the international community. Admittedly, as it cannot hold trials in absentia, the ICTY is dependent on international cooperation to arrest and transport indicted persons. To date, many such persons remain at large, notably Bosnian Serb leader Radovan Karadzic and his fellow Bosnian Serb General Ratko Mladic, raising questions about the commitment of all states to the work of the ICTY. In contrast, the Special Tribunal in Iraq has been enacted by the Iraq Governing Council in December 2003 and will derive authority from the Iraqi national government due to be elected in January 2005 (Human Rights First, 2004). As the legitimacy of these elections is contested by some factions within Iraqi society, it is highly probable that the Tribunal's work also will come under scrutiny. It will try Saddam Hussein, the former president, and many high-ranking members of the former Ba'ath regime. The Judges and Investigative Judges are to be Iraqi nationals, though they can take assistance from non-Iraqis. In the present state of flux in Iraq and opposition to the occupation by the Allied forces, the prospect remains that the forthcoming trials may bring further societal instability.

CONCLUSION

In the wake of 11 September, human rights and fundamental freedoms are imperilled by the strategies used to prosecute the 'war on terror'. Ironically, counter-terrorism measures run the very real risk of undermining precisely the freedoms that they are said to protect. At both the systemic and the regional level, institutions have called upon state authorities and organizations to ensure that 'measures taken in the struggle against terrorism do not discriminate in purpose or effect on grounds of race, colour, descent or national or ethnic origin' (UNHCR, 2002). The UN Secretary General, Kofi Annan, has demanded that the Commission on Human Rights guarantees that counter-terrorist strategies are not used as a guise for the repression of rights. Also within the UN forum, Mexico presented a draft resolution to the UN Commission on Human Rights during its 2002 session asking that all counter-terrorist measures paid due heed of prevailing international human rights law. In the face of strong opposition from states such as Algeria, Egypt, India, Pakistan and Saudi Arabia, notably states that have used counter-terrorism to repress internal political and civil dissent, and the USA, the draft resolution was withdrawn by Mexico. The EU, through statements to the UN Commission on Human Rights, and at both its Extraordinary Council of 21 September 2001 and the European Council of Laeken in the following December, also stressed the need for measures tackling terrorism to be in accordance with respect for human rights (von Schorlemer, 2003 p. 278). As noted, however, such pleas have gone unheard as states have either derogated from some laws or disregarded them completely. In the anarchical international system, there is no power higher than the state that can command observance of and commitment to international law. The UN Commissioner for Human Rights has the requisite remit but his capacity is dependent upon the political will of states: 'in the end, national governments must make these rules happen, in name and in fact' (Joyner, 2004, p. 255). This political will, especially in terms of core states within the system, is obviously lacking. The reliance on states for enforcing human and civil rights norms is especially problematic 'in cases where the state is simultaneously the perpetrator of rights abuses and the institution through which grievances should be reported and addressed' (Schwarz, 2004, p. 203). This has severe consequences for the provision of comprehensive security – both for states and for individuals. As Kofi Annan has correctly observed, 'we cannot achieve security by sacrificing human rights. To try to do so would hand the terrorists a victory beyond their dreams' (Annan, 2002). When we witness core states suspending and/or violating their international obligations to defend and promote fundamental freedoms and rights – and rewarding other states for doing so, then we forsake both our humanity and our security:

> Sacrificing rights for 'security' may seem tough and pragmatic, but it is fraught with peril. By breeding new resentments, foreclosing avenues of peaceful dissent, and undermining the international standards that help explain why terrorism is wrong, it risks exposing us to still greater dangers. It is time for the right kind of sensitivity. (Roth, 2004).

12. Agriculture

Wyn Grant

The 2004 enlargement of the European Union (EU) took place at a time when a debate was occurring among analysts about whether substantial progress had at last been made in reforming the Common Agricultural Policy (CAP). The CAP had been devised at a time when policy makers had very different preoccupations from those that concerned them at the beginning of the twenty-first century. For policy makers the aftermath of the Second World War was a very real recent memory. Large segments of the European population had had insufficient food to eat and, against the background of the Cold War, food security seemed to be a major priority. The possibility that the communist states of Eastern Europe might one day become democratic countries with liberal market economies with a union of European states would have seemed an impossible dream. Hence agricultural policy was governed by a 'productionist' philosophy in which the emphasis was on encouraging farmers to maximize their output. The CAP was set up with a financial structure that rewarded farmers for successfully increasing their production. The mechanization of European agriculture, a process still taking place at the time that the CAP was being established, and the possibilities offered by the chemical revolution offered by fertilizers and agrochemicals, made higher levels of output relatively easy to achieve, assisted by the dissemination of new knowledge by state-funded agricultural advisory services and the 'fieldsmen' of the leading agrochemical companies. Improvements in veterinary medicine and in animal husbandry techniques also made their contribution. The possibility that more intensive forms of agriculture might lead to unacceptable levels of environmental damage or that animal welfare might become a policy consideration did not enter into the minds of decision makers.

There was a real concern about the gap in the standard of living in urban and rural areas. There were real fears that a marginalized peasantry might provide a reservoir of support for extremist movements, either the Communist Party or, more likely, populist 'Poujadiste' movements or other parties of the extreme right. It is therefore something of a paradox that the entry of Poland into the EU has reintroduced a significant group of subsistence or semi-subsistence farmers into the EU population and that they have provided a basis of electoral support for radical populist and nationalist parties. The story of European farming since the 1950s has, however, been one of a larger amount of output being produced on a smaller number of larger farms by fewer farmers. In countries such as France, however, family links with the countryside are still cherished and farming is seen as making a contribution to visions of the nation out of line with its economic importance.

The CAP has been widely criticized for absorbing a disproportionate share of the EU budget (still around 45 per cent in 2004) and distorting world trade patterns in agriculture, particularly to the disadvantage of least developed countries. It has sometimes been defended as a social policy, but in fact most of the financial benefits go to large-scale farmers, including members of Europe's royal families. A large-scale arable farmer could easily receive over one million euros a year in subsidies. The policy has also pushed up the price of land, making it hard for new entrants to come into farming and producing an elderly farming population. Intensive farming practices made a particularly significant contribution to water pollution in rivers and lakes, while large-scale arable farming on 'prairie' fields produced unattractive landscapes and undermined biodiversity. The complexity of the CAP has made it open to systematic attempts at fraud, sometimes involving organized criminal activity. Some of the more notorious examples of fraud include the herd of cows supposedly located on the fifth floor of an office block in Rome and the arable fields supposedly to be found deep under water near Rockall in the North Atlantic. Although the share of a household budget spent on food fell as per capita incomes increased, the general effect of the CAP was to push food prices in Europe above world market levels.

Analysts of agricultural policy have taken different views about whether the CAP has experienced significant reform. The optimistic view is that promulgated by the Commission but also shared by some analysts (Ackrill, 2000). In summary form, this perspective accepts that the reforms undertaken in the 1980s, driven by budgetary pressures, did little to change the shape of the CAP. The introduction of milk quotas in 1984 dealt with a serious budgetary crisis by effectively capping the level of milk production. However, it failed to eradicate the structural surplus of milk in Europe which still had to be dumped on world markets, endangering the livelihoods of small-scale dairy producers in countries such as Jamaica. Particularly in those member states that did not permit quota transfers, it ossified existing market structures and did nothing to enhance the competitiveness of the European dairy industry on world markets. Milk produced by a small-scale farmer in Bavaria, Brittany or the English west country could cost two-and-a-half times as much to produce as in Australia, New Zealand, the Argentine or Uruguay. Similarly, the so-called 'budgetary stabilizers' reform of 1988 did little to stabilize the CAP budget and was open to the 'fudges' typical of any budgetary reform given the complexity of the CAP.

The 1992 MacSharry reform was, however, significantly different from earlier reforms, and optimists claim that it set the CAP on a new path. It was driven by the need to secure agreement in international trade negotiations which brought a new range of actors into decisions about agricultural policy, not just trade ministers but also industrial and service companies concerned about the implications of a failure to secure agreement in the Uruguay Round (UR) of trade negotiations. Accounts of exactly how the reform was brought about differ, but essentially MacSharry seized a window of opportunity to force through a reform that changed the way in which farmers were paid under the CAP. The reform was largely confined to the arable sector, although some changes were made in livestock regimes and agri-environmental schemes were introduced as a discretionary element of the CAP.

The key innovative element of the reform was to at least partially break the link between production and subsidy for the key arable crops, something referred to in the jargon as 'decoupling'. For wheat, for example, farmers henceforth received an area aid payment based on the area under cultivation. The payment they received was calculated on a very generous basis so it increased rather than reduced the cost of the CAP. However, the intervention price was reduced, eventually to near the world market level, so it was no longer attractive to produce surplus crops that could be sold into a risk-free, publicly provided market. As part of the 2003 and subsequent reforms, this concept was rolled out into other crops, in particular a range of Mediterranean products such as rice and olive oil. Steps were also taken to start to reform the dairy sector through projected reductions of the intervention crisis and per capita payments to farmers based on the 'virtual cow'.

The Agenda 2000 reforms agreed in 1999 were intended to prepare the EU for eastern enlargement, but many commentators saw them as designed to enable the EU to fulfil the commitments it had made in the UR. At the last moment, following an agreement between France and Germany, the EU backed away from a radical commitment to 'degressivity', that is, a real annual reduction in the level of agricultural subsidy. The agriculture commissioner, Franz Fischler, used a commitment in the 1999 package to a 'mid-term review' of the reforms to leverage a renewed discussion of policy change. Steps had earlier been taken in the direction of a more vigorous rural development policy and the concept of 'modulation' provided for the diversion of funds from the so-called 'first pillar' of the policy, essentially farm subsidies, to the 'second pillar' covering rural development and environmental programmes. The 2003 reform package also provided for cross-compliance, which meant that farmers would not be eligible for aid unless they complied with a range of environmental, animal welfare, occupational safety and other standards. All these changes were presented by the Commission as a move towards a 'multifunctional' agricultural policy in which the role of agriculture was not simply to provide food, but to contribute towards other public policy goals such as preventing rural depopulation, maintaining valued landscapes and contributing towards the achievement of environmental goals.

The 'optimistic' view of the reform process is that there has been real progress towards a renewed policy, made possible not by a 'big bang' reform, but by a series of incremental changes building on the new direction signalled by the MacSharry reforms in 1992. The CAP in 2010 will thus be considerably different from the CAP in 1990. Commission officials often feel that they have not been given sufficient credit for their long-term planning and for the extent to which they outmanoeuvred a Farm Council often resistant to reform, although they have been helped by the decline of the traditional agricultural lobby that has increasing difficulty in agreeing a common position as the EU has become larger. Certainly most analysts would agree that Franz Fischler, who left office in the autumn of 2004, has been an exceptional agriculture commissioner, both in terms of having a new strategic vision of the CAP and his possession of the tactical political skills necessary to put that vision into practice. Accounts of EU policy often underestimate the extent to which an individual commissioner can make a difference. There was much speculation about whether his successor in the agriculture portfolio would be appointed from one of the accession states or from one of the six original member states such as the Netherlands.

The 'pessimistic' view of reform points out that farmers in the EU still receive, according to OECD figures, over one-third of their income from subsidies, tax breaks and other forms of public support. (For a sceptical view of the reform process, see Daugbjerg, 1999.) From this general perspective, the emphasis on multifunctionality is seen as a way of placing subsidies in the 'green' or non-trade-distorting box in international negotiations, thus evading trade policy challenges to those traditional forms of farm support. EU policies still have a distorting effect on the world market faced by developing countries, with Oxfam pointing out that what it calculates as the average $2 per day subsidy received by a European dairy cow is more than some people have to live on in the least developed countries. For all the emphasis on the 'second pillar', most of the EU's agriculture budget is still being spent on traditional support policies. Spending on rural development and environmental schemes is unlikely to reach more than the low teens in terms of a percentage of all EU spending on agriculture by 2010. 'Decoupled' subsidies can still distort patterns of production because they mean that farmers have available to them sums of money they wouldn't otherwise have to use on capital investment or maintaining otherwise unprofitable ventures.

So where does the balance lie? Has there been real reform, or are the changes mere window dressing that allows 'business-as-usual' policies to continue? The CAP has changed, but not fundamentally. It is a more Janus-faced policy, pointing in two directions. This is not entirely accidental. It is possible to interpret the current CAP as a dual policy. On the one hand, large-scale, intensive farming that can compete on international markets, particularly with decoupled subsidies and intervention buying still available as a safety net, should be able to continue much as it always has done in areas such as Eastern England, the Paris basin or the plains of Northern Germany. On the other hand, remoter areas of Europe with more marginal forms of farming, including large areas of the accession states, will engage in more 'multifunctional' forms of agriculture. Traditional farming practices will continue and help to prevent depopulation in these politically sensitive areas, but will increasingly be combined with rural tourism (especially 'green' tourism) and value-added niche production of regional food processing and other products.

Indeed, there is a long-term structural change across Europe away from farming as a sole occupation, exemplified by the fact that even the grain barons of Eastern England are increasingly contemplating diversification. Many farmers are increasingly part time, including a number of 'hobby farmers' who have farms as country residences that offer sporting opportunities or produce niche products after leaving their lifetime occupations. Long-established farmers increasingly have to enhance their revenues from agricultural contracting, rural tourism and refurbishing outbuildings for use as offices or storage. These and other forms of diversification will become increasingly important in the accession states, which offer particularly good opportunities for 'green tourism' if current levels of biodiversity can be maintained.

The reform options are also not as straightforward as they sometimes appear. The sugar regime is the last unreformed commodity regime in the CAP. Through a combination of import protection and export subsidies, it allows beet sugar to continue to be grown in substantial areas of Europe (it is an important crop in many accession states). Producers of cane sugar, a tropical grass, are allowed only limited access to the European market despite the fact that their product is more competitive, although that will eventually change as a result of the 'Everything But Agriculture' agreement. However, complete liberalization is not a panacea. In Northern Europe, sugar beet can be the most suitable crop for certain soils. Beet sugar factories are an important source of jobs in rural areas where industrial employment is often lacking. Removing existing arrangements would not necessarily benefit countries such as Mauritius, where sugar exports are a key element of the national economy and where preferential access is available to the European market under special arrangements made originally under the Lomé agreements. Indeed, a liberalized international sugar regime would probably largely benefit emerging countries such as Brazil and Thailand, with Brazil in particular benefiting from economies of scale, climate and cross-subsidization from ethanol production. In the longer run, it may be that biofuel production will offer a new future for the European sugar beet industry.

The CAP turned Europe from an agricultural importer into an agricultural exporter, with a consequent impact on patterns of world agricultural trade to the annoyance of the USA and medium-sized agricultural exporting countries in the Cairns Group led by Australia. In the longer run, international trade negotiations have probably been the most important single factor forcing change in the CAP. In the context of the Doha Round negotiations in 2004, the EU made an offer to phase out its export subsidies, conditional upon reciprocal moves on export credit schemes and 'single-desk' commodity trading companies. Export subsidies have particularly disadvantaged some developing countries, but even if they are eventually removed, that would still leave unresolved the question of the large amounts of import protection provided by the EU for agricultural products. Export subsidies are in any case dwarfed in size by the agricultural subsidies provided by the EU and, although the form of those subsidies may have changed, they are unlikely to disappear.

THE 2004 ENLARGEMENT AND THE CAP

The 2004 enlargement of the EU saw its 7 million farmers increased by 4 million to 11 million, some 2.5 million of them in Poland. In the ten accession countries in 2002, 13.4 per cent of the employed population was engaged in agriculture compared with 4 per cent in the EU15. Accession added 38 million hectares of farmland to the EU, a 30 per cent rise on 130 million hectares. Yet the value of agricultural production was estimated to rise by only 6 per cent.

Given these marked differences in agricultural structure and productivity, and what was at one time seen as the very high financial cost of admitting Central and East European states, enlargement of the EU to the East was for long seen as a potential major driver of change in the CAP. In fact, the reforms that occurred in 2003 were driven as much as anything by German budgetary concerns and a French desire to maintain the CAP as much as possible in its present form, combined with the insistence of the UK and other North European states such as Sweden that the reform impetus should be maintained. The accession states turned out to be policy takers rather than policy makers, obliged to accept a phased entry to the CAP. However, the longer-term impact of accession may yet be significant. Once the accession states in effect become full members of the CAP, there may be a renewed 'reform crunch' stimulated by budgetary pressures. Budgetary pressures remain, however, an uncertain stimulant for real change (Moyer and Josling, 1990) and much in practice may depend on how the Doha Round of trade negotiations turns out. There is also uncertainty about what the stance of the accession states will be in the Farm Council and how effectively they will advance their policy preferences. For example, will there be a Franco-Polish alliance to resist reform or will the different commodity interests of the two countries pull them apart? Certainly the new member states may well group together and block any deal on sugar reform that disadvantages them.

The accession states are a very heterogeneous group in terms of the political economy of their agricultures. However, a considerable number of them need not be considered in depth in an analysis of this type either because they are small countries with relatively small agricultural economies (Malta being the extreme example) or because they are predominantly industrial countries in which agriculture is not a major part of the economy (the Czech Republic). The real story about enlargement as far as agriculture is concerned is a narrative about Hungary, and especially about Poland.

Hungary has considerable potential as an agriculture producer because of its topography (much of the country is a plain), its fertile soils, its continental climate and its central location in Europe on the Danube. In the days of autarchic trading within the communist bloc under COMECON, it had an important role as a supplier of food to the Soviet Union, which took 90 per cent of its grain crop, but was held back by the inefficiencies of the communist system. The author recalls visiting a large food processing plant in Hungary in the days of the communist regime where he was shown with some pride a computer-controlled salami production plant purchased from the Netherlands. Next door, meat was being processed by large numbers of workers using knives as the main implement. After the end of communist rule, Hungary joined the Cairns Group as a grain-exporting country, although it had to resign when it became a candidate for EU membership. Hungary's gross agricultural trade surplus is greater than that of the UK and ranks it sixth among member states. Structural problems remain as a hangover of communism, not least questions of land title, but there has been some inward investment by farmers from Britain and elsewhere who have found ways of coping with the complexities of the legal system. Hungary has the potential to be a major supplier to the rest of Europe of a wide range of goods from grain to fruit and vegetables, although the implication is that less efficient producers elsewhere in Europe will lose out as a result.

Poland presents the paradox of a country that is not especially suitable for farming, yet has 18.8 per cent of its population engaged in agriculture. In part this reflects the fact that there is high unemployment in rural areas, much of it unregistered, and that there is nowhere else for farmers to go. At least on the land they receive a state pension and tax and social security benefits, with the prospect of a windfall payment from the EU, initially €44.46 per cultivated hectare, although many of them appeared unwilling to register for this benefit, either because they lacked proper title to their land or because they were suspicious of the authorities. Indeed, the Catholic hierarchy had to intervene to encourage them to apply for EU funds.

Poland has poor natural conditions for agriculture, with land quality 'among the poorest in Europe' (Kowalski, 1991, p. 57). Soils are predominantly light, leading to a susceptibility to drought, and high levels of acidity are a problem in many areas. The winters are harsh and the summers hot, producing a short growing season. Because the climate is intermediate between the maritime climates of Western Europe and the continental climates of the East, it displays unpredictable weather and important changes from one year to another. These problems with soil and climate are compounded by farm structure. A total of 57 per cent of farms, especially those in the south and east of the country, are less than five hectares in size. In 2003, 3 per cent of holdings produced nothing (presumably occupied by infirm pensioners), about 12 per cent of farms cater only for family food requirements, and 49 per cent market less than £190 of products per year. In part, this reflects the presence under communism of 'industrial peasants' in some parts of Poland on a model also seen in Germany. A worker might have a position in a steel plant, but he would also have a smallholding which would feed his family and produce a small surplus for sale by the roadside or in local markets. In some cases workers have lost their industrial jobs and been forced back on the smallholding as a means of subsistence. Collectivization was much less extensive in Poland than in most other communist states. There were, however, a large number of former state farms in the north-west of the country which have proved to be financially viable. Those close to the German border have been a target for foreign investment from Germany, although investors from other member states are also present. Outright ownership of Polish land by foreigners is not permitted for the time being in order to respect nationalist sentiments, but just before accession, the Polish government made it easier for foreign investors to farm in Poland, recognizing that this is an important way of achieving modernization as not just capital, but also business and technological skills, are in short supply.

THE ACCESSION PROCESS

Early forecasts of the financial impact of accession on the CAP were very pessimistic. 'Early estimates suggested that extending the CAP to cover just the countries of Poland, Hungary and the then Czechoslovakia, the so-called Visegrad states, would require an increase in contributions by EU members of 60 per cent' (Gaisford et al., 2003, p. 16). Clearly such a financial burden would have been unacceptable to the existing member states, and the EU sought to deal with the problem both by reducing the funds made available to the new member states and, second, by seeking further reform of the CAP itself. Indeed, the EU's initial negotiating position appeared to be that arable aid payments would be denied to the new member states altogether on the grounds that they were compensation for the removal of subsidies which these countries had never received. Clearly, this position was untenable and the final settlement reached means that grain farms on either side of the Austro-Hungarian border will receive substantially different amounts of subsidy from the CAP in the years up to 2013 in spite of the fact that they are supposedly members of the same common internal market.

The deal reached at the Copenhagen Summit in 2002, sweetened at the last minute by some side payments direct into the Polish treasury, provided for CAP direct payments to be phased in over a ten-year period. The starting point is 25 per cent of the full rate in 2004, 30 per cent in 2005 and 35 per cent in 2006. However, it was agreed that new member states will be able to top these sums up by 30 per cent, partly using EU funds that would otherwise go into rural development and partly with cash from their own treasuries. This means that most accession countries (but not the Czech Republic) will be paying 55 per cent of the full rate of direct payments in 2004, rising to 60 per cent in 2005 and 65 per cent in 2006. It is possible that farmers in the new member states could be receiving the same direct payments as EU15 farmers in 2010, rather than 2013 for countries that don't top up.

It may be questioned whether the diversion of funds from rural development is entirely sensible as most of these countries have defective rural infrastructures. Communist regimes tended to concentrate expenditures on urban areas and industry or on massive structures on the collective farms themselves which are now of little use. Rural areas often lack good roads, agricultural advisory and consultancy services are generally absent or inadequate, skills training programmes particularly for supervisory roles do not exist and there are generally few arrangements for providing capital for rural projects. On the other hand, there was an initially poor take-up of the pre-accession SAPARD programme (Special Accession Programme on Agriculture and Rural Development), in large part because there was no administrative infrastructure to publicize it and run it in a proper fashion. These problems reared their head again, with difficulties in setting up accredited payments agencies in the member states in time for accession so that the correct payments could be made to eligible producers. Proper records of farmland to enable the Commission's Integrated Administration and Control System (IACS) to be operated were generally absent and titles to the ownership of land often did not exist or were disputed. It is perhaps just as well that eight of the ten new member states decided to operate a simplified single area payment scheme for the first three years of membership. Under this arrangement all of a country's aid is spread over its whole agricultural area to produce a single flat-rate payment.

Dairy quotas also had to be negotiated for each of the new member states. In the case of Poland, there was considerable unhappiness about the 9.38 million tonne quota negotiated with the EU, even though this figure is greater than the volume delivered to creameries at the time of accession. However, around 40 per cent of the milk produced in Poland is sold directly to consumers or is used by farming families or for rearing calves. It is quite likely that accession will lead to restructuring of dairying, with marginal farmers going out of production and milk increasingly going to processors. Large-scale dairy farming could well be a viable proposition in Poland given the country's potential for producing grass and high-protein crops such as alfalfa.

The phasing in of CAP payments has been a source of considerable resentment in the accession states. The Commission's justification was that if the payments were too generous they would simply be diverted into household consumption by small-scale farmers and that they would lead to income disparities that would generate resentment in rural areas (Daugbjerg and Swinbank, 2004, pp. 101–2). However, initial reports from Poland suggested that farmers were investing in machinery, fertilizers and chemicals with the Ursus tractor factory in Warsaw selling 1600 tractors in the first five months of 2004 compared with 1000 in the whole of 2003 (www.agra-net.com, 18 June 2004). The real reason for phasing in the payments, however, was to keep the budgetary costs of enlargement down to a tolerable level, against the background of the Chirac–Schröder deal of 2002 which limited increases on expenditure on CAP subsidies to 1 per cent per year after 2006 with no allowance for inflation. The hope of CAP policy makers was that by the time subsidies were fully phased in for the accession states, further reforms would have reduced their level, thus avoiding a budgetary crisis.

SCENARIOS FOR THE FUTURE

In discussing the future likely impact of eastern enlargement on the CAP, it is necessary to distinguish between the effect on the EU15 and the consequences for the accession states themselves. In some respects this is a positive sum game because, as the accession states become more prosperous, domestic consumers will be able to purchase more locally produced, high-value-added food products. One of the paradoxical consequences of the European Agreements signed on a bilateral basis following the collapse of the communist regimes was that they led to the transition states importing what were seen as high-quality food products from the West to replace domestic products, rather than succeeding in exporting food to the West. At the time of accession all of the new member states had substantial agricultural trade deficits with the EU15, with the exception of Hungary.

In Western Europe, particularly among farmers, accession has often been perceived as a zero sum game in which cheaper products from Central and Eastern Europe will displace food products from Western Europe. The greatest potential advantage of the accession states in the short run is in labour-intensive products such as fruit and vegetables, with Poland being a major potato producer. The mushroom industry is particularly labour intensive, with British and Irish growers under pressure from imports from Poland which, it has been alleged, have sometimes been produced making use of even cheaper labour from the Ukraine. In general, however, the ability of producers from the accession states to compete effectively in West European markets will be constrained for some time by their much lower rates of productivity in agriculture. This gap is unlikely to be closed for some time if the experience of southern accession offers any guidance. The stylized facts are that Spanish productivity levels have generally reached EU standards, but those in Greece and Portugal still lag well behind. Farmers will, of course, have additional funds available for investment, but some of this will be diverted into consumption, particularly by smaller-scale farmers. There are a number of uncertainties involved in forecasting how rapidly productivity gaps will close, including the rate of foreign investment, the extent to which skill shortages are resolved and how quickly deficiencies in rural infrastructure are overcome. No doubt progress will be more rapid in some accession states (e.g. Estonia, Hungary, Slovenia) than in others. Domestic markets should benefit from a faster GDP growth than in the EU15 and will therefore absorb a considerable proportion of any increased production. Under transitional arrangements, some products are not allowed to enter the EU15 because of unacceptable hygiene standards and so on, but producers regard the 'for domestic consumption only' label as a barrier to local sales and this has given them an increased incentive to improve standards.

Analysts are concerned that one of the most negative impacts of membership will be on land prices in the accession states. There can be little doubt that land prices will rise in the new member states, just as they were forced up by the introduction of the CAP in Western Europe. 'The supply of land is basically fixed and therefore the price of land tends to be bid up when governments increase agricultural support.' As a consequence, 'the next generation of farmers will have to pay high prices for farmland, reflecting the right to receive future subsidies. Thus the lock-in effect will be transmitted to the new Member States, which could further hinder the process of CAP reform' (Daugbjerg and Swinbank, 2004, p. 109). Concern has been expressed that 'the combination of inadequate farm incomes and high land values will slow the pace of consolidation and condemn existing farmers to relative poverty and isolate them from the benefits others in society will receive from EU membership' (Gaisford et al., 2003, p. 196). Whilst the kind of bond scheme advocated by Daugbjerg and Swinbank offers an alternative to the negative effects of direct payments, the political chances of it being adopted are slim.

The environmental impact of accession on agricultural practices could be substantial. As farmers make more use of fertilizers and agrochemicals, the problems of diffuse source water pollution from farms encountered in the EU15 could very well be replicated. Pig farming offers relatively quick returns from comparatively low start-up costs and uses more labour than some other forms of farming so that it is an attractive option for countries with limited capital and low labour costs. Unfortunately, it can be a major polluter of watercourses. However, perhaps the greatest potential impact of membership of the CAP in the accession states is on biodiversity. Many of the accession states are rich in a variety of flora and fauna, including mammals not generally found in the EU15 in some remoter regions. The sort of problem that can develop is shown by the case of the rare Iberian lynx that has been brought to the verge of extinction in Spain and Portugal. Favourable habitats for biodiversity are threatened in the accession states in a number of ways. Grasslands that support rare or attractive plants, insect life and hence a diverse bird population may be ploughed up for crops. Wetlands depend on the proper maintenance of drains and dykes and have already suffered in the Baltic states in the transition period. Land abandonment, which has already happened on an extensive scale in a number of countries, for example Estonia, threatens biodiversity as unmanaged scrub is much less supportive of a range of species than farmland used on an extensive basis. Unfortunately, there are doubts about whether the enthusiasm or the administrative capacity exists to support effective agri-environmental schemes in most of the accession states, even though they could bring financial rewards if combined with an effective 'green tourism' strategy.

Future accessions also pose considerable problems. Romania has a larger population on the land than even Poland, reflecting the fact that many people returned to their villages when industry collapsed. It is difficult for the land to sustain this increased population, hence the resort to illegal emigration to the EU. The author recalls driving through a large area of rural Romania at harvest time and feeling that he had travelled back 50 years in a time machine: horses working in the fields, chickens and other animals all over the road in villages, peasants carrying bundles of wood on their back and people selling small quantities of berries by the roadside. Careful thought will have to be given to the state of agriculture in Bulgaria and Romania before accession negotiations are completed.

CONCLUSIONS

There are considerable uncertainties surrounding the impact of the 2004 enlargement on the CAP, not least in relation to any agreement reached in the Doha trade round. An enlarged EU will be vulnerable to any Doha Round agreement that eliminates export subsidies and flattens tariff peaks. It is particularly difficult to forecast the outcome of the Doha Round, given the reduced political impetus for agricultural trade liberalization in the USA and the role of the new G20 grouping led by emerging countries such as Brazil, India and China.

Because of the productivity gap, and the effect of increased domestic consumption, enlargement is unlikely to have a dramatic effect on the supply–demand balance in agriculture and food products in the EU. This is not to say that surpluses may not appear in political commodities, but the areas in which the accession states are most competitive are either outside the CAP as food products (potatoes) or have relatively light regimes (fruit and vegetables). Indeed, the benefits of accession for farmers in the new member states may be offset by higher land prices. The potential impact of enlargement as a reform impetus has been blunted by the phasing in of support and further adjustments to the CAP. This does not mean that there will not be a budgetary problem by the time that full phasing in has occurred, and this may be exacerbated by the consequences of the Doha Round. A new 'reform crunch' stimulated in part by enlargement may therefore occur at some time in the future, for example towards the end of the first decade of the twenty-first century.

13. Environmental policy

Pamela Barnes

INTRODUCTION

The European Union (EU)'s environmental policy is a field of action that is characterized by a high degree of Europeanization. More than 80 per cent of national environmental policy has been made at EU level. There is thus a considerable sharing of the norms of the EU's environmental discourse among the policy makers at supranational, national and sub-national levels within the EU15. For the new member states, the conditions of accession have driven the development of their national environmental policies since the early 1990s. However, the EU's environmental discourse has not yet become the dominant ideology among the policy makers and policy implementers within the new states. As a result the dynamism and innovation of EU environmental policy making in the 1990s may slow down after 2004. It is to be hoped that actions will not be taken after enlargement that will undermine what has already been achieved. It would not be in the interest of any EU state, nor would it be in the long-term interests of future member states (including Turkey), to allow this to happen.

This chapter begins with a review of the development of the EU's environmental *acquis*, followed by discussion of the policy issues and debates surrounding the search for mechanisms to achieve sustainable development. The main focus of attention is the impact of the 2004 enlargement and the factors that will facilitate the process of Europeanization of the national environmental policies of the new states. The environmental *acquis* was transposed into the national bodies of legislation of the new member states before accession, but substantial changes are required at the national and sub-national levels for the environmental *acquis* to be accepted as the norm of their environmental discourse.

THE EVOLUTION OF THE EUROPEAN UNION'S ENVIRONMENTAL *ACQUIS*

By the 2004 enlargement the European Union had a firmly established and extensive environmental policy based on more than 200 major legislative acts covering horizontal legislation (such as strategic environmental impact assessment), water and air pollution, management of waste and chemicals, biotechnology, nature protection, industrial pollution and risk management, noise and radiation protection legislation. The Policy had been launched in 1973 in the first of a series of Environment Action Programmes (EAPs).[1] The measures contained in the early action programmes of the 1970s and 1980s were the EU's response to a number of pressures. First there was an increased international awareness of the problems of environmental degradation and the necessity for the EU states to respond. Second, the measures were aimed at ensuring that differences in national environmental policies amongst the EU's member states did not act as barriers to trade. Third, there was increasing evidence of the need for action against the damage that was being done to human health by environmental degradation. These early years of policy developments spawned a great deal of regulatory action. However, the directives and measures adopted tended to be focused on specific problems with solutions that were primarily 'end-of-pipe'[2] measures.

Because the EU is a Treaty-based organization, its institutions may only act if the Treaty gives them the power to do so. The 1957 European Economic Community Treaty did not include any articles that specifically related to the environment. The early measures had been introduced on the basis of interpretation of three Treaty articles relating to free trade and the market and improving the quality of the lives of the citizens. The Single European Act (SEA) revision of the Treaty in 1987[3] enabled the EU to introduce wider-ranging and more holistic policy measures. Articles specifically focusing on the environment were included in the Treaty for the first time. The basic principles included in articles 130r–130t SEA (renumbered in 1999 as 174–176 TEC) established an explicit legal basis for environmental policy developments.

The SEA also included changes to the institutions that gave the European Parliament (EP) an increased opportunity to act in the legislative process. The European Parliament is frequently regarded as the most environmentally concerned of the EU's institutions. By giving a clear legal basis and by introducing changes to the policy-making process, the Single European Act was the most important step forward in the history of the development of the environmental *acquis*.

Following the 1987 World Commission on Environment and Development Report – the 'Brundtland Report' – sustainable development became established on the global agenda. The Brundtland Report's definition of sustainable development: 'development that meets the needs of the present without compromising the ability of future generations to meet their own needs'[4] is deceptively simple! It is now a very well-known definition to the general public and policy makers alike, but that does not mean that its implications are necessarily understood. Sustainable development requires progressive changes to be made to the global economy and society to address the problems of poverty without causing further environmental degradation and loss of resources. This challenges policy makers to find instruments that offer sufficient flexibility to achieve a balance between the economic, environmental and social dimensions that underlie this concept.

The Treaty on European Union (TEU)[5] was negotiated in 1991 at the same time as the EU's Fifth Environmental Action Programme was being developed. The TEU contained a commitment to economic growth respecting the environment, a phrase criticized for its lack of definition. The Action Programme on the other hand was less ambiguous on the issue, including the Brundtland definition in its preamble and using as its title the phrase 'Towards Sustainability'. Taken together the TEU and the Fifth EAP established the European Union as an active participant in the global debate about how the objectives of sustainable development could be achieved. The Action Programme was also very influential in its approach. It replaced the reactive approach that had characterized the four earlier action programmes with a three-'pillared' strategy that combined command-and-control methods with an appropriate use of a range of economic instruments and increased funding for environmental programmes. The five sectors of economic activity that were the most potentially damaging to the environment (energy, agriculture, transport, industry and tourism) were targeted.

By the time of the 1995 enlargement to include the Nordic States of Finland and Sweden and Austria (regarded as environmental 'leaders'),[6] the basis was in place for a period of dynamic, wide-ranging and innovative policy action. The Amsterdam Treaty in 1999[7] included a clear statement of commitment to 'harmonious, balanced and sustainable development …' (Art. 2 TEC). Protection of the environment was put on to the same basis as economic development as a core objective of the EU. (This commitment has been reaffirmed in the Treaty of Nice, 2003, and the Constitutional Treaty.)

The Sixth Environmental Action Programme (2002–12) came into force when enlargement looked secure. It covered the immediate period post enlargement. The objective of the programme was to build a comprehensive environmental 'roadmap' for the EU25. The strategic targeting approach of the Fifth Environmental Action Programme was continued, but the method of targeting changed. The sector-specific targeting approach of the Fifth EAP did have its benefits, but sustainable development requires the opportunity for dealing with a number of issues and problems in a multidimensional way. The targets identified in the Sixth EAP include issues such as climate change, the loss of biodiversity, the impact of environmental degradation on human health and the quality of life, and the maintenance of natural resources (including waste reduction and management). The EAP was accompanied by a series of sector-specific strategies, identifying key environmental objectives, priorities and targets for a significant number of areas of the EU's action.[8]

The EU's environmental policy began in the 1970s as remedial regulatory action to deal with specific problems, moving after 1987 into an increasingly effective and coherent policy with a wide-ranging body of legislation and accompanying measures. It was this *acquis* that the accession states had to transpose into their national environmental policies. After 2004 the priority for the EU25 is to meet the challenges of sustainable development. Adding an environmental pillar to the Lisbon Strategy[9] for economic and social growth brought the requirements for sustainable development to a higher position on the EU's policy agenda.

In many respects, the concept of sustainable development remains elusive. Policy makers sometimes wrongly interpret it as a repackaging of environmental policy. They often fail to equate it with a balanced approach to the economic, social and environmental pillars, and with the need to place the three dimensions on an equal footing (CEC, 2003c, p. 5).

The 2004 enlargement has clearly increased the diversity of environmental problems that must be dealt with. But it has not brought failures of implementation, lack of commitment to a strategy of sustainable development or ineffective implementation to the EU. Even where there was clear agreement and understanding of the issues and need for action, the EU's environmental policy is not effective because of these failures at national and sub-national levels. 'The last few years have seen a growing difficulty in the timely and correct implementation as well as proper practical application of EC environmental legislation … the number of new complaints (of infringement) remains higher than 500 per year …' (CEC, 2004c, p. 5).

These problems were already there because many of the 'low hanging fruits of integration have already been picked …' (CEC, 2004b, p. 3) and the more difficult political decisions remain to be made. In the early stages of EU environmental policy development it was easier to gain agreement about measures because national policies were in embryonic stages of development and a 'policy space' existed into which the supranational policy could penetrate. The policy issues were immediate, pressing pollution problems that required limited and targeted action. Solutions to these problems appeared to present a very good return on any investments made.

Having dealt with these soft targets, the EU15 moved into a phase where agreements for action became more difficult, and the targeted problems and the solutions more complex. The European environment has continued to deteriorate. The policy therefore appears to provide a poorer return on the massive commitments that have been made to it. Environmental 'fatigue' has set in as a result, commitment is lower and implementation of action has become more limited. What the 2004 enlargement has done is to highlight the importance of the problems of failure to implement action because of its potential impact on all the member states of the EU25, both 'old' and 'new'. The problem has been given more 'visibility', but this visibility will have to be transformed into positive action. Strengthening the mechanisms for effective implementation is an urgent challenge for all the EU25's policy makers to confront.

SUSTAINABLE DEVELOPMENT POLICY – COMING TO TERMS WITH A 'FUZZY' BUZZWORD?

Among the many environmental issues that have emerged in recent years are global warming and climate change, greenhouse gas emissions, unsustainable use of natural resources such as fish stocks and forests, the generation of municipal waste, increased use of transport and energy, loss of biodiversity, groundwater pollution and agricultural practices. All of these have significant economic, social and financial costs, including costs to human health, but climate change and global warming represent the biggest threat to the goal of sustainable development. In order to meet these environmental challenges the EU's environmental policy agenda is wide-ranging. It carries significant implications at the sub-national, national and supranational levels within the EU itself and also for the role of the EU as an international environmental actor.

Of particular importance for sustainable development is the de-coupling of environmental pressures from economic growth. This requires a major shift to take place in advanced economies so that economic policy produces an outcome ensuring growth at the same time as environmental improvement. In designing measures and policy tools to produce this shift, policy makers must take the following criteria into account:

1. Renewable resources must not be utilized in a way that will exceed their long-term capacity for regeneration.
2. Non-renewable resources should be used efficiently and ways to substitute them by renewable resources found.
3. Emissions of polluting substances should not exceed the assimilative capacity of the environment into which they are released.
4. Irreversible impacts of human activities on ecosystems should be avoided.

5. All measures should be implemented in a cost-effective way and contribute to the application of the polluter-pays principle and the user-pays principle.

Within the European Union these criteria provide the basis of the policy framework for action until 2012. They are found in the initiatives of the Cardiff Process for the integration of environmental objectives to all EU policies (1998),[10] the adoption of the EU's Sustainable Development Strategy (SDS) (2001), and the Sixth Environment Action Programme (CEC, 2001a). The AC10 states were included in the deliberations about both SDS and the Sixth EAP with its accompanying strategic programmes targeting the priorities for action, although they were not included in the final decision-making procedures.

Recognition of the importance of integrating environmental objectives to all policies to achieve the goals of sustainable development has grown within the EU. Article 6 TEC provide a firm legal basis for the commitment that 'environmental objectives must be integrated into the definition and implementation of the Community policies ... with a view to promoting sustainable development' which is reaffirmed in the Constitutional Treaty. The different Council formations were asked to produce sector specific de-coupling strategies for presentation during the European Council meeting in June 1998.

By 2004 all EU25 states had introduced national environmental plans of action for the implementation of strategies of sustainable development and integration of environmental objectives. There has not yet, however, been a significant impact on the ground (EEA, 2003, p. 272). The initial strategies did not contain all the elements expected, nor did they include many new measures. The national plans based on the strategies were varied in their structures, as is the progress on their implementation. On the plus side the plans do provide frameworks for the national and sub-national policy makers and implementers. Regular progress reports must be submitted to the Commission and these provide an opportunity to bring consistency into policy measures across the EU25.

THE EU AS AN INTERNATIONAL ENVIRONMENTAL LEADER – HOLDING THE MORAL 'HIGH' GROUND?

During the 1990s the European Union gained a reputation as a leader in global environmental agreements, particularly those associated with climate change. The United Nations Framework Convention on Climate Change (UNFCC) was adopted in May 1992 and came into force in March 1994.

The Convention obliged signatories to establish national programmes to reduce the greenhouse gas emissions that were recognized as responsible for climate change and global warming.[11] In December 1997 a Protocol was added to the Convention in Kyoto that set legally binding limits for the six most damaging greenhouse gases. The aim was to reduce emissions by 5.2 per cent below 1990 levels during the first commitment period of 2008–12. The EU15 as a group played an active role in this international action to curb emissions by setting a target of 8 per cent reduction in its emissions, based on a burden-sharing agreement among the member states. Within this agreement some EU15 states committed to a more stringent reduction and this gave others the opportunity to proceed more slowly to achieve their target. The AC10 states had targets set for them individually.

The ratification of the Protocol was not without its problems. Two thresholds had to be met. More than 55 of the parties to the Convention from the industrialized states had to sign. Between them they had to have produced more than 55 per cent of the global carbon dioxide emissions (CO_2) in 1990. The EU15 and the AC10 states were among the 111 states that had ratified the Protocol by May 2004 but between them these states had not produced 55 per cent of the CO_2 emissions in 1990. The USA, a major producer, refused to ratify the Protocol in 2001 because of the potential costs of introducing implementing measures to US industries.

Russia was the other major producer of significant amounts of greenhouse gases. The Russian government was initially expected to ratify the Protocol, but in October 2003 President Putin announced that it did not intend to do so as 'an increase of two or three degrees would not be so bad for a northern country like Russia' (Pearce, 2004). The Russian government was concerned about the long-term implications of the Protocol. Kyoto required the participants to meet rigid emissions targets to a fixed timetable. In autumn 2003 Russia, because of the collapse of the post-communist economy, was producing less carbon dioxide than it had in 1990. For Russia this meant a high level of uncertainty about the costs of implementing the Protocol if their levels of emissions were falling in any event.

However, following agreements made during the EU–Russia Summit held in Moscow in May 2004, the Kyoto Protocol was presented to the Russian Parliament for ratification in late September 2004.[12] In return the EU had supported Russian membership of the World Trade Organization and made commitments to introduce measures that would mitigate the economic impact of the 2004 enlargement for Russia. As a result the Protocol gained the legal force required for it to become effective in 2005.

When the US government announced its withdrawal from the Kyoto Protocol the EU assumed the lead, encouraging other states to support its objectives by continuing with its own package of measures to curb emissions. The European Climate Change Programme (ECCP) had been launched in June 2000, to establish a framework of support for EU action. Somewhat disappointingly, despite the ECCP initiatives not all EU states were able to cut their emissions. By May 2004 the EU15 appeared to be on track for a reduction of emissions of 4.7 per cent by 2008 not the 8 per cent EU Kyoto target! So while the EU has remained committed to the rhetoric of the Kyoto Protocol, it will not be able to retain the moral 'high' ground of global leadership in its implementation without strengthening its own measures to achieve the agreed target. Furthermore, the Kyoto Protocol is time-limited and the EU did not appear to be exerting additional pressure to ensure that mechanisms were introduced to replace it.

Commitment to the goal of sustainable development implies a commitment to solving the problems of inequalities in the distribution of resources contributing to poverty in the Third World states. Initiatives such as the EU Water Initiative, with accompanying financial support for development of clean water supplies, especially in Africa, the Johannesburg Coalition on Renewable Energy and the EU Initiative for Poverty Eradication and Sustainable Development are a direct result of proposals made during the 2002 World Summit on Sustainable Development (WSSD). The EU15 was also the driving force behind ensuring that environmental issues were on the agenda of the World Trade Organization (WTO)'s meetings in Doha, Qatar in 2001, even if the outcomes were not as clear-cut or as far-reaching as many environmental groups had hoped.

The EU25 is moving into an era of considerable reorientation of its policies with regard to its nearest neighbours. The CE8 states have links with states in the Western Balkans, Russia and the Commonwealth of Independent States (CIS), Cyprus and Malta with Southern Mediterranean neighbours. The EU's Wider Europe Policy Initiative and Strategy (CEC, 2003a) includes an environmental dimension. It will provide an opportunity to take action on environmental problems that have cross-border and wider regional implications, for example initiatives in the Danube River Basin region or the Baltic and Mediterranean seas.

Globally the linkage between security issues and the environment has become increasingly evident in recent years. Indeed the EEA has concluded:

> Recent evidence suggests that military activities are among the world's most environmentally destructive activities. The environmental impacts of the war begin with disturbance and destruction of natural habitats and progress to contamination of land, air and water with wastes of people and machines. In most war zones the impacts on the environment are long term or permanent. (EEA, 2003, p. 219)

Other issues that have gained prominence on policy agendas include the linkage of availability and access to scarce resources and conflict, and the necessity to prepare to take action against terrorist attacks which have environmental implications.

The EU has taken up opportunities to play a leading role in many international environmental agreements, particularly those on climate change. However, it may be that the EU has gained its reputation as an environmental leader in the face of weak competition from other sources for the title. Despite this there are nevertheless clear benefits from the actions that have been taken by the Commission and the representatives of the EU's national governments working together in these agreements and international fora. Enlargement to 25 states has increased the potential for effective international action. At the same time it has increased the potential for the EU25 to look inward and concentrate on the environmental problems of the wider geographical region that it now occupies. It will require careful management of the policy tools that the EU has to ensure that this does not happen.

POLICY INSTRUMENTS – GETTING THE PRICE 'RIGHT'?

Regulatory instruments will remain the predominant form of EU action for the foreseeable future. Legally binding instruments are needed to ensure compliance from all member states. But a wide range of economic policy instruments has been and is being developed to supplement the legislation and bring a market orientation into future measures. These include getting the price of environmental degradation 'right', by removing national government subsidies to polluting industry, encouraging the use of environmental taxes and incentives, the introduction of tradable permits, improved consumer knowledge, environmental management and procurement systems, and sustainable land use in urban, coastal and other environmentally sensitive regions.

These have implications for the national and sub-national authorities. The roles of the administrative authorities and institutional frameworks associated with these measures are varied and complex. For example:

- The Eco-labelling Regulation requires national agencies to be in place for companies to register for the scheme. Enforcement by the national authorities includes the monitoring, imposition of national sanctions and 'on-the-spot' investigations and controls of the registered companies.

- General Directive 90/313/EEC 'on the freedom of access to information on the environment' contains a requirement for the national authorities to respond to requests for environmental information from the public.
- Directive 96/61/EC 'on integrated pollution prevention and control' (IPPC) is a major piece of environmental legislation to control the environmental impacts of mainly industrial activities with high pollution potential. It is based on a comprehensive permitting system and assessment regime for each environmental medium simultaneously and requires a high level of expertise among the national authorities.
- Directive 2003/87 EC 'establishing the EU's scheme for greenhouse emissions trading', begun in 2005, is intended to limit carbon dioxide emissions from 4000 to 5000 large-scale producers such as power generation stations. The national authorities will provide the regulatory framework for the scheme. Allowances will be allocated to the large emitters on an annual basis outlined in agreed national allocation plans. If emissions are reduced below the level of the allowance, the excess may be 'sold' to another polluter or saved for future use. Companies that exceed their limits may invest in pollution abatement technology or buy allowances on the market, whichever is cheapest. Information and monitoring by national authorities is essential to the scheme and supporting EU legislation has also been introduced to ensure that accurate data are available.

Encouraging the development of a wide range of policy instruments in addition to legislation has brought a large number of additional actors into the policy process. To enthusiastic environmentalists the EU's policy has already proved to be disappointing. Many believe that a lack of political will among the policy makers is the reason for policy failures, as governments and sectoral interests 'defend' their positions. However, in reviewing the extent of the EU's environmental policy developments it is difficult to imagine alternative structures that could have produced similar positive results. This does not mean that policy makers and implementers are able to complacently accept the *status quo*. Increasing the number of actors in the policy process to include the general public, local authorities and non-governmental organizations could lead to further fragmentation of effort. Reliable and comparable information flows have to be established with stringent reporting and monitoring procedures to ensure that this more flexible and inclusive approach does produce effective policy. This in turn requires the high level of Europeanization of the national policies to be maintained and the development of shared environmental norms within all the EU25 states.

MEETING THE CHALLENGE OF ENLARGING THE ENVIRONMENT?

All the states of Central and Eastern Europe have very specific environmental problems associated with their history of economic development before 1989. There has been environmental improvement since the early 1990s in the CE8. However, this improvement has been the result of economic recession and not a positive restructuring of the economy so that the goal of sustainable development may be reached! Decreasing levels of domestic extraction of raw materials are leading to an improved environmental situation. On the other hand these gains are being lost as transport volumes rise and transport use becomes more road-oriented.

For the island states of Cyprus and Malta the recent history of development is different from that of the CE8 states and other problems are evident. Cyprus developed mass tourism as the focus of its economic activity and there has been considerable environmental damage as a result. The confused and unstable political position of the island as a result of its division has undermined the development of a coherent approach to the environmental problems affecting the whole island. Many problems in Malta originate in the fragmented and often complex duplication of action by the national and sub-national authorities responsible for implementation of environmental policy.

For all the new states the search is for mechanisms to maintain their new and fragile competitiveness and de-couple economic development from environmentally damaging activities. It is evident that economic growth in the AC10 requires a significant increase in resource productivity that is not yet apparent. Consequently the new states will find it difficult to avoid moving towards unsustainably high levels of direct material input (EEA, 2003). Economic growth rates of 3.7 per cent average in the AC10 states contrasted in 2004 with EU15 average rates of 0.9 per cent. If these high rates of economic growth are maintained without more efficient use of resources, the potential for environmental damage will intensify, particularly if the economic growth is biased towards traditional environmentally damaging practices and not based on more eco-efficient and eco-friendly alternatives.

During the early years of the 1990s the governments of the CE8 states moved quickly to embed their countries in the economic and political systems of Western Europe. The goal of EU membership provided the main strategy for the policy makers. It became the justification for action, calming the concerns of the populations of the states as changes were introduced. The conditions for EU membership were the practical frameworks towards which the changes were geared. As a result the content of evolving national environmental policies was driven by the content of the EU's environmental *acquis*. Although the political and economic situations in Malta and Cyprus were different, the same requirements for membership have driven national environmental policy developments since the mid-1990s.

There had been significant growth in the impact of the EU's environmental policy on the domestic policies of all the EU15 member states by 2004. Jordan has demonstrated that even in the Eurosceptic state of the UK, 'Europeanization affects most if not all aspects of national environmental policy' (Jordan, 2002, p. 208). 'Europeanization consists of processes of a) construction b) diffusion and c) institutionalization of formal and informal rules, procedures, policy paradigms, styles, "ways of doing things" and shared beliefs and norms which are first defined and consolidated in the EU policy process and then incorporated in the logic of domestic (national and sub-national) discourse, political structures and public policies' (Radaelli, 2004, p. 35). Introducing the EU's 'way of doing things' into the new states initially required the inclusion of the content of the EU *acquis* in the national bodies of environmental legislation. Apart from the derogations and transition periods agreed to 2017, this transfer was accomplished and the environmental chapter of the Treaty provisionally closed with all the accession states during the 2002 round of negotiations.

In the new states the process of domestic policy change for membership of the EU has resulted in radical transformation of the national policies as there was a high degree of policy 'misfit' between the EU's environmental *acquis* and the emerging environmental policies of the new member states (Borzel and Risse, 2000 as cited in Jordan, 2002, p. 16). A warning must be sounded as a result for future developments. Whilst the *acquis* set targets and objectives, because there was no alternative in order to fulfil the conditions for membership, the *acquis* has not emerged as the basis for environmental ideology in the new states (EEB, 2004, p. 18).

The new member states have received a great deal of support to introduce the *acquis* and prepare the national administrative and institutional capacities during the pre-accession period. But the AC10 states have been required to import a body of legislation that is the outcome of a process of evolution and development begun elsewhere since 1973. Meeting the conditions for membership was the single most important driver in the development of national environmental policies in the states of Central and Eastern Europe throughout the pre-accession period. Similarly in Cyprus and Malta the *acquis* was dominant in developing national environmental policy and raised environmental concerns on to the national policy agendas in a way that had not been apparent before.

Overall EU policy was a step forward, but it was not received with enthusiasm in all the AC10 states in its entirety. The implementation of the legislation carries with it a significant number of costs. In the new states the environmental *acquis* was used as a 'ceiling' target for action in the preparation of national policies, not as a 'floor'. In Latvia and the Czech Republic legislation on water quality was poorly implemented before 1989 but did in fact contain stringent standards that were changed as a result of the transposition of the environmental *acquis*. These issues raised concerns that the most effective national environmental policies were not being introduced in the new states.

Europeanization of the national environmental discourse in the AC10 states requires a number of conditions to be met. First the national politicians must be able to form alliances with other member states in the preparation of new policy measures. This will enable the governments of AC10 states to feel that they are active partners in the policy deliberations. Second, there must be a degree of consensus about environmental issues among all the groups involved in policy formulation at national and sub-national level. This will drive the approach and attitude of the national politicians and determine the partners they will seek within the EU's decision-making system. Third, the AC10 states must be able to develop effective and reliable national public administrative capacity and the institutions necessary for implementation of the environmental *acquis* quickly.

BUILDING NATIONAL ALLIANCES

The AC10 states, particularly the CE8 states, were perceived somewhat simplistically as a group within the overall context of enlargement, but there is considerable variation of national interests among the group. After enlargement, a number of possible coalitions are beginning to emerge, not all of which will bring benefits to the development of environmental policy. Enlargement will no doubt increase the number of laggard states in the EU overall. However, there may be some surprises as EU15 states and the AC10 form strategic policy coalitions within the Council of Ministers. EU15 environmental 'leaders' must develop new tactics to ensure that the objectives of sustainable development remain on the policy agenda.

There is a possibility of increased cooperation emerging between Sweden and Finland (among the environmental leaders) and the Baltic states of Latvia, Lithuania and Estonia that will bring benefits to the northern region of the EU. On the other hand the latest version of the 'tomato' pact,[13] the seeming coalition of Poland and Spain that emerged during the debate on Council voting weightings in the Constitutional Treaty in early 2004, carries with it some disquieting signals. Both states are medium-sized states and are concerned to be counted among the major players within the EU25 and not included with the group of small states. Spain is considered to be among the EU's environmental laggards! Poland, the largest of the AC10 states, has some of the most deep-rooted and costly-to-resolve environmental problems. The governments of both states have similar concerns about the impact of environmental legislation on the development of their fragile economies. If Poland allies with Spain on some issues, will it also ally with Spain on environmental ones to the detriment of future policy developments?

Hungary, Slovakia and the Czech Republic are states where there are high levels of biodiversity and good soil quality, coupled with commitment to ensuring that there is no slowing of overall environmental policy development. The major concerns for these states appear to lie in the environmental pressures that may result from changes in consumption pattern with increased economic growth and affluence. Partly as a function of low levels of income, Hungary, the Czech Republic, Slovakia and Poland, for example, had lower levels of household waste per capita during the socialist era than in the EU15. The widespread use of integrated intermodal public transport systems, as there were few alternatives, was also of benefit to the environment. With growing affluence in all four states the disposal of domestic waste packaging has become a major problem and the demand for private car ownership has dramatically increased. Poland, the Czech Republic, Slovakia and Hungary, collectively seen as the 'Visegrad 4'[14] by the EU during the enlargement negotiations, do have similar environmental concerns. But the stance of Poland in negotiations about the agricultural chapter in 2002 left the other three states clear that any alliance in the region was a fragile one when national self-interests become important. These four states are very unlikely to form a stable coalition on environmental issues!

Despite deep differences over environmental issues in the past, given their geographical location close to Germany and particularly Austria, Hungary, the Czech Republic and Slovakia may find common ground in the future with these environmental 'leaders'. Successive Hungarian governments have prioritized water policy and favour the identification of the Danube river basin as a unit for environmental protection. Advantages will come for Hungary from opportunities for closer cooperation in the region as Bulgaria and Romania become EU member states and the Ukraine strengthens its agreements with the EU.

On nuclear issues differences between the Visegrad 4 states are apparent. The Czech Republic and Slovakia favour building programmes for new reactors. France is also a supporter of the nuclear industry. The Polish government has indicated that it would seek to maintain nuclear energy as an option in future developments. The UK has indicated that nuclear energy developments are not ruled out completely for the future. Hungary, on the other hand, has adopted a more negative view and may ally on these issues with Germany.

Of the two new island states, Malta in particular appeared to be able to very effectively use the small-state 'advantage' during the accession negotiations. The Maltese government was able to obtain more concessions to its national concerns than any of the other states. It may be that remaining outside any clear pattern of coalitions will be the way for Malta to continue to gain most from its position as the smallest state in the EU25.

INVOLVING CIVIL SOCIETY

Europeanization of the national policies in the new states is important to ensure that all the parties in the policy deliberations understand the 'language' of the environmental discourse. At the national level it was apparent that 'Environmental issues were an important catalyst demonstrating the failure of the political system we shared in Central and Eastern Europe until the end of the eighties. They were a rallying point for democratic opposition in many countries' (Stritih, 2000, p. 2). This did not necessarily mean that the environmental groups in the new states were ecologically interested – often they were more interested in establishing opportunities for democratic opposition to the state. There has been a change since the mid-1990s. The accession process, coupled with financial support from the EU institutions, strengthened the position of the environmental organizations in the new states. They are acquiring the 'green' credentials of the groups within the EU15 and becoming an important part of the policy process. This has been particularly the case in Slovenia and Hungary.

There is a high level of transnational interest group involvement in the policy process within the EU. Eighty per cent of proposals from the Commission may survive into the final text of legislation. The ability of environmental groups to participate in the policy process is an important aspect of ensuring that the new states are able to develop a more active role as policy makers. Industrial and business groups are able to access the policy-making system through European employers' associations and industrial groups more readily and effectively than many of the environmental groups. The Commission relies on environmental interest groups to provide information and advice. For this reason the Commission is open and prepared to support groups in the interests of maintaining balance and transparency in decision making. The European Environment Bureau (EEB), which brings together a large number of small and medium-sized environmental interest groups within the wider European geographical region, has received EU funding since the early 1970s to ensure that there is a counter-weight to the industrial interests in policy making.

BUILDING THE NATIONAL ADMINISTRATIVE AND INSTITUTIONAL CAPACITIES

The problems of national administrative and institutional capacity are not merely technical niceties but are crucial if the AC10 states are to make the change from the passive policy importers of the accession process to active contributors to a dynamic environmental policy in the future. 'Domestic institutions play a key role in absorbing, rejecting or domesticating Europe' (Bulmer and Radaelli, 2004, p. 9) with 'departments … in effect the main policy "fitters" in the EU' (Jordan, 2002, p. 5). As long as developments of strong administrative and institutional frameworks remain absent at national level, then the new member states will not be able to strengthen their positions in policy making. The ability of the new member states to affect policy development will have an important impact on net benefits of enlargement. The speed at which the process of change takes place is very important.

The governments of the AC10 states worked intensively during the pre-accession period to prepare for involvement in the EU decision-making process. However, 'EU accession management capacity is notably greater at the central, higher levels of government than in line ministries (especially at lower echelons)' (Nunberg, 2000, as cited in Apap et al., 2003, p. 25). Staff needs at the centre were prioritized during the accession procedures. The accession institutions stood out from the overall public administration organs in quality and efficiency, and had multilingual staff with higher educational qualifications than in other civil service departments. Concerns were raised among the new states that as opportunities emerged after enlargement those staff that had gained in understanding and expertise in EU policy making would relocate to Brussels, taking that expertise with them. If European policy continues to be restricted to small teams of well-trained civil servants and diplomats based either at the centre of government or relocating to Brussels, the process of Europeanization will take longer to accomplish and the overall development of environmental policy will be undermined.

The environmental *acquis* established the objectives that had to be achieved, but it is then left to the individual member states to ensure that the requisite institutional and administrative structures are in place to check that standards of permitting, monitoring, inspecting, notification are met. There are considerable constraints imposed on the national arrangements for environmental protection as a result of requirements of the legislation, but the institutions will continue to reflect the institutional and administrative culture of the nation-state. If the norms of environmental discourse are not shared within the EU25, then environmental protection will be undermined by the national differences.

Administrative departments will be dealing with different mechanisms for differing regulatory frameworks. Regulations covering traded products in the market will be easier to implement, for example standards for paint products. They will also have a higher level of visibility in terms of trade across the borders of the EU25. But legislation on the protection of groundwater or the requirement to conduct environmental impact assessments for which the national governments have greater responsibility will present more problems for the national implementers. Legislation of this type will leave the nation-states that are less committed to the EU legislation with opportunities for delays to implementation and enforcement.

During the accession negotiations the Commission identified a number of issues for the new states to take into account in order to implement the environmental *acquis*. The AC10 states were required to identify the number and type of national ministries which were in place, whether the implementation of specific directives was to be undertaken by national, regional or local institutions, whether there was a separation of departments responsible for the differing environmental media and what were the formal and informal mechanisms in place for implementation of legislation. Other issues that were discussed during the pre-accession negotiations included the numbers of staff involved in the protection of the environment and how they were deployed. Information was requested also about the levels of technical support and expertise in organizations acting in an advisory capacity to the relevant departments. Even the morale of the staff was questioned.

Staff training needs became apparent with the problem of significant costs to provide them in some of the AC10 states. Essential integration and communication infrastructures across and within departments had to be established and required further financing by the national governments. As funding of EU environmental programmes comes through the LIFE[15] fund and it is also an integral part of the Structural Funds, financial control and independent auditing mechanisms had to be identified within the AC10. The competent authorities for implementation, assessment and licensing, and notification for certification had to be shown to be separate from inspectorate authorities.

For the AC10 states with generally weak and developing administrative structures there was openness among the political élites to ideas for appropriate administrative and institutional models for the effective implementation of legislation. While the EU remained tough on ensuring that the AC10 states had the institutional and administrative capacities in place, there was an almost complete lack of an institutional template for the new states to follow. The result is that the influence of the EU has not been as wide-ranging in the new states as it might have been. Schemes such as the twinning of relevant authorities from an EU15 state with those of an AC10 state, and the encouragement of the AC10 authorities responsible for implementation to join the IMPEL network, certainly helped. But the conclusion remains that, despite the measures introduced to support the accession states before May 2004, the AC10 states have still to absorb the ideology and discourse of EU environmental policy.

CONCLUSION – THE FUTURE OF ENVIRONMENTAL POLICY IN EU25

Enlargement of the EU may cause a slowing of the dynamic and creative environmental policy making of the 1990s. Europeanization of the national environmental policies in the AC10 states has been facilitated by their drive to comply with the conditions for EU accession. However, if comparisons are made with other phases of enlargement, there is a considerable degree of misfit between the requirements of the policy and the ability of the AC10 states to adapt their administrative and institutional structures to deliver on its operation. There are more new states and the environmental *acquis* is more extensive than in earlier phases of EU enlargement. The new states have been undergoing extensive rapid and radical changes in order to meet the accession conditions of liberal democracies with functioning market economies during the period of accession.

Substantial changes will be needed to the domestic systems to absorb the changing policy style, to adapt the policy tools and instruments of the legislation and ensure that the environmental standards are met. Europeanization will affect the development of the domestic systems in the AC10 states at different speeds. There will be a difficult period of transition as all those involved in environmental policy making within the AC10 states at national and sub-national level adopt the norms of the discourse of EU policy. As economic development in the new member states proceeds, opportunities will occur that will result in long-term commitment to environmental improvements. The new states have within them many environmental advantages as a result of rich biodiversity and areas of natural beauty and wilderness regions. Developments of civil society and opportunities for greater public participation in processes of policy formation are emerging from the democratization process in the new member states. The potential exists for the enlarged EU to make an increasingly significant contribution to European and global environmental developments in the future.

It was not the argument of this chapter that EU environmental policy is the best tool to provide sustainable development within the EU25, nor that Europeanization of the national environmental policies of the AC10 states is the best way forward. Rather the argument is that Europeanization of the national environmental policies of the EU25 provides the basis for discourse among the group of 25 states which have very different backgrounds of economic and political history as well as environmental endowments. As such it provides a framework for future developments to deal with the difficult political decisions that exist about how to achieve the goal of sustainable development.

NOTES

1. First Environment Action Programme 1973–77, Second 1977–82, Third 1982–87, Fourth 1987–92, Fifth 1992–2002, Sixth 2002–12.
2. 'End-of-pipe' measures are those which target specific pollution problems without looking at the causes of the pollution, for example fitting a filter to a chimney to stop emissions into the atmosphere rather than considering changes to the production processes giving rise to the emissions.
3. Agreed by the heads of government at the Luxemburg European Council, December 1985, ratified by national governments and came into effect in July 1987.
4. WCED (1987), p. 43.
5. Agreed by the heads of government during the Maastricht European Council, December 1991 and came into effect in November 1993.
6. The environmental 'leaders' among the EU15 states are considered to be Germany, the Netherlands, Denmark, Austria, Sweden and Finland; and the environmental 'laggards' Spain, Greece, Portugal and Italy.
7. Agreed 1997, ratified in 1999.
8. Soil (September 2004) Marine Environment (May 2005), Pesticides (Sept 2004), Air Quality (2004), Waste Management and Recycling (mid-2005); others to follow include the Urban Environment and Natural Resource Management.
9. At the European Council meeting held in Lisbon in 2000 the EU heads of government stated that their objective was to make the EU 'the most competitive and dynamic knowledge-based economy in the world, capable of sustainable economic growth with more and better jobs and greater social cohesion by 2010'. The environmental dimension to this commitment was added in the adoption of the Sustainable Development Strategy at the Gothenburg European Council meeting in June 2001.
10. The title given to the initiatives launched by the Cardiff European Council in 1998 that have led to an increased awareness of the importance of integration by the EU's policy makers.
11. Carbon dioxide (80 per cent of emissions), methane, nitrous oxide, hydrofluorocarbons, perfluorocarbons and sulphur hexafluoride are considered to be the six most damaging of the greenhouse gas emissions in industrialized countries. Some of the gases are more damaging than others. Carbon dioxide produces the largest volume but sulphur hexafluoride is 20,000 times more damaging by volume.

12. In his concluding remarks during the press conference following this summit Russian President Putin commented, 'I must say that we did not link the WTO and the Kyoto Protocol … But one of the biggest concerns was that we have to face several issues all at once … EU enlargement, Kyoto itself … and the process of our accession to the WTO. The EU has made some concessions on some points during the negotiations on the WTO. This will inevitably have an impact on our positive attitude to the Kyoto Protocol.'
13. The somewhat derogatory term applied to the poorer Mediterranean states of Spain and Portugal following their accession in 1986.
14. Named for an agreement reached by the four states in Visegrad, the old capital of Hungary.
15. LIFE – Financial Instrument for the Environment.

14. EU regional policy: from side payment to societal security

Mike Mannin

Enlargement has changed the arena and agenda of structural funding. The foreseeable expansion of the EU by 10–12 new member states during the 1990s produced an integrated response by the Commission. Agenda 2000 (1997) included explicit recommendations for EU financial and policy frameworks to incorporate enlargement as well as a message for the Council of Ministers to hasten institutional reforms commensurate with enlargement and its consequential new policy arrangements (Commission, 1997).[1]

This, together with the implementation of Stage III of Economic and Monetary Union (1999), a persistently disappointing economic performance from several member states in recent years and, a consequently defensive intergovernmental atmosphere, was the arena for the future discussion of regional policy in the early years of the millennium. In such circumstances the role of structural funding, the main financial agent of an EU Regional Policy (EURP), took on a new significance.

This begs the question of what the EURP agenda is. Can a complexity of policy objectives and budgetary envelopes, of inter-institutional responsibilities, of EU-wide and member state initiatives and funding arrangements, amount to a coherent policy agenda? It is perhaps worthwhile briefly defining the notion of EURP before attempting to answer this question.[2]

WHAT IS EURP?

When applied at nation-state level the term regional policy refers to the intervention of a centrally directed public sector in the market and in social processes of specially denominated arenas, in order to reduce economic inequalities that exist within the state as a result of market forces. While the drivers for such interventions – of social equity, economic growth and political cohesion – are shared factors in the creation of EURP, the application of the term to a union of states, with sub-federal status, is inevitably tenuous. With a limited central capability, indirect and disaggregated communication with 25 member state public sectors, the task of implementation is problematic. The resources for EURP remain miniscule when compared to the weight of the EU economy as a whole and, as we indicate below, the task of reducing huge regional disparities is daunting; and the concept of region is definitionally complex and empirically varied. Categorized simply, the term region may be applied to: groups of nation-states – the EU, the Eurozone, Visigrad; transnational regions – Transmanche, the Atlantic Region; sub-national regions – Nord-Pas de Calais, Scotland, Hamburg. Such a vertical categorization may be supplemented by a 'horizontal' counterpoint: regions defined in terms of identity, administration or structure (Schmitt-Egner, 2002). In each categorization, however, region is defined by both external and internal actions and 'regional policy can be described as a strategy and tool to implement and control the regional programme from the outside together with, without or against the regional actor' (ibid., p. 186).

EURP, as we shall see, applies not just to sub-national and transnational regions but in a looser sense internationally – the EU as a regional actor involved in redistributive actions to other non-EU regions, nations and transnational regions. Our point here is that the EU has regional policy dimensions that range from the international to local and, notwithstanding the complexity of such interventions, these policies need some form of coordination. However, the identification of regional policy with one Commission Directorate, Regional Policy (DG Regio) is only partly appropriate. The search for this coordination takes place within such conceptual frameworks as cohesion, convergence, subsidiary, sustainability, cooperation and development. Regional policy must also pay attention to competitiveness and labour flexibility – the mantra of the Lisbon process since 2001. Consequentially Directorates such as Agriculture, Social Policy, Competition, Environment, Enlargement, Economic Policy and Development all have an interest in EURP. The role of DG Regional Policy in shaping and coordinating EURP is complicated by these overlapping arenas of interest and the tasks of EURP within the European project are consequentially diverse.

The term regional policy therefore is used here as an umbrella within which a range of EU objectives, policies and related financial envelopes are partially connected and coordinated by DG Regional Policy (DG Regio). Those policies more directly under the auspices of DG Regio are known as structural policy, and are described within the periodic reports on economic and social cohesion produced by DG Regio, the third was produced in 2003. Structural policy is composed of those programmes funded through Structural Funds (SF), the majority of which have a 'regional' focus (see

Table 14.1). The concept of region embraces member state (Cohesion Fund) sub-state (Objective 1); border regions (Intereg IIIc) transnational (Intereg III); and structural (rural/coastal development, city regeneration, labour inequalities).[3]

Table 14.1 Structural and cohesion funding: sources (1958–2002)

European Social Fund (ESF) 1958	Action in the field of vocational training and finding employment for the unemployed
European Regional Development Fund (ERDF) 1975	Action to promote regional investment and innovation and develop the infrastructure in regions with severe economic difficulties
European Agricultural Guidance and Guarantee Fund (EAGGF) (Guidance Section) 1964 and Fisheries Guidance 1994	Action to improve, strengthen and adapt agricultural and fisheries structures
European Investment Bank (EIB) 1957 and The EU Solidarity Fund, 2002	In collaboration with above, to grant loans and issue guarantees consistent with the aims of community regional policy
Cohesion Fund (1992)	Action to improve transnational transport and communications networks, the environment and infrastructure in Eire, Spain, Portugal and Greece

The objectives of structural policy are to assist EU economic and social cohesion, in particular to reduce 'disparities between the various regions, including rural areas' (Art. 130a SEA; Art. 130a TEU; Art. III–II6 Draft Constitution). Cohesion has not just economic and social components but also political and cultural overtones (Tarschys, 2003). Suffice to say that 'cohesion' emerged as a codeword for a social antidote to the market-oriented elements of the SEA and also emerges more specifically as a name for one aspect of structural policy – the Cohesion Fund. In searching for economic cohesion, the convergence of territorial economies, enhanced by the redistributive impact of EURP, particularly via the structural funds, is an obvious aim. Convergence, or rather the 'convergence criteria', is also utilized as a set of macroeconomic conditions associated with EMU and spelled out in the Stability and Growth Pact 1997 (see chapter X). Although there are obviously points of intersection between the two fields, here we are concerned with the debate over whether EURP through structural funding has made any major contribution to regional economic convergence.[4] To say the least the issue is controversial, with conflicting expert analysis often based on unresolved economic data (Sapir et al., 2003; Rodriguez-Fuentes and Daw, 2003; Rodriguez-Pose and Frates 2004). In crude summary, the Commission in its most recent Cohesion Report points to an evident success in the growth and catch-up rate of the cohesion countries, a general narrowing of economic divergence between member states but a growing disparity between regions within member states (1999–2003) (Commission, 2003a; Tarschys, 2003, pp. 32–54). Much of the debate regarding EURP future is shaped by this calculation, which itself reflects the themes of this section – the role of the state *vis-à-vis* the EU, the struggle for a balance of policies within limited resources, the nature of policy-making networks and their influences in EURP, and the impact of enlargement.

After examining the development of structural policy the chapter moves to an examination of the SF policy process. There follows an evaluation of EURP and European integration from a conceptual and institutional position. This in turn takes us towards the evaluation of the impact of EURP on the governance of New Europe. Finally, and by way of summary, the future of EURP is examined against these internal and external challenges.

THE DEVELOPMENT OF STRUCTURAL FUNDING POLICY: FROM REGIONAL SIDE PAYMENT TO ECONOMIC AND SOCIAL COHESION

Like many Community policies a European regional policy was long in gestation. The Treaty of Rome (1957) included in its preamble aims 'reducing the differences existing between the various regions and the backwardness of less favoured regions', as implicitly part of the move towards 'ever closer union'. Article 92 of the Treaty was more explicit in promoting the economic development of areas where the standard of living is abnormally low, or where there is serious underemployment. This was conditional on any redistributive policy not seriously distorting markets and trading conditions. Aid was to be limited, selective and investment-oriented. No Regional Fund or Directorate was created at this time, with the European Investment Bank (EIB), European Social Fund (ESF) (not specifically regional in its objectives) and the Common Agricultural Policy

(CAP) (the most important budgetary policy area) having only a general commitment to reducing regional disparities.

Ten years on, however, the economic miracle of the 1950s had failed to trickle down with much effect to the most southerly reaches of the Community, and a Directorate for Regional Policy (DGXVI) was established (1968). It was not until the Paris Summit (1972), however, that discussion of economic and monetary union and enlargement to include Britain, Eire and Denmark resulted in a definitive commitment to the establishment of a Regional Fund (George, 1991). As we shall see, further enlargements were also to prove a catalyst for subsequent and more notable policy changes.

The first instrument of an EU regional policy, the European Regional Development Fund (ERDF), was created in 1975. The size of the fund (ECU 1.3 billion) was less than half what was proposed by Commissioner Thomson, and though doubled by 1977, ERDF amounted to only 5 per cent of the Community budget in 1978. A national fixed quota system was applied, with Italy (40 per cent) and the UK (28 per cent) receiving the largest shares. The period 1975–85 was thus characterized by a funding policy that fitted the intergovernmentalist character of the Community then prevalent. Regional policy was limited in size and scope, primarily subject to national rather then Commission initiative, and amounted to little more than a subsidy for the adverse impact of the EC budget and/or policies on particular member states.

During the mid-1980s two factors provided a political and economic catalyst for a re-evaluation of the role of regional policy. First, the accession of Greece (1981), Spain and Portugal (1986), reinforced member state demands for regional redistributive policies and strengthened the negotiating position of existing peripheral and agricultural regions within the Community.[5]

Second, the negotiation of the SEA, as with other EU policies, also encouraged a policy rethink by the Commission and member states (Cecchini, 1988; Delors, 1989; PA Cambridge Economic Consultants, 1988). In the context of these economic unknowns, regional policy was to gain considerable attention as a counterweight to potentially disruptive and disintegrating aspects of the SEA. In 1988 agreement was reached to double the size of the Structural Funds by 1992 and, by 1989, radically amended mechanisms for its redistribution were in place. In effect, the SEA acted as a catalyst for the upgrading of EC regional policy and the 1988 reforms set the framework and character of subsequent policy reformulation.

The 1988 Reforms

The 1988 reforms began a process that has contributed to slow reform of the Union budget and, associated with this, CAP. More than this, however, the organization and implementation of SF represented a significant shift in decision taking from the Council to the Commission. The (then) five objectives of SF (see Table 14.2) were based on attempts by the Commission to:

- coordinate both national and community policy more effectively, via multi-annual programming, transparency, additionality and regular project evaluation;
- concentrate redistributed resources on areas facing the greatest need and with evident problems of structural adjustment associated with the SEA;
- develop regional policies with a substantial and long-lived economic impact;
- provide assurance of medium terms funding so as to assist the development of a programmatic approach to regional policy.

This meant a shift away from project-based support (for example road building), towards a framework that coordinated available resources from the various sources of SF with national regional policies. The title of the objectives clearly indicated the main characteristics of community regional inequalities as identified in the late 1980s, as did the proportion of funding allocated to each of the objectives, with 70 per cent going to Objective 1 Regions.

Implementation of the new system involved the creation by national governments, with the consent of the Commission and assistance of regional and local 'partners', of Community Support Frameworks (CSF); the Commission provided the general priorities for a particular region, and national and local partners an Operational Programme for intervention, including a commitment to provide an agreed proportion of programme resources – partnership funding. In the period 1989–93 there were 110 CSFs spending ECU 46 billion on approximately 1000 Operational Programmes.

Further financial support came from a system of Community Initiatives worth approximately ECU 3 billion (1989–93) that could be accessed if community-wide issues were evidently part of a region's problems, for example, regional research, cross-border cooperation, environmental problems, radical economic restructuring because of over-reliance on traditional industries and/or the impact of the SEA.

The reforms focused 28 per cent of the Community budget on 'poor areas'; this meant that, rather than being perceived as a compensatory side payment to member states which were net budget contributors, structural funds were to be investments, especially in those areas with a per capita GDP that amounted to 75 per cent or less than the EU average. In practice only Eire

Table 14.2 Changes in Structural Fund Programme objectives, 1988–2004

Objective	1988	1994	1998	2004
1	The development of structurally backward regions		To include Objective 6 regions	Convergence: supporting growth and job creation in least developed regions
2	The conversion of regions in industrial decline		To include rural coastal and urban zones of decline/ deprivation	Anticipating change in urban rural and industrial arenas. Support for full employment productivity and competition
3	Combating long-term unemployment	Combating long-term and youth unemployment and assisting the socially excluded	To promote: • Social inclusion • Lifelong education/ training • Anticipation of social/economic change • Female employment opportunities	Promoting European territorial cooperation through cross-border interregional and external frontier programmes
4	Increasing employment opportunities for young people	Adaption of employees to industrial change and restructuring		
5 (a)	Adjustment to agricultural structures	To include both agriculture and fisheries		
5 (b)	Promoting rural development	To include both agriculture and fisheries		
6		To assist in the development of areas of sparse population		

and Northern Ireland of the Northern states fell into this category. Objective 1 status fell most easily to the 'Mediterranean' countries. There emerged, therefore, a greater political competition for funding that manifested itself more in the Objective 2 classification, as the Southern accessions (1981–86) had clearly altered the relative poverty ladder of the Community. This competition was heightened by the decline in nationally resourced regional assistance, especially in the Northern member states (Bachtler and Michie, 1993). Monies received from the EU to be identified as additional to national regional expenditure were perceived by some members, especially the then British Conservative Administration, as a means of compensating a declining commitment to regional aid (McAleavy, 1992).

Delors II and the Edinburgh Council 1992: From Structural Funding to Economic and Social Cohesion

Problems of additionality, area designation and the size of the structural fund were addressed in the negotiations before and after the Edinburgh Conference (1992) and during discussions before the Nordic/Austrian enlargement. The Edinburgh Council revisions, as part of the 'Delors II package', included an increase in the budget by 26 per cent (ECU 66.8 billion in 1992 to ECU 84 billion by 1999), of which ECU 27 billion would be funding through a Cohesion Fund set at ECU 15 billion for 1993–99. The elevated position of SF to meet the intentions of Article II of the TEU was the inevitable outcome of its identification as an integral aspect of economic and social cohesion.

With regard to the spatial distribution of this expanded budget, the five East German *Länder* and East Berlin were given Objective 1 status, as was Cantabria in Spain. More controversial was the inclusion of several Northern European regions whose GDP was, in 1992, above the 75 per cent criterion. Thus Hainault (Belgium); Merseyside and Highlands and Islands (UK); Nord-Pas de Calais (France) and Flevoland (Netherlands) were so designated. Some of these are densely populated in core areas, bringing the proportion of EU population in Objective 1 areas to 26.6 per cent (21.7 per cent 1986), so raising the general criticism that the aim of resource concentration was weakened by the political deals struck to produce an 'acceptable' outcome to the Edinburgh Summit and subsequent budgetary negotiations (Bachtler and Michie, 1994). Allocations agreed in July 1993 for the 1994–99 period were also subject to tough intergovernmental negotiations. The Irish government threatened to veto the new regulations unless guaranteed a 13.5 per cent share of Objective 1 monies. Spain sought to exclude any diminution of the Cohesion Fund.[6] Negotiations leading to the enlargement of the Community (1995) led to the designation of an Objective

6 for regions with sparse populations (less than 8 per square kilometre). In this way Finland and Sweden also gained access to the SF pot.

In effect a larger geographic and demographic area of the EU received funding from an increased SF but within a more specifically targeted range of 'approved' programme activities. Other changes included clear (transparent) evidence of the addition of national/regional resources to ERDF proportions of funding; a simplified application procedure; the inclusion of education and health projects; the revision of the framework for Community Initiatives and an enhanced monitoring process that involved member states more closely in evaluation/accountability of expenditure; and extension of the programme period for Objective 1 to six years together with an increase in the (potential) proportion of community contributions to Objective 1 initiatives to 85 per cent. Finally a series of environmental requirements were attached to the criteria for regional development planning (Bachtler and Michie, 1994).

Summary

In tracing the development of SF so far we have observed its increasingly significant economic and social role within the EU 'cohesion' agenda. From its emergence in the 1970s as 'little more than a channel for relatively minor side payments between national governments' (Ansell et al., 1997, p. 351), SF was transformed into a vital component of '*espace organisé*' and was to provide the cohesion for '*espace libre*', the single market (Hooghe, 1996, p. 5). This transformation was enhanced by three factors external to any intrinsic values of a European regional policy: the three periods of enlargement negotiation, each of which introduced new national agendas, so reshaping the policy arena itself; the SEA, from which emerged real (or anticipated) economic consequences for EU peripheries; and institutional changes and policy extensions that were justified as vital components of a 'fulfilled' single market. In the late 1990s, however, the imminent and unknown impacts of Economic and Monetary Union (EMU) and enlargement to a group of economically depressed applicants provided a climate for EU policy review in which RP was to play its part.

FROM AGENDA 2000 TO E25: REGIONAL POLICY IN THE TWENTY-FIRST CENTURY

> In an enlarged EU territory, economic and social cohesion should be taken into account more than ever in the formulation and implementation of every Community Policy. (Commission, 1997)

The salience of SF to the enlargement process and the internal cohesion of the existing Union was clearly recognized by the Commission. With a GDP of 32 per cent of EU 15 average (1995 base), the ten CEEC applicants were far behind the average of the existing four Cohesion countries, whose GDP averaged 74 per cent of the Community average. Thus, on the basis of existing regulations for structural funding, the eligible EU population for Objective 1 at EU25 would increase to 42 per cent (25 per cent EU15), manifestly conflicting with the aims of concentration and thus effectiveness of SF application and outcome.[7] Inevitably a further reform of SF was necessary before enlargement; and inevitably, a pre-accession strategy for aspiring member states would run in parallel to SF reform as part of the preparation of the CEECs to absorb their responsibilities in this and other *acquis*.

Agenda 2000 presented an integrated intellectual persuasion to the Council and an opportunity for member states to 'discount' particular national interests within a generally accepted framework solution (Smyrl, 1998). The strict enforcement of the 75 per cent GDP criterion clawed back the 1992 member state horse-trading associated with Objective 1 status which was to be 'technically decided'. This resulted in a reduction of EU population coverage from around 25 to 20 per cent on 1997 data (Hall, 1997). The proposals for Objective 2 also reduced coverage to around 18 per cent of the EU's population, but extended its scope to rural coastal and urban areas. The criterion for eligibility, however, particularly those associated with unemployment, remained contended by member states, as was regional eligibility, which remained a member state/Commission negotiation. This, together with the broad focus of the objective, proffered the opportunity for a 're-nationalization' of structural policy (Fothergill, 1997). Similar arguments can be made in regard to Objective 3 (15 per cent average coverage), whose overall aim was to ensure a minimum participation (for ESF intervention) while at the same time permitting each member state to decide its priorities for ESF investment (Commission, 1998a).[8]

The Commissions proposals, with new SF regulations, were agreed by the Council of Ministers in June 1999 (Council, 1999). There were a number of small but significant changes to the Commission's Agenda 2000 recommendations, the most notable being the reduction in the recommended SF budget envelope from €218 billion to €195 billion. The member states' influence over the final outcome for 2000–2006 financial arrangements was also evident in their concern to sustain transitional arrangement for the regions losing their Objective 1 status and a greater role in mid-term and performance review[9] (Sutcliffe, 2000). The political context, however, must not be forgotten. The resignation of the Santer Commission, in March 1999, together with the general concerns of existing member states for the impact of enlargement, was scarcely a climate for an enhanced role for the Commission. However, their role continued to be strong in drafting CSF and single programme documentation and as partners in implementation and monitoring SF processes within the concept of partnership and thus Multi-level Governance (MLG) (ibid., p. 306).

As well as €195 billion SF appropriation for 2000–2006, the Berlin Council also agreed to an €18 billion Cohesion Fund and €22 billion for pre-accession structural assistance (0.45 per cent of EU15 GNP), a sum that the Commission in its Second Cohesion Report perceived as the minimum by which an EURP would achieve credibility (Commission, 2001). The Report also provided a glimpse of the state of economic and social conditions in an EU of 27 member states.[10] This, together with the disappointing growth of EU15 and the unknown regional impact of EMU, implied a period of transition for regional policy until the resolution of these economic and political uncertainties. In the Second Progress Report for the period 2000–2006, the Commission had a clearer medium-term perspective to guide its assessment of RP to 2006. With the date for EU25 set for May 2004, the Commission was able to stipulate how structural funding would be applied to the ten new member states in the interim period of 2004–2006. Additional resources for new member states in this period were agreed at the Copenhagen Council, though the sum €21 billion was inferior to the ceiling fixed three years before in Berlin (Commission, 2003a).

The guarded optimism of the Progress Report with regard to the evident general trend towards economic convergence among the EU15 was tempered by a stark assessment of the impact that enlargement to EU25 would bring. Regional disparities would nearly double with two-thirds of disadvantaged regions situated in the new member states. Only 30 (EU15) regions would remain under the 75 per cent threshold after the 'statistical effect' of enlargement in 2004. Thus 18 existing Objective 1 regions were set to lose status.[11] Given the slow growth of the EU15 economy and the consistent decrease in employment within candidate countries, especially in rural and industrial areas, approximately 3 million new jobs within a five-year period needed creating in order to align new member states with the EU15 average employment rate (Commission, 2003a). This scenario, together with the Commission's concern regarding the ability of the new member states to adequately implement SF *acquis* from January 2004 (the eligibility start-date), added to the continuing debate regarding the viability of regional funding within the budgetary and policy assumptions of Agenda 2000. (For a summary of actors' positions on the future of regional policy see Bachtler and Taylor, 2003; Tarschys, 2003).

The Sapir Report (July 2003), an 'independent high level study group' established by Romano Prodi, was tasked with advising how the EU economic system might deliver more effectively. The Report criticized both the policy process and the effectiveness of EU regional subsidies, recommending the creation of new funding pools based on clearly directed objectives (growth, convergence and restructuring) with resources directed either to member states most in need or individuals anywhere in the EU based on their economic circumstances (Sapir et al., p. 166). The de-emphasis of a regional dimension in their recommendations, together with their support for a re-nationalization of structural funding, was not well received by the then Commissioner for Regional Policy, Michael Barnier, who claimed the report conclusions 'have not taken account of reality' (Euroactive.com, 2003). Reality was better presented according to the M. Barnier in the Third Cohesion Report (January 2004), which 'confirms that Europe's added value has been significant at many levels' and that cohesion policy has been the catalyst for new forms of partnership involving the regional and local authorities, national governments and the Union, working both within and across national borders (Commission, 2004a; foreword, p. iii).

THE THIRD COHESION REPORT

The main thrust of the Third Report was reflected in earlier Council and Commission papers. An informal ministerial meeting in October 2003 pointed to a 'paradigm shift' in development policies of industrialized nations that emphasized 'place-based policies', that is, full exploitation of local actors in designing and implementing policies and thus a move towards multi-level governance which makes, 'institution building a crucial part of cohesion policy' (Council of Ministers, 2003, p. 1). The aim is thus to increase the potential of regions, as EURP should now be about growth not redistribution, and as such cohesion policy 'should become even more Lisbon oriented' (ibid., p. 4).

These strategic perspectives for cohesion policy reform were also reflected in the Commission's budgetary statement (Commission, 2004b). Reform 'must focus on competitiveness, sustainable development and employment ... [so as] to ensure that the Lisbon and Gothenberg objectives and anticipation of change stemming from the new international divisions of labour are systematically incorporated from the outset into the design of all national and regional development strategies' (ibid., pp. 15–16). Thus the three priorities replacing the previous objectives would be convergence, with a focus on the less developed member states and regions, regional competitiveness and employment to cover other member states and regions, and territorial cooperation around cross-border and transnational programmes (see Table 14.3).

Table 14.3 The Third Periodic Report on Economic and Social Cohesion

Proposals for Reform, February 2004; a new architecture after 2006 (to assist competitiveness, sustainable development and economic/social restructuring)	
Targeted interventions	• Innovation and the knowledge economy • Environment and risk prevention • Accessibility and services of general economic interest
Community priorities	• *Regional competitiveness and employment*: to assist the Lisbon Agenda and cohesion throughout EU25 especially in industrial/urban/rural areas and in national programmes for change adaptation • *Territorial cooperation*: supporting cooperation on issues of community importance at cross-border, transnational and inter-regional level, including external frontiers and outermost regions
Reformed delivery system	• A single strategic policy document, annually revised • More subsidiarity • MS–Commission negotiated development policy • National–regional outline member states' programmes • Effective coordination with other Community programmes
Financial control	• Reduced to 3 fund sources. (ERDF–ESF–Cohesion Fund) • One fund source per programme • Commission/MS financial control based on proportionality • Additionality verified by Commission within convergence objective only • Automatic decommitment ('*n*+2' rule) maintained
Financial resources (2007–13)	• €345 billion allocated over period (0.46 per cent GNI of EU27) – of which 78 per cent for convergence; 18 per cent regional competitiveness/ employment; 4 per cent territorial cooperation • 50–50 split between new and old MS • Relative importance of Cohesion Fund enhanced (third of financial allocation for new member states)
Concentration and performance	• Emphasis on new member states • Focus on Lisbon and Gothenberg agendas • Focus on institution-building priorities in convergence regions • Regional competitiveness programmes • Annual dialogue with EU institutions • MS/region trade impact assessment • Community performance reserve

The political context of the Third Report explains 'tiller adjustments' rather than radical alteration in the direction of EURP. Impending EP elections in 2004 and the creation of a new Commission, together with the sceptical perspective presented by some member states on the viability of the EU budget proposals, implied a response of 'due consideration' rather than major innovation. The tone of the Report was guardedly upbeat, stressing relative success especially in Cohesion Fund states; incorporative of external critical performance appraisals; and pragmatic in relation to its proposals for the 2007–13 cohesion programme. Thus the relative success of the 1988 principles – programming, partnership, co-financing and evaluation, were to be maintained. They were to be enhanced in EU25 by more evidenced strategic planning, further decentralization and partnership 'on the ground in member states, regions and local authorities'; more transparent partnerships and monitoring and the simplification of management, while ensuring sound financial accountability (Commission, 2004b, p. xxxiv). A revised and simplified set of objectives and funds, yearly EU institution progress debates, strategic priorities (oriented around the Lisbon and Gothenburg agendas) and added member states' responsibilities in financial controls (based on proportionality), was evidence of Commission recognition of the renationalization debate. The impact of enlargement was indicated in the favourable allocation of resources for new member states but also in the maintenance of a maximum national receipt of structural funding, the 4 per cent GDP ceiling; the '*n*–2' rule[12] and a stress on the importance of 'institution building' and effective management. The broader global perspective is also contained in new demands for trade assessment evaluations, change adaptation strategies, transnational border cooperation and neighbourhood programmes.

Regional Policy 2007–13 as proposed in the Third Cohesion Report owed much to the 1988 Framework proposals and the preparatory analysis of Agenda 2000 for an EU25 and its attendant problems. If there is a difference to be noted in the latest strategy, it is in the recognition that EURP has not only internal but also external dimensions, associated with the globalist perspectives of the Lisbon and Gothenburg agendas as well as security and development dimensions, emerging from the new borders and neighbours of EU25. This will be discussed in the concluding sections of the chapter.

THE SF POLICY PROCESS: WHO DOES WHAT, WHY, WHEN AND HOW?

This section seeks to analyse the policy process associated with SF. It contains a brief description of the current formal processes associated with the 1999–2006 Programme; there follows an examination of the application of SF in several countries and their regions.

The Components of Structural Funding Policy

We can identify, initially, several levels of policy process that begin with decisions about: the size of the SF cake (its budgetary 'envelope') and its distribution (which member states get what amount); the principles of funding distribution (the institutional SF framework); and the application of the SF framework (territorial programming). The last falls into four stages: nationally agreed regional development plans; contractual relationships – the Operational Programmes (OP); and finally the implementation and evaluation/monitoring of individual contracts. Each of these stages involves both formal and informal processes at several levels, from the supranational to the local.

With regard to the budgetary envelope of SF and with the share of the EU budget increasing from 5 per cent in 1975 to 34 per cent during the period 2000–2006, the structural contribution to member states' regional economies amounts to 0.46 per cent of the EU's GNP. Access to SF has, literally, 'high stakes' and in this financial context the member states as donors and recipients would be expected to play a significant role in its allocation. We have already observed the political bargaining evident during the 1992 budgetary negotiations, whereby recipients negotiated an additional Cohesion Fund as a 'side payment' for their acquiescence to monetary convergence and market deregulation, as well as the reduction in budget at the Berlin Council (1999), in the light of emerging enlargement negotiations. More recently debate surrounding the 2007–13 budgetary package seems to have resulted in its containment, with Germany, Austria, Netherlands, Sweden and the UK arguing for a budgetary reduction as well as renationalization of its distribution (HM Treasury, 2003). In effect the positioning of the SF debate in relation to other budgetary considerations, such as the British rebate or CAP, are indicative of the continuing state-centric character of the SF process at this macro stage of policy formulation (Allen, 1996; Begg, 2004).

It is contended, however, that the examination of SF budgetary politics is more than a simple game of fixed recipient/donor negotiation. This is especially apparent given the dynamic nature of regional economic disparities, for example Ireland's notable progress economically contrasted with Germany's 'eastern' *Länder* difficulties. Moreover, the range of objectives and sources of funding produced situations where countries became both winners and losers, depending on which aspect of regional policy was at stake (Marks, 1996, p. 391; Bachtler et al., 2003, p. 26). Finally the uncertainties and imperatives of economic integration have produced a moral dimension to the debate that individual actors and EU institutions such as the European Parliament and the Committee of Regions have raised as a motivating dimension for sustaining SF policies. The role of state executives in this most evidently intergovernmental aspect of the policy process is undeniable; yet its character is circumscribed by both domestic and supranational factors that allow an important role for the Commission as initiator and mediator and for sub-national and supranational public and private interests that pressurize both the Commission and member states. Thus it can be argued that the Commission is provided with 'a vital if politically delicate source of political leverage in its dealings with member state governments' (Marks, 1996, p. 392).

With regard to the establishment of a framework of principles within which SF are to be allocated, a state-centric explanation may also seem appropriate. The Delors I package (1998) and amendments through the SEA to the Treaty of Rome (Title V, Arts 130a–e) had strengthened the hand of the Commission in the SF reform process as well proffering responsibility for coordination and partnership within the process. The Maastricht negotiations and Delors II (1991–2), Allen argues, arrested this slide towards the Commissions ascendancy by detaching the financing of TEU objectives from their negotiation. This, together with the Protocol on Economic and Monetary Cohesion, represented a considerable 'steer' towards the retention of member state control over both budgetary size and setting SF objectives (Allen, 1996, p. 217).[13]

This is also evident in more recent decisions. Thus, some of the decisions taken at the March 1999 Berlin European Council were clearly for reasons of efficiency and simplification or to stress the then current agenda (e.g. equal opportunity, social inclusion, sustainable development and environmental protection) (Sutcliffe, 2000, p. 304). Other decisions, as well as those taken by the Berlin Council later in June, illustrate the centrality of intergovernmental bargaining to the emergence of structural funding regulations and its financial framework for the 2000–2006 period. A reduction in the performance reserve to 4 per cent, constraints to Community Initiatives allocation, and the 13 special arrangements for certain member states' regions were illustrative of the intergovernmentalist impact on the 2000–2006 programme. The Lisbon and Gothenburg Council agendas are clearly evident in the Commission's revised guidelines for the programme (Commission, 2003b). Other influences from evolving Community policies such as the reformed CAP (June 2003), fisheries policy (January 2003) and energy and transport are further illustrations of the Commission's responses to evolving Council positions. We have already noted a similar responsiveness to intergovernmental agendas in recommendations to the Commission included in the Third Cohesion Report (2004a).

There is less contestation of the appropriateness of Commission influence rather than intergovernmentalism to explain the character of the application/implementation and monitoring stages of EURP. First, the 1988 principles of concentration, partnership, additionality and programming are a Commission-initiated 'code' enhanced and legitimized by the Maastricht Treaty Protocol on Economic and Social Cohesion. Re-commitment to these principles is made periodically in both Council and Commission documentation (Commission, 2003a; 2004a; Council of Ministers, 2003). The principles, intrinsically, offer the Commission wide scope to formulate and implement SF policy in conjunction with member state officials and other actors necessary to achieve principal objectives. As applied to member states there are three elements to programming – the Cohesion Fund, Community Initiatives and the Community Support Frameworks (national development policy documents). In effect the four stages associated with SF operationalization in member states – national development planning, contract negotiations, operational programming and implementation/monitoring – are policy stages that give opportunities for sub-national actors to interact with their national governments and the Commission in order to facilitate SF objectives.

Marks (1996) presents a framework of analysis to explain variation within these stages that identifies four institutional levels in each of several member states (between 1989 and 1993) as they interrelated with each other at each of the states above.[14] As Marks points out, influence is most evenly spread where information necessary for the achievement of particular stage objectives is not controlled by central government. This is most evident at the implementation/monitoring stage – where sub-national government has greater opportunity for influence – than at the contract negotiation stage – a central government/Commission dialogue.

One other factor, especially significant in examining the strength of Commission influence on the application of SF, is the resource dependence of member states on EU funding. It is noticeable that the 'Cohesion' countries – whose regional spending budgets are massively enhanced by SF – are those where Commission influence is greater. A combination of constitutional pluralism, information symmetry and SF dependence present the opportunity for Multi-Level Governance (MLG) emerging as a consistent feature of the SF process in different member states, as evidenced below.

Policy at Sub-state Level: A Comparison

When observed more closely, variations in sub-national involvement in the policy process are also evident within as well as between member states. A few examples illustrate this point. Despite the extension of federal autonomy to Eastern Germany and thus an important role in federal and regional policy making, the new *Länder* exhibited 'a pattern' of policy relationships akin to member states within 'resource poor regional actors' (Anderson, 1996, p. 189). Though less true for the programme period after 1994–99, the gatekeeper role of the Federal government was less evident than was the case with the old *Länder*, which sought central support to avoid what they perceived as Commission encroachment on their regional independence (ibid.; Conzelmann, 1995; Bachtler et al., 2003, p. 25).

For different reasons, Spanish regions also provide divergent examples of Commission/national government relationships. Spain's 17 regions enjoy considerable responsibility and some financial autonomy; there is, however, no overreaching central body, no *Bundesrat*, that would allow a centrally coordinated regional response to national government, which retains field agencies to coordinate regional/local issues not transferred to the regions. Spanish regional autonomy rests heavily on the lead given by the ethnic/national pressures exerted in the Catalan and Basque regions that demand special and direct representation in Brussels.[15] As against this, the Spanish government's control over the Cohesion Fund and its reluctance to allow regional rather than national CSFs contribute to what remains still a mainly centrally directed policy process.

While a similar conclusion can be reached in observing the UK, several examples of partnership and intervention have cut across a uniform portrait of a centrally directed SF process. Up until devolved government in Scotland, Wales and Northern Ireland, and the establishment of Regional Development Agencies, the character of a regional policy in the UK was reflected in primarily administrative regional structures of central government – Integrated Regional Offices, now Government Offices (GOs) that since 1993 act as coordinators of SF bids, monitor the Single Programme Documents (SPD) and maximize the 'efficient' use of both EU regional and UK government-derived regeneration budgets. Notwithstanding the lack of a democratically elected tier of regional government, or the persistent weakening of the financial independence of local authorities in the UK, there evolved several examples of networking among UK partners that one commentator termed a 're-engineering' of administrative processes and political channels within the SF policy process (Jacobs, 1997). While GOs create an environment for considerable central government control, bottom-up responses to advance regional and local interests were evident in the emergence of regional associations encouraged by the Commission to assist in the provision of regional strategies.[16]

After 1997 the creation of devolved governments in Scotland, Wales and Northern Ireland, Regional Development Agencies (RDA) and appointed Regional Chambers extended the range of partners involvement in the

EURP process. This, together with the consolidation of the coordinative role of GOs, presents a paradoxical vision of a regional Britain under the current Labour administration. On the one hand GOs were tasked with 'gatekeeping' on behalf of central government; on the other there was a clearly government-encouraged role for RDAs and Regional Chambers 'to take a leading role' in programming activities (Burch and Gomez, 2002, p. 772).[17] But while a regional dimension is now formally recognized, it would be misleading not to conclude that 'despite the ongoing reform of regional governance, Whitehall has maintained its dominant position' with the ERDF process through the GOs (ibid.).

The emergence of full English Regional Assemblies may establish the political dimension missing from the current situation. Evidence from the Scottish and Welsh experiences would suggest that such a dimension might help resolve the current indeterminate status of English regions within EURP. Despite limits on its legislative capacity and financial dependence on the UK Treasury, the Welsh Assembly has achieved a political presence previously lacking in the principality.[18] For Bache and Bristow (2003), the 'key difference between a policy challenge from the [Welsh] National Assembly rather than the Welsh Office is the more effective political weight of the former' (p. 424).

In Scotland a different scenario was also apparent after devolution. The new Scottish Executive and Parliament took over an already well-established system of programme management through partnerships (Bachtler et al., 2003, p. 15), as well as a considerable range of domestic policies within a limited financial autonomy. However, the 2000–2006 SF budget (£636 million) was some £220 million less than for the previous period; the O1 status for Highlands/Islands changed to that of transitional programme. In effect the Scottish Executive and Parliament were charged with the management of a declining SF contribution and as such the primary issue is the management of that decline, with a deleterious impact on partner involvement in strategic decision.[19] This is in contrast to the Welsh and some English regions, whose economic interests in the medium term imply a more coherent representation of their interests via new partnerships and their emergent public assemblies.

These brief examples illustrate the diversity of interactions between actors in EURP process. The effect of EURP over time has been to 'Europeanize' local regional and national actors to deal with the complex regulatory framework of regional policy laid down periodically through mainly intergovernmental negotiation over a Commission-laid table. Thus MLG as a conceptual tool gives us 'a provisional coherence to contributions sharing criticism of state centre assumptions regarding EU policy analysis'

(Gualini, 2003, p. 618). More than this it can also be seen as a 'catalyst' for institutional change as well as the analysis of policy processes.

CONCEPTUALIZING EU REGIONAL POLICY

As EURP has grown in budgetary and political significance within the EU, so its academic analysis has increased in importance: the explanation of European integration cannot ignore and must seek to include so significant a policy arena if it is to claim any comprehensive utility or conceptual weight.

An examination of the changes in SF would suggest a contest between intergovernmental and neofunctional interpretations of integration which has in more recent years veered towards a neofunctionalist interpretation of the development of SF. As we have already pointed out, the 1970s were characterized by a series of member state trade-offs within a national quota system of grants that augmented nationally derived regional policies. In such conditions the Commission's role in regional policy was minimal and fragmented.

Consequently, the 1988 reforms represented a reconfiguration of the EURP process away from an intergovernmentalist, state-centric conception of decision taking. But it did not follow that a neofunctional explanation fell axiomatically from the decline in state-centric control over regional policy. The neofunctionalist model postulates the development of a sub-national/supranational relationship that transcends the nation-state; the EU agenda is manipulated by pluralist, mainly private sub-national and transnational interests interacting with the supranational processes contained and controlled, in particular by the Commission. In the case of EURP we have already argued that neither model accurately and usefully explains the development of this policy arena, for in certain spatial and temporal situations governments have exercised this function in cooperation with either sub-state or EU institutions while maintaining an integral agenda-setting role; in effect a complex picture of political and technical interrelationships has emerged that is most usefully examined by the conceptual frameworks of MLG or (relatedly) network analysis.

Before attempting to verify these conceptual interpretations, it is worthwhile stating the implications of adopting such an approach. In the case of both multi-level governance and network analysis our attention is on meso theory – in this particular case, policy analysis. Such a shift of theoretical focus explicitly takes us away from the broader macro-theoretical focus of integration theory. Implicitly, however, such a focus assumes a level of integration that allows what amounts to fairly well-worked political science tools of policy analysis to effectively analyse a growingly significant arena of the EU. A *de facto* recognition of integration is therefore part of the analysis of SF; in this sense the somewhat tired debates surrounding intergovernmentalism and neofunctionalism became less significant (Caporaso and Keeler, 1995; Bache, 1998).

So if MLG has a relevance for conceptualization of the current and future SF policy process, we would expect this to be reflected in emerging formal policy processes. The 1988 and successive regulations contain principles (of partnership, programming, coordination and prioritization) that required the Commission to provide and monitor a framework for SF policy; and of necessity gave meso-level public and quasi-public bodies and official capability within the framework. It can be argued that these circumstances emerged only at the behest of member states (Hooghe, 1996, p. 99); however, the principles themselves originated from within the Commission and were based on the concepts developed in the Commission-led Integrated Mediterranean Programme (Smyrl, 1998). In the case of EURP we have already argued that neither model accurately and usefully explains the development of this policy arena. In certain spatial and temporal situations governments have exercised this function in cooperation with either sub-state or EU institutions while maintaining an integral agenda setting role. In effect, despite successive revisions to the original 1988 regulations through to the Third Cohesion Report (2003), the Commission has been pivotal in the design and implementation of regional funding in the new century. The formal collaborative framework of SF, whereby the perspectives and objectives of Commission, member state and designated sub-national actors are to be incorporated and achieved, allows the application of appropriate policy analysis frameworks, especially MLG, to explain EURP (Rhodes and Marsh, 1992; Peterson, 1995: Kassim, 1994).

Marks et al. (1996) described how MLG's decision-making competences are shared by actors at various levels. Thus national governments are 'one among a variety of actors contesting decisions that are made at a variety of levels' and 'the separation between domestic and international politics … is rejected by the multi-level governance model' (ibid,. pp. 346–7). The basis for these changes is in the broadening of EU policy arenas, especially since the SEA and the corresponding increase in the supranational capacity of the EU that was to be further extended at Maastricht. The principles of the SF framework specifically enhance both the supranational and sub-national component of regional policy decision taking, through its processes of partnership, programming and coordination. In the past ten years there has been a substantial increase in sub-national authorities that now 'mobilize' in Brussels (Marks et al., 2002; Inforegio Panorama, 2004). This, together with the official consultative status of the Committee of the Regions, or the advisory Council for Local and Regional Authorities, has given both a *de facto* and *de jure* status to sub-national governments within the several stages of the SF policy process.

As we have already suggested, there is no necessary assumption with the MLG model that member state governments have yielded their gatekeeping control of access to the various policy agendas, including SF, nor that they remain still the most powerful actors in most policy-making circumstances. There may be, however, situations where member state officials actively seek to shift decision-making responsibilities to either supranational or sub-national partners; there may also be constitutional/legal/technical situations where there is no choice (Bache, 1998). Differences between and within policy arenas may be examined in the light of these circumstances. As with network analysis, the MLG model describes a process of decision making rather than explains policy outcomes. In effect MLG, when applied to regional policy, becomes a process that is not much different from the situation in some national politics, particularly those organized federally (Marks, 1996, p. 359).

We may argue from much the same perspective when considering the appropriateness of network analysis to SF. Organizations that are identified operating within a network may be seen to have a set of interrelated characteristics: resource dependency (on other organizations within the network); resource 'richness' (to a lesser or greater extent); dominance/supplicancy, within an accepted system of resource exchange; thus variations in resource richness of interdependent organizations explain power relations within the network and its type (Rhodes, 1981). Thus policy communities that are limited to a membership that is professional and technocratic and where resources for exchange (informational, economic, legal, and so on) are held by all participants – contrast with the more broadly based issue network – are mainly consultative in character. In the case of policy communities, there is a high degree of resource interdependence and in terms of goal achievement for actors involved, every chance of a positive-sum game. The issue-based network with a range of participants with unequal possibly fluctuating research/weakness is more likely to produce a zero-sum game. Both examples of these networks may be seen operating within the SF arena (Bretherton and Sperling, 1996; Conzelman, 1995; Ansell et al., 1997).

It is evident that network analysis is more appropriately focused on policy implementation rather than policy initiation. Other limitations are claimed to be the problem of identifying network boundaries, especially within the EU bureaucracy and its constitutional fluidity and complexity (Kassim, 1994). It can also be argued that for network theory to operate convincingly it needs to be applied within an established theory of the state, so far not available to the EU. Finally the divergencies between EU policy arenas, and indeed within them, make for only a limited application of network analysis as an accurate descriptor of EU policy processes. However, the conditions that sustain policy networks have been established since the 1988 reforms and, indeed, consolidated within the objectives and implementation requirements of the 2000–2006 programme (Rhodes et al., 1996, p. 385; Commission, 2004a).

The same *de facto* assumption regarding integration is made when considering the impact that regional policy has had on the Europeanization of governance in member states and the relationship between EURP development and institutional change, both at EU and member state levels. These phenomena are considered below, but here we note that their analysis as concepts relating to integration theory lead us in the theoretical direction of neo-institutionalism (Bulmer, 1994; 1998) and the new constitutionalism (Nentwich and Weale, 1998). While an examination of these concepts is outside the scope of this chapter, the point here is that EURP has impacted on the European project so as to play a role in 'state re-structuring as part of the construction of a new European Policy space' (Gualini, 2003, p. 619). Its conceptualization may already be moving away from the (relatively) comfortable fit of MLG and network analysis towards frames seeking explanation of the structural dynamics and institutional change within the EU.

REGIONAL POLICY, INSTITUTIONAL CHANGE AND EUROPEANIZATION

In 1975 James Cornford wrote of the 'failure' of both West and East European states to deal with a growing policy demand, against a rising wave of ethnic–national aspirations and the inability to adjust to international and (emerging) supranational economic and political pressures. His analysis of state and sub-state institutional transformation recognized several likely responses to the 'sandwich' of upward and downward pressures that the European state was likely to experience (Cornford, 1975). Some 25 years on, the responses of EU member states, particularly those associated with the demands for and impact of EU cohesion policy, were examined in an edited volume (Hooghe, 1996). The establishment of a 'regional' tier to assist in adjustment to international market pressures, to meet local/ethnic/national demands for economic and political recognition of their problems, and now to sustain the cohesion of the Union reflects the 'significant change which has taken place in the organization of production and the growing competitiveness of regional markets' (Nanetti in Hooghe, 1996 p. 68). Regional/local actions are required to shield own interests (a traditional role), but also develop the necessary linkages (interregional, national, trans-regional) for their survival in such circumstances. The 1998 SF regulations encouraged, indeed expected, sub-national involvement in development planning. Cornford's 1975 characterization of several nation-state responses to 'failure' was recognized in the objectives of Union cohesion policy and the pressures exerted by Union institutions, not least the Commission. We can observe political, administrative and institutional changes, formal and informal, that have enhanced the significance of local/regional authorities and interests at national and EU level.

A EUROPE OF REGIONS

As well as the general commitment to subsidiarity (Art. A), the Treaty of Union recognized the need for formal regional representation in the creation of the Committee of Regions (COR) that was not always apparent in the legal–institutional frameworks of member states. Despite the favourable circumstances of the 'Europe of Regions' vision in the mid-1990s and the welcome it received from DG Regio and its then Commissioner, Monika Wulf-Mathies (Jeffrey, 2002, p. 34), COR has received little recognition from the Council (Warleigh, 1999). Its disparate membership, with often competing 'local' and 'regional' viewpoints, has led to sub-national representation continuing in the plethora of Brussels-based trans-regional/local associations including the Assembly of Regions, and the European Council of Local and Regional Authorities.[20] There is little evidence to suggest that COR will be in the foreseeable future anything more than secondary for representation of regional interests at the supranational level.

A more direct channel is the plethora of a sub-national representational offices set up by most EU regions. Excluding the long-established *Länder* lobbies, their members have increased from 15 permanent Brussels-based offices (1988) to 218 in 2004. The increase reflects two phenomena – the recognition of financial and economic regional/local interests and the trend towards decentralization in member states during the 1990s. It is the UK that has the most Brussels sub-national offices; new member states have also sought to establish sub-regional representation with 16 offices (*Inforegio Panorama*, 2004). The Commission recently expressed a wish to establish a 'more systematic dialogue' with these offices, which are seen as important allies as well as partners, 'particularly as regards regional policy and structural funds' (ibid., p. 24). There has also been Commission encouragement for interregional and trans-regional cooperation through the INTEREG programmes. This is reinforced within proposals contained within the Third Cohesion Report in the form of a 'European cooperation structure' to help 'address the traditional legal and administrative problems encountered in the management of cross border programmes and projects' (Commission, 2004a, p. xxxi). Also regions are 'to incorporate actions in the field of interregional cooperation within their national programmes' (ibid.). Has the EU, therefore, wrestling with the tension created between economic integration and political and cultural diversity, acted as an instigator of 'state-hollowing' and devolved power?

Member states have responded, and continue to respond, to EURP requirements in the search for optimum benefits from funding opportunities and regional/national advantage from a single market. A Brussels strategy for member states seeking to maximize their advantage from SF or sub-national regions competing with each other implies a proactive policy (Vos et al., 2002). This has entailed a range of tactical moves to enhance a region's 'international representation'. This is especially appropriate for long-established and/or constitutionally strong regions such as the German *Länder*, or those politically powerful areas such as Catalonia or Scotland. Member states have also taken the initiative in maximization of regional presence to meet Community expectations. Thus Ireland, as it lost its Cohesion status, created regions to sustain Objective 1 funding for the 2000–2006 programme. Central and East European member states responded to pressure to meet strict *acquis* associated with structural and social funding by developing regional levels of administration, as indeed did successive British governments during the 1990s (Burch and Gomez, 2002). The 'new regionalism' does not, however, automatically augur the diminution of the gatekeeper role of the state. Olivier Nay argues that 'by retooling and reasserting itself on the regional and local levels' so as to best arbitrate and coordinate French sub-national interest at Union level in response to EURP – the state gains an opportunity to reposition itself and to gain new strength' (Downs, 2002, p. 176; Nay, 2002, pp. 245–60).

The examples of the development of English as distinct from Scottish and Welsh decentralization illustrates a similar complex picture of institutional change associated with EURP. As mentioned earlier, developments post 1997, the most recent being the halting moves towards regional government (for electorally assenting northern regions), built on pre-'New Labour' innovations. Despite the ambivalence of Labour's drive towards constitutional reforms in the shape of decentralized government, Cornford's analysis of institutional change, driven by both external (EU) and parochial (regional) interests, remains apposite as there now exists 'a Europeanization effect that has assisted the development of New English regionalization so far and will continue in the future' (Burch and Gomez, 2002, p. 777).

THE EUROPEANIZATION OF EURP

This brings us on to a final area of conceptualization of EURP – the burgeoning reference to 'Europeanization' as a phenomenon of post-Maastricht integration (Kohler-Koch, 1999; Bulmer and Burch, 2000; Bache, 2003). In the case of EURP the term encompasses patterns of discourse, institutions and policies at sub-national and national level and the way they are affected and in turn affect the dynamics of supranational (EU) political, social and economic priorities (Burch and Gomez, 2003). Here the stress is on an interaction between top–down and bottom–up processes that may emanate from horizontal and vertical policy relationships. Thus Europeanization through EURP can take place via the presentation of (evolving) SF regulations that hone the management of EURP at national and local level. Conversely Europeanization may take place via its civil society component (ibid., p. 607); through shared good practice between regions, for example the English Regions Network (Burch and Gomez, 2002); or by sharing informational or lobbying processes so as to facilitate intervention at national and Brussels levels, such as Medcités – an environment network of 30 Mediterranean coastal towns and a regional network for knowledge and technical innovation. These and other examples of 'cross-loading' (Burch and Gomez, 2002) illustrate the multidimensional avenues of EURP through Europeanization that are dynamic and cumulative. In effect the concept impacts on all components of a policy – from civil society to political and bureaucratic actors and at various points of the institutional framework.

Applied to English regions, Burch and Gomez explore and evaluate Europeanization in a manner applicable to any member state – how it impacts on a polity's system of constitutional rules; the organizational dimension on offices and bureaucratic structures; on regulations and on the policy process itself. However, central government agendas cannot be excluded from the change agenda and are evident in the shape of systemic change rather than in the regulative or process dimensions more readily susceptible to a Brussels' influence. EU-related activities such as environmental, agricultural, employment and internal market policies and their coordination with EURP have made the sources and the impact of Europeanization complex. As such, 'Europeanization has been an important and persistent factor in the story of English (and other MS) regionalism though the full extent of its cumulative effect is too early to gauge' (Burch and Gomez, 2003, p. 21).

ENLARGEMENT AND THE FUTURE OF EURP

By way of conclusion to this chapter there follows a discussion of the impact of enlargement on EURP and its future as an instrument of cohesion and convergence in the EU. As we suggested in the opening paragraphs, the arena and agenda of regional policy has changed in the past few years in no small measure as a result of the decision at the Amsterdam Summit (1997) to open simultaneous negotiations with 12 applicant countries. Agenda 2000 presented a composite framework within which EU27 might be accomplished. This included a pre-accession strategy (ISPA) outlining priorities and measures for financial assistance (Mannin, 1999). That built on other assistance programmes offered by the Union since 1990, particularly under the PHARE Programme (Poland and Hungary: Assistance for Economic Reconstruction) directed at microeconomic change through sectoral transformation. A less well-funded programme, Technical Assistance for the Commonwealth of Independent States (TACIS), reflected a 'European Policy' that differentiated between countries in a manner that implied a 'near/far' EU perspective towards new neighbours (Mannin, 1999, p. 16).[21] From 1989 to 1996 PHARE funding amounted to ECU 6636 to 13 partner countries, covering a population of 105 million, supporting activities in sectors such as agriculture, the environment, infrastructural renewal, equal opportunities for women and democratic capacity. In effect PHARE and related programmes may be seen as regional policies in the broader definitional sense suggested above and retained many of the objectives and principles associated with post-1988 Structural Funding.

Between 2000 and 2006 ISPA, PHARE and SAPARD (Assistance to Modernize Agriculture) totalled approximately €3 billion. Transitional cohesion funding arrangements for acceding countries (2004–2006) included a financial framework amounting to €40.7 billion that included €21.8 billion for cohesion (14.7 billion in Structural Funds and €7.1 billion from the Cohesion Fund). Since all the new member states receive SF support, population coverage increased from 40 per cent (EU15) to 49 per cent (EU25). Poland received over 50 per cent of the overall commitment. The expanded Cohesion Fund now accounts for over one-third of total EU cohesion support (previously 18 per cent); similarly Objective 1 funding (EU25) amounts to over 90 per cent of SF itself (compared with 70 per cent previously). This is scarcely surprising given that 'some 92 per cent of the population of the 10 accession countries meet Objective 1 criteria' (Bachtler, 2004, p. 11). The 4 per cent GDP cap (see ibid., p. 11) means, however, that aid per capita for the new member states (2004–2006) remains likely to be substantially less than per capita receipts in what were the previously poorest (Cohesion) states of EU15.

The debate surrounding SF and previous enlargements resulted in policy change, as the strengths and weaknesses of EURP were exposed to the challenges of new economic social and political conditions. The 2004 enlargement is profoundly important by virtue of the scale of its challenge to the viability of EU governance. In consequence the value of SF as an agent of cohesion and convergence came under close scrutiny as its cost and its effectiveness in an expanded EU were predicted.

'Structural Fund support' says the Third Cohesion Report 'will be of central importance to the new member states in strengthening their economic competitiveness and catching up with the rest of the EU in terms of GDP per head' (Commission, 2004a, p. 170). Notwithstanding economic growth rates that have often outstripped those of EU15 in the past few years, Table 14.4 illustrates the enormity of the convergence objective at member state level.

Table 14.4 GDP growth and unemployment, EU15–27

	GDP growth, % per annum (1995–2001)	GDP 1999–2001 (EU15, 100)	Unemployment (2002), %, Total	Unemployment (2002), %, Female
EU15	2.5	100	7.8	8.8
New 10 (NI0)	4.8	45.5	14.9	15.6
EU25	2.6	91.0	9.0	10.0
EU27	2.6	86.8	9.1	10.0
Ireland	9.2	115.0	4.3	3.8
Netherlands	3.3	111.5	2.8	3.1
Britain	3.0	103.0	5.1	4.5
Germany	1.6	102.0	9.4	9.1
Spain	3.7	83.9	11.4	16.4
Greece	3.5	66.3	10.0	10.0
Slovenia	5.1	67.1	6.3	6.8
Czech Rep.	1.5	59.8	7.3	9.0
Poland	6.3	41.1	19.9	20.9
Estonia	5.2	37.1	10.3	9.7
Bulgaria	0.0	24.9	18.2	17.3
Romania	–0.1	23.7	8.4	7.7

Source: Commission (2004a).

Estimates of the time to achieve national convergence vary. However, 'there is a general recognition that it will require a significant and sustained commitment by the EU to the accession countries over a 30–40 year period, while at the same time enabling the poorer EU15 member states to make further progress on closing the development gaps with richer countries' (Bachter, 2004, p. 13).

Table 14.5 indicates a further complexity to this problem by showing highest/lowest GDP rates in selected E27 regions (NUTS2).

Table 14.5 NUTS2 regional GDP (average 1999–2001: EU15=100)

	Highest	Lowest
Germany	148.7 (Oberbayern)	60.5 (Dessau)
Britain	251.4 (Inner London)	59.1 (Cornwall)
Spain	106.2 (Navarra)	53.8 (Extremadura)
Greece	86.7 (Sterea Ellada)	52.9 (Anatolika)
Poland	62.2 (Mazowieckle)	28.6 (Lubelski)
Czech Republic	129.8 (Prague)	47.8 (Stfedni Moravia)
Slovakia	97.4 (Bratislava)	33.1 (Vychodne)
Romania	46.5 (Bucharest)	18.8 (Nord-Est)

Source: As Table 14.4.

Despite considerable structural reform and corresponding institutional adjustments and mainly impressive annual economic growth, serious economic imbalances remain for new member states. Government deficit spending is high, as is public expenditure relative to EU15. There is a notably higher proportion of workers in agriculture (13 per cent N10: 4 per cent EU15), with the industrial sectors heavily skewed towards older sectors, for example mining and steel production 'that present some of the most serious economic social, political and environmental challenges to the transformation process' (Bachter, 2004, p. 13).

While the structural problems of new member states have allowed for immediate access to Structural and Cohesion Funds, existing member states are squeezed by the 'statistical effect' and by economic indications that show slow relative national convergence but continuing and, in some cases, alarming divergence when viewed from a sub-national level. Other factors contribute to the tension between member states' view of enlargement and SF. Despite the experience of pre-accession EU programmes, Central and East European countries have been slow to create an institutional process adapted to successfully receive and implement EURP. The latest Cohesion Report reiterates a perennial Commission concern over their administrative capacity that remains 'questionable' (Commission, 2004a, p. 175; also Mannin, 1999, p. 55; Baun, 2002; Bailey and De Propis, 2002a). As Bailey and De Propis state, 'by the end of the 1990s ... no CCE country – with the exception of Hungary – had developed a comprehensive regional policy' (p. 309). The legacy of democratic centralism has meant that decentralization has met with scepticism (Baun, 2002, pp. 274–5). A tendency to rely on strong central government gatekeeping has not assisted a relatively low disbursement ratio (between funds allocated and funds received) of 50–70 per cent commitments (Sapir et al., 2003, p. 104). Sapir also asserts that there is a 'chronic deficit of well prepared projects' that reflects the low level of sub-national competence to play a full partnership role. 'EU assistance is urgently needed' to enhance such capacity (ibid.).

Recent EURP is also bound up in the geo-political challenges associated with the 2004 enlargement. Post-Cold-War Europe during the 1990s offered opportunities to the EU to assist in the management of a 'return' to liberal politics and market economics for CEECs, all of whom emerged as willing partners. EU12/15 was in a sense 'buffered' by its new neighbours from the backwash of instability emanating from the imperfections of the post-Soviet CIS. Slovenia in the south-east offered a similar geo-political buffer from the tragedy of ex-Yugoslavia. The Copenhagen (1993) and Essen (1994) summits presented criteria for political and economic renewal leading to full membership. In effect regional policy instruments available to EU15 were extended to third-party states: PHARE as a form of structural funding; SAPARD for agricultural restructuring and ISPA to shadow Cohesion Fund aims. A new European external paradigm was perceived not just in political and security terms but included economic, environmental and societal sectors (Buzan et al., 1998; Bretherton, 1999).

Enlargement in 2004, however, pushed back EU boundaries to new neighbours: Belarus, Moldavia, the Ukraine and, by 2007, the EU will surround ex-Yugoslavia. New issues of economic, environmental and social stability in those states have imposed themselves in the shape of border politics that requires a new transnational policy response. This is reflected in emergence of the Commission's European Neighbourhood Policy (Commission, 2004b) that seeks to integrate existing TACIS and as MEDA initiatives via a European Neighbourhood Instrument (ENI). This initiative funds border cooperation at sub-state level so as 'to complement external and internal funding instruments able only to operate on one side of the Union's borders' (ibid., p. 27). Transnational cross-border cooperation is also evidenced in the 2007 EURP Objective European Territorial Cooperation designed to strengthen relationships between regions 'so as to further harmonious and balanced integration of the territory of the Union by supporting cooperation ... on issues of community importance at cross-border transnational and interregional level' (Commission, 2004a). In its Budget Communication for 2007–13, the Commission again stresses the role of the EU as a (world) regional leader and thus the need to establish partnerships to stabilize the 'wider neighbourhood' through cooperation and, where appropriate, 'integration' in such areas as regulatory convergence, transport energy and environmental security and inevitably migration and crime (Commission, 2004b, p. 23). For neighbouring countries a 'policy mix on sharing stability and prosperity' must include the 'important impact of EU internal policies' (ibid., p. 25) in a search for a community of 'everything but institutions'. The ENI, included within the heading, 'The EU as a Global Partner', would build upon the principles of existing cross-border programmes – partnership, multi-annual programming and co-financing (ibid., p. 33) – reinforcing the role of sub-national actors in the application of what remains formally EU external policy arenas. EURP, in several guises, has consequently emerged as a component of societal security within the New Europe.

CONCLUSION: THE FUTURE OF EURP

It is worth reiterating the stark factors that bear heavily on the EURP debate since 2004 enlargement: EU25 increases the Union's population by 20 per cent, bringing with it only a 5 per cent increase in GDP, per capita has fallen by more than 12 per cent, and 92 per cent of the ten new member states' population live in Objective 1 regions. The number of regions below 75 per cent GDP has increased from 48 to 67; they cover a population of 166 million (25 per cent) compared with 68 million (18 per cent of EU15). Inevitably questions remain regarding the financial viability of EURP. The Commission assumption of an EU financial package of 0.46 per cent (EU27 GNI) for 2007–13 is currently still to be agreed by member states, with counter-proposals from the 'gang of six' demanding a capping of the budget for the period at 1.00 GNI.[22] Negotiations over the budget settlement may well last into 2005, and should there not be agreement on radical proposals, one commentator suggests that real reform would be on the agenda for the next decade (Begg, 2004, p. 5). In this scenario the substance of the Commissions proposals for cohesion policy through to 2013 will be sustained in their incrementalist form by default, and the general principles for cohesion established in 1988 will, as amended, continue into the second decade of the twenty-first century.

In a review of the current and future developments (September 2000), Olivier Guersent, a member of the DG Regional Policy Cabinet, listed the main principles of regional policy in the first years of the twenty-first century: financial 'consolidation', a recognition that the SF budget was unlikely to benefit from any major increase in support from member states or a reduced CAP in the foreseeable future; concentration, within 'themes' and towards targeted poorer areas, and more effective, decentralized and simplified implementation. A priority that shaped these 'principles' was preparation for enlargement – 'one of the most challenging tasks assigned to EU regional policy' (Guersent, 2001, p. 162). In effect SF priorities are now being shaped by both the political and economic needs of existing member states (especially employment generation, sustainability and environmental impact and information technology) and the recognition of a massive change to the regional panorama within a limited time frame, with the accession of new member states. Subsequently the Lisbon (2001) and Gothenburg (2002) summits added a global dimension to Guersent's assessment of the priorities and constraints of regional policy in the twenty-first century.

The Third Cohesion Report may thus reflect a watershed in SF development. SF, the most visible of EU policies, has contributed to the economic convergence of member states within EU15. Its role in reducing regional economic disparities within member states is less clear. The contribution to the creation of a European policy space and to the Europeanization of processes through the frame of MLG is easier to acknowledge. As such it may be argued that political and cultural cohesion is an emerging by-product of EURP despite calls for its consolidation and nationalization (Tarschys, 2003). This is made all the more pressing when observing the pressures on Union cohesion engendered by new members and new neighbours in the foreseeable future. As such, policies that encompass the broader concepts of 'region' outlined in the introduction to this chapter are emerging, as the cohesion of the Union is perceived in terms of pan-European societal security as well as EU economic progress. Thus regional policy is asked to play its part in the EU's response to global economic opportunity and threat.

NOTES

1. The Commission's recommendation to include five CEECs plus Cyprus triggered Article II of the Amsterdam Protocol on Institutional Reform, which required that, 'at least one year before EU membership exceeds 20', a comprehensive review of the Union's institutions must be undertaken.
2. Regional policy is formally a European Community (EC) policy contained within pillar 1 (social and economic) of the Treaty of Union (TEU). The term EU will be used for sake of simplicity.
3. There is a common classification for sub-national-level governance (NUTS): NUTSI level must have a population sized between 3 and 7 million and thus may be member state size, e.g. Latvia or sub-state (Scotland; Catalonia). NUTS II: 8 million to 3 million (Merseyside; Calabria); NUTS III: 150 000 to 800 000 (French departments; Italian provinces).

4. In making a case for EURP that is additional to the separate member state policies, one writer lists six distinct arguments, ranging from 'vested interest' (of EU citizens, member states and capital); 'financial targeting' (of disadvantaged regions/member states), 'coordination' (as mentioned above), 'effects of integration' (the avoidance of negativities that may emerge); the 'effect of other policies' (again as an antidote to the negative impact on some regions of CAP or the expense of EU environmental standards); and 'further integration' (as a contribution to establishing an integrative coalition of the willing) (Armstrong, 2002).
5. The new three, plus Italy and Ireland, were potentially a negating bloc in the negotiation process leading to the Single European Act (SEA) which, once agreed, enhanced the likelihood of reformed and larger structural funds in budgetary negotiations at the beginning of 1987. Thus regional policy breakthrough 'came as part of an old fashioned package deal' (George, 1991, p. 199) that involved a relative decrease in agricultural expenditure (at the behest of Britain), acceptance of a timetable for implementation of the SEA (France and Germany) and a doubling of the structural funds by 1993 (Spain, Portugal, Greece and Ireland).
6. Other controversies surrounded the merging of Objectives 3/4 and the creation of a new Objective 4 and aimed to assist adaptation of workers to industrial/technological change. The then Conservative Administration in Britain refused to participate in the funding process for this objective. A proposed Objective 6 associated with regions heavily dependent on the fishing industry was not agreed, though the issue was later absorbed within slightly amended regulations for Objectives 1, 2 and 5b.
7. Before the publication of *Agenda 2000* estimated costs of applying an unreformed SF suggested a doubling of the 1993–99 allocation, depending on numbers of CEEC entry (Grabbe and Hughes, 1998, p. 100).
8. The reduction of Community Initiatives to three, and its budget from 9 per cent to 5 per cent of the total SF, was both 'an admission of the somewhat mixed appreciation of their contribution' (Hall, 1997, p. 181) and the Commission's wish to enhance cross-border, transnational and interregional cooperation in a more focused programme. The concept of a 10 per cent performance reserve from the total SF budget to be allocated on criteria defined by the Commission was an innovation that clearly enhanced the '*dirigiste*' aspect of the proposals.
9. Member states remained responsible for the provision of statistical information on which Objective 2 regions were selected and played a powerful part in the Commission's final choice. Also, while the 1999 regulations stressed the importance of partnership, it is the member state that selects those partners. This, together with the reduction in the number of, and budget for, Community Initiatives, and the continuing role of member states in establishing their own additionality baselines, was seen as further evidence of a gradual and piecemeal 'renationalization' of the SF process.
10. EU27 was likely to fall into three distinct economic groupings: 'the well off' – the 12 existing member states; a middle group to include Greece, Spain, Portugal and Cyprus, Malta, Slovenia and the Czech Republic, with GNP at 80 per cent of the EU average; and a 'lagging group' of eight new entrants with a GNP of around 40 per cent of the EU average, accounting for 10 per cent of the EU population.
11. These were accessed as: Brundenburg; Mecklen–Vorpommern; Dresden; Halle; Magdenburg; Thuringen (Germany); Burgenland (Austria); Ita-Suomi (Finland) Asturias Murcia; Centa Y Melilla (Spain); Basilicata (Italy); Madeira (Portugal); Hainault; Namur (Belgium), Merseyside, West Wales, South Yorkshire (Britain).
12. 'n+2' relates to a three-year rolling spend requirement where n = yr 1 + following two years, so year 1 spend must be committed and defrayed by the end of year 3. The critical element is that the amount of spend must be achieved but it is not necessary for that spend to relate to projects approved in year 1. Any spend that falls short of the required spend profile is 'decommitted', that is, taken from the programme and returned to Brussels.
13. This view, however, is strongly contested (Smyrl, 1998; Sutcliffe, 2000; Marks, 1996). The design of the SF framework in 1988, 1993 and 1999 'reflected the blue prints the

Commission drew up' (Marks, 1996, p. 393). One DG region official termed this 'the magnet effect of the Commission's tabled agenda' (Interview, October 1998).

14. Thus Belgium, with a constitutionally powerful regional structure, demonstrated weak levels of political influence for its central government in all stages of SF operationalization; by contrast Belgian regions demonstrated moderate to strong influences at all stages. In Germany, the *Länder* enjoy a uniformly strong influence on SF programming that extended even to contract negotiation with the Commission – for the most part dominated in other member states by central governments. Also worthy of general comment is the relatively weak position of local governments in all stages of the process. Only Belgian local government demonstrated a strong influence (at the development planning and implementation stage) and German, Irish and Greek local government a moderate influence (in implementation/monitoring) (Marks, 1996).
15. This has encouraged other regions to establish Brussels regional offices, though it is Catalonia and to a lesser extent the Basque region that have gone further in this respect. Both have an interest in taking full advantage of cross-border cooperation, for example: Catalan and Basque involvement in INTEREG and Catalan interest in the trans-Pyrenean euro region (to include Languedoc–Roussillon and Midi Pyrénées); trans-regional cooperation – the 'Four Motors for Europe' – initiative (to include Lombardy, Rhône-Alpes and Baden-Württemberg); early and leading participation in the Committee of Regions (Morata and Munoz, 1996).
16. Where a Regional Association exists, their use of the SPD process since 1994 assisted in the influence of region-wide perspectives on regional strategy; thus the West Midlands Regional Economic Consortium, via a Regional European and Regional Innovation Strategy, contributed to strategic policy 'through politically neutral partnerships' (Jacobs, 1997, p. 42). Thus the North West Regional Association (NWRA), a broadly based partnership of public, voluntary and private bodies, brought some coherence to the bidding process, especially after the politically divisive and somewhat negative responses of some local authorities during the late 1980s (Boland et al., 1995; Wallace, 1993).
17. Thus the NWRA has a permanent presence on ERDF strategy and monitoring committees; the South West RDA enjoys a similar leading position within the strategic aspects of SF programming.
18. A minority Labour Administration (May 1999) took over responsibility for developing and managing the Objective 1 West Wales and Valleys Programme (2000–2006). SF monies granted for this period (£1.46 billion) were nearly twice the allocation in the previous period. However, because of a disjuncture in budgetary timetables between central government support and the availability of Objective 1 monies for 2000–2001, the Assembly found itself unable to meet matching funding requirements. The ensuing political debate produced a gradual weakening of the minority Labour Administration as it cleared to fail in getting cast-iron guarantees for additional Treasury funding. The minority executive was defeated in a no-confidence vote (February 2000) and, assisted by a critical Commission appraisal, the reformed Labour executive was able to negotiate sufficient additional funding beyond sums previously negotiated.
19. Another perspective is that after some 20 years of successful partnership, its embeddedness within economic development practice in Scotland would continue in whatever regional development policies are to emerge (Bachtler et al, 2003, p. 34).
20. The Constitutional Treaty (June 2004) confirms COR's consultative status and the Committee's involvement in the application of the principles of subsidiarity and proportionality. There are also proposals to allow COR direct access to the Court of Justice to defend its prerogatives and lengthen the terms of office to members to five years (COR, 2003).
21. Similar differentiation can be observed in the extension of association (European Agreements) and Trade and Cooperation Agreements (TCAs), the former amounting to enhanced trade and political opportunities to those countries on a rapid path toward democratic and market transformation (Mannin, 1999).
22. Austria, France, Germany, the Netherlands, Sweden and the UK.

15. Health policy challenges in a uniting Europe: the intriguing cases of health security and tobacco

Graham Moon

INTRODUCTION

> Good health is a state of physical and mental well-being necessary to live a meaningful, pleasant and productive life. Good health is also an integral part of thriving modern societies, a cornerstone of well-performing economies, and a shared principle of European democracies.
>
> Achieving good health for all means not just reacting to ill-health, but proactively promoting health, preventing diseases and helping people make healthy choices.
>
> It also means successfully tackling important challenges currently facing the European Union. These challenges include ageing-related conditions, high levels of lifestyle related diseases linked for example with obesity or tobacco consumption, a resurgence of serious communicable diseases, such as HIV/AIDS and the threat of new diseases such as SARS. (Byrne, 2004)

This chapter starts with a statement from European Commissioner Byrne of his views on the directions that should be taken by the emerging health strategy of the European Union. Commissioner Byrne adopts a broad definition of health, akin to that used by the World Health Organization (WHO, 1946). Health is much more than medical intervention and much more than biomedical treatment systems centred on hospitals and health professionals. Such matters are, of course, national concerns and, though converging around a consensus involving mixed public–private health systems (Saltman and Figueras, 1997; Elola, 1996), the European nations differ in the ways in which they organize health care intervention. Byrne's focus is, in contrast, on the bigger public health picture, on a concern for the broad health of the European population. This focus inevitably transcends the boundaries of nation-states and has thus been the concern of EU health policy since its emergence in the 1990s (Moon and Curtis, 1998; Moon, 1999). A similarly broad perspective also characterizes much of the policy of other trans-governmental organizations that impact on the health of Europeans, for example the WHO and the World Bank.

Byrne goes on to mention specific challenges facing health policy makers. He cites demography, tobacco, obesity and emergent diseases. It is undoubtedly the case that Europe, perhaps more than any other world region, faces health-related demographic pressures. The population structure is ageing and this has multiple policy implications that extend beyond health. There are consequences for the size, availability and capability of the workforce and, thus, for the state of economies. There are carer needs to consider and an emergent crisis in pension funding. More directly, the health impact relates to people living lives that are longer but often, particularly in extreme old age, characterized by disability and multiple costly health problems. Obesity is similarly an important issue. Europeans are generally getting bigger as a result of a combination of factors that include eating habits, sedentary lifestyles and low levels of exercise.

While not denying the importance of demography and obesity as health issues in contemporary Europe, this chapter focuses on the other two issues highlighted by Byrne: tobacco and emergent diseases. These are chosen as particularly significant topics for a monograph concerned with matters of policy and governance across the European space. They are assuredly important health issues; Byrne selected wisely and well. However, they are also the subject matter of political debate, embodying fascinating contradictions and opening up agendas that extend well beyond population health enhancement. Thus, in choosing emergent diseases as case studies, this chapter is able to engage with the laudable policy goal of restricting the spread of 'new' diseases within and into Europe. At the same time, it can also consider how the protection of Europeans' health can be linked to restrictions on the mobility of people from places deemed less healthy and to associations with bio-terrorism – the use of disease as a threat to European health. In the case of tobacco, a case study enables an analysis of the contradiction inherent in the simultaneous deployment of measures to restrict smoking, and thus reduce levels of mortality and morbidity, and the continuing subsidies that are paid to tobacco farmers. Further issues that arise from the tobacco theme include cigarette smuggling and the considerable revenue accruing to governments as a consequence of sales and import tax on tobacco.

The aim of this chapter is to use the twin case studies of emergent diseases and tobacco to highlight and examine critically the extended impact of health matters within a European context. Of necessity this context extends beyond the EU to include the Balkan states and those of the western parts of the former Soviet Union. The chapter's key contribution lies in the arguments that are developed concerning the politics of health protection and promotion. Two substantial sections of the chapter are thus devoted to the case studies. These are preceded and succeeded by, respectively, a brief assessment of current cross-national health policy in Europe, and a concluding assessment on the wider implications of the case study topics.

CROSS-NATIONAL HEALTH POLICY IN CONTEMPORARY EUROPE

Pan-European health policy is complex and can take many forms. Its complexity derives substantially from the web of influences on patterns of disease (McKee et al., 2004). Put simply, these influences extend from biomedical and genetic factors at one extreme, to contextual determinants such as poverty at the other. It is the contextual determinants of health that have provided the focus of cross-national policy towards health.

The European Union's health policy is thus centrally concerned not with medical intervention or with treatment services but with health protection and a social rather than medical model of public health. For the European Office of the World Health Organization, the policy focus is similarly broad and societal:

> Our work supports countries in developing health policies, health systems and public health programmes both to improve people's health and to reduce inequities in health within and between countries. We also work to strengthen international solidarity for health, especially to support countries in need, and to anticipate and facilitate collaboration on transboundary health threats. (WHO, 2004)

The World Bank, with its focus on the development of Central and Eastern Europe, gives rather more attention to the reform of the health care sector, but, none the less also subscribes, through selective application of its millennium development goals, to the importance of prevention:

> the importance of establishing effective and sustainable surveillance, vital registration, and health information systems to provide valid data for local decisions and international comparisons, and the continued need for interagency collaboration in support of all these objectives. (Rechel et al., 2004, p. 16)

The EU, WHO and the World Bank each have distinct but overlapping impacts on pan-European health policy (Moon, 1999). The WHO European Office has provided thematic input and valuable oversight over many years. In a very broad sense it would be possible to characterize the EU's concern as being with standardization and harmonization. On a similarly general level, the Bank's focus is on the health consequences of economic reconstruction.

The processes of transition in Eastern and Central Europe and the related matter of EU enlargement have meant that both the EU and the Bank have seen considerable changes to their roles in recent years.

The case of the EU exemplifies this process of change. It is widely acknowledged that considerations of health really only appeared substantively on the EU agenda with the Treaty of Maastricht (Mossialos and McKee, 2002). That Treaty committed the EU to making a contribution to a high level of health protection for its citizens. Through Article 129 provision was made for Community-wide action to prevent major disease scourges. It was also intended that an awareness of health protection should come to pervade other EU policies. The scope for implementing these two goals was, in theory, limited. The emphasis was on coordination and persuasion rather than legislative change. Only in specific circumstances was genuine concerted Community-wide action anticipated: when a health problem was significant and an appropriate preventive response could be identified, when a transnational solution was essential and in harmony with the approaches of other agencies, and when the action would enhance other EU goals.

By the time of the Amsterdam Treaty revision (1997), there had been something of a metamorphosis in EU health policy. The implementation of Article 129 had taken health policy rather further than might have been anticipated by the letter of EU law. In particular, the range of diseases and determinants of disease had been widened, with implications for the role of both national governments and the EU. Many health professionals welcomed this development, but it was not always seen as appropriate by governments or even by the European Commission. The extension of the Article was thus the subject of debate and dispute that was, in the event, resolved largely by the advent of an external stimulus: the mid-1990s emergence of Bovine Spongiform Encephalopathy (BSE – 'mad cow' disease).

BSE, or more specifically its species-hop to humans, provided a textbook example of a situation under which cross-EU action could be initiated under Article 129. The appearance of chronic degenerative brain disorders in previously healthy young people raised important questions about disease surveillance, food safety and health promotion that definitively crossed borders and demanded cross-national action. Yet vested interests, nationalism and protectionism resulted in a very ineffective response. The Treaty revision at Amsterdam, Article 152, can be interpreted as the EU's subsequent reaction to the lessons of the BSE crisis (McKee et al., 1996). It had many of the limitations of its predecessor and was undoubtedly a compromise between public health and national governmental lobbies. Article 152 did, however, give a clearer steer towards recognizing the health implications of wider EU policy and has contributed to positioning health higher up on the EU political agenda.

This slowly increasing importance has been carried through in the draft of the EU Constitution (Bonde, 2005). Article III-179–1 provides a general context:

> Action by the Union, which shall complement national policies, shall be directed towards improving public health, preventing human illness and diseases, and obviating sources of danger to physical and mental health. Such action shall cover:
>
> (a) the fight against the major health scourges, by promoting research into their causes, their transmission and their prevention, as well as health information and education;
> (b) monitoring, early warning of and combating serious cross-border threats to health.

More specific measures provide for the possibility that

> European laws or framework laws may also establish incentive measures designed to protect and improve human health and in particular to combat the major cross-border health scourges, as well as measures which have as their direct objective the protection of public health regarding tobacco and the abuse of alcohol ... (Article III-179–5)

Direct action is envisaged on 'measures in the veterinary and phytosanitary fields which have as their direct objective the protection of public health' (Art. III-179–4c) and 'measures concerning monitoring, early warning of and combating serious cross-border threats to health' (Art. III-179-d). The paramount role of national governments with regard to health care is reaffirmed and, overall, a clear commitment to the primacy of national governments remains in most circumstances.

At present, health thus appears to be a rising theme in EU policy but one that has some way to go before it becomes a major issue. Movement towards that higher position is centrally about putting health at the centre of EU policy making: the recognition that achieving good health requires cross-sectoral action extending beyond health services and beyond the input of health professionals. Placing health policy in this broader context is, at root, grounded in economic functionalism. A healthy population and, by extension, a healthy workforce, is necessary for economic growth and sustainable development. To this end, the European Commission committed itself to integrating health into the post-Lisbon agenda as a driver of competitiveness and sustainable development, seeing health action as a long-term investment rather than a short-term cost. The European Council of March 2004 similarly encouraged national governments to strengthen health reforms as a means to improve macroeconomic performance.

General conclusions that can be drawn from this brief assessment of cross-national health policy in Europe include the importance of the coordination across an increasingly diverse Europe, the scope for conflict with national states and the focus on specific themes, notably within the public health arena. The EU's emergent recognition of health development as an element of macroeconomic policy is not specifically shared with the WHO, but resonates well with the concerns of the World Bank. The less functionalist policy objective of placing health at the centre of public policy is, however, a perspective shared by all players in pan-European health policy. It is the potential for contradiction that lies in the juxtaposition of economy, health and policy centring, as well as emergent notions of a social Europe (Commission of the European Communities, 2005), that underlie the case studies that follow.

EMERGENT DISEASES AND EUROPEAN SECURITY

> Europe also needs to build on the lessons learned with SARS and invest in EU-wide resource planning and capacity to provide better protection at lower cost against major threats to public health, from influenza or other pandemics and bio-terrorism. Health threats for example from infectious diseases may have very heavy consequences for the population and the economy of the EU as a whole. (Byrne, 2004, p. 7)

The visibility of public health in world politics has increased, in part because of the global span of new epidemics such as HIV/AIDS and SARS/Avian flu (Fidler, 2003). This visibility has been accompanied by a conundrum in which public health is torn between a global and internationalist objective and one that is more nationalist and isolationist. As Forrest (1996) notes, the control of imported disease has long been based on notions of exclusion and quarantine. These ideas are inconsistent with economic globalization and European integration. Nor do they acknowledge the potential for rapid borderless disease diffusion in modern society. International cooperation for research, surveillance, prevention and response appears essential. This section explores the contrasting impulses of integration and exclusion as exemplified by the developing role of public health in European security policy.

Following King (2004), the concept of scale politics provides a useful analytical framework to begin this exploration. In the European context, contrasts can be drawn between security inside Europe and security issues concerning entry to Europe from 'outside'. Public health campaigns around newly emerging diseases and other perceived threats to European health exhibit both similarities and differences in their construction of this insider–outsider differentiation. The campaigns are seldom simply about health, however; they demonstrate a wider ambivalence about change and difference as well as the implications of economic globalization.

This tendency was evident even in the early days of modern European integration. The 1957 Treaty of Rome created freedom of movement among member states. The movement of people, services and goods carried direct implications for health and for disease control. Freedom of movement was thus qualified, with member states permitted to restrict movement for the protection of health. By the late 1980s, it became clear that these safeguards were no longer adequate. As the integration of a larger Europe proceeded, the remittance of the health element of security to national governments became simultaneously a restriction on further integration and a barrier to more effective measures for health protection. Existing surveillance and control systems, based on national structures, were inadequate in the face of outbreaks that crossed borders.

The focus that emerged from this realization was initially focused within Europe. Article 129 of the Maastricht Treaty provided a legal basis for the development of a common EU-wide approach to epidemic surveillance, mainly focused on HIV/AIDS. A programme of short-term project funding was also initiated to support networks of national surveillance centres. The success of these networks demonstrated the need for more sustained action but also contributed to shifting some attention from intra-European matters towards Europe's borders and beyond. Lever and Joseph (2001) showed, for example, that cases of legionnaires' disease within Europe could not be understood without considering causal origins outside Europe, extra- and intra-European travel patterns and pooling international data.

Although action within Europe has remained crucial, the concern with borders and 'outside' has escalated in recent years. A number of factors lie behind this development. First, the enlargement of the EU has brought parts of the outside that had been subject to marked health deficits into the inside. Coker et al. (2004) show that screening policies to detect tuberculosis among new entrant countries to the EU are extremely varied, although infection rates are increasing. While rates of HIV infection remain low in new member states of the EU, they are also rising fast. The clear implication is that EU enlargement has brought internal health threats. The allied issues are wider ranging, including themes as diverse as the costs of modernizing health care provision in the face of significant health challenges, and the social impact of the health–poverty nexus.

Second, Europe remains a migration target; widening borders are perceived by some to increase the contrast between a healthy inside and an unhealthy outside (Coker, 2003; for a contrasting perspective see Migration Watch UK, 2003). The expanded EU has borders with countries (Belarus, Ukraine) where levels of communicable disease are very much higher than the differential between new and old member states. For the new island members, Cyprus and Malta, there are issues centred on their bridging location between Europe and Asia and Africa respectively. Further EU expansion, particularly the Turkish candidature and expansion into the Balkans and non-Baltic former Soviet Union, is likely to exacerbate this issue. Continuing migration from former colonial spaces provides a further angle on this theme, with its underlying assumption that the extended borders of the new EU may have made Europe more vulnerable to external health threats as well as heightening the health inequalities within Europe.

The impact of the equation of migration with health problems is perhaps best seen in proposals and policies concerning health screening for immigrants. Although notions such as quarantine originated in Europe, immigrant screening has actually featured infrequently as a formal policy of European states. Indeed, in strictly epidemiological terms the very notion flies in the face of growing evidence that immigrant populations tend to be healthier than average, at least initially (Bentham, 1988). Those European countries with screening requirements tend to focus on refugees and asylum seekers and screen on entry to the country. Others require screening as part of citizenship application. In 2001 the Parliamentary Assembly of the Council for Europe called for processes to be standardized across Europe (International Organization for Migration, 2003).

The global resurgence of tuberculosis (TB) has been the catalyst for a reconsideration of the current relatively liberal position. For example, the Netherlands now imposes TB screening on applicants for stays of over three months. Exceptions are made for applicants from selected countries deemed low risk. Other countries, including Britain, are taking a similar stance: Britain is endeavouring to implement screening as part of the immigration application process and the Conservative opposition propose more severe measures that would deny visas to prospective immigrants who test positive for TB and extend testing to migrants from new EU member states (*Lancet*, 2005).

The third way in which borders, 'inside' and 'outside', enable the construction of health as an aspect of European security relates to political concerns about the potential threat of bio-terrorism. The impact of bio-terrorism can of course cross borders both within and into Europe in the same way as any (other) disease. At the same time its initiation links straightforwardly to discourses that link particular migrant communities with terrorism. At EU level, current capacity to respond to these is based on four pillars. The Health Security Committee (HSC), created in 2001, brings together high-level representatives and experts to foster cooperation. Bio-terrorism response plans were initially a national responsibility and seldom shared or coordinated more widely. After 11 September 2001 this situation began to change as European countries and the EU faced up to the prospect of bio-terrorism and the role of the HSC developed. Networks of national and international public health surveillance provide the third element in the response to bio-terrorism. Bio-terrorist acts differ from 'normal' epidemics only in the nature of their source: deliberate release as opposed to natural occurrence. 'Normal' epidemic surveillance networks are therefore of value. Personnel numbers involved specifically in bio-terrorism surveillance in Europe dramatically increased in October 2001. Finally, cross-EU standards in laboratory testing also constitute a crucial element in the management of bio-terrorist threats. A far more centralized approach was progressively adopted after 11 September 2001.

The threat of an attack using postal diffusion of anthrax provides a case study of the current EU approach to bio-terrorism in action (Coignard, 2001; Maclehose et al., 2001, 2004). Twenty cases of anthrax inhalation were identified in the USA in late 2001, all associated with the deliberate release of anthrax. European countries anticipated copycat action and had to manage numerous suspected instances of contaminated mail. In the event, all proved to be hoaxes, mistakes or cases of justifiable caution. National bio-terrorism response plans had, however, not always been fully developed at the time and were often classified, thus limiting coordination across Europe. Differences were also revealed in case definitions or data collection procedures, indicating the need for standardized procedures. Public health surveillance in the form of mail testing varied greatly by country, with a suggestion that most testing occurred where the numbers of threats were lowest. In countries facing a greater number of threats, national laboratory capacities were probably exceeded. They focused on the identification of potential rogue substances and would have been less effective had they been concerned with matching symptoms to cause in a post-release scenario. Finally, there was some evidence that the response, while adequate for anthrax, would have been less satisfactory for other potential threats. This might indicate a need for action at EU level rather than the dispersal of scarce resources in multiple countries.

The prospect of bio-terrorism thus represents a case for partnership across Europe and across policy sectors within Europe: it concerns not only the health sector, but also security, justice and the police, among others. Information sharing and action coordination appear essential to avoid duplicated efforts. Liaison with international agencies such as the EU Directorate General for Health and Consumer Affairs (DG-SANCO) or the WHO Regional Office for Europe was limited in relation to the anthrax scare and subsequent moves have sought to ensure that it is now in place and future activity, particularly activity crossing borders, will be coordinated, proactive and capable of calling on Europe-wide expertise.

The new European Centre for Disease Prevention and Control should have a key role in the prevention of such health threats.

As King (2002) has argued, public health has a clear link with national security. During the 1990s, American public health experts capitalized on this historical association, arguing that 'emerging diseases' presented a threat to American political and economic interests. This claim applies equally to the European situation. The pressures of integration, immigration and territoriality in the form of discourses of inclusion and exclusion ensure that health offers a distinctive and important angle on national and European security (Council of the European Union, 2003).

TOBACCO AND EUROPEAN HEALTH

> The European Region of WHO, with only 15 per cent of the world's population, faces nearly one third of the worldwide burden of tobacco related diseases. At the end of the 1990s tobacco products were responsible for 1.2 million deaths (14 per cent of all deaths), and unless more effective measures are implemented it is estimated that they will cause 2 million deaths (20 per cent of all deaths) each year by 2020. While it has fallen from 45 per cent to 30 per cent over the past 30 years and has currently stabilized, smoking prevalence in the European Region still remains at a level that is devastating for public health and future generations. The negative trends in smoking prevalence among young people, women and lower socioeconomic groups, as well as the gap in tobacco control policies between member states, are of a particular concern. (WHO, 2002, p. 5)

Tobacco consumption represents a very serious health problem across Europe. It is the single largest cause of preventable disease and premature death in the European Union and has been estimated to cause about one-third of all cancers and 90 per cent of lung cancers, and cost some €100 billion each year through the disease burden of lung morbidities (Loddenkemper et al., 2003). This impact varies geographically. For example, there is a marked genderization to smoking. This has led to increases in tobacco-related health problems in Southern Europe where, due in part to cultural factors, smoking by women is continuing to rise rapidly. In Central and Eastern Europe, the aggressive entry of international tobacco companies to new markets has also increased prevalences (Connolly, 1995). The risk of tobacco-related premature mortality is estimated to be 200 per cent higher in former socialist states compared to the EU (Peto et al., 1994).

Given the clear and stark impact that smoking has on the health of the European population, it might be expected that both national governments and the EU would see smoking and tobacco in a negative light. In a general sense this is indeed the case but it is not solely the case. Public policy towards tobacco is not solely a matter of health; indeed there are aspects of tobacco policy within Europe that seem perverse in the light of the health impact of tobacco. To understand this, it is necessary to acknowledge that the tobacco industry represents a powerful economic lobby. Not only does it provide an addiction that is popular with sections of the electorate; it also generates jobs in cigarette manufacture and, via corporation and similar industrial taxes, represents a source of revenue and an income stream for other industries, notably advertising. Tobacco addiction also levers revenue for governments through the tax element in the price of cigarettes. Two more issues further complicate the paradoxical position of tobacco in public policy: some European countries grow tobacco and some are involved as state owners in the manufacture of cigarettes. Notwithstanding the popularity of smoking, these industries are generally in receipt of state subsidies. The second issue concerns another threat to the revenue stream represented by tobacco: a significant proportion of the cigarettes smoked in Europe are smuggled. Countering this illicit trade can be seen as both health promotion and revenue protection. The following paragraphs address these issues.

Cigarette manufacturers were thought to employ some 64 000 full-time job equivalents in 2000 in processing and direct manufacturing (Aspect Consortium, 2004). The enlargement of the EU has presented both opportunities and threats. Europe is a major market for any industry and no less so for the tobacco industry. The structuring of opportunities and threats facing the tobacco industry as it encountered enlargement reflected the nature of that industry (Gilmore et al., 2004). International tobacco companies such as British American Tobacco (BAT) foresaw increased demand and an opening market for a product that could be advertised as representative of a globalizing, aspirational new order. This market opportunity was arguably sufficient to counter the disadvantages of tax harmonization and the loss of duty-free sales. National companies and state monopolies were more threatened. Without the shelter of protection and exposed to far greater markets, such operations would be vulnerable to competition. While a health perspective might see this as a basis for reducing the size of the industry, the economic reality has been one of merger and takeover by international tobacco. Thus, in October 1999, Tabacalera (Spain) and Seita (France) merged to form Altadis and, in July 2003, BAT acquired Ente Tabacchi Italiano. Enlargement, and possible future accessions, notably that of Bulgaria, are likely to see an escalation of this process.

In a perverse sense, it therefore seems that European economic integration has contributed to the tobacco industry becoming more efficient and more able to market its products. There is some empirical evidence to show that removing barriers to trade in tobacco products leads to increased consumption (Bettcher et al., 2001). General increases in living standards have brought higher salaries and consequent disposable income. Finally, a more uniform and more stable business environment has been created.

A productive cigarette manufacturing industry undoubtedly represents a source of revenue for governments, not least through the excise tax element of cigarette pricing. Figure 15.1a illustrates the range of excise levels across a sample of European countries. This factor, together with similar differentials in the pricing of cigarettes (Figure 15.1b), underpins the parallel, and from a revenue point of view less satisfactory, illicit market for tobacco products. Together the figures contrast a low-tax, low-price regime in Central Europe and a high-tax, high-price one in the 'old' EU. This situation provides a basis for smuggling and bootlegging that is exacerbated by the economic differentials between the old and new EU. There is strong evidence that both organized crime and multinational tobacco companies are deeply implicated in this process (Joosens and Raw, 1998; Joosens, 1999), with the latter benefiting by increasing its market and entering new markets at advantageous prices. On average illicit tobacco comprises between 10 and 15 per cent of the cigarette market across Europe (Joosens and Raw, 1995); a figure of 40 per cent has been officially suggested for Albania (WHO, 2003a). It is estimated that one in five cigarettes smoked in the UK and almost 80 per cent of hand-rolling tobacco are smuggled, costing £2.5 billion in lost tax tobacco revenue (HM Customs and Excise and HM Treasury, 2000). Spain provides a rare example of a country that has successfully tackled smuggling and bootlegging.

Perhaps the most controversial and paradoxical aspect of European policy towards tobacco is the extent of the agricultural subsidy paid to tobacco growers by both national governments and by the EU. The WHO (2003a) states that subsidies are currently paid to tobacco farmers in Albania, Andorra, Belarus, Belgium, Bosnia, Bulgaria, Croatia, France, Georgia, Hungary, Italy, Moldova, Portugal, Romania, Serbia, Spain, Macedonia and Turkey. Grower nations also include Germany, Austria, Slovakia, Poland, Greece and Cyprus, although only the last three are reported to have subsidies from the EU (Aspect Consortium, 2004). In total some 125 000 full-time equivalents are employed in tobacco farming. Although the quality of the tobacco and the extent of production are both low, tobacco is the most heavily subsidized crop per hectare in Europe. Growers get €7800 per hectare and the EU spent around €1000 million annually on subsidies through the 1990s (about 2.3 per cent of the Common Agricultural Policy (CAP) budget) and 1.1 per cent of the total Commission budget. Over the same period EU spending on smoking prevention amounted to just €2 million per annum (Gilmore et al., 2004). This incongruity has

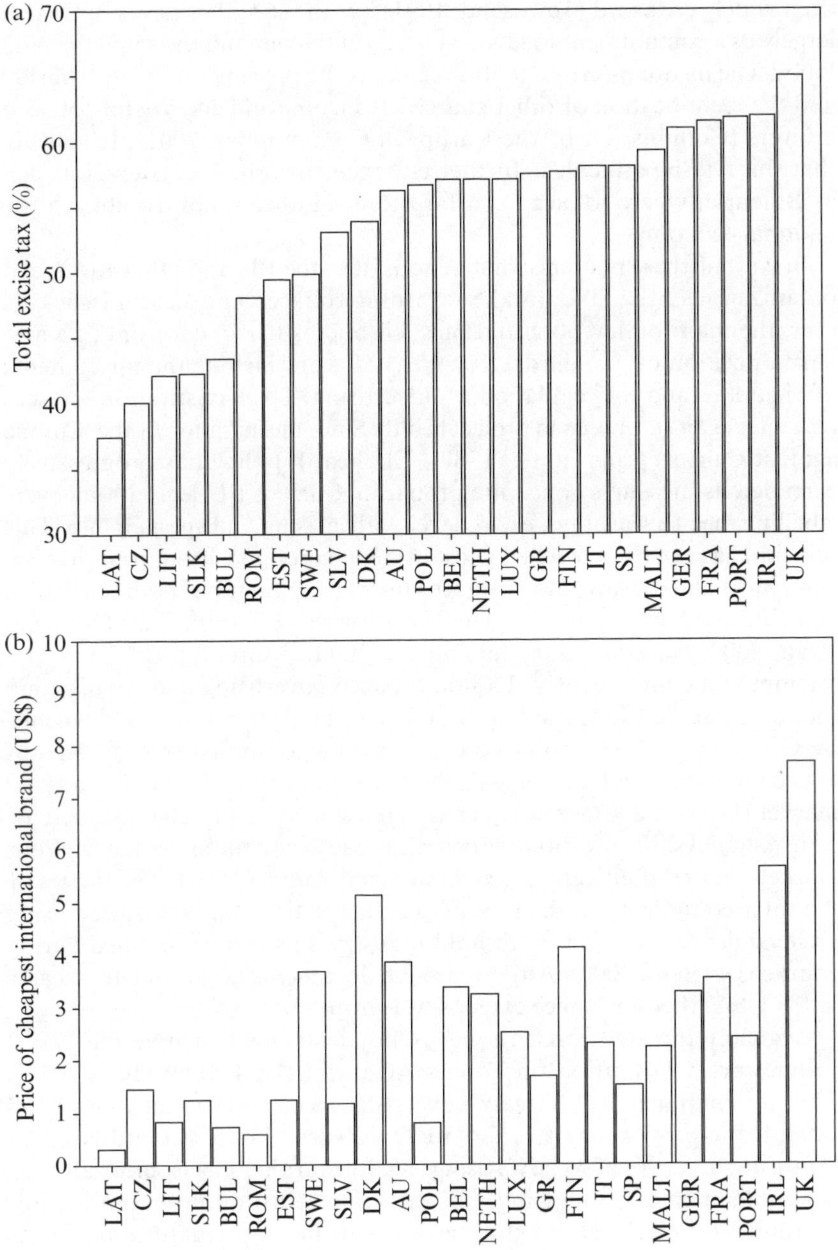

Source: WHO (2003a).

Figure 15.1 Tax and pricing in the European cigarette market

been widely criticized (Townsend, 1991) but the subsidies have continued, largely as a commitment to less-favoured rural areas and the small farming lobby. The medium-term intention remains the phasing out of the subsidy and the identification of other sources of income and activity for tobacco growers (Commission of the European Communities, 2001). It is likely that this will be difficult if further enlargement brings in countries such as Bulgaria, where tobacco is a far more significant contributor to the national economy.

In view of these matters, what actions have the EU and other European organizations been able to take regarding tobacco as a health issue? As ever, the main policy potential of such bodies lies in coordinating and harmonization of standards. Key areas of work include the tar contents of cigarettes and the regulation of advertising. The Constitution foresees measures against tobacco to protect health. Since the initiation of the 'Europe against Cancer' programme (1987), EU health policy has progressively extended its measures concerning tobacco. Current EU legislation covers labelling, health warnings, excise levels, advertising and sponsorship. This position has not been reached without trenchant opposition from tobacco companies and prevarication by governments. For example, both the British and German governments have had issues with advertising bans (Neuman et al., 2002; Hastings and MacFadyen, 2000). Moreover, the EU's first attempt at a comprehensive ban on tobacco advertising and sponsorship foundered in the European Court of Justice in 2000 following a challenge by Germany and four tobacco companies who argued that a ban was anti-competitive and contrary to the EU's remit to facilitate the internal market (Hervey, 2001). A weaker version was passed in 2002 because of transnational shifts in attitudes towards tobacco and the ascendancy of less market-focused political parties (Duina and Kurzer, 2004). The tactics of the tobacco industry in the face of such legislation can be assessed using archival depositories set up to hold industry documents obtained during court cases (Bero, 2003). Although these documents largely relate to cases in the USA, their relevance extends to Europe.

Arguably the key transnational policy instrument is now the WHO Framework Convention on Tobacco Control (FCTC) (WHO, 2003b). This 'international health treaty' covers all aspects of tobacco control and extends the provisions of other WHO policies (Anderson and Hughes, 2000). It covers tobacco advertising, health warning labels, price and tax issues, illicit trade (smuggling) and smoking cessation programmes. For example, Article 11 states that health warnings on cigarette packages should occupy no less than 30 per cent of the principal display areas and bans the use of descriptors such as 'low tar', 'light', or 'mild'. Article 13 requires a comprehensive ban on tobacco advertising, promotion and sponsorship. It recognizes that individual states can no longer effectively control the global factors that drive the tobacco epidemic, and coordination is needed. The FCTC has to be both signed and ratified by both the EU and individual member states. The EU is unable to ratify until all member states have ratified. By early 2005, 17 of the 52 member states of the European Region of the World Health Organization had ratified: Norway, Armenia, Denmark, Finland, France, Germany, Hungary, Iceland, Latvia, Lithuania, Malta, Netherlands, San Marino, Slovakia, Spain, Turkey and the UK. The remaining states can largely be equated with those in which there is a tobacco-growing lobby or where multinational tobacco companies are particularly active.

In summary, tobacco policy provides a clear illustration of the difficulties of policy formulation in a transgovernmental context, particularly when that context is dominated by economic imperatives. The evidence for the harmful health consequences of tobacco is incontrovertible, and policy aimed at mitigating these effects has increased markedly in recent years. Yet both national governments and the EU persist in subsidizing tobacco growing as part of their agricultural policy. This apparent contradiction can be understood in terms of political expediency, historic inertia and the power of multinational tobacco companies, but it also indicates something of the gap between the social and economic policy drivers.

CONCLUSION

This chapter has argued that 'health' is more than a narrow concern with the apparatus of medical care and the control of disease. It provides a construct that features in policy development across a much wider arena. What may appear to be straightforward health issues can also link to policy outcomes with wider and even contradictory implications. Thus the concern to combat emergent diseases can metamorphose from a desire to protect the public health goal to a tool for restricting mobility and controlling entry within the European space. In the case of tobacco, the chapter has demonstrated the paradoxes thrown up by the encounters of the EU and national governments with the simultaneous presence of a threat to health and the provision of employment and revenue. Together, the two case studies suggest that health needs to be recognized as an important element in the European policy environment.

16. Change, pensions and ageing in Europe: discourses of risk and security

Kay Peggs

INTRODUCTION

The changing demographic structure of the European Union (EU), with older people comprising an increasing proportion of its population, has been allied with discourses of individual and collective risk. Negative discourses, for example focusing on the age dependency ratio, present this increasing proportion of older people as a growing burden to employees and governments alike. Much has been said about the risks that an increasing number of older people pose, with a focus on societal ageing and the future pensions bill in Europe. Risk is central to these assumptions since enormous sums of money are involved. Thus 'it's all fertile ground for the alarmists' (Littlewood, 1998, p. 1). The purpose of this chapter is to consider such discourses and to draw attention to the ways in which government policies and initiatives pose a risk to the security (both financial and otherwise) of this significant and increasing proportion of the population of the EU.

Change and the risks associated with change are an important feature of this chapter, not least in its focus on the recent enlargement of the EU. In EU countries separately, and in combination, discourses connected with societal ageing have caused alarm, leading to government, pressure group, media, academic, and individual engagement with these risk discourses. However, such engagements are differentially aligned. For example, concern about hugely increased future pension costs has induced governments and other commentators to engage in debates about policy changes and individual financial security as a route to the protection of government funds. However, proposed policy changes have led to worker and pensioner demonstrations in European Union countries[1] because of fears about lost pension benefits. In addition, younger citizens[2] have protested against what they see as the unfair burden of state pension payments linked to taxation. Fears about the consequences of EU enlargement have further excited this already agitated risk debate, for example with worries about further increases in pensions bills due to supposed enormous leaps in immigration through arrivals from the new EU countries, and concerns about new EU member states which are deemed to have ill-conceived and unsustainable pension systems. Of particular interest here is the perceived pension consequences of enlargement involving the most recently established Eastern European countries. These countries have undergone considerable and rapid transition, and this has negatively affected older people (Hinchliff and Hall, 2002). Thus I am interested to tease out how discourses of the risks of an ageing society are combined with discourses of the risks of EU expansion to fuel an already alarmist debate.

This chapter begins with a brief outline of how discourses of risk have been incorporated into discussions about ageing and pensions and how the marketization of pensions has been posited as a solution. I then move on to a discussion of ageing in Europe focusing on theoretical perspectives on discourses of risk associated with pensions and ageing. After a brief outline of ageing in Europe I present and analyse the consequences of EU expansion. This leads me to a critical appraisal of suggested reforms to pension policy in the EU. The chapter concludes that the financial security of older people in the EU is an urgent issue that should be fundamental to discussions about pension issues and central to pension policy reforms in EU countries.

RISK DISCOURSES AND PENSIONS: 'PROBLEMS' AND 'SOLUTIONS'

Discourses associated with ageing and pensions draw heavily on notions of risk and security. Foucault's discussion of governmentality points to the ways in which discourses are influential in constructing issues such as risk as phenomena, with areas of life problematized as areas of risk (Gordon et al., 1980). Foucault is interested in 'seeing historically how effects of truth are produced within discourses which in themselves are neither true nor false' (ibid., p. 118). Such risk discourses, presented as truths, influence our perceptions of ageing and pensions. Discourses associated with ageing, which often focus on what Hawksworth et al., among others, call the 'burden of an ageing population' (2000, p. 6), emphasize the apparently negative consequences associated with demographic ageing. Using typically militaristic imagery, Hawksworth et al. conclude that in Europe 'the demographic time bomb is real enough – from 2010 onwards it will begin to explode' (ibid., p. 4). Expert judgements are essential to the formulation of the 'truth' of such 'risks', with groups of individuals being established as high risk, requiring expert knowledge and interventions (Gordon et al., 1980). Expert discourses such as those provided by Holzmann et al. (2003) for the World Bank provide an example. In their forward to a World Bank Report on pensions in Europe, Linn and Rischard suggests that 'unless changes are implemented fairly soon in the current retirement income systems, this burden on workers and on public budgets will become more and more overwhelming, and will result in defaults on past promises. This would hurt the very vulnerable elderly' (2003, p. vii). Although the problems for the 'vulnerable elderly' are mentioned, here the key focus is the *burden* on budgets of governments and workers, with pensioners and governments, and workers and pensioners, pitted against each other in conflict over scarce resources.

Foucault shows how individuals are relied upon to willingly conform to the interests and needs of the state. Individuals attempt to 'transform themselves in order to attain a certain state of happiness, purity, wisdom, perfection or immortality' (Foucault, 1988, p. 18). In this respect financial security in later life is seen as a matter of individual responsibility that requires constant work. Indeed, modified risk discourses broaden the debate to encompass the risks to older people that lack of engagement with pensions problems will have (cf. Holzmann et al., 2003). Here the notions of choice and trust are important. The expansion of choice is said to be one of the positive aspects of living in the 'risk society' we are said to live in (Giddens, 1998). Leaving aside for one moment that 'choice is differentially distributed according to class and income' (ibid., 1998, p. 30) and life-course position, gender and ethnic origin (Peggs, 2000), we know that in the UK there is an array of pensions from which to choose, and an informed choice depends on an increasing amount of knowledge about a very complex field. Of course, individuals want to maximize their financial well-being in later life, so often take on this task of finding out about pensions. Moreover, since we live in a moral climate where we are expected to make choices and assume responsibility for our fate (Smart, 1999), and where we take increasing responsibility for our own welfare (Aldridge, 1998), to resist such work is tantamount to admitting carelessness. Thus non-engagement with risk avoidance is considered 'a failure of the self to take care of itself – a form or irrationality, or simply a lack of skilfulness' (Greco, 1993, p. 361). So an important feature in several neo-liberal societies is an increasing focus on the importance of individuals managing their own risks by taking out private insurance rather than participating in the social insurance schemes offered by the state (Dean, 1999). Thus individuals are encouraged to take out seemingly 'superior' non-state pensions rather than state pensions. Consequently the solution to pensions problems is presented as the marketization of pensions. Thus, coming back to Foucault, risk avoidance is a form of self-government, which converges with the needs of national governments to relieve their budgets.

The typical retirement income has three pillars: basic government provision, workplace or private schemes and all other voluntary savings (Littlewood, 1998, p. 4). It is a combination of access to and benefit from these different pillars that establishes the financial security of older people (Walker and Maltby, 1997, p. 44). Regarded as unsustainable, the increasing costs of pillar 1 are deemed to be due in part to demographic changes associated with slower population growth, longer life expectancy and reduced economic growth (ibid., p. 4). Thus pension reform is high on the agenda of most European countries (Linn and Rischard, 2003, p. vii) and the emphasis has been put on individuals' needs to secure workplace or private schemes in order to secure financial security in old age. This is evident in the UK.

In the UK this marketization of pensions is part of the rolling back of the welfare state with risks and costs being passed on to consumers (Aldridge, 1998), with successive governments being less willing to guarantee financial security during pension years (Falkingham, 1998). A recent report by the World Bank suggests that newly embraced EU countries will have to adopt pension systems like those in the UK to make them viable (Holzmann et al., 2003b). However, the UK pension system epitomizes some of the problems associated with the marketization of pensions in neo-liberal economies. Since 1988 there has been a range of changes to the UK pension system that have been defended by a rhetoric of choice, which have themselves incorporated what can be seen as increasing risks for individuals (Peggs, 2000). Since the state has been declared a barrier to choice and freedom in pensions, the 'burden of the state' was removed in order to maximize consumer power (Gabriel and Lang, 1995). Through these Thatcherite discourses of 'choice' and 'power to choose' (Phillips, 1998, p. 854), individual responsibility has become a prominent feature of social and political discourses (Smart, 1999). The emphasis is on the need to be self-sufficient and owe as little as possible to others (Leadbetter, 1989). Thus financial risks have been passed on to consumers (Aldridge, 1998), and choice has been linked to notions of good and evil and right and wrong (Gabriel and Lang, 1995).

Although it is not appropriate here to provide details of the pension system in the UK, it is worth mentioning that employees paying National Insurance Contributions (NICS) have no choice but to make pension contributions. However, within this constraint, since 1988 those with access to all second-tier pension options can choose from an increasing range of state and non-state schemes. Those such as occupational final salary have a set relationship between earnings and pensions, whereas others, such as money purchase approved pensions and money purchase occupational schemes, are dependent on investment performance (Waine, 1995). Choosing a second-tier pension is complicated and risky. Pension choice has often been based on limited information, lack of knowledge and fear. Fears about the future of state pensions have meant that many have switched from state to non-state schemes (Vincent, 1995). Occupational pensions are often taken up with very little thought, and scheme members have very little knowledge about them (Field and Farrant, 1993; Williams and Field, 1993). So the complex literature associated with occupational schemes does little to aid understanding (Field and Farrant, 1993). Only a minority of those with an approved private pension feel they have a very good understanding of them (Williams and Field, 1993), and the advice that women receive takes little or no account of their disrupted employment lives (Davies and Ward, 1992). In addition, pension choice is not available in the same proportions to all and the notion of choice is often meaningless to those with limited financial resources (Nettleton and Burrows, 1998).

In summary, discourses associated with ageing and pensions draw heavily on notions of risk and security. Reports by a range of experts have emphasized the apparently negative consequences associated with demographic ageing and the costs to governments and employees alike. The marketization of pensions in the UK has been put forward as a model for how other EU countries might deal with their purported impending pensions crisis. However, this marketization of pensions is the result of successive UK governments being less willing to guarantee financial security during pension years, and it has passed the risks and costs on to pension consumers. I now consider these issues by turning my attention more specifically to pensions and ageing in the EU.

AGEING AND PENSIONS IN EUROPE

Each of the EU member states is experiencing societal ageing. The main factors underlying this are the weak birth rates and declining mortality rates evident in recent decades (Walker and Maltby, 1997, p. 13; European Community, 2005, p. 1). The fertility rate has been below replacement level (that is, some 2.1 children per woman) since the 1970s in West Europe and since the 1980s in East Europe (Holzmann et al., 2003a, p. 3). Over the next 50 years life expectancy is anticipated to increase for women (by 4.2 years) and for men (by 5 years) (ibid.). In addition, over the next 15 years the baby boom generation will reach retirement age (European Community, 2005, p. 1). However, the rate of ageing differs among member states. Figures for the year 2000 show that of the countries in the EU, Greece had the largest percentage (23.4 per cent) of people aged 60 and over and Ireland (15.2 per cent) had the smallest (Carnell, 2001). These transformations in national age structures have subsidiary effects. For example, as each member state ages it becomes increasingly feminized because women's life expectancy exceeds that of men in all EU member states (Walker and Maltby, 1997, pp. 11–13).

How has the EU responded to these transformations? Although member states are responsible for forming and executing their own pensions policies, in December 2001 member states sanctioned a proposal for 'open coordination' of pension policies, which involves 'agreeing broad common objectives, translating these objectives into national policy strategies and … monitoring progress periodically' (European Older People's Platform, 2003, p. 1). Eleven common objectives were agreed which can be grouped under three headings: the adequacy of pensions (e.g. ensuring that older people are not 'placed at risk of poverty and can enjoy a decent standard of living'); the financial sustainability of pensions (i.e. by placing 'pension systems on a sound financial footing'); and the modernization of pension systems (in response to the 'changing needs of the economy, society and individuals') (ibid., pp. 2–3). To be sure, these policy initiatives draw on discourses of risk that highlight the financial security of pensioners; however, the focus remains on societal ageing, which is represented as a threat to economic well-being at a national level. As the European Older People's Platform notes, 'the agenda has been driven to a large extent by official fears about the future cost of pensions to national budgets …' (European Older People's Platform, n.d. p. 1). Thus it seems that the concern about hugely increased future pension costs has induced governments and other commentators to engage in debates about policy changes and individual financial security as a route to the protection of government funds.

Although pension systems differ across the EU, the first pillar, or state system, is the main source of income for older people in Europe (Walker and Maltby, 1997, p. 45). However, governments argue that state pensions are unsustainable and thus pension reforms are needed. Pension expenditure for the 15 EU member states before enlargement is estimated to peak at 13.6 per cent of GDP in 2040, constituting a rise from 10.4 per cent in 2000 (Whiteford, 2003, p. 7). Thus reforms are said to be needed due to budgetary pressure and European economic integration (Holzmann et al., 2003a, p. 1). In this respect information detailing, for example, that Western European countries have a higher proportion of GDP spent on public pensions than richer countries such as Australia, Japan and New Zealand (ibid., p. 2) encourage this assertion.

Even though there are high poverty rates among older people in the UK, Greece, Portugal and Spain, above all such reform is 'equated with cost containment' and 'increasing the role of the private sector rather than addressing longstanding distributional issues' (Walker and Maltby, 1997, p. 46). Using a comparative analysis, non-governmental sources note what they see as the different degrees of 'strain' for each EU country, attributed to the proportion of the total pension mix in each country that the first pillar (basic state) covers. In this respect Hawksworth et al. suggest that Germany and Italy will have more severe problems than countries such as the UK because of relatively high state pensions compared to earnings (2000, p. 2). However, although in the UK there has been an improvement in couples' and single persons' pension incomes, these have deteriorated when compared with average incomes, with both single and couple pensioners being over-represented in the bottom two-fifths of the income distribution (Walker and Maltby, 1997, p. 47). In addition, compared with their counterparts in other leading industrial societies, older people in the UK are financially disadvantaged and there is polarization among UK pensioners (ibid.). The reduction in the basic state pension and the promotion of occupational and private pensions will lead to increased economic polarization among future pensioners, with the low paid and women having the poorest prospects (ibid., p. 50). Thus, Walker and Maltby conclude, UK pensioners are likely to remain worse off than their Northern European Union counterparts for the foreseeable future (ibid., p. 49). In addition to the UK, there are high poverty rates among older people in Greece, Portugal and Spain (ibid., p. 50). However, such financial insecurity does not seem to be the major source of alarm for Hawksworth et al:. their concern is 'an explosion of government debt …' (2000, p. 6). They note that 'Ultimately the choice for all European countries is stark: higher taxes and social security contributions, or less generous state pensions' (ibid.).

State pensions are financed by means of the contributions made by current employees. Thus low birth rates, for example the record low population growth in Southern European countries (Geddes, 2002, p. 2), are emphasized as a major problem. Anna Diamantopoulou, a European Union commissioner, argues that 'We need to bring our population back into balance' because as life expectancies rise there will be 'fewer workers [to] … support more pensioners' (Belt, 2004, p. 64). As referred to above, Italy and Germany have been singled out as having potentially more pressures. Italy has a fertility rate of 1.2 children per woman, which is among the lowest in the world, and has an unemployment rate of around 10 per cent (Geddes, 2002, p. 2). The problem in Germany is seen to go further than a low fertility rate, with young, qualified people leaving in search of jobs elsewhere (Henley, 2004, p. 2). A number of suggestions have been put forward for dealing with the purported 'future catastrophe'. Hawksworth et al. suggest that nations need to: increase labour force participation rates, particularly among women, and reduce unemployment rates; reform state pensions to make them more affordable; encourage increased involvement in private pensions and increase economic productivity rates with other reforms (2000, p. 9). Other bodies have reached similar conclusions.

Governments have responded to such risk discourses in expected ways. In July 2004 the Italian government passed a pension reform bill that aimed to lower spending on pensions (which ran at about 14 per cent of GDP) to make annual savings of 0.7 per cent from about 2013 to the early 2030s (Barber, 2004, p. 1). The bill also requires employees to pay 40 years of contributions before retirement and has increased the pension age from 57 to 60 (ibid.). Recent reports show that one-third of Germany's population is heading towards old age and suggest that Germany 'is waking up to an impending pensions crisis' (Henley, 2004, p. 1). The government has responded by, for the first time, freezing state pensions (which run at double the amount that they do in the UK). There are also moves to shift the responsibility for pensions much further into the private sector (ibid., p. 2). This has been accompanied by a public outcry.

In summary, the problems highlighted by non-governmental and governmental commentators focus on a combination of differences within each state. Although each EU member state is experiencing societal ageing, some have more aged populations than others. In addition, differences in policies mean that some states rely more heavily on state pensions than others. However, there is a 'policy of deficit' between the needs and demands of older people and the social and economic policies of governments (Walker and Maltby, 1997, p. 122). Although poverty is the reality of many current older people's lives, and is the destiny for many future older people in the EU, the focus of government debates has been on cost containment. Although policy initiatives draw on discourses of risk that highlight the financial security of pensioners, the focus remains on societal ageing, which is represented as a threat to economic well-being at a national level. Countries with a proportionately older population and high state pensions are presented as having the most severe problems regarding government cost containment. Governments have generally responded accordingly by cutting the level of state pension benefits available. This means that an increasing proportion of older people living in EU member states have the prospect of a less financially secure retirement. Let us now turn to the implications highlighted since EU enlargement.

RISK DISCOURSES, AGEING AND EUROPE IN TRANSITION

Thus far we have seen that changes associated with societal ageing in EU member states have been infused with risk discourses that highlight the economic problems associated with an increasingly aged population. Such discourses have largely focused on the containment of costs to governments, with much less regard for the financial well-being of older people. This has resulted in policy changes that often have negative implications for the financial security of older people, an increasing proportion of the population of the EU. Here I want to take these issues further by discussing them in the light of seemingly unrelated changes in the EU, those associated with EU enlargement. Fears about the consequences of EU enlargement have exacerbated this already agitated risk debate, for example concerns about new EU member states that are judged to have ill-conceived and unsustainable pension systems. Of particular interest here are the apparent pension consequences of EU enlargement involving the most recently established Eastern European countries.

Since 1957 the number of countries in the EU has expanded from six to 25, with the most recent expansion occurring in May 2004, when ten new countries joined.[3] In addition, Bulgaria, Romania and Turkey have ongoing applications to join, and Croatia has recently applied. Already enlargement has been greeted with risk discourses. For example, 'the prospect of adding 10 new countries, 74 million people, and 280,000 square miles to the European Union all at once strikes some current members as a reckless gamble …' (Belt, 2004, p. 56). Enlargement makes the European Union 'a larger single market than Japan and America combined' (The European Commission and the Foreign Commonwealth Office, 2003, p. 1); however, the economic consequences of expansion have been greeted with expressions of alarm. The external context to the EU was transformed by the collapse of the communist regimes in Central and Eastern Europe, the dismantling of the USSR and the end of the Iron Curtain and the Cold War (Henig, 1997). Six of the countries in the newly expanded EU underwent these major economic transitions. Estonia, Latvia and Lithuania are former Soviet Union countries and Hungary, Poland and Czechoslovakia are former Soviet bloc countries. Additionally, the reunification of Germany meant a physical and geographical enlargement of the community itself (ibid.). Comments such as Belt's 'to succeed, they'll need to get communism out of their system' (2004, p. 56) point to risk discourses that problematize the very heart of the economic systems of these countries. Such risk discourses interact with those about ageing to intensify apprehension about the impending 'pensions problem'.

As with pre-enlargement EU member states, each accession state is experiencing societal ageing. Figures for 2000 show that of the ten accession countries[4] Latvia had the largest proportion of the population over 60 (20.9 per cent) and Slovakia the smallest (15.4 per cent) (see Carnell, 2001). Thus EU enlargement is not expected to avert the supposed demographic 'crisis' caused by ageing since, although enlargement means that there are 455 million people now in the EU, low birth rates mean that the population will decline to 431 million by 2050 if current birth rates are maintained (Belt, 2004, p. 64). Such discourses focus on the strain that this will have on what are deemed to be ill-conceived and unsustainable pension systems in Central and Eastern EU new member states. Economic transition has resulted in a large increase in unemployment and falls in employment and population ratios (Whiteford, 2003, p. 7), with concomitant 'financial instability, unemployment and crises in public funding …' (Hinchliff and Priestley, 2001, p. 1). One reaction to this has been early retirement, thus increasing the number of pensioners (Whiteford, 2003, p. 8). Many of these countries had 'close to universal coverage of retirement pensions in the 1980s' (ibid., p. 7) and although, on average, state pension spending increased from just under the EU average in 1990 to just over the average in 1998, the proportion of the population aged 65 and over is higher in EU countries (ibid., p. 8). The longer-term projection is unfavourable; thus pressures for reform were even stronger in many countries of Central and Eastern Europe (ibid.). With the exception of Romania (5.1 per cent) all other accession countries in Central and Eastern Europe have pension expenditures close to (and in Croatia, Poland and Slovenia well above) the EU average and much higher than non-European OECD countries despite an income level of a quarter or less (Holzmann et al., 2003a, p. 2). Poland (with an expenditure of nearly 15 per cent) rivals Austria and Italy as having the world's highest figure (ibid.). In the absence of changes to the system and with projected increases in life expectancy, public pension spending in for example Latvia is projected to increase by 16 per cent of GDP by 2050 (Whiteford, 2003, p. 8). Hinchliff and Priestley conclude that older people in these countries face a changed world in which former levels of state provision are unlikely to be restored (2001, p. 5).

The rapid transition and extensive changes that Eastern and Central European countries have experienced since 1989 have negatively affected older people in these countries (Hinchliff and Priestley, 2001; Hinchliff and Hall, 2002; Whiteford, 2003). Even though they now live in democratically elected regimes, very high levels of economic insecurity have accompanied this, since the value of pensions has plummeted, making them so inadequate that they are a major source of dissatisfaction (Hinchliff and Priestley, 2001, p. 4). Opportunities for older people to supplement their incomes have been seriously reduced, further aggravating their financial security, and these changes have occurred alongside changes in older people's roles in kinship and community systems (ibid., pp. 4–5). Thus the economic and social security of older people has been negatively affected by the economic transition but their needs have not been considered by most national governments and they have not been consulted about planned policies (ibid., p. 1). However, each country faces its own specific challenges (ibid., p. 6). For example, Estonia has made economic progress and has relatively well-funded provision for older people aged 65 and over (ibid.). But older people in the country still face a number of problems. Before transition, the Soviet system provided state basic pensions; however, the collapse of that system resulted in a period of hyperinflation that plunged pension funds into crisis (ibid., p. 17). Thus financial insecurity and hardship characterize the lives of a significant proportion of older people, who comprise about 14 per cent of the population (ibid.). However, more positively, they are more affluent than their counterparts in other former Soviet bloc countries due to age-related subsidies for vital items such as medicines and public transport (ibid.). In 1992 the Estonian government decided to raise the retirement age and in 2000 it began reforming its pension system to the three-pillar pension model (ibid.). Other European accession countries such as Bulgaria, Hungary, Latvia and Poland have introduced, or intend to introduce, pension reforms along similar lines (Linn and Rischard, 2003, p. viii). These reforms include strengthening the relationship between pension benefits and contributions, extending the contribution period needed to qualify for a full pension, and ensuring that private pensions play a larger role in retirement income (ibid.).

In summary, risk discourses associated with societal ageing have interacted with risk discourses associated with EU enlargement, in particular the supposed negative consequences for government budgets of including the most recently established Eastern European countries in the EU. However, the rapid transition and extensive changes that Eastern and Central European countries have experienced since 1989 have negatively affected the financial security of older people in these countries, and these issues have had little public exposure.

PENSIONS, AGEING AND FUTURE FINANCIAL SECURITY IN THE NEW EUROPE

Risk discourses associated with societal ageing focus on perceptions of the long-term negative effects of having higher proportions of older people in populations than before. Thus expert observations, often in the form of reports, advocate a long-term strategy and urge considerable economic reforms in Europe. One such example is the Economist Intelligence Unit (EIU) report, published in June 2004. The EIU warns that 'The pension system is at risk of collapse unless people retire later, start saving more into pensions and accept a cut in state benefits ...' (Loveless, 2004, p. 1). Thus the pension position of most EU members is seen as unsustainable, with urgent reforms being needed (McRae, 2004, p. 16). The EIU editorial director, Daniel Franklin, makes clear that the case is urgent since the 'demographic decline will be the biggest social challenge that Europe will face over the next five years' (ibid.). The report makes clear that this is a global issue, but emphasizes that the 'problem' is particularly severe in Europe (EIU, 2004). The EIU reports that Europe's dependency ratio is set to double by 2040, a change that raises difficult questions about the future of retirement funding (ibid.). The report concludes that most Europeans will have to work longer and save harder before retiring (ibid.).

Although this report does not cover all countries in the EU, we can use it to see how risk discourses have been fully incorporated into projections for the well-being of some EU nations in the future. Developing a meteorological discourse, a major part of the report focuses on results related to the EIU 'barometer' of demographic risk, which compares the severity of the problem that each of the 20 countries faces, with their willingness to address demographic change. On the basis of this, each of the 20 European countries is placed into one of three categories as follows. For the UK, Ireland, the Netherlands and the Nordics the outlook is seen as fair (the best prospects the report gives) because, in these countries, the populations are ageing more slowly and they are felt to be in the best position to 'manage the challenge of population ageing' (EIU, 2004). By 2050 the EIU forecasts that the UK will have the lowest old age dependency ratio and the lowest public pension burden of any European country included in the report (ibid.). As in the Netherlands, the strong position of private pensions in overall retirement income counts in the UK's favour. However, uncertainty over the future of occupational pensions and the need to boost saving rates are highlighted as issues that must be addressed.

None of the accession countries included in the EIU report has a fair outlook: all are in the unsettled or stormy categories. The outlook is seen as unsettled for Belgium, France, Germany, Hungary, Poland, Portugal and Slovakia (EIU, 2004). This is because, the report suggests, France and Germany face a steeper demographic decline than the UK, and both countries have state pension schemes that are unsustainable in the long term. Although reforms have been made, for example in Germany, as mentioned above, the EIU suggests that such reforms have developed slowly in the face of strong public opposition. The EIU concludes that for all countries with an unsettled outlook the trend towards early retirement will need to be reduced and more efforts will need to be made to attract women and older workers into employment. The countries that face the biggest 'threat' over the next 45 years have a stormy outlook. Austria, the Czech Republic, Greece, Italy and Spain have rapidly ageing populations and 'a mountain to climb' in reforming their economies and welfare systems. On current trends the EIU predicts that Italy's old age dependency ratio will decline to where there will be 1.5 active workers for each person over 65 by 2050. Spain and Greece are experiencing population ageing on a similar scale. Austria state pensions consume 14 per cent of GDP, the highest proportion of any country in the report, while the Czech Republic must undertake a root-and-branch change to its healthcare reform to avert a steep rise in costs as people live longer. However, although the report concludes that Southern Europe, Austria and the Czech Republic have the greatest 'threats' from population ageing, far-reaching reforms are required across the region to avert the threat of economic decline.

The EIU groups its conclusions for needed reforms under three headings: 'the challenges of ageing' for governments, for companies and for individuals. The report maintains that the challenge for governments is that for most European countries further reforms are needed to pensions and healthcare; in most countries retirement ages will need to be raised and governments will need to ensure that individuals take greater responsibility for their own healthcare and financial security in old age. The UK government's pensions czar, Adair Turner, has already suggested that the retirement age either be scrapped or raised from 65 to 70 years (Loveless, 2004, p. 2). To sustain employment, labour market reform is needed to attract more people into the labour market. The report suggests that increased immigration and initiatives to increase low birth rates may also be required. The EIU recognizes that many of these measures are deeply unpopular with electorates, 'but failure to act now will store up greater pain for future generations' (EIU, 2004). The EIU proposes that the challenge for companies is the need to minimize their future pension liabilities, with the result that more defined benefit schemes should be replaced with defined contribution schemes. The EIU report also suggests that companies need to attract more skilled workers and bring more women and older workers into employment. For the EIU the challenge for individuals is the need to move away from the notion that retirement as a 'permanent holiday' that begins at 60. To ensure a comfortable income for old age, the report emphasizes that many individuals will have to save more during longer working lives. In addition, individuals will have to learn to invest wisely and will need to regularly update their skills to improve prospects for late-life careers. In this respect the EIU sees a role for governments and the financial services industry in providing more incentives for saving and opportunities for lifelong learning (EIU, 2004).

These suggested reforms do not address the 'policy of deficit' (Walker and Maltby, 1997) between the needs and demands of older people and the social and economic policies of governments. Financial security in later life is a matter for individuals who need to retrain, reskill and understand complex investment information. Rather than providing a good model, the UK spends less as a nation on pensions than any other country in Europe (Loveless, 2004, p. 2), and this plunges many pensioners into financial insecurity and poverty. The marketization of pensions in the UK has passed risks and costs on to individuals (Aldridge, 1998). Pension 'mis-selling' has created little trust in financial advisers (Peggs, 2000), and money purchase schemes, an EIU suggested move for companies, a move that they are already taking, are dependent on investment performance (Waine, 1995) and thus are less advantageous than defined benefit schemes. Thus an increasing number of older people in Europe will face a future of financial security, a financial insecurity for which they will be held responsible.

SOME CONCLUDING COMMENTS

There can be no doubt that ageing must be integrated into wider government planning and that all European countries must plan systematically for increasing numbers of older citizens (Hinchliff and Priestley, 2001, p. 4). Pension systems, pensioners and future retirees are coping with discourses of discontent and risk and are managing constant change. The EU encompasses an increasing number of people and on average the population of the EU is ageing. Societal ageing has been greeted with negative discourses of risk which seem to celebrate little the advances made in life expectancy but rather focus on the seeming 'burden' of older citizens. The UK pension system has been put forward as a model, though it is itself in need of reform. Many older people in the UK, particularly women (who make up the majority of older people) have been disadvantaged by this system (e.g. Peggs, 2000). Moreover, ageing societies in the EU are increasingly feminized, and conflicts in many accession countries have increased this feminization further; older women are often the biggest pension losers. If other EU countries adopt this model, governments might save in pension expenditure (though might have to divert extra monies into, for example, means-tested benefits), but older people are likely to lose the little financial security they currently have.

Reforms are often difficult to carry through (McRae, 2004, p. 16). Val Koromzay, the Director of Country Studies in the OECD's Economics

Department, argues that to achieve real reform two factors must come together: a popular awareness that 'things have to change' and a leadership that can translate broad dissatisfaction into policies (McRae, 2004, p. 16). He argues that real reforms are those that remove the inefficiencies in the system – including the benefits that come to the richer few, such as tax loopholes (ibid.). Although reforms are necessary, the call for reform needs to be accepted and this seems unlikely when, as Linn and Rischard admit, 'older people and all of us who hope to retire with a pension fear that reforms will make pensions insecure' (Linn and Rischard, 2003, p. viii). The financial security of older people in the EU is an urgent issue that should be fundamental to pension policy reforms in EU countries. However, discourses about the risks to financial security in later life largely focus on the need for individuals to invest in pensions, retrain, reskill and understand complex investment information; government policy initiatives thus far focus more keenly on the risks associated with societal ageing and ways of cutting down the costs of the future pensions bill in Europe.

NOTES

1. For example, see Barber T. (2004), Italy passes bill on pensions reform, http://new.ft.com/servlet/ContentServer?pa…/FullStory&c=StoryFt&cid=108737405863.
2. For example, see Conradi, P. (2003), Pension revolt simmers among Europe's young', *Sunday Times*, 29th June.
3. The ten countries that joined in May 2004 are Cyprus, Czech Republic, Estonia, Hungary, Latvia, Lithuania, Malta, Poland, Slovakia and Slovenia.
4. Figures are not available for Cyprus.

17. Conclusion

Fergus Carr and Andrew Massey

In concluding this volume, it is useful to remind ourselves how the grand project of the European Union began: it was in the context of a continent ruined by the devastation of the Second World War, a devastation wrought by the conflict between fascism, Nazism, Soviet communism and liberal democracy. As a maimed Western Europe began to reconstruct itself, it lay wounded and threatened by Stalin's tanks to the East and in thrall to the overwhelming economic hegemony of US power to the West. Western Europe lay trapped in the middle, with Germany in particular seen as the prize to be 'won' by either side. Jean Monnet, the successful French businessman, state planner and later 'father' of the EU, saw clearly what needed to be done. He wrote that for France there was an obvious path to take: 'I could see only one solution: we must bind ourselves inextricably to Germany in a common undertaking in which our other neighbours could join. A European-wide territory of prosperity and peace would thus be created' (www.jean-monnet.ch/anglais/pMonnet/monnet5.htm). From the outset this was to be both a political and economic project, an approach repeated with the accession of ten new states in 2004. But it was not the first time Monnet had been closely involved with such an undertaking.

In the autumn of 1939 the concept of a European federation based on the UK and France had already been proposed, with the intention that a newly democratic Germany would join, after the defeat of the Nazis (Wistrich, 1994, p. 23). Monnet, working on coordinating allied war supplies, knew of the proposal and supported it enthusiastically. It was developed in London by a committed team of British Foreign Office officials, with the full approval of Prime Minister Neville Chamberlain. An Act of Perpetual Association was drawn up and approved by Lord Halifax, the Foreign Secretary (ibid.). By the spring of 1940, with the collapse and occupation of the Low Countries, France was on the point of defeat; Monnet persuaded the new prime minister, Winston Churchill, to declare that Britain and France should merge their governments and parliaments, in effect to establish an Anglo-French federation (ibid., pp. 23–4). The proposal was too late to prevent the fall of France, but Monnet had developed an approach that was to find a more fertile soil in the period of postwar reconstruction, and Europe's destiny for the next 50 years was set.

The evolution of the EU, its expansion and the steady Europeanization of new members and those outside of the Union represent a remarkable transformation of the continent of Europe within a period of little more than two generations. It took place in the early years simultaneously with decolonization by Britain, France, Belgian and the Netherlands, and a scattering of colonial wars that further drained the treasuries of Europe. By the 1990s the postwar world had been again transformed by the collapse of the Soviet empire and the subsequent widening and deepening of the European project into a social market (but thoroughly liberal-democratic) model. It may be seen in some ways as a triumph of the liberal ideal (Fukuyama, 1992). The challenges to Europe, however, have not gone away; they have simply changed, and the contributions to this volume have sought to discuss and analyse these evolving issues. Some are problems that may or may not be solved, but the EU and its Commission are seeking to predict and plan for them.

An example of this preparation may be found in the Mid-Term Report on the EU's Lisbon strategy for growth and employment by a 'High Level Group'. Chaired by the former Dutch prime minister, Wim Kok, it contains an analysis that reflects many of the concerns we have identified within this volume. While the future of the EU must be seen as a separate issue from the future of Europe, none the less the two are clearly entwined and located within a rapidly changing global context. The Report assesses the strengths and weaknesses of progress towards reform within the EU in order to enable the emergence of a unified and competitive European economic entity, with a clear commitment to delivering opportunities to the citizens of the EU. It notes the difficulties of achieving this in the current political, administrative and social complexity of European national vested interests, international competitor blocs and emergent economic behemoths, wryly suggesting:

> at risk – in the medium to long run – is nothing less than the sustainability of the society Europe has built. Europeans have made choices about how to express the values they hold in common: a commitment to the social contract that underwrites the risk of unemployment, ill-health and old age, and provides opportunity for all through high-quality education, a commitment to public institutions, the public realm and the public interest, and that a market economy should be run fairly and with respect for the environment. These values are expressed in systems of welfare, public institutions and regulation that are expensive in a world where low cost and highly efficient producers are challenging the old order. If Europe cannot adapt, cannot modernize its systems and cannot increase its growth and employment fast enough then it will be impossible to sustain these choices. Europe, in short, must focus on growth and employment. (Kok, 2004, p. 17)

In essence, the EU's political élite are aware that a significant element of the motivation for the development and expansion of the EU's membership and competencies, that is the efficient delivery of a social as well as economic benefit to its citizens (with the former underwritten by the latter), is under threat.

The problems set to ambush the EU's grand project are not particularly obscure; indeed, in the case of the so-called pensions time bomb (as discussed by Peggs, Chapter 16 in this volume) they are less an ambush and more a very obvious cliff towards which the Union is heading. Kok also makes clear that the internal challenges to the EU include the twin challenge of

> declining birth rates and rising life expectancies [which] are interacting to produce a dramatic change in the size and age structure of Europe's population. The total population size is projected to fall by 2020. By 2050, the working-age population (15–64 years) is projected to be 18 per cent smaller than the current one, and the numbers of those aged over 65 years will have increased by 60 per cent. As a result, the average ratio of persons in retirement compared with those of the present working age in Europe will double from 24 per cent today to almost 50 per cent in 2050. This dependency ratio will vary in 2050 from 36 per cent in Denmark to 61 per cent in Italy. This development is already at work and in 2015 the EU average dependency ratio will increase to 30 per cent. The impact is then compounded by the low employment rate of older workers. These developments will have profound implications for the European economy and its capability to finance European welfare systems. (Kok, 2004, p. 14)

As the polls seeking to discover the reasons for the rejection of the EU's Constitution make clear, however, the EU's citizens are wedded to the welfare and employment benefits of the Union and it is the sustainability of these that is most clearly threatened in the future. But threatened it is, since if the system remains unreformed this ageing will result in 'an increase in pension and healthcare spending by 2050, varying between 4 and 8 per cent of GDP' (ibid.). Indeed:

> already from 2020, projected spending on pension and healthcare will increase by some 2 per cent of GDP in many member states and in 2030 the increase will amount to 4–5 per cent of GDP. On top of this, the lower economic growth rate will impact negatively on public finances, and this negative impact will commence from 2010. (Ibid.)

In other words, even current welfare and social contract arrangements are unsustainable, yet if these are diluted, the popular support for the European project will be in deep political trouble, as will Europe itself. It is conceivable (though unlikely) that the Union could unravel into something akin to a simple 'common market' rather than a grand social and political project.

In this volume we have explored the policies, dynamics and motivations across a range of activities and old and emerging issues. A series of cross-cutting themes is apparent:

1. Policy making is complex and grows ever more sophisticated as the range of competencies claimed by the EU and the number of member states increases.
2. We have returned constantly to the problems of ensuring proper accountability, that is democratic accountability over officials, and those charged with making and implementing policy.
3. The enlargement of the EU and the dynamics for reform are constant themes across states and across policy areas, as is the attendant problem of national administrations seeking to reform to a sufficiently high level of competency in order to properly implement and oversee EU policy.
4. The continuing impact of 9/11.
5. And partly connected to this, but running far deeper in both economic and political terms, the question as to whether transatlanticism is ending.

It is to each of these issues that we now turn.

THE COMPLEXITY OF POLICY MAKING

The increasing complexity of policy is reflected in the multiplicity of terms being used to analyse and describe the developments taking place in Europe. Of these, the concepts of the differentiated polity and multi-level governance as outlined by Andrew Massey (Chapter 1), provide the perspective from which many observers write, although as Paul Flenley (Chapter 8) makes clear, Russia has turned its back on this approach, seeing the resurrection of a strong central state as a prerequisite to its own modernization. Europeanization, combined with regionalization/devolution and varieties of modernization such as New Public Management and the marketization of state services, has shown the limitations to the power and competence of the individual nation-state; it is 'hollowed out' with the levers of power no longer connected in ways ensured by old-fashioned welfare state bureaucracies (Rhodes, 1994). But although we need to beware of over-theoreticizing these developments (Schmitter, 2004), it is obvious that in this age of governing through governance, the interpenetration of the state and national and global civil society (Omelicheva, 2004), and the formulation and delivery of policy and policy outputs through a mix of state, private and NGO institutions, has seen an exponential rise in the complexity of the policy process.

With the diffusion of power and accountability that multi-level governance induces (and reflects), the importance of technocratic élites becomes more pronounced in specialist and limited areas, such as energy policy or banking. Overall, there is a seeking by politicians and public alike for a neutral umpire in the case of disputes, and this has led to a huge increase in the role and influence of the EU's judicial system, and national judges and lawyers seeking to apply European law. For example, Cherie Booth QC, addressing an audience of lawyers, civil servants and diplomats in Malaysia, said judges made rulings in a way that taught citizens and government about the 'ethical responsibilities' of participating in a true democracy committed to 'universal human rights standards'. She said courts should be 'guardians of the weakest, poorest and most marginalized members of society against the hurly-burly of majoritarian politics'. A good example of this working was the decision by the UK's highest court, the House of Lords law lords, that the UK's policy of holding foreign terrorist suspects indefinitely without charge broke human rights laws (http://news.bbc.co.uk/1/hi/uk_politics/4719977.stm).

It is notable that Ms Booth should choose to castigate *majoritarian* politics. Another definition of such a form of politics would be 'democratic' politics, and it may be argued that for a nation's judiciary to seek to interfere with the proper workings of national democratic decision-making processes may be one reason why EU politics is seen as remote and irrelevant (or worse) by so many citizens. The proper separation of powers between the judiciary and the executive has been tilted more towards unelected judges in the age of the differentiated polity.

The complexity of policy making is further illustrated within the EU when we explore the delicate issues of collective defence and national interest. Fergus Carr, in Chapter 2, shows clearly that although the EU has become an economic superpower, it remains a military pygmy when contrasted to the USA. The Atlanticist pull through NATO is most keenly felt by the UK and the new member states to the East, while the old axis of France and Germany continues to seek to carve out a 'European' way. In assessing whether the EU can perform as a major international actor, Fergus Carr demonstrates that there can be no straight answer. In economic, industrial and commercial terms there is a clear EU role. In international relations and military matters the EU's ambition to assert its presence as an international actor was impaired by its inability to maintain common positions (Kintis, 1997). In Carr's view, the EU has 'a legal personality in specifically defined policy areas' (Bretherton and Vogler, 1999, pp. 16–18). It has representation, conducts negotiations and has detailed decision-making procedures. It is at best, however, quasi-autonomous in that the 'Europeanization' of foreign policy is a matter of degree and affected by policy area. In other words, the policy process has a temporal, institutional and issues-based context that varies so convolutedly that the tortuous negotiations from Maastricht onwards to forge a common policy have succeeded only in obscuring further that which was already opaque. Thus what we are observing in the EU is an imperfect political entity that is essentially a good forum for intergovernmentalism, but it is a 'cracked' federal structure. As such the clear institutional structures and procedures that would be expected in a 'proper' federal structure to allow more transparent and accountable policy making are stunted and in need of remedial treatment.

The policy study chapters by Pamela Barnes (Chapter 13) and Mike Mannin (Chapter 14) underscore this complexity. Barnes explains how by the 2004 enlargement the EU had an extensive environmental policy 'based on more than 200 major legislative acts covering horizontal legislation (such as strategic environmental impact assessment), water and air pollution, management of waste and chemicals, biotechnology, nature protection, industrial pollution and risk management, noise and radiation protection legislation'. It was a policy that dated back to the 1970s when it was conceived as remedial regulatory action to deal with specific problems. After 1987 the EU moved towards a more coherent policy rooted in a body of legislation: an *acquis* that the accession states had to adapt to and 'transpose into their national environmental policies'. Barnes notes the difficulties engendered by this complicated process in that after 2004 the priority for the EU 'is to meet the challenges of sustainable development. Adding an environmental pillar to the Lisbon Strategy' as economic and social growth raised the profile of the requirements for sustainable development. As Barnes shows, however, politicians and civil servants in national administrations sometimes wrongly interpret the concept of sustainable development as a repackaging of environmental policy and fail to equate it with 'a balanced approach to the economic, social and environmental pillars, and with the need to place the three dimensions on an equal footing'.

Barnes quotes the official document to show that problems were already there because many of the 'low hanging fruits of integration have already been picked …' (CEC, 2004, p. 3) and the more difficult political decisions remain to be made. In the early stages of EU environmental policy development it was easier to gain agreement about measures because national policies were in embryonic stages of development and a 'policy space' existed into which the supranational policy could penetrate. In other words environmental policy is a good illustration of the increasing complexity of the policy process and the reasons for it, as layers upon layers of dynamics, regulations, legislation and precedents are overlain to form a Byzantine addition to the *acquis*. This experience is repeated across most, if not all, policy areas within the EU.

If the initial environmental policy issues were urgent pollution problems requiring action, the subsequent solutions to these problems appeared to present a very good return on any investments made. Yet Barnes argues:

> having dealt with these soft targets the EU15 moved into a phase where agreements for action became more difficult, the targeted problems and the solutions more complex. The European environment has continued to deteriorate. The policy therefore appears to provide a poorer return on the massive commitments that have been made to it.

Thus a kind of 'environmental fatigue' has set in; as a result, commitment is lower and implementation of action has become more limited. Enlargement of the EU has highlighted not a continuing success here, but considerable failure, further demonstrating how it is the very complexity of the process and the intractability of the problems that has brought about this failure. The process of the Europeanization of the national environmental policies in the ten new accession states 'has been facilitated by their drive to comply with the conditions for EU accession', yet as Barnes shows, 'there is a considerable degree of misfit between the requirements of the policy and the ability of the ten new accession states to adapt their administrative and institutional structures to deliver on its operation'. We return to this problem of technical competency in a later section of the chapter.

Mannin's chapter further illustrates and deepens our understanding of the complexity of the policy process. In his study of the labyrinthine structures and procedures of the EU's regional policy, especially as it interacts with social policy, he explores the myriad of ways through the maze of the policy process. In his conclusion he explains that

> 92 per cent of the ten new member states' population live in Objective 1 regions. The number of regions below 75 per cent GDP has increased from 48 to 67; they cover a population of 166 million (25 per cent) compared with 68 million (18 per cent of EU15). Inevitably questions remain regarding the financial viability of EURP. The Commission assumption of an EU financial package of 0.46 per cent (EU27 GNI) for 2007–13 is currently still to be agreed by member states, with counter proposals from the 'gang of six' demanding a capping of the budget. (Chapter 14, p. 327).

In other words, we are having to live with the paradox that one of the modernizing implements used by post-communist politicians in dealing with their citizens was that reforms aimed at Europeanization would reap short-term pain, but long-term benefits from membership of the EU. One of those benefits included a set of regional and social policies that would transfer funds from the richer Western and Northern nations to the accession states in order to raise their standard of living and provide adequate levels of social care. As Mannin (and indeed Wyn Grant and Kay Peggs) demonstrate, the paradox is that in seeking to make good on this, the transfer of resources from other common policies (or from national treasuries) threatens the stability of existing structures and institutions.

Therefore there is a need to reform (a subject dealt with later), but there is also a need to construct an almost infinite number of trade-offs and compromises, each one of which further complicates the policy process and makes future change (even of an incremental nature) more difficult as it becomes entrenched within a series of 'national positions'. Mannin argues that 'in this scenario the substance of the Commission's proposals for cohesion policy through to 2013 will be sustained in their incrementalist form by default and the general principles for cohesion established in 1988 will as amended continue into the second decade of the twenty-first century'; that is, things have by necessity become so complex that there is a sclerosis within the EU body politic leading to an *immobilism* caused by competing centrifugal political forces that at times seem reminiscent of the French Fourth Republic. Such complexity ensures that the search for transparency and accountability is made more difficult, and it is to this we now turn.

DEMOCRATIC ACCOUNTABILITY

The challenge of democratic accountability is identified in several chapters within this study. Massey, in Chapter 1, looked at the problems of accountability in a policy process of networks of multi-level governance in the European polity. His argument was not focused on the erosion of parliamentary scrutiny, but the complexity of policy making where sovereignty is 'pooled' and Europeanized. In Chapter 2, Fergus Carr made similar points with regard to EU external relations, which are conducted through two pillars, while state-level outputs sit alongside European. While it can be agreed that foreign policy has always been élitist, concerns about European accountability are likely to grow with the adoption of a greater security agenda under ESDP (see Wagner, 2005). In Chapter 3, Petr Drulák argued for the recognition of the significance of ideas, values and attitudes in the 'return to Europe'. By implication the importance of future public opinion in Central and Eastern Europe towards the evolving European project cannot be overestimated. As we shall see below, public opinion in the original member states has, in the form of the French and Dutch referendums, delivered a veto on the proposed European Constitution. In Chapter 9, Paul Norman explored the post-9/11 development of JHA and pointed to the need for enhanced accountability in what is often a relatively 'closed' policy area.

The challenge of democratic accountability in the EU has normally been presented as a 'democratic deficit': the 'growing gap between the essential requirements of modern democratic government and the actual conditions upon which the governance of the Union is largely based ...' (Chryssochoou, 1998, p. 10). The democratic deficit is seen as a product of the lack of accountability of EU institutions and the 'gap between the powers transferred to the EU and the ability of the European Parliament to oversee and control those powers' (McCormick, 1996, p. 130). Moravcsik argues that procedural qualms 'might be tolerable were it not for the perceived bias in the outputs of European policy-making ... EU directives and regulations promote wider and deeper markets, while providing only a truncated range of compensating and counterbalancing policies of regulatory protection or social welfare guarantees' (Moravcsik, 2002, p. 605). While Moravcsik questions this notion of bias, evidence in this text helps explain the perception. Mike Mannin reveals cohesion funds were really a 'social antidote' to the single market and Kay Peggs contrasts the growing vulnerability of state pension provision with the absence of EU responsibility. If the Union is not responsive to its citizens' needs, a wider notion of the deficit results. Indeed, it has been argued that there is a 'missing link between domestic political life and the realm of transnational relations, and between the currently fragmented European citizen body and a transnational demos conscious of its political identity' (Chryssochoou, 1998, p. 14).

It is possible to argue that 'constitutional checks and balances, indirect democratic control via national governments and the increasing power of the European Parliament are sufficient to ensure that EU policy-making is, in nearly all cases, clear, transparent, effective and politically responsive to the demands of European citizens' (Moravcsik, 2002, p. 605). It is equally possible to interpret the policy process in a more negative manner, but the tests of social legitimacy are provided in polls, elections and referenda. The French and Dutch referendums on the proposed European Constitution provide valuable evidence of citizen attitudes.[1] The French referendum took place on 29 May 2005 and the Netherlands vote took place on 1 June 2005. In France the turnout was 69.3 per cent of eligible voters which, when compared to the 42.8 per cent for the June 2004 European elections, indicates the significance of the issue for the electorate. In the Netherlands turnout was marginally lower at 62.8 per cent, but still considerably higher than participation rates in the 2004 elections. In France, 54.7 per cent voted no and in the Netherlands 61.6 per cent rejected the Constitution. The 'No' votes in both countries effectively ended the constitutional ratification process despite its approval in ten other member states although only in one, Spain, by referendum. The UK suspended its plans for a referendum, as did the Danish, Portuguese and Polish governments. The European Council in June 2005 agreed to a period of reflection and debate involving citizens with a review in the first half of 2006.

The French rejection of the Constitution had a number of reasons, but economic issues were clearly most important. Of the 'No' voters 31 per cent believed the Constitution would have negative effects on employment in France, 26 per cent felt the economic situation in France was too weak and unemployment too high, 19 per cent saw the draft as economically too liberal and 16 per cent rejected the Constitution because it lacked a social focus. In addition 12 per cent found the Constitution too complex, and 6 per cent did not want Turkey as an EU member.

Of the 'Yes' votes, 39 per cent saw the Constitution as essential to pursue the European construction and 16 per cent voted 'Yes' because they had always been in favour of the European project. In addition 12 per cent believed the Constitution strengthened the role of France within the Union and 11 per cent saw the Constitution as strengthening the EU over the USA.

In the Netherlands, unlike France, a significant reported response was lack of information. Some 51 per cent of those who abstained believed they were insufficiently informed to vote, and 32 per cent of all 'No' voters cited lack of information as their reason. Other factors in the 'No' vote were concerns at the loss of national sovereignty (19 per cent), opposition to the national government or certain political parties (14 per cent) and 13 per cent saw the cost of Europe as too high for Dutch taxpayers.

The French and Dutch votes do not reflect disenchantment with EU membership. In France all 'Yes' voters and 83 per cent of 'No' voters consider membership to be a good thing. In the Netherlands similar responses have been recorded, with 78 per cent of 'No' voters believing in EU membership. In both countries a majority of voters agreed that the rejection of the Constitution would enable its renegotiation in order to place a greater emphasis upon social aspects. Similarly, in both countries majorities see the referendum rejection as enabling renegotiation to better defend the respective interests of France and the Netherlands. However, the Dutch are less convinced than the French or the Spanish that a Constitution is essential for the European project.

The response to the impasse created by the rejection of the Constitution was led by the UK, which took over the EU presidency in July 2005. Prime Minister Tony Blair believed the Constitution had become a vehicle for 'the people to register a wider and deeper discontent with the state of affairs in Europe' (Blair, 2005a, p. 2). He saw the Constitution as a 'perfectly serviceable set of rules to govern a Europe that is no longer 15 countries but 25 and perhaps 30 or more but the question that is being debated by the people in Europe is how do we in this era of globalization make our economies stronger and competitive, what is the European social model of social protection in today's world?' (Blair, 2005b, p. 1). The British Foreign Secretary, Jack Straw, saw the need for change:

> the EU must adapt to survive and to prosper in a world quite changed from when it was founded some 50 years ago. It needs, first, better to respond to the sense among European citizens that the EU is remote from the concerns of their daily lives. That was brought into sharp relief by the 'no' votes on the EU Constitution in two of its founder members. (Straw, 2005, p. 1)

The challenge for the British Presidency and its successors is to make the EU relevant to its citizens. Tony Blair believes the problem 'is not a crisis of political institutions, it is a crisis of political leadership' (Blair, 2005a, p. 2). The problem is that the reform agenda is contentious and potentially contradictory, with neoliberal economic strategies sitting alongside concerns for social protection and a budget weighted in favour of CAP. The process had an inauspicious start when EU leaders failed to agree budgetary plans for 2007–13. The issues on the table were proposed changes to the British budget rebate, first secured in 1984, and the British response demanding reform of all expenditure including agricultural plans agreed in 2002. The deadlock was described by the French president, Jacques Chirac, as placing Europe in a 'deep crisis' and he deplored 'the fact that Britain refused to pay a fair and reasonable share of the cost of enlargement' (*The Independent on Sunday*, 19 June 2005). Tony Blair's riposte was that 'a modern Budget for Europe is not one that ten years from now is still spending 40 per cent of its money on CAP' (Blair, 2005a, p. 3). The constitutional crisis, the concerns of French and Dutch voters and the budget deadlock point to the challenges confronting a reform agenda in the EU.

ENLARGEMENT AND THE DYNAMICS OF REFORM: PROBLEMS OF NATIONAL ADMINISTRATIONS

The Kok Report of 2004 was explicit about the benefits of EU expansion and the need for reform across a range of areas. It employed equal clarity to explore the barriers to reform and to posit the problems of EU expansion. In this volume we have similarly identified the problems and the urgent need for reform of the EU's policies and institutions in the fields of:

- the Common Agricultural Policy (Grant, Chapter 12);
- pensions (Pegg, Chapter 16);
- health care (Moon, Chapter 15);

- environmental policy (Barnes, Chapter 13);
- regional policy (Mannin, Chapter 14);
- economic policy (McVeigh, Chapter 7);
- structural reform of the Commission and the Council and of their workings in a range of policy areas (Carr, Chapter 2; Carr and Callan, Chapter 6; Drulák, Chapter 3; and Lippert, Chapter 5).

It is often the case, as Lippert demonstrates, that although the need for reform is understood and the principle even agreed upon, it is the nature and extent of reform that is disputed, with entrenched national interests vetoing change until such time (often after an expansion of membership, but not before) as the EU enters a crisis and circumstances conspire to force through treaty amendments or indeed new treaties. Such a crisis, inspired by allegations of corruption, led to the fall of the Santer Commission and the attempt at a root-and-branch reform of the Commission and its civil service by Commissioner Neil Kinnock (Massey, 2003, pp. 59–74). This process remains unfinished.

The Kok Report argued that improved economic growth and increased employment provide the means

> to sustain social cohesion and environmental sustainability. In their turn, social cohesion and environmental sustainability can contribute to a higher growth and employment. For Europe to increase its living standards, it needs to accelerate employment and productivity growth via a wide range of reform policies as well as a wider macroeconomic framework as supportive as possible of growth, demand and employment. (Kok, 2004, p. 7)

The authors of the Report were aware of the hurdles to attaining these goals and of the need for concerted, coordinated and coherent action to achieve them via transformative reforms of the EU. They observed that:

> No single action will deliver higher growth and jobs. Rather, there are a series of interconnected initiatives and structural changes that through concurrent action in the European Union will release its undoubted potential. This requires urgent action across five areas of policy:
>
> 1. **the knowledge society**: increasing Europe's attractiveness for researchers and scientists, making R and D a top priority and promoting the use of information and communication technologies (ICTs);
> 2. **the internal market**: completion of the internal market for the free movement of goods and capital, and urgent action to create a single market for services;
> 3. **the business climate**: reducing the total administrative burden; improving the quality of legislation; facilitating the rapid start-up of new enterprises; and creating an environment more supportive to businesses;

4. **the labour market**: rapid delivery on the recommendations of the European Employment Taskforce; developing strategies for lifelong learning and active ageing; and underpinning partnerships for growth and employment;
5. **environmental sustainability**: spreading eco-innovations and building leadership in eco-industry; pursuing policies which lead to long-term and sustained improvements in productivity through eco-efficiency. (Kok, 2004, pp. 7–8)

The Report noted that 'individual member states have made progress in one or more of these policy priority areas but none has succeeded consistently across a broad front' (ibid., p. 8).

In part this reflects the different backgrounds of national administrations and their differentiated levels of technical skill. Earlier work has demonstrated how, in the run-up to accession, states subject their administrations to the effects of mimetic isomorphism and coercive isomorphism (Massey, 2003, pp. 59–74). That is, in order to prepare for entry to the EU, nations modernize/Europeanize their administrations, sometimes by simply transposing the European 'way of doing things' into their own administrations, sometimes by doing so because that is the only way they will be able to adopt the *acquis* and gain sufficient credit to release funding from the Commission or indeed to gain entry to the Union (see the chapters in this volume by Barnes, Callan, Mannin, Grant and Moon). On occasion this coercive isomorphism works in reverse, as in the example of the Kinnock reforms when the examples of good governance and modernization provided by the British and Northern European central government administrations were used as a model on which to attempt reform of the Commission. Kok argues that the task 'is to develop national policies in each member state, supported by an appropriate European-wide framework, that address a particular member state's concerns and then to act in a more concerted and determined way' (Kok, 2004, p. 8).

Such a reform requires 'more coherence and consistency between policies and participants, improving the process for delivery by involving national parliaments and social partners, and clearer communication on objectives and achievements' (ibid.). The motivation for the reform not only includes the need to cater for the effects of expansion due to the unprecedented accession of ten new members, but also to meet the challenge posed to Europe by a resurgent US economy and the new economic giants of China and India. For example, the US has used its lead in ICTs to kick-start its economy and has begun to outperform nearly all Europe's leading economies (Kok, 2004, p. 9). The view of the Kok Report (and the Commission generally) is that 'a jointly created economic tide would be even more powerful in its capacity to lift every European boat. The more the EU could develop its knowledge and market opening initiatives in tandem, the stronger and more competitive each member state's economy would be' (ibid.). The EU's attempt to operationalize this strategy, under the Lisbon agreements, 'was a comprehensive, interdependent and self-reinforcing series of reforms' intended to achieve these aims (ibid.). The 2004 enlargement, although a sound political development designed to reward members of the former Soviet bloc for modernizing and ensure their continued development in the EU model, has made Europe-wide achievement of these aims more difficult. This is because 'the new member states tend to have very much lower employment rates and productivity levels; achieving the R and D goals, for example, from a lower base is even tougher than for the EU of the original 15 who signed' the original Lisbon accord (ibid., p. 12).

Enlargement has brought with it many challenges, not least of which is the realization that it has 'made inequality and the problems of EU cohesion more pronounced' (ibid., p. 14). The figures here are illustrative, in that previous enlargements (from six to nine) have either made the EU considerably richer and improved GDP, or in the case of the accession of Spain, Portugal and Greece, been of a scale that could be more readily absorbed (Mannin above, and Knill, 2001; Andersen and Eliassen, 1993). In the most recent major accessions, as Mannin noted, the EU population

> has increased by 20 per cent while the addition to European GDP is only 5 per cent, resulting in a drop of output per head of 12.5 per cent in the EU 25. Moreover, the new member states are characterized by strong regional disparities with wealth concentrated in a small number of regions. The population living in regions with output per head of less than 75 per cent of the EU has increased from 73 million to 123 million. Equally … the EU 25 average employment rate has dropped as a consequence of enlargement by almost 1.5 percentage points. The long-term unemployment rate for the EU 25 is 4 per cent compared with 3.3 per cent for the EU 15. Some of the environmental targets will also be more difficult to achieve. (Kok, 2004, pp. 14–15)

But because the new member states have so much further to catch up, it is likely they will emulate the rapid growth of Ireland, Spain and Greece, creating an 'area of economic dynamism in eastern Europe' (ibid., p. 15). The evidence that this is already happening may be found in Estonia, Lithuania, Latvia, Hungary, Poland, Slovenia, Slovakia and the Czech Republic, whose growth rates have been above that of the USA over the last five years (ibid.). The contributors to this volume have highlighted these issues and shown how the problems of expansion also bring with them problems of convergence that have the potential to create a great deal of discord.

Conversely, if negotiated intelligently and in good faith, expansion and the inevitable reform it will engender may be a positive and constructive commitment to the next phase of the grand European project. As noted at the start of this chapter:

> the principle underpinning the European Union is well established: Europeans better hang together or they will hang separately. The single market in goods and services promotes trade that benefits every member state. The euro creates a monetary union of predictable, stable low interest rates and low inflation that benefits every member state. No single European country can achieve an improved environment in isolation; and the better the European economy performs, the more investment flows to every member state to take advantage of the improved general European business climate. In the same way, the effects of building a European knowledge economy spill over to benefit all. (Kok, 2004, pp. 15–17)

The contributors to this volume have demonstrated the opportunities and difficulties that expansion has brought with it; many of the new states seeing it as a return to Europe (Drulák) and concerned at the way in which having 'escaped' the embrace of Russia, they now perceive the climate post 9/11 to suggest a somewhat closer relationship with their erstwhile partners than they had envisaged (Carr and Callan; Flenley). The contributions of Schimmelfenig (Chapter 4) and Barnes have pointed out the problems of smaller accession states having, or developing, the technocratic capacity to deliver on all they have signed up to, reiterating the need to include modernization of national administrations in terms of technical competence, as well as (in some cases) ethical 'competence'.

The Commission, indeed the EU's political élites, are struggling with these issues, especially the need to ensure that proper technocratic and institutional competence is part of the reform process in the wake of the expansion eastwards and southwards. Kok argued that, in order to ensure the benefits of reform are realized and shared across the EU:

> member states must take their responsibility and take ownership of the process. The European Commission must be prepared to 'name and shame' those that fail as well as to 'fame' those that succeed. Too much is at stake to respect the sensibilities of those who hinder the pursuit of the common European good. … If Europe is to achieve its goals, it must act single-mindedly and with focus … One of the most persistent obstacles is the failure of too many member states to act on the commitments they make in the Council within the agreed time limit. There is little benefit in governments agreeing to measures in Brussels if they do not then show the same commitment when it comes to implementing those measures at national level. In spite of the European Council's repeated calls for zero tolerance for excessive delays in transposition, this remains a huge problem. Every directive that is late in being implemented by a member state reduces the competitiveness of the entire Union. (Kok, 2004, pp. 15–20)

In other words, the problems engendered by expansion, complexity, the democratic deficit and so forth cannot be used as an excuse to resist comprehensive reform of the kind identified as essential by the contributors to this volume: to do so is to risk losing the greater part of the project. The issues generated post 9/11, and transatlanticism generally, are inherent parts of this debate, and it is to this we now turn.

THE CONTINUING IMPACT OF 9/11

The 9/11 attacks upon the USA had a number of consequences for European politics. For the EU, solidarity with the USA was the first priority and policy direction. Carr and Callan have shown in Chapter 6 that these bonds of transatlanticism began to fracture as the war against terror turned to the axis of evil agenda. The prospect of regime change in Iraq divided the Western alliance and split NATO, aligning France and Germany with their Cold War adversary, Russia. Britain remained staunchly in support of Washington and was joined by the accession states of Central and Eastern Europe. As Drulák has shown in Chapter 3, the East Europeans were concerned that transatlanticism remained as the cornerstone of European security. The division of European opinion over Iraq and the Franco-German clash with the USA have at face value been resolved in demonstrations of solidarity such as the convening of a NATO Defence Ministers' meeting in Nice. Underlying problems remain, however, with, as we shall see below, more fundamental divisions over approaches to international order. In contrast to disputes over the strategic responses to rogue states, Paul Norman has shown in Chapter 9 that the terrorist attacks accelerated changes in the field of JHA and cemented links to the USA. This development was in parallel to the growing political fallout in foreign policy. The consequences for human rights were examined by Elspeth Guild in Chapter 10 and Theresa Callan in Chapter 11. Guild demonstrated that after 9/11 states increasingly conceptualized security in a territorial sense, with the border given a new salience. The result has been to problematize the relationship between human rights conventions which, in part, seek to safeguard the rights of asylum seekers and forced migrants with the anti-terrorist barricades of European frontiers. Theresa Callan develops this theme, showing the tensions between state security and the protection of the individual. Callan, like Guild, points to the consequent insecurity of the non-national. The European Council has stressed the need for counter-terrorism to respect human rights principles, but enforcement rests with states and, as Callan demonstrates, the core powers, including the USA, have eroded the key principle of the indivisibility of human security.

THE END OF TRANSATLANTICISM?

The differences between the USA and Europe have been seen to reflect differences in power and, consequently, preferences in diplomatic strategy. In Kagan's view, 'Europeans focus on issues – "challenges" – where European strengths come into play, but not on those "threats" where European weakness makes solutions elusive' (Kagan, 2003, pp. 32–3). The uni-polar character of the international system affords the USA great opportunities for power projection, which it has increasingly been willing to utilize in a unilateral manner. The USA can 'act alone'; its military capability is not matched by any other state or organization. The EU, as argued in Chapter 2, is characterized by 'soft power' and seeks to nurture an international order in which normative principles prevail. European commitments to multilateralism, to the pacific resolution of disputes and to the United Nations, in part reflect this resource base. EU strategy is also constructed in this manner because normative principles are valued. The USA, in contrast, remains 'mired in history, exercising power in an anarchic Hobbesian world where international laws and rules are unreliable, and where true security and the defence and promotion of a liberal order still depend on the possession and use of military might' (Kagan, 2003, p. 3). The comparison for some is between the 'modern' and 'postmodern' (Cooper, 2003, pp. 21–54) or 'Mars and Venus' (Kagan, 2003, p. 3). It is a contrast between the classical states system, realpolitik and force, with states in 'a highly developed system for mutual interference in each other's domestic affairs, right down to beer and sausages' (Cooper, 2003, p. 27). The typologies may be exaggerated, but they capture the essential features of the transatlantic divide – a divide that can be seen in a range of issues from regime change in Iraq to the International Criminal Court and the Kyoto Protocol.

The post-Cold-War order in Europe enabled the EU to realize its security agenda. The demise of the Soviet threat left a Europe where economic and political stability were key priorities. The EU was uniquely placed to be the key 'security provider' in this context, directly assisted by the aspirations of the Central and Eastern European countries for membership. Russian policy under both Yeltsin and Putin has positively accommodated the EU, while arms control agreements such as the Conventional Forces in Europe (CFE) Treaty cemented the new diplomatic order. Europeans were in effect granted an opportunity to determine their own affairs in comparison to Cold War dependence on the USA and its leadership of the Atlantic Alliance.

European strategic reliance on the USA has, however, not ended in the post-Cold-War world. The Balkan Wars soon exposed the fragile limits of the EU's capacity for crisis management. The consequences have, on the one hand, facilitated transatlantic partnership with NATO's strategic adaptation while, on the other hand, made for more turbulent politics as the EU has attempted to redress its weakness in military capabilities. The post-St-Malo development of ESDP has been both welcomed by Washington as a necessary European contribution to NATO and criticized when it purports to be an autonomous European centre of decision making. The European position on this issue is far from cohesive, with Britain, in particular, supporting the drive to enhance European capabilities but asserting that nothing should be done to undermine NATO. The new East European NATO member states which have joined the EU are equally concerned not to sever their bonds, so recently acquired, with Washington. A sense of ambivalence may be detected between the recognized need for Europe to advance its own crisis management capabilities and the desire to retain the role of the USA. The challenge for the Europeans is to find the appropriate institutional means to accommodate both sets of interests and for Washington to accept limitations on its leadership.

The lure of the USA as a strategic partner is not confined to the EU. In Chapter 8, Paul Flenley revealed how 9/11 accelerated Putin's policy changes and provided the means to explicitly identify Russia with the USA. Russia became a partner in the war on terror, linking Chechnya with the US campaign. Moscow provided practical assistance with military action against the Taliban and, while standing with France and Germany over Iraq, still sought to cement its new relationship with Washington. This pragmatic recognition of interest has also driven the EU's JHA agenda with regard to Washington and, as Paul Norman reports in Chapter 9, towards Moscow.

The recognition of mutual interests between Europe and the USA should not be surprising. Paul McVeigh, in Chapter 7, depicts Washington's leadership of the post-1945 economic order within which Europe's recovery was secured. Europe and America also share a common cultural and intellectual tradition:

> the real point is that the United States was born of Europe's rib. We have common roots in the European Enlightenment, and we share the body of ideas that emerged from that period of emancipation from received authority. We have worked together over the last half-century to fashion an international legal order covering not just trade and security, but human rights, too, and fundamental freedoms. (Patten and Lamy, 2003)

The advent of global terrorism brought Europe and the USA closer in alliance. As in the Cold War, mutual threats overrode policy drift and disagreement. The difference with the Cold War era is that the EU is developing a sense of political autonomy. While the Union is yet to realize a full range of resources to support that autonomy or to sustain a common

European voice across the spectrum of global issues, Europe's views are increasing in salience. At the same time the USA has unparalleled power and the uni-polar moment permits unilateralism in Washington's strategy. It would be far too premature to sound the death knell of transatlanticism, but the challenge, as US Secretary of State Condoleezza Rice has recognized, is to try to move beyond a 'partnership based on common threats' and focus instead upon 'common opportunities, beyond the transatlantic community' (Rice, 2005).

NOTE

1. The statistics are taken from the European Commission Eurobarometer post-referendum surveys in France and the Netherlands (EB171 and EB172), published in June 2005.

References

CHAPTER 1

Adshead, M. (2002), 'Conceptualizing Europeanization: Policy Networks and Cross-National Comparison', *Public Policy and Administration*, **17** (2), 25–42.
Berger, P. and Luckman, T. (1967), *The Social Construction of Reality: a Treatise in the Sociology of Knowledge*, New York: Anchor Books.
Buchanan, J. (1999), *The Logical Foundations of Constitutional Liberty*, Indianapolis: Liberty Fund.
Buller, J. and Gamble, A. (2002), 'Conceptualizing Europeanization', *Public Policy and Administration*, **17** (2), 4–24.
Butcher, T. and Massey, A. (eds) (2003), *Modernizing Civil Services*, Cheltenham, UK and Northampton, MA, USA: Edward Elgar.
Carr, F. and Massey, A. (eds) (1999), *Public Policy in the New Europe: Eurogovernance in Theory and Practice*, Cheltenham, UK and Northampton, MA, USA: Edward Elgar.
Christiansen, T. and Piattoni, S. (eds) (2003), *Informal Governance in the European Union*, Cheltenham, UK and Northampton, MA, USA: Edward Elgar.
Chryssochoou, D. (1999), 'Eurogovernance and the Policy Process', in Carr, F. and Massey, A. (eds), *Public Policy in the New Europe: Eurogovernance in Theory and Practice*, Cheltenham, UK and Northampton, MA, USA: Edward Elgar.
Chryssochoou, D. (2001), *Theorizing European Integration*, London: Sage.
Commission of the European Communities (2003), *First Report of the Implementation of the Framework Action 'Updating and Simplifying the Community Acquis'*, Brussels, COM (2003) 623.
Cutler, C. (1999), 'Locating "Authority" in the Global Political Economy', *International Studies Quarterly*, **43**, 59–61.
Diez, T. and Wiener, A. (2004), 'Introducing the Mosaic of Integration Theory', in Wiener, A. and Diez, T. (eds), *European Integration Theory*, Oxford: Oxford University Press, pp. 1–21.
Dunford, M., Louri, H. and Rosenstock, M. (2001), 'Competition, Competitiveness, and Enterprise Policies', in Hall, R., Smith, A. and

Tsoukalis, L. (eds), *Competitiveness and Cohesion in EU Policies*, Oxford: Oxford University Press, pp. 109–46.

Dunleavy, P. (1997), 'The Globalization of Public Services Production: Can Government be "Best in World"?', in Massey, A. (1997), *Globalization and Marketization of Government Services: Comparing Contemporary Public Sector Developments*, Basingstoke: Macmillan, pp. 16–46.

Dunsire, A. (1973), *Administration: The Word and the Science*, London: Martin Robertson.

Egan, M. (2001), *Constructing a European Market*, Oxford: Oxford University Press.

Ekengren, M. (2002), *The Time of European Governance*, Manchester: Manchester University Press.

European Policy Forum (2003), *NGOs, Democratization and the Regulatory State*, London: European Policy Forum, pp. 5–22.

Fraser Moleketi, G. (2005), *The World We Could Win: Administering Global Governance*, Amsterdam: IOS Press.

Fukuyama, F. (1992), *The End of History and the Last Man*, London: Penguin.

Gray, J. (2004), *Al Qaeda and What It Means to Be Modern*, London: Faber and Faber.

Greenwood, J., Pyper, R. and Wilson, D. (2002), *New Public Administration in Britain*, 3rd edn, London: Routledge.

Gruber, K. (2002), 'Globalization, Regions, Nations and Integration: Central and Western European Perspectives', *Perspectives on European Politics and Society*, **3** (2), 200–28.

Halabi, Y. (2004), 'The Expansion of Global Governance into the Third World: Altruism, Realism, or Constructivism?', *International Studies Review*, **6**, 21–48.

Hall, R., Smith, A. and Tsoukalis, L. (2001), *Competitiveness and Cohesion in EU Policies,* Oxford: Oxford University Press.

Hay, C. (2004), 'Theory, Stylized Heuristic or Self-Fulfilling Prophecy? The Status of Rational Choice Theory in Public Administration', *Public Administration*, **82**, 39–62.

Haynes, B. and Melville Jones, H. (1999), 'Ethics and Public Sector Management: The Western Australian Experience', *Australian Journal of Public Administration*, **58** (2), 70–82.

Held, D. and McGrew, A. (2002a), *Governing Globalization: Power Authority and Global Governance*, Cambridge: Polity Press.

Held, D. and McGrew, A. (2002b), 'Introduction', in Held, D. and McGrew, A. (2002a), *Governing Globalization: Power Authority and Global Governance*, Cambridge: Polity Press.

Howse, R. and Nicolaidis, K. (2003), 'Enhancing WTO Legitimacy: Constitutionalization or Global Subsidiarity?', in *Governance: An International Journal of Policy, Administration and Institutions*, **16** (1), 73–94.

Jachtenfuchs, M. and Kohler-Koch, B. (2004), 'Governance and Institutional Development', in Wiener, A. and Diez, T. (eds), *European Integration Theory*, Oxford: Oxford University Press, pp. 97–116.

Kickert, J.M. and Stillman, R.J. (1999), *The Modern State and its Study: New Administrative Sciences in a Changing Europe and United States*, Cheltenham, UK and Northampton, MA, USA: Edward Elgar.

Kooiman, J. (2003), *Governing as Governance*, London: Sage.

Lipschutz, R. with Mayer, J. (1996), *Global Civil Society and Global Environmental Governance*, Albany: State University of New York Press.

Lodge, M. (2002), 'Varieties of Europeanization and the National Regulatory State', *Public Policy and Administration*, **17** (2), 43–67.

Maesschalck, J. (2004), 'What Difference Does the Organization Make?', EGPA, Proceedings of the Annual Conference, *Administering the New Europe*.

Mairate, A. and Hall, R. (2001), 'Structural Policies', in Hall, R., Smith, A. and Tsoukalis, L. (2001), *Competitiveness and Cohesion in EU Policies*, Oxford: Oxford University Press, pp. 315–46.

Margetts, H. (1997), 'The Automated State', in Massey, A. (1997), *Globalization and Marketization of Government Services: Comparing Contemporary Public Sector Developments*, Basingstoke: Macmillan, pp. 87–104.

Massey, A. (1988), *Technocrats and Nuclear Politics*, Aldershot: Avebury Press.

Massey, A. (1993), *Managing the Public Sector: A Comparative Analysis of the United Kingdom and the United States*, Aldershot, UK and Brookfield, US: Edward Elgar.

Massey, A. (1999), 'The Joint European Torus: An Historical Case Study in European Public Policy', *Public Policy and Administration*, **14** (4).

Massey, A. (2003, 'Modernization as Europeanization', in Butcher, T. and Massey, A. (eds), *Modernizing Civil Services*, Cheltenham, UK and Northampton, MA, USA: Edward Elgar.

Massey, A. (2005), 'Multilevel Governance: Administering Global Governance in a Differentiated Political Context', in Fraser Moleketi, G. (2005), *The World We Could Win: Administering Global Governance*, Amsterdam: IOS Press.

Massey, A. and Pyper, R. (2005), *Public Management and Modernization in Britain*, Basingstoke: Palgrave Macmillan.

Omelicheva, M. (2004), '"Global Civil Society?" An Empirical Portrayal', paper to the Annual Meeting of the American Political Science Association, APSA.

Plant, R. (2003), 'A Public Service Ethic and Political Accountability', *Parliamentary Affairs*, 560–79.

Price, D.K. (1983), *America's Unwritten Constitution*, Baton Rouge: Louisiana State University Press.

Rhodes, R.A.W. (1994), 'The Hollowing out of the State', *Political Quarterly*, **65** (2), 138–51.

Rhodes, R., Carmichael, P., McMillan, J. and Massey, A. (2003), *Decentralizing the Civil Service: From Unitary State to Differentiated Polity in the United Kingdom*, Buckingham: Open University Press.

Richards, D. and Smith, M. (2002), *Governance and Public Policy in the UK*, Oxford: Oxford University Press.

Rose, R. (2005), *Learning from Comparative Public Policy: A Practical Guide*, Abingdon: Routledge.

Sabatier, P. (1988), 'The Advocacy Coalition Framework: Revisions and Relevance for Europe', *Journal of European Public Policy*, **3** (1), 98–130.

Salway, P. (2001), 'Reporting on Public Sector Ethics and Values: A New Public Management Model in Practice', *International Review of Administrative Sciences*, **67**, 567–70.

Sandholtz, W. and Stone Sweet, A. (1998), *European Integration and Supranational Governance*, Oxford: Oxford University Press.

Schimmelfennig, F. (2000), 'International Socialization', *European Journal of International Relations*, **6** (1), 109–39.

Schmitter, P. (2004), 'Neo-neofunctionalism', in Wiener, A. and Diez, T. (eds), *European Integration Theory*, Oxford: Oxford University Press.

Spragia, A. (1998), 'Institution-Building from Below and Above: The European Community in Global Environmental Politics', in Sandholtz, W. and Stone Sweet, A., *European Integration and Supranational Governance*, Oxford: Oxford University Press.

Stillman, R. (1999), 'Conclusion: American versus European Public Administration', in Kickert, J.M. and Stillman, R. (eds), *The Modern State and its Study: New Administrative Sciences in a Changing Europe and the United States*, Cheltenham, UK and Northampton, MA, USA: Edward Elgar.

Stone Sweet, A. (2000), *Governing With Judges: Constitutional Politics in Europe*, Oxford: Oxford University Press.

Stone Sweet, A. and Sandholtz, W. (1998), 'Integration, Supranational Governance, and the Institutionalization of the European Polity', in

Sandholtz, W. and Stone Sweet, A. (1998), *European Integration and Supranational Governance*, Oxford: Oxford University Press.
Tarditi, S. and Zanias, G. (2001), 'Common Agricultural Policy', in Hall, R., Smith, A. and Tsoukalis, L. (2001), *Competitiveness and Cohesion in EU Policies*, Oxford: Oxford University Press, pp. 179–216.
Vogel, D. (1989), *Trading Up: Consumer and Environmental Regulation in a Global Economy*, Cambridge, MA: Harvard University Press.
Wiener, A. and T. Diez (eds) (2004), *European Integration Theory*, Oxford: Oxford University Press.
Wildavsky, A. (1995), *But is it True? A Citizen's Guide to Environmental Health and Safety Issues*, Cambridge, MA: Harvard University Press.

CHAPTER 2

Aliboni, R. (2005), 'The Geopolitical Implications of the European Neighbourhood Policy', *European Foreign Affairs Review*, **10**, 1–16.
Allen, D. and Smith, M. (1990), 'Western Europe's Presence in the Contemporary International Arena', *Review of International Studies*, **16**, 19–37.
Alpher, J. (2000), 'The Political Role of the EU in the Middle East: Israel: Aspirations', in Behrendt, S. and Hanett, C.P. (eds), *Bound to Cooperate – Europe and the Middle East*, Gütersloh: Bertelsmann Foundation Publishers.
Aoun, E. (2003), 'European Foreign Policy and the Arab–Israeli Dispute: Much Ado About Nothing?', *European Foreign Affairs Review*, **8**, 289–312.
Asseburg, M. (2003), 'From Declarations to Implementation? The Three Dimensions of European Policy Towards the Conflict', in Ortega, M. (ed.), *The European Union and the Crisis in the Middle East*, Chaillot Papers, No. 62, Institute for Security Studies, European Union.
Babarinde, O. and Faber, G. (2004), 'From Lomé to Cotonou: Business as Usual?', *European Foreign Affairs Review*, **9**, 27–47.
Barcelona Declaration (1995), *The Euro-Mediterranean Partnership – Barcelona Declaration*, http://europa.eu.int/comm/external-relations/euromed/bd.htm.
Bill, J. (1988), *The Eagle and the Lion: The Tragedy of American–Iranian Relations*, New Haven, CT: Yale University Press.
Brotherton, C. and Vogler, J. (1999), *The European Union as a Global Actor*, London: Routledge.
Bull, H. (1982), 'Civilian Power Europe: A Contradiction in Terms', *Journal of Common Market Studies*, **21** (2), 149–64.

Bush, G.W. (2002), *The President's State of the Union Address 29/1/02*, http://www.whitehouse.gov.news/releases/2002.

Commission of the European Communities (2003), *Paving the Way for a New Neighbourhood Instrument*, Brussels, COM (2003) 393 final, 1 July.

Commission of the European Communities (2005a), *Communication from the Commission to the Council, the European Parliament and the Economic and Social Committee: Speeding Up Progress Towards the Millennium Development Goals, the European Union's Contribution*, Brussels, COM (2005) 132 final, 12 April.

Commission of the European Communities (2005b), *Communication from the Commission to the Council, the European Parliament and the Economic and Social Committee: Policy Coherence for Development*, Brussels, COM (2005) 134 final, 12 April.

Cooper, R. (2003), *The Breaking of Nations: Order and Chaos in the Twenty-First Century*, London: Atlantic Books.

Cotonou Agreement (2000), *The Cotonou Agreement*, http://europa.eu.int/comm/development/body/cotonou/agreement.

Council of Ministers (2001), *General Affairs, Brussels 26/27 February 2001 Duty Free Access for Least Developed Countries*, http://ue/eu.int/vedocs/cms_Data/docs//pressdata/en/.geena/ACF1314.html.

Croci, O. (2003), 'A Closer Look at the Changing Transatlantic Relationship', *European Affairs Review*, **8**, 469–91.

Delors, J. (1991), 'European Integration and Security', *Survival*, **33** (2), 99–109.

DFID (2004), *Department for International Development: Country Assistance Plan for Palestinians*, www.dfid.gov.uk.

Dosenrode, S. and Stubkjær, A. (2002), *The European Union and the Middle East*, London: Sheffield Academic Press.

Duchêne, F. (1973), 'The European Community and the Uncertainties of Interdependence', in Kohnstamm, M. and Hager, W. (eds), *A Nation Writ Large? Foreign Policy Problems Before the European Community*, Basingstoke: Macmillan.

Duke, S. (2002), 'CESDP and the EU Response to 11th September: Identifying the Weakest Link', *European Foreign Affairs Review*, **7**, 153–69.

Ehteshami, A. (2000), 'Europe, the US and Iran', in Behrendt, S. and Hanett, C.P. (eds), *Bound to Cooperate – Europe and the Middle East*, Gütersloh: Bertelsmann Foundation Publishers.

EMP (2005–6), *MEDA Regional Indicative Programme*, http://www.europa.eu.int/comm/external-relations/euromed/rsp/.

European Commission (2004), *A World Player*, europa.eu.int/comm./world.

European Commission (2005), *Overview of EU Relations with the Palestinians*, http://www.delwbg.CEC.eu.int/en/eu_and_Palestine/overview.htm.

The European Community's Development Policy (2000), *The European Community's Development Policy: Statement by the Council and the Commission*, http://europa/development.

European Council (1980), *Venice Declaration*, http://www.medea.

European Council (1993a), *European Council in Brussels 29 October 1993, Presidency Conclusions*, http://europa.eu.int/rapid/press.

European Council (1993b), *European Council in Brussels 10 and 11 December 1993, Presidency Conclusions*, http://europa.eu.int/rapid/press.

European Council (1993c), *Conclusions of the Presidency*, European Council in Copenhagen, 21–22 June.

European Council (2000a), *Presidency Conclusions Nice European Council, December 2000*, http://ue.eu.int/uedocs/cms_data/docs/pressData/en/ec.

European Council (2000b), 'Common Strategy of the European Council of 19 June 2000 on the Mediterranean Region' (2000/458/CFSP), *Official Journal of the European Communities*.

European Council (2001a), *Laeken Declaration on the Future of the European Union*, Presidency Conclusions, European Council Meeting in Laeken, SN300/1/01/REV1.

European Council (2001b), *Conclusion and Plan of Action of the Extraordinary European Council Meeting on 21st September 2001*, http://UE.evint/vedocs/cms-data/docs/pressdata/en/ec/140.enpdf.

European Security Strategy (2003), *A Secure Europe in a Better World*, Brussels, 12 December, http://europa.

European Union Bulletin (2001), 'EU 9–2001 Joint EU-US Ministerial Statement on Combating Terrorism', http://Europa.EU.int/abc/doc/off/bull/en/200109/p106047.htm.

Eurostat (2004), *Portrait of the European Union*, http://www.europa.eu.int/comm/eurostat.

Ginsberg, R.H. (2001), *The European Union in International Politics: Baptism by Fire*, Lanham, MD: Rowman and Littlefield.

Gnesotto, N. (2002), 'Preface', in Ehrhart, H.G., *What Model for CFSP?*, Chaillot Papers No. 55, European Union. Paris: Institute for Security Studies.

Hill, C. (1993), 'The Capability–Expectations Gap, or Conceptualizing Europe's International Role', *Journal of Common Market Studies*, **31** (3), 305–28.

Hill, C. (2004), 'Renationalizing or Regrouping? EU Foreign Policy since 11 September 2001', *Journal of Common Market Studies*, **42** (1), 143–63.

Hiro, D. (1985), *Iran under the Ayatollahs*, London: Routledge and Kegan Paul.

Keohane, R. (1984), *After Hegemony: Cooperation and Discord in the World Political Economy*, Princeton, NJ: Princeton University Press.

Keohane, R.O. and Hoffmann, S. (1991), *The New European Community: Decision-making and Institutional Change*, Boulder, CO: Westview Press.

Kharrazi, K. (2005), *Statement by H.E. Dr. Kamal Kharrazi, Minister of Foreign Affairs of the Islamic Republic of Iran to the Seventh NPT Review Conference*, http://www.un.int.iran/statements/generalassembly/session 59/19.htm.

Kintis, A. (1997), 'The EU's Foreign Policy and the War in the Former Yugoslavia', in Holland, M. (ed.), *Common Foreign and Security Policy: The Record and Reforms*, London: Pinter.

Laqueur, W. and Rubin, B. (eds) (1984), *The Israel–Arab Reader*, Harmondsworth: Penguin.

Leonard, M. (2005), *Why Europe Will Run the 21st Century*, London: Fourth Estate.

Manners, I. (2002), 'Normative Power Europe: A Contradiction in Terms?', *Journal of Common Market Studies*, **40** (2), 235–58.

Manners, I. and Whitman, R.G. (eds) (2000), *The Foreign Policies of European Union Member States*, Manchester: Manchester University Press.

Marr, P. (2000), 'US Policy of Sanctions: Prospects for Revision', in Behrendt, S. and Hanelt, C.P. (eds) (2000), *Bound to Cooperate – Europe and the Middle East*, Gütersloh: Bertelsmann Foundation Publishers.

Matthews, A. (2004), 'The EU and the Developing World', in El-Agraa, A.M. (2004), *The European Union: Economics and Policies*, Harlow: Pearson.

Migliorsi, S. (2003), *The Consequences of Enlargement for Development Policy*, migliorsi@dev-strategies.com.

Nielson, P. (2000), *Speech by Paul Nielson European Commissioner for Development Cooperation and Humanitarian Aid, ACP-EC Partnership Agreement, Cotonou, Benin*, http://europa.eu.int/rapid.

NSS (2002), *The National Security Strategy of the United States of America*, The White House, available at http://www.whitehouse.gov/nsc/nss.html.

Nuttall, S. (1992), *European Political Cooperation*, Oxford: Clarendon Press.

Nuttall, S. (2000), *European Foreign Policy*, Oxford: Oxford University Press.

Nye, J. (2002/3), 'Limits of American Power', *Political Science Quarterly*, **117** (4), 545–59.

OLAF (2005), *OLAF Investigation into EU Assistance to the Palestinian Authority Budget*, http://europa.eu.int/comm/externaal-relations/gaza/news/olaf05–03.htm.

Patten, C. (2003), *Europe in the World: CFSP and its Relation to Development*, http://europa.eu/int/comm/external-relations/news/patten/sp07–11–03.htm.

Patten, C. (2004a), *Speech for EP Plenary Debate on the Greater Middle East Region*, 30 March, http://europa.eu.int/comm/external-relations/news/patten/sp04–165.htm.

Patten, C. (2004b), *Reply to EP Debate on Iran*, http://europa.eu.int/comm/external-relations/news/patten/speech04.

Santer, J. (1995), 'The European Union's Security and Defence Policy', *NATO Review*, **43** (6), 3–6.

Shawcross, J. (2003), *Allies: The US, Britain, Europe and the War in Iraq*, London: Atlantic Books.

Sjöstedt, G. (1977), *The External Role of the European Community*, Farnborough: Saxon House.

Smith, M. (2004), 'Institutionalization, Policy Adaptation and European Foreign Policy Cooperation', *European Journal of International Relations*, **10** (1), 95–136.

Solana, J. (2004), *Summary of Remarks, Conference of Ambassadors, La Farmesina, Rome 27 July 2004*, http://ue.eu.int/newsroom.

Stein, A. (1993), 'Coordination and Collaboration: Regimes in an Anarchic World', in Krasner, S. (ed.), *International Regimes*, Ithaca, NY: Cornell University Press.

Ueta, T. (1997), 'The Stability Pact: From the Balladur Initiative to the EU Joint Action', in Holland, M. (ed.), *Common Foreign and Security Policy: The Record and Reforms*, London: Pinter.

United Nations (2002), *The Impact of Closure and Other Mobility Restrictions on Palestinian Productive Activities*, Office of the United Nations Special Coordinator.

United Nations Millennium Declaration (2000), *Resolution Adopted by the General Assembly*, http://www.un.org/millennium/declaration.

White, B. (2001), *Understanding European Foreign Policy*, Basingstoke: Palgrave Macmillan.

The White House (2002), *National Security Strategy of the United States*, http://www.usinfo.state.gov/topical/pol/tterror/secstat.htm.

Whitman, R. (1998), *From Civilian Power to Superpower?*, Basingstoke: Macmillan.

Woodward, B. (2002), *Bush at War*, New York: Simon and Schuster.

World Bank (2003), *Twenty-Seven Months of Intifada, Closures and Palestinian Economic Crisis: An Assessment*, http://www-wds.worldbank.org.

Young, A. (2004), 'The EU and World Trade: Doha and Beyond', in Cowles, M. and Dinan, D., *Developments in the European Union*, Basingstoke: Palgrave Macmillan.

Young, O.R. (2002), 'Are Institutions Intervening Variables or Basic Causal Forces? Causal Clusters versus Causal Chains in International Society', in Brecher, M. and Harvey, F.P. (eds), *Realism and Institutionalism in International Studies*, Michigan: The University of Michigan Press.

CHAPTER 3

Bailey, D. and De Propris, L. (2004), 'EU Pre-Accession Aid and Capacity-Building in the Candidate Countries', *Journal of Common Market Studies*, **42** (1), 77–98.

Beichelt, T. (2004), 'Euro-Scepticism in the EU Accession Countries', *Comparative European Politics*, **2** (1), 29–50.

Bilčík, V. (2002), 'Developments in the EU Foreign and Security Policy – the Candidates' Perspectives', in Martin Brusis and Janis A. Emmanoulidis (eds), *Thinking Enlarged: The Accession Countries and the Future of the European Union*, Bonn: Europa Union Verlag, pp. 89–102.

Boruta, I. (2002), 'Some Observations on the Changes in Accession Negotiation Strategy', in Barcz, Jan and Michonski, Arkadiusz (eds), *Negotiations on Poland's Accession to the European Union*, Warsaw: Ministry of Foreign Affairs, pp. 61–8.

Brusis, M. (2001), 'Conclusions: European and National Identities in the Accession Countries – the Role of the European Union', in Drulák, P. (ed.), *National and European Identities in EU Enlargement: Views from Central and Eastern Europe*, Prague: Institute of International Relations, pp. 195–208.

Dimitrova, A. (ed.) (2004), *Driven to Change: The European Union's Enlargement Viewed from the East*, Manchester: Manchester University Press.

Drulák, P. (ed.) (2001), *National and European Identities in EU Enlargement: Views from Central and Eastern Europe*, Prague: Institute of International Relations.

Drulák, P. (2002), 'A Look at the Future EU from the Candidate Countries', in Brusis, M. and Emmanoulidis, J.A. (eds) *Thinking Enlarged: The Accession Countries and the Future of the European Union*, Bonn: Europa Union Verlag, pp. 29–46.

Drulák, P. (2004), *Metaphors Europe Lives By: Language and Institutional Change of the European Union*, Working Paper, Department of Social and Political Sciences, Florence: European University Institute.

Drulák, P. and Drulákoví, R. (2004), 'What do the Elections to the European Parliament Tell Us about New Member Countries?', in Adebahr, M. et al. (eds), *EuroMission: Neue Perspektiven für die erweiterte Europäische Union*, Münster–Hamburg–Berlin: LIT Verlag.

Drulák, P. and Königová, L. (2005), 'The Czech Republic – From Socialist Past to Socialized Future', in Flockhart, T. (ed.), *Socializing Democratic Norms: The Role of International Organizations for the Construction of Europe*, London: Palgrave, forthcoming.

Drulák, P., Česal, Jiří and Hampl, Stanislav (2003), 'Interactions and Identities of Czech Civil Servants on their Way to the EU', *Journal of European Public Policy*, **10** (4), 637–54.

Fierke, K. and Wiener, A. (1999), 'Constructing Institutional Interests: EU and NATO Enlargement', *Journal of European Public Policy*, **6** (5), 721–42.

Freiberga, Elga (2001), 'European Values and Latvian Identity', in Drulák, P. (ed.), *National and European Identities in EU Enlargement: Views from Central and Eastern Europe*, Prague: Institute of International Relations, pp. 113–28.

Fris, L. (2002), *Countdown to Copenhagen. Big Bang or Fizzle in the EU's Enlargement Process?*, Copenhagen: Danish Institute of International Affairs.

Goetz, Klaus H. (2001), 'Making Sense of Post-Communist Central Administration: Modernization, Europeanization or Latinization?', *Journal of European Public Policy*, **8** (6), 1032–51.

Goetz, Klaus H. and Wollmann, H. (2001), 'Governmentalizing Central Executives in Post-Communist Europe: A Four Country Comparison', *Journal of European Public Policy*, **8** (6), 864–87.

Grabbe, H. (2001), 'How does Europeanization Affect CEE Governance? Conditionality, Diffusion and Diversity', *Journal of European Public Policy*, **8** (6), 1013–31.

Gyárfášová, O. (2001), 'From Defence Against the Others to the Formulation of its Own Interests: The Case of Slovakia', in Drulák, P. (ed.), *National and European Identities in EU Enlargement: Views from Central and Eastern Europe*, Prague: Institute of International Relations, pp. 39–56.

Havel, V. (1993/1999), 'Spoluodpovědnost Západu', in *Projevy a jiné texty z let 1992–1999*, Spisy VII, Praha: Torst, pp. 162–71.

Ivanov, A. (2001), 'The Crystallization of European Identities: The Bulgarian Case', in Drulák, P. (ed.), *National and European Identities in EU Enlargement: Views from Central and Eastern Europe*, Prague: Institute of International Relations, pp. 161–78.

Klaus, V. (2003), Projev při obědě podávaném prezidentem Rauem, Berlín, zámek Bellevue, 10.4.2003, http://www.klaus.cz/klaus2/asp/clanek.asp?id=7SqFVdjxYhIQ.

Königová, L. (2004), 'Geneticky modifikované organizace? Twinning jako příklad transnacionální interakce', *Mezinárodní vztahy*, **39** (1), 7–26.

Kopecký, P. and Mudde, C. (2002), 'Two Sides of Euroscepticism. Party Positions on European Integration in East Central Europe', *European Union Politics*, **3** (3), 297–326.

Krzeminski, I. (2001), 'The National Identity and European Consciousness of Poles', in Drulák, P. (ed.), *National and European Identities in EU Enlargement: Views from Central and Eastern Europe*, Prague: Institute of International Relations, pp. 57–68.

Lippert, B., Umbach, G. and Wessels, W. (2001a), 'Europeanization of CEE Executives: EU Membership Negotiations as a Shaping Power', *Journal of European Public Policy*, **8** (6), 980–1012.

Lippert, B., Hughes, K., Grabbe, H. and Becker, P. (2001b), *British and German Interests in EU Enlargement*, London: The Royal Institute of International Affairs.

Ludlow, P. (2004), *The Making of the New Europe: The European Councils in Brussels and Copenhagen 2002*, Brussels: EuroComment.

Majcen, B. (1999), 'Measurement of Costs and Benefits of Accession to the EU for Selected CEECs: Country Report Slovenia', *Research Reports*, 256, Vienna: The Vienna Institute for Comparative Economic Studies.

Marek, D. and Baun, M. (2002), 'The EU as a Regional Actor: The Case of the Czech Republic', *Journal of Common Market Studies*, **40** (5), 895–920.

Mayhew, A. (1998), *Recreating Europe: The European Union's Policy Towards Central and Eastern Europe*, Cambridge: Cambridge University Press.

Meyer-Sahling, J.-H. (2001), 'Getting on Track: Civil Service Reform in Post-Communist Hungary', *Journal of European Public Policy*, **8** (6), 960–79.

Moravcsik, A. (1998), *The Choice for Europe: Social Purpose and State Power from Messina to Maastricht*, Ithaca, NY: Cornell University Press.

Plavšak, K. (2001), 'Coming Home to Europe: The Reconstruction of Slovene National Identity in Relation to Europe', in Drulák, P. (ed.), *National and European Identities in EU Enlargement: Views from Central and Eastern Europe*, Prague: Institute of International Relations, pp. 79–94.

Ray, J.L. (1992), *Global Politics*, 5th edn, Boston, MA: Houghton Mifflin.

Schimmelfennig, F. (1998), 'The Community Trap: Liberal Norms, Rhetorical Action, and the Eastern Enlargement of the European Union', *International Organization*, **55** (1), 47–80.

Schimmelfennig, F. and Sedelmeier, U. (2002), 'Theorizing EU Enlargement: Research Focus, Hypotheses, and the State of Research', *Journal of European Public Policy*, **9** (4), 500–528.

Telička, P. and Barták, K. (2003), *Kterak jsme vstupovali*, Praha: Paseka.
Vinogradnaite, I. (2001), 'The Construction of National and European Identity in Lithuania', in Drulák, P. (ed.), *National and European Identities in EU Enlargement: Views from Central and Eastern Europe*, Prague: Institute of International Relations, pp. 95–112.

CHAPTER 4

Ágh, A. (1998), *The Politics of Central Europe*, London: Sage.
Andonova, L.B. (2005), 'The Europeanization of Environmental Policy in Central and Eastern Europe', in Schimmelfennig, F. and Sedelmeier, U. (eds), *The Europeanization of Central and Eastern Europe*, Ithaca, NY: Cornell University Press, in press.
Avery, G. (2004), 'The Enlargement Negotiations', in Cameron, F. (ed.), *The Future of Europe. Integration and Enlargement*, London: Routledge, pp. 35–62.
Brusis, M. (2003), 'Instrumentalized Conditionality: Regionalization in the Czech Republic and Slovakia', paper presented at the workshop 'The Europeanization of Central and Eastern Europe', European University Institute, Florence, 4–5 July.
Bruszt, L. and Stark, D. (2003), 'Who Counts? Supranational Norms and Societal Needs', *East European Politics and Societies*, **17** (1), 74–82.
Grabbe, H. (2001), 'How Does Europeanization Affect CEE Governance? Conditionality, Diffusion and Diversity', *Journal of European Public Policy*, **8** (6), 1013–31.
Grabbe, H. (2005), 'Regulating the Flow of People', in Schimmelfennig, F. and Sedelmeier, U. (eds), *The Europeanization of Central and Eastern Europe*, Ithaca, NY: Cornell University Press.
Grzymala-Busse, A. and Innes, A. (2003), 'Great Expectations: The EU and Domestic Political Competition in East Central Europe', *East European Politics and Societies*, **17** (1), 64–73.
Ham, P. van (1993), *The EC, Eastern Europe and European Unity. Discord, Collaboration and Integration Since 1947*, London: Pinter.
Jacoby, W. (2005), 'External Incentives and Lesson-Drawing in Regional Policy and Health Care', in Schimmelfennig, F. and Sedelmeier, U. (eds), *The Europeanization of Central and Eastern Europe*, Ithaca, NY: Cornell University Press.
Jasiewicz, K. (1998), 'Elections and Voting Behaviour', in White, S., Batt, J. and Lewis, P.G. (eds), *Developments in Central and East European Politics*, Basingstoke: Macmillan, pp. 166–87.

Kaldor, M. and Vejvoda, I. (1999), 'Democratization in Central and Eastern European Countries: An Overview', in Kaldor, M. and Vejvoda, I. (eds), *Democratization in Central and Eastern Europe*, London: Pinter, pp. 1–24.

Kelley, J.G. (2004), *Ethnic Politics in Europe. The Power of Norms and Incentives*, Princeton, NJ: Princeton University Press.

Kopstein, J. and Reilly, D. (2000), 'Geographic Diffusion and the Transformation of the Postcommunist World', *World Politics*, **53** (1), 1–37.

Kubicek, P.J. (ed.) (2003), *The European Union and Democratization*, London: Routledge.

Lavenex, S. (1998), '"Passing the Buck": European Union Refugee Policies towards Central and Eastern Europe', *Journal of Refugee Studies*, **11** (2), 126–45.

Majone, G. (1996), *Regulating Europe*, London: Routledge.

Maniokas, K. (2002), 'EU Enlargement and Europeanization: When a Patchwork Becomes a Blueprint. Summary', mimeo.

March, J. and Olsen, J. (1989), *Rediscovering Institutions. The Organizational Basis of Politics*, New York: Free Press.

McFaul, M. (2002), 'The Fourth Wave of Democracy and Dictatorship. Non-Cooperative Transitions in the Postcommunist World', *World Politics*, **54** (2), 212–44.

Pravda, A. (2001), 'Introduction', in Zielonka, J. and Pravda, A. (eds), *Democratic Consolidation in Eastern Europe. Volume 2: International and Transnational Factors*, Oxford: Oxford University Press, pp. 1–27.

Reus-Smit, C. (1997), 'The Constitutional Structure of International Society and the Nature of Fundamental Institutions', *International Organization*, **51** (4), 555–89.

Risse, T. and Sikkink, K. (1999), 'The Socialization of International Human Rights Norms into Domestic Practices: Introduction', in Risse, T., Ropp, S.C. and Sikkink, K. (eds), *The Power of Human Rights. International Norms and Domestic Political Change*, Cambridge: Cambridge University Press, pp. 1–38.

Schimmelfennig, F. (2000), 'International Socialization in the New Europe. Rational Action in an Institutional Environment', *European Journal of International Relations*, **6** (1), 109–39.

Schimmelfennig, F. (2003), *The EU, NATO and the Integration of Europe. Rules and Rhetoric*, Cambridge: Cambridge University Press.

Schimmelfennig, F. and Sedelmeier, U. (2005a), 'Introduction: Conceptualizing the Europeanization of Central and Eastern Europe', in Schimmelfennig, F. and Sedelmeier, U. (eds), *The Europeanization of*

Central and Eastern Europe, Ithaca, NY: Cornell University Press, in press.

Schimmelfennig, F. and Sedelmeier, U. (2005b), 'Conclusions: The Impact of the EU on the Accession Countries', in Schimmelfennig, F. and Sedelmeier, U. (eds), *The Europeanization of Central and Eastern Europe*, Ithaca, NY: Cornell University Press, in press.

Schimmelfennig, F., Engert, S. and Knobel, H. (2003), 'Cost, Commitment and Compliance: The Impact of EU Democratic Conditionality on Latvia, Slovakia and Turkey', *Journal of Common Market Studies*, **41** (3), 495–518.

Schimmelfennig, F., Engert, S. and Knobel, H. (2005), 'The Impact of EU Political Conditionality', in Schimmelfennig, F. and Sedelmeier U. (eds), *The Europeanization of Central and Eastern Europe*, Ithaca, NY: Cornell University Press, in press.

Sissenich, B. (2002), 'The Diffusion of EU Social and Employment Legislation in Poland and Hungary', in Linden, R.H. (ed.), *Norms and Nannies. The Impact of International Organizations on the Central and East European States*, Lanham, MD: Rowman and Littlefield, pp. 287–315.

Sissenich, B. (2005), 'The Transfer of EU Social Policy to Poland and Hungary', in Schimmelfennig, F. and Sedelmeier, U. (eds), *The Europeanization of Central and Eastern Europe*, Ithaca, NY: Cornell University Press.

Smith, K.E. (2001), 'Western Actors and the Promotion of Democracy', in Zielonka, J. and Pravda, A. (eds), *Democratic Consolidation in Eastern Europe. Volume 2: International and Transnational Factors*, Oxford: Oxford University Press, pp. 31–57.

CHAPTER 5

Ahner, D. (2004), *CAP Reform and EU Enlargement. The Future of European Agricultural Policy*, European Commission, DG Agriculture, Sofia, 14–16 March 2004, available at http://europa.eu.int/comm/agriculture/events/sofia/ahner.pdf, 27 September.

Allen, D. (2000), 'Cohesion and Structural Funds', in Wallace, H. and Wallace, W. (eds), *Policy-Making in the European Union*, Oxford and New York: Oxford University Press, pp. 243–65.

Baldwin, R. and Widgrén, M. (2004), *Council Voting in the Constitutional Treaty: Devil in the Details*, 23 June 2004, available at http://www.cepr.org/content/en/articles/showarticle.php? ArticleID=10, 27 September.

Bengel, B., Boüske, H.-G., Garthe, M., Korte, K.R., Schmucker, O., Schultz, H., Vornbäumen, A. and Weidenfeld, W. (1983), *Nur verpaßte Chancen?*

Die Reformberichte der Europäischen Gemeinschaft, Bonn: Europa Union Verlag.

Blair, T. (2000), 'Superpower not Superstate', speech by British Prime Minister Tony Blair to the Polish Stock Exchange, 6 October.

Brunn, G. (2002), *Die Europäische Einigung von 1945 bis heute*, Stuttgart: Reclam Verlag.

Commission of the European Communities (1979), *Proposal for the Reform of the Commission of the European Communities and its Services (Spierenburg Report)*, 24 September, Luxembourg.

Conference of the Representatives of the Governments of the Member States (2004), *Treaty Establishing a Constitution for Europe*, Brussels, 6 August (CIG 87/04).

Dahrendorf, R. (1979), 'A Third Europe?', Third Jean Monnet Lecture, Florence, 26 November.

Dehaene, J.-L., Weizsäcker, R. von and Simon, D. (1999), *The Institutional Implications of Enlargement. Report to the European Commission*, 18 October.

Dinan, D. (1998), 'The Commission and Enlargement', in Redmond, J. and Rosenthal, G.F. (1998), *The Expanding European Union*, Boulder, CO and London: Lynne Rienner Publishers, pp. 17–41.

Dinan, D. (1999), *Ever Closer Union. An Introduction to European Integration*, second updated edn, Basingstoke: Palgrave.

Edwards, G. (1998), 'The Council of Ministers and Enlargement: A Search for Efficiency, Effectiveness, and Accountability?', in Redmond, J. and Rosenthal, G.F. (1998), *The Expanding European Union*, Boulder, CO and London: Lynne Rienner Publishers, pp. 41–64.

European Commission (1985), *Completing the Internal Market: White Paper from the Commission to the European Council*, COM (85) 310 final.

European Commission (1992), *European Commission Report on the Criteria and Conditions for Accession of New Members to the Community*, in Europe/Documents, 1790, 3 July.

European Commission (1997a), *Agenda 2000: For a Stronger and Wider Union*, COM (97) 2000 final, Vol. I.

European Commission (1997b), *Agenda 2000: The Challenge of Enlargement*, COM (97) 2000 final, Vol. II.

European Commission (2004a), *Communication from the Commission: Building our Common Future: Policy Challenges and Budgetary Means of the Enlarged Union 2007–2013*, COM (2004) 101 final.

European Commission (2004b), *Proposal for a Council Regulation Laying Down General Provisions on the European Regional Development Fund, the European Social Fund and the Cohesion Fund*, COM (2004) 492 final.

European Commission (2004c), *A New Partnership for Cohesion. Convergence, Competitiveness, Cooperation. Third Report on Economic and Social Cohesion*, Brussels: EUR-OP.

European Commission (2004d), *Enlargement and Agriculture,* available at http://europa.eu.int/comm/agriculture/publi/enlarge/text_en.pdf, 27 September.

European Council (1993), *Conclusions of the Presidency, European Council in Copenhagen, 21–22 June 1993*, SN 180/1/93.

European Council (2001), *Conclusions of the Presidency, European Council in Laeken, 14–15 December 2001*, SN 300/1/01.

European Parliament (1992), 'Report of the Committee on Institutional Affairs on the Draft Uniform Electoral Procedure for the Election of Members of the European Parliament', rapporteur: Mr de Gucht, *Official Journal* C 176/72.

European Parliament (1995), *Report on the Functioning of the Treaty on European Union with a View to the 1996 Intergovernmental Conference: Implementation and Development of the Union*, Committee on Institutional Affairs, Co-rapporteurs: Mr Bourlanges and Mr David W. Martin, 4 May 1995, A4–0102/95.

Fischer, Joschka (2000), 'From Confederacy to Federation – Thoughts on the Finality of European Integration', Speech at Humboldt University, Berlin, 12 May.

Fischler, F. (2004), *Enlargement and Agriculture*, European Commission, DG Agriculture, http://europa.eu.int/comm/agriculture/publi/enlarge/text_en.pdf.

Grabitz, E. (ed.) (1984), *Abgestufte Integration. Eine Alternative zum herkömmlichen Integration*, Kehl am Rhein and Straßburg: N.P. Engel Verein.

Hill, C. (2000), *The Geo-political Implications of Enlargement*, EUI Working Paper RSC No. 2000/30, Florence.

Hughes, K. (2004), *Turkey and the European Union: Just Another Enlargement? Exploring the Implications of Turkish Accession*, A Friends of Europe working paper, June 2004, available at http://www.friendsofeurope.org/pdfs/TurkeyandtheEuropeanUnion-WorkingPaperFoE.pdf, 27 September.

Joerges, C., Meny, Y. and Weiler, J. (eds) (2000), *The Fischer Debate*, Harvard Law School 2000, Jean Monnet Working Paper 7/00.

Jopp, M. (2002), *Germany's European Policy: Perceptions in Key Partner Countries*, Bonn: Europa Union Verlag.

Jopp, M., Lippert, B. and Schneider, H. (eds) (2001), *Das Vertragswerk von Nizza und die Zukunft der Europäischen Union*, Bonn.

Josling, T. (1998), 'Can the CAP Survive Enlargement to the East?', in Redmond, J. and Rosenthal, G.F. (eds), *The Expanding European Union*, Boulder, CO and London: Lynne Rienner Publishers, pp. 89–106.

Keohane, R.O. and Hoffmann, S. (1991), *The New European Community. Decision-Making and Institutional Change*, Boulder, CO and Oxford: Westview Press.

Kerremans, B. (1998), 'The Political and Institutional Consequences of Widening: Capacity and Control in an Enlarged Council', in Laurent, P.-H. and Maresceau, M. (eds) (1998), *The State of the European Union. Vol. 4. Deepening and Widening*, Boulder, CO and London: Lynne Rienner Publishers, pp. 87–109.

Laffan, B. and Shackleton, M. (2000), 'The Budget', in Wallace, H. and Wallace, W. (eds) (2000), *Policy-Making in the European Union*, Oxford and New York: Oxford University Press, pp. 211–41.

Lippert, B. (2004), 'Glanzloser Arbeitserfolg von epochaler Bedeutung: Eine Bilanz der EU-Erweiterungspolitik 1989–2004', in Lippert, B. (ed.) (2004), *Bilanz und Folgeprobleme der EU-Erweiterung*, Baden-Baden, Germany: Nomos, pp. 13–71.

Lippert, B. and Umbach, G. (2004) 'EU-Beitritt als Herausforderung für die Verwaltungen in Mittel- und Osteuropa: Uniformer Europäisierungsdruck – individuelle Entwicklungspfade', in Lippert, B. (ed.) (2004), *Bilanz und Folgeprobleme der EU-Erweiterung*, Baden-Baden: Nomos, pp. 111–38.

Maurer, A. (2000), 'Die institutionelle Ordnung einer größeren Europäischen Union – Optionen zur Wahrung der Handlungsfähigkeit', in Lippert, B. (ed.) (2000), *Osterweiterung der Europäischen Union – die doppelte Reifeprüfung*, Bonn: Europa Union Verlag, pp. 31–59.

Maurer, A. (2004), *Ordnung, Effizienz und Demokratie. Verfahren und Normenhierarchie im Verfassungsvertrag*, Diskussionspapier, Stiftung Wissenschaft und Politik, Berlin.

Neunreither, K. (1998), 'The European Parliament and Enlargement, 1973–2000', in Redmond, J. and Rosenthal, G.F. (eds), *The Expanding European Union*, Boulder, CO and London: Lynne Rienner Publishers, pp. 65–88.

Nugent, N. (2003), *The Government and Politics of the European Union. Institutional Dynamics and Prospects for Democracy*, Basingstoke, UK and New York: Macmillan.

Pinder, J. (1991), *European Community. The Building of a Union*, Oxford and New York: Oxford University Press.

Preston, C. (1997), *Enlargement and Integration in the European Union*, London and New York: Routledge.

Redmond, J. and. Rosenthal, G.F. (1998), 'Introduction', in Redmond, J. and Rosenthal, G.F. (eds), *The Expanding European Union*, Boulder, CO and London: Lynne Rienner Publishers, pp. 1–14.

Scharrer, H.-E. (1984), 'Abgestufte Integration – Eine Einführung', in Grabitz, E. (ed.) (1984), *Abgestufte Integration. Eine Alternative zum herkömmlichen Integration*, Kehl am Rhein and Straßburg: N.P. Engel Verein, pp. 1–30.

Schäuble, W. and Lamers, K. (1994), *Überlegungen zur Europäischen Politik*, Bonn, 1 September.

Schimmelfennig, F. (2003), *The EU, NATO, and the Integration of Europe: Rules and Rhethoric*, Cambridge: Cambridge University Press.

Schröder, G. and Blair, Tony (2002), *Reform of the European Council. Joint Letter to Prime Minister Aznar*, 25 February 2002.

Sedelmeier, U. (2000), 'East of Amsterdam: The Implications of the Amsterdam Treaty for Eastern Enlargement', in Neunreither, K. and Wiener, A. (eds), *European Integration After Amsterdam*, Oxford and New York: Oxford University Press, pp. 218–36.

Spence, D. (1991), *Enlargement without Accession: The EC's Response to German Unification*, RIIA Discussion Paper No. 36, London.

Tindemans Report (1976), 'European Union. Report by Mr Leo Tindemans, Prime Minister of Belgium, to the European Council', *Bulletin of the European Communities*, Supplement 1/76.

Wallace, H. (1985), *Europe: The Challenge of Diversity*, Chatham House Papers No. 29, London: Routledge & Kegan Paul.

Wallace, H. and Wallace, W. (1995), *Flying Together in a Larger and More Diverse European Union*, Working Documents W 87, Netherlands Scientific Council for Government Policy, The Hague, June.

Wessels, W. (2004), 'Die institutionelle Architektur der EU nach der Europäischen Verfassung: Höhere Entscheidungsdynamik – neue Koalitionen?', *Integration*, 3, Baden-Baden: Nomos, pp. 161–75.

Wiener, A. (2004), 'Die Verfassung Europas: Konturen eines europäischen Konstitutionalismus', *Integration*, 3, Baden-Baden: Nomos, pp. 176–85.

CHAPTER 6

Allin, D.H. (2004), 'The Atlantic Crisis of Confidence', *International Affairs*, **80** (4), 649–63.

Allot-Marie, M. (2005), *Greetings to the Media, NATO Defence Ministers Informal Meeting, Nice, 9 February 2005*, http://www.defense.gov.

Anderson, J. and Goodman, J. (1994), 'Mars or Minerva? A United Germany in a Post-Cold War Europe', in Keohane, R., Nye, J. and Hoffmann, S. (eds) (1994), *After the Cold War: International Institutions and State Strategies in Europe, 1989–1991*, Cambridge, MA: Harvard University Press.

Annan, K. (2004), 'Interview with United Nations Secretary General', BBC World Service, 16 September, http://news.bbc.co.uk/1/hi/world/middle_east/3661640.stm.

Bartholomew, R. (1991), 'Bartholomew Memorandum', quoted in Duke, S. (2000), *The Elusive Quest for European Security: from EDC to CFSP*, Basingstoke: Macmillan.

Blair, T. (1999), *NATO, Europe and our Future Security*, http://www.fco.gov.uk/text-only/news/speechtext.

Blair, T. (2003a), *Doorstep Interview by the Prime Minister on the European Union Constitution*, http://www.number-10.gov.uk/output/Page4673.asp.

Blair, T. (2003b), *EU Agreement must be Workable and Effective*, http://www.number10.gov.uk/output/pate4989.asp.

Blair, T. and Bush, G.W. (2003), *UK and US Publish Joint Statement on Multilateralism*, http://www.number-10.gov.uk/output/paage4879.asp.

Borger, J. (2004), 'A Global Intelligence Failure', *Guardian*, 10 July.

Burns, R.N. (2003), *The New NATO: Healing the Rift*, http://www.state.gov/p/eur/rls/rm/2003.

Bush, G.W. (2001a), *Remarks by the President and Prime Minister in Joint Press Conference*, http://www.whitehouse.gov/news/releases/2001.

Bush, G.W. (2001b), Press Availability with President Bush and NATO Secretary General Lord Robertson, http://www.whitehouse.gov/news/releases/2001.

Bush, G.W. (2002), *President's Remarks at the United Nations General Assembly*, http://www.whitehouse.gov/news/releases/2002.

Calleo, D. (1970), *The Atlantic Fantasy*, Baltimore, MD: The Johns Hopkins Press.

Calleo, D.P. (2001), 'Imperial America and its Republican Constitution', in Gardner, H. and Stevanova, R. (eds), *The New Transatlantic Agenda: Facing the Challenges of Global Governance*, London: Ashgate, pp. 7–16.

Cleveland, H. (1970), *NATO: The Transatlantic Bargain*, London: Harper Row.

Cohen, W. (2000a), *36th Munich Conference on Security Policy: European Security and Defence Identity*, http://www.defenselink.mil/speeches.

Cohen, W. (2000b), *Speech at Western European Union's Transatlantic Forum*, http://www.defenselink.mil/speeches.

Cohen, W. (2000c), Press Conference at NATO Headquarters, December 5, United States Department of Defense News Briefing.

Cook, R. (1999), Speech by the Foreign Secretary, House of Commons, 1 December, http://www.fco.gov.uk/news/speechtext.

Cooper, R. (2003), *The Breaking of Nations: Order and Chaos in the Twenty-First Century*, London: Atlantic Books.

Cox, M. (2003), 'Martians and Venutians in the New World Order', *International Affairs*, **79** (3) 523–32.

Crockatt, R. (1996), *The Fifty Years War: The United States and the Soviet Union in World Politics*, London: Routledge.

Daalder, I. (2001), 'Are the United States and Europe Heading for a Divorce?', *International Affairs*, **77** (3), 553–67.

Deighton, A. (1997), *On the Cusp: Britain, Maastricht and European Security*, Working Paper RSC, No. 97/59: European University Institute.

Duke, S. (2003), 'The Hyperpower and the Hype: Reassessing Transatlantic Relations in the Iraqi Context', European Institute of Public Administration Working Paper W/1.

European Commission (2002), *Afghanistan Reconstruction Steering Groups (ARSG) Ministerial Pledging Conference*, Tokyo, 21–22 January 2002, MEMO/02/3, Brussels.

European Council (1999), *Presidency Conclusions Helsinki European Council*, http://europa.eu.int/comm/external_relations/news/12–99.

European Council (2000), *Presidency Conclusions Nice European Council*, http://ue.eu.int/uedocs/cms-data/docs/pressdata.

European Security Strategy (2003), *A Secure Europe in a Better World*, http://europa.

Foreign and Commonwealth Office (1998), *Joint Declaration on European Defence*, http://www.fco.gov.uk/text.

Freedman, L. (ed.) (2002), *Superterrorism: Policy Responses*, London: Blackwell Publishing.

Gardner, H. and Stefanova, R. (eds) (2001), *The New Transatlantic Agenda: Facing the Challenges of Global Governance*, Aldershot: Ashgate.

Gellman, B. and Pincus, W. (2003), Iraq's Nuclear File: Inside the Pre-war Debate, 'Depiction of Threat Outgrew Supporting Evidence', *Washington Post*, 10 August, p. A1.

Ginsberg, R.H. (2001), *The European Union in International Politics: Baptism by Fire*, Oxford: Rowman and Littlefield.

Hoffman, B. (2004), *Insurgency and Counterinsurgency in Iraq*, Occasional Paper, Santa Monica, CA: RAND: National Security Research Division.

Hoffmann, S. (2003), 'US–European Relations: Past and Future', *International Affairs*, **79** (5), 1029–35.

Holbrooke, R. (1999), *To End a War*, New York: McGraw-Hill.

Howard, M. (1995), 'Ethnic Conflict and International Security', *Nations and Nationalism*, **1** (3), 285–95.

Howorth, J. (2000), 'Britain, France and the European Defence Initiative', *Survival*, **42** (2), 33–55.

Howorth, J. (2003), 'France, Britain and the Euro-Atlantic Crisis', **45** (4), November, 173–92.

Howorth, J. (2004a), 'Discourse, Ideas and Epistemic Communities in European Security and Defence Policy', *West European Politics*, **27** (2), 211–34.

Howorth, J. (2004b), 'The European Draft Constitutional Treaty and the Future of the European Defence Initiative: A Question of Flexibility', *European Foreign Affairs Review*, **9**, 483–508.

Hunter, R. (2002), *The European Security and Defense Policy: NATO's Companion or Competitor?*, Santa Monica, CA: Rand.

Hyde-Price, A. (2000), *Germany and European Order: Enlarging NATO and the EU*, Manchester: Manchester University Press.

Joffe, J. (1981), 'European–American Relations: The Enduring Crisis', *Foreign Affairs*, **59** (4), 835–51.

Judah, T. (1999), 'Kosovo's Road to War', *Survival*, **41** (2), 5–18.

Judah, T. (2000), *Kosovo: War and Revenge*, New Haven, CT and London: Yale University Press.

Kagan, R. (2003), *Paradise and Power: America and Europe in the New World Order*, London: Atlantic Books.

Kissinger, H. (1965), *The Troubled Partnership: A Re-appraisal of the Atlantic Alliance*, New York: McGraw-Hill.

Litwak, R.S. (2003/04), 'Non-proliferation and the Dilemmas of Regime Change', *Survival*, **45** (4), 7–32.

Loeb, V. (2003), 'Rumsfeld seeks better Intelligence on Iraqi Insurgents', *The Washington Post*, 11 December, p. A43.

Makins, C.J. (2003), *Renewing the Transatlantic Partnership: Why and How?*, Washington, DC: Atlantic Council of the United States.

Menon, A. (2000), *France, NATO and the Limits of Independence 1981–1997*, Basingstoke: Macmillan.

Menon, A. (2004), 'From Crisis to Catharsis: ESDP after Iraq', *International Affairs*, **80** (4), 631–48.

Mettler, A. (2001), *From Junior Partner to Global Player? The New Transatlantic Agenda and Joint Action Plan*, Discussion Paper, Bonn: Centre for European Integration Studies.

Moravsik, A. (2003), 'Striking a New Transatlantic Bargain', *Foreign Affairs*, **82** (4) 74–89.

NATO Security General and the EU Presidency (2003), *Joint Press Statement*, http://www.state.gov/p/eur/rls/prsrl/2003/26890.htm.

North Atlantic Council (1990), *London Declaration on a Tranformed North Atlantic Alliance*, Brussels: NATO Office of Information and Press.

North Atlantic Council (1991a), 'The Alliance's Strategic Concept', in *NATO Handbook 1995*, Brussels: NATO Office of Information and Press.

North Atlantic Council (1991b), 'Declaration on Peace and Cooperation', *NATO Communiqués 1991–1995*, Brussels: NATO Office of Information and Press.

North Atlantic Council (1994), *Declaration of Heads of State and Government Participating in the Meeting of the North Atlantic Council, Brussels*, Press Communiqué M-1 (94), 3.

North Atlantic Council (1996), *Ministerial Meeting of the North Atlantic Council*, Berlin, Brussels: NATO Office of Information and Press.

North Atlantic Council (1999), *Washington Summit Communiqué*, NATO Press Release NAC-S (99), 64.

NSC68 (1950), 'National Security Council Paper No. 68', in Maidment, R. and Dawson, M. (eds) (1994), *The United States in the Twentieth Century: Key Documents*, London: Hodder and Stoughton.

NSS (2002), *The National Security Strategy of the United States of America*. The White House, available at www.whitehouse.gov/nsc/nss.html.

Nye, J. (2002–2003), 'Limits of American Power', *Political Science Quarterly*, **117** (4), 545–59.

Patten, C. (2002), *Iraq: Speech by the Rt Hon Chris Patten, European Parliament, Plenary Session*, http://europa.eu.int/comm/external-relations/news/patten/sp.2.

Peterson, J. (2004), 'America as a European Power: The End of Empire by Integration?', *International Affairs*, **80** (4), 613–29.

Peterson, J. and Pollack, M. (2003), *Europe, America and Bush: Transatlantic Relations in the Twenty-First Century*, London: Routledge.

Pew Research Centre for the People and the Press (2004), *Bush Margin Widens Again, Despite Vulnerabilities*, 28 September, http://people-press.org.

Pollack, M. (2003), 'Unilateral America, Multilateral Europe?', in Peterson, J. and Pollack, M. (2003), *Europe, America, Bush: Transatlantic Relations in the Twenty-First Century*, London: Routledge.

Polling Report (2004), *Iraq*, www.pollingreport.com/iraq.htm.

Powell, C. (2003), 'Powell Presents US Case to Security Council of Iraq's Failure to Disarm', *UN News Centre*, 5 February, http://www.un.org/News/.

Robertson, G. (1999), *Speech to the Annual Session of the NATO Parliamentary Assembly Amsterdam*, http://www.nato.int/docu/speech/1999.

Schake, K., Bloch-Lainé, A. and Grant, C. (1999), 'Building a European Defence Capability', *Survival*, **41** (1), 20–40.

Schulzinger, R.D. (2002), *US Diplomacy Since 1900*, New York and Oxford: Oxford University Press.

Select Committee on Intelligence (2004), 'Report on the US Intelligence Community's Pre-War Intelligence Assessments on Iraq', Select Committee on Intelligence, United States Senate, 108th Congress, http://intelligence.senate.gov/iraqreport2.pdf.

Stavenhagen, R. (1998), 'Ethnic Conflicts and their Impact on International Society', *International Social Science Journal*, **157**, 433–45.

Stevanova, R. (2001), 'Balkan Clutter: American and European Handling of a Powder Keg', in Gardner, H. and Stevanova, R. (eds), *The New Transatlantic Agenda: Facing the Challenges of Global Governance*, London: Ashgate, pp. 81–101.

Tenet, G.J. (2004), 'Remarks by Director of Central Intelligence Agency George J. Tenet to Employees of the Central Intelligence Agency and US Intelligence Community', Central Intelligence Agency, Press Releases and Statements, 3 June, http://www.cia.gov/public_affairs/press_release/2004/pr06032004.

Thomas, R. (1999), *Serbia Under Milosevic: Politics in the 1990s*, London: Hurst.

Treverton, G. (1985), *Making the Alliance Work: The United States and Western Europe*, London: Macmillan.

Vedrine, H. (2002), 'Speech' quoted in Hiro, D. (2002), *War Without End*, London: Routledge.

Vulliamy, E. (ed.) (1994), *Seasons in Hell: Understanding Bosnia's War*, New York: St Martin's Press.

WEU (1992), *Petersberg Declaration*, WEU: Press and Information Service.

Wijk, R. (1997), *NATO on the Brink of the New Millennium*, London: Brassey's.

Wörner, M. (1991), The Atlantic Alliance in a New Era', *NATO Review*, **39** (1), 1–10.

CHAPTER 7

Ainger, K. (2003), 'Sweet Nothings in Cancun', *New Internationalist*, **363**, 20–21.

Ainger, K. (2004), 'The Scramble for Africa', *New Internationalist*, **367**, 9–12.

Albert, M. (1993), *Capitalism against Capitalism*, trans. Paul Haviland, London: Whurr.

Amin, A. (1994), *Post-Fordism: A Reader*, Oxford: Blackwell.

Amin, S. (1977), *Imperialism and Unequal Development*, Hassocks: Harvester Press.

Anon. (2003), 'Tricks of the Trade', *New Internationalist*, **353**, p. 16.

Armstrong, P., Glyn, A. and Harrison, J. (1991), *Capitalism Since 1945*, Oxford: Oxford University Press.

Arrighi, G. (1982), 'A Crisis of Hegemony', in Amin, S., Arrighi, G., Frank, A.G. and Wallerstein, I. (eds), *Dynamics of Global Crisis*, London: Macmillan.

Atkinson, R. and Divoudi, S. (2000), 'The Concept of Social Exclusion in the European Union: Context, Development and Possibilities', *Journal of Common Market Studies*, **38** (3), 427–47.

Bauman, Z. (1998), *Globalization: The Human Consequences*, Cambridge: Polity.

Beland, D. and Hanson, R. (2000), 'Reforming the French Welfare State: Solidarity, Social Exclusion and the Three Crises of Citizenship', *West European Politics*, **23** (1), 47–64.

Biel, R. (2000), *The New Imperialism: Crisis and Contradictions in North–South Relations*, London: Zed.

Boyer, R. (1978), *Accumulation, Inflation, Crises*, Paris: Presses Universitaires de France.

Bunsha, D. (2003), 'Sugar Daddies', *New Internationalist*, **363**, 14–15.

Burbach, R. (2004), 'Can't Pay, Won't Pay!', *New Internationalist*, **374** December, 26–27.

Burchill, S. (2001a), 'Liberalism' in Burchill, S. et al., *Theories of International Relations*, 2nd edn Basingstoke: Palgrave, pp. 29–69.

Burchill, S. (2001b), 'Realism and Neo-realism', in Burchill, S., Linklater, A., Devetak, R., Donnelly, J., Paterson, M., Reus-Smit, C. and True, J. (eds), *Theories of International Relations*, 2nd edn, Basingstoke: Palgrave, pp. 70–102.

Callinicos, A. (2001), *Against the Third Way: An Anti-Capitalist Critique*, Cambridge: Polity.

Cecchini, P. (1989), *The European Challenge 1992: The Benefits of a Single Market* (The Cecchini Report), Aldershot: Wildwood House.

Cerny, P. (1993), 'American Decline and the Emergence of Embedded Financial Orthodoxy', in Cerny, P. (ed.), *Finance and World Politics: Markets, Regimes and States in a Post-Hegemonic Era*, Aldershot, UK and Brookfield, US: Edward Elgar, pp. 155–85.

Cerny, P. (1996), 'Paradoxes of the Competition State: The Dynamics of Political Globalization', *Government and Opposition*, **32** (2), 251–74.

Coates, D. (1999), 'Models of Capitalism in the New World Order: The UK Case', *Political Studies*, **47**, 643–60.

Crouch, C. and Streeck, W. (eds) (1997), *Political Economy of Modern Capitalism: Mapping Convergence and Diversity*, London: Sage.

Davis, M. (1984), 'The Political Economy of Late-Imperial America', *New Left Review*, **143**, 6–38.

Dicken, P. (2004), *Global Shift*, 4th edn, London: Sage.

Dinan, D. (2004), *Europe Recast: A History of European Union*, Basingstoke: Palgrave.

Dore, R. (2000), 'Will Global Capitalism be Anglo-Saxon Capitalism?', *New Left Review*, **6**, 101–19.

Dos Santos, T. (1970), 'The Structure of Dependence', *American Economic Review*, **60**, 231–6.

Economist Survey (1998), 'A Survey of World Trade – Where Next?', *Economist*, 3 October.

Economist Survey (1999), 'A Survey of France – The Grand Illusion', *Economist*, 5 June.

Economist Survey (2000), 'A Survey of European Business – Lean, Mean and European', *Economist*, 29 April.

Economist Survey (2001), 'A Survey of Globalization – Globalization and its Critics', *Economist*, 29 September.

Economist Survey (2002), 'A Survey of France – A Divided Self', *Economist*, 16 November.

Economist Survey (2003), 'A Survey of Global Finance – A Cruel Sea of Capital', *Economist*, 3 May.

Economist Survey (2004a), 'A Survey of Ireland – The Luck of the Irish', *Economist*, 16 October.

Economist Survey (2004b), 'A Survey of Sub-Saharan Africa – How to Make Africa Smile', *Economist*, 17 January.

Elwood, W. (2004), 'The World Trading System is Corrupt and Unjust', *New Internationalist*, December, 9–11.

Esping-Anderson, G. (1990), *The Three Worlds of Welfare Capitalism*, Cambridge: Cambridge University Press.

Europa (a) 'Bilateral trade relations – USA', available at: www.europa.eu.int/comm./trade/issues/bilateral/countries/usa/index_en.htm, date accessed: 28 March 2005.

Europa (b) 'Bilateral trade relations', Available at: http://www.europa.eu.int/comm/trade/issues/bilateral/index_en.htm, date accessed: 28 March 2005.

Europa (c) 'Corporate Social Responsibility', available at: www.europa.eu.int/comm./trade/issues/global/csr/index_en.htm, date accessed: 28 March 2005.

Europa (d) 'Trade and Social Conditions', available at: www.europa.eu.int/comm./trade/issues/global/social/index_en.htm, date accessed: 28 March 2005.

Europa (e) 'Trade and Development', available at: www.europa.eu.int/comm./trade/isssues/global/development/index_en.htm, date accessed: 28 March 2005.

Europa (f) 'Generalised System of Preferences', available at: www.europa.eu.int/comm./trade/issues/global/gsp/index_en.htm, date accessed: 28 March 2005.

Europa (g) 'ACP and EU: A Long and Preferential Relationship', available at: www.europa.eu.int/comm./trade/issues/bilateral/regions/acp/lprel_en.htm, date accessed: 28 March 2005.

Europa (h) 'Negotiations of Economic Partnership Agreements', available at: www.europa.eu.int/comm./trade/issues/bilateral/regions/acp/lprel_en.htm, date accessed: 28 March 2005.

Europa (i) 'Textiles – What's New', available at: www.trade-info.cec.eu.int/textiles/index.cfm, date accessed: 28 March 2005.

Europa (j) 'Changes in EU Agricultural Policy', available at: www.europa.eu.int/comm./trade/issues/sectoral/agri_fish/agri/apt_en.htm, date accessed: 28 March 2005.

Europa (k) 'Trade in Agricultural Goods and Fishery Products', available at: www.europa.eu.int/comm./trade/issues/sectoral/agri_fish/agri/apt_en.htm, date accessed: 28 March 2005.

Europa (l) 'New Round Negotiations on Trade and Competition', available at www.europa.eu.int/comm./trade/issues/sectoral/competition/index_en.htm.

European Central Bank (2005), 'Review of the International Role of the Euro', available at: www.ecb.int/pub/pdf/other/euro-international-role2005en.pdf.

European Commission (2004), *Facing the Challenge: The Lisbon Strategy for Growth and Employment* (Report from the High Level Group chaired by Wim Kok), Luxembourg: Office for Official Publications of the European Commission.

Ferrera, M. and Gualmini, M. (2000), 'Reforms Guided By Consensus', *West European Politics*, **23** (2), 187–208.

Frank, A.G. (1978), *Dependent Accumulation and Underdevelopment*, London: Macmillan.

Gerschenkron, A. (1962), *Economic Backwardness in Historical Perspective*, Cambridge, MA: Belknap Press.

Gill, S. (1998), 'European Governance and New Constitutionalism: Economic and Monetary Union and Alternatives to Disciplinary Neo-liberalism in Europe', *New Political Economy*, **3** (1), 5–26.

Gill, S. and Law, D. (1998), 'Global Hegemony and the Structural Power of Capital', in Gill, S. (ed.), *Gramsci, Historical Materialism and International Relations*, Cambridge: Cambridge University Press.
Gilpin, R. (1995), 'Three Ideologies of Political Economy', in Kegley, C. and Wittkopf, E. (eds), *The Global Agenda: Issues and Perspectives*, 4th edn, New York: McGraw-Hill, pp. 141–58.
Grahl, J. (2001), 'Social Europe and the Governance of Labour Relations', in Thompson, G. (ed.), *Governing the European Economy*, London: Sage, pp. 133–64.
Grahl, J. (2003), 'Globalized Finance: The Challenge to the Euro', *New Left Review*, **8**, 23–48.
Green-Pederson, C. (2001), 'The Puzzle of Dutch Welfare State Retrenchment', *West European Politics*, **24** (3), 135–49.
Haas, E. (1958), *The Uniting of Europe: Political, Social and Economic Forces 1950–57*, Stanford, CA: Stanford University Press.
Habermas, J. (1999), 'The European Nation-State and the Pressures of Globalization', *New Left Review*, **235**, 46–59.
Hall, P. (1986), *Governing* the *Economy: The Politics of State Intervention in Britain and France*, Cambridge: Polity.
Hamilton, A. (2003), Excerpts from 'Report on Manufactures', in Roe, G.C., Cronin, P. and Dash, K. (eds), *International Political Economy*, 2nd edn, Basingstoke: Palgrave, pp. 85–98.
Hanson, B. (1998), 'Whatever Happened to Fortress Europe? External Trade Policy Liberalization in the European Union', *International Organization*, **32** (1), 55–85.
Hart, J. (1992), *Rival Capitalists: International Competitiveness in the United States, Japan and Western Europe*, Ithaca, NY: Cornell University Press.
Haseler, S. (2004), *The New Europe and Its Challenge to America*, London and New York: IB Tauris.
Hayward, J. (1986), *The State and the Market Economy: Industrial Patriotism and Economic Intervention in France*, Brighton: Wheatsheaf.
Held, D., McGrew, A.G., Goldblatt, D. and Perraton, J. (1999), *Global Transformations: Politics, Economics, Culture*, Cambridge: Polity.
Henderson, J. (1993), 'The Role of the State in the Economic Transformation of East Asia', in Dixon, C. and Drakakis-Smith, F. (eds), *Economic and Social Development in Pacific Asia*, London: Routledge, pp. 85–110.
HSBC (2003), 'The Euro as a Reserve Currency: Limits and Limitations', available at http://www.eurolegal.org/yurp/eurocurr.htm.
Hutton, W. (1995), *The State We're In*, London: Jonathan Cape.
Jessop, B. (1991), 'Thatcherism and Flexibility: The White Heat of a Post-Fordist Revolution', in Jessop, B., Kastendiek, H., Nielsen, K. and

Pedersen, O.K. (eds), *The Politics of Flexibility: Restructuring State and Industry in Britain, Germany and Scandinavia*, Aldershot, UK and Brookfield, US: Edward Elgar, pp. 135–61.

Jochem, S. (2000), 'Nordic Labour Market Policies in Transition', *West European Politics*, **23** (3), 115–38.

Johnson, C. (1982), *MITI and the Japanese Miracle: The Growth of Industrial Policy 1925–1975*, Stanford, CA: Stanford University Press.

Katzenstein, P. (1985), *Small States in World Markets: Industrial Policy in Europe*, Ithaca, NY: Cornell University Press.

Krugman, P. (ed.) (1986), *Strategic Trade Policy and the New International Economics*, London: Cambridge, MA: MIT Press.

Krugman, P. (1996), *Pop Internationalism*, Cambridge, MA and London: MIT Press.

Kuhnle, S. (2000), 'The Scandinavian Welfare State in the 1990s: Challenged but Viable', *West European Politics*, **23** (2), 209–28.

Lash, S. and Urry, J. (1987), *The End of Organized Capitalism*, Cambridge: Polity.

Ledebur, K. (2004), 'Ring of Fire', *New Internationalist*, December, 24–5.

Linklater, A. (2001), 'Marxism', in Burchill, S., Linklater, A., Devetak, R., Donnelly, J., Paterson, M., Reus-Smit, C. and True, J. (eds) (2001), *Theories of International Relations*, 2nd edn, Basingstoke: Palgrave, pp. 129–55.

Lochner, D. (1999), 'Embedded Liberalism, Disembedded Markets: Reconceptualising Pax Americana', *New Political Economy*, **4** (3), 343–59.

Loomba, A. (1998), *Colonialism/Postcolonialism*, London: Routledge.

McVeigh, P. (1999), 'Globalization and National Economic Strategy: The Case of Spain', *Journal of European Area Studies*, **7** (1), 74–90.

Meidner, R. (1992), 'The Rise and Fall of the Swedish Model', *Studies in Political Economy*, **39**, 159–71.

Menz, G. (2003), 'Reregulating the Single Market: National Varieties of Capitalism and their Responses to Europeanization', *Journal of European Public Policy*, **10** (4), 532–55.

Modelski, G. (2003), 'Globalization', in Held, D. and McGrew, J. (eds), *The Global Transformations Reader: An Introduction to the Globalization Debate*, 2nd edn, Cambridge: Polity, pp. 55–9.

Moravcsik, A. (1998), *The Choice for Europe: Social Purpose and State Power from Messina to Maastricht*, Ithaca, NY: Cornell University Press.

Nolke, A. (1999), 'Transnational Economic Relations and National Models of Capitalism: Institutional Investors and the "Disembedding" of German Corporate Finance', unpublished paper presented at ECPR Joint Sessions of Workshops, 26–31 March 1999, Mannheim, Germany.

Olson, M. (1982), *The Rise and Decline of Nations: Economic Growth, Stagflation and Social Rigidities*, London and New Haven, CT: Yale University Press.

Padoa-Schioppa, T. (2002), 'Reserve Currencies: New Choices', available at: www.frankfurt-ebc.de/pdf/padoa-schioppa_2002.pdf.

Palier, B. (2000), 'Defrosting the French Welfare State', *West European Politics*, **23** (2), 113–36.

Perez, S. (2000), 'From Decentralization to Reorganization: Explaining the Return to National Bargaining in Italy and Spain', *Comparative Politics*, **32** (4), 437–58.

Petitbò, A. (1993), 'Globalización, Política Industrial y Competencia', *Economía Industrial*, **292**, 15–30.

Portillo, M. (2005), 'The Escape Door's Open but Blair Stays on as EU Hostage', *Sunday Times*, 27 March, p. 17.

Ransom, D. (1999), 'Banana Split', *New Internationalist*, **317**, 7–10.

Ransom, D. (2000), 'Fair Trade – Small Change, Big Difference', *New Internationalist*, **322**, 9–12.

Redwood, J. (2001), *Stars and Strife: The Coming Conflicts Between the USA and the European Union*, Basingstoke: Macmillan.

Rodney, W. (1982), *How Europe Underdeveloped Africa*, Washington, DC: Howard University Press.

Rodrik, D. (2003), 'Has Globalization Gone Too Far?', in Held, D. and McGrew, J. (eds), *The Global Transformations Reader: An Introduction to the Globalization Debate*, Cambridge: Polity, pp. 379–83.

Salmon, K. (2000), 'The Spanish Economy: From the Single Market to EMU', *Mediterranean Politics*, **5** (2), 17–43.

Schmidt, V. (2002), *The Futures of European Capitalism*, Oxford: Oxford University Press.

Smith, A. (2003), 'Excerpts from "The Wealth of Nations"', in Roe, G.C., Cronin, P. and Dash, K. (eds), *International Political Economy*, 2nd edn, Basingstoke: Palgrave, pp. 33–48.

Stiglitz, J. (2002), *Globalization and its Discontents*, London: Penguin.

Strange, S. (1986), *Casino Capitalism*, Oxford: Basil Blackwell.

Streeck, W. (1999), 'German Capitalism: Does it Exist? Can it Survive?', *New Political Economy*, **2** (2), 237–56.

Streeck, W. and Schmitter, P. (1991), 'From National Corporatism to Transnational Pluralism: Organized Interests in the Single European Market', *Politics and Society*, **19** (1), 133–64.

Therborn, G. (1987), 'Does Corporatism Really Matter? The Economic Crisis and Issues of Political Theory', *Journal of Public Policy*, **7** (3), 259–84.

Tsoukalis, L. (1997), *The New European Economy Revisited*, Oxford: Oxford University Press.
van Apeldoorn, B. (2002), *Transnational Capitalism and the Struggle over European Integration*, London and New York: Routledge.
van der Pijl, K. (1984), *The Making of an Atlantic Ruling Class*, London: Verso.
van der Pijl, K. (1998), *Transnational Classes and International Relations*, London and New York: Routledge.
Wade, R. (1990), *Governing the Market: Economic Theory and the Role of Government in East Asian Industrialism*, Princeton, NJ: Princeton University Press.
Warren, B. (1980), *Imperialism: Pioneer of Capitalism*, London: Verso.
WTO (n.d.), 'Trade Statistics', available at: http://www.wto.org/english/res_e/statis_e/statis_e.htm, date accessed: 11 November 2004.

CHAPTER 8

Arbatova, N.K., Gutnik, V.P., Khesin, E.S., Yudanov, Y. (eds) (2003), *Rasshirenie ES na Vostok: Preposylki, Problemy, Posledstviya*, Moscow: Nauka.
Archer, C. (2000), *The European Union: Structure and Process*, London: Continuum.
Averre, D. and Cottey, A. (eds) (2002), *New Security Challenges in Postcommunist Europe: Securing Europe's East*, Manchester: Manchester University Press.
Babaeva, S. (2002), 'Prishli na bazu', *Izvestiya*, **90**, 29 May, p. 1.
Babkin, V. (2002), 'Investitsii tol'ko na gigienu', *Izvestiya*, 29 May, p. 4.
Baranovsky, V. (2000), 'Russia: A Part of Europe or Apart from Europe?', *International Affairs*, **76** (3), 443–58.
Bordachev, T. (2000), 'Russia and the Expanded Europe: New Risks and New Opportunities', *Briefing Papers*, **2** (12), December, Moscow Carnegie Centre. Retrieved on 7/1/04 from http://pubs.carnegie.ru/english/briefings/2000/issue12–00.asp.
Bovt, G. (2002), 'Konkretnoe dzhentl'menskoe soglashenie', *Izvestiya*, 23 November, p. 3.
Burlatskii, F. (2002), 'Voina otlozhena – nadolgo li?', *Izvestiya*, 15 November.
Burns, N., Steinbruner, J., Matlock, J. and Winston, V. (1995), 'Four Years after the Collapse of the USSR', *Post-Soviet Affairs*, **11** (4), October–December, 295–304.

Carr, F. and Flenley, P. (1999), 'NATO and the Russian Federation in the New Europe: The Founding Act on Mutual Relations', *Journal of Communist Studies and Transition Politics*, **15** (2), June, 88–110.

Coalson, R. (2004), 'The End of the Russian Federation', *Russian Political Weekly*, 24 September, Vol. 4, No. 37, http://www.rferl.org/reports/rpw/2004/09/37-240904.asp.

Cottrell, R. (2002), 'Kim Meeting Puts Russia's Balancing Act to the Test', *Financial Times*, 24 August.

Crow, S. (1994), 'Why has Russian Foreign Policy Changed?', *RFE/RL Research Report*, **3** (18), 6 May, pp. 1–6.

Dempsey, J. (2003), 'Moscow Uneasy at Proposals for Bases', *Financial Times*, 15 December.

Denisov, A.I. (2003), 'Non-Visa Regime and the EU', *Diplomaticheskii Vestnik*, 24 July.

EUPolitix.com (2004), *Prodi Defends Offensive EU Beslan Statement*, 6 September, retrieved from http://eupolitix.com/EN/News/200409/aa81f16f-d/b9–4c93-aa7d-elc20925a6c6.htm.

European Commission (2004a), *EU and Russia Confirm the Extension of the PCA to the Enlarged EU*, 27 April, retrieved from http://europa.eu.int/com/external_relations/russia/intro/ip04_549.htm.

European Commission (2004b), *Joint Statement on EU Enlargement and EU–Russia Relations*, 27 April, retrieved from http://europa.eu.int/com.russia/russia_docs/js_elarg270404htm.

European Commission (2004c), *Russia–WTO: EU Russia Deal Brings Russia a Step Closer to WTO Membership*, 21 May, retrieved from http://europa.eu.int/comm.external_relations/russia/intro/ip04_673.htm.

European Commission (2004d), *Communication from the Commission to the Council and the European Parliament on Relations with Russia*, COM (2204) 106, 9/2/04, Brussels.

European Commission (2004e), *The EU's Relations with Russia*, retrieved on 11 August from http://europa.eu.int/com/external_relations/russia/intro/.

Flenley, P. (1998), 'Russia in the New Europe', in Carr, F. (ed.), *Europe: The Cold Divide*, Basingstoke: Macmillan, pp. 105–36.

Foundation for Prospective Studies and Initiatives (2003), *Russian Expert View*, 1 July, p. 14.

Fritch, P. (2002), 'Analysis: New Beginnings', *NATO Review*, Summer, retrieved from http:/nato.int/docu/review/2002/issue_2/English/analysis.html.

Gedmin, J. (2002), 'Transatlantic Ties After 9/11: An American View', *Internationale Politik*, **3**, 13–18.

Gomart, T. (2003), 'Les dilemmas de la coopération: prévention des conflits, gestion des crises et règlement des conflits', in Dov Lynch (ed.), *EU–Russian Security Dimensions*, occasional paper, No. 46, July, Paris: European Union–Institute for Security Studies, pp. 20–41.

Gower, J. (2004), 'Russian Foreign Policy Towards the European Union', in Ross, C. (ed.), *Russian Politics under Putin*, Manchester: Manchester University Press, pp. 236–54.

Grigor'evna, E. (2002), 'Ne v piku Evrope, no zhest budet sil'nyi', *Izvestiya*, 22 November, p. 3.

Herd, G.P. and Aldis, A. (eds) (2003), *Russia and the Regions: Strength through Weakness*, London: Routledge Curzon.

Herd, G. and Moroney, J. (eds) (2003), *Security Dynamics in the Former Soviet Bloc*, London: Routledge Curzon.

Herspring, D. R. (2003), 'Putin and the Armed Forces', in Herspring, D.R. (ed.), *Putin's Russia*, Oxford: Rowman and Littlefield, pp. 155–75.

Hoffman, D. (2002), *The Oligarchs: Wealth and Power in the New Russia*, New York: Public Affairs.

Ivanov, I. (2001), 'The Enlargement of the European Union and Russian Interests', *Contemporary Europe* (Russian Academy of Sciences), **3**, July–September in *Russian Expert View*, 1 July 2003, 24–6.

Ivanov, I. (2003), 'A New Foreign Policy Year for Russia and the World', *International Affairs: A Russian Journal of World Politics, Diplomacy and International Affairs*, **49** (6), 33–8.

Joint Declaration of Germany, France and Russia on Iraq (2003), *Internationale Politik*, **4**, Spring, p. 104.

Jones, A. and Fallon, G. (2003), 'The Political Economy of Cooperation, Trade and Aid between the European Union and Russia', *Journal of Contemporary European Studies*, **11** (2), November, 253–77.

Karaganov, S. (2002), 'Maximizing Russia's Engagement with the West', *Internationale Politik*, **4** (3), Winter issue, 39–43.

Kelin, A. (2004), 'Attitude to NATO Expansion: Calmly Negative', *International Affairs: A Russian Journal of World Politics, Diplomacy and International Affairs*, **50** (1), 17–25.

Kerr, D. (1995), 'The New Eurasianism: The Rise of Geopolitics in Russia's Foreign Policy', *Europe–Asia Studies*, **47** (6), 977–88.

Kleveman, L. (2003), *The New Great Game*, London: Atlantic Books.

Kortunov, S. (2003), 'Kaliningrad and Russia–Europe Partnership', *International Affairs: A Russian Journal of World Politics, Diplomacy and International Affairs*, 111–31.

Kozin, V. (2000), 'The Kremlin and NATO: Prospects for Interaction', *International Affairs: A Russian Journal of World Politics, Diplomacy and International Affairs*, **46** (3), 12–20.

Legvold, R. (2001), 'Russia's Unformed Foreign Policy', *Foreign Affairs*, **80** (5), 62–75.

Lepingwell, J.W.R (1994), 'The Soviet Legacy and Russian Foreign Policy', *RFE/RL Research Report*, **3** (23), 10 June, 1–8.

Light, G., Lowenhardt, J. and White, S. (2000), 'Russian Perspectives on European Security', *European Foreign Affairs Review*, **4**, 489–505.

Mahncke, D. (2001), 'Russia's Attitude to the European Security and Defence Policy', *European Foreign Affairs Review*, **6** (4), Winter, 427–36.

Makarychev, A. (2003), 'One Language, Multiple Discourses: The Kaliningrad Issue as a Russian Speech Act', *Russian Expert Review*, **1**, July, 16–19.

Matser, W. (2001/2002), 'Towards a New Strategic Partnership', *NATO Review*, Winter, 19–21.

McFaul, M. (2003), 'Proekt Putina Pochti Zavershen', *Nezavisimaya gazeta*, 8 December, No. 265.

Mihalka, M. (1994), 'European–Russian Security and NATO's Partnership for Peace', *RFE/RL Research Report*, **3** (33), 26 August, 34–45.

Moroney, J. (2003), 'Western Approaches to Security Cooperation with Central Asian States: Advancing the Euro-Atlantic Security Order in Eurasia', in Herd, G.P. and Moroney, J. (eds), *Security Dynamics in the Former Soviet Bloc*, London: Routledge Curzon, pp. 168–84.

NATO Update (2002), *Lord Robertson in Poland*, 14 February, retrieved from http://nato.int/docu/update/202/eo213a.

NATO (2002), *NATO–Russia Relations*, 11 June, retrieved from http://nato.int/docu/facts/nato-rus.htm.

Olsen, G.R. (2000), 'Promotion of Democracy as a Foreign Policy Instrument of Europe: Limits to International Idealism', *Democratization*, **7** (2), Summer, 142–67.

Parrish, S. (1996), 'Chaos in Foreign Policy Decision-making', *Transition*, **2** (10), 17 May, 30–33, 64.

Piontkovski, A. (2003), 'The Yukos Case', *Russian Foreign and Security Watch*, **44** (4), retrieved on 12 November from http://rferl.org/securitywtach/2003/11/44–051103.html.

Plekhanov, S. (1999), 'NATO Enlargement as an Issue in Russian Politics', in David, Charles-Philippe and Levesque, Jacques (eds), *The Future of NATO: Enlargement, Russia and European Security*, McGill: Queens University Press.

Polikanov, D. and Timmins, G. (2004), 'Russian Foreign Policy under Putin', in Ross, Cameron (ed.), *Russian Politics under Putin*, Manchester: Manchester University Press, pp. 223–35.

Primakov, Ye (2004), 'Saddam Hussein was Advised to Resign and Hold Democratic Elections', *International Affairs: A Russian Journal of World Politics, Diplomacy and International Affairs*, **50** (1), 26–30.

Prodi, R. (2004), *Russia and the European Union: Enduring Ties, Widening Horizons*, European Commission, 23 April, retrieved on 11 August from http://europa/eu.int/comm…rnal_relations/news/prodi/sp04_198.htm.

Puglisi, R. (2003), 'The Normalisation of Russian Foreign Policy', in Herd, G. and Moroney, J. (eds), *Security Dynamics in the Former Soviet Bloc*, London: Routledge Curzon, pp. 63–79.

Russian Foreign Policy and Security Watch, 5 November 2003, Vol. 4, No. 44, http://www.rferl.org/reports/securitywatch/2003/11/44-051103.asp.

Russian Foreign Policy and Security Watch, 21 November 2003, Vol. 4, No. 46, http://www.rferl.org/reports/securitywatch/2003/11/46-211103.asp.

Safonov, A. (2003), 'The World Needs a Global Anti-terrorist System', *International Affairs: A Russian Journal of World Politics, Diplomacy and International Affairs*, 28–34.

Sherr, J. (1996), 'Doomed to Remain a Great Power', *The World Today*, **52** (1), January, 8–9.

Shevtsova, L. (2003), *Putin's Russia*, Washington: Carnegie Endowment for International Peace.

State Council of Russia (2003), 'New Security Architecture in Russia: State Council of Russia Meeting, 22 January 2003', *International Affairs*, **49** (2), 1–27.

Steele, J. (2004a), 'Putin Promises to Put Lives of Hostages First', *Guardian*, 3 September, p. 4.

Steele, J. (2004b), 'Same Boots, Same Flak Jackets, Different Attitude', *Guardian*, 1 October, p. 28.

Steen, A. (2003), *Political Elites and the New Russia: The Power Basis of Yeltsin's and Putin's Regimes*, London: Routledge.

Stent, A. and Shevtsova, L. (2002/3), 'America, Russia and Europe: A Realignment?', *Survival*, **44** (4), Winter, 121–34.

Stepanov, A. (2003), 'The Ministry of Foreign Affairs of Russia: Glimpses from the Past and the Present', *International Affairs: A Russian Journal of World Politics, Diplomacy and International Affairs*, **49** (2), 174–85.

Stratfor Analysis (2003), *Net Assessment: Former Soviet Union – In Search of Revivial*, Strategic Forecasting Inc, retrieved on 22 October from http://stratfor.com/corp/Corporate.neo?s=SUB.

Tikhonov, A. (2002), 'Budushchee irakskoi nefti opredeleno. Rossii dostonetsya men'she, chem khotelos' by', *Izvestiya*, 12 November, p. 3.

Traynor, I. (2002), 'Russia and NATO Reach Historic Deal', *Guardian*, retrieved from http://guardian.co.uk/russia/article.

Trenin, D. (2003), 'Russia in the New Global Order', *Internationale Politik*, **4** (1), Spring, 47–52.

Trubnikov, V. (2003), 'A New Philosophy to Combat Terrorism is Emerging', *International Affairs: A Russian Journal of World Politics, Diplomacy and International Affairs*, **49** (6), 39–45.
Umbach, F. (2003), 'Russia's Changing Threat Perceptions', *Internationale Politik*, **4** (1), Spring, 53–7.
Utkin, A. (2003), *Vyzov Zapada i otvet Rossii*, Moscow: Algoritm-Kniga.
Wallander, C.A. (2002), 'Lost and Found: Gorbachev's New Thinking', *Washington Quarterly*, Winter, 117–29, retrieved 8 December 2003 from http://twg.com/02winter/wallander.pdf.
Webber, M. (ed.) (2000), *Russia and Europe: Conflict or Cooperation?*, New York: St Martin's Press.
Webber, M. (2001), 'Third-Party Inclusion in European Security and Defence Policy: A Case Study of Russia', *European Foreign Affairs Review*, **6**, 407–26.
Yasmann, V. (2002), 'Russia and NATO: In Search of a New Dimension', *Russian Security Watch*, **11** (41), retrieved on 12 December 2003, from http://rferl.org/securitywatch/2002/11/41-191102.html.
Yasmann, V. (2004), 'Russia and the EU: A Problematic Future', *Russian Political Weekly*, 5 May, Vol. 4, No. 17, retrieved on 19 June from http://rferl.org/reports/rpw/2004/05/17-050504.asp.
Young, H. (2002), 'Perhaps a Russia–British Lobby against War on Iraq', *Guardian*, 19 February.

CHAPTER 9

Anderson, S.S. and Burns, T.R. (1998), 'The European Union and the Erosion of Parliamentary Democracy: A Study of Post-Parliamentary Governance', in Anderson, A.S. and Eliassen, K.A. (eds), *The European Union: How Democratic Is It*?, London: Sage Publications, pp. 227–51.
Commission (2001a), *European Governance: A White Paper*, COM (2001) 428 final, Brussels: Commission of the European Communities.
Commission (2001b), *Proposal for a Council Framework Decision on Combating Terrorism*, COM (2001) 521 final, Brussels: Commission of the European Communities.
Commission (2001c), *Proposal for a Council Framework Decision on the European Arrest Warrant and the Surrender Procedures Between the Member States*, COM (2001) 522 final, Brussels: Commission of the European Communities.
Commission (2001d), *Proposal for a Council Regulation on Specific Restrictive Measures Directed Against Certain Persons and Entities with a View to Combating International Terrorism (Presented by the Commission)*, COM

(2001) 569 final, 2 October, Brussels: Commission of the European Communities.

Commission (2002a), *Biannual Update of the Scoreboard to Review Progress on the Creation of an 'Area of Freedom, Security and Justice' in the European Union (first half 2002)*, COM (2002) 261 final, Brussels: Commission of the European Communities.

Commission (2002b), *Regional Cooperation Programme in the Field of Justice, in Combating Drugs, Organized Crime ad Terrorism: Framework Document*, EuroMed Report Issues No. 44, Brussels: Commission of the European Communities.

Council of the EU (1997), *Achievements in the Field of Justice and Home Affairs in 1997*, Report for the Council to the European Council, 13191/1/97, Brussels: Council of the EU.

Council of the EU (1999), *EU Commitments vis-à-vis Third Countries*, Note from Secretariat to Delegations, 9848/99, Brussels: Council of the EU.

Council of the EU (2000), *The Prevention and Control of Organized Crime: A European Union Strategy for the Beginning of the New Millennium*, Note from Article 36 Committee to COREPER/Council, 6611/00, Brussels: Council of the EU.

Council of the EU (2001), 'Council Common Position of 27 December 2001 on the Application of Specific Measures to Combat Terrorism', *Official Journal*, L344, 28 December, Brussels: European Communities, pp. 93–6.

Council of the EU (2002a), *European Union Action to Combat Terrorism – Update of the Roadmap*, Presidency Note to the Council (General Affairs), 10773/2/02, Brussels: Council of the EU.

Council of the EU (2002b), *Working Methods in the Council (JHA Area): JHA Activities other than Legislative Work*, Note from General Secretariat to COREPER, 5515/02, Brussels: Council of the EU.

Council of the EU (2002c), 'Council Framework Decision of 13 June 2002 on Joint Investigation Teams', *Official Journal of the European Communities*, L162, Brussels: European Communities, pp. 1–3.

Council of the EU (2002d), *Council Decision on the Signing ... of the EuroMediterranean Agreement Establishing an Association between the European Community and its Member States... and the People's Democratic Republic of Algeria... 6786/02*, Brussels: Council of the EU.

Council of the EU (2002e), 'European Union Action Plan on Common Action for the Russian Federation on Combating Organized Crime (2000/C 106/02)', *Official Journal of the European Communities*, C106, Brussels: European Communities, pp. 5–12.

Council of the EU (2003), *Relations with Russia*, Note from Council to the European Council, 10554/03, Brussels: Council of the EU.

Council of the EU (2004a), *EU Commitments vis-à-vis Third Countries,* Note from Secretariat to Delegations, 9166/04, Brussels: Council of the EU.

Council of the EU (2004b), *Council Report on the Implementation of the Common Strategy of the European Union on Russia*, Note from Council to the European Council 10601/04, Brussels: Council of the EU.

Curtin, D. (1993), 'The Constitutional Structure of the Union: A Europe of Bits and Pieces', *Common Market Law Review*, **30**, 17–69.

den Boer, M. and Monar, J. (2002), '11 September and the Challenge of Global Terrorism to the EU as a Security Actor', *Journal of Common Market Studies*, **40** (Supplement 1), 11–28.

Duff, A. (ed.) (1997), *The Treaty of Amsterdam: Text and Commentary*, London: Federal Trust.

EU Russia (2003), *EU Russia Summit, Rome, 6 November 2003*, Council Press Release 13990/03 (Presse 313), Brussels: Council of the EU.

EU USA (1995), *New Transatlantic Agenda and Action Plan*, Council Press Release 12296/95, Brussels: Council of the EU.

EU USA (2001), *Joint US–EU Ministerial Statement on Combating Terrorism, 20 September 2001*, Council Press Release, Brussels: Council of the EU.

EU USA (2004), *EU US Declaration on Combating Terrorism, Dromoland Castle, 26 June 2004*, Council Press Release 10760/04 (Presse 205), Brussels: Council of the EU.

European Council (1999a), *Tempere European Council: Presidency Conclusions*, Brussels: Council of the EU.

European Council (1999b), 'Common Strategy of the European Union on Russia of 4 June 1999', *Official Journal*, L157, Brussels: European Communities, pp. 1–9.

European Council (2001a), *Conclusions and Plan of Action of the Extraordinary European Council Meeting on 21 September 2001*, Brussels: Council of the EU.

European Council (2001b), *Presidency Conclusions: European Council Meeting in Laeken*, Brussels: Council of the EU.

European Council (2002), *Presidency Conclusions: Seville European Council 21 and 22 June 2002*, Brussels: Council of the EU.

European Council (2004), *Declaration on Combating Terrorism*, Brussels: Council of the EU.

European Union (2003), *A Secure Europe in a Better World: European Security Strategy, Brussels, 12 December 2003*, Brussels: Council of the EU.

Grabbe, H. (2001), 'Breaking New Ground in Internal Security', in Bannerman, E., Everts, S., Grabbe, H., Grant, C. and Murray, A. (eds),

Europe After September 11th, London: Centre for European Reform, pp. 63–75.

Hayes-Renshaw, F. and Wallace, H. (1997), *The Council of Ministers*, Basingstoke: Macmillan.

Home Affairs Committee (1990), *Practical Police Cooperation in the European Community*, 7th Report, House of Commons, Session 1989–90, HC 363-I and II, Vol. I and Vol. II, London: HMSO.

Horeth, M. (1999), 'No Way Out for the Beast? The Unsolved Legitimacy Problem of European Governance', *Journal of European Public Policy*, **6** (2), 249–68.

International Press Institute (2000), *Veronica Guerin. International Press Institute Report*, Missouri, USA: International Press Institute, **6** (2), retrieved 1 October 2004 from http://www.freemedia.at/IPIReport/Heroes_IPIReport2.00/20Guerin.htm.

JHA Council (2001), *Conclusions Adopted by the Council (Justice and Home Affairs) Brussels*, SN 3926/6/01, Brussels: Council of the EU.

Monar, J. (2000), 'Justice and Home Affairs', *Journal of Common Market Studies*, **38** (Annual Review), 125–42.

Monar, J. (2001), 'The Dynamics of Justice and Home Affairs: Laboratories, Driving Factors and Costs', *Journal of Common Market Studies*, **39** (4), 747–64.

Monar, J. (2002), 'Justice and Home Affairs', *Journal of Common Market Studies*, **40** (Annual Review), 121–36.

Norman, P. (1999), 'European Union Police Policy Making and Cooperation', in Carr, F. and Massey, A. (eds), *Public Policy in the New Europe: Eurogovernance in Theory and Practice*, Cheltenham, UK and Northampton, MA, USA: Edward Elgar, pp. 104–22.

Norman, P. (2001), 'Policing "high tech crime" in the Global Context: The Role of Transnational Policy Networks', in Wall, D.S. (ed.), *Crime and the Internet*, London: Routledge, pp. 184–94.

O'Keefe, D. (1995), 'Recasting the Third Pillar', *Common Market Law Review*, **32**, 893–920.

Peers, S. (2003), *The Exchange of Personal Data Between Europol and the USA*, Statewatch Analysis No. 15, London: Statewatch.

Presidency of the Council of the EU (1999), *German Presidency Programme for External Relations in the Field of Justice and Home Affairs*, Note from German Presidency to K.4 Committee, 14414/98 ADD1, Brussels: Council of the EU.

Presidency of the Council of the EU (2000), *European Union Priorities and Policy Objectives for External Relations in the Field of Justice and Home Affairs*, Item Note from COREPER to General Affairs Council/European Council, 7653/00, Brussels: Council of the EU.

Presidency of the Council of the EU (2001), *Presidency Programme Concerning External Relations in the JHA Field (2001–2002)*, Note from Swedish Presidency to Council, 5146/01, Brussels: Council of the EU.

Presidency of the Council of the EU (2002), *European Union Action Plan to Combat Terrorism – Update of the Roadmap*, Presidency Note to Council (General Affairs), 10773/2/02, Brussels: Council of the EU.

Presidency of the Council of the EU (2004), *JHA External Relations Multi Presidency Programme*, Presidency Note to Council (Article 36 Committee/Strategic Committee on Immigration, Frontiers and Asylum), 11044/04, Brussels: Council of the EU.

Statewatch (1996), 'Council of Justice and Home Affairs: Beef Ban Conflict Dominates the Meeting in Luxembourg on 4 June', *Statewatch Bulletin*, **6** (3), 18–19.

Statewatch (2002), *Secret EU US Agreement on Criminal Cooperation Being Negotiated*, Statewatch Analysis No.12, London: Statewatch.

Wallace, H. (2001), *The Future of Europe Debate: Opportunities for British Policy*, One Europe or Several Policy Paper 05/01, Brighton: University of Sussex, retrieved 1 October 2004 from http://www.one-europe.ac.uk/pdf/p5wallace.pdf.

Wrench, P. (1997), 'The G8 and Transnational Organized Crime', in Cullen, P.J. and Gilmore, W.C. (eds) (1998), *Crime Sans Frontiers: International and European Legal Approaches*, Edinburgh: Edinburgh University Press, pp. 39–43.

CHAPTER 10

Please see endnotes, pp. 246–8.

CHAPTER 11

Amnesty International (2004), '"War on Terror" Human Rights Issues', www.anestyusa.org/waronterror/patriotact/.

Annan, K. (2002), Secretary General to Commission on Human Rights, 'Human Rights Must Not be Sacrificed to Counter-Terrorism', Commission on Human Rights, 58th Session, 12 April 2002, www.unhcr.ch.

Bishara, M. (2001), 'With Its New Muslim Alliance, US Risks Further Instability', *International Herald Tribune*, 24–25 November, p. 6.

Buergenthal, T. (1990), 'The Copenhagen Meeting: A New Public Order for Europe', *Human Rights Law Journal*, **2**, 213–25.

The Century Foundation (2004), *The USA PATRIOT ACT: The Basics*, New York: The Century Foundation Press.
The Charter of Fundamental Rights of the European Union (2000/C, 364/01), Brussels: The European Parliament.
Chandler, D. (1994), 'The OSCE and the Internationalisation of National Minority Rights', in Forsythe, D.P. (ed.), *Human Rights in the New Europe*, Lincoln: University of Nebraska Press.
Davis, M. (2003), 'Introduction: Law and Politics in the Pinochet Case', in Davis, M. (ed.), *The Pinochet Case: Origins, Progress and Implications*, London: Institute of Latin American Studies, pp. 1–14.
Fischer, J. (2002), Federal Minister for Foreign Affairs, 'Anti-Terrorism Measures Are No Excuse for Human Rights Violations', 58th Session of the Commission on Human Rights, Geneva, 20 March, www.unhcr.ch.
Fitchett, J. (2001), 'US Policy on Terrorism: Think Globally and Don't Interfere Locally', *International Herald Tribune*, 28 September, p. 10.
Hathaway, J.C. (2000), 'America, Defender of Democratic Legitimacy?', *European Journal of International Law*, **11**, 121–34.
Human Rights First (2004), 'Iraqi Special Tribunal: Questions and Answers', www.humanrightsfirst.org/international_justice/w_cont_10.htm.
Human Rights Watch (2002), World Report, www.hrw.org/wr2k2/print.cgi?intro.html.
Human Rights Watch (2004a), 'Background Note on the Russian Operation in Chechyna', www.hrw.org/reports/2001/chechnya/Disapfin-01.htm.
Human Rights Watch (2004b), 'Opportunism in the Face of Tragedy: Repression in the Name of Anti-Terrorism', www.hrw.org/campaigns/september11/opportunismwatch.htm.
Huntington, S.P. (1999), 'The Lonely Superpower', *Foreign Affairs*, **78**, 35–49.
Ignatieff, M. (2002), 'Will the Quest for Security Kill the Human Rights Era?', *International Herald Tribune*, 6 February, p. 7.
Jimeno-Bulnes, M. (2004), 'After September 11th: The Fight Against Terrorism in National and European Law. Substantive and Procedural Rules: Some Examples', *European Law Journal*, **10** (2), 235–53.
Johns, M. (2003), '"Do As I Say, Not As I Do": The European Union, Eastern Europe and Minority Rights', *East European Politics and Societies*, **17** (4), 682–99.
Joyner, C.C. (2004), 'The United Nations and Terrorism: Rethinking Legal Tensions Between National Security, Human Rights, and Civil Liberties', *International Studies Perspectives*, **5**, 240–57.
Lobe, J. (2004), 'House Republicans Fight International Criminal Court', 20 July, www.antiwar.com/lobe/?articleid=3058.

Moravcsik, A. (2000), 'The Origins of Human Rights Regimes: Democratic Delegation in Postwar Europe', *International Organisation*, **54** (2), Spring, 217–52.

Pinelli, C. (2004), 'Conditionality and Enlargement in Light of EU Constitutional Developments', *European Law Journal*, **10** (3), May, 354–62.

Risse-Kappen, T. (1996), 'Exploring the Nature of the Beast: International Relations Theory and Comparative Policy Analysis Meet the European Union', *Journal of Common Market Studies*, **34** (1), 53–80.

Roberts, A. (2004), 'Righting Wrongs or Wronging Rights? The United States and Human Rights Post-September 11', *European Journal of International Law*, **15** (4) 2004, 721–49.

Roth, K. (2004), Executive Director of Human Rights Watch, 'Human Rights in the War on Terrorism', 22 September, http://hrw.org/english/docs/2004/09/usdom9376_txt.htm.

Sadurski, W. (2004), 'Accession's Democracy Dividend: The Impact of the EU Enlargement upon Democracy in the New Member States of Central and Eastern Europe', *European Law Journal*, **10** (4), July, 371–401.

Schwarz, R. (2004), 'The Paradox of Sovereignty, Regime Type and Human Rights Compliance', *International Journal of Human Rights*, 8 (2), Summer, 199–215.

Smith, R. (2003), *Textbook on International Human Rights*, Oxford: Oxford University Press.

Spiro, P.J. (2000), 'The New Sovereigntists: American Exceptionalism and Its False Prophets', *Foreign Affairs*, **79**, 9–15.

UNHCR (2002), Statement of the Committee of the International Convention on the Elimination of all Forms of Racial Discrimination (CERD), 8 March, www.unhcr.ch.

Von Schorlemer, S. (2003), 'Human Rights: Substantive and Institutional Implications of the War Against Terrorism', *European Journal of International Law*, **14** (2), 265–82.

Washington Post (2001), 'China and Terrorism', editorial reprinted in *the International Herald Tribune*, 22 October 2001, p. 8.

Williams, A. (2003), 'Mapping Human Rights, Reading the European Union', *European Law Journal*, **9** (5), 659–76.

CHAPTER 12

Ackrill, R.W. (2000), *The Common Agricultural Policy*, Sheffield: Sheffield Academic Press.

Daugbjerg, C. (1999), 'Reforming the CAP: Policy Networks and Broader Institutional Structures', *Journal of Common Market Studies*, **37**, 407–28.

Daugbjerg, C. and Swinbank, A. (2004), 'The CAP and EU Enlargement', *Journal of Common Market Studies*, **42**, 99–119.

Gaisford, J.D., Kerr, W.A. and Perdikis, N. (2003), *Economic Analysis for EU Accession Negotiations: Agri-Food Issues in the EU's Eastward Expansion*, Cheltenham, UK and Northampton, MA, USA: Edward Elgar.

Kowalski, A. (1991), 'Agriculture', in Blazycouer, C. and Rapacki, R. (eds), *Poland in the 1990s*, London: Pinter.

Moyer, H.W. and Josling, T.E. (1990), *Agricultural Policy Reform: Politics and Process in the EC and USA*, Hemel Hempstead: Harvester Wheatsheaf.

CHAPTER 13

Apap, J., Kaniewska, M., Sitck, M., Walewski, M. and Szczygielski, K. (eds) (2003), *Policy Makers or Policy Takers? – Visegrad Countries Joining the EU*, Centre for Social and Economic Research, Warsaw, Poland.

Barnes, P.M. (1996), 'The Nordic Countries and EU Environmental Policy', in Miles, L. (ed.), *The European Union and the Nordic Countries*, London and New York: Routledge.

Barnes, P.M. and Barnes, I.G. (2000), *Environmental Policy in the European Union*, Cheltenham, UK and Northampton, MA, USA: Edward Elgar.

Bond, M. et al. (2004), *Contributions by the Ambassadors of the EU Accession States to Mark EU Enlargement in 2004*, European Essay no. 29, Federal Trust, London.

Borzel, T. and Risse, T. (2003), *Shaping and Taking EU Policies – Member States' Responses to Europeanization*, Queen's Papers on Europeanization, No. 2/2003, Queen's University, Belfast.

Bulmer, S. and Radaelli, C. (2004), *The Europeanization of National Policy*, Queen's Papers on Europeanization, No. 1/2004, Queen's University, Belfast.

Burchell, J. and Lightfoot, S. (2004), 'The EU and Sustainable Development', in Barry, J., Baxter, B. and Dunphy, R. (eds), *Europe, Globalization and Sustainable Development*, London and New York: Routledge.

Commission of the European Communities (CEC) (1992), *Towards Sustainability – the Fifth Environmental Action Programme*, COM (1992) CEC, Luxembourg.

CEC (2001a), *Environment 2010: Our Future, Our Choice – Sixth Environment Action Programme of the European Community*, COM (2001) 31 final, Brussels, 24 January.

CEC (2001b), *White Paper – Strategy for a Future Chemicals Policy*, COM (2001) 88 final, Brussels, 27 February.
CEC (2001c), *Consultation Paper for the Preparation of a European Strategy for Sustainable Development*, SEC (2001) 517, Brussels, 27 March.
CEC (2001d), *A Sustainable Europe for a Better World (Strategy for Sustainable Development)*, COM (2001) 264 final, Brussels, 15 May.
CEC (2001e), *The Challenge of Environmental Financing in the Candidate Countries*, COM (2001) 304 final, Brussels, 8 June.
CEC (2001f), *Twinning in Action*, DG for Enlargement, Brussels, October.
CEC (2003a), *Communication on Wider Europe Policy and Strategy*, COM (2003) 104 final, Brussels, 11 March.
CEC (2003b), *Developing an Action Plan for Environmental Technology*, COM (2003) 131 final, Brussels, 25 March.
CEC (2003c), *Environment Policy Review – 2003*, COM (2003) 745 final, Brussels, 3 December.
CEC (2004a), *Delivering Lisbon: Reforms for the Enlarged Union*, COM (2004) 2 final, Brussels, 20 February.
CEC (2004b), *Integrating Environmental Considerations into Other Policy Areas*, COM (2004) 394 final, Brussels, 1 June.
CEC (2004c), *Fifth Annual Survey on the Implementation and Enforcement of Community Environmental Law 2003*, SEC (2004) 1025, Brussels, 27 July.
Cremona, M. (ed.) (2003), *The Enlargement of the European Union*, Oxford and New York: Oxford University Press.
Dom, A. and de Ridder, W. (2002), *Paving the Way for EU Enlargement – Indicators of Transport and Environment Integration*, Copenhagen, Denmark: EEA.
European Environmental Agency (2003), *Europe's Environment: The Third Assessment*, Copenhagen, Denmark: EEA.
European Environmental Bureau (2004), *The Environmental Results of the Accession Process – Special Report*, European Environmental Bureau, April, Brussels.
Featherstone, K. and Radaelli, C. (2003), *The Politics of Europeanization*, Oxford and New York: Oxford University Press.
Fiedler, J. and Janiak, P. (2003), *Environmental Financing in Central and Eastern Europe 1996–2001*, Regional Environmental Centre for Central and Eastern Europe, Hungary.
Grabbe, H. (2004a), *CER Bulletin No. 34 Feb/March*, Centre for European Reform, London.
Grabbe, H. (2004b), *The Constellations of Europe*, Centre for European Reform, London, April.

Jehlicka, P. (2002), *Environmental Implications of Eastern Enlargement of the EU*, Robert Schuman Centre for Advanced Studies, Working Paper RSC No. 2002/23, European University Institute, Florence.
Jordan, A. (2002), *The Europeanization of British Environmental Policy*, Basingstoke, UK and New York: Palgrave Macmillan.
Pearce, F. (2004), 'Russia Set to Approve Climate Change Plan', New Scientist.com news service, 30 September.
Radaelli, C.M. (2004), 'Britain in Europe, Europe in Britain', unpublished paper presented at UACES/ERSC conference, organized by University of Sheffield held at the Town Hall, Sheffield, 16 July.
Stritih, J. (2000), 'Enlargement and the New EU Environmental Action Programme', *Metamorphosis*, EEB Newsletter no 26, May, EEB, Brussels.
World Commission on Environment and Development (WECD) (1987), *Our Common Future* (the 'Brundtland' Report), Oxford and New York: Oxford University Press.

CHAPTER 14

Allen, D. (1996), 'Cohesion and Structural Adjustment', in Wallace, H. and Wallace, W. (eds), *Policy-Making in the European Union*, Oxford: Oxford University Press, pp. 209–34.
Anderson, J. (1996), 'Germany and the Structural Funds, Reunification Bends to Bifurcation', in Hooghe, L. (ed.), *Cohesion Policy and European Integration: Building Multi-Level Governance*, Oxford: Oxford University Press.
Ansell, C., Parsons, C. and Darden, K. (1997), 'Dual Networks in European Regional Development Policy', *Journal of Common Market Studies*, **35** (3), 374–75.
Armstrong, H.W. (2002), 'European Regional Policy: Reconciling the Evaluation and Convergence Evidence', in Cuadrado-Rouva, J. and Parellada, M. (eds), *Regional Convergence in the European Union: Facts, Prospects and Policies*, Amsterdam: Springer-Verlag (Advances in Spatial Sciences Series).
Bache, I. (1998), *The Politics of European Union Regional Policy*, Sheffield: Sheffield Academic Press.
Bache, I. and Bristow, G. (2003), 'Devolution on the Gate Keeping Role of the Core Executive: The Struggle for European Funds', *British Journal of Politics and International Relations*, **5** (3), 405–27.
Bachtler, J. (2004), 'Enlargement and Cohesion Policy – Reshaping the Union', *Inforegio panorama*, **13**, Brussels, April, pp. 7–13.

Bachtler, J. and Michie, R. (1993), 'The Restructuring of Regional Policy in the European Community', *Regional Studies*, **27** (4), 719–25.

Bachtler, J. and Michie, R. (1994), 'Strengthening Economic and Social Cohesion. The Revision of the Structural Funds', *Regional Studies*, **28** (8), 789–96.

Bachtler, J. and Taylor, S. (2003), *The Added Value of Structural Funds: A Regional Perspective*, Strathclyde 1 Qnet report, University of Strathclyde, pp. 57–9.

Bachtler, J., Josserand, F. and Michie, R. (2003), *EU Enlargement and the Reform of Structural Funds: The Implications for Scotland*, Scotecom, University of Stirling.

Bailey, D. and De Propris, L. (2002), 'The 1988 Reform of the European Structural Fund: Entitlement or Empowerment', *Journal of European Public Policy*, **9** (3), 408–28.

Bailey, D. and De Propris, L. (2002a), 'EU Structural Funds, Regional Capabilities and Enlargement: Towards Multi-level Governance', *European Integration*, **24** (4), 303–24.

Baun, M. (2002), 'EU Regional Policy and the Candidate States: Poland and the Czech Republic', *Journal of European Integration*, **24** (3), 261–80.

Begg, I. (2004), 'The EU Budget: Common Future or Stuck in the Past?', Centre for European Reform, Briefing Note.

Boland, P., Mannin, M. and Wallace, J. (1995), 'Merseyside, The Regional Office and Structural Funding', *Regional Studies*, **29** (7), 698–706.

Bretherton, C. (1999), 'Security Issues in the Wider Europe: The Role of EU–CEEC Relations', in Mannin, M., *Pushing Back the Boundaries*, Manchester: pp. 183–216.

Bretherton, C. and Sperling, E. (1996), 'Women's networks and the European Union: Towards an Inclusive Approach', *Journal of Common Market Studies*, **34** (4), 487–500.

Bulmer, S. (1994), 'The Governance of the European Union – A New Institutionalist Approach', *Journal of European Public Policy*, **13** (4), 351–80.

Bulmer, S. (1998), 'New Institutionalism and the Governance of the Single European Market', *Journal of European Public Policy*, **5** (3), 365–86.

Bulmer, S. and Burch, M. (2000), 'The Europeanisation of British Central Government', in R.A.W. Rhodes (ed.), *Transforming British Government, Volume 1: Changing Institutions*, Basingstoke: Macmillan, pp. 46–62.

Burch, M. and Gomez, R. (2002), 'The English Regions and the European Union', *Regional Studies*, **36** (7), 767–78.

Burch, M. and Gomez, R. (2003), 'Europeanization and the English Regions', ESRC Seminar and Europeanization, University of Sheffield, 2 May (unpublished paper).

Buzan, B., Weaver, O. and De Wilde, J. (1998), *Security – A New Framework for Analysis*, Boulder, CO: Lynne Reinner.

Caporaso, J. and Keeler, J. (1995), 'The European Union and Regional Integration Theory', in Mazey, S. and Rhodes, C. (eds), *The State of the European Union*, Boulder, CO: Lynne Reinner/Longman.

Commission (1997), *Agenda 2000: For a Stronger and Wider Europe*, Vol 1. COM (97) 2000 final, Brussels, 15 July.

Commission (1998), *Agenda 2000 – The Legislative Proposals*, DN: IP/981258, 18th March, Brussels.

Commission (2001), Unity, Solidarity and Diversity for Europe, Its People and Territory – The Second Report on Economic and Social Cohesion, 31 January 2001, COM (2001) 24 final, Brussels.

Commission (2003a), *Second Progress Report on Economic and Social Cohesion*, COM (2003) 34 Final – 30 January, Brussels.

Commission (2003b), *The Structural Funds and their Coordination with the Cohesion Fund – Revised indicative guidelines*, COM (2003) final, 25 August.

Commission (2004a), *Third Report on Economic and Social Cohesion*, COM (2004) 107, 18 February, Luxembourg Office for Official Publication of the European Communities.

Commission (2004b), *Building a Common Future. Policy Challenges and Budgetary Means to the Enlarged Union 2007–2013*, Communication from the Commission to the Council and the European Parliament, COM (2004) 101 final, Brussels, 10 February.

Committee of the Regions (2003), Opinion on the COR Proposals for the Intergovernmental Conference, Brussels CDR 169/03 FIN, 9 October.

Conzelmann, T. (1995), 'Networking and the Politics of the EU Regional Policy, Lessons from North-Rhine Westphalia, Nord-Pas de Calais and the North West of England', *Regional and Federal Studies*, **5** (2), 134–72.

COR (2003), Opinion on the COR proposals for the Intergovernmental Conference, Brussels CDR 169/03 fin.

Cornford, J. (1975), *The Failure of the State*, London: Croom Helm.

Council of the European Communities (1999), 'Council Regulation (EEC) No. 1260/1999 of 21 June Laying Down General Provisions of the Structural Funds', *Official Journal of the European Communities* 116, 26/1/99, 1–42 Luxembourg.

Council of Ministers (2003), Cohesion and Competitiveness: Background Document for Discussion, Informal Ministerial Meeting on Cohesion Policy, Rome, 20 October.

Croxford, G.J., Wise, M. and Chalkley, J. (1987), 'The Reform of the European Regional Development Fund: A Preliminary Assessment', *Journal of Common Market Studies*, (26), 25–38.

Downs, W.M. (2002), 'Regionalism in the European Union: Key Concepts and a Project Overview', *Journal of European Integration*, **24** (3), 171–8.

Euroactive.com (2003), Controversial Expert Report Upsets Several Commissioners, http:www.euroactive.com/portal-News nr 1505948.

Fothergill, S. (1997), 'The Premature Death of EU Regional Policy?', *European Urban and Regional Studies*, **5** (2), 183–8.

George, S. (1991), *Politics and Policy in the European Community*, 2nd edn, Oxford: Oxford University Press.

Grabbc, H. and Hughes, K. (1998), *Enlarging the European Union Eastwards*, London: Pinter/RIIA.

Gualini, E. (2003), 'Challenges to Multi-level Governance: Contradictions and Conflicts in the Europeanization of Italian Regional Policy', *Journal of European Public Policy*, **10** (4), 616–38.

Guersent, O. (2001), 'The Regional Policy of the European Union: A Balance and Outlook', *Regional Studies*, **35** (2), 163–80.

Hall, R. (1997), 'Agenda 2000 and the European Cohesion Fund', *European Urban and Regional Studies*, **5** (2), 176–83.

HM Treasury (2003), 'A Modern Regional Policy for the United Kingdom', http://www.hm-treasury.gov.uk/newsroom-and-speeches/press/2003/press-35-03.cfm.

Hooghe, L. (1996), 'Building a Europe with the Regions: The Changing Role of the European Commission', in Hooghe, L. (ed.), *Cohesion Policy and European Integration*, Oxford: Clarendon Press, pp. 89–126.

Inforegio Panorama (2004), 'Brussels' Sub National Representation Offices', *Inforegio Panorama*, **13**, April, Directorate General for Regional Policy, Brussels, pp. 22–4.

Jacobs, B. (1997), 'Networks, Partnerships and European Regional Economic Development Initiatives in the West Midlands', *Policy and Politics*, **25** (1), 39–50.

Jeffrey, C. (2002), 'Social and Regional Interests: ESC and the Committee of the Regions', in Peterson, J. and Shackleton, M. (eds), *The Institutions of the European Union*, Oxford: Oxford University Press, pp. 326–46.

Kassim, H. (1994), 'Policy Networks, Networks and European Union Policy-making: A Sceptical View', *West European Politics*, **17** (4), 15–27.

Kohler-Koch, B. (1999), 'The Evolution and transformation of European Governance', in Kohler-Koch, B. and Eising, R. (eds), *The Transformation of Governance in the European Union*, London: Routledge, pp. 14–35.

Mannin, M. (ed.) (1999), *Pushing Back the Boundaries – The European Union and Central and Eastern Europe*, Manchester and New York: Manchester University Press.

Marks, G. (1996), 'Exploring and Explaining Variation in EU Cohesion Policy', in Hooghe, L. (ed.), *Cohesion Policy and European Integration*, Oxford: Clarendon Press, pp. 388–422.

Marks, G., Haesly, R. and Mbaye, H. (2002), 'What do Subnational Offices Think They are Doing in Brussels?', *Regional and Federal Studies*, Autumn, 1–23.

McAlevy, P.C. (1992), *The Politics of European Regional Development Policy: The EC's RECHAR Initiative and the Concept of Additionality*, Strathclyde Papers on Government and Policies no. 88, Glasgow: University of Strathclyde.

Morata, F. and Munoz, X. (1996), 'Vying for European Funds: Territorial Restructuring in Spain', in Hooghe, L. (ed.), *Cohesion Policy and European Integration – Building Multi-Level Governance*, Oxford: Clarendon Press, pp. 195–218.

Nanetti, R.Y. (1996), 'EU Cohesion and Territorial Restructuring in Market States', in Hooghe, L. (ed.), *Cohesion Policy and European Integration – Building Multi-Level Governance*, Oxford: Clarendon Press, pp. 59–88.

Nay, O. (2002), 'European Community Policy in France: the State Bounces Back', *Journal of European Integration*, **24** (3), 245–60.

Nentwich, M. and Weale, A. (eds) (1998), *Political Theory and the European Union*, London: Routledge.

Peterson, J. (1995), 'Decision making in the European Union: Towards a Framework for Analysis', *Journal of European Public Policy*, **2** (1), 69–93.

Rhodes, R. (1981), *Control and Power in Central Local Relationships*, Farnborough: Gower.

Rhodes, R. and Marsh, D. (1992), 'New Directions in the Study of Policy Networks', *European Journal of Political Research*, **21** (1), 181–205.

Rhodes, R., Bache, I. and George, S. (1996), 'Policy Networks and Policy Making in the European Union: A Critical Appraisal', in Hooghe, L. (ed.), *Cohesion Policy and European Integration*, Oxford: Clarendon.

Rodriguez-Fuentes, C. and Daw, S. (2003), 'EMU and the Regional Impact of Monetary Policy', *Regional Studies*, **37** (9), 969–80.

Rodriguez-Pose, A. and Frates, U. (2004), 'Between Development and Social Policies: The Impact of European Structural Funds in Objective 1 Regions', *Regional Studies*, **38** (1), 97–113.

Sapir, A. et al. (2003), *An Agenda for a Growing Europe: Making the EU Economic System Deliver*, Report: High Level Study Group for The President of the European Commission (Sapir Report), July.

Schmitt-Egner, P. (2002), 'The Concept of Region: Theoretical and Methodological Notes on its Reconstruction', *Journal of European Integration*, **24** (3), 179–200.

Smyrl, M. (1998), 'When (and How) do the Commission's Preferences Matter?', *Journal of Common Market Studies*, **36** (1), 79–99.

Sutcliffe, J.B. (2000), 'The 1999 Reform of the Structural Funds Regulation: Multi-level Governance or Renationalization?', *Journal of European Public Policy*, **7** (2) 290–309.

Tarschys, D. (2003), *Reinventing Cohesion: The Future of European Structural Policy*, Swedish Institute for European Policy Studies, University of Stockholm, September.

Vos, H., Boucké, T. and Devos, C. (2002), 'The *Conditio sine qua non* of the Added Value of Regions in the EU: Upper Level Representation as a Fundamental Precondition', *Journal of European Integration*, **24** (3), 201–18.

Wallace, J. (1993), 'European Regional Funding and Merseyside: The Politics of ERDF', unpublished M. Phil. Thesis, Liverpool: John Moores University.

Warleigh, A. (1997), 'A Committee of No Importance? Assessing the Relevance of the Committee of the Regions', *Politics*, **17** (2), 101–7.

CHAPTER 15

Anderson, P. and Hughes, J. (2000), 'Policy interventions to reduce the harm from smoking', *Addiction*, **95**, S9–S11.

Aspect Consortium (2004), *Tobacco or Health in the European Union*, Brussels: European Community.

Bentham, G. (1988), 'Migration and morbidity: implications for geographical studies of disease', *Social Science and Medicine*, **26**, 49–54.

Bero, L. (2003), 'Implications of the tobacco industry documents for public health and policy', *Annual Review of Public Health*, **24**, 267–88.

Bettcher, D., Subramaniam, C., Guindon, E., Perucic, A.-M., Soll, L., Grabman, G., Joosens, L. and Taylor, A. (2001), *Confronting the Tobacco Epidemic in an Era of Trade Liberalization*, Geneva: WHO.

Bonde J.-P. (2005), *The EU Constitution: The Reader-Friendly Edition*, Brussels: EU Observer, retrieved from http://www.euabc.com/upload/rfConstitution_en.pdf (accessed 10 April 2005).

Byrne, D. (2004), *Enabling Good Health For All: A Reflection Process for a New EU Health Strategy*, Brussels: European Commission for Health and Consumer Protection Brussels, retrieved from http://europa.eu.int/comm/health/ph_overview/Documents/byrne_reflection_en.pdf (accessed 10 April 2005).

Coignard, B. (2001), 'Bioterrorism preparedness and response in European public health institutes', *Eurosurveillance Monthly*, **6**, 159–66.

Coker, R. (2003), *Migration, Public Health and Compulsory Screening for TB and HIV*, Asylum and Migration Working Paper 1, London: Institute for Public Policy Research.

Coker, R., Bell, A., Pitman, R., Hayward, A. and Watson, J. (2004), 'Screening programmes for tuberculosis in new entrants across Europe', *International Journal of Tuberculosis and Lung Disease*, **8**, 1022–6.

Commission of the European Communities (2001), *A Sustainable Europe for a Better World: A European Union Strategy for Sustainable Development*, Brussels,15 May, COM (2001) 264 final.

Commission of the European Communities (2005), *Communication from the Commission on the Social Agenda*, Brussels, 9 February, COM (2005) 33 final.

Connolly, G. (1995), 'Tobacco, trade and Eastern Europe', in Slama, K. (ed.), *Tobacco and Health*, New York: Plenum Press.

Council of the European Union (2003), *A Secure Europe in a Better World: European Security Strategy*, Brussels: Council of the European Union.

Duina, F. and Kurzer, P. (2004), 'Smoke in your eyes: the struggle over tobacco control in the European Union', *Journal of European Public Policy*, **11**, 57–77.

Elola, J. (1996), 'Health care system reforms in western European countries: the relevance of health care organization', *International Journal of Health Services*, **26**, 239–51.

Fidler, D.P. (2003), 'Disease and globalized anarchy: theoretical perspectives on the pursuit of global health', *Social Theory and Health*, **1**, 21–41.

Forrest, D. (1996), 'Control of imported communicable diseases: preparation and response', *Canadian Journal of Public Health*, **87**, 368–75.

Gilmore, A., Osterberg, A., Heloma, A., Zatonski, W., Delcheva, E. and McKee, M. (2004), 'Free trade versus the protection of health: the examples of alcohol and tobacco', in McKee, M., MacLehose, L. and Nolte, E. (eds), *Health Policy and European Union Enlargement*, Maidenhead: Open University Press, pp.198–224.

Hastings, G. and MacFadyen, L. (2000), 'A day in the life of an advertising man: review of internal documents from the UK tobacco industry's principal advertising agencies', *British Medical Journal*, **321**, 366–71.

Hervey, T. (2001), 'Up in Smoke? Community (anti) tobacco law and policy', *European Law Review*, **26**, 101–25.

HM Custom and Excise and HM Treasury (2000), *Tackling Tobacco Smuggling*, London: The Stationery Office.

International Organization for Migration (2003), *World Migration 2003: Managing Migration*, Geneva: IoM.

Joossens, L. (1999), *Smuggling and Cross-border Shopping of Tobacco Products in the European Union: A Report for the Health Education Authority*, London: Health Education Authority.

Joossens, L. and Raw, M. (1995), 'Smuggling and cross border shopping of tobacco in Europe', *British Medical Journal*, **310**, 1393–97.

Joossens, L. and Raw, M. (1998), 'Cigarette smuggling in Europe: who really benefits?', *Tobacco Control*, **7**, 66–71.

King, N. (2002), 'Security, disease, and commerce: ideologies of postcolonial global health', *Social Studies of Science*, **32**, 763–89.

King, N. (2004), 'The scale politics of emerging diseases', *Osiris*, **19**, 62–76.

Lancet (2005), 'Editorial: disease is not a justification for discrimination', *The Lancet*, **365**, 9461.

Lever, F. and Joseph, C. (2001), 'Travel associated legionnaires' disease in Europe in 1999', *Eurosurveillance Monthly*, **6**, 53–61.

Loddenkemper, R., Gibson, G. and Sibille, Y. (eds) (2003), *The European Lung White Book*, Sheffield: European Respiratory Society/European Lung Foundation.

Maclehose, L., Coker, R. and McKee, M. (2004), 'Communicable disease control: detecting and managing communicable disease outbreaks across borders', in McKee, M., MacLehose, L. and Nolte, E. (eds), *Health Policy and European Union Enlargement*, Maidenhead: Open University Press, pp. 185–97.

Maclehose, L., Brand, H., Camaroni, I., Fulop, N., Gill, O. and Reintjes, R. (2001), 'Communicable disease outbreaks involving more than one country: systems approach to evaluating the response', *British Medical Journal*, **323**, 861–3.

McKee, M., Lang, T. and Roberts, J. (1996), 'Deregulating health: policy lessons of the BSE affair', *Journal of the Royal Society of Medicine*, **89**, 424–6.

McKee, M., MacLehose, L. and Nolte, E. (eds) (2004), *Health Policy and European Union Enlargement*, Maidenhead: Open University Press.

Migration Watch UK (2003), *Health Consequences of Current Immigration Policy*, London: Migration Watch UK. Retrieved from http://www.migrationwatchuk.org/pdfs/Health_consequences.pdf (accessed 10 April 2005).

Moon, G. (1999), 'The health of nations: structures and discourses in pan-European health policy', in Carr, F. and Massey, A. (eds), *Eurogovernance in Theory and Practice*, London, UK and Northampton, MA, USA: Edward Elgar, pp. 146–63.

Moon, G. and Curtis, S. (1998), 'Health and health care', in Unwin, T. (ed.), *A European Geography*, London: Longman.

Mossialos, E. and McKee, M. (2002), *EU Law and the Social Character of Health Care*, Brussels: Peter Lang.

Neuman, M., Bitton, A. and Glantz, S. (2002), 'Tobacco industry strategies for influencing European community tobacco advertising legislation', *The Lancet*, **359**, 1323–30.

Peto, R., Lopez, A.D., Boreham, J., Thun, M. and Clark, H. (1994), *Mortality from Smoking in Developed Countries 1950–2000*, Oxford: Oxford University Press.

Rechel, B., Shapo, L. and McKee, M. (2004), *Millennium Development Goals for Health in Europe and Central Asia: Relevance and Policy Implications*, New York: World Bank.

Saltman, R. and Figueras, J. (eds) (1997), *European Health Care Reform: Analysis of Current Strategies*, Copenhagen: WHO Regional Office for Europe.

Townsend, J. (1991), 'Tobacco and the European common agricultural policy', *British Medical Journal*, **303**, 1008–9.

WHO (1946), *Preamble to the Constitution of the World Health Organization*, as adopted by the International Health Conference, New York, 19–22 June 1946; signed on 22 July 1946 by the representatives of 61 States (Official Records of the World Health Organization, no. 2, p. 100) and entered into force on 7 April 1948.

WHO (2002), *European Strategy for Tobacco Control*, Copenhagen: WHO European Regional Office.

WHO (2003a), *Tobacco Control Database*, Copenhagen: WHO European Regional Office, retrieved from http://data.euro.who.int/tobacco/ (accessed 10 April 2005).

WHO (2003b), *Framework Convention on Tobacco Control*, Geneva: WHO, retrieved from http://www.who.int/tobacco/fctc/text/en/fctc_en.pdf (accessed 10 April 2005).

WHO (2004), *About WHO: Evidence-based Policy*, Copenhagen: WHO Regional Office for Europe, retrieved from http://www.euro.who.int/aboutwho/about/20020908_2 (accessed 10 April 2005).

CHAPTER 16

Aldridge, A. (1998), '*Habitus* and cultural capital in the field of personal finance', *The Sociological Review*, **46** (1), 1–23.

Barber, T. (2004), 'Italy Passes Bill on Pensions Reform', http://new.ft.com/servlet/ContentServer?PA.../fullStory&c=StoryFT&cid=108737405863.

Belt, D. (2004), 'Europe's big gamble', *National Geographic*, **205** (5), 54–65.

Carnell, B. (2001), *Population Age Distribution – Europe and the New Independent States*, http://www.overpopulation.com/print/faq/Basic_Information/age_distribution/europe.html.

Davies, B. and Ward, S. (1992), *Women and Personal Pensions*, London: HMSO European Community (2005), *Pensions*, http://europa.eu.int/comm/mediatheque/photo/select/pensions_en.htm.

Dean, M. (1999), 'Risk, Calculable and Incalculable', in Lupton, D. (ed.), *Risk and Sociocultural Theory: New Directions and Perspectives*, Cambridge: Cambridge University Press, pp. 131–59.

The European Commission and the Foreign Commonwealth Office (2003), *Enlargement: South East England*, London: The European Commission and the Foreign Commonwealth Office.

EIU (Economist Intelligence Unit) (2004), *Old Europe: Population Ageing and the Looming Pensions Crisis*, London: The Economist Intelligence Unit.

European Community (2005), *Pensions*, http://eurpoa.eu.int/comm/mediatheque/photo/select/pensions_en.htmeborah.

European Older People's Platform (2003), *Briefing on European Union Policy Coordination on Pensions*, http://ue.eu.int/newsroom/GR2003/index.asp?lang=EN.

European Older People's Platform (n.d.), *Age: Welcome to the EU Pensions Debate*, http://www.seniorweb.nl/eu-pensions/

Falkingham, J. (1998), 'Financial (in)security in later life', in Bernard, M. and Phillips, J. (eds), *The Social Policy of Old Age: Moving into the 21st Century*, London: Centre for Policy on Ageing, pp. 93–111.

Field, J. and Farrant, G. (1993), 'Public perceptions of occupational schemes', in Goode, R. (ed.), *Pension Law Reform: The Report of the Pension Law Reform Committee, Vol 2, The Research*, London: HMSO.

Foucault, Michel (1988), 'Technologies of the self', in Martin, L., Gutman, H. and Hutton, P. (eds), *Technologies of the Self: A Seminar with Michel Foucault*, London: Tavistock, pp. 16–49.

Gabriel, Y. and Lang, T. (1995), *The Unmanageable Consumer: Contemporary Consumption and its Fragmentations*, London: Sage.

Geddes, A. (2002), 'Europe's Ageing Population', http://news.bbc.co.uk/I/hi/world/2053581.stm.

Giddens, A. (1998), 'Risk society: the context of British politics', in Franklin, J. (ed.), *The Politics of Risk Society*, Cambridge: Polity, pp. 23–34.

Gordon, C. (ed.) (1980), *Michel Foucault Power/Knowledge: Selected Interviews and Other Writings 1972–1977*, trans. Colin Gordon, Leo

Marshall, John Mepham and Kate Soper, New York and London: HarvesterWheatsheaf.

Greco, M. (1993), 'Psychosomatic Subjects and the "Duty to be Well": Personal Agency within Medical Rationality', *Economy and Society*, **22** (3), 357–72.

Hawksworth, J., Vause, N., Pettitt, D., Lee, J. and Barker, T. (2000), *The European Pensions and Savings Revolution: Our Vision of the Future*, London: PricewaterhouseCoopers.

Henig, S. (1997), *The Uniting of Europe: From Discord to Concord*, London: Routledge.

Henley, P. (2004), 'Population Earthquake hits Germany', http://news.bbc.co.uk/2/hi/programmes/crossing_continents/3910821.stm

Hinchliff, P. and Hall, C. (2002), *A Generation in Transition: Older People's Situation and Civil Society's Response in East and Central Europe*, London: HelpAge International.

Hinchliff, P. and Priestley, B. (2001), *Making Our Voices Heard: Older People and Decision-making in East and Central Europe*, London: HelpAge International.

Holzmann, R., MacKellar, L. and Rutkowski, M. (2003a), 'Accelerating the European pension reform agenda in need, progress, and conceptual underpinnings', in Holzmann, R., Orenstein, M. and Rutkowski, M. (eds), *Pension Reform in Europe: Process and Progress*, Washington, DC: The World Bank, pp. 1–46.

Holzmann, R., Orenstein, M. and Rutkowski, M. (eds) (2003b), *Pension Reform in Europe: Process and Progress*, Washington, DC: The World Bank.

Leadbetter, C. (1989), 'Power to the person', in Hall, S. and Jacques, M. (eds), *New Times: The Changing Face of Politics in the 1990s*, London: Lawrence and Wishart, pp. 137–49.

Linn, J. and Rischard, J.-F. (2003), 'Foreword', in Holzmann, R., Orenstein, M. and Rutkowski, M. (eds) *Pension Reform in Europe: Process and Progress*, Washington, DC: The World Bank, pp. vii–viii.

Littlewood, M. (1998), *How To Create a Competitive Market in Pensions: The International Lessons*, London: Institute of Economic Affairs.

Loveless, H. (2004), 'Pensions collapse warning', *This is Money*, 24 June.

McRae, Hamish (2004), 'Everyone agrees Europe needs pensions reform. So why is it so hard to accomplish?', *The Independent on Sunday*, 27 June, p. 16.

Nettleton, S. and Burrows, R. (1998), 'Individualization processes and social policy: insecurity, reflexivity and risk in the restructuring of contemporary British health and housing policies', in Carter, J. (ed.), *Postmodernity and the Fragmentation of Welfare*, London: Routledge, pp. 153–67.

Peggs, K. (2000), 'Which pension?: women, risk and pension choice', *The Sociological Review*, **48** (3), 349–64.
Phillips, L. (1998), 'Hegemony and political discourse: the lasting impact of Thatcherism', *Sociology*, **32** (4), 847–67.
Smart, B. (1999), *Facing Modernity: Ambivalence, Reflexivity and Morality*, London: Sage.
Townsend, Abigail (2004), 'CBI calls for pensions overhaul', *The Independent on Sunday*, 27 June, p. 4.
Vincent, J.A. (1995), *Inequality in Old Age*, London: UCL Press.
Waine, B. (1995), 'A disaster foretold? The case of the personal pension', *Social Policy and Administration*, **29** (8), 317–34.
Walker, A. and Maltby, T. (1997), *Ageing Europe*, Buckingham and Philadelphia: Open University Press.
Whiteford, P. (2003), 'Introduction: learning from pension reform experiences', in OECD, *Reforming Public Pensions: Sharing Experiences of Transition and OECD Countries*, Paris: OECD.
Williams, T. and Field, J. (1993), *Pension Choices: A Survey on Personal Pensions in Comparison with Other Options*, London: HMSO.

CHAPTER 17

Andersen, S. and Eliassen, K. (1993), *Making Policy in Europe: The Europeification of National Policy-Making*, London: Sage.
Blair, T. (2005a), *Address to the European Union Parliament, 23 June 2005*, http://www.number-10.gov.uk.
Blair, T. (2005b), *Doorstep Interview in Tuscany, 30 May 2005*, http://www.number-10.gov.uk.
Bretherton, C. and Vogler, J. (1999), *The European Union as a Global Actor*, London: Routledge.
CEC (2004), *Delivering Lisbon: Reforms for the Enlarged Union*, COM (2004) 2 final, Brussels, 20 February.
Chryssochoou, D. (1998), *Democracy in the European Union*, London: Tauris.
Cooper, R. (2003), *The Breaking of Nations: Order and Chaos in the Twenty-First Century*, London: Atlantic Books.
Fukuyama, F. (1992), *The End of History and the Last Man*, London: Penguin.
Kagan, R. (2003), *Paradise and Power: America and Europe in the New World Order*, London: Atlantic Books.

Kintis, A. (1997), 'The EU's foreign policy and the war in the Former Yugoslavia', in Holland, M. (ed.), *Common Foreign and Security Policy: The Record and Reforms*, London: Pinter.

Knill, C. (2001), *The Europeanization of National Administrations: Patterns of Institutional Change and Persistence*, Cambridge: Cambridge University Press.

Kok, W. (2004), *Facing the Challenge: The Lisbon Strategy for Growth and Employment*, Report of the High Level Group Chaired by Wim Kok, Brussels: European Communities.

Massey, A. (2003), 'Modernization as Europeanization: the impact of the European Union on public administration', in Butcher, T. and Massey, A. (eds), *Modernizing Civil Services*, Cheltenham, UK and Northampton, MA, USA: Edward Elgar.

McCormick, J. (1996), *The European Union: Politics and Policies*, Oxford: Westview Press.

Moravcsik, A. (2002), 'In defence of the democratic deficit: reassessing legitimacy in the European Union', *Journal of Common Market Studies*, **40** (4), 603–24

Omelicheva, M. (2004), 'Global civil society? An empirical portrayal', paper to the Annual Meeting of the American Political Science Association, APSA.

Patten, C. and Lamy, P. (2003), 'Let's put away the megaphones: a transatlantic appeal', *International Herald Tribune*, http://www.iht.com/articles.

Rhodes, R.A.W. (1994), 'The hollowing out of the state', *Political Quarterly*, **65** (2), 138–51.

Rice, C. (2005), *Rice woos Paris with call to build bridges*, http://www.guardian.co.uk/print.

Schmitter, P. (2004), 'Neo-neofunctionalism', in Wiener, A. and Diez, T. (eds), *European Integration Theory*, Oxford: Oxford University Press.

Straw, J. (2005), *EU White Paper Released on Eve of UK Presidency 30/6/05*, http://www.fc.

Wagner, W. (2005), *The Democratic Legitimacy of European Security and Defence Policy*, Occasional Paper, No. 57, April 2005, European Union Institute for Security Studies.

Wistrich, E. (1994), *The United States of Europe*, London: Routledge.

Index